GOVERNING THE UK

Fourth Edition

GOVERNING THE UK

British Politics in the 21st Century

Fourth Edition

Gillian Peele

Blackwell
Publishing

© 1980, 1985 by Max Beloff and Gillian Peele
© 1995, 2004 by Gillian Peele

350 Main Street, Malden, MA 02148-5020, USA
108 Cowley Road, Oxford OX4 1JF, UK
550 Swanston Street, Carlton, Victoria 3053, Australia

The right of Gillian Peele to be identified as the Author of this Work has been asserted in accordance with the UK Copyright, Designs, and Patents Act 1988.

First edition published in 1980 by Weidenfeld and Nicolson, as *The Government of the UK* by Max Beloff and Gillian Peele.
Second edition published 1985 by Weidenfeld and Nicolson
Third edition published 1995 by Blackwell Publishing Ltd
Fourth edition published 2004

Library of Congress Cataloging-in-Publication Data

Peele, Gillian, 1949–
    Governing the UK / Gillian Peele. – 4th ed.
    p. cm.
Includes bibliographical references and index.
    ISBN 0-631-22681-8
1. Great Britain – Politics and government – 1945– I. Title.

    JN231.P44 2004
    320.441dc21   2003009295

A catalogue record for this title is available from the British Library.

Set in 10/12pt Sabon by Kolam Information Services Pvt. Ltd, Pondicherry, India.

For further information on
Blackwell Publishing, visit our website:
http://www.blackwellpublishing.com

Contents

Figures

Tables

Boxes

Maps

Preface

The period since the last edition of this book appeared in the mid-1990s has been one of rapid and extensive change in the United Kingdom's political system. The introduction of devolved government for Scotland and for Wales as part of the government's devolution strategy is perhaps the most obvious example of the way the contemporary British political landscape has been transformed in the last decade. Several other new institutions, such as the Electoral Commission and the Committee on Standards in Public Life, have already demonstrated their potential to alter the conduct of British politics. In addition to institutional innovation, there have been profound changes in the United Kingdom's political behaviour as New Labour, in two successive landslide general election victories, has established itself in a seemingly impregnable ascendancy.

In rewriting the book to take account of these changes, I have taken the opportunity to improve its format. The amount of historical material has been trimmed to allow space for discussion of contemporary developments. There is more visual material than in previous editions, which I hope enhances the original character of the book. Thus I have added some discussion of key concepts and political terms to each chapter. These are highlighted in bold on their first occurrence and defined in the margin as well as in a separate list at the back of the book. The chapters also contain a number of tables and boxes designed to illuminate the textual discussion. In order to make the book easier to use for teaching purposes, I have replaced the notes that appeared at the end of each chapter with a guide to further reading, a list of relevant websites and a suggested set of key questions that may be used to take the discussion further. A full list of references may be found at the back of the book, as well as a list of general websites. Legal cases referred to in the text are listed in an appendix.

As well as the material contained within the covers of the book, there is also a website http://www.blackwellpublishing.com/peele provided by Blackwell Publishing to help students and teachers of British politics keep up to date. This site will be regularly updated between editions. We hope it will prove a useful resource. Authors and publishers are always heavily dependent on their customers for feedback about their products. I very much hope that anyone who has suggestions for inclusions or additional material will get in touch, either with me directly or with the publishers.

Gillian Peele

Acknowledgements

The author and publishers gratefully acknowledge the following for permission to reproduce copyright material: tables 1.11, 9.2, 9.4, 9.8, 9.12, 13.4 reproduced with kind permission of MORI; table 3.2 reproduced with kind permission of British Market Research Association; tables 6.5, 8.1, 9.7, 15.3 reproduced with permission of Palgrave Macmillan; table 6.12 reproduced by permission of·Oxford University Press. The publishers apologize for any errors or omissions in this list and would be grateful to be notified of any corrections that should be incorporated in the next edition or reprint of this book.

In the course of writing this book I have been helped by a very large number of long-suffering friends, colleagues and students as well as by many organizations and individuals who have answered queries. Although I cannot thank them all personally, I want to record here my gratitude to them all.

A series of wonderful research assistants provided help at various stages of the production of the book. In particular I want to thank Catherine Needham, who provided extensive advice and scholarly insights over the whole project. She organized the tables and cheerfully coped with the range of tasks associated with completing the manuscript. At earlier stages of the book Teresa Curristine, Jonathan Treadwell, Hamish Dibley, Marc Glancy, Gavin Cameron, David Coleman, Mark Robson, Chris Ballinger and Alexander Hodbod all provided research help. In college Ben Bridle helped avoid a succession of computing catastrophes and provided timely assistance. Roberta Staples was patient about my demands on the library.

Nicholas Owen and Nicholas Baldwin read the whole manuscript and helped me avoid many errors. Stephen Hickey, Matthew Kelly and Ewan McKendrick read individual chapters. Paul Evans, David Butler, Lord Norton, Alan Ware and Joni Lovenduski generously answered queries.

I must also thank Blackwell for their support in producing this book. In particular I want especially to thank Angela Cohen, Justin Vaughan and Brigitte Lee. Of course, I alone am responsible for any errors.

Gillian Peele
December 2003

Abbreviations

ACAS	Advisory and Conciliation and Arbitration Service
ACC	Association of County Councils
ACPO-TAM	Association of Chief Police Officers Unit on Terrorism and Allied Matters
ADC	Association of District Councils
AEF	Aggregate External Finance
ALA	Association of Local Authorities
AM	Assembly Member (Wales)
AMA	Association of Municipal Authorities
AMS	Alternative Member System
AV	Alternative Vote
AWS	All-Women Shortlist
BES/BGES	British Election Study/British General Election Study
BIC	British–Irish Council
BMA	British Medical Association
BME	Black Minority Ethnic
CAP	Common Agricultural Policy
CBI	Confederation of British Industry
CFER	Campaign for the English Regions
CLP	Constituency Labour Party
CLPD	Campaign for Labour Party Democracy
CND	Campaign for Nuclear Disarmament
COREPER	Committee of Permanent Representatives
CPRS	Central Policy Review Staff
CPS	Centre for Policy Studies
CPSA	Civil and Public Services Association
CRE	Commission for Racial Equality
CRO	Commonwealth Relations Office
CSR	Comprehensive Spending Review
CSPL	Committee on Standards in Public Life
DCA	Department for Constitutional Affairs
DEFRA	Department for the Environment, Food and Rural Affairs
DfES	Department for Education and Skills
DoH	Department of Health
DPP	Director of Public Prosecutions

DTI	Department of Trade and Industry
DTLR	Department for Transport, Local Government and the Regions
DUP	Democratic Unionist Party
DUS	Deputy Under-Secretary
DWP	Department for Work and Pensions
EC	European Community
ECHR	European Convention on Human Rights
ECJ	European Court of Justice
EEC	European Economic Community
EU	European Union
EFTA	European Free Trade Area
EMS	European Monetary System
EMU	Economic and Monetary Union (or European Monetary Union)
EPC	European Political Cooperation
EOC	Equal Opportunities Commission
ERDF	European Regional Development Fund
ERM	Exchange Rate Mechanism
ESC	Economic and Social Committee
Euratom	European Atomic Energy Community
FCO	Foreign and Commonwealth Office
FM	First Minister
FMI	Financial Management Initiative
FPTP	First Past the Post
FSA	Financial Services Authority
GICS	Government Information and Communication Service
GLA	Greater London Authority or Greater London Assembly
HMSO	Her Majesty's Stationery Office
HRA	Human Rights Act
HSC	Health and Safety Commission
HSE	Health and Safety Executive
IEA	Institute of Economic Affairs
IGC	Intergovernmental Conference
IGR	Intergovernmental Relations
ILP	Independent Labour Party
IMF	International Monetary Fund
INLA	Irish National Liberation Army
IOD	Institute of Directors
IPPR	Institute of Public Policy Research
IRA	Irish Republican Army
JCPC	Judicial Committee of the Privy Council
JIC	Joint Intelligence Committee
JMC	Joint Ministerial Committee
JP	Justice of the Peace
LEA	Local Education Authority
LGA	Local Government Association
MEP	Member of the European Parliament
MLA	Member of the Legislative Assembly (Northern Ireland)

MOD	Ministry of Defence
MORI	Market Opinion Research Institute
MP	Member of Parliament
MPA	Ministerial Parliamentary Aide
MPC	Monetary Policy Committee
MSP	Member of the Scottish Parliament
NAO	National Audit Office
NATO	North Atlantic Treaty Organization
NDPB	Non-departmental Public Body
NEC	National Executive Committee (Labour Party)
NEDC	National Economic Development Council
NFU	National Farmers Union
NHS	National Health Service
NICRA	Northern Ireland Civil Rights Association
NICS	Northern Ireland Civil Service
NIO	Northern Ireland Office
NPM	New Public Management
ODPM	Office of the Deputy Prime Minister
OECD	Organization for Economic Cooperation and Development
OFGEM	Office of Gas and Electricity Markets
OFLOT	Office of the National Lottery
OFSTED	Office for Standards in Education
OFTEL	Office of Telecommunications Supply
OFWAT	Office of Water Regulation
OMOV	One Member One Vote
ONS	Office for National Statistics
OPCS	Office of Population and Census
OPSS	Office of Public Service and Science
ORR	Office of the Rail Regulator
OSCE	Organization for Security and Cooperation in Europe
PC	Plaid Cymru
PCA	Parliamentary Commissioner for Administration (Ombudsman)
PFI	Private Finance Initiative
PLP	Parliamentary Labour Party
PMO	Prime Minister's Office
PMOS	Prime Minister's Official Spokesperson
PMQs	Prime Minister's Questions
PPERA	Political Parties, Elections and Referendums Act
PPP	Public–Private Partnership
PPS	Parliamentary Private Secretary
PSA	Public Service Agreement
PSNI	Police Service of Northern Ireland
PUS	Permanent Under-Secretary
QC	Queen's Counsel
QMV	Qualified Majority Voting
Quango	Quasi-autonomous Non-governmental Organization
RDA	Regional Development Agency

RPI	Retail Price Index
SASC	Senior Appointments Selection Committee
SDLP	Social and Democratic Labour Party
SDP	Social Democratic Party
SNP	Scottish National Party
SSA	Standard Spending Assessment
STV	Single Transferable Vote
SV	Supplementary Vote
TAM	Terrorism and Allied Matters
TUC	Trades Union Congress
UDA	Ulster Defence Association
UKREP	UK's Permanent Representative to the European Community
UUP	Ulster Unionist Party
WTO	World Trade Organization

1 The Changing Structure of British Government

Governing the United Kingdom has always been a complex and multi-faceted process. Understanding that process at the beginning of the twenty-first century is, however, a much more daunting but exciting task than it was even when the last edition of this book was published in 1995. Although the interpretation of the British system of government offered in that edition, as in earlier ones, emphasized the fundamental changes that were occurring in the British polity, developments since the advent of the 1997 Labour government have had further wide-ranging effects on the country's administrative and political structures. In this introductory chapter, we examine in outline some key aspects of the British governmental system and its politics in order to provide some initial context for the reader, to offer a road map for what follows in subsequent chapters, and to highlight themes which run through the book as a whole. More specifically, we identify important sources of change in the British system and discuss the extent to which traditional patterns of political behaviour and values have come under challenge in recent years.

The chapter first provides a necessarily brief overview of some key developments in the British social and economic structure in recent years and relates them to the broader political system. (Many of these changes are examined in greater depth later in the book.) It looks at the position of the Labour Party and at the structure of party competition in the United Kingdom. In particular, it examines briefly the cluster of ideas and policies associated with **New Labour** and examines how they are shaping contemporary British government and politics. Since 1997 New Labour under Tony Blair has tried to modernize the workings of British democracy to make its institutions and processes more responsive to the needs of contemporary British society. A series of wide-ranging constitutional reforms (including **devolution**, the incorporation of most, though not all, of the European Convention on Human Rights (ECHR) into British law and the partial reform of the House of Lords) had a significant impact on many of Britain's traditional institutional arrangements. These reforms are still at a relatively early stage and have not yet fully bedded down in the routine workings of government. Nor is it easy yet to calculate their long-term effect on the British system of government as a whole. Clearly, the new constitutional arrangements, by creating a more complex governmental system and a **multi-layered polity**, demand greater coordination

New Labour Name given to the Labour Party under the leadership of Tony Blair after 1994. As New Labour, the party repositioned itself in the centre of British politics, abandoning support for traditional Labour policies such as nationalization and high rates of taxation.

devolution The transfer of legislative and executive powers to subordinate bodies within the state, e.g. the Scottish Parliament, the Welsh Assembly, the Northern Ireland Assembly 1921–72, the regions.

multi-layered polity A model of policy making which focuses on bargaining and negotiation between governmental actors (at the national, subnational and supranational levels) and private and voluntary sector organizations. The model emphasizes the extent to which powers overlap in the modern state.

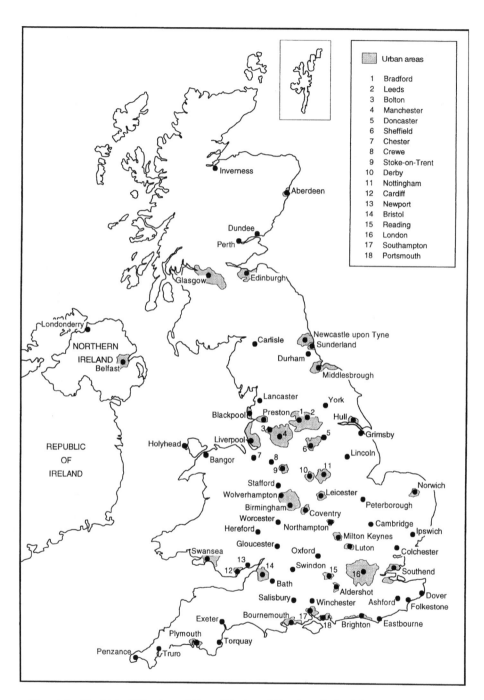

Map 1.1 The United Kingdom of Great Britain and Northern Ireland showing urban areas.

from the centre. Equally importantly, this burst of constitutional engineering was intended to reshape the country's political values – for example, by highlighting the significance of individual rights in the policy process. However, the process of reshaping the **political culture** was not one that the government could entirely control and the constitutional reforms may be expected to have a much more profound if unpredictable impact than was originally intended.

In addition to its constitutional reforms, New Labour initiated a number of strategies intended to renew British democracy and to make government more responsive to the public. Many of these strategies took advantage of the rapid developments in technology – the spread of the Internet, e-mail and personal computers – which have revolutionized so many people's lives and working habits. Other strategies – especially in relation to consultation with the public about its policy preferences – exploited the increasingly sophisticated techniques available for ascertaining public opinion. Thus there was a marked increase in the use made by local and central government (through the Cabinet Office) of **people's panels** and **focus groups**.

Despite these innovations in consultation and the identification of opportunities for the use of new technology to spread democratic **participation** and bring government closer to the people, more orthodox aspects of participation declined – for example, in electoral turnout and in levels of party membership. Equally, observers who surveyed the whole range of the British governmental system – who in effect carried out a democratic audit of the United Kingdom – found that it still displayed features that were difficult to reconcile with democratic values (Beetham, Byrne, Ngan and Weir, 2002). These themes of apparent public disengagement from the democratic process and the lack of democratic control in many areas of public life are ones that will recur throughout the book.

Governing the United Kingdom in the twenty-first century is qualitatively different from governing the country in an earlier period in at least one major respect. Many of the decisions that affect British citizens are taken not inside the United Kingdom but outside it – by public and private individuals and entities who are not responsible to the British public. Arguments about (and mobilization against) **globalization** are one face of that process. Another is the increasing integration of so much of the United Kingdom's policy-making process with the institutions of the European Union. Virtually every element of British government now has a European dimension, despite the continuing controversy over European issues in domestic politics.

political culture The attitudes, beliefs and values which underpin a political system, and which can help to account for the differences between countries with similar political institutions.

people's panel A representative panel of 5,000 people set up by the Labour government after the 1997 election as a way of testing responses to the government's proposed public service reform programme. It was dropped in 2002 when a Cabinet Office evaluation decided that its work had been done.

focus group A group which is used in public opinion polling and which involves intensive monitoring of attitudes over time through observation of group discussions and interviewing. It was used extensively by the Labour Party after 1994 to test policy options with swing voters.

political participation The engagement of the population in political action. There are various forms of participation ranging from voting through membership of parties and pressure groups to direct action.

globalization An umbrella term for the expansion of economic, political, cultural and environmental issues beyond national borders into issues of global importance.

A Changing Society

Developments in the economic and social structure of the United Kingdom over the last quarter of the twentieth century and on into the twenty-first century are likely to have profound consequences for the politics and government of the country. The size of the population is 58.8 million – a figure that gives the UK the third largest population of the current (2003) EU members (see tables 1.1 and 1.2). Within the UK England is by far the largest unit (see table 1.3).

Table 1.1 Population of the UK, 2001

	England	Wales	Scotland	Northern Ireland	United Kingdom
Population (thousands)	49,181	2,903	5,064	1,689	58,837
Per cent of population aged:					
Under 5	5.9	5.8	5.5	6.8	5.9
5–15	14.2	14.5	13.7	16.7	14.2
16 to pension age[a]	61.5	59.7	62.2	61.0	61.4
Above pension age	18.4	20.1	18.6	15.5	18.4
Population density (people per sq. km)	377	140	64	124	242
% population change 1981 to 2001	5.0	3.2	2.2	9.5	4.4

[a] Pension age is 65 for males and 60 for females.
Source: Office for National Statistics, *UK 2003 Yearbook*; http://www.statistics.gov.uk/downloads/theme_compendia/UK2003/UK2003.pdf

Table 1.2 Population of EU member states, 2001

EU member state	Population in 2001 (000s)
Austria	8,121
Belgium	10,263
Denmark	5,349
Finland	5,181
France	59,040
Germany	82,193
Greece	10,565
Irish Republic	3,781
Italy	57,884
Luxembourg	441
Netherlands	15,987
Portugal	10,243
Spain	40,122
Sweden	8,833
United Kingdom	58,837

Source: Office for National Statistics, *UK 2003 Yearbook*; http://www.statistics.gov.uk/downloads/theme_compendia/UK2003/UK2003.pdf

Table 1.3 England, population by region, 2001

	Population (000s)	Change in population, 1981–2001 (%)
North-east	2,517	−4.5
North-west	6,732	−3.0
Yorkshire and the Humber	4,967	1.0
East Midlands	4,175	8.4
West Midlands	5,267	1.6
East	5,395	11.1
London	7,188	5.6
South-east	8,007	10.5
South-west	4,934	12.6
England	49,181	5.0

Source: Office for National Statistics, *UK 2003 Yearbook*; http://www.statistics.gov.uk/downloads/
theme_compendia/UK2003/UK2003.pdf

Several features of the British population structure deserve comment. First, the 2001 census suggests that the population has once again started to grow slightly after remaining static for much of the previous quarter century. Secondly, it is an ageing population. Like many western European countries, the UK has a high percentage of its population in the over-65 age range (15.7 per cent in 1999). Although the numbers under 16 at present exceed those of pensionable age, the cohorts of pensionable age will exceed those under 16 in 2007. By 2025, it is estimated there will be 2 million more people of pensionable age than people under 16, with profound consequences for the ability of the country to support extensive welfare programmes and equally profound implications for the health and personal social services.

Thirdly, there have been major changes in the structure of British families in the period even since 1979. In common with many other European countries, there was an increase in births outside marriage, from 10.9 per cent in 1979 to 36.6 per cent in 1997. By 1999, nearly two-fifths of all births were outside marriage (Government Statistical Service, 2001). Almost one in five children were in single-parent families, mainly families headed by the mother. This development was one that had many implications for political debate. Some observers argued that this demographic change would inevitably damage the fabric of society and produce further social problems. In the early 1990s, the Conservatives attempted to reassert the virtues of traditional morality with a 'back to basics' campaign that was an embarrassing failure, not least because it was difficult to reconcile with a series of sexual scandals involving Conservative politicians which hit the headlines at the same time. Labour, by contrast, has tried to reinforce support for families not so much by moral campaigning as by restructuring benefits to direct additional help to those with children.

These new family patterns raised questions for the system of housing provision, welfare support and public spending. In particular, there was concern that a rise in the number of children being reared in single-parent families would increase further the level of child poverty. In 2003 it was reckoned that about one-third of all children were living in poverty, which was defined as living in families with 60 per cent or less of the median income (Child Poverty Action Group, 2003). Children in ethnic minority families were particularly affected. Labour in 1999 made the elimination of child poverty within a generation an explicit target and it is one of the issues that has been most significant in Labour's emphasis on gearing administrative reform to improving policy making and delivery.

Fourthly, the United Kingdom is now very definitely a **multi-racial and multi-ethnic society** with a significant ethnic minority population that represents nearly 8 per cent of the total population. Put slightly differently, about 1 UK citizen in 15 is from an ethnic minority group (see table 1.4). The age of the ethnic minority population is relatively young by comparison with the population as a whole and it tends to be concentrated in a few, mainly urban, areas.

Although Britain had experienced waves of Jewish immigration from eastern Europe prior to the First World War, and there was a small addition to the numbers of Jewish immigrants immediately before (and indeed after) the Second World War, the acquisition of a substantial ethnic minority population is very much a product of the post-1945 period. After 1945 there was extensive migration into the United Kingdom, first from the Caribbean, and then from the Asian subcontinent and Africa. These immigrants were attracted by the prospects of better living standards and some were directly recruited to fill labour shortages – in the British transport system and National Health Service (NHS), for example. Their ability to enter the United Kingdom freely (before restrictions were imposed) was a legacy of Britain's imperial past. Although the years after the Second World War saw a gradual

multi-racial/multi-ethnic society Model of society which has within it a series of diverse groups and ethnicities all of which are accorded equal legitimacy and recognition.

Table 1.4 Ethnic minorities in the UK, 2001–2

	%	Number of people (millions)
White	92.2	53.0
Asian or Asian British		
Indian	1.7	1.0
Pakistani	1.2	0.7
Bangladeshi	0.5	0.3
Other Asian background	0.5	0.3
All Asian groups	4.0	2.3
Black or black British		
Caribbean	1.0	0.6
African	0.9	0.5
Other black background	0.2	0.1
All black groups	2.1	1.2
Mixed	0.9	0.5
Chinese	0.3	0.2
Other ethnic groups	0.5	0.3
All ethnic groups	100.0	57.5

Source: Office for National Statistics, *UK 2003 Yearbook*; http://www.statistics.gov.uk/downloads/theme_compendia/UK2003/UK2003.pdf

transformation of Empire into Commonwealth, the British Nationality Act of 1948 initially maintained the broad principle of free entry and the right to settle in the United Kingdom for all Commonwealth citizens.

Although political reaction to the rising numbers of post-war Commonwealth immigration was at first muted, by the late 1950s it had become a political issue in part as a result of racial tensions in some areas. However, it was not until the 1960s that race and immigration issues gained any currency in mainstream political debate, largely because the two major British parties found them difficult to handle. Increasingly, however, ethnicity has become an important factor in British society and many aspects of politics and policy making in the United Kingdom have acquired an ethnic dimension. In 1962, the UK's traditional policy of allowing free access to Britain for all Empire and Commonwealth citizens was reversed (Hansen, 2000). New immigration was drastically reduced and was further tightened by subsequent legislation even though the imposition of controls meant limiting the rights of British passport holders. This issue became especially sensitive when British passport holders wished to settle in Britain to escape political danger. Such a situation arose with the Ugandan Asians in the 1970s and in the 1990s in relation to many Hong Kong residents who feared the consequences of the colony's return to China. In the latter case, the rights of settlement were removed.

Although primary immigration became progressively more difficult after the 1962 policy reversal, some new immigration did, and does still, occur. There is also outward migration. There has been a net inflow of migrants to the UK of approximately 73,000 per year over the late 1990s (Government Statistical Service, 2001). However, in general British immigration policy is now extremely restrictive. This tough approach to immigration was underlined by the Blair government's determination to win concessions to the European Union's policy of free movement of people (which might have limited the United Kingdom's ability to police entry effectively). It has also been evident in policies designed to make the right of **asylum** more difficult to claim and changes to the benefits system to make asylum in the UK less 'attractive'.

Alongside restrictions on new immigration, British governments have become increasingly conscious of the need to foster good race relations and to ensure that Britain's ethnic minorities enjoy equal opportunities and are protected from discrimination.

There has been extensive legislation against race discrimination since 1965 as well as legislation to combat other forms of discrimination such as sex discrimination and discrimination against the disabled (see box 1.1). Although there is discussion about merging the various agencies dealing with different forms of discrimination into a single body to promote equality, each area of anti-discrimination regulation is at present separately organized. The Commission for Racial Equality (CRE) is the key body charged with monitoring efforts to combat race discrimination and to deal with complaints and its mission has been reinforced by the passage of the Human Rights Act of 1998.

asylum Process in which immigrants claim the right to stay in the United Kingdom because of political oppression or other threat in their home country. The increase in asylum seekers since the 1990s turned the issue into one of intense political controversy and generated successive revisions of the laws governing asylum. There was also criticism of the provisions for appeal against decisions to refuse asylum from the agencies with responsibility for the well-being of asylum seekers.

Box 1.1 Discrimination legislation

Equal Pay Act 1970: Gives an individual the right to the same contractual pay and benefits as a person of the opposite sex in the same employment, where the man and the woman are doing work of 'equal value'.

Sex Discrimination Act 1975: Prohibits sex discrimination against individuals in the areas of employment, education and the provision of goods, facilities and services and in the disposal or management of premises.

Race Relations Act 1976: As amended by the **Race Relations (Amendment) Act 2000,** makes it unlawful to discriminate against anyone on the grounds of race, colour, nationality (including citizenship) or ethnic or national origin. It is also unlawful for public bodies to discriminate while carrying out any of their functions.

Disability Discrimination Act 1995: Gives disabled people rights in the areas of employment, access to goods, facilities and services, and buying or renting land or property.

Source: Equal Opportunities Commission; Commission for Racial Equality; Disability Rights Commission

Whether enough is being done to combat racial discrimination is now a matter of urgent political debate. Complacency was jolted by a series of race riots which broke out in 2002 in Oldham, Burnley and Bradford, a group of Lancashire and Yorkshire towns, and which were the worst examples of racially motivated public disorder since the early 1980s. There was also comprehensive analysis of the adequacy of police handling of racially motivated attacks after the Stephen Lawrence case, in which the police investigations into the death of a black teenager appeared negligent. Certainly, policing has been one area of British life where there have been extensive charges of discrimination and insensitivity in relation to ethnic minorities. Recently these have been countered with strenuous efforts to improve ethnic minority recruitment and diversity within the police. None the less, ethnic minority confidence in the police remains low.

The political self-consciousness of ethnic minorities had grown during the 1990s, as had the efforts made by the major parties to field ethnic minority candidates in elections. The 2001 general election saw 66 ethnic minority candidates, which was an increase on the 47 fielded in 1997. However, these candidates were not evenly distributed between the parties and many were fielded for unwinnable seats. Consequently, following the 2001 general election there were only 12 ethnic minority MPs in the House of Commons, and all them were Labour (see table 1.5).

Class and social change

In addition to becoming a multi-racial society, the United Kingdom has changed in a number of other important respects. In particular the size of the working class has

Table 1.5   Ethnic minority MPs, 1945–2001

Election	Total elected	% of all MPs
1945	–	–
1950	–	–
1951	–	–
1955	–	–
1959	–	–
1964	–	–
1966	–	–
1970	–	–
1974 (Feb)	–	–
1974 (Oct)	–	–
1979	–	–
1983	–	–
1987	4	0.6
1992	6	0.9
1997	9	1.4
2001	12	1.8

declined in Britain – as it has in many other advanced industrial societies – and its character has changed. In the 1960s it had been noted that affluence had affected working-class attitudes, making workers more instrumental and less solidaristic in their approach to politics (Goldthorpe, 1968). By the twenty-first century, other significant social changes had further reshaped political identities and assumptions. Some of these key social changes – most notably the growth of home ownership and the decline of trade union membership – had been encouraged by Conservative policy between 1979 and 1997; but they were also a reflection of broader cultural transformations and specific changes in the pattern of employment (see figure 1.1, table 1.6). The shrinking of Britain's manufacturing base and the rise of the service economy (see table 1.7) created a different social environment even from that of the 1960s.

The blurring of traditional class identities has significant political implications. These have been especially important for the Labour Party. With the shrinkage of its traditional working-class base, it became evident that Labour would have to appeal to a much broader range of voters than hitherto and would have to reduce or eliminate the emphasis on class issues. This analysis formed an important part of the rationale for rebranding the Labour Party as New Labour and underpinned the reforms of structure and policy which greatly contributed towards Labour's land-slide victory of 1997.

The New Labour Ascendancy

The results of the 2001 general election confirmed the existence of a new party political order in the United Kingdom. By achieving a second overwhelming electoral

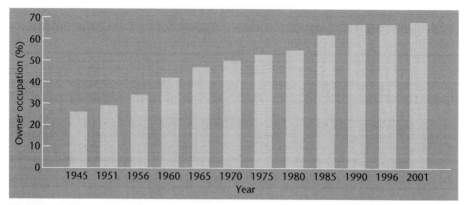

Figure 1.1 Home ownership in Great Britain, 1945–2001. *Source*: Butler and Butler (2000); Office for National Statistics, *UK 2003 Yearbook*, http://www.statistics.gov.uk/downloads/theme_compendia/UK2003/UK2003.pdf

Table 1.6 Trade union membership in the UK, 1971–2001

Year	Membership (000s)
1971	11,135
1976	12,386
1981	12,106
1986	10,539
1991	9,585
1996	7,987
2001	7,600

Source: Office for National Statistics, Annual Abstract of Statistics.

Table 1.7 The changing occupational structure in the UK

Occupation	Workforce jobs (000s)	% of workforce jobs	% change 1982–2002
Agriculture and fishing	455	2	−28
Energy and water	192	1	−70
Manufacturing	3,959	13	−33
Construction	1,975	7	12
Services total	22,918	78	38
Distribution, hotels and restaurants	6,754	23	24
Transport and communication	1,761	6	10
Finance and business services	5,692	19	91
Public administration, education and health	6,963	24	28
Other services	1,748	6	57
All jobs	29,499	100	16

Source: Office for National Statistics, *UK 2003 Yearbook*, p. 128, http://www.statistics.gov.uk/downloads/theme_compendia/UK2003/UK2003.pdf

victory in terms of parliamentary seats, Labour's position as the dominant party was secure (see table 1.8). Never before had Labour won two general election victories in a row on a scale that guaranteed it could govern confidently for two consecutive full terms and could consequently plan policy for an extended period (see table 1.9). The 2001 electoral triumph not only gave Labour the prospect of a full second term; it also resulted in it being difficult to see how the major opposition party, the Conservative Party, could recover sufficiently to mount a realistic challenge to Labour's hegemony even at the next election. Indeed, the scale of the Labour victory and the magnitude of the Conservative defeats in 1997 and 2001 raised the question of whether some fundamental change amounting to a political **realignment** was occurring in the United Kingdom. Certainly, Tony Blair had made clear that such a change in the landscape of British politics was his long-term goal or project so that what were called the 'forces of progressivism' (Labour and the Liberal Democrats) could dominate the twenty-first century as the forces of conservatism had dominated much of the twentieth.

realignment Concept used to analyse long-term shifts in the pattern of support in a competitive party system and which usually identifies a reconfiguration or fundamental change in the political loyalty of key social groups.

Labour's successive electoral triumphs in 1997 and 2001 were the product of a long period of party rebuilding. Although Labour in 2001 claimed continuity with the party which had won the 1945 general election and those of 1950, 1964, 1966 and the two elections of 1974, in many respects it was a quite different entity. From the loss of the general election of 1983, successive Labour leaders – Neil Kinnock, John Smith and Tony Blair – together with a faction of Labour modernizers had increasingly designed and implemented a programme intended to make Labour capable of winning elections once more (see boxes 1.2, 1.3 and 1.4). That programme involved changing Labour's image and electoral appeal, changing the Labour Party structure to give greater emphasis to individual members as opposed to unions, and changing some of Labour's core beliefs which were deemed no longer to resonate with the British public.

Table 1.8 Election results, 2001

Political party	MPs elected	% share of UK vote
Labour	412	40.7
Conservatives	166	31.7
Liberal Democrats	52	18.3
Scottish National	5	1.8
Plaid Cymru	4	0.7
Ulster Unionist	6	0.8
Democratic Unionist	5	0.7
Social Democratic and Labour	3	0.6
Sinn Fein	4	0.7
Speaker	1	0.1
Others	1	0.1

Source: Office for National Statistics, *UK 2003 Yearbook*; http://www.statistics.gov.uk/downloads/theme_compendia/UK2003/UK2003.pdf

Table 1.9 Twentieth-century governments

Election	Majority party	Prime minister
1900	Conservative	Marquis of Salisbury (3rd) (1900–2)
		Arthur Balfour (1902–5)
		Henry Campbell-Bannerman (1905–6)
1906	Liberal	Henry Campbell-Bannerman (1906–8)
		Herbert Henry Asquith (1908–10)
1910 (Feb)	Liberal	Herbert Henry Asquith
1910 (Dec)	Liberal	Herbert Henry Asquith (1910–16)
1918	Liberal–Conservative coalition	David Lloyd George (1916–22)
1922	Conservative	Andrew Bonar Law (1922–3)
		Stanley Baldwin (1923)
1923	Labour (minority government)	Ramsay MacDonald (1924)
1924	Conservative	Stanley Baldwin
1929	Labour (minority government)	Ramsay MacDonald
1931	Conservative/National Government	Ramsay MacDonald (1931)
		Stanley Baldwin (1935)
1935	Conservative	Stanley Baldwin (1935–7)
		Neville Chamberlain (1937–40)
1940	Coalition	Winston Churchill (1940–5)
1945	Labour	Clement Attlee
1950	Labour	Clement Attlee
1951	Conservative	Winston Churchill (1951–5)
		Anthony Eden (1955)
1955	Conservative	Anthony Eden (1955–7)
		Harold Macmillan (1957–9)
1959	Conservative	Harold Macmillan (1957–63)
		Alec Douglas-Home (1963–4)
1964	Labour	Harold Wilson
1966	Labour	Harold Wilson
1970	Conservative	Edward Heath
1974 (February)	Labour	Harold Wilson
1974 (October)	Labour	Harold Wilson (1974–6)
		James Callaghan (1976–9)
1979	Conservative	Margaret Thatcher
1983	Conservative	Margaret Thatcher
1987	Conservative	Margaret Thatcher (1987–90)
		John Major (1990–2)
1992	Conservative	John Major
1997	Labour	Tony Blair
2001	Labour	Tony Blair

Source: Dod's Parliamentary Companion 1994 (London: Dod's Parliamentary Companion, 1994), p. 760; Butler and Butler (2000), p. 55; Butler and Kavanagh (2002), p. 260.

These changes not only succeeded in creating a new image for the Labour Party but also altered the framework of political debate in the United Kingdom. New Labour shed much, if not most, of its commitment to socialism and it abandoned its

Box 1.2   Neil Kinnock (1942–)

Kinnock was elected to Parliament in 1970, taking on the shadow education portfolio in the early 1980s, and succeeding Michael Foot as leader of the party after the calamitous defeat of 1983. He was committed to purging the Labour Party of extremists from the **Militant Tendency**, and to moving the party away from an unpopular hard-left agenda. He recognized the importance of good communications to the party's success, appointing Peter Mandelson as the party's director of communication in 1985. In the policy review of the late 1980s, he also moved Labour away from some of their more unpopular policies such as unilateral nuclear disarmament. Despite his success in repositioning the Labour Party as a viable party of government, Labour lost the 1987 and 1992 elections. After the 1992 defeat, Kinnock resigned, and has since then been active as an EU Commissioner in Brussels.

Militant Tendency A Trotskyist party which used a policy of entryism to gain control of several local Labour parties in the 1970s. Militant was particularly powerful in Liverpool, where it dominated the Labour-controlled city council. After the 1983 election, Neil Kinnock pursued a policy of expulsion against Militant and it had declined as a force by the late 1980s.

Box 1.3   John Smith (1938–94)

Smith took over the Labour leadership from Neil Kinnock after Labour's 1992 defeat. A Scottish lawyer from the right of the party, Smith continued Kinnock's internal modernization, for example moving to One Member One Vote (OMOV) for leadership elections. His approach to policy reform was conservative, appearing to support a 'one more push' approach to electoral success, rather than assuming Labour needed fundamental policy reform. He was a popular leader in the party and in the country, and was widely mourned following his sudden death in April 1994.

commitment to Clause 4 of the Labour Party constitution, which had committed the party to socialism and public ownership. New Labour accepted and even celebrated the triumph of liberal capitalism – now global in character – engaging with it through the concept of the **third way**, an approach that appeared to blend ideas from neo-liberalism and social democracy in a pragmatic and eclectic manner. The rhetoric of class-based politics, egalitarianism, redistribution and public ownership was eliminated from Labour's statements and there was a new emphasis on community and citizenship. Even in relation to the **welfare state** there was a different language, signifying a move away from a commitment to universalism and towards a more pragmatic approach.

The rhetoric that New Labour employed, particularly after Tony Blair became leader in 1994, was also the rhetoric of modernization. That rhetoric not only proved popular in electoral terms but also provided an intellectual rationale for many of the diverse policy programmes and strategies adopted by Labour in government. It also meant that many of the traditional patterns and practices of the British system of government were subjected to reappraisal and, in some cases, radical reform.

third way Doctrine associated with Anthony Giddens which argues for a new intellectual synthesis that transcends the ideological cleavage between capitalism and socialism and takes account of globalization. Third-way thinking had an impact on the policy choices of President Clinton and Tony Blair.

welfare state State which recognizes an obligation to provide an extensive level of welfare services to its citizens.

pluralism The idea that power is and should be spread extensively through society and the political system. In political science, pluralists argue that as broad a spread of interest group activity as possible is necessary if democracy is to be maximized.

Box 1.4   Tony Blair (1953–)

After training as a barrister, Tony Blair entered Parliament in 1983 as MP for the safe seat of Sedgefield. He entered Labour's shadow cabinet in 1988 as shadow spokesman for employment, demonstrating a formidable skill at the dispatch box. After the 1992 election, he took on the shadow Home Office brief in John Smith's shadow cabinet, and took steps to reverse the perception that the Labour Party was soft on crime. John Smith's sudden death in 1994 pushed Blair into the limelight as a leadership contender and Blair put his name forward in place of Gordon Brown, a close friend of Blair's who had been seen as the more likely successor to Smith. After becoming leader in July 1994, Blair set about the reform of Labour Party policy that Smith had eschewed. His first step was to announce a review of Clause 4 of the party's constitution which included a commitment to public ownership. Despite opposition from trade unions and party activists, Blair was able to convince party members of the need to redraft the clause. Blair's leadership marked a continuation and intensification of the reforms begun by Neil Kinnock. He accepted much of the Thatcherite legacy, embraced low taxes, distanced the party from the trade unions and christened it New Labour to mark a decisive break with the past. His centrist agenda took Labour to power with a majority of 179 in the 1997 election. As prime minister he has displayed a commitment to constitutional reform and **pluralism**, whilst at the same time consolidating more power into his own office. He remained very popular throughout most of his first term and oversaw a second decisive victory for Labour in the 2001 election.

The transformation of the Labour Party into a powerful new political machine was in large part the product of the efforts of successive Labour leaders who grasped the political significance of underlying trends in the social and political system. In particular, changes in the character and size of the working class meant that no party could afford to pitch its appeal primarily to the traditional working class. Labour thus needed to become a **catch-all party**, drawing support across the country, connecting with the aims and aspirations of the majority of the population and not just with isolated sectional interests. New Labour fashioned its message on the reality of electoral preferences as revealed by systematic polling and focus groups. Tony Blair also appreciated the extent to which the mass media, rather than the party activists, shaped the political agenda and the need to communicate the party's message powerfully and effectively.

catch-all party A type of party which appeals to all voters rather than concentrating on one sector of society. Such parties tend to de-emphasize any ideological or rhetorical characteristics which would prevent them from maximizing their vote and they typically seek the centre-ground of politics. The term is associated with Kirchheimer and is widely used to explain the tactics of modern political parties such as New Labour.

Blair understood how much personality and leadership mattered in the new political landscape. In opposition Blair asserted the prerogative of the party leadership. This focus on the leadership continued a process by which the traditional centres of party authority – the trade unions, the Conference and the National Executive Committee (NEC) – were marginalized in the party's policy making. This new approach to policy making altered the emphasis of Labour's constitutional processes and went against the grain of much of its **collectivist** traditions, to the dismay of old Labour stalwarts such as Tony Benn (see box 1.5).

collectivism General theory that social and economic policy should be organized for the good of the community as a whole rather than for private enterprise or individuals.

Box 1.5 Tony Benn (1925–)

Since he was a hereditary peer, Viscount Stansgate, it required a change in the law before Tony Benn could renounce his peerage and enter the Commons in 1963. He held cabinet positions in the 1964–70 Wilson governments, and was Energy Minister in the 1974–9 Labour government. His left-wing views clashed with those of the party leadership, particularly under James Callaghan, and he led a faction of Labour MPs opposed to the leadership position on Europe and economic reform. After the 1979 defeat he played a role in moving the party further to the left. He stood for the leadership and deputy leadership in the early 1980s, but narrowly failed to be elected to either position, and remained on the backbenches until he retired from Parliament in 2001. He has remained in the public eye as a writer and broadcaster and critic of New Labour.

Bennites Left-of-centre group associated with Tony Benn, especially in the period 1979–83 when he was actively supportive of the Campaign for Labour Party Democracy's agenda of reform in the Labour Party.

Not surprisingly, many of the lessons learned in opposition were carried into office. From the beginning Blair's Labour government paid enormous attention to the media and to the presentation of policy, so much so that critics and satirists accused it of being obsessed with **spin** rather than substance. A new unit to manage presentation and communication was established in No. 10 Downing Street and Blair's media adviser, Alastair Campbell, became one of his most influential advisers in government. Above all, Blair made it clear that his was to be a government with a strong centre, meaning that his conception of the premiership entailed giving Downing Street the institutional infrastructure to support its strategic role.

Tony Blair's style of government with its emphasis on prime ministerial leadership had much in common with the style adopted by Margaret Thatcher. And it stood in marked contrast to that of Blair's immediate predecessor, John Major, whose attempts to assert a more collegial style of government had ended up simply with him looking weak (Foley, 2000). Blair differed from Thatcher in a number of ways, however. For example, he was much more systematic about administrative change, especially at the centre of government, than Thatcher had been. The cabinet that Blair formed in 1997 was one dominated by the prime minister rather than a cabinet of equals. Only Gordon Brown had any comparable political strength.

In addition to his admiration for Margaret Thatcher's highly personalized prime ministerial style, Blair and New Labour were also the beneficiaries of the radical policies which she had implemented and which had altered so much of the political landscape between 1979 and 1990 (Heffernan, 2000). It would be difficult to exaggerate the difference between the world Blair inherited in 1997 and the one left by the previous Labour prime minister, James Callaghan, in 1979, not least the reduced role of the trade unions whose series of public sector strikes in 1978–9 had so damaged Labour (see box 1.6). In addition, a range of state-owned industries and utilities (coal, water, rail, gas and electricity) had been **privatized** and there was a much greater emphasis on market-based solutions and consumerism.

spin Term denoting the systematic attempt to influence the reception by the media and public of news and information.

privatization A term usually associated with the sale of shares in publicly owned industries to the private sector. Companies such as British Gas and British Telecom were sold off in this way during the 1980s.

Box 1.6 James Callaghan (1912–)

Becoming prime minister following Harold Wilson's surprise resignation in 1976, Callaghan inherited a country riven by industrial conflict and in economic turmoil. He negotiated a loan from the International Monetary Fund (IMF), which came with stringent conditions for cutting public spending and restricting the money supply. The winter of 1978–9 saw widespread strikes in public services, leading it to be dubbed 'The Winter of Discontent'. In a general election in the spring of 1979, Callaghan and the Labour Party lost decisively to Margaret Thatcher's Conservative Party, and Labour remained out of power for the next 18 years.

new public management (NPM) An umbrella term for the introduction of new forms of management into public administration in the 1980s, based on private sector values of risk taking, entrepreneurship, market testing and emphasis on results rather than traditional bureaucratic values of hierarchy and formality.

executive agencies Organizations created following the 1988 Ibbs Report to reform the civil service and produce greater executive efficiency. Effectively, these agencies are single-purpose bodies which operate at a degree of distance from the parent department. The minister retains responsibility for policy, but the chief executive of the agency is responsible for their day-to-day management.

benchmarking Comparing the quality of products, services and practices against best practice – for example, using the best-performing local authorities as a guide to the standard of performance (or benchmark) that other local authorities are expected to achieve.

core executive A network of interdependent actors at the centre of government, who govern through building alliances rather than through command. The core executive includes the prime minister, ministers and senior civil servants and focuses on resource mobilization and informal contacts rather than on formal organizational structures.

New Labour's domestic agenda reflected the new consensus and its own new ideological stance. The competent management of the economy became the overriding goal of the Blair administration, dominating demands for higher spending on public services. New Labour's approach to the organization of government and to issues of public administration mirrored these priorities. Blair as prime minister endorsed most of the administrative reforms initiated by previous Conservative governments that have been collectively dubbed the **new public management (NPM)**. Of especial significance here was a series of reforms to the organization of government through the creation of **executive agencies** operating at one remove from the traditional departmental structures and the importation into government of a range of management tools and techniques derived from the private sector, such as performance-related pay and **benchmarking** (see chapter 5).

Underlying this approach was the belief that government should draw a distinction between policy making and the delivery of services. Central government could set objectives and regulate the provision of services, but it would not itself deliver them. There were several advantages to this model. By separating the core functions of central government from the detailed administration of policy, a government could concentrate on key strategic functions and not become overloaded in managing the detail of service delivery which could equally well be devolved. Certainly, Blair's conception of the premiership was of a strong and centralizing force, but this activist conception demanded that the range of the **core executive** be limited. Secondly, this model of government fits well with the notion of policy making and administration that emphasizes the technical and apolitical nature of much decision making as opposed to emphasizing policy choice and discretion. Finally, drawing a distinction between central policy making and administration had the convenient feature of allowing the government to dissociate itself from responsibility for many policy failures that might occur. However, Blair's government was also increasingly committed to improving the quality of public services and the efficiency of the policy-making process. It created its own modernizing agenda, which emphasized the need for 'joined-up' or **holistic** government, implementation and flexibility. There was thus a tension between the desire to devolve and decentralize decision making in the name of efficiency and the determination to control and improve the policy process in the name of political credibility.

Constitutional Reform

Little of Labour's policy agenda in government could be characterized as radical in the sense of being inspired by the ideas of equality or the redistribution of wealth in British society. Indeed, it seemed to accept much of what had been done by previous Conservative governments, although placing a more technocratic rather than free-market gloss on its approach. Yet in one sphere, that of constitutional reform, the Blair government did produce in its first term a programme of very radical change that affected a number of key political structures and relationships. The detail of these changes is discussed in later chapters (see especially chapter 2). None the less, it is necessary here to underline some of the systemic implications of the reforms and to indicate some of their internal ambiguities.

First, it is important to note that the effect of the constitutional changes introduced under the Blair governments has been to alter the structure and the values of the British state. With the creation of devolved governments for Scotland and Wales, a directly elected mayor and Assembly in London, and an enhanced regional dimension (as well as the attempt to reintroduce devolved government for Northern Ireland), what was once a heavily centralized state has become much more decentralized. The creation of these additional tiers of government has also added to the multi-layered character of the British polity.

Secondly, as a result of devolution, Scotland and increasingly Wales have become much more autonomous subsystems within the United Kingdom with their own distinctive policies, political agendas, elites and institutional arrangements. Politics and policy in Northern Ireland had long been very different from those of the rest of the United Kingdom; with devolution, Scotland and Wales acquired increasingly divergent characters from each other and from England.

Thirdly, the coordination of policy making became an increasingly important task for the centre of government, generating new integrating bodies in the Cabinet Office and causing a reorganization of the responsibilities of both the territorial departments and the parliamentary bodies dealing with devolved areas.

Finally, the changes had the potential to rebalance institutional power within the system. Thus the Human Rights Act of 1998 and the partial incorporation of the European Convention on Human Rights into the domestic legal system seemed likely to

joined-up government Style of government which emphasizes that greater efficiency and effectiveness in policy making require greater integration at all levels and the reform of structural and other barriers that encourage fragmentation. The approach was endorsed by the Blair government on coming to power in 1997. Also called holistic government.

dissent Disagreement and opposition which can appear at many different levels of the political system. One powerful measure of dissent within the context of an organized parliamentary party is the frequency with which MPs have voted against the instructions given by the leadership in a whipped division.

cabinet government In Britain a form of government in which a group of senior ministers has executive responsibility. It is buttressed by the twin conventions of collective responsibility and individual ministerial responsibility. The way it works in practice has changed significantly over the years. Trends such as the enhanced power of the prime minister and the greater use of committees and informal procedures have caused many observers to argue that cabinet government has been so seriously undermined that it no longer serves as a useful description of how Britain is governed.

civil service In the UK the name given to the officials who are appointed to support the government, advising on policy and implementing it. Reform of the civil service in recent years has placed great emphasis on managerial skills.

strengthen the judiciary and to weaken the powers of both Parliament and the executive.

The role of the state and policy making

Labour came to power in 1997 at the end of a period in which there had been much questioning of the proper role of the state. Unlike the Conservative Party, which had placed great emphasis on the role of markets as instruments of policy delivery, Labour, it was assumed, would strengthen the role of state provision. Yet Labour's revised doctrinal beliefs made it much more pragmatic on questions of public and private provision of services and much more open to experiment with partnerships across the two sectors. Blair's governments accordingly maintained many of the administrative innovations that had occurred under Margaret Thatcher and John Major even though they relied heavily on ideas derived from the private sector and often reduced the role of the public sector. As a result, the role of the state remains a contested and lively question and there is considerable debate about how to improve policy making and policy delivery. (For an examination of the changing role of the state and the mechanisms by which public policy is coordinated, see chapter 3.)

When Labour returned to power in 1997 it did so with a determination to avoid the internal **dissent** which had damaged it in government and opposition from at least the early 1970s. Equally, it was determined to avoid the problems which John Major had encountered as a result of intra-party dissent. Blair wanted to project an image of strong leadership and consequently was anxious to make Britain's system of **cabinet government** a sharper tool for the central direction of government. (Chapter 4 examines in detail the role of the prime minister and cabinet and the operation of central government departments.)

One feature of Labour's administrative reform agenda was the need to ensure improved methods of policy making (which it was thought suffered from too much fragmentation). There was a search for ways of joining up government, namely, of overcoming the natural tendency of government policy to reflect departmental and organizational difference rather than focus on the totality of a policy problem. The same search occurred in relation to the delivery or implementation of policy. This objective led to the creation of a number of cross-departmental task forces, renewed emphasis on administrative reform and a new concern with enforcement. There was also continued effort to ensure that the **civil service** – the people who staffed the various departments of central government and

Box 1.7   Developments in the debate about standards in public life, 1990–2003

1994, July	Two Tory MPs (David Tredinnick and Graham Riddick) discovered to have accepted cash for putting down **parliamentary questions**.
1994, October	*Guardian* newspaper publishes material on the relationship between Neil Hamilton MP and Mr Mohammed Al-Fayed, owner of Harrods.
1994, October	Tim Smith and Neil Hamilton resign as ministers.
1994, October	(**Nolan**) Committee on Standards in Public Life announced.
1995, May	Nolan First Report proposes extensive new machinery and enunciates seven principles of public life.
1995, October	Select Committee on Standards in Public Life (CSPL) established to deal with Nolan recommendations (several subsequent reports on various aspects of conflict of interest).
1995	Code of Conduct for MPs embraces seven principles of public life.
1997	Labour government elected. Terms of reference of CSPL extended to cover political funding.
1997	Row about link between the exemption of Formula One racing from a projected ban on sports sponsorship by tobacco companies and a £1 million donation to Labour prior to the 1997 election by Formula One chief Bernie Ecclestone. Following embarrassing publicity and on the advice of the Committee on Standards in Public Life (CSPL), Labour hands the money back. The following year the CSPL begins its hearings on party funding.
1997	Home Office publishes working paper on preventing corruption.
1997, December	Surcharge of £31.6 million upheld against Dame Shirley Porter for her part in a complex homes for votes scandal in Westminster City Council.
1999	Jeffrey Archer withdraws as candidate for London mayoralty and is prosecuted for perjury.
1999	Jonathan Aitken jailed for perjury and perverting the course of justice.
1999	Hamilton loses libel case against Al-Fayed.
1999/2000	CSPL reviews impact of its First Report.
2000	Political Parties Elections and Referenda Act (PPERA) establishes Electoral Commission to regulate party spending at national level and donations.
2001	Keith Vaz exonerated by Standards and Privileges Committee on nine allegations of improper conduct.
2001/2	Elizabeth Filkin not offered automatic new contract as Parliamentary Commissioner for Standards.
2002	Sir Philip Mawer appointed as Standards Commissioner.
2002	Eighth Report of CSPL reviews standards in House of Commons.
2003	Standards and Privileges Committee suspends Michael Trend MP for two weeks in connection with his expenses claim.

parliamentary questions Written and oral questions from MPs and peers to ministers. Answers to written questions are printed in *Hansard*; oral questions are answered by ministers at departmental question time in the chamber.

Nolan Lord Nolan chaired the Committee on Standards in Public Life from its inception in 1994 to 1997. The Committee's first report into standards in public life (the Nolan Report) recommended substantial restrictions on MPs working for outside interests, which were adopted by the Major government in 1995.

the executive agencies – had the right skills and attitudes for the tasks involved. (The role of the British civil service is discussed in chapter 5.)

It has already been emphasized that one of the Blair government's major concerns was the modernization of the British system of government and that this concern was also a driving force in its approach to the workings of British democracy. In 1997, Blair inherited a situation in which there was a good deal of distrust in government, to a large extent the result of sleaze and corruption, which had become increasingly evident under the Conservative governments of the 1990s (see box 1.7). Although the Committee on Standards in Public Life has been vigorous in trying to set standards of probity across the many areas of British public life, and new machinery for monitoring ethics has been established (see box 1.8), the public still appears distrustful of politicians.

Alongside the distrust evidenced by opinion polls went a decline in participation in the country's political life. Turnout at British elections showed a decline in the 1997 general election (it was to fall still further in 2001), and it was extremely low at local and European elections (table 1.10; see also tables 2.5 and 15.3, pp. 66 and 498). Membership of political parties declined sharply. The public interest in, and awareness of, political issues is also limited.

Box 1.8 New machinery for monitoring ethics and standards in public life

A series of episodes of questionable conduct by MPs in the 1990s (for example, the 'cash for questions' affair in which two MPs appeared willing to take cash for putting down a parliamentary question and another MP, Neil Hamilton, was revealed to have had extensive financial dealings with Mohammed Al-Fayed, the owner of Harrods) led to the establishment of the Committee on Standards in Public Life. Originally chaired by Lord Nolan but now chaired by Sir Nigel Wicks, the Committee has issued a range of reports covering such topics as MPs' conduct, standards in local government and standards in the House of Lords. Its first report (published in 1995) prompted the establishment of new machinery to monitor the conduct of MPs. This new machinery, by imposing stricter rules and new enforcement mechanisms, represents a significant change from the much more informal regime of self-regulation which endured prior to 1995.

The key changes from 1995 were:

1 A ban on paid advocacy, i.e., putting down a question or raising a matter with a minister for payment.
2 A new office of Parliamentary Commissioner for Standards. The Commissioner has the responsibility of keeping the Register of MPs' interests. He or she also advises MPs on conduct and may investigate complaints.
3 A new Standards and Privileges Committee to oversee the work of the Parliamentary Commissioner and to investigate complaints against individual members.
4 A Code of Conduct for MPs which was first agreed in July 1996. A new code was agreed by the House of Commons in May 2002.

Source: Adapted from House of Commons information.

Table 1.10 Turnout at general elections since 1945

Election	Turnout (%)
1945	72.6
1950	83.6
1951	81.9
1955	76.8
1959	78.7
1964	77.1
1966	76.0
1970	72.2
1974 (Feb)	79.0
1974 (Oct)	73.0
1979	76.0
1983	72.8
1987	75.4
1992	77.8
1997	71.5
2001	59.4

Source: Institute for Democracy and Electoral Assistance, http://www.idea.int/vt/country_view.cfm

electoral reform A term usually used to refer to moves to abandon Britain's first past the post or simple plurality system.

In one way the programme of constitutional reform was a response to the declining interest in and commitment to political involvement, although it was noticeable that the one constitutional reform which many thought would aid political engagement – **electoral reform** for Westminster elections – was studiously ducked. In 2003 Charles Kennedy, the Liberal Democrat leader, virtually admitted that the prospect of electoral reform at Westminster had receded way beyond the horizon of political reality.

On other levels the Blair government attempted to supplement the constitutional reforms with innovative measures designed to enhance the democratic process. There was a radical overhaul of the machinery of electoral administration to facilitate participation (see chapter 7, which discusses the electoral system). There was a much-increased use of new technologies to consult the public on policy proposals. And there was a drive to increase civic education in schools.

There was, however, a tension running through much of the Labour government's efforts to enhance democratic participation. Blair and his cabinet professed a commitment to greater democracy but on a number of occasions the actions of the government appeared calculated to maximize government control, not genuine democratic choice. This fatal flaw ran through much of the constitutional reform effort as Blair's attempts to impose control on the Labour candidate selection process in Scotland, Wales and in London (using methods he had condemned in his modernization of Labour) belied his commitment to a greater pluralism. This ambiguity explained the omission or delay of certain items of constitutional reform – electoral reform and freedom of information – and it seemed to many critics that it marked the Blair government's approach to the reform of Parliament (Commission on Strengthening Parliament, 2000).

prime minister's questions (PMQs) A 30-minute weekly session in the Commons in which the prime minister answers oral questions from MPs. Questions are not given in advance so the prime minister must be prepared to answer on a wide range of subjects.

hollowing out of the state Theory associated with Professor Rhodes and with B. G. Peters that organizational and structural changes to the state (decentralization, devolution and deconcentration) have changed fundamentally the nature of modern governance.

Parliament

Parliament is in theory the source of authority and legitimacy in the British system of government. However, there are extensive problems with the way Parliament functions in practice. Parliament lacks resources to challenge the executive and the tight organization of political parties has long meant that it has found it difficult to exert an independent influence. Constitutional trends – including the growing power of supranational organizations such as the European Union and the devolution of power to subnational bodies – appeared to reduce the scope of parliamentary authority while the increasing concern with the media meant that many ministers preferred to announce their policy innovations on the radio or television rather than before Parliament (Riddell, 2000). Its hours and procedures often seemed archaic and irrelevant to mainstream policy debates. There was concern about the quality of representation within Parliament and worry that the important function of holding the executive accountable to the public was no longer possible via the use of parliamentary mechanisms.

The 1997 Labour government's approach to Parliament was like much of its other reforming and modernizing agenda – contradictory. On the one hand an extensive overhaul of parliamentary procedures was set in motion, generating interesting experiments with new forms of committee, with reforms of hours of sitting and an innovative use of Westminster Hall as a parallel debating chamber to the House of Commons. On the other hand, Labour continued to impose extremely tight discipline on its own parliamentary members, resisted initially at least any dilution of the power of party managers and made unilateral changes to the organization of **prime minister's questions (PMQs)**. Ministers and especially the prime minister reduced the amount of time spent in Parliament, which often appeared to be of marginal significance by comparison with the political world of government and the media.

The Impact of Europe

It is of course increasingly apparent that the British government's scope for autonomous decision making is limited both by the global economic environment and by the effects of British membership of the European Union (EU). This process of shrinkage in the role of the national state as a result of a growth in transnational policy making may be seen as part of a more general **hollowing out of the state**. Britain's role in Europe is one of the most bitterly contested issues of contemporary politics. Yet it is one which appears to engage political elites to a much greater extent than ordinary voters. In so far as citizens do have views about Europe, however, they appear to have become much more Eurosceptic in recent years (see table 1.11). And even as politicians and the media debate, often in strident tones, the future course of Britain's relationship with Europe, the reality of British participation in the European venture has been increasingly felt. Few aspects of British government can now be adequately

Table 1.11 Public attitudes to Europe

(a) Membership of the European Union

Q: If there were a referendum now on whether Britain should stay in or get out of the European Union, how would you vote?

Year	Stay in (%)	Get out (%)	Don't know (%)
1977	47	42	11
1980	26	65	9
1983	36	55	9
1987	48	39	13
1990	62	28	9
1992	52	35	13
1994	52	36	12
1997	40	40	19
1999	41	37	22
2000	53	32	15
2001	43	41	16

(b) Membership of the single currency

Q: If there were a referendum now on whether Britain should be part of a Single European Currency, how would you vote?

Year	In favour (%)	Against (%)	Don't know (%)
1991	33	54	13
1994	33	56	11
1995	29	60	11
1996	23	60	17
1997	22	58	19
1998	31	54	16
1999	31	53	15
2000	25	60	14
2001	28	57	15
2002	31	53	16
2003	31	57	11

All figures have been rounded down.

Source: MORI, http://www.mori.com/europe/index.shtml

discussed without reference to the European dimension that permeates the country's policy making and politics. Although British membership of the EU initially appeared to have only a limited impact on its domestic policies and governmental practices, it always contained the potential to challenge traditional constitutional customs. By 2003 many of the tensions produced by British membership of the 15-member union had become painfully apparent. Specifically, there was tension as the EU's agenda developed into new areas of policy, as enlargement required a revamping of the EU institutions and a convention to devise a constitution for the EU highlighted the quickening pace of integration.

The United Kingdom had opted to join the European Community (as the EU was then known) in part as a remedy for Britain's post-1945 comparative economic decline, a decline that was reflected in low growth rates and a host of economic ills. But Britain's late membership (in 1973 as opposed to 1955), together with her distinctive imperial past and her continuing strong ties to the United States, meant that she was never seen as entirely committed to the European project. The extent to which the United Kingdom's perspective on world affairs aligned her more closely with the United States than with the other members of the European Union was again underlined in 2003, when Britain strongly supported the US in the war against Iraq while most other members of the EU opposed it. Nor did the United Kingdom completely share the underlying philosophy of the other member states. Moreover, the organization which Britain joined in 1973 itself experienced rapid change in the 1980s and 1990s. It increased in size so that the original six members had become nine in 1973 and stood at 15 by 2003, with definite plans to become 25 in 2004 (see table 1.12). As other states signalled their desire to join, it was inevitable that the character of the EU should become uncertain.

There was also a change of pace in the internal dynamics of the EU in the period after 1980. The goal of an internal market was pursued with vigour and there was a quickening of progress towards political and financial integration. One element of the agenda of closer integration that proved peculiarly divisive in the United Kingdom was the drive towards Economic and Monetary Union (or European Monetary Union, EMU) and the introduction of a single European currency. Originally advocated in the 1988 Delors Report, EMU gained tangible form in 2002 when 12 of the 15 EU countries abandoned their separate national currencies for the euro. The United Kingdom – along with Denmark and Sweden – stayed

Table 1.12 EU members and candidates for membership

(a) Current members

Countries	Date of membership
France	1951
Germany	1951
Italy	1951
Netherlands	1951
Belgium	1951
Luxembourg	1951
United Kingdom	1973
Denmark	1973
Ireland	1973
Greece	1981
Spain	1986
Portugal	1986
Austria	1995
Finland	1995
Sweden	1995

(b) Candidates

Countries	Expected date of membership
Hungary	mid-2004
Poland	mid-2004
Czech Republic	mid-2004
Slovakia	mid-2004
Slovenia	mid-2004
Estonia	mid-2004
Latvia	mid-2004
Lithuania	mid-2004
Malta	mid-2004
Cyprus	mid-2004

out. The question of whether or not the United Kingdom joins the single currency remains a pressing one, not least because the decision as to whether or not to do so involves the assessment of complex economic criteria and political judgement.

Over the period 1973–2003 the European issue became increasingly disruptive to the internal cohesion of the parties. In the early 1970s and 1980s it was Labour that was most divided over European issues. But New Labour increasingly became pro-European and from the 1980s disagreements over European policy inflicted massive damage on the Conservative Party. On one level the disruptive impact of European issues on the Conservative Party might seem surprising. After all, the Conservatives have generally valued party unity so highly that both the leadership and the party as a whole developed a common interest in avoiding faction and moderating issue conflict (see chapter 8, which provides further discussion of internal party factionalism). It was the Conservative Party that under Macmillan and Heath sought to take the UK into Europe in the first place. Increasingly, however, European policies provoked Conservative opposition. Few Conservatives liked the idea of a federal Europe and most felt more comfortable leaving power in the hands of a strong nation state. In addition, the style of European policy making with its emphasis on negotiation and brokerage rather than **adversarial politics** was alien to many Tory politicians. The **corporatist** flavour of European social policy was also viewed with suspicion by many free marketeers and the keystone European policies of the Common Agricultural Policy (CAP) and the Common Fisheries Policy (CFP) were also greatly disliked.

Increasingly, Conservative leaders began to legitimize anti-European sentiments within the party. Although Edward Heath had been a committed European, Margaret Thatcher especially towards the end of her premiership became closely associated with anti-integrationist perspectives. Her hostility towards the EU was by no means shared by all her cabinet colleagues, so that European issues repeatedly divided her government in its final years. So acute had the intra-party divisions become by the 1990s that John Major's 1992–7 government was effectively crippled by the wrangling over European issues that touched all levels of the party. (See boxes 1.9, 1.10, 1.11) After the loss of the 1997 election the Conservatives became even more hostile to Europe, committing themselves to a policy of exclusion from the single European currency and electing three successive leaders (William Hague, Iain Duncan Smith and Michael Howard; see boxes 1.12, 1.13 and 1.14) who were clearly opposed to further European integration.

Labour's landslide victory in 1997 brought to power a prime minister who was enthusiastic about putting Britain at the heart of Europe. This Labour victory did not mean, however, that British positions were immediately aligned with those of other EU members. The issue of British membership of EMU exposed internal divisions within the new Labour government about the wisdom of joining.

adversarial politics Style of politics in which the need to oppose government policy is emphasized rather than building consensus. Closely associated with the Westminster model of parliamentary democracy and two-party dominance.

corporatism A system of government in which key interest groups representing labour and capital are included in the policy-making process. Although the state loses its autonomy, it gains the support of these groups in the implementation of policy as well as enhanced legitimacy.

Box 1.9   Edward Heath (1916–)

Heath was the Tories' first working-class prime minister. He entered Parliament in 1950, rose to the Conservative Party leadership in 1965, and was prime minister from 1970 to 1974. He entered 10 Downing Street with a right-wing agenda, pledging to reduce state involvement in the economy and weaken the unions, but his premiership floundered under economic recession and industrial unrest. His most memorable achievement was taking Britain into Europe in 1973. He refused striking miners a wage rise, preferring to suffer a three-day week and then call an early poll in February 1974, which the Conservatives narrowly lost. In a subsequent election in October 1974, Labour won a clear victory. Heath was challenged as party leader in 1975 and lost to Margaret Thatcher, a defeat which he bitterly resented. In later years he became a leadership critic and ardent pro- European on the backbenches.

Box 1.10   Margaret Thatcher (1925–)

The daughter of a grocer, Thatcher trained as a chemist before entering Parliament in 1959. She held the pensions portfolio under Macmillan, and was Secretary of State for Education in the Heath administration of 1970–4. In the leadership election that followed the Conservatives' defeat in 1974, Thatcher won a surprise victory and began to develop a free-market critique of the so-called post-war consensus (see box 3.1, p. 91). When the Conservatives came to power in the 1979 election, Thatcher began to implement a radical agenda of monetarist economics, privatization and anti-trade unionism. She won three successive general elections –

poll tax A form of local government taxation introduced in Britain in the late 1980s, formally called the community charge. The poll tax was levied on all adults rather than on a household basis, and was deeply unpopular.

in 1979, 1983 and 1987 – and was widely commended for her handling of the Falklands War with Argentina in 1982. Her autocratic leadership style brought her into conflict with cabinet members, however, and her imposition of the **poll tax** policy despite public protest was seen as damaging to the party's electoral prospects. In 1990, in a leadership challenge, which she perceived as a great betrayal, Conservative MPs failed to back her in sufficient numbers and opted for the more conciliatory John Major to replace her.

Gordon Brown, Blair's powerful Chancellor of the Exchequer (see box 1.15), and the Treasury exhibited greater scepticism than the prime minister about the idea of joining the euro. In part this was because the UK's position made the economic advantages of joining difficult to calculate (see box 1.16). In part it was because there was also uncertainty about the process by which entry could be achieved without damaging the government's standing. Labour has promised that the issue of entry will be put to a referendum. Given that public opinion had moved in a Eurosceptic direction, a referendum seemed to combine the likelihood of

Box 1.11   John Major (1934–)

Coming from a poor south London background with little formal education, Major was elected to the Commons in 1979 as MP for Huntingdon. He held the positions of Foreign Secretary and Chancellor of the Exchequer under Thatcher. When Conservative MPs failed to give decisive support to Thatcher during the leadership contest of 1990, he emerged as the frontrunner to succeed her. He was prime minister from 1990 to 1997, winning a surprise victory for the Conservatives in the 1992 election. The period from 1992 to 1997 was a difficult one for Major as he struggled to lead a party riven by splits on Europe and destabilized by sleaze. In 1995 he resigned as party leader and put himself forward in a leadership contest, challenging Conservative MPs to 'put up or shut up'. He won, but without the decisive mandate from backbenchers that he had hoped for. His administration limped along until 1997, when it lost heavily to Blair's New Labour Party in the May general election.

Box 1.12   William Hague (1961–)

After making his name with a speech to the Conservative Party conference aged 16, Hague entered Parliament in 1989 as MP for Richmond in Yorkshire. He held the Welsh Portfolio under Major. When Major stood down after the 1997 election defeat, Hague stood for the leadership. His Eurosceptic stance won him the support of Conservative MPs who rejected his better-known rival, Kenneth Clarke, for his pro-European views. As leader of a party coming to terms with the scale of the 1997 defeat, he was faced with the difficult job of turning the party around. He introduced significant intra-party reforms, unifying the party organization for the first time and devolving power to individual members. He was considered an impressive performer at the dispatch box but opinion polls indicated that he was failing to impress the public. When the Conservatives lost the 2001 general election by almost the same margin as the 1997 defeat, Hague resigned as leader.

Box 1.13   Iain Duncan Smith (1954–)

MP for Chingford and Woodford Green since 1992, Duncan Smith was best known during the 1990s for his opposition to European integration. He was one of nine Conservative MPs who resigned the party whip under Major in the mid-1990s in protest at the ratification of the Maastricht Treaty. When Hague resigned as leader after the 2001 election defeat, Duncan Smith fought off challenges from high-profile candidates such as Michael Portillo and Ken Clarke to emerge as the surprise winner. His anti-European views appeared to be in accordance with those of fellow Conservative MPs and party members. As leader he struggled to establish a distinctive position for the Conservative Party and provoked criticism for his luke-warm approach to modernization. His failure to raise electoral support for the party over 2003 led to a vote of no confidence, which he lost, thereby triggering his resignation.

Box 1.14   Michael Howard (1941–)

Michael Howard was unanimously elected leader of the Conservative Party in November 2003 following a vote of no confidence in Iain Duncan Smith. The son of immigrants from eastern Europe, Howard was educated at grammar school and Cambridge University. He established a successful practice at the bar and became an MP in 1983. Thereafter he held a succession of offices in Margaret Thatcher's and John Major's governments. As Home Secretary from 1993 to 1997 he acquired a controversial reputation for his approach to penal policy. Michael Howard's emergence as the Conservative leader was in many ways a surprise. He had come last in the leadership contest of 1997 and, although appointed shadow Foreign Secretary in 1999, he had retired from the Conservative front bench in 1999. However, with the election of Iain Duncan Smith in 2001, Howard was appointed shadow Chancellor, a position in which he was able to use his financial expertise and debating skills. The decision to elect Howard as leader indicates the Conservative Party's frustration at its continuing inability to make an impact with the public, but it also marks a shift back to someone with extensive experience in government even at the risk of reviving associations with the Thatcher–Major years. For his part, Michael Howard appears keen to shed his right-wing image and to move in the direction of those who argue for modernization. He has also moved swiftly to assert his power over the party machine and over a reduced shadow cabinet in an effort to eliminate the factionalism that has so weakened the Conservatives in recent years.

Box 1.15   Gordon Brown (1951–)

Entering Parliament in the 1983 election as MP for Dunfermline East, Brown shared an office with Tony Blair. He entered the shadow cabinet in 1985 as trade and industry spokesperson, but it was his handling of the shadow Treasury portfolio from 1992 onwards that brought him to prominence. When John Smith died in 1994, he agreed not to run as a candidate to allow Blair the best chance of winning, a decision which is said to have soured the relationship between the two men. As Chancellor of the Exchequer since 1997 he has been famous for his 'prudence' in running the economy. His stature in the cabinet is second only to Blair's and he enjoys large amounts of autonomy in the appointment of junior ministers. Friends and foes claim that he hopes to become prime minister when Blair retires.

Box 1.16   The five economic tests for joining the euro

The five economic tests set out by Gordon Brown in October 1997 are:

- sustainable **convergence** between Britain and the economies of a single currency;
- whether there is sufficient **flexibility** to cope with economic change;
- the effect on **investment**;
- the impact on our **financial services** industry;
- whether it is good for **employment**.

Source: HM Treasury, http://www.hm-treasury.gov.uk/Documents/The_Euro/euro_index_index.cfm

political disruption with a limited likelihood of success. Thus, although the question of close integration into the European Union was nowhere near as divisive for the Labour Party as it was for the Conservative opposition, it was still not straightforward.

Despite the heated debates about the direction of the European project, behind the scenes, as we have noted, the processes of British government had increasingly adapted to the challenges of membership of the European Union. At the level of central government, ministers and civil servants had developed increasingly close ties with their opposite numbers within the EU. Parliamentary procedures had been adapted to try to allow British parliamentary opinion to be taken into account in the formative stages of policy. The British judiciary increasingly found themselves applying the developing body of European law and having to resolve cases of conflict between domestic and EU law.

From the perspective of the British system of government as a whole, membership of the European Union inevitably makes the policy-making process itself more complex because it engages different layers of government and involves more actors. Obviously, the extent of the European dimension of British government also varies considerably between policy sectors. Thus it is extensive in matters relating to competition, trade, agriculture and employment but is relatively limited as yet in such policy areas as education, law and order and health. This growing impact of Europe and what has been described as the advent of a multi-layered polity is reflected in all of the chapters of the book, although, as in previous editions, there is a separate chapter which looks in more detail at the operation of European institutions (see chapter 15).

Pressures arising from membership of the European Union are not, however, the only international influences on British government. There are a host of other international organizations in which Britain participates (see box 1.17). Ultimately, the United Kingdom's political system has to adjust to the realities of an economic environment that is increasingly global. A global economy means that not merely are financial markets becoming more and more integrated across national boundaries, they also operate in a way that is outside the control of the national government's authority. From the perspective of the British citizen, the growing power of the European Union (as indeed of other transnational and international bodies) raises important issues of **accountability**. Not only are the structures of British democracy increasingly ill-fitted to control the vast array of governmental activity that takes place beyond the borders of the nation state; there are also some areas where it is difficult to see any mechanism for inducing control or responsiveness.

Conclusions

Recent years have seen growing criticism of many traditional aspects of British government as well as a series of pressures from outside the system on its policy-making processes. The Blair government in 1997 initiated some major changes in the country's institutional arrangements, believing that a controlled

accountability System of control and answerability which is seen as an inherent part of democratic and representative government. The mechanisms by which accountability is enforced vary, but may include political, legal and informal methods.

> **Box 1.17** Major international organizations in which the UK participates
>
> - European Union
> - Council of Europe
> - Organization for Security and Cooperation in Europe
> - Commonwealth
> - United Nations
> - NATO
> - G8
>
> *Source*: Foreign Office, http://www.fco.gov.uk

and selective process of constitutional reform would modernize the British political system and refresh its democratic practice. Whether these reforms could be grafted onto the existing patterns of government remains an open question and, even if they can be, it is not at all clear that the government's agenda is sufficient to re-engage the public with the country's political life. In the next chapter we examine the United Kingdom's constitutional framework in order to see how well traditional concepts and understandings have meshed with the major reforms of the Blair years.

 Key Questions

1 What would you expect to be the political impact of recent social and economic changes in the United Kingdom?
2 How far is the United Kingdom able to set its own policy agenda?
3 What factors encourage individuals to participate in the political process?

 Further Reading

Excellent historical analyses of the United Kingdom can be found in K. O. Morgan, *The People's Peace* (Oxford: Oxford University Press, 1999) and in D. Childs, *Britain since 1945: A Political History* (5th edn; London: Routledge, 2001). David Marquand and Anthony Seldon, *The Ideas that Shaped Post-war Britain* (London: Fontana, 1996) looks at the intellectual influence on post-1945 British history. M. Foley, *The Politics of the British Constitution* (Manchester: Manchester University Press, 1999) traces the evolution of the debate about the constitution.

Two studies by journalists offer illuminating perspectives on the demand for change in the organization of the British state: Andrew Marr, *Ruling Britannia* (London: Penguin, 1996) focuses primarily on political issues, while Will Hutton's *The State We're In* (London: Vintage, 1996) is a survey with a strong economic argument.

The weaknesses of the British system of democracy are explored in D. Beetham, I. Byrne, P. Ngan and S. Weir, *Democracy Under Blair: A Democratic Audit of the United Kingdom*

(London: Politicos in association with Democratic Audit, Human Rights Centre, University of Essex, 2002).

Issues related to ethnicity and culture can be investigated further in David Mason, *Race and Ethnicity in Modern Britain* (2nd edn; Oxford: Oxford University Press, 2000). Immigration is covered well in Randall Hansen, *Citizenship and Immigration in Post-war Britain: The Institutional Origins of a Multicultural Nation* (Oxford: Oxford University Press, 2000). The political aspects of ethnic diversity are examined in Shammit Saggar, *Race and Politics in Britain* (London: Harvester Wheatsheaf, 1992).

Popular attitudes are reviewed in the various volumes of the *British Social Attitudes* survey. See for example A. Park, J. Curtice, K. Thomson, L. Jarvis and C. Bromley, *British Social Attitudes: The 19th Report* (London: National Centre for Social Research, 2002). A wealth of statistical data and basic information about the United Kingdom compiled by the Office for National Statistics is to be found in the official publication *UK 2003 Yearbook* (London: HMSO, 2003).

Websites

See also the list of general websites at the back of the book.

- www.statistics.gov.uk – Office for National Statistics
- www.cre.gov.uk – Campaign for Racial Equality
- www.eoc.org.uk – Equal Opportunities Commission

2 The Constitution

One of the most marked features of British political life in the last decade has been the extent to which constitutional issues have become a prominent part of the political agenda. As noted in chapter 1, a number of factors fuelled dissatisfaction with the United Kingdom's traditional constitutional arrangements and generated diverse demands for reform. The advent of a Labour government in 1997 saw the introduction of a number of radical changes to many fundamental aspects of the British governmental system as part of an unusually wide-ranging and explicit programme of constitutional modernization. Among the most important changes of the Blair 1997–2001 term were the passage of a Human Rights Act in 1998, the creation of devolved governmental systems in Scotland, Wales and Northern Ireland, regional decentralization, a new directly elected London mayor, reform of the House of Lords, freedom of information legislation, and the use of different electoral systems at the subnational level.

These changes grafted onto Britain's traditional institutions and politics a number of new decision-making structures, introducing new procedures and methods of working. They created powerful new political arenas which generated new patterns of political competition and cooperation. And they further stimulated debate about the core democratic values of legitimacy, accountability and representation. In this chapter we shall examine the role of the constitution and of constitutional argument in the British political system. We shall also examine in some detail the extensive constitutional reform measures introduced since 1997 as well as continuing points of constitutional tension within the system. Finally, we will attempt an assessment of the impact of constitutional change on the whole process of British government and its style of politics. First, however, it is necessary to examine the role of constitutions in modern states and the distinctive character of the British constitution.

bill of rights Statement of civil liberties or individual rights. The Bill of Rights of 1689 established parliamentary supremacy over the Crown. It did not, however, provide the kind of comprehensive statement of civil liberties found in many modern states. By incorporating most of the European Convention on Human Rights, the Human Rights Act of 1998 gives the UK a statement of rights and liberties.

What is a Constitution?

A constitution provides the basic framework for a country's system of government by prescribing the principles, rules and procedures within which power will be exercised. Specifically, a constitution will usually define (at least in outline) the relationship between the key institutions within a state (for example between the legislature and the executive) and it will often also define the relationship between the state and its citizens, for example by reference to a **bill of rights** or a statement of civil liberties. A constitution is thus in part about operating procedures and values as well as about institutional arrangements. For most countries the constitution is a single document which provides a starting point for understanding the character of the political system, although a full understanding of the way any political system operates requires knowledge of much additional formal legal material and of the role of informal institutions and forces such as **pressure groups** and parties in the system. In most political systems also there will be a single authoritative body, usually in the form of a constitutional court, to resolve disputes about the meaning of the constitution.

The Distinctive Character of the British Constitution

Any attempt to understand the British constitution is subject to greater difficulties than confront the observer of the character and impact of the constitution in other democratic systems. In virtually all other countries (though New Zealand and Israel are to some extent exceptions), the basic principles of the constitutions are not only formally set out in a single text but are also recognized as superior rules which bind the players in the political game. In the United Kingdom, where there is no single comprehensive constitutional document, constitutional principles have to be gleaned from a number of sources; and there is often no agreement about their meaning nor any mechanism to enforce them. Some disputes with a constitutional dimension do reach the courts and, as we shall see, recent constitutional changes may be expected to increase the number of issues that are **justiciable**. But there remain many areas of constitutional doubt where it is not possible to settle the dispute definitively. As a result, the British constitution is more amorphous and contested than is normal in other modern democracies.

Instead of a formal constitutional document, the United Kingdom's constitution is frequently analysed in terms of historical evolution and organic growth. In part the reason why the United Kingdom has no single comprehensive constitution indeed reflects the fact that there has been no major point of regime change since the seventeenth century and no revolution or founding moment at which a new constitution might have been written. Instead, major changes in the character of the political system have occurred slowly. Thus the evolution of the political system from a personal monarchy to a parliamentary democracy occurred incrementally over the period from 1689 (see box 2.1).

Many of these radical changes in the basis of authority within the polity occurred not merely without a revolution but also without changing the outward form of many of Britain's institutions. The limitation of royal power, the expansion of the franchise to full adult suffrage, the dismantling of the Empire and membership of the European Union have all occurred without any formal break in the continuity of the state, even though these momentous changes

pressure group An organization which is formed to promote a cause or interest. Such organizations have a limited agenda and do not themselves seek to govern the country, though they may run candidates for office as part of their general strategy to change public opinion and influence the policy process. Alternative terms may be interest groups or lobbying organizations.

justiciability Term used to describe issues which properly fall within the jurisdiction of the courts. The concept is sometimes also used in a prescriptive manner to describe issues which are capable of being resolved by legal means and which therefore should be resolved by a court. Justiciable issues are often contrasted with 'political' or policy issues for which courts might seem inappropriate decision-making bodies.

Westminster model System of parliamentary government found in the UK and a number of Commonwealth countries which has a number of distinct features and which contrasts with the parliamentary systems found in continental Europe. The government (which consists of a prime minister and cabinet) is formed from the majority party. The second largest party forms the opposition. Politics is adversarial. The British version is widely seen as promoting stable government, although its use of the simple plurality system is criticized for its unfairness to minorities.

prime minister The head of the government and leader of the cabinet. A prime minister's position usually derives from his or her position as leader of the majority party in Parliament. The role is an extremely powerful one, although there are substantial variations in authority and style among individual holders of the office.

concentration of powers/separation of powers The extent to which powers within a state are divided between different institutions and people – especially between the executive, legislative and judicial powers – and the extent to which powers are concentrated in the same institutions and personnel. In a democracy it is often considered preferable to separate these powers, although in the UK they are largely concentrated through the cabinet, which is drawn for the most part from the House of Commons and controls it through the party system.

Box 2.1   The evolution of the British system of parliamentary democracy

Magna Carta 1215: Limited the absolute power of the monarch. The king agreed to consult his barons and to abide by a charter of liberties. Led to the establishment of the House of Lords.

Bill of Rights 1689: Established a constitutional monarchy, subject to laws passed by a sovereign Parliament.

Act of Union 1707: Established Great Britain by the union of England and Scotland.

Representation of the People Act 1832 (sometimes known as the First Reform Act): Modest reform of the electoral law, extension of the franchise to some adult male property owners and redistribution of seats. Followed by further extensions of the franchise in 1867 and 1884, which enfranchised all male property owners.

Parliament Act 1911: Lords' power to reject legislation reduced to a two-year delaying power, with no power to delay money legislation.

Representation of the People Act 1918: Abolished property qualification for voting, extending franchise to all men over 21 and women over 30. Voting age equalized in 1928.

Parliament Act 1949: Lords' delaying power over bills other than money bills reduced to one year.

Life Peerages Act 1958: Introduced life peers into the House of Lords.

Representation of the People Act 1969: Reduced voting age to 18.

House of Lords Act 1999: Removed the right of all but 92 hereditary peers to sit in the House of Lords.

have had significant repercussions on the theory and practice of British government.

The *form* of the British system of government has long provided a distinctive model of constitutional government – the so-called **Westminster model** – which has been exported to many other countries especially within the Commonwealth, although those countries have added their own variations to it. The executive (a **prime minister** and cabinet) is selected from, and answerable to, a democratically elected and, in the case of the United Kingdom, legally sovereign Parliament. It is thus very different from a **separation of**

powers model as found in the United States, where the executive (the president) is separately elected from the legislature. Indeed, as Geoffrey Marshall has written,

> Much of the world's constitution-making reflects the competing claims of the English **concentration of powers** and the American separation of powers – one featuring a theory of legislative sovereignty with ideological roots in Hobbes; the other a doctrine of equal and semi-autonomous authorities, in part derived from the Lockean philosophy of restricted governmental power and natural law. (Marshall, 1971)

The emphasis on the Westminster model's concentration of powers is of crucial importance for understanding both the character of the United Kingdom's constitutional inheritance and the reasons for recent demands for constitutional reform. In the United Kingdom, the formal and theoretical concentration of power in the hands of the legislature became identified with the country's adherence to **responsible and representative government**. Yet in practice that concentration of power in the legislature became a concentration of power in the hands of the government of the day because from the late nineteenth century the executive was able to control the legislature through a disciplined party system. The expansion of the franchise led directly to increased **party cohesion** in Parliament as well as enhanced party organization to secure the voters' support. Although **whipped votes** were not the norm in the first half of the nineteenth century, by 1900 some 90 per cent of the divisions were organized on party lines. Thus a government which had perhaps gained power as a result of only a slender electoral advantage could govern for the lifetime of the Parliament with few serious checks on its power.

It is also important to note that some of the checks on executive power which exist in other systems (and which certainly mark the United States) are not prominent features of British democracy. For example, by the end of the twentieth century the United Kingdom had become a highly centralized state in the sense that there was no strong independent system of local government to challenge the central government's authority. Nor was there much room for a strong judicial role, although as will be seen later significant developments in the late twentieth century are now creating a potentially much more powerful judiciary. The benefits attributed to the British system of democracy were that it allowed a government with a working majority the opportunity to implement its programme and that it allowed a government to be held accountable to the electorate for its stewardship. The disadvantage of the system was that it could easily produce what Lord Hailsham in the 1970s called an '**elective dictatorship**'.

responsible government System of government in which the executive is formally answerable and accountable to the legislature, representative assembly or Parliament. The effectiveness of responsible government depends on a number of factors, including the resources of the legislature, the techniques of scrutiny available and the extent to which it itself is controlled by the executive through patronage or party discipline.

representative government System of government in which the people elect members of a legislature or other body to represent them.

party cohesion The extent to which a political party votes together in legislative divisions.

whipped votes Votes or divisions in Parliament in which the party instructs its members how to vote.

elective dictatorship Phrase coined by Lord Hailsham to refer to the ability under the British constitution of a party elected with only a small plurality of the votes or seats to exercise untrammelled power because of the absence of checks and balances on the executive.

The Sources of the Constitution

The absence of a single written constitutional document has meant that recourse has to be had to a variety of sources for the rules and

convention Unwritten rules which govern political conduct but which do not have legal force. Their strength is that they are flexible, their weakness that they can be broken and are often unclear. Traditionally there has been a wide use of conventions in the British constitution, although the period since 1979 has seen an expansion of the use of written statements of practice.

Crown Monarch personally but usually used in a governmental context to refer to ministers and departments.

principles of the British constitution. These sources are of many different types, including prerogative power, judicial decisions, statute and **conventions**. In addition, reference may be made to a range of secondary authorities such as A. V. Dicey, Walter Bagehot and Ivor Jennings. Unfortunately, such secondary authorities are unlikely to resolve hard constitutional issues or to provide a complete guide to the workings of the British political system, not least because all these writers have their own particular concerns and values which may not be shared by the courts or the country's political elites. It is also the case that in many secondary works on the constitution the descriptive and prescriptive elements are difficult to disentangle. In addition, the passage of time may render some constitutional writings less relevant, just as contemporary writing from authorities such as Geoffrey Marshall, Vernon Bogdanor and Robert Hazell may suffer from being too close to the events they are interpreting.

The sources of the British constitution themselves reflect the country's historical continuity and the weight put on both precedent and pragmatism in British political life. Here we examine briefly five constitutional sources:

1 prerogative powers
2 judicial decisions
3 statute
4 convention
5 texts and secondary authorities

Prerogative powers

The United Kingdom is a monarchy and the monarch traditionally had a very wide range of powers. Battles between the monarch and Parliament resulted in the imposition of restrictions on monarchical absolutism and the evolution of the United Kingdom into a parliamentary democracy. However, although the monarchy is now a constitutional one and the queen exercises virtually no political power in her own right, the **Crown** has retained its wide-ranging prerogative powers. Today all of these powers are exercised either by ministers individually on the Crown's behalf or by ministers collectively. The executive thus has at its disposal a highly convenient source of authority.

Important examples of prerogative powers include the prerogative of mercy (exercised on the monarch's behalf by the Home Secretary), the conduct of foreign affairs and the power to declare war. As a result, the government enjoys a considerable amount of freedom in the field of foreign policy so that it can make treaties, recognize foreign governments and issue passports without need for parliamentary approval. The deployment of troops may be done by prerogative power, as was the case with the Falklands conflict in 1982. Parliament would normally expect to be notified of new treaty arrangements and it would have to pass legislation if the treaty involved any alteration to domestic law. Similarly, Parliament would expect to be offered an immediate opportunity to debate the commitment of armed forces abroad. The 2003 decision to invade Iraq was highly controversial within the Labour Party and the government regarded Parliament's support as politically necessary even if not legally essential. Accordingly, the government allowed a debate in March 2003 prior to the invasion and that debate was widely seen as crucial both to authorizing the commitment of British troops and to Blair's own political survival. Whether the handling of the Iraq crisis constitutes a precedent remains to be seen; but it suggests that a government will hesitate to commit the armed forces to military action where political support is less than certain.

The ability of a government to use these powers with little parliamentary oversight and limited judicial control is seen by some observers as evidence of the way the British system of government has ingeniously retained the instruments of a pre-democratic period for use by a democratically elected government. Certainly, the prerogative powers can prove extremely convenient when action needs to be taken quickly or when no statutory authority exists.

Other critics regard prerogative powers as anomalies in a modern democratic system and think they should be abandoned or at least codified. Indeed, some critics are concerned that British membership of the European Union has generated an increase in the use of prerogative power because of the extensive power which ministers have to assent to or dissent from European legislation in the Council of Ministers. This executive participation in European legislation occurs independently of parliamentary approval, although the executive's actions may be constrained informally by parliamentary opinion.

Prerogative power is thus enormously important across the range of government activities, providing a constitutional basis among other things for the executive's power to make judicial appointments or to organize the civil service. Prerogative power gives the executive an independent source of legislative power in that the monarch may issue so-called **Orders in Council**, which have the force of law. During the seventeenth and eighteenth centuries the monarch's power to legislate without parliamentary approval was the subject of intense constitutional controversy. The Bill of Rights of 1689 limited the power of the monarch to legislate by **royal prerogative** but did not abolish it entirely. Thus the Crown has retained the power to legislate independently of Parliament, although today that power is limited in scope and is always exercised by the monarch on the advice of her elected ministers meeting as the Privy Council. Prerogative powers, including the power to legislate, thus provide a very broad authority for the executive to use in a range of situations in the modern state (see boxes 2.2 and 2.3).

There are, however, two important constitutional prerogative powers that are seen as being personal to the monarch. These are the power to appoint a prime minister and the power to grant a **dissolution** of Parliament within its five-year term. (The maximum life of a Parliament has been set at five years since 1911 when the Parliament Act reduced the maximum life of a Parliament from

Orders in Council Decree or order made by the monarch with the advice of the Privy Council. The power to issue such orders effectively gives the executive a broad legislative power, although it is only used as an alternative to primary legislation in extreme circumstances. Orders in Council are widely used as a form of delegated legislation.

royal prerogative Power which was exercised by the monarch without parliamentary oversight – such as the ratification of treaties and the issuing of passports. Most of these powers have now passed to the government and the prime minister.

dissolution Formal name given to the process of ending the life of one Parliament and calling a general election. Theoretically the decision is taken by the monarch, but in fact the choice is that of the prime minister of the day. The maximum life of a Parliament is five years in normal circumstances, although in exceptional circumstances Parliament may be continued.

Box 2.2 Different types of prerogative power

The royal prerogative powers include:

- Making Orders in Council.
- Declaring war or committing the United Kingdom forces to armed conflict.
- Making treaties.
- Recognizing foreign governments.
- Appointing ambassadors, permanent secretaries of departments, the heads of the security services, members of the Defence Staff, Royal Commissions and members of public bodies.
- Declaring a state of emergency.
- Issuing pardons and detaining felons or the insane during her majesty's pleasure.
- Instituting or quashing legal proceedings.

Box 2.3 Parliamentary question to the prime minister on royal prerogative powers

Mr Allen: To ask the Prime Minister if he will list the power which he may exercise under the Royal Prerogative; and if he will make it his policy to (a) keep a list of his use of Royal Prerogative powers and (b) place it in the Library each year.

The Prime Minister: Records are not kept of the individual occasions on which powers under the Royal Prerogative are exercised, nor could it be practicable to do so.

Source: House of Commons, *Hansard*, 18 November 2002, Vol. 394, Col. 19W.

seven years to five. However, in cases of national emergency the life of Parliament may be extended.) The monarch normally has no personal discretion in the exercise of these powers. In the case of the appointment of a prime minister after an election, the monarch sends for the leader of the party with a majority in the House of Commons. In the case of a dissolution, there will rarely be any question but that the monarch will accept a prime minister's request for a dissolution of Parliament and for a consequent general election. Nevertheless, there remains an element of uncertainty surrounding the use of these powers and commentators have speculated about the extent to which they could be used in a political crisis or extreme situation. Of course, such circumstances are rare and those who speculate about whether the prerogative remains available for use in an emergency are divided over the existence and desirability of acknowledging any residual role for the monarch even in the most hypothetical of situations (see box 2.4). Some critics of the prerogative power have therefore suggested ways both of transferring to Parliament some of the powers currently available to the executive and of codifying the procedures to be followed by the monarch in the event of such a crisis (Hennessy, 1995; Hennessy and Anstey, 1992). For the moment, however, prerogative powers remain important mainly as a

Box 2.4   The role of the monarch

- Symbolizes continuity of the state, e.g. opening Parliament.
- Personalizes government, e.g. award of honours, reception of visiting heads of state, attendance at ceremonial and civic functions.
- Performs key political functions, e.g. appoints prime minister, dissolves Parliament.
- Law-making powers – royal assent to legislation; use of prerogative power.
- Presides over Privy Council.
- Personal advice to prime minister.
- Head of Commonwealth.

source of flexible constitutional authority for the government rather than as mechanisms by which the monarch could exert her personal influence.

Judicial decisions

Judicial decisions have long formed an important source of rules on constitutionally important issues. In the seventeenth, eighteenth and nineteenth centuries the courts were important institutions protecting the liberties of the individual – including freedom from arbitrary arrest and from arbitrary search and seizure. The courts performed this task in the absence of a codified bill of rights, and indeed for a long period the common law was seen as a powerful protector of the rule of law and a barrier against executive power. However, much of the power of the courts in relation to civil liberties consisted historically of asserting the somewhat residual right of the individual in the absence of a law to the contrary. Such an approach, as that adopted in the 1882 case of *Beatty* v. *Gillbanks*, was not supportive of positive rights; thus the courts could not offer much protection against statutory invasion of civil rights and freedoms (see box 2.5). As a result of the expanding tendency of governments to regulate extensive areas of public life, the effectiveness of this kind of approach to

Box 2.5   *Beatty* v. *Gillbanks*

The *Beatty* v. *Gillbanks* (1882) case arose from attempts to restrict members of the Salvation Army from marching in the streets of Weston-super-Mare, because their presence attracted a hostile crowd. Limits on their freedom to march were overturned on appeal where it was held that persons who lawfully and peaceably assembled could not be convicted of the offence that they did 'unlawfully and tumultuously assemble with divers other persons ... to the disturbance of the public peace, and against the peace of our sovereign Lady the Queen'. They did nothing unlawful and the evidence showed that the disturbances were caused by other people antagonistic to the appellants.

Source: Judgements of the House of Lords, http://www.parliament.the-stationery-office.co.uk

Box 2.6   Controversial statutes affecting civil liberties

Official Secrets Act 1911: Wide-ranging pre-First World War legislation designed to protect official information.

Police and Criminal Evidence Act 1984: Comprehensive legislation strengthening police powers to arrest without a warrant.

Human Rights Act 1998: Landmark legislation designed to provide legal protection for human rights in the UK.

Anti-Terrorism, Crime and Security Act 2001: Legislation introduced after the 9/11 attacks on New York. Allows detention of foreign nationals suspected of being a threat to national security.

Regulation of Investigatory Powers (Extension) Act 2000 (with extensions): Enables government to acquire information about individuals' Internet and electronic communications.

judicial review Process by which the courts scrutinize administrative or legislative acts to see if they are legal. In the UK, courts may examine an Act of Parliament to see if it conforms to the Human Rights Act or if it is in conflict with EU legislation. Subordinate legislation and administrative action are frequently reviewed by the courts.

civil liberties diminished. In the last quarter of the twentieth century, concern grew about the government's powers in such areas as censorship, public order, policing and surveillance (see box 2.6). Given that the courts displayed only a limited determination or ability to protect civil liberties, especially when national security issues were involved, the case for a formal statement of civil rights became increasingly persuasive. In 1998 the government incorporated much of the European Convention on Human Rights (ECHR) into British law with effects which will be fully discussed later in this chapter.

Historically, British judges have not exercised a significant amount of independent constitutional power, deferring for the most part to Parliament and the executive. Nevertheless, judicial decisions may be important when there is a dispute about the meaning of a constitutional rule or practice. However, because so much of the constitution is governed by informal convention, the courts have by definition played only a limited role in relation to such crucial areas as the operation of cabinet government.

It is, however, important not to underestimate the potential for judicial intervention in the political and administrative process. The period since the 1960s saw the development by the judges of the doctrines of administrative law and **judicial review** in a way that has provided greater opportunity to challenge decision making by public authorities, including ministers. This increasingly important area of administrative law complements other developments that have expanded the role of the courts and legal issues in British political and administrative life – notably, the growing jurisdiction of European Community law and the increasing salience of the European Convention of Human Rights (see box 2.13, p. 74).

The United Kingdom does not at the time of writing have a single body that is clearly a constitutional court. Nor does it have a completely separate system of administrative courts as some other countries do for dealing with cases involving the state, though reorganization of the High Court has given it a specialist administrative division. Disputes about constitutional issues (in so far as they are justiciable at all) for the most part have to be resolved in the ordinary courts and the most important cases will reach the House of Lords, the highest court in the United Kingdom system. However, in June 2003 the government announced that it intended to create a new constitutional court that would exercise the functions currently discharged by the House of Lords and the Judicial Committee of the Privy Council (JCPC). The devolution legislation had given a new role to the JCPC by placing jurisdiction over devolution disputes there rather than with the House of Lords. The case for a new specialized constitutional court (which could hear human rights as well as devolution issues) had gained increasing support since 1997, including from senior judges such as Lord Bingham and Lord Steyn. One important feature of the new court which will be a marked departure from current practice is that the senior judiciary will no longer sit as part of the legislature.

Statute

Parliamentary statute governs many basic constitutional relationships in the United Kingdom. For example, the powers and composition of the House of Lords, the rules of the electoral system and the structures and powers of local government are largely set out in statutes (see box 2.7). Parliamentary legislation dealing with such topics as official secrecy, criminal procedure and the powers of the police also has an important impact on civil liberties. It has been noted that there is no special status accorded to a parliamentary measure which deals with matters of constitutional significance except that important constitutional **bills** will usually be given detailed scrutiny (known as the **committee stage**) by a Committee of the Whole House rather than in a smaller **standing committee**. It is also worth noting here that since the passage of the Human Rights Act of 1998, any legislative measure brought before Parliament has to be accompanied by a statement that the legislation is, in the view of the minister, compatible with the Human Rights Act.

It has generally been thought impossible to **entrench** (i.e., give special protection to) legislation in the British system because of the doctrine of **parliamentary sovereignty**. This doctrine, which we will have occasion to review at the end of this chapter and to refer to throughout the book, is traditionally one of the key principles of the constitution. The doctrine asserts that each elected Parliament is able to pass any law it wishes so that no Parliament can bind its successors. As will be seen later, the doctrine of parliamentary sovereignty is now less convincing than it once was whether as a descriptive statement of the basic rule of the constitutional system or as a normative principle with a claim to dominate other constitutional values. Theoretically, however, formal entrenchment remains an impossibility in the system because a subsequent Parliament could simply repeal earlier legislation. There are, however,

bill Legislative proposal that will normally be introduced by the government of the day (or Scottish executive). Bills are usually to be considered in principle and in detail. Amendments to bills may be made during legislative passage. After a bill has gone through all its parliamentary stages and receives the royal assent, it becomes law.

committee stage Stage of a legislative measure at which it is considered in detail rather than in principle. Often carried out in a small committee rather than in the full legislative body, although in certain cases the whole legislative body may examine a bill in detail.

standing committee Committee of the British Parliament used for a variety of legislative business, including the detailed consideration of bills and the handling of delegated legislation.

entrenchment Protections built into powers or functions so that, for example, a bill of rights might be repealed only by a two-thirds majority or after a referendum.

parliamentary sovereignty The doctrine that no outside body can overrule the will of Parliament, described by A. V. Dicey as one of the pillars of the British constitution. The doctrine has been challenged by membership of the EU, devolution and the extension of judicial review but remains formally central to the British constitution.

Box 2.7 Constitutionally significant statutes since 1900

Parliament Act 1911: Lords' power to reject legislation reduced to a two-year delaying power, with no power to delay money legislation.

Representation of the People Act 1918: Abolished property qualification for voting, extending franchise to all men over 21 and women over 30. Voting age equalized in 1928.

Irish Free State (Agreement) Act 1922: Creation of an independent Ireland, with the six counties of Northern Ireland remaining part of the United Kingdom.

Equal Franchise Act 1928: Voting age for women reduced to 21.

Statute of Westminster 1931: Divested Westminster of its powers to legislate for the Dominions and transferred legislative authority to the Parliaments of Australia, Canada, New Zealand and South Africa.

Parliament Act 1949: Lords' delaying power over non-money bills reduced to one year.

Life Peerages Act 1958: Introduced life peers into the House of Lords.

Representation of the People Act 1969: Reduced voting age to 18.

European Communities Act 1972: Took Britain into the European Community.

Single European Act 1987: Opened the way for an internal market of goods, services, capital and people in the European Community, and limited the veto powers of national governments.

Scotland Act 1998: Created a Parliament for Scotland with legislative and tax-raising powers.

Wales Act 1997: Created a Welsh Assembly with executive authority.

Human Rights Act 1998: Incorporated European Convention on Human Rights into British law.

House of Lords Act 1999: Removed the right of all but 92 hereditary peers to sit in the House of Lords.

Freedom of Information Act 2000: Granted individuals the right of access to government documents, with some exemptions.

referendum A vote of the national, regional or local electorate to settle a particular policy issue. Referendums have been an increasingly popular tool at local and regional level in the UK.

some laws, for example the Statute of Westminster of 1931, the European Communities Act of 1972 and, more recently, the Scotland Act of 1998 and the Human Rights Act of 1998 which would be very difficult to repeal on political grounds. Similarly, statutes which have been passed after a **referendum** (such as the Scotland Act) may be assumed to be protected against repeal without a further referendum or support from a general election.

Box 2.8 Important conventions of the British constitution

Conventions play a central role in British constitutional life, although they may be subject to varying interpretations. Examples of conventions are:

- The monarch always gives her assent to legislation.
- The monarch acts only on the advice of her ministers.
- The monarch dissolves Parliament on the request of the prime minister.
- The prime minister must be a member of the House of Commons.
- The House of Lords will not oppose a measure contained in the government's election manifesto (**Salisbury convention**).
- After a general election the monarch asks the leader of the party with an overall majority to form a government.
- Members of the cabinet must accept its collective decisions or resign.
- Ministers are personally responsible to the House of Commons for anything that happens in their departments.
- Proceedings of the cabinet are secret.
- A government which loses the support of the House of Commons in a vote of no confidence must resign.
- The Speaker of the House of Commons is impartial.

Salisbury convention The practice that the House of Lords will not vote down legislative proposals contained in the election manifesto of the winning party after an election.

Convention

Judicial decisions and statutes are part of the formal legal system. Disputes about the meaning of legal rules can be resolved by the courts. Much more difficult is the status of convention that governs a large part of the constitution (see box 2.8). Thus it is a *convention*, rather than a formal law, that the monarch always gives her consent to bills which have passed through Parliament and it is by convention that after an election the monarch sends for the leader of the largest party in the House of Commons to form a government. Much of cabinet government depends on convention, although some of the rules have been written down in a document called the **Ministerial Code** (formerly Questions of Procedure for Ministers), which is now published. This extensive reliance on convention has both positive and negative features. It has had the advantage of giving the British system of government a good deal of flexibility to adapt to different personalities and leadership styles as well as to different circumstances, including of course war. On the other hand, the reliance on convention also means that much of British political life is governed by rules which cannot be legally enforced and may be subject to reinterpretation by the very people they are meant to regulate. Examples of key areas of British constitutional practice where the rules appear to be what the strongest

Ministerial Code Essentially a handbook for ministers, which covers such issues as how to bring business to cabinet, relations with the media and ethical issues such as how to handle gifts. Although elements of the code date back to 1917, the modern document may be traced to Attlee's 1945 administration and the desire to promote efficient procedure in government. It was made public in 1992. Recently there has been some pressure to make the code enforceable against ministers, but at present it remains dependent on the prime minister for its implementation, an informal compendium of practice rather than a rulebook. (There is a separate Ministerial Code for Scotland.)

players say they are include the balance between prime minister and cabinet and the doctrines of collective cabinet and individual ministerial responsibility. It is worth having a preliminary look at these areas of uncertainty, although many of them will be considered in more detail in later chapters.

The power of the prime minister

One of the constitutional relationships which came under sustained scrutiny in the 1980s was that between the prime minister and cabinet. Concern had long been expressed that the prerogatives concentrated in the prime minister's hands were too great and could lead to a highly personal rather than collective form of government. Mrs Thatcher's political style – with its emphasis on strong leadership and its apparent denigration of extended debate over policy – generated accusations that her conduct of cabinet government was improper (Hennessy, 1986). Critics pointed to reductions in the frequency of cabinet meetings, to the fall in the number of papers coming to full cabinet and, above all, to the prime minister's preference for by-passing cabinet structures altogether.

Similar criticisms have been made of Tony Blair's style of premiership, although in many ways the approach of the current Labour administration to the conduct of government is as much the result of analysis of the need for strengthened central direction in government as it is the product of personality and prime ministerial style. A detailed discussion of the British cabinet system and the increasingly powerful (some would say presidential) role of the prime minister within it can be found in chapter 4. Here it is worth noting four preliminary and general points about the constitutional role of the cabinet.

First, the style of individual prime ministers varies considerably. Some, like David Lloyd George and Margaret Thatcher (and, for all his informality of style, Tony Blair), appear imperial in the sense that they expanded the powers of the premiership at the expense of collective structures. Others, such as James Callaghan and John Major, had a more collegial style. Nevertheless, all prime ministers have to work within the confines of a cabinet system which has its own operating procedures and established norms and which exists to support a governing process that is necessarily collective rather than personal. A prime minister may enjoy substantial resources in terms of the powers at his or her disposal, but for a government to be successful its various members have to be drawn together as a team.

Secondly, the prime minister holds that position in most cases by virtue of being the leader of a political party with a majority in the House of Commons. (This was not true of Lloyd George between 1916 and 1922 or Ramsay MacDonald between 1931 and 1935.) However great the powers available to a British prime minister, he or she will hold office only so long as he or she enjoys the confidence of the cabinet and the parliamentary party, a fact brought home to Mrs Thatcher when she was successfully challenged for the leadership at the end of 1990.

Thirdly, the institutional structure at the centre of British government is designed to support the cabinet as a whole rather than the prime minister. Although there has been a substantial strengthening of the institutional support for the prime minister since Tony Blair entered No. 10 Downing Street and a massive expansion of advisers located there, there is still an ambiguity about the role of the prime minister's office.

The series of readjustments to the central institutions of command – the prime minister's office and the cabinet office – underline the balance that has to be struck between recognizing the dominant role of the prime minister and the constitutional position of the cabinet and the need to provide machinery for the government as a whole.

Finally, it is worth underlining the shifts in the style of cabinet government over the years. In the eighteenth century cabinet was an informal and flexible grouping which would, according to Bogdanor, have been recognizable to late twentieth-century premiers, though it would have been in marked contrast to the style employed by a prime minister such as Clement Attlee (Bogdanor, 2003).

The debate about the role of the prime minister highlights the advantages and dangers of the British constitution's dependence on convention and practice. The malleability of the system can accommodate very different prime ministerial types – a terse and efficient committee man such as Clement Attlee or an idiosyncratic operator such as Winston Churchill. It can adapt to the changing pressures of war and peace. Yet its very flexibility inevitably means that the system can become highly personalized, especially if – as Mrs Thatcher did – a prime minister remains in power for a long time and loyalties develop to the individual rather than to the system as a whole. That said, it is hard to see how a written constitution could prescribe the relationship between cabinet and prime minister in terms that would be comprehensive. It is doubtful if any party leader with realistic hopes of becoming prime minister would willingly advocate the removal of prime ministerial prerogatives. Such a trimming of the prime minister's formal powers would make little difference to the management of cabinet, the internal dynamics of the executive and the increasingly demanding leadership role of the prime minister.

Collective responsibility

Other features of the British system of cabinet government raise difficulties for those who would like constitutional precision in government. The doctrine of collective responsibility is an established principle of British government. It imposes on all the members of a government the requirement that they support the policies of the government as a whole regardless of the views taken by individual ministers. If a minister cannot support the final decision of the government on a policy matter, he or she is expected to resign. The doctrine does not require members of the government (from members of the cabinet to unpaid parliamentary private secretaries) to agree on policy; it merely requires them to defend established decisions in public.

The way this principle works in practice is, however, far from clear-cut. The modern cabinet rarely discusses issues collectively so that members of the government are increasingly likely to be bound by decisions in which they took no part. The confidentiality which is seen as the corollary of collective responsibility is increasingly breached as a result of media briefings by individual ministers and by the prime minister himself. The spin that is put on a story may be aimed at the media in an attempt to set the terms of the debate; but it may equally be aimed at warring ministers inside a government. Strategic leaks of cabinet discussions and coded hints to journalists have long been a weapon that a dissident minister could use to signal disagreement about a policy. Increasingly, these tactics have become a routine part of the governing

ministerial responsibility
The convention that ministers should be held accountable to Parliament for the conduct of their department. In recent years accountability has been interpreted as a requirement to give an account rather than to resign if problems occur.

dignified/efficient parts of the constitution A distinction made by Walter Bagehot in *The English Constitution* (1867) between those parts of the constitution where formal power resided (e.g. the Crown) and those parts where it was really located (e.g. the cabinet).

process. As a result, although the principle of collective responsibility formally still operates, in practice divisions within the government are constantly exposed to view. Differences over the conduct of the economy and above all over European policy deeply and publicly divided John Major's 1990–7 governments. While Tony Blair's governments have not been as publicly divided over issues as his predecessor's, their personal fissures – especially the rivalry between Tony Blair and Gordon Brown and their respective supporters – have been extensively exposed (Naughtie, 2002; Rawnsley, 2001).

The point is not that such open policy divergence hinders the effectiveness of government, but rather that one of the features of conventions – even one ostensibly so central to the operation of government as collective responsibility – is that they are liable to change with successive governments. Similar uncertainty surrounds the convention of individual **ministerial responsibility** where, although a minister who is involved in personal misconduct will usually be obliged to resign, the extent to which a minister will shoulder the blame for what occurs inside his or her department varies with political circumstance.

Sometimes a political challenge to a convention or the emergence of doubts about its meaning will lead to legislation to settle the point. Thus although it had been assumed for many years prior to 1909 that the unelected House of Lords would always defer to the popularly elected House of Commons in matters of finance, the House of Lords in 1909 defied the convention and threw out the budget. The Parliament Act of 1911 was then passed to reduce the legislative powers of the House of Lords and to enshrine its lack of authority in matters of finance.

Texts and commentaries

Some influential writers on the constitution have left their own mark on the British system. Thus Walter Bagehot, a Victorian journalist, in his writings on the constitution underlined the distinction between what he called its paper description and its living reality. Bagehot saw the genius of the constitution in its ability to combine historical continuity with functional adaptation. The famous contrast between the **dignified** and the **efficient** parts of the constitution is a distinction between outward form and inner reality. In essence, the constitution, Bagehot argued, 'is strong with the strength of modern simplicity, its exterior is august with the Gothic grandeur of a more imposing age' (Bagehot, 1995).

Although Bagehot himself recognized the extent to which frequently repeated constitutional maxims might with time cease to be wholly true, his essay on the English constitution itself yielded a very large number of maxims and aphorisms that were perhaps more often repeated than analysed. Bagehot's insights were particularly influential on two issues – the role of the monarchy and the role of the cabinet. On the monarchy, Bagehot observed the impact of democracy on the political power of the monarch. By 1872 when the second edition of *The English Constitution* was published, Bagehot noted that the monarchy retained only three rights: the right to encourage, the right to be consulted and the right to warn.

Bagehot's assessment of the cabinet was that it was the constitution's efficient secret, the key to understanding the working of the whole constitution. Rather than operating on a separation of powers principle, the British system of government *combined* powers and it was the cabinet which embodied that fusion. The cabinet was 'the hyphen that joins and the buckle that fastens' the British executive to the legislative branch. In the twentieth and twenty-first centuries the role of the cabinet has been subject to extensive examination as political analysts have tried to assess the extent to which it has increasingly lost power to other actors, especially the prime minister, within the British executive (see chapter 4). None of that subsequent discussion, however, detracts from the extent to which Bagehot's incisive exposition of the role of the cabinet illuminated the political and constitutional reality of his own day.

A rather different kind of interpretation of the British constitution was offered by A. V. Dicey, the Victorian jurist. Dicey emphasized the supremacy of Parliament as an omnipotent law-making body. His analysis also emphasized the accountability of the government to Parliament and of Parliament to the electorate. On this theory Parliament was thus the sole source of democratic legitimacy and the only machinery for securing accountability within the state. The model entailed a subordinate role for the judiciary. Certainly, it did not allow judges to review parliamentary legislation to see if it accorded with the constitution.

Dicey's exposition of the constitution (which was highly influential not least among lawyers) rested then upon the notion of parliamentary sovereignty. This principle will be examined more fully later, especially because Dicey's formulation of it has so frequently operated to exclude wider discussion of constitutional values. Here it is worth mentioning the extent to which Dicey highlighted two other distinctive features of the British constitution. One was the extent to which the least formal source of constitutional norms – political practice – had proved a source of constitutional understandings. This point has already been highlighted as one of the factors accounting for the British constitution's apparent lack of precision. The other is the **rule of law**, which requires further examination here briefly because, although it is frequently cited as an important principle in the British constitution, some modern critics of Britain's constitutional arrangements have pronounced the idea vacuous and empty of content.

Dicey's own formulation of the rule of law involved three notions. First, Dicey was hostile to broad uses of executive power. He argued that no one should suffer either bodily or financial punishment except for a distinct breach of law established in the ordinary courts of the land. This formula clearly precluded arbitrary executive action and retrospective law but also the use of wide **discretionary power** by the government. The second sense in which Dicey understood the rule of law was also controversial. No man, whatever his status, was above the law; all were subject to the ordinary law of the land and the jurisdiction of the ordinary courts. Here the emphasis on the ordinary courts may have contributed to the blindness in the British legal tradition (which survived late into the twentieth century) to the special character of disputes between individuals and the state. Special jurisdictions, different methods and a distinct expertise are needed for cases with a public law element; but the English courts were slow to

rule of law According to A. V. Dicey, the second pillar of the British constitution, alongside parliamentary sovereignty. The rule of law protects individuals from arbitrary government, requiring that all be equal before the law, and that government act in accordance with the law.

discretionary power A power vested in an administrative body or minister. Discretionary power is an essential tool of executive activity. Although broad, such powers are not unlimited and in recent years the courts have supervised their exercise increasingly closely to see, for example, if they have been used reasonably.

ombudsman Generic name given to an official who hears complaints against public authorities.

develop these tools for protecting the citizen against public authorities, partly because of the suspicion that to create separate jurisdictions for administrative cases would favour the state (see also chapters 13 and 14).

Thirdly, Dicey suggested that the rule of law – or what he called the 'predominance of the legal spirit' – could be described as a special attribute of English institutions. Thus in the United Kingdom the general principles of the constitution were thought to derive from judicial decisions about the rights of private individuals rather than from any abstract statement about the powers of public authorities.

Dicey's views on the rule of law were shaped in part by his opposition to collectivism and they were subject to critical analysis by a number of important twentieth-century constitutional theorists such as Ivor Jennings and William Robson, who both argued for an interpretation of the constitution that took a much more positive view of government and its expanding role in society.

In the post-1945 period the doctrine of the rule of law has been given more substantive form by emphasizing the linked ideas of equality before the law and procedural fairness. The desire to enhance these values also led to the creation of new institutions for reviewing governmental decisions. These new institutions included the Council on Tribunals and the various **ombudsmen** who investigate appeals against decisions in both the public and the private sector. The judiciary also contributed to the control of discretion by strengthening administrative law and applying its principles to a wide range of decision-making bodies, including the Crown. In addition, there were efforts (for example through legal aid schemes) to ensure that the cost of litigation did not impede access to justice. These developments to some extent gave fuller meaning to many of the ideas associated with the rule of law. For many critics, however, such improvements were insufficient to counter the enormous imbalance between the individual citizen and the powers of the state. Indeed, it could be argued that many recent developments in the political system, especially the fragmentation of authority, have exacerbated the difficulty of holding government accountable for its use of power. This is a question that will be addressed in subsequent chapters.

Parliamentary Sovereignty

Parliamentary sovereignty was long seen by the majority of observers as the most important, if not the defining, characteristic of the British constitution. Even today, when fundamental constitutional changes brought about by UK membership of the European Union appear – to some at least – to have weakened the doctrine fatally, support for it can still be found especially in the rhetoric of politicians.

The classic doctrine of parliamentary sovereignty was expressed by Dicey in the form of two propositions that gave it a positive and a negative aspect. On the positive side, Dicey argued that under the British constitution Parliament has the right to make or unmake any law whatever. The negative aspect was that under the British constitution no body or person would be recognized as having a right to set aside the legislation of Parliament.

The positive aspect of Dicey's formula reflected his belief that in the British political system Parliament was legally the supreme body and that its law-making power could not be fettered either by morality or by international law. Equally importantly, no Parliament could bind its successors because legal sovereignty was an attribute of every Parliament. The negative aspect reflected his belief that no national or international tribunal or court could review the legality or constitutionality of an **Act of Parliament**. In the early seventeenth century, it had seemed possible that the judiciary would set aside parliamentary legislation which did not conform to 'right reason'. Yet by the middle of the eighteenth century the supremacy of parliamentary legislation was established, and the doctrine of parliamentary sovereignty had become judicial orthodoxy by the middle of the nineteenth century. The doctrine was formally stated in an 1842 case – *Edinburgh and Dalkeith Railway Company* v. *Wauchope* – and although there were several challenges to it, particularly from Scotland, none was successful.

One consequence of the traditional doctrine of parliamentary sovereignty was that it was thought legally impossible for one Parliament to bind itself or its successors. Later statutes took precedence over earlier ones so that if a later statute contradicted a statute passed earlier, either expressly or implicitly, the earlier statute was assumed to be repealed. That assumption explains why initially there was much scepticism about the value of incorporating a statement of rights in the British system. If, for example, a bill of rights was passed but Parliament later legislated in a way that was in conflict with the provisions of the bill of rights, it was assumed that the later law would prevail. Nor under the traditional doctrine was it thought possible to entrench legislation to protect it against direct repeal.

Controversy has surrounded the seriousness of obstacles to entrenching legislation. Some authorities argued, for example, that a distinction could be drawn between sovereignty that was self-embracing and sovereignty that was not (Hart, 1972). Others have argued that, although Parliament could not bind itself or its successors with respect to the substance of legislation, it might be possible to bind future Parliaments with respect to the manner and form of legislation. Parliament on this theory could limit its own sovereignty by providing, for example, that all bills with a certain sensitive subject matter (such as civil liberties or the relationship between the component parts of the United Kingdom) should be subject to a referendum or required a two-thirds majority for passage.

The academic debate about whether Parliament could bind itself as to the manner and form of legislation invoked twentieth-century instances of Parliament appearing to change its own legislative competence. The Parliament Act of 1911 restricted the power of the House of Lords over financial issues and removed the Lords' right to veto legislation. The Parliament Act did this by amending the existing constitutional procedure for legislation, imposing restrictions of substance and manner and form. The 1911 Act also made it easier to pass legislation and, if alterations could be made to parliamentary procedure to achieve that end, why, some have asked, should it not also be possible to alter parliamentary procedure to make the passage of legislation more difficult (Le Sueur and Sunkin, 1997). Another example that was brought into the debate was the Statute of Westminster of 1931. This legislation divested Westminster of its powers to legislate for the then Dominions and transferred the legislative au-

Act (of Parliament, of Scottish Parliament) Legislative measure which has passed through all its formal stages and become law. In the case of Westminster legislation, this means that normally a bill must be passed by both Houses of Parliament and must have received the royal assent. In the case of Scottish legislation, a bill must have gone through the Scottish Parliament and received the royal assent. The majority of public legislation is introduced by the government.

practice statement Direct-ive issued on the authority of a court or its judges. Such a statement may relate to the way business will be handled or to the rules of interpret-ation which the court will follow.

reference Request from a national court or tribunal for a preliminary ruling to the European Court of Justice on the interpretation of the European law and the validity of acts of the various EU bodies.

thority to the Parliaments of Australia, Canada, New Zealand and South Africa (Marshall, 1957).

Both pieces of legislation presented other puzzles. Was Parliament redefining itself in the Parliament Act of 1911 or simply delegating legislative power to a subset of its component parts? Was the Statute of Westminster ceding sovereignty forever or binding itself not to legislate for the Dominions but retaining the legal power to legislate if necessary? What would happen if a subsequent Parliament wished to change either the Parliament Act of 1911 or the Statute of Westminster?

The question of what would happen if Parliament at any time chose to depart from the restrictions imposed upon itself is a difficult one, which depends for its answer on the attitude of Parlia-ment itself, on political circumstances and on the attitude of the judiciary. Ultimately, however, the attitude of the judiciary is the most important factor because parliamentary sovereignty is a rule of *statutory interpretation* – a rule which may be applied to determine which law or rule should take precedence in the event of a conflict. These rules may be changed by the judges themselves. Traditionally, the courts would not question the validity of a statute; nor would they look beyond the bare facts of an Act's existence on the Parliament roll or inquire into its legislative history either to establish that the proper procedure had been followed or to clarify the meaning of a clause. However, the House of Lords in an important precedent and a **practice statement** in the 1992 case of *Pepper* v. *Hart* changed their rules of interpretation to enable the courts to use parliamentary material to illuminate legislative intent.

Clearly, British membership of the European Union – which took effect in 1973 – was intended to alter the powers of the United Kingdom in a number of policy areas. The fundamental constitutional issue was whether British membership of the Euro-pean Union was compatible with the notion of parliamentary sovereignty. As a condition of membership, British courts had to give effect to legislation emanating from the European Community. Membership was achieved both by signature of a range of treaties and by the passage of an Act of Parliament, the European Communities Act of 1972. The legislation is novel in its intent. By section 2 of the European Communities Act of 1972, parliamentary statutes both past and future take effect subject to Community law. By prescribing the rules for the future, the European Communities Act was binding future Parliaments. The European Com-munities Act of 1972 thus clearly defined the rules in cases of conflict: disputes about the validity, effect or interpretation of legislation were to be treated by British judges as questions of law. Such conflicts could not be avoided on grounds of political sensitivity.

Rules were also prescribed for legal issues with a European element. Article 177 of the Treaty of Rome stated that if a dispute reached the final court of appeal in the domestic system, there had to be a **reference** (a formal request for a ruling) to the European Court of Justice (ECJ). The ECJ has the task of implementing Community law within the member states and ensuring that the interpretation of European law across the Community is harmonized. Its jurisprudential approach reflects the ECJ's mission to promote the development of the European Union. Although a reference to the ECJ may also be made if a lower court in the domestic judicial hierarchy requests a ruling, the doctrine of **acte clair** also permits judges to apply the law without reference to the ECJ where the precedent is straightforward. Increasingly, lower courts and tribunals in the UK have been applying European law without the need for further reference. Thus not only was a new hierarchy of law put in place from 1973, but British courts were also involved in the process of implementing European law directly. (Under Article 12 of the Treaty of Amsterdam, the Treaty of Rome [the treaty establishing the European Community] and the Maastricht Treaty [the treaty establishing European Union] have been renumbered. I have used the original numbers but a table of equivalences should be consulted for the post-Amsterdam reference.)

It is doubtful whether the full implications of membership for the doctrine of parliamentary sovereignty were squarely faced either by British politicians or by judges at the time of accession to the European Community (Nicol, 2001). In the early period of British membership judges tended to rely on the British law to resolve conflicts, but from the late 1970s judges became increasingly willing to rely on the structure of the European Community and the priority of the treaties for their reasoning. Reference to parliamentary sovereignty gave way to reference to a new legal order.

The full constitutional significance of British membership was initially masked also by the tendency of some early conflicts between British and European law to be over **delegated** rather than **primary legislation**. The conflict between European and national law was therefore often at one remove from the Act of Parliament itself. Equally, the British government often chose not to pursue its arguments where a conflict between national and European law arose. Thus when students from the EU argued that they were entitled to pay the same university fees as British nationals, the government chose to amend its regulations rather than continue litigation before the ECJ.

There were a number of indications of the courts' growing awareness of their need to adapt to new pressures on their jurisprudence (see box 2.9). Frequently, the judges expounded their intention to construe provisions of parliamentary statutes in a manner that was consistent with European law. Thus Lord Diplock in *Garland* v. *British Rail* (1983) noted that nothing short of an express positive statement that a particular provision was intended to be in breach of European legal obligation would justify an English court in construing the law in a way that was inconsistent with a Community treaty obligation *however wide a departure from the prima facie meaning of the language of the provision might be needed to achieve the consistency* (my italics). This approach was adopted in *Pickstone* v. *Freemans PLC* (1987), where regulations amending the Equal Pay Act of 1979 were interpreted against their literal meaning to comply with the relevant European Community law.

acte clair Doctrine which allows national courts not to refer an issue of European law to the European Court of Justice because the answer to that issue is sufficiently clear. It is a technique which the UK courts have used to resist pressure from the ECJ.

primary legislation/secondary legislation Acts of the Westminster and Scottish Parliaments constitute primary legislation. Secondary legislation (also called delegated legislation and statutory instruments) modifies the provisions of the Act in a way permitted by the original legislation – for example, by increasing the levels of benefit payment authorized by a Social Security Act.

direct effect The process by which European law comes into immediate effect and binds individuals and states. The Van Gend en Loos case (1963) clarified the doctrine of direct effect.

directive Form of European legislation which is very widely used. It specifies the goals of a policy's objectives but allows individual member states discretion about the means to achieve those goals.

regulation (1) Legislative instrument used by the European Community. Regulations are directly effective and specify both the goal of the regulation and the method of securing it. (2) System of rules applied to private bodies (especially to privatized industries) as a way of ensuring that they operate in a manner that conforms to the public interest.

Box 2.9   Some key cases in the development of European Community law

NB This is a tiny selection of cases at the European and national levels.

Van Gend en Loos v. Nederlandse Tariefcommissie (1963) ECR 3

A major case which established the principle that European law had **direct effect**, i.e., will have immediate legal force without subsequent national government legislation.

Costa v. ENEL (1964) ECR 585

A decision in which the ECJ explains the distinctive nature of the legal order created by the treaties.

Amministrazione della Finanze v. Simmenthal (1978) ECR 629

A case which establishes that the rules of Community law must be fully applied in all member states from the time a **regulation** or **directive** enters into force.

Van Duyn v. Home Office (1974) ECR 1337

Reinforced the assumption that provisions of European law are directly effective.

Bulmer (H.P.) Ltd v. J. Bollinger S.A. (No. 2) 1974 3 WLR

Influential British case in which Lord Denning gives guidelines for courts (other than the House of Lords) in deciding when a case with a European element for a preliminary ruling needs to be referred to the ECJ. Superseded by Lord Bingham's formulation in *R. v. International Stock Exchange ex parte Else* (1993) 1 AER, which emphasized that if a national court has any real doubt about the application of Community law, it should refer the issue to the ECJ.

R. v. Secretary of State for Transport ex parte Factortame 1990 AC

House of Lords accepts the primacy of directly effective European law over subsequently enacted provisions of a UK Act of Parliament.

Until 1990, however, there had been no instance of a piece of legislation being set aside (or **disapplied**) as a result of a conflict with European Community law. Then in the case *R. v. Secretary of State for Transport ex parte Factortame* the extent to which European legislation had altered the doctrine of parliamentary sovereignty was underlined as a piece of British legislation was found incompatible with European Community law. In *Factortame* Spanish fishermen (who had registered their vessels as British under the 1894 Merchant Shipping Act) challenged the provision of a 1988 Act which set up a new register to exclude non-British nationals from

disapplication Process by which a statute that does not comply with European Community law is effectively suspended.

registering their vessels as British. The purpose of this legislation was in part to prevent quota-hopping, which enabled other countries to use British fishing quotas. The Spanish fishermen challenged the validity of the legislation as contrary to Community law.

The challenge was something more than a simple conflict of laws issue. The plaintiffs did not wish to wait for a lengthy resolution of the substantive issue before stopping the Act from taking effect (the case could have taken two years); and so they asked for an order prohibiting the implementation of the legislation and sought interim relief pending the final judgement of the issues. Effectively, they wanted an injunction that would suspend the 1988 Act, although this legal remedy was not available in British law.

When the case reached the House of Lords the judges followed the principle that they could not question an Act of Parliament, although the issue of interim relief had to be referred to the ECJ. The ECJ held that the full effectiveness of European Community law required the national court to set aside any rule of national law that prevented it from granting a remedy that ought to be available – in this case, interim relief. In complying with the European opinion, the House of Lords had to take the unprecedented step of restraining the Secretary of State from obeying an Act of Parliament pending the final ruling of the Court.

The *Factortame* case thus threw into sharp relief the extent to which the *grund-norm* or basic rule of the British legal system had been changed by entry into the European Community. The Advocate General underlined that it was 'quite clear' that a Community provision having immediate effect within the member states of the Community 'confers enforceable legal rights on the individual from its entry into force and for so long as it continues in force, irrespective and even in spite of' prior or subsequent national provisions which might seek to negate those rights. In other words, the doctrine of parliamentary sovereignty had been superseded by a new hierarchy of legal rules and the Community treaty obligations had indeed made it possible not merely for Parliament to bind its successors, but for the courts to overrule parliamentary legislation.

Three further points should be noted here about the impact of European Community law. First, it has been made very evident that the simple non-implementation of national law found to be in conflict with Community law is not likely to satisfy the ECJ, which requires such legislation to be removed from the statute book in the interests of clarity. This means that the ECJ has acquired substantial and strong powers of judicial review of European legislation. Secondly, because of the doctrine of direct effect, national courts became the key agents for applying and interpreting European law and thereby have acquired the power to modify or even set aside parliamentary legislation in the process of resolving legal conflicts. Thirdly, damages are available for individuals against governments which infringe Community law – for example by the non-implementation of directives.

The incremental strengthening of European Community law and the erosion of the doctrine of parliamentary sovereignty as traditionally understood has implications for the constitutional balance of the British political system. Clearly, it empowers the courts and enhances the role of law in a system that had hitherto accorded legal factors little weight. The success of other constitutional changes – notably the Human Rights Act of 1998 – will be affected by the changing role of the

think tank Organization formed to conduct independent research and to press for the adoption of new policies. Think tanks became especially important in the period after 1970, when a clutch of organizations such as the Institute of Economic Affairs and the Centre for Policy Studies pushed for radical changes in social and economic policy and exerted intellectual influence on Conservative thinking. Think tanks associated with progressive and left-of-centre politics include Demos and the Institute of Public Policy Research.

judiciary within the political system, not least the growing impact of transnational influences on British jurisprudence. As the scope of the European Union spreads and deepens, many aspects of the British state are likely to be further affected as the EU interlocks British structures with those shaped by European values. To that extent, the simple demolition of Dicey's theory of parliamentary sovereignty may be less significant than the acquisition of new influences on British decision makers, including on the British judges themselves.

The Erosion of Constitutional Complacency

Untidy though the British constitution might be, it appeared to work well enough for much of the twentieth century. Yet in the last twenty years or so, there has been a rash of constitutional debate and discussion, so much so that those who seek to defend the traditional constitutional arrangements appear very much in a minority (Foley, 1999; Norton, 1992). Why did this intellectual about-turn occur?

There were several reasons for the surge in interest in constitutional matters from the 1980s. Awareness of the concentrated and centralized nature of power in the United Kingdom was heightened dramatically by the unusually long period of government by one party between 1979 and 1997. Moreover, for much of that period a dominant prime minister, Margaret Thatcher, pursued a radical programme based on free-market principles and adopted a highly personal governing style. As a result, key institutions such as the cabinet, local government and the civil service found their role and power challenged. Critics of the Conservative government in these years also detected a pattern in the strengthening of police powers, which some argued was part of a systematic strengthening of the state and consequent erosion of civil liberties (see, for example, Ewing and Gearty, 1990). Not surprisingly, there was an explosion of interest in formalizing the United Kingdom's hitherto informal constitutional arrangements as **think tanks** and special interest groups, as well as academics and the liberal media, rushed to condemn the rickety character of the British constitutional design. Among the think tanks some (such as Charter 88, the Constitutional Reform Centre and the Constitution Unit) promoted discussion across the whole range of constitutional issues. Others, such as the Electoral Reform Society and the Commission for Local Democracy, had a specialized agenda.

The debate about constitutional reform was also joined by the judiciary. Traditionally, British judges had been cautious about direct involvement in political controversy, but the 1980s and 1990s saw individual judges becoming increasingly outspoken on a range of issues and disagreeing with the government of the day (see also chapter 13). On the specific issue of a bill of rights, opinion moved in favour of introducing one. Lord Scarman was especially eloquent in the cause of constitutional reform. 'Time and the development of our society', he wrote, 'have rendered the checks and balances such as they now are of our constitution of no avail...to restrain an oppressively minded executive if it should win control of the House of

Commons. The path to an "elected dictatorship" is open and must be blocked now before the bad boys realise their opportunity and organise a takeover of the British constitution' (Scarman, 1989).

Among the political parties the Liberal Democrats had long been committed to constitutional reform, especially to reform of the electoral system, which in their view unfairly disadvantages minor parties. For constitutional reform to succeed, however, it needed the support of one of the two major parties. Although the Conservative Party had flirted with some elements of constitutional reform when in opposition between 1974 and 1979, Mrs Thatcher was not really interested in the topic. Once in government she wanted to strengthen the central state to deliver her free-market initiatives and she certainly had no interest in devising constitutional barriers to her freedom of action (Gamble, 1988).

Labour had historically regarded constitutional reform with suspicion. Labour valued the power which the British system gave to a duly elected government. Institutional checks and balances would inevitably make it more difficult for a reforming Labour government to implement a radical programme. Moreover, Labour was traditionally antagonistic to any reform that might transfer power to the judges, who were generally regarded as unsympathetic to progressive values (Griffiths, 1991). During the 1990s, however, Labour's attitude began to change. First, the experience of a long period of opposition underlined the merits of a more balanced system. Secondly, the successive election as party leader of two lawyers – John Smith and Tony Blair – reflected the erosion of Labour's visceral dislike of the legal profession and legal processes. Thirdly, Labour would have had to devise a radical policy to meet Scotland's demand for greater autonomy and some parallel strategy would therefore have had to be devised for Wales. Approaching a number of specific policy issues from the standpoint of a general commitment to constitutional modernization enabled Labour to make common cause with a range of pressure groups and with the Liberal Democrats. Thus for Labour, constitutional reform was a mixture of principle and pragmatism.

The relationship with the Liberal Democrats was especially important in the gestation of Labour's constitutional reform proposals. After Tony Blair became leader of the Labour Party in 1994, the Liberal Democrats were consulted on many aspects of constitutional reform and in the first year of the Blair government the unusual step was taken of including some Liberal Democrats on a cabinet committee on constitutional reform.

As a result of these efforts not merely were individual constitutional issues such as freedom of information and reform of the House of Lords made increasingly salient for the general public, but there was also renewed interest in the idea of introducing a bill of rights for the United Kingdom and of substituting a fully codified consti- tution for Britain's unwritten one. To some extent, of course, constitutional reform was an issue which resonated more with the political elite than with the electorate as a whole and the Blair government itself by 2001 had refocused its energies on the mainstream electoral issues of service provision. Nevertheless, by that stage Labour had already advanced a substantial portion of its reform agenda, making its first term in office one of the most concentrated periods of constitutional change since the early twentieth century.

The 1997 Reforms

The Blair government that came into office in 1997 was determined to modernize the machinery of government and sought to associate itself with the cause of constitutional reform. But the reforms that were brought forward were not derived from a single constitutional blueprint. Rather, they were developed piecemeal, reflecting a range of different influences on the administration, differences between the lead departments and a different degree of enthusiasm for the separate items on the reform agenda.

There was also a tension at the core of the reform agenda. Many of Blair's reforms entailed a major dispersal of power within the UK system. At the same time, the new Labour government was determined to strengthen its strategic hold on government and policy making. Thus at the level of the cabinet, what emerged was a much more personalized and centralized system affording more direction and control to the prime minister and to his immediate aides and a corresponding reduction in the role of the cabinet as a collective entity (see chapter 4). At the level of parliamentary reform, it was clear that, while the Blair administration intended to reform the House of Lords, it was also determined to maintain tight control over the House of Commons through revised rules of party discipline for Labour MPs and other management techniques. Efforts to give the House of Commons a substantially greater independence of the executive through procedural reform were received unenthusiastically by the government, at least until Robin Cook's brief period as Leader of the House in the second Blair administration. There was doubt about how far the executive was really committed to any substantial enhancement of Parliament's powers if such strengthening involved giving Parliament greater capacity to check the executive.

In the field of territorial relations within the United Kingdom, Labour moved quickly to fulfil its specific manifesto commitments to set up a Scottish Parliament, a Welsh Assembly and a directly elected mayor and assembly for London. But the government also tried – unsuccessfully as it turned out – to control the candidate selection process for those bodies to ensure that the regimes that emerged in these new political arenas reflected New Labour values.

In relation to both human rights and freedom of information legislation, the measures brought forward fell short of what many constitutional advocates had wished, while on the question of electoral reform for the House of Commons the government beat a hasty retreat from its 1997 manifesto commitment of a referendum on the topic. Thus, while it set up a Commission under Lord Jenkins to examine the alternatives to the **first past the post** system for Westminster, Blair's government has to date ignored its findings.

Devolution: Scotland and Wales

One of the most dramatic changes to the structure of British government brought about by the Blair administration was the creation of two new sub-governments in Scotland and Wales. Under the Scotland Act 1998, Scotland (which had last had a separate Parliament in 1707) regained its own Parliament and its own administration in the form of a cabinet and **first minister**. Wales gained an Assembly with an administration also headed by a cabinet and first secretary, although the title first minister has been used increasingly in Wales, but not a Parliament with the power to pass primary legislation.

Devolution for Scotland and Wales had been an issue intermittently in British politics since the late nineteenth century. Labour in the period 1974–9 had brought forward legislation to provide devolved government for Scotland and Wales; but these schemes had failed in referendums in the two countries. During the long period of Conservative government between 1979 and 1997, sentiment in favour of devolved government grew massively in Scotland, reflecting the sharp contrast between Scottish political and cultural values and **Thatcherite** Conservatism. A Scottish Convention called in 1987 demonstrated the depth of civic and cross-party support for a Scottish Parliament. While Wales never displayed the same degree of enthusiasm for devolution as Scotland, the renewed interest in constitutional reform, together with a slight reassertion of Welsh political consciousness, made it appropriate to bring forward some measure of devolution for Wales.

The Scottish and Welsh were not treated equally in the Labour government's devolution strategy, not least because the support for greater self-government was evidently so much stronger in Scotland than in Wales. Given that Northern Ireland's arrangements were necessarily different again to reflect the special circumstances of the province, devolution was from the beginning asymmetrical (Bogdanor, 2003; McEldowney, 2002). Under the Scotland Act of 1998, Scotland acquired a fixed-term 129-member Parliament (whose members were to be known as MSPs) with powers to pass primary legislation on a wide range of domestic matters. The executive – first minister and cabinet, junior ministers and civil servants – were to be responsible to the Parliament. The Scottish Parliament was given a small independent tax-varying power (it could add or subtract up to 3p to the basic rate of income tax); but the bulk of the money for Scotland's government was to come from a **block grant** transferred from Whitehall. Wales by contrast was given a 60-member Assembly (whose members were to be known as AMs) with no powers of primary legislation but the power to debate matters of interest to Wales and to vary secondary (i.e., delegated) legislation. The Welsh Assembly was given no independent taxing power so it was dependent on the block grant from the central government in London. Although it had been anticipated initially that the executive would operate through a committee structure, the final legislation established a cabinet system responsible to the Assembly. The separation of powers between the executive and the Assembly was increasingly emphasized as the Welsh system took root.

Before either the Scotland Act or the Wales Act could come into force, the devolution schemes had to be approved by two referendums. There was no necessity for this procedural hurdle, but it was thought that referendums would have the advantage of providing an additional political barrier to repeal by a future Conservative government as well as adding legitimacy to the new institutional

first minister Equivalent of the prime minister in the devolved systems of Scotland, Wales and Northern Ireland.

Thatcherism Name given to the mix of free-market and populist policies associated with Margaret Thatcher.

block grant Method of payment of grant from one authority to another that merges payments for different purposes in a way which allows the recipient body maximum discretion in the allocation of spending. Block grants have been employed in the UK since 1929 for a large portion of central government grant to local authorities and are used to transfer money to the devolved governments of Scotland and Wales.

arrangements. It was also suggested that the Welsh scheme – which occasioned much less enthusiasm than the Scottish – might be aborted if there was no popular support for it.

In the Scottish referendum two questions were put: on whether there should be a Scottish Parliament and whether it should have limited tax-varying powers. Both questions were answered in the affirmative: by 74.3 per cent to 25.7 per cent the Scots voted for a Scottish Parliament; and they gave it tax-varying powers by only a slightly smaller majority of 63.5 per cent to 36.5 per cent. In Wales the referendum outcome was much less clear, with a mere 50.3 per cent voting yes to the Welsh Assembly with 49.7 per cent voting no (see table 2.1). The first elections to the Scottish Parliament and the Welsh Assembly were held in May 1999. Both representative bodies were given electoral systems different from Westminster's simple plurality system. Instead, the elections took place under a version of the alternative member system (AMS) which is used in Germany and New Zealand. Under this system the voter casts two votes – one for a member to be elected on the first past the post basis, the other from a party list used to adjust any imbalance in the ratio of votes to seats in the simple plurality system. As a result, the first elections for both the Scottish Parliament and the Welsh Assembly helped a range of smaller parties strengthen their representation and weakened the hold of the Labour Party, which had previously been dominant in both regions (see table 2.2).

Table 2.1   Results of the devolution referendums in Scotland and Wales

Scotland 11 Sept 1997	Creation of Parliament	Tax-varying powers
Agree	74.3%	63.5%
Disagree	25.7%	36.5%
Turnout:	60.2%	
Wales 18 Sept 1997	Creation of Assembly	
Agree	50.3%	
Disagree	49.7%	
Turnout:	50.1%	

Source: Adapted from Butler and Butler (2000).

Table 2.2   Results of elections to the Scottish Parliament and Welsh Assembly, 1999

	Lab	Con	Lib Dem	SNP/PC	Green	Other
Elections to the Scottish Parliament						
% share of votes	34	15	13	27	4	8
% share of seats	43	14	13	27	1	2
Seats	56	18	17	35	0	3
Elections to the Welsh Assembly						
% share of votes	36	17	13	31	3	2
% share of seats	47	15	10	28	0	0
Seats	28	9	6	17	0	0

Source: Dunleavy (2002); Cowley (2002).

The absence of a single party able to command an overall majority in either the Scottish Parliament or the Welsh Assembly created an opening for a new style of politics. In Scotland Labour and the Liberal Democrats formed a coalition which proceeded to develop a different policy agenda from that of Westminster on a number of key issues, including university tuition fees, care for the elderly and hunting. In Wales, where Labour was the single largest party but without an overall majority, a minority Labour administration initially took office. But after a rather unstable first year, the first secretary Alun Michael resigned and was replaced by Rhodri Morgan, who moved towards a coalition with the Liberal Democrats.

Both the Scottish and the Welsh systems of devolution had been established against the background of tension within the Labour Party as the government in London sought to exert control over the outcome of candidate selection in the two areas. In Scotland the attempt to manipulate the outcome of the elections had a less damaging effect than in Wales, where Blair's imposition of his own preference, Alun Michael, on the Welsh Labour Party as first secretary created a backlash. Ultimately, Michael was forced to resign after a vote of no confidence was carried in February 2000 (see also chapter 12).

Devolution: Northern Ireland

The issue of devolution for Northern Ireland was an infinitely more complex question than that of devolution for Scotland and Wales. Northern Ireland's status as part of the United Kingdom remained controversial and the region was marked by bitter communal violence. It had experienced devolved government from 1921 until 1972, but the treatment of the minority nationalist population inside the province led to extensive disorder and a resurgence of terrorism which in turn led to the restoration of direct rule from London. Re-establishing devolved government as part of a more general settlement to the Northern Ireland conflict had been a goal of successive governments since 1972. Any comprehensive agreement had, however, proved elusive because of bitter sectarian divisions between the unionist and nationalist communities, even though there was increasing cooperation between the British government in London and the Irish government in Dublin over Northern Ireland issues.

The election of the Labour government in 1997 provided a new opportunity to try to find a framework for agreement. The details of the so-called Good Friday Agreement (the Belfast Agreement) are discussed in more detail in chapter 12. Here it is sufficient to note that one part of the agreement involved the establishment of a new set of devolved institutions with their own Assembly and executive.

Unlike the Parliament of Scotland and Wales, however, the Northern Ireland Assembly and executive had to be organized in a way which ensured that the new institutions operated in a manner which could command consent from both the unionist and nationalist populations. As a result, an Assembly of 108 members (MLAs) was elected by **proportional representation** (using the single transferable vote or STV) to ensure a fair representation of all the parties. The executive included representation of all the parties and the passage of certain

proportional representation (PR) Methods of election which attempt to ensure that the seats gained by each party accurately reflect their support in the electorate.

weighted consent/parallel consent System used in Northern Ireland to ensure that decisions on some issues require more than a simple majority and must achieve a level of cross-community agreement.

key issues requires cross-community consent in the Assembly. This was to be demonstrated either in a process known as **parallel consent** (which requires a majority of those present and voting *plus* a majority of unionists and nationalists) or **weighted consent** (which requires support from 60 per cent of those present and voting *plus* a 40 per cent majority of both unionists and national-ists). This rather unwieldy system was designed to prevent either community using its power to disadvantage the other. Unfortu-nately, the emphasis on consent meant that it gave minorities a veto and a power to bring the operation of government and Assembly to a standstill.

The devolved institutions were only one part of a series of interlocking new arrangements for handling Northern Ireland's government. Others covered relation-ships among the several parts of the British Isles and between the UK and the Republic of Ireland. The referendum in May 1998 endorsing the Belfast Agreement was designed to test support for the agreement as a whole and a simultaneous referendum was held in the Republic of Ireland. In Northern Ireland on an extremely high turnout of 81.1 per cent, an overwhelming 71.1 per cent of those voting were in favour of the agreement and 29 per cent against (see table 2.3). However, within the two communities there was a marked imbalance of enthusiasm, with the nationalist/ Catholic population registering much greater support than the unionist segment of the electorate. Elections for the Northern Ireland Assembly were held on 25 June 1999. The results registered a growth in support for the two nationalist parties, the Social and Democratic Labour Party (SDLP) and Sinn Fein (SF). The unionist vote, which was already fragmented, was split further between pro- and anti-agreement parties (see table 2.4).

The British government had wanted the Northern Ireland Assembly to take power on 1 July 1999 so that all three component sub-units of the United Kingdom would achieve devolution on the same day. Disagreements between the parties about

Table 2.3 Results of the Good Friday Agreement referendum in Northern Ireland

Northern Ireland 22 May 1998	Good Friday Agreement
Agree	71.1%
Disagree	29%
Turnout:	81.1%

Source: Adapted from Butler and Butler (2000).

Table 2.4 Results of elections to the Northern Ireland Assembly, 1999

	UUP	SDLP	DUP	SF	Others
% share of votes	26	22	19	17	17
% share of seats	26	22	19	17	17
Seats	28	24	20	18	18

Source: Cowley (2002).

whether the establishment of an executive should wait until there had been some progress on **decommissioning** meant, however, that the devolved institutions were not properly up and running until December 1999.

> **decommissioning** Process of putting weapons held by paramilitary forces in Northern Ireland beyond use.

The decommissioning issue continued to hang over the workings of the new Northern Ireland system as David Trimble's Unionists demanded evidence that the Irish Republican Army (IRA) were really committed to disarming. Sinn Fein, the political wing of the IRA, accused the Unionists of using decommissioning as a diversionary tactic and of wanting a veto over the peace process. In February 2000, the absence of progress on the decommissioning front caused the British government to suspend the executive. It was reconvened in May 2000 following an indication that the IRA would be seeking to put its weapons beyond use. By November 2000 the evidence of progress in this respect remained slim and David Trimble was experiencing increasing difficulty holding his wing of the unionist movement together behind the Belfast Agreement. The discovery of an IRA cell operating within Stormont itself in 2002 caused the Unionists to withdraw from the executive and the devolved institutions once again to be suspended. Although a new round of elections to the Northern Ireland Assembly was held in November 2003, these resulted in gains for the hard-line anti-Agreement DUP as well as for Sinn Fein at the expense of the more moderate parties. In consequence, the resumption of devolved government on a power-sharing basis looks remote.

The impact of devolution

The advent of devolved systems of government for Scotland, Wales and Northern Ireland created important new political structures and arenas within the United Kingdom and introduced a new diversity to the pattern of politics. The way these new structures operate is discussed in more detail later in the book. But devolution is inevitably likely to have other knock-on effects of profound political and constitutional significance.

Devolution inevitably also had important consequences for governing the United Kingdom as a whole and has prompted substantial adjustments within both Whitehall and Westminster. Devolving power to Scotland, Wales and Northern Ireland presented new challenges to administrators and policy makers. The coordination of government between the several parts of the United Kingdom inevitably became more complicated, demanding a greater percentage of central government's time. At the Whitehall level, the machinery for coordinating policy shifted as the new institutions became established. During the first phase of the devolution process there was a Devolution Policy Committee chaired by the Lord Chancellor; but in 2001 this cabinet committee was replaced by a Committee on the Regions and Nations, chaired by John Prescott, who as deputy prime minister had acquired a strengthened enforcement and coordinating role.

During the first year of devolution special machinery in the form of a new joint ministerial committee (JMC) was established to bring together the ministers of the different governments on matters of joint concern. This JMC framework was

concordat Agreement made between London and a devolved government as to how powers shall be exercised.

select committee Parliamentary committee which is established with a strong scrutiny role and which in the United Kingdom attempts to operate on a bipartisan basis.

designed to provide a formal setting for resolving problems but in fact after the first year its meetings became very infrequent. Such problems and issues as arose tended to be handled instead at lower and less formal levels and in ad hoc ministerial meetings. Initially these committees had been serviced by a new division of the Cabinet Secretariat within the Cabinet Office, which took the lead role in developing appropriate coordinating machinery to handle relations between the devolved governments and the centre. (The new constitutional secretariat also provided the secretarial support for the British–Irish Council, one of the institutions established under the Belfast Agreement.) Reorganization of the Cabinet Office staff in 2001 saw a merger of the constitutional secretariat into a new Regions and Nations division.

Underpinning the new devolved structures is a series of **concordats**, memorandums of understanding and devolution guidance notes which attempt to codify the relationships between the central and the devolved governments. Although these formalized procedures for coordinating relationships were seen by many as the tip of the iceberg and in many ways less important than the multiple informal relationships between officials in the various governments, they introduced a massive new dimension of written material into Britain's constitutional arrangements (Hazell, 2003).

There had been some speculation that with devolution the roles of the three territorial Secretaries of State and their departments would become redundant, but all three were kept in being, despite a major reorganization in Whitehall after the 2001 election and again in June 2003. It is unlikely that there will be any move to abolish the Northern Ireland Office (NIO), which may have to resume responsibility for governing Northern Ireland for the long term. The argument for reorganizing the work of the other two 'territorial' departments – the Scottish Office and the Welsh Office – did, however, prove persuasive. Merging them into a single department was strongly advocated by a report of the House of Lords Constitution Committee in 2002–3 (see box 2.10). The Committee was also concerned that the arrangements for intergovernmental cooperation were not strong enough to withstand a change of political regime in London (see also chapter 12). In the event, the government brought the posts of Secretary of State for Scotland and for Wales within the ambit of the newly enhanced Department for Constitutional Affairs, which in 2003 replaced the Lord Chancellor's Department and which brought devolution within its remit. Although these territorial posts may be combined with other roles, the civil servants and their office are for the moment to be kept separate and permanent.

The sequence of constitutional changes required adjustments to be made at Westminster, not least because, with the establishment of the Scottish Parliament, MPs at Westminster could no longer put down questions about matters for which responsibility had passed to Edinburgh. Although at the time of writing there has been no major change to the select and other committees that deal exclusively with Scotland, Wales and Northern Ireland, the logic of the reform establishing a Department of Constitutional Affairs suggests a single **select committee** to monitor that department, with separate subcommittees to scrutinize Scottish and Welsh policy.

Box 2.10 Recommendations of the Select Committee on the Constitution's 2nd Report, Devolution: Inter-Institutional Relations in the United Kingdom

1 Greater use should be made of formal mechanisms for intergovernmental relations – such as the Joint Ministerial Committee (JMC) – even if they seem to be excessive at present in order to provide a framework for informal contacts and as a fall-back if either informal relations fail or governments of different political persuasions have to deal with each other.

2 The criteria for holding a JMC should be resolved and published and there should be at least one 'functional' JMC each year covering areas of where policy is devolved for two or three devolved administrations but exercised by the UK for the rest or where there is substantial overlap between functions that are devolved and those retained at the UK level. Existing meetings of agriculture ministers should become JMC meetings.

3 There should be greater openness achieved via an agreed press statement after each JMC and a statement in the House of Commons by the prime minister after each JMC plenary to cover both that meeting and intergovernmental meetings generally.

4 Concordats should be made for fixed terms and capable of being varied.

5 The devolution and English regions teams within the ODPM [Office of the Deputy Prime Minister] should be merged with the parts of the Scottish and Wales Office dealing with intergovernmental relations to create a single group of officials to deal with intergovernmental issues.

6 Consideration should be given to replacing the Secretaries of State for Scotland and Wales with a single cabinet minister to deal with intergovernmental relations.

7 The Office of the Deputy Prime Minister should be strengthened in anticipation of a formal liaison between Westminster and the devolved institutions.

8 There should be greater information available about public spending decisions for England and for the devolved institutions. If there is a review of the **Barnett formula** it should be undertaken by an independent body. Disputes about payments *outside* the Barnett formula should be referred to an independent body.

9 There should be a review of intergovernmental relations at least once every Parliament preferably by a Joint Committee of both Houses.

10 There should be greater consistency in how Westminster legislates for Wales. An explanatory memorandum should be attached to any bill affecting the functions of the National Assembly for Wales or a policy area where the Assembly has responsibilities. Further consideration should be given to legislation applying specifically in Wales and to how members of the Welsh Assembly can consider Westminster legislation affecting the Assembly or its functions.

11 Westminster should consider the lessons from the legislative process in Edinburgh and the use of business committees.

12 The civil service should remain as a single Home Civil Service.

Barnett formula Formula named after Joel Barnett, Treasury Secretary in the late 1970s, for allocating public expenditure between England, Scotland, Wales and Northern Ireland. Originally introduced in 1888 as the Goschen formula, it allocated 11/80ths of public expenditure to Scotland. Under Joel Barnett that percentage was changed to 10/80ths. The Barnett formula is controversial because it is based on population rather than need.

West Lothian question The anomaly of Scottish, Welsh and Northern Irish MPs voting in Westminster on English issues, while English MPs are prevented by devolution from voting on Scottish, Welsh and Northern Irish issues. The question was repeatedly raised by Tam Dalyell, West Lothian MP.

English question The broad question of whether devolution to Scotland, Wales and Northern Ireland should be complemented by a parallel devolved body for England or should be matched by a series of regional authorities.

The devolution schemes themselves have an inherent instability. Institutional patterns including conventions and practices will develop so that the paper arrangements may end up looking very different from the actual behaviour of those who have to work the system. Already, for example, Welsh members of the executive have changed their titles from secretaries to ministers and Rhodri Morgan has proved active in pushing for a review of the framework of Welsh devolution. In addition to the natural evolution that may be expected, there is thus likely to be an effort on the part of the Welsh to move towards the Scottish model.

A third question raised by the form of devolution introduced in 1998 was the question of fairness to England. One element of this issue was the so-called **West Lothian question**, named after Tam Dalyell, the Labour MP who repeatedly pointed to the anomalous position of Scottish MPs at Westminster after devolution. Once the Scottish Parliament started to function, Dalyell observed, MPs from Scottish constituencies at Westminster would have no influence on a range of domestic matters affecting their own constituencies because those matters had been transferred to Edinburgh. Nor could English MPs affect those policy areas. But Scottish MPs could influence laws in these policy areas for England.

The West Lothian question triggered the broader problem of how best to govern England after devolution. Put rather differently, the introduction of a Scottish Parliament and a Welsh Assembly created an anomaly for the residents of England who had no Parliament solely dedicated to English affairs and whose laws were written by a Parliament in which the Scots and the Welsh MPs were overrepresented by comparison with English MPs. How far this anomaly troubled the English is open to question, though poll evidence suggests a slight raising of English consciousness on the issue.

There were varied solutions offered to the **English question**. Some Conservatives such as Theresa Gorman argued for an English Parliament. An all-party Procedure Committee recommended in a May 1999 report, entitled *The Procedural Consequences of Devolution*, that bills relating only to England or England and Wales should go to a second reading committee composed wholly of members from the relevant part of the UK – a recommendation that was curtly rejected by the government. The then Conservative leader William Hague, by contrast, endorsed the idea of procedural reform within the House of Commons to preclude Scottish and Welsh MPs from voting on purely English matters. Thus a Conservative-commissioned enquiry in 2000 (*Strengthening Parliament*) suggested a procedure by which bills could be certified as relating only to England and would then effectively be handled only by English MPs.

The Labour government (in addition to acknowledging that there would have to be some reduction in the number of Scottish MPs at Westminster from 2005) favoured splitting England into regions and creating elected regional assemblies. Labour's commitment to strengthening the regional dimension of government in the United Kingdom was underlined when in 1999 it established regional development agencies (RDAs) and regional chambers throughout the country. This initiative was followed by an announcement by John Prescott in 2002 that elective regional authorities could be established where there was demand for them. It remains to be seen how much enthusiasm there is for a new dimension of government outside Yorkshire, the north-east and the south-west.

Local government

The creation of a regional tier of government in England inevitably has implications for the structure of local government. Labour returned to power in 1997 after a long period in which local government had been at the centre of political controversy as Conservative governments clashed with councils (often but not exclusively Labour) over such policies as the sale of council houses and the direction of education policy. The short-lived experiment with the poll tax as a way of financing local government not only provoked violence but in many ways contributed to the removal of Mrs Thatcher from the premiership (Adonis, Butler and Travers, 1994). In opposition Labour had been sympathetic to arguments which urged a strengthening of local government and a revitalization of its contribution to democratic representation. One major reform that the Blair government did implement was the restoration to London of its own **strategic authority** and the creation of a directly elected mayor. This was an important and generally popular move since London had been without a strategic authority as a result of Mrs Thatcher's abolition of the Greater London Council (GLC) and six other metropolitan counties in 1986. The government's attempt to exclude the former leader of the GLC – Ken Livingstone – from running as the Labour candidate, although successful in the short run, ultimately proved a dismal failure. Livingstone, though denied the official Labour nomination, stood as an independent candidate and was duly elected in May 2000.

The election of the London mayor along with that of the newly constituted Greater London Authority (GLA) of 25 members took place using the **supplementary vote** system for the mayor and the **alternative vote** system for the GLA. Local government had been seriously weakened in its battles with central government by low turnout (see table 2.5) and it was hoped that the use of a different electoral system to that employed for Westminster elections might increase electoral participation.

The idea of a directly elected mayor (which had been canvassed during Michael Heseltine's time at the Department of the Environment in the 1990s) appealed to Blair and some others in the cabinet for several reasons. It was hoped that the position might attract high-calibre candidates and that the reform would thus enhance the executive capacity of local authorities. Equally, it was hoped that the identification of a mayor with a major city would inject new interest into local government and provide greater accountability. There was, however, powerful opposition, especially within the Labour Party, to the idea of a directly elected mayor. Directly elected mayors were thought to encourage personality politics and to strengthen the role of leader at the expense of internal party democracy. Thus when legislation was brought forward to strengthen the executive capacity of local government through reform

strategic authority Authority such as the Greater London Authority which has powers to set long-term policy goals at a high level (usually in such areas as transport) but which has relatively few powers of direct service provision.

alternative vote (AV)/supplementary vote (SV) Voting method in which the elector indicates his or her preference among the candidates in the order 1, 2, 3 etc. If any candidate receives 50 per cent + 1 of the total vote on first count, that candidate is elected. If not, the candidate with the fewest first preferences is eliminated and that candidate's second preferences are redistributed. The process continues until a candidate reaches 50 per cent + 1 of the vote.

Table 2.5 Turnout in local government elections since 1973

Year	Turnout (%)
1973	42.6
1974	36.0
1975	32.4
1976	46.4
1978	40.3
1980	39.1
1982	41.8
1983	47.6
1984	40.3
1986	42.4
1987	49.5
1988	40.6
1990	48.4
1991	47.2
1992	36.8
1994	42.5
1995	38.4
1996	34.2
1998	28.2
1999	31.2
2000	29.6
2001	62.1
2002	35.0

Source: Department of the Environment, Transport and the Regions (2000),
Turnout at Local Elections, http://www.elections.dtlr.gov.uk/turnout/; LGC Elections Centre
http://www.lgcnet.com/pages/products/elections/elec.htm

of its leadership structures, it was felt necessary to offer a choice of models on which reform could be based. While the introduction of a directly elected mayor was one such model, it was not one that commanded great support among local authorities and by 2003 only a handful had opted for directly elected mayors. Apart from the initiative to reform leadership structures, there was very little evidence that Labour, despite its commitment to devolution and regionalism, had any great desire to see more political autonomy for local government (see chapter 11).

The use of the referendum

One interesting feature of the legislation designed to strengthen local authority leadership structures was that it required a referendum to be held if a council wanted to introduce a directly elected mayor. As a result there has been an increased use of referendums across the United Kingdom in recent years. As noted earlier, the devolution schemes for Scotland and Wales and the introduction of a directly elected mayor for London were also put to referendums prior to the passage of the legislation. And further referendums were promised on changing the British electoral system and, when the time was judged right, on entry into the single European currency.

Although the use of a referendum to ascertain the support for constitutional change was not formally required, it was thought (especially by Blair himself) that the visible endorsement from a referendum would make the reforms more difficult to repeal. (The complex settlement in Northern Ireland was also put to referendums on both sides of the border, although there its use fulfilled a rather different function in that it both demonstrated public support for the settlement and provided some momentum to the process of by-passing the regular parties.) Thus since 1997 there have been four referendums in different parts of the United Kingdom and many at a local level.

The use of the referendum (which is common in Switzerland, Ireland and the United States at the state level) has thus become a more familiar part of British constitutional life, although it should be noted that to date only one *nationwide* referendum has been held. This occurred in 1975 when the issue of Britain's continuing membership of the European Community was put to voters. However, it is assumed that any decision to adopt the single European currency would require prior endorsement at a referendum. Consideration of a new constitution for the European Union has led many critics of the enterprise on the Conservative side to push for a referendum on the issue.

The referendum has the advantage that it enables the government to ascertain public opinion on important issues and allows that test to occur without putting the government's own political life at stake. It allows parties that may be split on fundamental questions to campaign openly without enforcing an artificial unity on them. Thus in 1975 members of the Labour government were able to campaign on different sides, despite the normal rules of collective cabinet responsibility. A referendum campaign may educate the public on a major issue. And, in the absence of any formal way of *legally* entrenching a measure under the British constitution, endorsement at a referendum provides a form of *political* entrenchment that may give practical protection against repeal. It could also be argued that the use of the referendum strengthens popular sovereignty and offers an opportunity for **direct democratic participation**.

There are, however, powerful arguments against the use of the referendum to settle political issues. An increase in popular sovereignty inevitably comes at the expense of parliamentary sovereignty and further weakens the role of Parliament. The government can determine the timing of a referendum (as it can the timing of a general election) and may manipulate the phrasing of the questions to obtain the result it wants. If the government is committed to a certain outcome, it may campaign on one side and its superior resources may skew the results. In the 1975 referendum campaign, the yes side easily outspent and outweighed the no side, an imbalance which some fear could occur again if the issue of joining the euro were put to a referendum.

The increased use of referendums but the lack of rules governing them caused the Committee on Standards in Public Life in 1998 to suggest bringing them under a coherent regulatory framework, and in 2000 the government included many of its recommendations in the Political Parties, Elections and Referendums Act (PPERA).

direct democracy The use of instruments such as the initiative, referendum and recall which allow citizens a direct say in law making rather than simply delegating the authority to make laws to an elected body.

ratification Process by which Parliament gives approval to an international treaty.

Most importantly, the legislation brought referendums under the supervision of a new Electoral Commission and set expenditure limits. It also attempted to secure greater equality between the sides by providing some core funding for each campaign and banning government intervention in a campaign within 28 days of the vote (see also chapter 7).

The Human Rights Act

One of the most profound constitutional developments which occurred as a result of the Labour government's constitutional reform programme was the adoption of a new bill of rights for Britain. The United Kingdom had **ratified** the European Convention on Human Rights (ECHR) in 1951 but had never incorporated it into British law. Individuals wishing to rely on the protections offered by the ECHR had to use the separate procedures provided for by the Court and the Commission on Human Rights at Strasbourg, and these procedures could prove time- consuming and costly. Although the United Kingdom had always thought of itself as having a strong record in the field of civil liberties, a series of judgements of the ECHR had gone against the UK in the last quarter of the twentieth century, when international consciousness of human rights issues was rising (see box 2.11). Concern about the absence of real protections for civil liberties in the British system created a strong movement for a bill of rights which found favour in the Labour Party in the late 1990s.

There were, however, practical difficulties about grafting a bill of rights onto a system that had for so long emphasized parliamentary sovereignty as being at the heart of its democracy. What rights should be protected in such a measure? Should a bill of rights simply adopt the rights protected by the ECHR? How could it be protected against repeal in a system with no obvious way of entrenching legislation? Above all, there loomed the question of how such a bill would work. Should it conform to the stronger models of the United States or Canada, where a judicial finding that legislation is incompatible with the bills of rights results in the invalidating of that legislation? Or should it conform more to the New Zealand model, where the judiciary has no power to invalidate legislation found to be incompatible with the bill of rights? Finally, there was the question of how the introduction of a bill of rights would affect a system in which the judiciary had traditionally played only a very limited political role.

The solution adopted was to incorporate most (but not all) of the rights contained in the ECHR into British law through the Human Rights Act of 1998. These rights include such important ones as the right to life, the right to a fair trial, the right to a private life and the right not to be subjected to degrading treatment or torture. Although the ECHR could not be entrenched, it was assumed that no political party would risk the public hostility that would result from repealing it. The compromise devised for enforcing the Act preserved the form of parliamentary sovereignty in that it did not allow judges to invalidate legislation as a result of a conflict with the Human Rights Act. Instead, judges

Box 2.11 European Court of Human Rights judgements issued against the UK since 1999

Date	Case	Subject Matter	Article Violation
1999 February	*Matthews* v. *UK*	Exclusion of Gibraltar residents from voting in European elections.	Article 3 of Protocol 1
1999 February	*Cable and Others* v. *UK*	Independence and impartiality of court martial.	Article 6 s. 1
1999 July	*Scarth and Others* v. *UK*	Lack of public hearing in arbitration proceedings.	Article 6 s. 1
1999 September	*Lustig-Prean and Beckett* v. *UK*	Dismissal of homosexuals from armed forces following investigation.	
1999 October	*Perks and Others* v. *UK*	Unavailability of legal aid for proceedings relating to non-payment of community charge.	Article 6 c. 3
1999 December	*T.* v. *UK*	(1) Absence of review of continuing lawfulness of detention.	Article 5 s. 4
		(2) Effective participation of child in trial in adult court.	Article 6 s. 1
		(3) Fixing by executive of minimum period to be served within discretionary sentence.	Article 6 s. 1
2000 February	*McGonnell* v. *UK*	Independence and impartiality of bailiff in Guernsey in proceedings relating to refusal of planning application.	Article 6 s. 1
2000 February	*Fitt* v. *UK*	Non-disclosure of material by prosecution on grounds of public interest immunity.	Article 6 s. 1
2000 March	*Curley* v. *UK*	(1) Absence of court review of detention 'at Her Majesty's pleasure'.	Article 5 s. 4
		(2) Absence of right to compensation.	Article 5 s. 5
2000 May	*Condron* v. *UK*	Drawing of adverse inferences from accused's failure to answer police questions.	Article 6 s. 1
2000 May	*Sander* v. *UK*	Alleged racial prejudice of jurors.	Article 6 s. 1

(Continues)

Box 2.11 *Continued*

Date	Case	Subject Matter	Article Violation
2000 May	*Khan* v. UK	(1) Absence of legal basis for interception of conversation by listening device installed on private property.	Article 8
		(2) Absence of remedy in respect of complaints about interception of conversation.	Article 13
2000 June	*Magee* v. UK	Denial of access to a lawyer during initial stages of detention.	Article 6 s. 1 and 3 (c)
2000 June	*Foxley* v. UK	Redirection of bankrupt's mail to the trustee in bankruptcy.	Article 8
2000 July	*A.D.T.* v. UK	Conviction for gross indecency between men.	Article 8
2000 September	*I.J.L., G.M.R. and A.K.P.* v. UK	Use at trial of statements made under threat of sanction to inspectors investigating company takeover.	Article 6 s. 1
2000 September	*Oldham* v. UK	Two-year period between reviews of detention after recall to prison.	Article 5 s. 4
2000 November	*Kingsley* v. UK	Impartiality of Gaming Board and scope of judicial review.	Article 6 s. 1
2001 March	*Hilal* v. UK	Threatened expulsion to Tanzania.	Article 3
2001 April	*Keenan* v. UK	(1) Treatment of prisoner with history of mental disorder.	Article 3
		(2) Lack of effective remedy.	Article 13
2001 May	*Hugh Jordan* v. UK	Effectiveness of investigation into shootings by soldiers.	Article 2
2001 May	*Z. and Others* v. UK	(1) Failure of social services to remove children from parents known to be neglecting them.	Article 3
		(2) Lack of effective remedy.	Article 13
2001 May	*T.P. and K.M.* v. UK	(1) Failure of social services to involve a parent in care of her child following removal of the child following suspected sexual abuse.	Article 8
		(2) Lack of effective remedy.	Article 13
2001	*S.B.C.* v. UK	(1) Lack of power of judge before whom detainee brought to order release on bail.	Article 5 s. 3

Box 2.11 *Continued*

Date	Case	Subject Matter	Article Violation
		(2) Absence of right to compensation.	Article 5 s. 5
		(3) Lack of effective remedy.	Article 13
2001 July	*Price* v. *UK*	Conditions of detention of severely handicapped person.	Article 3
2001	*Hatton and Others* v. *UK*	(1) Noise nuisance from night flights.	Article 8
		(2) Scope of judicial review.	Article 13
2001 October	*O'Hara* v. *UK*	(1) Failure to bring detainee promptly before a judge.	Article 5 s. 3
		(2) Absence of compensation.	Article 5 s. 5
2001 October	*Brennan* v. *UK*	Police supervision of consultation with lawyer.	Article 6 s. 1 Article 3 (c)
2001 October	*Devlin* v. *UK*	Access to court – issue of national security certificate precluding operation of non-discrimination in employment.	Article 6 s. 1
2002 March	*Paul and Audrey Edwards* v. *UK*	(1) Killing of detainee by mentally ill cellmate.	Article 2
		(2) Lack of effective investigation.	Article 2
		(3) Lack of effective remedy.	Article 13
2002 June	*Faulkner* v. *UK*	Interference with prisoner's correspondence.	Article 8
2002 June	*Willis* v. *UK*	Unavailability of widow's allowances to widower.	Article 14 Article 1 of Protocol 1
2002 July	*Wilson, National Union of Journalists and Others* v. *UK*	Offering of incentives to employees to renounce trade union rights.	Article 11
2002 July	*Christine Goodwin* v. *UK*	(1) Lack of recognition of transsexual.	Article 8
		(2) Impossibility of allowing transsexual to marry.	Article 12
2002 July	*Davies* v. *UK*	Length of period of disqualification of company director.	Article 6 s. 1
2002 July	*P.C. & S.* v. *UK*	(1) Absence of legal representation in childcare proceedings.	Article 6 s. 1

(Continues)

Box 2.11 *Continued*

Date	Case	Subject Matter	Article Violation
		(2) Taking of child into care at birth on an emergency basis.	Article 8
		(3) Procedures concerning care and freeing for adoption.	Article 8
2002 September	*Cuscani* v. *UK*	Failure to provide an interpreter for hearing on sentence.	Article 6 s. 1 and 3 (e)
2002 September	*M.G.* v. *UK*	Refusal of access to records of time in public care as a child.	Article 8
2002 October	*Somjee* v. *UK*	Length of time of sets of proceedings relating to employment.	Article 6 s. 1
2002 October	*Foley* v. *UK*	Length of civil proceedings.	Article 6 s. 1
2002 November	*Allan* v. *UK*	(1) Absence of legal basis for covert recording of remand prisoner at police station.	Article 8
		(2) Use in criminal proceedings of evidence obtained by police informer in suspect's cell.	Article 6 s. 1
		(3) Absence of effective remedy for covert recording.	Article 13
2002 November	*E. & Others* v. *UK*	(1) Failure to prevent physical and sexual abuse of children by mother's partner.	Article 3
		(2) Absence of an effective remedy.	Article 13

declaration of incompatibility Declaration by the judges that a statutory provision is incompatible with the human rights protected under the Human Rights Act 1998. Such a declaration does not in itself quash legislation, but it sends a strong signal to government that it should either amend the offending provision or justify its retention.

must (under section 3) strive to interpret all pre- and post-Convention legislation in a manner compatible with the Human Rights Act. Where they cannot do so, the higher courts (currently the House of Lords and JCPC) can issue a **declaration of incompatibility** (under section 4). The expectation is that where possible the government will take quick steps to amend the offending incompatible legislation. Initially it had been envisaged that a new fast-track procedure would allow ministers to amend primary legislation by order; but that was thought to grant too great a legislative power to the executive and the Human Rights Bill was amended so that new primary legislation would be required to repeal a law deemed incompatible with the Human Rights Act, unless there was a compelling reason to use secondary legislation.

How effective this process will prove to be is as yet unclear. Inevitably, the approach of the courts to the Human Rights Act will develop with time. One question that arises is how the courts will draw the boundary between sections 3 and 4 – that is to say, how far they will prefer to solve a conflict by interpretation rather than by a declaration of incompatibility. Another is how easy it will be for governments faced with a heavy legislative timetable to make swift amendments to legislation deemed incompatible with the Human Rights Act. At the time of writing, there have been only a few declarations of incompatibility, most notably the decision that the Mental Health Act of 1983 was not compatible with article 5 of the ECHR (*R. (On the application of H.)* v. *Mental Health Review Tribunal for North and East London Region*). Legislation was brought forward to correct the position (see box 2.12).

The adoption of this model of a bill of rights, of course, leaves open the possibility that the government may choose to resist a declaration of incompatibility. Examples of the sort of circumstances where such a resistance might be necessary would be if the judiciary used the ECHR to restrain access to abortion by extending the right to life to the unborn. Parliament might then need to make a different public policy judgement. And the government continues to have the power to derogate from an article of the ECHR if it deems the circumstances warrant it. Thus in 2001 it issued an order allowing it to derogate from article 5, which would have been incompatible with the Anti-Terrorism (Crime and Security) Act passed in the wake of the September 11 attacks on the United States.

Box 2.12   Important cases since the Human Rights Act 1998

- *R. (H.)* v. *Mental Health Review Tribunal for North and East London Region* (2002) QB 1 (CA): First use of remedial order. Case concerned Mental Health Act which placed burden of proof on patient to show that (s)he was safe for release. Declared incompatible with section 5 of the Convention (right to personal freedom).
- *Douglas* v. *Hello Ltd* (2001) QB 967: Court acknowledges the right to privacy.
- *R.* v. *Mental Health Review Tribunal and Secretary of State for Health, ex parte KB and others* (2002) EWHC (Admin): Delays in Mental Health Tribunals in review of detention due to lack of resources unacceptable under the Convention and must be dealt with by central government.
- *R. (Alconbury Developments Ltd)* v. *Secretary of State for Environment, Transport and Regions* (2001) 2 WLR 1389: Court finds planning procedures compatible with Article 6(1) guarantee of fair trial.
- *Starrs* v. *Procurator Fiscal* (1999): Scottish case challenging the appointment of part-time judges.

How far will the adoption of a bill of rights change the legal position of the citizen? The Human Rights Act makes it unlawful for any public authority to act in a way which is incompatible with a Convention right and provides judicial remedies where rights have been violated. It thus imposes an obligation on a large number of public bodies (and private bodies exercising public functions) to comply with the ECHR. The Act also means that Convention rights can be used as a defence in judicial proceedings. The Act thus covers a large number of public bodies, including central and local government, and has a potentially dramatic impact. It has been suggested, for example, that the law of medical negligence could be profoundly affected by the ECHR's emphasis on the right to life. Discrimination on the grounds of sexual preference may fall foul of the right to a private life. Privacy and confidentiality are likely to receive stronger protection, and indeed in two significant cases the courts recognized that the Human Rights Act required greater protection of privacy even in a case involving individuals rather than public authorities. (This so-called *horizontal effect* arises because of the obligation on courts and tribunals under section 6 to uphold ECHR rights.) And the Convention is likely to produce challenges to many aspects of the legal system because of the rights that it provides in relation to access to justice (see box 2.13).

In addition to the specific rights created and extended by the Human Rights Act, the government indicated that it wanted more generally to promote a culture of rights. Certainly, introducing the Human Rights Act has

---

Box 2.13   Rights protected by the ECHR and the Human Rights Act

Article 2 The right to life

Absolute right which may be removed by the state only in limited circumstances. Includes the right to an effective public investigation on behalf of the victim or the victim's family if the right is invaded. Important protection for prisoners and detainees, and those facing extradition. Has implications for hospitals, potentially increasing their liability in negligence suits. It does *not* as yet protect the unborn.

Article 3 Freedom from torture or inhuman or degrading treatment

A fundamental right which protects suspects under questioning and precludes physical and mental abuse. Important protection against child abuse and corporal punishment. Has implications for the level of care available in such institutions as hospitals and old people's homes.

Article 4 Freedom from slavery or forced labour

A fundamental right but one which is not breached by military service or community service. There are few situations in the UK where this right has implications.

Box 2.13 *Continued*

Article 5 Personal freedom

Limited right not to be arrested or detained even for a short period except in certain specified circumstances, for example in connection with the commission of a criminal offence. Even if lawful, detention must be carried out in a manner which is not arbitrary or discriminatory. There are other rights under the article which provide a broad due process protection, including the right to be brought before a court promptly and the right to be tried in a reasonable time, the right to bail and the right to have a sentence reviewed at reasonable intervals.

Article 6 Right to a fair trial

This article gives a broad right to a trial which involves a fair and public hearing before an independent and impartial tribunal within a reasonable time. It has important implications for the whole range of tribunals and courts in the United Kingdom and has already resulted in the reform of such practices as appointing temporary judges.

Article 7 No punishment without law

This article protects against retrospective trials.

Article 8 Private life and family

This article gives a broad protection to private life and personal privacy. It limits the extent to which the state can intercept personal communications and correspondence and places an obligation on public authorities to maintain the confidentiality of personal records. It protects the freedom to choose a sexual identity. It has implications for the extent to which the state can interfere with these rights. The protection of family life is the right to live as a family (whether formally married or not) and to enjoy a home. The right to enjoy a home has implications for public authorities, which must ensure that homes are not threatened by noise or environmental pollution.

Article 9 Freedom of belief

This article offers a broad protection to beliefs, religion and conscience. It has implications for the extent to which employers must accommodate religious and other beliefs of their employees and to which public authorities can invade the religious or other beliefs of individuals, e.g. through requiring the wearing of uniform or sitting examinations on a holy day.

Article 10 Free expression

This article protects free expression, which is given a broad meaning to include political opinions, demonstrations and cultural expression. However, it may be restricted – for example by law designed to protect national security and to prevent the expression of opinions offensive to racial or religious minorities. It has important implications for individuals, trade unions and other pressure groups and the media as well as for public order. It effectively makes censorship and prior restraint more difficult.

(Continues)

Box 2.13 *Continued*

Article 11 *Free assembly and association*

This article protects both freedom to engage in peaceful protest and the right to belong to a party or to form a trade union. It also protects the right *not* to join a party or trade union.

Article 12 *Marriage*

This article protects the rights of men and women to marry and to found a family. The article has important implications for the regulation of adoption and access to reproductive techniques, which the state may not restrict unreasonably. The state must also allow transsexuals to be recognized in law, to marry and to found a family.

Article 14 *Freedom from discrimination*

This article protects against discrimination in the exercise of other Convention rights. It makes it unlawful to discriminate on grounds of sex, race, colour, language, religion, political or other opinion, national or social origin, association with a national minority, property or birth or on any other grounds or other status, such as sexual orientation, legitimacy, disability, marital status or age. At the moment the article is tied to the exercise of pre-existing Convention rights, but a new protocol (which the British government has not signed) is designed to make this a free-standing article intended to eradicate discrimination. It may thus in due course become a major protection against all discrimination within the ECHR area.

Protocol 1.1 *Property*

This protocol gives the right to enjoy property peacefully.

Protocol 1.2 *Education*

This protocol provides the right of access to the educational system and the right to an effective education.

Protocol 1.3 *Free elections*

This protocol provides that where there is a right to vote the elections must be free and fair.

Protocol 6 *The death penalty*

This protocol abolishes the death penalty.

Articles 17 and 18

These articles are interpretative. Article 17 provides that the ECHR is not to be read as allowing any person or group to engage in any activity calculated to destroy ECHR rights. Article 18 states that restrictions on ECHR rights are not to be used for purposes other than those specially set out in the ECHR.

Source: LCD Study Guide to the Human Rights Act, 2nd edition

important implications across the governmental system. The Human Rights Act became operative throughout the United Kingdom in October 2000 but had already come into effect in Scotland and Wales. In anticipation of the Act, the government had established small ad hoc committees in each department to examine the implications of the new legislation and at the cabinet level there were dedicated committees covering the Human Rights Act. It seems that central government was reasonably well prepared for the change, though other public bodies, including local and health authorities, may find its implications more demanding.

The judges, who now have the responsibility for developing the legislation, are faced with a novel task. Although they are to be guided by the jurisprudence of the Court and Commission on Human Rights in interpreting and applying the Human Rights Act, they are not bound by that jurisprudence. As a result, they will have considerable freedom to adapt the principles of the ECHR to British circumstances. But in so doing, they will inevitably risk the accusation that they are imposing their own values on the legal system. And the increased salience of the judiciary will also focus attention on the character and composition as well as the skills of the judiciary.

The period since the implementation of the Human Rights Act has seen a major rise in the number of times the ECHR has been cited in the courts. And, although it is perhaps too early to get a real estimate of the caseload, it is clear that the Act is being used. Thus according to the Lord Chancellor's Department, of 297 cases analysed in the period between 2 October 2000 and 2003, Human Rights Act claims were upheld in just over a fifth of cases and made a difference to the outcome, the reasoning or the procedure.

Dramatic though the adoption of the ECHR might seem in a British context, it disappointed some critics and is very dependent upon the attitude of the judiciary for its effectiveness. One omission from the Human Rights Act was the establishment of any kind of Commission which could monitor the working of the legislation. A **joint committee** of the House of Lords and the Commons was set up to oversee human rights issues and especially the human rights implications of bills and remedial orders. Although the committee cannot investigate individual cases, it can take up thematic issues as well as contentious topics such as derogation. It has also itself set in motion an enquiry into the desirability of a Human Rights Commission for the United Kingdom as a whole.

The 1998 Human Rights Act is to some extent in danger of being overtaken by events. The EU has been signalling a growing interest in human rights and it has placed a new charter of rights on its agenda. Such a charter if adopted would be far stronger than the Human Rights Act because judges would have to give effect to the rights created under it even at the expense of directly striking down legislation. Not surprisingly, the British government is resisting any such move from Brussels and has adopted a stance which wishes to limit EU involvement to declaring existing rights rather than developing, expanding or enforcing them.

joint committee Committee containing members of both Houses of Parliament, usually as a means of achieving better coordination.

Reform of the House of Lords

Radical though devolution and the incorporation of the ECHR were, they proved more straightforward than Labour's commitment to reform the House of Lords. In the nineteenth century it had gradually become apparent that the House of Commons as the elected chamber was the dominant one and statute and convention effectively limited the House of Lords' role over the twentieth century. Nevertheless, Labour had long regarded any continuing exercise of political influence by the hereditary aristocracy in the House of Lords as an affront to democracy. Yet earlier efforts to reform the composition and powers of the second chamber had foundered (see box 2.14). Although Labour had in 1983 committed itself to outright abolition of the House of Lords, the 1997 manifesto promised reform not abolition. In office, Labour approached reform not as a single task but as a two-stage challenge in order to avoid the fate of many previous reform efforts where failure to reach a consensus on an alternative composition for the House of Lords derailed all change. First, the right of hereditary peers to sit in the House of Lords was abolished by legislation brought forward in 1999. At the same time, the government announced the establishment of a royal commission under a Conservative peer, Lord Wakeham, to make recommendations about the long-term future of the House.

The removal of hereditary peers from the House of Lords was intended to leave the United Kingdom with a second chamber consisting entirely of life peers, judges and bishops until such time as the royal commission could make its recommendations about the composition of the Lords. However, a compromise between the then Conservative leader of the Lords, Viscount Cranbourne, and the government ensured that 92 representatives of the hereditary peers were able to remain until the implementation of the second stage of reform.

When Wakeham reported in 2000 (*A House for the Future*), it was evident that securing agreement on the long-term reform of the Lords was not going to be easy. Wakeham accepted that the second chamber was to be subordinate to the House of Commons and not a rival to it. It would complement the House of Commons, not control it. And it took it as axiomatic that in order to be legitimate it should be as representative as possible. The problem was how to secure that representative quality without thereby giving it a legitimacy that would enable it to challenge the House of Commons. Wakeham considered four methods of determining the composition of a reformed chamber – direct election, indirect election, nomination and a mix of nomination and election. Ultimately the Commission opted for a mix of election and nomination but was divided over what the mix should be.

Nor did the government itself find agreement any easier. A proposal from the then Lord Chancellor Lord Irvine's cabinet committee for a 20 per cent elective element found no consensus either inside the government or in the Labour Party; and pressure mounted for a wholly elected chamber. In May 2002, the government announced its intention to hand the problem to a joint committee of the Lords and the Commons to see if such a committee could reach agreement on the composition and role of the second chamber. In February 2003, seven options for Lords reform were put before the House of Commons and all were rejected (see box 2.15).

Box 2.14 Reform of the House of Lords, 1900–2003

Parliament Act 1911: After battle over Lloyd George's budget, the Lords' power to reject legislation reduced to a two-year delaying power, with no power to delay money legislation. Preamble to the bill envisages an elected House in the near future.

Parliament Act 1949: Lords' delaying power over non-money bills reduced to one year, after Lords block Labour's steel nationalization plans.

Life Peerages Act 1958: Introduced life peers into the House of Lords, allowing women members for the first time.

Peerage Act 1963: Peers allowed to disclaim peerages for life and thus become eligible for membership of the House of Commons.

Parliament (No. 2) Bill 1969: Labour government proposes to phase out the hereditary element but is defeated by an alliance of Labour (who favour more extensive reform) and Conservative backbenchers (who favour the status quo).

House of Lords Act 1999: Removed the right of all but 92 hereditary peers to sit in the House of Lords.

January 1999: Labour publishes a **white paper** proposing to abolish 'hereditary peers with no democratic legitimacy' from the House of Lords. A Royal Commission headed by Lord Wakeham set up 'to consider and make recommendations on the role and functions of a second chamber'.

January 2000: Wakeham Report published outlining several options for reform, and favouring an option in which 87 of 550 members of the second chamber are elected. The rest to be appointed by an independent commission.

November 2001: White paper published, proposing 20 per cent elected element in the Lords. Draws heavy criticism from MPs and the media.

January 2002: In response to criticism of its proposals, the government appoints a Joint Committee on Lords Reform to allow Lords and MPs to identify options for a reformed second chamber.

February 2003: Lords and Commons vote on the seven options for reform proposed by the Joint Committee (see box 2.15). All options are defeated in the Commons. A fully appointed House gets support in the Lords.

Thus for the moment progress on reform of the Lords' composition has ground to a halt.

Meanwhile, the process of reform has produced four significant changes to the upper chamber. The first – the abolition of all but a vestige of the hereditary element – has removed one anomaly in the system, though at the price of creating a chamber heavily dependent on prime ministerial patronage. (As of June 2000, Tony Blair had created 202 peers, a rate which if sustained would be higher than

white paper Document which sets out the government's thinking in a policy area. Although there is usually time for consultation before legislation is introduced, the proposals in a white paper are normally indicative of the government's intentions and much firmer than in a green paper.

Box 2.15 Options for reform of the House of Lords, February 2003

Options for reform of the House of Lords	House of Commons		House of Lords	
	In favour	Against	In favour	Against
Fully appointed	245	323	335	110
80% elected; 20% appointed	281	284	93	339
60% elected; 40% appointed	253	316	91	318
50% elected; 50% appointed	No vote	No vote	84	322
60% appointed; 40% elected	No vote	No vote	60	359
80% appointed; 20% elected	No vote	No vote	39	376
Fully elected	272	289	106	329
Abolition	172	390	No vote	No vote

Source: BBC, http://news.bbc.co.uk/1/hi/uk_politics/2725769.stm

peerage General term given to group of nobles whose titles are conferred by the Crown. There are hereditary peers (whose titles pass to their heirs) and life peers. Until 1999 all hereditary peers and life peers of the UK could sit as members of the House of Lords, the second chamber of the British Parliament. After 1999 only a small number of hereditary peers could sit as members of the House of Lords as of right.

any prime minister since 1958 when life **peerages** were introduced.) It also slightly reduced the numerical strength of the Conservatives in the upper House (from 41 per cent to 34 per cent) and increased the percentage of Labour peers from 15 per cent to 28 per cent (see figure 2.1).

The second change was the introduction of a new appointments commission designed to secure the appointment of non-partisan peers from as broad a spectrum of British society as possible, some on the basis of self-nomination. The third change was the creation of a new select committee on the constitution, which has produced a series of useful reports including an overview on devolution with special reference to the impact on the British constitution as a whole. Finally, the logic of constitutional reform persuaded the government that the role of the Lord Chancellor should be radically changed and that the House of Lords should in due course have the opportunity to elect its own independent presiding officer. Part of this package was a new supreme court, whose members would not sit in the House of Lords but constitute an independent judicial body.

The threat of reform did not prevent the Lords from challenging the government. Despite the assumption embodied in the Salisbury convention that the Lords will not defeat at second reading a legislative measure that has been in the manifesto, the House of Lords has from time to time locked swords with the House of Commons on matters where it has considered it has special expertise or where it views the issue as one removed from the central partisan debate. (As table 2.6 shows, for example, the House of Lords felt justified in challenging a minority Labour government

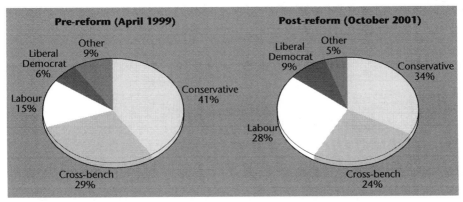

Figure 2.1 Composition of the House of Lords by party, pre- and post-reform. *Source:* House of Commons Library Research Paper, 01/77, *House of Lords: Developments since 1997*, http://www.parliament.uk/commons/lib/research/rp2001/rp01-077.pdf

between 1974 and 1979.) The House of Lords has inflicted defeat on a number of aspects of Labour's legislation since 1997, and that pattern has been maintained in the period since the removal of most hereditary peers. Thus, for example, the Lords defeated the Commons on a range of issues in the 1999–2000 **session** including the right to a jury trial, the discussion of homosexuality in schools, the electoral system and the Learning and Skills Bill. In July 2003 the Lords also revised government legislation designed amongst other things to reduce the right to a jury trial. On one argument such challenges to the will of the Commons are undemocratic and illegitimate; on another, the Lords are providing a necessary check on a government with a virtually invulnerable Commons majority.

Modernizing the House of Commons

By comparison with Labour's radical approach to the second chamber, the Blair government's approach to the reform of the House of Commons was remarkably cautious. This caution was hardly surprising given the government's determination to keep control of the legislative process and to protect itself from political criticism. Those who hoped that the House of Commons might develop a greater degree of independence from the executive were therefore disappointed. Blair made it clear that the Parliamentary Labour Party (PLP) would be expected to maintain tight discipline and, although there were changes in the workings of the House, they were not intended to alter the balance between legislature and executive, which remained overwhelmingly in the executive's favour. The Liaison Committee (which consists of the chairs of the select committees) in 2000 was highly critical of the government's refusal to consider its modest proposals for increasing the independence of select

session Annual sitting of Parliament, usually from November to November.

Table 2.6 Government defeats in the House of Lords, 1974–2003

Session	Defeats
	Labour government
1974–5	not available
1975–6	126
1976–7	25
1977–8	78
1978–9	11
	Conservative government
1979–80	15
1980–1	18
1981–2	7
1982–3	5
	Conservative government
1983–4	20
1984–5	17
1985–6	22
1986–7	3
	Conservative government
1987–8	17
1988–9	12
1989–90	20
1990–1	17
1991–2	6
	Conservative government
1992–3	19
1993–4	16
1994–5	7
1995–6	10
1996–7	10
	Labour government
1997–8	39
1998–9	31
1999–2000	36
2000–1	2
	Labour government
2001–2	56
2002–3	21

Source: Parliament website, House of Lords, Frequently Asked Questions, http://www.parliament.uk/faq/faq2.cfm

committees from party control (*Shifting the Balance: Select Committees and the Executive*, March 2000; *Independence or Control?*, July, 2000). Debate about the relative weakness of the House of Commons was further stimulated by reports from outside bodies such as the Hansard Society (*The Challenge for Parliament: Making Government More Accountable*, 2001) and from the Norton Commission (*Strengthening Parliament*, 2000) established by William Hague.

Debate about the scope and purpose of reform of the House of Commons is very much an ongoing one. The appointment of Robin Cook as Leader of the House of Commons in 2001 suggested that there was a greater opportunity for radical reform of the Commons, and indeed he presented a major set of reform proposals to the House of Commons in December 2001. What is not clear, however, is the extent of the will among MPs to push for extensive radical change. The proposal to make the appointment of select committee members more independent of the **whips** and thus to emphasize that the ownership of the select committee system of scrutiny belonged to the Commons was, for example, rejected on a free vote by MPs in May 2002. Since Cook's resignation in March 2003, it appears unlikely that there will be any great push for further major reform. That said, there have been significant reforms to the hours of the House, to the handling of legislation as well as to such central procedures as PMQT (see also chapter 6). In addition, the House of Commons is now operating in an environment where there are within the British Isles alternative models of legislative organization. The Scottish Parliament in particular has shown what can be achieved with a strong committee system and a less adversarial style. It is possible that these newer legislative bodies may provoke emulation at Westminster.

Electoral reform

Many critics of the executive's dominance of the legislature argued that the only fundamental remedy to this situation was electoral reform, meaning a change from the FPTP system. Any shift towards a more proportional system would be likely to strengthen minority parties in the House of Commons, perhaps necessitating coalition-style government rather than single-party government. Reform of the electoral system had been on the agenda of many of the groups who participated in the constitutional reform movement before the 1997 election. For the Labour Party, however, the issue was a difficult one. The long years of Conservative government between 1979 and 1997 had converted some Labour supporters – especially younger ones – to the cause of electoral reform; but many others totally rejected the idea.

Electoral reform was a key item of concern to the Liberal Democrats and the promise of a referendum on the issue was part of the price which Labour was prepared to pay prior to the 1997 election for cooperation with the Liberal Democrats. Despite a lack of commitment to electoral reform for Westminster, Labour once in office moved to establish an enquiry into the electoral system under Lord Jenkins; but by the time it reported (recommending a change to a new electoral system based on the alternative vote; see box 2.16), opposition to change had grown. Given that the Conservative Party and a majority of the Labour Party appears to be against change at the moment, it seems unlikely that any further move towards electoral reform will occur in the future.

Though advocates of reform of Westminster's electoral system were disappointed, the period after 1997 saw a number of changes to the electoral system for elections apart from Westminster. A regional list system was introduced for the European elections; AMS was used to elect the new Scottish Parliament and Welsh

whip Name given to the officials who manage the supporters of their party in a legislature. Also the notice of business which requires attendance to vote with the party.

Box 2.16   Recommendations of the Jenkins Commission

- 80–85 per cent of MPs to be elected under the alternative vote system.
- A top-up of 15–20 per cent of additional MPs distributed among the parties to achieve proportionality.
- Voters to cast two ballots: one for 530–560 constituency MPs, the other for a 'top-up' of a hundred or so MPs.
- Constituency MPs require the support of at least 50 per cent of those voting.
- Top-up MPs would be chosen from an open list, so that the elector could vote for a party or candidate on that list.
- Only registered political parties would be entitled to an allocation of 'top-up' candidates.
- Electoral commission to oversee electoral administration and independent commission to run the referendum on voting systems.

Source: Report of the Independent Commission on the Voting System, Cmnd 4090, October 1998.

Assembly; the supplementary vote was used to elect the new London mayor and London Assembly; and Northern Ireland's Assembly was elected by STV. In addition, there was much discussion of introducing a form of proportional representation into local government elections. Apart from the anomaly of having a number of different electoral systems in use at the same time, these innovations at the very least made alternative methods of choosing representatives more familiar to the general public, although it is doubtful if they did much to recommend reform to the leaders of the major parties, or indeed to their followers (see box 7.1, p. 245).

Modernizing government

In addition to the major constitutional reforms brought in by the Blair administration, there was after 1997 a new approach to government and policy making. Blair's prime ministerial style was much more dominant and personal than that of his predecessor, John Major, and, while Gordon Brown as Chancellor was also seen as exercising a good deal of power within the administration, there was little sense that the cabinet as a whole exercised directive force. Instead, Blair opted for more informal means of decision making (including bilateral meetings with ministers, task forces and policy groups) which could, if necessary, be ratified in cabinet committee afterwards.

As prime minister Blair was anxious to promote a more strategic approach to government. The goal was to overcome what were seen as inefficiencies resulting from the fragmentation of policy making and to modernize the governing process, for example by using new electronic means of communication and consultation. To ensure better coordination at the centre of government, there was a series of efforts to reshape the Prime Minister's Office and integrate it more closely with the Cabinet Office. Special units such as the Social Exclusion Unit were introduced to deal with cross-cutting issues, and the devices of task forces and working groups were employed to overcome departmentalization and to produce joined-up government that focused on users.

All of this resulted in a new set of priorities for ministers and for the civil service and a number of innovations in the organization of the core executive. Yet in many ways these innovations were simply giving a new twist to the changes in the public service culture generated during the Thatcher years. And in some respects the promised changes turned out to be less radical than had been anticipated. Thus, for example, a reform to give a legal right to freedom of information, when finally brought forward by the Blair government, deeply disappointed many observers, who had hoped it would go further than the informal code put in place by John Major. Instead, there were many exemptions and the powers given to the Information Commissioner were weak. Its full implementation was also delayed until 2005. And, of course, there was a recurrent tension between the prime minister's concern to strengthen his command of the strategic heights of British government and the implications of many of the constitutional reforms of the first term, which inevitably fragmented and dispersed political authority.

Conclusions

Labour's post-1997 constitutional reforms were an ambitious attempt to modernize and democratize the British constitution and its workings. They were driven in part by the need to respond to new political demands but also by the recognition that constitutional arrangements that had relied on informal understandings, trust and pragmatism had lost credibility. Although they fell short of providing a comprehensive written constitution, they greatly extended the areas of political and administrative life governed by legal rules and written codes. Clearly, these changes were expected and intended to have an impact on the United Kingdom's manner of government and its political culture. How far these constitutional changes have altered the quality of British democracy or created new political patterns are questions that will recur throughout the book. By 2003, it was clear that some of these reforms – notably, devolution to Scotland and Wales and the introduction of the Human Rights Act – had already 'bedded down' and were unlikely to be reversed. It was also clear that the institutions created as a result of these reforms – for example, the Scottish Parliament and the Welsh Assembly – were developing their powers and had the potential to generate further change within the system. Westminster to some extent lost control of the constitutional reform agenda.

On other fronts, efforts to reform the system had either unravelled (as in Northern Ireland) or stalled (as with House of Lords reform), creating a sense of frustration and unfinished business (Richard and Welfare, 1999). Certainly, by its second term the Labour government seemed to be diverting its energies to the problems of policy making and policy delivery and the more routine dilemmas of managing the administrative process.

Key Questions

1 Does the United Kingdom have a constitution?
2 Is further change needed to modernize and/or democratize the constitution? If so, what would those reforms be?
3 How well are individual rights and civil liberties protected in the United Kingdom?

Further Reading

There is now a massive literature on constitutional reform. Classic accounts of the British constitution can be found in Walter Bagehot, 'The English Constitution', in N. St John Stevas (ed.), *The Collected Works of Walter Bagehot*, vol. 5 (London: Routledge, 1995) and in A. V. Dicey, *Introduction to the Law of the Constitution* (10th edn; London: Macmillan, 1995). Ivor Jennings, *The British Constitution* (5th edn; Cambridge: Cambridge University Press, 1966) offers a different perspective.

The strengths and weaknesses of the pre-1997 constitution are addressed in Rodney Brazier, *Constitutional Practice* (Oxford: Clarendon Press, 1988) and in Vernon Bogdanor, *Politics and the Constitution: Essays on British Government* (Aldershot: Dartmouth, 1996), especially 'The Political Constitution'. Vernon Bogdanor's *Power and the People: A Guide to Constitutional Reform* (London: Gollancz, 1997) is also very useful.

K. D. Ewing and C. A. Gearty, *Freedom under Thatcher: Civil Liberties in Modern Britain* (Oxford: Clarendon Press, 1990) and Ian Harden and N. Lewis, *The Noble Lie: The British Constitution and the Rule of Law* (London: Hutchinson, 1986) offer sceptical analyses of traditional constitutional practice.

Peter Hennessy, *The Hidden Wiring: Unearthing Britain's Constitution* (London: Gollancz, 1995) provides a lively account of the constitutional system. Geoffrey Marshall, *Constitutional Conventions* (Oxford: Oxford University Press, 1984) analyses a number of familiar conventions. A valuable overview is given by Ferdinand Mount, *The Constitution Now: Recovery or Decline?* (London: Heinemann, 1992).

The constitution after 1997 is increasingly well covered. Special mention should be made of the publications from the Constitution Unit at University College London and work derived from them. See, for example, Robert Hazell, *Constitutional Futures: A History of the Next Ten Years* (Oxford: Oxford University Press, 1999) and Hazell et al.'s 'The constitution: Coming in from the cold', *Parliamentary Affairs*, 55: 2 (2002). Different perspectives on the merits of constitutional reform may be found in Keith Sutherland's edited collection *The Rape of the Constitution* (Thorverton, Devon: Imprint Academic, 2000) and in A. Barnett, *This Time: Our Constitutional Revolution* (London: Vintage, 1997). R. Blackburn and R. Plant, *Institutional Reform: The Labour Government's Constitutional Reform Agenda* (London: Longman, 1999) provides much insightful discussion. Anthony King's *Does the United Kingdom Still Have a Constitution?* (London: Sweet and Maxwell, 2001) is a stimulating essay, while J. Jowell and D. Oliver (eds), *The Changing Constitution* (4th edn; Oxford: Oxford University Press, 2000) brings together a series of illuminating articles on different aspects of constitutional change. (Earlier editions are also worth consulting.) J. Morrison, *Reforming Britain: New Labour, New Constitution?* (London: Pearson, 2001) is a valuable survey. Among several useful shorter articles, good analyses can be found in Nevil Johnson, 'Then and now: The British constitution', *Political Studies*, 48: 1 (2000), which provides a more critical analysis, and Diana Woodhouse, 'New Labour and a new constitutional settlement', *Parliamentary Affairs*, 52: 2 (1999), which looks at constitutional reform in general terms.

 Websites

See also the list of general websites at the back of the book.

- www.ucl.ac.uk/constitution-unit/ – Constitution Unit, University College London
- www.charter88.org.uk – Charter 88
- www.cfoi.org.uk – Campaign for Freedom of Information
- www.liberty-human-rights.org.uk – Liberty
- www.dca.gov.uk – Department for Constitutional Affairs
- www.echr.coe.int/Eng/BasicTexts.htm – European Convention on Human Rights

3 The Character of the Modern British State

The modern British state impinges on the lives of its citizens in innumerable ways. In addition to the delivery of such crucial services as health care and education, government in the United Kingdom has a role in relation to matters as diverse as environmental protection, food safety and animal welfare. Many aspects of these varied responsibilities of the state are taken for granted, at least until some disaster occurs, such as the bovine spongiform encephalopathy (BSE) crisis in the mid-1990s and the foot and mouth epidemic of 2001. The BSE crisis constituted what has been called a 'paradigm of policy failure', not just because of the scale of the damage done by the epidemic but also because of the way it highlighted the problems for British government of policy making when the subject matter has a strong scientific component and the process of risk assessment is controlled by politicians (Van Zwanenberg and Milstone, 2003). The efficiency with which government manages its public services and the competence with which it steers the economy will be key factors in deciding whether it will get re-elected. Not surprisingly, therefore, improving both policy making and policy delivery are likely to be issues high on every prime minister's agenda. In this chapter we shall be examining some of the characteristics of the modern British state by looking in very general terms at the role of government and the public sector in the United Kingdom. We shall examine some of the factors that caused the state historically to take on new functions as a prelude to discussing the quality of the policy process and of service delivery in the United Kingdom. The chapter will thus provide an overview of the part played by government in British society in the early twenty-first century and will highlight some of the problems of governing the country, especially the problems of coordination and accountability. This discussion is intended to set the stage for the more detailed examination of the British core executive and such related questions as the role of the civil service and Parliament in chapters 4, 5 and 6. It is also intended to raise a number of normative questions about the organization of the public sector, including the extent to which changes of structure and policy style aid or impede the promotion of other governmental goals such as efficiency or democratic responsiveness.

The Growth of the State

The range of responsibilities of the British state has expanded enormously since the nineteenth century. Whether we measure the growth of government's role by

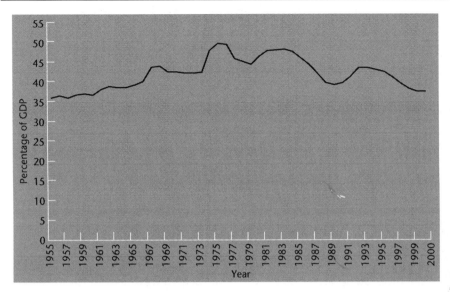

Figure 3.1 Government expenditure as percentage of GDP, 1955–2000. *Source*: Office for National Statistics

Table 3.1 Expenditure of EU governments as percentage of GDP, 2001

Countries	Government expenditure as % of GDP
Austria	52.3
Belgium	49.4
Denmark	55.3
Finland	49.0
France	52.7
Germany	48.3
Greece	48.2
Ireland	33.6
Italy	48.4
Luxembourg	40.4
Netherlands	46.4
Portugal	46.3
Spain	39.9
Switzerland	57.0
United Kingdom	40.4
EU 15	47.2

Source: Eurostat, The European Commission, http://www.europa.eu.int/comm/eurostat/

legislative output, by personnel employed or by the percentage of national income taken by the public sector, the trend has been upwards. The period since 1975, however, has seen an effort to halt this growth and the United Kingdom government's spending as a percentage of GDP now ranks behind all but two of the current EU countries (see figure 3.1 and table 3.1).

night-watchman state
Term associated with the political philosopher Robert Nozick (1974), who called for a minimal state that would provide nothing beyond a basic framework of laws and security for its citizens.

The question of when and where the state should intervene to provide a service or control an activity is one that has long been, and to some extent still is, central to ideological debate within the United Kingdom (Fry, 1979). For much of the nineteenth century the dominant ideological position was that of *laissez-faire* liberalism, which attributed a relatively minor role to government and left much to the free market and to civil society. The limited role of government in the nineteenth century meant that it was sometimes described as a **night-watchman state**, though the British state's role grew incrementally over the nineteenth century (Greenleaf, 2003). From the last quarter of the nineteenth century, accelerating over much of the twentieth century, there was a steady trend towards collectivism as the state came to be seen as the best mechanism for managing the economy and addressing major social problems. Government accordingly intervened in more and more areas of public policy and its responsibilities became more extensive. By the same token, the role of the market became more constrained by regulation. The role of private philanthropy in such fields as welfare and education (which had been extensive in the nineteenth century) became more limited.

The growth of the state in the United Kingdom (and the acceptance of the notion of a welfare state) was a matter of broad inter-party consensus for much of the twentieth century (Fraser, 2000). Although there is considerable academic debate about the character and extent of that consensus, there was certainly a cumulative growth of governmental responsibilities over the twentieth century (Pimlott, 1989). Thus, although first the Liberal governments of the early twentieth century and then Labour governments saw state intervention as the obvious remedy for a range of social and economic problems, the trend towards an expanding state role continued even when Conservatives were in office. This convergence of approach between the two major parties after the Second World War prompted the use of the term **Butskellism** to describe their shared assumptions.

From the mid-1970s, however, there was a major reassessment of the role of the state, spurred both by disillusion with the fruits of the post-war consensus (see box 3.1) and by a renewed interest in free-market economics. The election of Margaret Thatcher as leader of the Conservative Party in 1975 and as prime minister in 1979 marked a turning point in Britain's post-1945 history, ushering in a period in which concerted efforts were made to reduce the scope of the public sector and to improve its efficiency. State ownership of industry was radically reduced through a series of privatization initiatives and there were successive reforms in the size of the civil service and its organization and working methods (see also chapter 5). As a result, the British state from 1979 became less directly interventionist and developed new tools for securing its objectives (Salamon, 2002).

The 1997 Labour government, despite its long association with an extensive commitment to welfare and public ownership, accepted much of the thrust of its predecessor's market-oriented changes. Although still committed to an ambitious agenda of social reform, the Blair government adopted a pragmatic position with regard to the role of the state. 'What matters is what works' became the guiding principle as to whether the state should itself deliver services or whether other strategies, especially market-based ones, should be used. And it accepted that in managing many aspects of social and economic policy, its role would be indirect rather than direct, or, in the

Box 3.1   The post-war consensus

The period following the Second World War was characterized by a high degree of consensus between Labour and the Conservatives over both constitutional conventions and broad policy objectives. Both parties pursued centrist policies that supported the welfare state, a mixed economy and the use of Keynesian economic management to maintain full employment. The term **Butskellism** was invented to capture the similarity of policy between the Conservative Chancellor R. A. Butler and his Labour counterpart Hugh Gaitskell. The consensus began to unravel in the economic crises of the late 1960s and 1970s, which sparked confrontations between government and trade unions. Critics of the consensus theory pointed to significant differences of emphasis between the parties, but there was certainly more consensus between the parties in the 1945–77 period than in the period that followed. Thatcher denounced the consensual politics of the post-war period and moved her party to the right, whereas Labour shifted to the left after its 1979 defeat. It has since been argued that Thatcher created a new consensus, based around monetarist economic policies, privatization and reduced welfare provision. There has been considerable continuity between the economic policies of the Conservative governments of 1979–97 and those of the Labour governments in power since 1997.

Butskellism Phrase used by *The Economist* to capture the overlap between the economic policies pursued in the 1950s first by Labour's Chancellor of the Exchequer, Hugh Gaitskell, and then by the Conservative Chancellor R. A. Butler, who accepted many of the Keynesian theories of his predecessor.

words of one well-known American analysis of the task of government, that it should be steering rather than rowing (Osborne and Gaebler, 1992).

Debates about the role of the state may focus not just on *what* the state should do but on *how* it should achieve its objectives. These controversies about method also have a macro- and a micro-level dimension. At the macro level, even the briefest of surveys of the various programmes undertaken by government will show that there have been frequent and profound changes in the organization of services. Sometimes these changes have reflected shifts in belief about the optimal size for a department. Thus, for example, there has at times been a preference for so-called 'super-departments' in which a group of related functions could be administered within a single department of the central government. This pattern was one that appealed to Edward Heath's government of 1970–4. At other times, in contrast, there has been an assumption that each department of the central government would be responsible for a sharply defined function.

Different prime ministers have also found it appropriate to link different programmes together. Thus education has sometimes been linked to employment and at other times (as now) employment has either been linked to welfare functions or to productivity. The periods of major change in the role of government frequently saw the creation of new departments to match new responsibilities or to reflect new thinking about the machinery of government or policy delivery. Thus a series of new departments was created in the First World War and its immediate aftermath to manage newly acquired governmental responsibilities – for example, in relation to pensions and health. Half a century later the Heath government of 1970–4 created a new Department of the Environment to reflect concern with the management of a range of disparate issues relating to the environment.

Best Value The duty of continuous improvement for local authorities as set by the Local Government Act 1999. To fulfil Best Value requirements, councils must consult local people, review all their functions periodically, measure their performance and produce a performance plan which is audited by an independent auditor.

public service agreements (PSAs) Performance targets negotiated between central government departments and the Treasury, or set for local government by central government. Future funding may depend on meeting the targets.

The Blair government in 2001 made substantial changes to the responsibilities and names of a number of central government departments in order to reflect its own emphasis on joined-up government and policy implementation. These changes brought into being the new departments of Education and Skills, Environment, Food and Rural Affairs, Transport, Work and Pensions, and an Office of the Deputy Prime Minister. In 2003 the government made a range of further changes in the field of constitutional and legal administration by creating a new Department of Constitutional Affairs to replace the Lord Chancellor's Department.

At the micro level, innovations in the techniques of public administration may have a transformative effect on wider political relationships. The period since the late 1970s saw a series of reforms designed to improve the efficiency of British government by importing into the public sector ideas and techniques from the private sector. These included managerial decentralization, the use of flexible pay and performance systems, and the introduction of new methods of measuring and evaluating results. This new thinking about British public administration (known as the new public management or NPM) was both a response to, and a catalyst for, new interpretations of the character of the British state (Hood, 1991). As a result, there have been profound changes in the structures and culture of British government at all levels. New public management ideas have also exerted influence beyond the UK and have been taken up by other national systems and by a range of international organizations.

Although conceived under a Conservative government, which preferred market-oriented to state-based solutions on ideological grounds, the NPM reforms were continued, albeit in modified form, by the Labour government elected in 1997. Labour, however, after 1997 added its own new tools and techniques (such as **Best Value** and **public service agreements**) in a drive to raise the standards of public services and their delivery. Indeed, as the Public Administration Committee noted in 2003, government by targets became a marked feature of the Blair government (Public Administration Select Committee, 2002–3).

The Multiple Dimensions of Governmental Activity

The task of providing an overview of what the state does is complicated by problems of definition. Even without the complexities introduced by the fragmentation and decentralization of government since the 1980s, any analysis of the role of the British public sector is beset by conceptual and empirical difficulties.

What do we mean by the state? Here the general term 'state' is used as convenient shorthand to refer to the whole range of governmental institutions and public authorities, although we of course recognize the variety of theoretical issues raised by the concept. Such issues include the relationship between the state and civil society and the extent to which the state can be held accountable in a liberal democracy. It should be noted also that the concept of the state is not one commonly used in British political discourse. Indeed, some authors have suggested that the

Box 3.2   Elected regional assemblies: Main aims

- Decentralizing power from central government and bringing decision making closer to the people.
- Giving regions the freedom and flexibility to meet their own priorities, within a national framework.
- Making government in the regions more accountable to people in the regions.
- Providing democratic representation in the regions and a new political voice.
- Improving delivery by ensuring better coordinated government at regional level.
- Giving regional stakeholders a clearer decision-making framework to engage with.
- Promoting sustainable development and improving quality of life.

Source: Office of the Deputy Prime Minister, *Your Region, Your Choice: Revitalising the English Regions* (2002).

United Kingdom, by contrast with continental European countries, lacks a state tradition (Dyson, 1980; Laborde, 2000).

Nor is the concept of the state used much in British constitutional law, where a series of more specific notions such as the Crown are employed to analyse public power (Daintith and Page, 1999; McEldowney, 2002). In some ways the lawyers' caution is justified. The British state was never monolithic and it has become even more fragmented as a result of devolution, which has created new layers of government and means that government departments have different territorial spans of responsibility. Administrative innovations such as executive agencies have complicated this picture further. Thus not only should the state not be seen as a single actor, but there is also a concern that this fragmentation has become a real impediment to coherent policy making. Certainly, many different institutions are involved in the making of public policy and in its implementation. In addition to the familiar levels of central government and local government, there is now an important dimension of regional government throughout England as a result of the creation of nine regional development agencies (RDAs) that were launched between 1999 and 2000. In 2002 a white paper anticipated that regional government might acquire a democratically elected regional element if that was wanted by a region (see map 11.2, p. 372 and box 3.2). And of course the transnational levels of government (such as the European Union) increasingly impinge on and constrain the nation state.

One further complication of identifying what we mean by the state should be noted. There has long existed in the United Kingdom a bewildering number of special purpose authorities including such significant organizations as the National Health Service (NHS). These specially constituted bodies have taken a number of forms and been given a range of different names. One popular label for them was the term **quango** (Barker, 1982); another, more neutral, term was non-departmental public bodies or NDPBs. In many ways both terms now conceal the variety and diversity of bodies that fall into this category. Thus specially constituted bodies may be

quango Publicly funded body operating at arm's length from a department. Quangos may perform executive, advisory or quasi-judicial functions. They have grown in number in recent years and are frequently criticized because they offer ministers extensive patronage and lack accountability.

executive or advisory in function. They may be national, local or hybrid bodies linking the state to the voluntary sector. And they may be appointed in a variety of ways. One recent attempt by the Public Administration Select Committee to map what it called the 'quango state' found over 530 advisory NDPBs in central government, over 5,300 in local government and a further 2,300 bodies that linked the voluntary and public sectors. A count in April 2002 of public bodies sponsored by government departments and regulators numbered 834.

One crucial feature of concern about these bodies is that their members are not elected but appointed – often by ministers who may choose them on grounds of political sympathy. Naturally, parties out of power tend to attack these bodies as undemocratic tools of ministerial patronage. Governments find them too useful a device to abandon. Thus despite their loud objections to quangos in opposition, the Conservative governments of 1979–97 increased their number, provoking cries of righteous indignation from Labour. Once in power, however, Labour maintained a large number of quangos, and indeed its innovative approach to public policy making has created new governmental devices such as task forces and ad hoc policy reviews which share some of the features of quangos (see box 3.3).

There have been some efforts to curb the worst excesses of patronage associated with quangos. Following the Nolan Report (which recommended that public appointments should be on merit and contain an independent element), a Commissioner for Public Appointments was established, supported by an office. This office now oversees some 11,000–12,000 of 26,000 or so appointments made by government each year. However, the Public Administration Select Committee thought there was still considerable room for reform and, as it pointed out in 2003, 'the appointment state runs far wider than the quango state'.

The organization of the functions of government has always displayed a good deal of fluidity. There is no obvious logic in the allocation of functions between departments of central government or between different tiers of government or agencies. Functions have also been moved between tiers of government, so that local government in particular has experienced substantial changes to its responsibilities (usually to its detriment), especially in the period since 1945. Moreover, the advent of what has been called a multi-layered polity or multi-level governance (not least as a result of Labour's creation of new layers of devolved government in Scotland, Wales and Northern Ireland and the expanding role of the European Union) has further complicated the distribution of responsibilities within the public sector. The determination to strengthen regional government in England promises further substantial administrative and organizational upheaval, as does the likely shift of power from exclusively national bodies to supranational and multinational ones. Thus, for example, environmental policy making involves a range of players at different governmental levels, most significantly the European Union level, which has increased its role in environmental regulation so that it now accounts for approximately 80 per cent of environmental legislation (Jordan, 2002).

Within central government itself, the formal framework of the government department has provided organizational stability since the structure of departments displays important regularities (see figure 3.2). But as already emphasized, the names, size, significance and distribution of functions and responsibilities for programmes *between* and *within* departments have been much more fluid (Clifford,

Box 3.3   Selected quangos

There are over a thousand quangos – non-departmental public bodies (NDPBs) – in the United Kingdom, although some 15 per cent are now responsible to the Scottish Parliament, the Assembly for Wales and (when operative) the Northern Ireland Assembly. Quangos are sponsored by a department but are not part of it and the staff are not civil servants. There are approximately 30,000 appointments to NDPBs and such appointments are generally within the gift of ministers. These bodies may be advisory, executive or semi-judicial in character.

NDPB	Department	Type	Function
Higher Education Funding Council	Education and Skills	Executive	Regulates and distributes funding of universities.
English Nature	Environment, Food and Rural Affairs	Executive	Conserves wildlife and geology.
Committee on the Safety of Medicines	Health	Advisory	Advises on the quality and safety of new products and monitors the marketing of licensed medicines.
Animal Procedures Committee	Home Office	Advisory	Advises on the use of protected animals in scientific research.
Special Needs Appeal Tribunal	Education and Skills	Tribunal/quasi-judicial	Hears appeals against local authority decisions on special educational needs.
General Commissioners of Income Tax	Lord Chancellor's Office[a]	Tribunal/quasi-judicial	Hears appeals against tax assessments.

[a] Now the Department for Constitutional Affairs.
Source: Adapted from *Vacher's Parliamentary Companion* 1109 (March 2003) and websites of the NDPBs.

McMillan and McLean, 1997; Pollitt, 1993; Rose, 1987). And even within the ostensibly integrated and uniform structures of central government departments, there are subtle but resilient differences of ethos or culture (Hennessy, 2001c). These differences will often reflect the historical legacies and traditions of a department and its position within the Whitehall structure; or they may reflect the character of the policy community of which the department forms a part. Sometimes reorganizations of a department's structure and responsibilities are motivated by an explicit desire to change the organizational culture of a particular department. Thus the old Ministry of Agriculture, Fisheries and Food (MAFF) was so identified with the producer organizations – especially the farmers – that it lacked credibility in relation

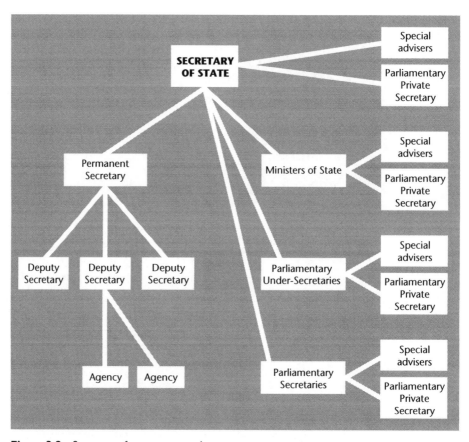

Figure 3.2 Structure of a government department.

to its food safety responsibilities. It was therefore reorganized in 1997 into a new Ministry (DEFRA) and a separate Food Standards Agency.

The late 1980s saw a major change even in the departmental structure with the administrative reforms based on the Ibbs Report (see box 3.4). These reforms saw the hiving off of discrete – often routine – areas of governmental responsibilities (such as the issuing of passports or the regulation of highways) to new administrative bodies known as agencies or Next Steps Agencies after the title of the Ibbs Report. The role of agencies will be examined in more detail in chapters 4 and 5; but here it is necessary to note the underlying philosophy of the reform, which was based on the belief that policy and administration could be separated organizationally. Although the minister would retain control of policy, the chief executive of each agency was to have control of operational matters. Over 75 per cent of civil servants now work in executive agencies and by 1998–9 there were 136 such agencies.

The reorganization of so many governmental functions into agencies complicates the structure of the British state, fragmenting the lines of control by ministers over many areas of administration. As a result, some commentators have suggested that it has blurred, if not fatally weakened, the constitutional accountability of those

Box 3.4   The Ibbs Report

Sir Robin Ibbs, *Improving Management in Government: The Next Steps* (1988):

- Stressed the need for more urgency in the search for better value for money.
- Criticized progress of management reforms since 1979. Argued that radical change was required to overcome obstacles to change.
- Recommended that executive functions of civil service (approximately 95 per cent of civil service tasks) be transferred to agencies. Sponsoring departments to contract with the agency for those services.
- Agencies to be headed by a chief executive and have significant managerial freedom from sponsoring department.
- Choice and definition of suitable agencies for ministers and senior management in departments to determine.

Source: Efficiency Unit, 1988.

agencies even though they still fall squarely within the remit of a named department and minister. One explicit purpose of the Next Steps reforms was to improve the quality and efficiency of administration by encouraging a focus on a single function in an agency, giving it a dedicated mission rather than having a multiple focus as occurs in a department. How far this has worked is unclear; and there is some evidence that smaller agencies (for example, within Transport) are being brought together again.

Agency status was also intended to allow greater operating freedom and flexibility from some of the standard rules and centralizing procedures and practices that have grown up in British government in relation to staffing, for example. Changes in the organizational culture of the civil service were also expected as a result of the reforms, making it more entrepreneurial and managerial and less risk averse. It was also hoped that by shifting the emphasis to management and service delivery the civil service would become less concerned with policy formulation, allowing ministers greater control. As will be seen in chapter 5, doubts have been expressed about the extent to which the agency initiative in fact has delivered the anticipated benefits as well as about the effects on the ethos of the civil service. For the purposes of this chapter it is important to notice that this change in the organizational structure of government, though introduced as part of the Conservatives' programme to reduce the role of the state after 1979, was accepted by Labour with only a few modifications. Agencies therefore must now be seen as a permanent feature of the British governmental scene.

The scale and impact of the state's activity are further complicated by the range of forms its intervention may take once government has decided to intervene in a policy area. The styles and modes of policy intervention are varied, and may include the direct provision of a service, regulation of a service provided by a third party, and a host of cooperative and negotiated agreements. Government policy may be effected through the use of financial incentives such as grants and subsidies. Changes in thinking about the role of the state (which became especially marked in the period after 1979)

contracting out Process of delegating activities and services previously performed directly to third parties or private providers.

public–private partnership (PPP) A joint venture between the public and private sectors, with investment often coming from the private sector and risk shared between the two sectors. Such partnerships may cover the management of services and small-scale enterprises as well as large-scale projects.

Private Finance Initiative (PFI) The contracting out of large public sector capital projects to the private sector, often used to build hospitals and schools. Private companies may lease buildings back to the public sector over a period of 30 years or more.

generated a shift towards policy styles, which emphasized the government's role as a regulatory agent rather than a direct service provider. Thus the Conservative governments of Margaret Thatcher (1979–90) and of John Major (1990–7) expanded the role of both markets and regulation in securing public policy objectives. The post-1979 period therefore saw an extended use of strategies that blur the distinction between the private and the public sector – for example, through **contracting-out** arrangements in many services such as community care. Although the Labour governments since 1997 were less explicitly enthusiastic about purely market solutions, their governing style has also involved a wide range of modalities to achieve their own policy goals, including controversially the use of **public–private partnerships** (see box 3.5) to raise new capital for schools, hospitals and the London Underground (see chapter 11).

Commentators have tried to capture the character of the modern British state in terms of this new indirect mode of intervention, which is increasingly replacing direct provision of services and public ownership. Thus the modern British state has been described as a 'regulatory state' to highlight the role of regulation as a preferred tool for government to promote its objectives (Majone, 1996; Hood, James and Scott, 2000). An alternative formula is that of an audit society (Power, 1997). What these accounts highlight is the extent to which we must look beyond the traditional institutions of central and local government to a series of new bodies such as regulatory agencies which have an important impact on public policy.

These shifts in policy style link to another preliminary point about the analysis of state activity in contemporary Britain. The shift towards a different mix of interventionist techniques underlines the extent to which the processes of government involve multiple actors. In addition to the familiar cast of ministers, policy advisers, civil servants and other officials at the central level of government, there is a range of significant decision makers at other levels of the governing process. Thus there are in every policy area networks of pressure groups and professional bodies with a crucial role in the processes of policy making and implementation. The use of such techniques as contracting out (at local and national government

---

Box 3.5   Public–private partnerships

Public–private partnerships are mechanisms for reforming the public services especially by injecting new capital into them through the **Private Finance Initiative (PFI)**, but also by injecting new energy and values into their organization. Public–private partnerships are seen as especially important to developing the NHS, where the private sector is being used to build new hospitals and to take some of the load from hospital waiting lists. Although logically different from privatization, public–private partnerships have incurred opposition from trade unions, and the Institute of Public Policy Research (IPPR) found the initial experiments flawed, not least because of their lack of accountability and protection for employees.

Box 3.6   Governance

The term 'governance' is usually encountered as part of a broad theoretical approach to the processes of politics and government. Its distinctive feature is that it emphasizes the way in which the contemporary governing process blurs public/private sector boundaries and cannot be accommodated by hierarchical models of decision making. Rather, it sees the process of governing as relying on the operation of markets and the existence of networks as much as on formal state institutions. It is thus a description of a governing style and sometimes a prescriptive theory about how collective decisions should be made. It can be applied to the national level of government but it has powerful appeal at both the subnational and local levels and at the supranational level. Its emphasis on a multi-faceted process of orchestrating interests and policies rather than on a single legitimate government makes it an attractive approach for analysts of the European Union.

levels) involves private sector firms and organizations in the processes of service delivery and adds a new complexity to the task of policy making. Thus public sector reforms have not just restructured the state but have made it smaller and involved the private sector in policy making to a much greater extent than before.

These networks of actors further blur the division between the private and the public sector, reinforcing the need to see government decision making less as a self-contained and insulated activity of command and control and more as a complex process of coordination. This shift has been seen by many observers as so substantial as to constitute a paradigm shift in our understanding of the governmental process. Authors such as Rhodes and others attempt to highlight this shift by using the notion of **governance** as opposed to 'government' to capture it (Rhodes, 1997; Salamon, 2002; see box 3.6). The important point for the purposes of the discussion here is that governing is a complex and multi-dimensional activity which intersects with the economic and social life of the country in a variety of ways, challenging formal and institutional arrangements for coordination and control. Indeed, one of the most important themes of the 1997 Labour government's approach to policy making was its desire to strengthen the mechanisms of coordination in order to achieve joined-up government and overcome the tendencies to fragmentation within the policy process.

Explaining Governmental Growth

Although we now take the big state for granted, it is worth remembering that until the early nineteenth century, government provided few services for its population and its principal functions were concerned with the provision of the core services of law and order, defence, trade and foreign affairs and raising the revenue to pay for these services. As industrialization and urbanization generated new social problems, the responsibilities of government gradually

governance A model of policy making which focuses not on formal governmental institutions but on policy making through bargaining and negotiation between governmental actors at the national level and private and voluntary sector bodies.

expanded, although the process was piecemeal and incremental rather than coherent and rational.

So what kinds of factors have generated changes in the role of government? Here we identify four broad causes of change: changes in the political order; changes in state capacity; crises in public policy; and external pressure.

Changes in the political order

A number of shifts in the political order may alter the role of the state. For example, there may be changes in the structure of party support which bring a party with a distinctively new policy agenda to power. The election of Labour in 1945 changed the responsibilities of the state because that party had a radical commitment to extending the welfare state and managing the economy to maintain full employment. The election of the Conservatives in 1979, by contrast, brought into government a party determined to expand the role of the free market and reduce the role of the state. Parties are not the only actors capable of altering the state's role. New interest groups such as trade unions or environmental groups may emerge or become stronger. Thus the extent to which an interest is able to mobilize behind a change in the role of the state (or indeed to oppose it) is always important.

Secondly, governmental growth may reflect changes in the public philosophy. Change in the climate of ideas can affect the role of the state in a number of ways, for example by changing the language in which a social problem is discussed or by predisposing policy makers to adopt one policy solution rather than another. The nineteenth century, although generally seen as one in which the *laissez-faire* model and classical liberalism were dominant influences, saw the state taking on a series of new regulatory responsibilities in such fields as labour law and public health. These interventions themselves generated further government intervention, as policies were refined and enforcement measures introduced or strengthened.

Fundamental shifts in the intellectual climate are historically rare and usually occur when some crisis or series of crises have cast doubt on pre-existing assumptions. We can identify three periods in the twentieth century in which there have been significant reassessments of the role of government. The first was the period between 1900 and 1914, when there was a marked movement towards a more positive role for the state in the promotion of welfare. This movement was associated with the rise of **new liberalism** and resulted in a range of major initiatives in the field of welfare, including the introduction of old-age pensions in 1908 as well as in significant changes in the machinery of government (Freeden, 1986). The second was the period immediately following the Second World War – the years of the Attlee Labour governments of 1945–51 – which saw the acceptance of a much more comprehensive role for the state in the management of the economy, in industry and in welfare. As noted earlier, the extent to which the ideas of this period constituted a consensus has been much debated. What is beyond doubt is that the dominant ideas of this crucial period

new liberalism Radical strand within British liberalism that emerged in the late nineteenth century and heavily influenced the Liberal governments of 1906–16. The new liberalism emphasized the positive role of the state and supported government intervention in the economy and in society, in contrast to the classical *laissez-faire* liberalism. Not to be confused with neo-liberalism, which was one strand in the movement to the right in the 1970s.

in British history, especially the economic theories of John Maynard Keynes and the social philosophy of William Beveridge, gave additional impetus to an expansion in the public sector's role and created an assumption that the state's activities would continue to increase. Only in the third crucial period – the 1970s – did this assumption come to be challenged. By the mid-1970s, although there were challenges from both the left and the right, it was the challenge from the right, specifically the neo-liberal or **new right**, which was politically the most important in terms of both its intellectual dynamism and its political success.

The period from the mid-1970s until 1997 saw an unusually coherent attempt to reduce the role of the government and to redress the balance between the state and the market (Helm, 1989; Jenkins, 1987). In this radical reappraisal, a number of significant policy changes occurred. The public ownership of several key industries taken into state ownership in the 1945–51 period was reversed; and many key utilities (telephone, water, gas, electricity and the railways) were privatized. In order to preserve the public interest in the running of these industries, a series of regulatory bodies was established. Thus as a result of the period 1979–97, not merely was the state's role as a direct provider of services and owner of industry cut back, but a whole new cluster of state bodies in the form of regulatory agencies was established (see box 3.7). These regulatory agencies (such as OFTEL, OFGEM and OFWAT) have become an important new part of the modern British state, joined by newer agencies such as the Financial Services Authority (FSA), established in 2001 to oversee the financial system, and OFSTED, which regulates school standards.

In addition to the radical reduction of the British state's direct ownership of industry, the state scaled down its role in some other areas of public policy. Thus housing policy was left much more to the market after 1979, as a result of both the Conservative government's forced sale of council housing and the gradual elimination of tax relief on mortgages. Also, a number of private sector techniques (such as **performance indicators** and benchmarking) were introduced into government in the effort to improve efficiency. More generally, the state increasingly appeared to employ methods that were more indirect and less coercive than previously.

Although the initiative for this rebalancing of the roles of state and market had been enthusiastically adopted by the Conservative Party, it had implications for Labour as the party was forced to reassess its own ideological thinking and approach to public policy. As a result, the Labour Party – or New Labour, as it explicitly became under Blair – adopted a much more pragmatic approach to policy. Under Blair, the specific commitment to public ownership (contained in Clause 4 of the Labour Party 1918 constitution) was discarded. Labour from the late 1990s expressed its policies in terms of a third way. This approach was seen by some as an amalgam of ideas employing state and market solutions and a halfway house between democratic socialism and capitalism, and by others as a new synthesis that transcends the capitalism–socialism dichotomy (Giddens, 1998; White, 2001).

new right A term attached to the coalition of neo-liberal economists, philosophers and politicians who rose to prominence in the 1970s, advocating a reduced role for the state and a market-oriented, *laissez-faire* approach to economics. The term may also be used to refer to their organized supporters and is often associated with the policies of Margaret Thatcher in the UK and Ronald Reagan in the United States.

performance indicators Criteria against which public bodies are judged. Local authorities, for example, are measured against a set of Best Value performance indicators, and the results are published in league tables. Failure to meet the required standard may lead to the imposition of penalties such as loss of grant or intervention by the Secretary of State.

Box 3.7   Regulatory agencies

Utility regulators

OFTEL (Office of Telecommunications)*
OFGEM (Office of Gas and Electricity Markets)
OFWAT (Office of Water Regulation)
ORR (Office of the Rail Regulator)

Other UK regulators

Broadcasting Standards Commission*
Civil Aviation Authority (CAA)
Data Protection Commission
Drinking Water Inspectorate
Electoral Commission
Financial Services Authority (FSA)
Food Standards Agency (FSA)
Health and Safety Executive (HSE)
Independent Television Commission (ITC)*
National Lottery Commission
Office for Standards in Education (OFSTED)
Office of the International Rail Regulator
Occupational Pensions Regulatory Authority (OPRA)
Postal Services Commission (POSTCOMM)
Radio Authority*
Radiocommunications Agency*

* These regulatory agencies were to be replaced by OFCOM (Office of Communications) at the end of 2003.

Source: Adapted from Brazier (2003).

Changes in state capacity

A second important factor affecting when the state will intervene is the capacity of government. Government cannot realistically take on a new function or meet new challenges unless it has certain tools at its disposal and has the appropriate knowledge, infrastructure, communications, money, personnel and leadership to intervene.

Changes in the knowledge at a state's disposal will alter its disposition to act. Doubtless, many governments would have liked to prevent outbreaks of disease such as the plague; but until the advances of science and technology in the nineteenth century, governmental intervention was ineffective. Advances in scientific knowledge and communication have greatly expanded the ability of modern governments, although there remains – as the BSE and foot and mouth crises showed – a good deal of doubt about the ability of government to interpret scientific data effectively and to integrate scientific advice into the policy process.

Table 3.2 Government spending on market research, 1990–2001

Year	Spending (£ million)
1990	9.3
1991	11.0
1992	13.2
1993	17.2
1994	16.3
1995	16.7
1996	18.3
1997	20.8
1998	21.3
1999	23.8
2000	33.9
2001	29.8

Source: British Market Research Association, http://www.bmra.org.uk/

State capacity is also expanded by its ability to ascertain and store large amounts of data about the characteristics of the society. The modern governmental machine is thus engaged in a range of investigative activities from collecting census data to surveys of household income and crime. The modern state increasingly has the ability to consult the population about its policy preferences through polling and through relatively recent devices such as focus groups and people's panels. The latter have been used at both central government and local government levels as ways of testing the reaction of the public to policies and services. The spread of information technology and the adoption of an e-government strategy have transformed the ability of both decision makers to consult citizens and citizens to access government information quickly (see table 3.2 and box 3.8).

Knowledge (whether of what the public wants or of how to deliver it) by itself is not, however, sufficient: there must be an adequate infrastructure to enable policy making and implementation to operate effectively. Until the nineteenth century central government lacked the tools to be able to perform much in the way of direct administration and therefore most governmental functions had to be performed locally, either by agents of the central government or by elected local officials. Today there is an increasing emphasis on the need to strengthen government's **strategic capacity**, by which is meant the ability to plan, direct and deliver policy in the long term. As a result – and this will be discussed in more depth in chapter 4 – there is constant concern both with the capacity of the central institutions of government and with the institutional support for key policy makers.

In addition to the basic knowledge and infrastructure, the state also needs personnel and money appropriate to the task in hand. The creation of a competent bureaucracy was an essential part of the expansion of the British state. Following the Northcote–Trevelyan reforms, Britain gradually put in place a neutral civil service recruited on merit rather than on patronage. The composition and culture of the British civil

strategic capacity Government's overall ability to plan, direct and deliver policy in the long term.

Box 3.8   Examples of government surveys

Census: Ten-yearly census of everyone in the UK, covering accommodation, relationships within households, migration, employment, qualifications, travel to work and the age, sex, marital status and ethnic composition of the UK population.

Labour Force Survey: Quarterly survey presenting data on labour market structure and activity, employment and unemployment rates, economic inactivity, earnings and subnational economic activity.

British Crime Survey: Annual survey measuring crime levels in England and Wales by asking people about crimes they have experienced in the last year and their attitudes towards crime and the criminal justice system. The survey includes crimes that are not reported to the police and also helps to identify those most at risk of different types of crime.

General Household Survey: A multi-purpose, continuous survey which collects information on a range of topics from people living in private households. It presents up-to-date information on a wide range of socio-demographic topics, providing a comprehensive picture of how people live in Britain today.

Family Expenditure Survey: A survey of household spending in England and Wales. Contains detailed analyses of expenditure on goods and services by household income, composition, size, type and location.

Source: National Statistics Handbook, 2002.

service are examined in greater detail in chapter 5. Here it is necessary only to note that the question of how far the British civil service is suited to the tasks of the modern state is one that has greatly concerned policy makers in recent years. As a result, the civil service has adopted a much more flexible approach to recruitment and a new concern with management skills and training. There have also been significant shifts in thinking about the personnel required for modern local government and for other parts of the state.

The provision of a service by government has to be paid for, whether out of money raised by taxation, by user fees or by borrowing. In recent years, governments in Britain as in many modern states have found a resistance to rising tax burdens. It was for this reason that the Labour Party in 1997 pledged that it would not increase direct taxation, although in government it did adopt a number of so-called 'stealth taxes', including in 2002 an increase in national insurance.

Finally, leadership is an important factor both in the political realm and inside the state machine (Theakston, 1999, 2000). The energy of a prime minister (such as David Lloyd George or Margaret Thatcher), of an individual minister (such as Michael Heseltine), a mayor (such as Joseph Chamberlain) or an administrator (such as Hubert Llewellyn Smith or William Beveridge) can make a real difference to the effectiveness of policy making and implementation.

Crises in public policy

Changes in the role of the state can be occasioned by the experience of a crisis in public policy. Such crises can take many forms. War is an obvious one. Thus the Boer War underlined the poor health of working-class recruits to the army, while the experience of the First World War prompted major reforms in the machinery of cabinet government and a general expansion of government intervention in the country's economic and social life. The Second World War of 1939–45 also prompted important moves in the direction of collectivism and a massive expansion in the role of government, both in order to win the war itself and in the aftermath of war when social reconstruction was undertaken. But war is not the only source of policy disjuncture. Economic crisis can prompt significant changes in the role of the state. Thus, for example, the experience of unemployment in the interwar years was one factor encouraging a commitment to full employment and state responsibility for economic management after 1945. Public health crises – cholera, HIV/AIDS and, most recently, BSE – have provoked substantial re-evaluation of the state's role in preventing disease. Internal disorder in the form of race riots prompted a reassessment of a range of state machinery and policies, including the culture of the police.

External pressure

Finally, although much of the impetus for government intervention has been domestic, some important changes in the role of the state have come from external sources. The British state operates in the context of a global economy and is thus always subject to competitive pressures which may in turn affect the government's role. Thus the use of incentives, grants and other subsidies to encourage research and development may arise because of the perception of international competition. The use of tariffs and industrial protection is another weapon that can be used by government to enhance its competitive position. In the modern world, the increased mobility of capital means that governments must adopt policies which investors will find favourable, including low corporate tax.

The government may also change its political agenda or alter its handling of a policy problem as a result of learning from another political system. Lloyd George's commitment to the introduction of sickness and invalidity insurance in 1908 was strongly influenced by the system he observed in Germany. Much more recently, reform of the system of child support in the 1990s and the introduction of 'welfare to work' owed much to policy learning from the United States and Australia.

Finally, membership of international organizations may shape not merely what the state does but how it does it. The European Union is an important source of new forms of regulation in such matters as environmental protection and food quality. This regulation, although generated by the European Union, is devolved to the member states for implementation in a process which transfers the costs downwards to the national and subnational levels (Moran, 2001).

In addition to the European Union, the United Kingdom is subject to other policy pressures from beyond its shores. Although much environmental regulation comes from the European Union, the United Kingdom is also bound by international agreements such as the Kyoto accords. The incorporation of the ECHR into British law via the Human Rights Act of 1998 intensified the impact of European human rights legislation on British practice, but even before 1998 the United Kingdom was subject to the jurisdiction of the European Court on Human Rights.

The extended range of international pressures on the governing process in the United Kingdom inevitably affects the style of policy making in a variety of ways. The increased fragmentation of the policy process puts a greater premium on effective coordination. The enhanced role of both the European Union and the incorporation of the ECHR have strengthened the legal dimension of government, making legal techniques and judicial attitudes more central concerns of the governmental process (Stone Sweet, 2000).

An Overview of the Modern British State

Enough has already been said to show that the responsibilities of government in the United Kingdom have been subject to continual change and redefinition. British government enjoys a good deal of flexibility over how to manage the allocation of functions because the transfer of function from one agency to another or between departments does not necessarily require parliamentary endorsement, although the introduction of a wholly new function does require parliamentary approval. And radical reorganization of government departments may occasion controversy if it appears that the changes have been made too hastily. Thus the sudden change to the remit of the Lord Chancellor's Department and the proposed abolition of that historic office were the subject of major controversy in 2003. Normally, however, shifting of functions from department to department generates little sustained interest beyond the world of Whitehall.

In providing a brief overview of the functions of government in contemporary Britain, it is convenient to start with the core functions of the state – those responsibilities that are essential to all governments. Managing foreign policy, defence, law and order, including the organization of the court system, have long been recognized as key characteristics of a state. Equally significant in the governmental process is the power to raise revenue to fund the various activities of government and to shape the broader economy and society. We shall then move on to discuss responsibilities which historically the state took on later. Finally, we shall highlight some of the problems involved in managing the modern British state, especially the problem of coordinating its multiple activities and securing its accountability to the governed.

Foreign affairs, defence, law and order

The management of the country's foreign relations has been a specialized function since the eighteenth century, although the nature of diplomacy has been subject to much recent debate. The responsible department – the Foreign and Commonwealth Office (FCO) – acquired its present title in 1968 following a merger between the Foreign Office and the department previously responsible for handling Commonwealth relations. The formal responsibilities of the FCO inevitably altered as a result of the United Kingdom's reduced role in the world after 1945. Similarly, a new international agenda and changing conceptions of the tasks of diplomacy have brought pressures for change on both the FCO and the diplomatic service, which is a separately organized staff for FCO at home and abroad. Although the United Kingdom still exerts unusual influence in the international arena for a country of its size, much of its foreign policy is now conducted within the framework of multi-national alliances and organizations, especially the North Atlantic Treaty Organization (NATO), the G8, the Council of Europe, the Organization for Security and Cooperation in Europe (OSCE), the Commonwealth and the European Union (EU). The G8 is an informal group of eight countries – Canada, France, Italy, Japan, Germany, the United States and the UK – which meets annually to address global issues such as environmental problems, terrorism and development. Although the role of the G8 has increased, it has deliberately retained its informal character and has no formal secretariat or rules of procedure. Membership of the European Union, by contrast, is very formal. It has transformed national policy processes and the foreign policy agenda, blurring the distinction between foreign and domestic policy.

While the traditional notion of diplomacy as the handling of alliances between states is still relevant, the substance of contemporary foreign policy is increasingly about coordinating external policy across a range of policy areas and promoting objectives such as human rights and trade (Clarke and Stewart, 1992). This broader conception of foreign policy involves not merely the departments traditionally responsible for overseas policy (such as the FCO and the Ministry of Defence (MOD)), but also a number of domestic departments that maintain external divisions (such as the Department of Trade and Industry (DTI) and the Department of Environment, Food and Rural Affairs (DEFRA), which in 2003 was the department with responsibility for agriculture and fisheries).

Of course some domestic departments, notably the Treasury and the Bank of England, have always had important international responsibilities. As the salience of the international aspects of economic policy (and relations with such bodies as the International Monetary Fund (IMF) and the World Trade Organization (WTO)) has increased, so the Treasury's role in foreign policy management has grown. The debate about whether or not the UK should join the euro is an issue in which the Treasury is centrally involved. Moreover, the new agenda of international relations necessarily involves a range of domestic departments and agencies beyond the FCO. Traditional diplomatic skills have had to be supplemented with a good deal of technical and economic expertise in a way which has generated challenges to the primacy of the FCO and the diplomatic corps as well as adjustment within the FCO to new roles. As a result, the FCO now operates in a world where its work is increasingly intertwined with that of other departments and agencies.

The growing importance of the European Union is likely to continue blurring this boundary between foreign and domestic policy. Although EU affairs are coordinated through the FCO itself and through the Cabinet Office's European Secretariat (which was established early in the 1970s), so much of the policy making and administration within domestic departments now has a European dimension that coordination between a number of departments including the FCO has become a matter of routine. The internal organization of the FCO has to some extent changed to reflect these new pressures. Instead of focusing on organization by area, there is increasing emphasis on functional organization around cross-cutting issues (see figure 3.3).

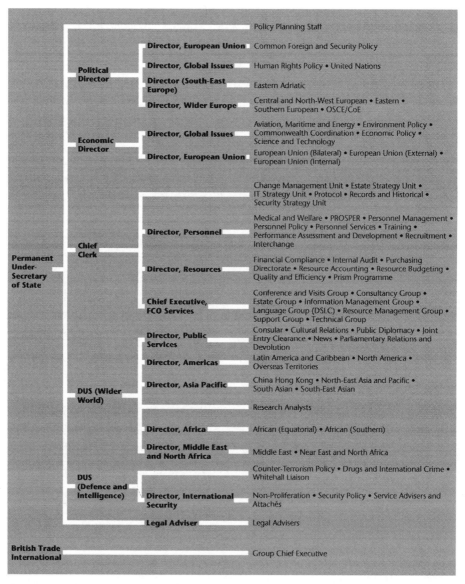

Figure 3.3 Organization of the Foreign and Commonwealth Office. *Source:* Adapted from *Civil Service Yearbook*, 37th edn, 2002.

The management of Britain's external relations was once the sole prerogative of the monarch. Although this has long ceased to be the case, the executive enjoys greater formal autonomy in this field than in domestic policy making. By the same token, Parliament's formal role in foreign affairs is not as prominent as in domestic policy matters, although opportunities will always be given for Parliament to debate foreign policy issues. In 2003 the war with Iraq was the subject of a number of dramatic debates in Parliament. The Select Committee on Foreign Affairs also plays an extremely useful role in probing the assumptions of British foreign policy and reviewing changes in its management. The same is true in relation to defence issues and the Defence Select Committee.

Within the executive there has been an increasing tendency for the prime minister to encroach on the traditional functions of the Foreign Secretary. This tendency, although not a new one, has been exacerbated by three related features of modern government. First, the centralization of political decision making has strengthened the hand of the prime minister in foreign policy. Secondly, the expanding role of the EU with its emphasis on regular meetings of Heads of Government in the European Council has been an important factor in enhancing the international role of the prime minister. Finally, the style of much modern diplomacy – with its emphasis on head-to-head meetings of key political leaders – has emphasized the role of personality in diplomacy. This has been reinforced by developments in the media where journalists find it more attractive to focus on the glamorous aspects of summitry than on detailed processes of diplomatic negotiation.

The advent of a Labour government in 1997 saw a renewed attempt to ground British foreign policy on moral and humanitarian values rather than the simple promotion of national self-interest. One manifestation of this approach was a mission statement which made explicit the government's efforts to frame an ethical foreign policy; another was the return to an organizational separation (with a seat in the cabinet) of overseas aid from the mainstream functions of the FCO in order to highlight aid's enhanced status. The newly formed Department for International Development (which also manages relations with the World Bank and other international agencies concerned with development issues) secured a tangible increase in its budget so that British spending on aid as a proportion of GDP rose from 0.2 per cent in 1996–7 to a projected 0.33 per cent for 2003–4.

The FCO's definition of its mission as the promotion of British interests abroad and contributing to a strong world community involves it in a range of cultural activities and requires cooperation with several agencies such as the BBC World Service, the British Council and Commonwealth Institute. Following a 1999 Cabinet Office review, the highly significant function of export promotion is now managed by British Trade International, an export promotion body run jointly by the FCO and the DTI.

Traditionally, the separate organization of the Foreign Office staff meant that it was seen as being somewhat apart from the rest of Whitehall with a culture that was less accessible than that of other departments. Today there is some evidence of modernization and adaptation through such measures as more flexible recruitment. Equally importantly, there has been an increased awareness of the multiple functions of diplomacy. From a position where a controversial Central Policy Review Staff (CPRS) report in the 1970s could question whether much of the Foreign Office activity was redundant, recent parliamentary investigations of the FCO role have tended to question whether there are not too many tasks for it to perform (see, for example, the Select Committee on Foreign Affairs' 1999 report, *Foreign and Commonwealth Office Resources*).

Defence is also one of the core functions of the British state. Historically, defence and the capacity to wage war were at the centre of the struggle for constitutional power, since many of the early battles between Crown and Parliament in the seventeenth century turned on the control and payment of the armed forces. In addition to its inherent importance, the organization of military provision and defence arrangements had an impact on the wider political system, not least because, as noted earlier, wars and military crises prompted major reappraisals of the role of government and its organization.

The United Kingdom's defence arrangements have naturally been affected by transformations in the country's international role and by the changing environment. The decline of Britain's world role after 1945 was reflected, albeit slowly, in its defence commitments and the end of the Cold War in 1989 saw further adjustments as Britain's defence strategy was reappraised. The incoming Labour government of 1997 carried out a strategic defence review, which attempted to link defence policies and priorities to the new world situation.

Until the post-1945 period the organization of British defence was not centralized and was handled through five separate defence-related departments, the three service ministries (War Office, Admiralty, Air Ministry) together with two others, Supply and Defence. These five ministries exhibited great rivalry with each other and the armed service personnel were often in conflict with the civilian politicians. In 1964, despite opposition from the service chiefs, the management of defence was restructured through the creation of a separate Ministry of Defence. Although this initial attempt to integrate all aspects of British defence was not completely successful, subsequent reforms have brought greater coherence and managerial effectiveness to a diffuse ministry and have limited the policy role of the separate service chiefs. The Secretary of State for Defence is supported by three junior ministers and has two senior advisers, the Permanent Secretary and the Chief of the Defence Staff, who is the professional head of the armed forces and the government's chief military adviser.

An important part of the arrangements for managing defence is the Defence Council (which has a number of formal powers vested in it and is chaired by the Secretary of State), the Defence Management Board (which is chaired by the Permanent Secretary) and the Chiefs of Staff Committee (which provides collective military advice under the chairmanship of the Chief of the Defence Staff). Altogether, defence consumes about 6.6 per cent of public expenditure and, although the period 1985–97 saw a drop in defence expenditure by about one-fifth, the 2001–2/2003–4 three-year comprehensive spending review (CSR) envisages a small increase in defence expenditure. The destabilized world situation after 11 September 2001 – including the war with Iraq – put increased upward pressure on UK defence spending, indicating the level of unpredictability that surrounds this area of government. The provision of defence expenditure has a number of other impacts on the wider political and economic system. The MOD is involved in a web of relationships that spread beyond central government because of its role as a major employer and as a purchaser of equipment through the Defence Procurement Agency. The MOD's concern to encourage the development of British weapons technology makes it also an important sponsor of scientific research and development.

The legal system, crime and national security

The maintenance of a legal system (covering both criminal and civil law), like the provision of foreign policy and defence, is a defining quality of a state. At present the United Kingdom has no single department to cover all legal questions, so that responsibilities for various aspects of the legal system are fragmented. Within England and Wales responsibility for handling legal issues is divided between a number of departments – notably, the Department for Constitutional Affairs (which replaced the Lord Chancellor's Department in 2003) and the Home Office. (The fragmentation of responsibilities for the legal system had earlier prompted the Blair government to take new initiatives to bring constitutional responsibilities and legal services together, resulting in an expansion of the Lord Chancellor's Department prior to the more radical reorganization of 2003; see figure 3.4.) In addition, however, important legal responsibilities are exercised by the two Law Officers (the Attorney General and Solicitor General) and by the Treasury Solicitor. Devolution has added further complexity to the administration of law, although the Scottish executive (which is responsible for criminal and civil law in Scotland) has taken the step of uniting responsibility for legal issues within Scotland in a single justice ministry.

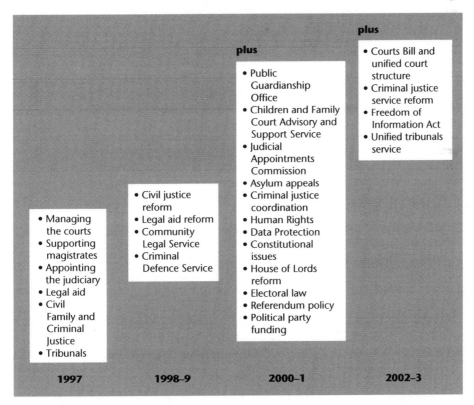

Figure 3.4 Changing responsibilities of the Lord Chancellor's Department (now the Department for Constitutional Affairs).

The Lord Chancellor's Office was once the key source of advice to the monarch. Today the office (renamed the Department of Constitutional Affairs) is responsible for the management of the court system in England and Wales and for the appointment of judges and magistrates as well as for a range of constitutional issues such as human rights. The Department of Constitutional Affairs is also responsible for such functions as legal aid, law reform and the custody of public records as well as freedom of information legislation and electoral law. As we noted in the last chapter, the multiple roles of the Lord Chancellor became highly controversial because the combination of executive, legislative and judicial functions breached the requirement of judicial independence. Although the traditional role of the Lord Chancellor was for a time robustly defended, a radical reorganization was set in train in 2003. The increasing role of the Lord Chancellor's Office had already prompted the setting up of a new select committee in 2003 with a remit to cover the department and constitutional affairs more generally (see figure 3.4).

Legal advice *within* government is given by the government's own lawyers, whether operating centrally through the Treasury Solicitor's Office or within the department. (Some but not all departments maintain their own legal teams.) These lawyers handle both the routine legal tasks of the government (such as conveyancing) as well as the tasks that arise because of the distinctive nature of government. The need for legal advice within government is increasing. Partly this increased demand is a result of the growth of legal challenges to government decision making as a result of the growth of judicial review (see chapters 13 and 14). Increased emphasis on legal issues has also occurred because of the expanding impact of European Community law on so many aspects of British policy and the growing importance of constitutional and legal factors inside government – for example, issues relating to human rights and the complexities produced by devolution.

There have been significant recent changes in the approach to the organization and delivery of legal services. A desire for enhanced economy and efficiency prompted a series of reviews of the operation of the courts themselves and of legal aid. Some aspects of the legal system (such as the handling of prosecutions) – have been reorganized into agencies. There has also been a limited attempt to contract out some routine legal tasks to private companies.

Although the Lord Chancellor historically provided unity in a diffuse and fragmented system, much of the effective responsibility for law and order has always been a local matter. There were two reasons for this. First, the lack of good communications meant that the 'King's Peace' had to be kept by those with local intelligence and the ability to respond quickly to disturbances. Thus there had to be reliable agents of the centre in each county – the lords lieutenant and the magistrates. Secondly, British political culture was traditionally hostile to the idea of a centralized policing regime. Local control of the police was therefore highly valued, although as will be seen in chapter 13, the reality of contemporary policing in Britain is that it is increasingly centralized in practice if not in name. Indeed, developments such as the Police National Computer provide a degree of central information greater than that possessed by many continental European countries.

The central government department which deals with police services and penal policy in England and Wales is the Home Office, which has a variety of responsibilities related to the criminal justice system (including the maintenance of prisons)

Box 3.9 Steps towards open government and freedom of information

1979	New select committee system established – extends flow of information to Parliament.
1983	National Audit Office established to scrutinize government accounts and bring irregularities to public attention.
1984	The Data Protection Act gives people the right to see records held about them on computer.
1988	Medical Records Act introduces patient access to reports prepared for insurance or employment purposes.
1989	Official Secrets Act narrows the scope of the criminal law in the protection of official information and introduces a harm test.
1992	Lord Chancellor changes policy on sensitive public records over 30 years old to allow more to be released.
1992	Terms of reference and membership of Ministerial Cabinet Committees published.
1992	Questions of Procedure for Ministers (now the Ministerial Code) published for the first time.
1992	Prime minister acknowledges existence of Security Intelligence Service (MI6) and names its Chief.
1992	White paper on open government sets out government policies.
1994	Code of Practice on Access to Government Information comes into effect. Appeals to be made to the Parliamentary Ombudsman.
1997	White paper *Your Right to Know* published promising a presumption in favour of openness and legally enforceable rights to seek documents from government and other public bodies. Contents-based exemptions: documents exempted where public body could demonstrate 'substantial harm' if disclosed.
1999	White paper published. Widened exemptions to include class-based exemptions; the release of policy advice limited.
2000	Freedom of Information Act passed, to be gradually phased in.
2002	Central government departments to implement Act, producing publication schemes, describing information they publish.
2003	Local government, police and armed forces to implement Act.
2005	All public authorities to comply with the Act.

as well as other domestic topics that do not clearly fall within the scope of another department. Thus the Home Office is responsible for immigration and nationality laws, for passports (through the Passport Agency) and for adoption proceedings. Its responsibilities were even more diverse before the Lord Chancellor's Office absorbed some legally related issues that were previously handled by the Home Office, such as election law, open government, data protection and freedom of information (see box 3.9).

At the intersection of law and order, foreign policy and defence are the three British security services. These consist of the Security Service (MI5), which deals with domestic subversion, and the Security Intelligence Service (MI6), which deals with overseas operations, together with GCHQ (the government monitoring service at Cheltenham). There is also Special Branch (the police division responsible for security matters) and a special counter-terrorism unit within the police (ACPO-TAM). MI5 and MI6 were founded as a single service in 1909 in the period of public concern about a possible war with Germany, but in 1910 MI5 and MI6 were divided.

Although the security services were once shrouded in total secrecy (to the point of denying their existence), in recent years some major steps have been taken to make them more open and accountable. In 1989 a Security Service Act established the accountability of MI5 to the Home Secretary. (MI6 and GCHQ are responsible to the Foreign Secretary, although in all security matters the prime minister and the Cabinet Office exercise a major role.) The 1989 legislation also established an independent tribunal to hear complaints against the service. In the 1990s a number of changes occurred, and significant legislation – the Intelligence Services Act – was passed in 1994. A parliamentary committee (the Intelligence and Security Committee) was created in 1994 to exercise oversight of the security service. At the same time there was a shift in attitude towards the role of MI5, with the then director Stella Rimington (who was named for the first time) giving the Dimbleby Lecture and, more controversially, publishing her memoirs (Rimington, 2001). Her successor is Eliza Manningham Buller. A further move towards openness came with the advertisement of vacancies in MI5's staff of nearly 2,000.

Even with these changes many commentators believe that there is insufficient accountability of the services, although the emergence of new security concerns following the events of September 11, 2001 has strengthened the ability of the services to resist further attacks on their autonomy (Hennessy, 2003; Thurlow, 1994).

Taxation, finance and the economy

The management of the government's finances and the control of economic policy are crucial functions in any modern government. In the United Kingdom the role of the Chancellor of the Exchequer and the position of the Treasury are central to politics and policy making (see figure 3.5). As the Treasury Select Committee put it in an unusually wide-ranging examination of the role and power of the Treasury, '[it] is one of the central offices of state, lying at the heart of Government' (Treasury Select Committee, 2001).

Control of the purse strings was always a source of power and an essential function of government. As soon as the British state acquired positive responsibilities, it had to find methods of paying for them. The two classic sources of government finance are borrowing and taxation. Taxation was initially spasmodic and ad hoc, and was usually the result of the need to finance a war. By the nineteenth century, however, taxation – whether direct or indirect – had become a regular feature of British life. Taxation fulfils many objectives in addition to the simple funding of public spending. For example, taxation is one mechanism used to regulate

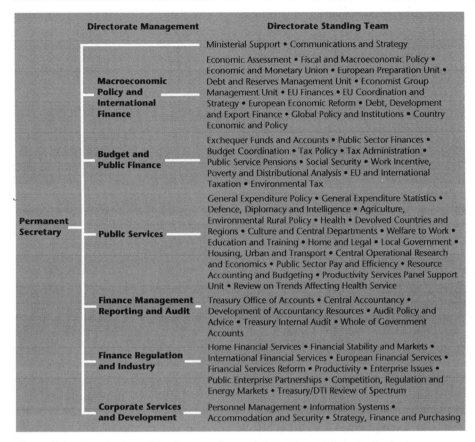

	Directorate Management	Directorate Standing Team
Permanent Secretary		Ministerial Support • Communications and Strategy
	Macroeconomic Policy and International Finance	Economic Assessment • Fiscal and Macroeconomic Policy • Economic and Monetary Union • European Preparation Unit • Debt and Reserves Management Unit • Economist Group Management Unit • EU Finances • EU Coordination and Strategy • European Economic Reform • Debt, Development and Export Finance • Global Policy and Institutions • Country Economic and Policy
	Budget and Public Finance	Exchequer Funds and Accounts • Public Sector Finances • Budget Coordination • Tax Policy • Tax Administration • Public Service Pensions • Social Security • Work Incentive, Poverty and Distributional Analysis • EU and International Taxation • Environmental Tax
	Public Services	General Expenditure Policy • General Expenditure Statistics • Defence, Diplomacy and Intelligence • Agriculture, Environmental Rural Policy • Health • Devolved Countries and Regions • Culture and Central Departments • Welfare to Work • Education and Training • Home and Legal • Local Government • Housing, Urban and Transport • Central Operational Research and Economics • Public Sector Pay and Efficiency • Resource Accounting and Budgeting • Productivity Services Panel Support Unit • Review on Trends Affecting Health Service
	Finance Management Reporting and Audit	Treasury Office of Accounts • Central Accountancy • Development of Accountancy Resources • Audit Policy and Advice • Treasury Internal Audit • Whole of Government Accounts
	Finance Regulation and Industry	Home Financial Services • Financial Stability and Markets • International Financial Services • European Financial Services • Financial Services Reform • Productivity • Enterprise Issues • Public Enterprise Partnerships • Competition, Regulation and Energy Markets • Treasury/DTI Review of Spectrum
	Corporate Services and Development	Personnel Management • Information Systems • Accommodation and Security • Strategy, Finance and Purchasing

Figure 3.5 Organization of HM Treasury. *Source:* Adapted from *Civil Service Yearbook,* 37th edn, 2002.

the general economic climate and it can be refined to redistribute wealth and reduce income inequalities. Indeed, under Gordon Brown the Treasury has become a key player in the welfare reform process (Thain, 2002).

The Treasury as a department has always enjoyed enormous prestige and power within the British system of government. Its two key strategic functions – the overall management of the economy and the detailed control of public expenditure (see figure 3.6) – are crucial to the success of any modern government (Brittan, 1971; Thain, 2002; Thain and Wright, 1995). Increasingly, the control of public expenditure (which always gave the Treasury a unique leverage over other departments) has drawn the Treasury into concern with the detailed implementation of policy in order to secure value for money and efficient administration. This aspect of the Treasury role has loomed larger since the Labour government's second election victory of 2001, which heralded a new emphasis on the delivery of improved public services.

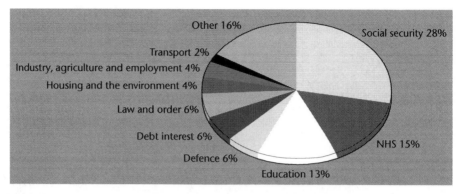

Figure 3.6 Government spending, 2001. *Source:* Office for National Statistics, *UK 2001 Yearbook.*

service delivery agreement Sets out in more detail than a public service agreement the detailed outputs on which a department must focus to meet its targets.

The combination of roles together with informal sources of influence make the Treasury one of the most powerful – if not the most powerful – government departments. It is, however, a relatively small department with its own distinct ethos. Traditionally seen as recruiting the most able of each generation of civil servants, the Treasury has produced a disproportionate number of 'high-fliers' who became permanent secretaries. When Labour came to power in 1997, Treasury influence was further enhanced by a combination of an unusually assertive and expert Chancellor of the Exchequer in the person of Gordon Brown and the effect of new arrangements for monitoring the effect of public spending on policy outputs.

The character of the Treasury's involvement in public expenditure control has thus changed markedly since 1997. Traditionally, the Treasury has been concerned mainly with overall spending totals. Since 1997, however, the Treasury has become much more concerned with the details of policy and with the efficiency of public spending in the promotion of the government's goals. The three-year CSR initiated by Gordon Brown in 1997 to replace the annual spending round involved departments closely in the spending review process and introduced a new device – public service agreements (later supplemented by **service delivery agreements**) – which tied the release of additional resources to departmental progress in achieving specific policy goals.

The novelty of public service agreements (PSAs) was the way in which ministers in major spending departments were made responsible for measurable improvements in the quality of services delivered to the public and progress tied to financial incentives. As the initial Treasury statement put it, if progress is found to be slipping, a Cabinet Committee chaired by the Chancellor will look at the problems with the minister. Although there is no crude threat to reduce resources from the budgets of departments that fail to meet their targets, there is a presumption that departments must earn additional revenue.

Until 1997 the Treasury in conjunction with the Bank of England set interest rates. (The Bank of England was founded as a private bank in 1694 but was nationalized in 1946.) This role in the management of monetary policy gave the Treasury another important lever over the British economy. In 1997, in a major initiative of the Chancellor of the Exchequer taken before Labour's new cabinet had even had a chance to meet formally, responsibility for setting interest rates was transferred to the Bank of England's Monetary Policy Committee (MPC). In an interesting innovation, the House of Commons Select Committee on the Treasury now regularly conducts confirmation hearings on senior appointments at the Bank of England, including on members of the MPC. These investigations form part of a wider strategy designed to impose a degree of accountability on the Bank of England.

That decision to give greater autonomy to the Bank of England (which was put into effect by the Bank of England Act 1998) represented a major move towards creating an independent central bank comparable to the European Central Bank or the Federal Reserve. It thus prepared the British economy for possible entry into the single European currency. The related issue of debt management was transferred to a new executive agency of the Treasury, the Debt Management Office.

The formidable concentration of power within the Treasury has led on occasions to attempts to reduce its influence by establishing alternative sources of power and/or dividing its responsibilities. Thus Harold Wilson in the period 1964–70 created two new departments which, for a brief period, seemed to threaten the power of the Treasury: the Department of Economic Affairs (DEA) and the Civil Service Department (CSD). Neither department lasted long and in many respects the central supervisory role of the Treasury is more firmly established than ever before. Indeed, the Treasury has become a more proactive agent inside government, using its power over public expenditure to influence not merely the implementation of government policy as a whole and the efficient delivery of services but also the detail of welfare policy (Deakin and Parry, 2000).

Although the overall levels of taxation are decided by the Treasury, the detailed working out of tax proposals and the responsibility for their implementation are in the hands of two non-ministerial departments distinct from the Treasury: the Board of Inland Revenue, which is responsible for direct tax, notably income tax, and the Board of Customs and Excise, which is responsible for the administration of value-added tax (VAT) as well as customs and excise duties. The latter task means that Customs and Excise has important international responsibilities in relation to such matters as drug smuggling. These Boards have always had a large degree of autonomy from the Chancellor of the Exchequer. Both became agencies under the Next Steps initiative.

The Inland Revenue has acquired an important new role in the period since 1999 because of new responsibilities in the field of social security and employment, specifically tax credits and the enforcement of the minimum wage as part of the government's general strategy for dealing with poverty. Whether these new functions of the Inland Revenue can be absorbed without loss of efficiency remains to be seen; but, by the middle of 2003, there was extensive concern about the possibility of administrative backlog in the department.

Trade, industry, agriculture, employment and education

The power of the Treasury over the other aspects of government was already established by the late nineteenth century. Although the extensive provision of welfare functions did not become a feature of the British state until the twentieth century, elements of government intervention in a variety of other policy areas can be found well before then. Thus although the state did not take positive responsibility for managing the economy until the Second World War, the United Kingdom's national government has a long history of attempting to regulate the economy. Committees of the Privy Council were concerned with the promotion of trade in the early seventeenth century and the Board of Trade which emerged in 1786 (and became a separate department in 1867) acquired a range of responsibilities relating to Britain's increasingly important commercial role. These responsibilities by the nineteenth century included railway regulation, merchant shipping, patent legislation, and bankruptcy and company legislation. The Board of Trade continued until 1970, when it was merged with the relatively new Ministry of Technology to form a new super-department, the DTI.

One sector of industry which has traditionally been given special government protection is agriculture. Although only a very small percentage of the British population is now engaged in agriculture, the importance of maintaining a strong farming industry has prompted government to make special arrangements to protect its interests. A Board of Agriculture was formed in 1889 and evolved into a separate ministry in 1919. From 1955 a single ministry exercised responsibility for agriculture, fisheries and food. Maintaining the pricing structure for agricultural products was a significant feature of government policy towards agriculture for much of the last century. Price supports were introduced during the Second World War and guaranteed prices were institutionalized over the immediate post-1945 period. British membership of the European Union radically altered the British government's ability to support its own agricultural industry since two key policies of the European Union – the Common Agricultural Policy (CAP) and the Common Fisheries Policy – were designed to protect fishing and agriculture throughout the European Union.

The Ministry of Agriculture acquired important responsibilities beyond the simple protection of the agricultural interest. These included responsibilities for environmental protection, food safety and animal welfare. Often there has been a tension between these policy areas and the ministry's responsiveness to the agricultural interest. In the area of food safety in particular, there appeared to be a direct conflict of interest between producers and consumers and the experience of a series of problems about food safety (including the controversy over BSE) led the Labour government in 1997 to set up a Food Standards Agency. In 2001 Labour reorganized the ministry to create a new department (DEFRA), not least in the hope that within such a new structure a better balance could be maintained between producer and consumer interests.

Labour issues had become increasingly a matter for government involvement since the nineteenth century, partly because of humanitarian concern about conditions of work in an industrializing society and partly because of the growing power of the trade unions. The need to direct manpower during the First World War led to the creation of a separate Ministry of Labour in 1916. Through that ministry the state was increasingly concerned both with the level of employment, which affected a range of other social issues, and with its conditions. The state also became involved in labour disputes, both directly and indirectly.

The government's approach to the maintenance of full employment has changed markedly even since 1945. In the period immediately after the Second World War the government was committed to maintaining full employment, and indeed the fact that unemployment was low for much of the period from 1945 to 1970 encouraged all parties to think that they had learned how to manage the economy to ensure full employment. By the 1970s, however, unemployment began to rise. Although at the time of writing unemployment is again low (at 5.2 per cent of the eligible work-force), there is an awareness that a national government may not be able to maintain traditionally high levels of employment in the increasingly competitive global economy. As a result, attention shifted to improving the competitiveness of Britain, especially through reform of trade union legislation, and to training.

The reorganization of the Ministry of Labour and the creation of a new Department of Employment and Productivity, subsequently renamed the Department of Employment, occurred in 1964. Until 1995 this department exercised responsibility for most aspects of employment, including national and regional manpower policy, the promotion of equal employment opportunity and the payment of unemployment benefits. It was also responsible for a wide range of industrial relations bodies, including employment tribunals and the Health and Safety Commission, the Advisory and Conciliation and Arbitration Service (ACAS), and the Manpower Services Commission (now the Training Agency). In 1995 the department's responsibilities for training and the labour market were merged with education to create a new Department for Education and Employment. Other functions of the old Department of Employment were transferred – industrial relations and pay issues went to the DTI, while safety issues went to the Department of the Environment. In a major reorganization in 2001, a different split was effected and the training and skills component of the department's work was transferred to a new Department for Education and Skills (DfES). Other employment-related functions were transferred to a new Department for Work and Pensions (DWP).The conditions of employment in the UK are no longer solely regulated by national laws. British employment conditions are also subject to EU regulations designed to promote the free movement of labour as well as by EU guarantees on such issues as hours of work.

Education became a major area of governmental involvement in the early nineteenth century. The state first made grants to schools in 1833, and in 1870 it made primary education free and compulsory. Free secondary education was not made universally available until R.A. Butler's 1944 Education Act. Alongside the provision of education went other state intervention through the provision of a range of ancillary services such as school meals.

Education is one of the major services where central government (operating first through a separate Board of Education in 1899 and then a Department of Education) does not itself provide the programmes but relies for delivery on other agents, notably local education authorities but also a range of private sector schools, voluntary societies, churches and universities. Until 1988 there was no formal or extensive control over what occurred inside schools, but the Education Reform Act of 1988 signalled a major change of direction as central government took new powers over the curriculum and imposed an obligation for regular testing of pupils. In addition, the government sought to encourage greater devolution of managerial power and budgetary responsibility to head teachers in schools that remained under local authority control.

Poverty, health and welfare

Care for the poor has been one of the responsibilities assumed by government since the seventeenth century, when the Poor Law of 1601 made parishes responsible for the relief of poverty. Attitudes towards poverty and the principles governing state support of the poor have, however, varied enormously since government first became involved in this policy area. Initially, public provision for the relief of poverty was limited and grudging, especially where the able-bodied poor were concerned. Thus the 1834 Poor Law provided relief in a manner that was harsh and demeaning. Liberals over the nineteenth century and later **Fabians** and other social reformers pressed for changes based on the view that poverty did not necessarily reflect moral failure.

The first steps towards a comprehensive prevention of poverty were taken by the Liberal and coalition governments of 1906–18, which introduced forms of social insurance and programmes providing for old-age pensions. New machinery (for example, a Ministry of Pensions created in 1916) emerged to administer these new programmes.

Concern for public health and planning for sanitation and the prevention of disease were major catalysts of administrative reform in the nineteenth century. The reforms of national insurance in the pre-1914 period improved the availability of medical treatment for workers. The election of a Labour government in 1945 signalled a radical extension in the state's welfare responsibilities. The Labour government was committed to implementing the principles of the Beveridge Report (see box 3.10). New programmes and policies were introduced to promote social justice and create a comprehensive welfare state. In education the commitment to free access in the 1944 Education Act was put into effect; a National Health Service free at the point of delivery was introduced; and a range of social security programmes was implemented. These programmes provided benefits for different categories of the population such as children, widows, the elderly and the disabled and were designed to provide everyone with a basic minimum income.

Fabianism Approach to political change that advocates gradual reform rather than revolution. Associated with a group of social reformers and intellectuals who founded the Fabian Society in 1884. Beatrice and Sidney Webb and George Bernard Shaw influenced the Liberals as well as the early Labour Party.

The broad outlines of the welfare state created in the immediate post-war period were accepted by both parties until the mid-1970s, although the detail of the programmes and the machinery for delivering underwent substantial amendment. In the mid-1970s a new debate about the role of the state emerged in the UK, triggered in part by concern about the rising cost of welfare and the extent to which an ever-expanding state threatened individual freedom and collective prosperity. There also emerged a debate about the extent to which welfare should be seen as an automatic right rather than a benefit

Box 3.10   The Beveridge Report

Written in 1942 by a committee headed by William Beveridge, the report proposed a 'cradle to the grave' scheme of social insurance covering all citizens irrespective of income. It aimed to tackle the five 'giants': illness, ignorance, disease, squalor and want.

The major recommendations of the report were:

- a comprehensive scheme of social insurance, including unemployment and sickness benefit, maternity benefit, widow's benefit and pension, retirement pension and other grants
- a free National Health Service
- a system of children's allowances
- an industrial injuries scheme
- training schemes for the unemployed

Although not entirely as Beveridge wished, the measures were adopted and formed the basis of the British post-war welfare state. Family allowances were enacted in 1945, and national insurance and the National Health Service in 1946; full employment became government policy. Together, these developments created the welfare state, a system of social security guaranteeing a minimum level of health and social services.

Source: Adapted from a range of sources, including the London School of Economics history website, http://www.lse.ac.uk/lsehistory/beveridge_report.htm

conditional upon the individual's contribution to the wider society. Some analysts in Britain and the United States suggested that far from reducing poverty, the provision of welfare encouraged it by creating a culture of dependency. Although the Thatcher and Major governments of 1979–97 promoted a more critical approach to the principles underpinning the welfare state, they faced formidable barriers to radical change in the structure of welfare provision, not least because public opinion remained supportive of existing welfare policies.

Labour's advent to power in 1997 brought significant changes in the role of the state in the field of welfare policy. First, following the ideas of the Social Justice Commission, which reported in 1994, as well as the approach of President Clinton's New Democrats, the government moved towards the modernization of social provision in a way that differed from both the traditional welfare state principles of Old Labour and the approach of the more market-oriented Conservatives. Thus it emphasized the extent to which social provision had to be made in the context of a global and competitive economy and highlighted the need for the welfare system to produce incentives to work and investment in skills. Secondly, it was recognized that many of the most intractable policy issues cut across departmental boundaries and required a much more integrated approach than hitherto. As the government focused its poverty strategy on social exclusion and child poverty, it put in place new administrative mechanisms to address these issues. Finally, under Labour after 1997, the management of welfare policy was altered as a result of the enhanced role taken by the Treasury and the shift towards using the tax system (and the use of tax

purchaser–provider split
Distinction which argues that it is more efficient to separate the purchase and regulation of a service from its direct provision.

credits) rather than traditional benefits as a major mechanism for guaranteeing income levels. Labour also introduced a formal minimum wage.

Welfare reform under both the Conservatives and Labour has followed a similar trajectory. It has placed great emphasis on getting people into work even at the expense of appearing punitive. And in the problematic area of health care policy there has been a concern to introduce greater competition in order to maximize efficiency. In 1990 the Conservatives reorganized the structure of health provision and community care in the National Health Service and Community Care Act. Instead of local authorities and health authorities providing services directly for a given locality, the legislation introduced a new regime in which purchasers of services would contract with providers for the services they required. This **purchaser–provider split** was intended to create an environment of greater competition and efficiency but also to make services more responsive to the needs of clients. In the area of health care, hospitals were formed into NHS Trusts which could compete for services from general practitioners. This introduction of quasi-markets into health care was highly controversial. The Blair government did not, however, abandon the purchaser–provider split but simply reformed the structure further to make primary health groups the 'purchasers' in the system rather than GPs. Thus both Conservatives and Labour have moved away from the old hierarchically organized and bureaucratic NHS structure to one which mimics the competition provided by the market.

Health care, education and welfare provision are at the cutting edge of any modern government's concerns because of their electoral salience and the problem of cost. Not surprisingly, it is in these areas that efforts to improve value for money, efficiency and responsiveness are concentrated.

Quality of life issues: The environment, leisure and culture

The introduction of a welfare state and economic prosperity meant that poverty and related issues became less prominent for most citizens in the post-1945 period. Instead of concern about economic survival, there emerged a series of concerns about the quality of life. As environmental issues became more salient, the Conservative government of 1970–4 set up a separate department to bring together areas with an environmental dimension within a single super-department. New Labour has in theory displayed heightened interest in an integrated approach to environmental issues, but as always there was and is a tension between environmental protection and such pressing concerns as the need for more affordable housing and the demands of motorists.

Equality issues

During the 1970s there emerged a new set of issues, which can be loosely grouped together as equality issues. At their heart is a concern for providing equality of opportunity for disadvantaged groups – for women, for ethnic minorities, for homosexuals and for the disabled.

Increasingly within the public sector, greater attention is paid to these equality issues. Two years after its return to power, Labour made the cause of equality a high-profile one with an equality statement, and it has taken a number of initiatives such as the appointment of a Minister for Women. Yet fundamental problems remain. Some would argue there is more presentation than substance to the government's approach and there was a lack of coordination between initiatives. Certainly, the government has moved from legislation to preclude discrimination against such groups to a much more positive promotion of their cause. Thus in relation to women, ethnic minorities and the disabled, the Labour government elected in 1997 launched a campaign to increase the employment of these groups in government.

Statistics, information technology and policy presentation

Qualitative changes in information technology – the e-government revolution – have had an important effect on the operation of the state. First, the state is increasingly able to handle and use very large amounts of statistical data. This improves the government's policy capacity, and indeed Labour has explicitly committed itself to a more evidence-based approach to policy making than existed before. Secondly, it is able to link the public with government in several new ways. Thirdly, it is able to present government policy much more effectively than ever before.

Nevertheless, these advances have come at a cost. The growing emphasis on the presentation of policy in particular has raised crucial issues about the proper boundary between information and propaganda and the extent to which government may legitimately promote its own policies by media manipulation.

New Labour came to office committed to a clear view of the need to project its policies and its image in government as it had in opposition. Indeed, it saw presentation as part of the seamless web of policy making. Part of this approach involved a new emphasis on coordinated handling of the media at the centre, and the combination of a forceful chief press secretary (Alastair Campbell) and the creation of a new Strategic Communications Unit in Downing Street greatly strengthened the government's ability to manage its presentation. All government departments after 1997 were required to clear media statements with the Downing Street Press Office and to link all announcements to a message that was determined centrally and reflected the government's corporate priorities. But the process backfired on the government, damaging its image. The government's so-called **spin doctors** became the story rather than the policies that were the object of the publicity. Indeed, the press itself increasingly focused on spin, which became indelibly associated with the Blair style of government (Jones, 1999, 2002).

In addition to allegations that the government was obsessed by the need to control information, concerns were expressed about the extent to which a hitherto neutral body (the Government Information Service (GIS)) had been politicized. In 1998 the GIS was renamed the Government Information and Communications Service (GICS) to reinforce the change in attitude 'from reactive information supply in response to media queries to proactive communications as

spin doctor One who is professionally concerned with ensuring that news and information are presented in the way that most benefits his or her client.

part of the normal business of government' (Scammell and Semetko, 2000: 522). Following a series of clashes over the position of information heads within the GIS, 25 heads of information or deputy heads in the main departments were replaced out of a total of 44 during Labour's first year in office. Many of them publicly criticized Labour's reforms of the GIS (Public Administration Select Committee, 6th Report, 1997–8). Yet in a sense the professionalization and politicization of the government's handling of policy presentation is an inevitable product of modern government and the desire to set the political agenda. However much the development has been criticized, it is unlikely to be reversed.

Conclusions

The British state has grown substantially since the late nineteenth century, despite the determined efforts of governments and politicians to reduce its role. Expansion of the state's policy responsibilities has presented greater challenges of coordination and direction. Ministers have frequently acknowledged a need for coordination but they have often been unable to devise methods adequate to the task. Sometimes also, governments have exacerbated the problem. Thus the need for more effective coordination was highlighted by the 1997 and 2001 Labour manifesto commitments to enhance public services; but their decision both to embrace the fragmenting reforms of NPM and to create new arenas of policy making at the subnational level inevitably made the goal of policy coherence harder to achieve.

Several strategies have been adopted to meet the challenge posed by an increasingly fissiparous state. New units of coordination were set up (in April 2000) to cope with the effects of regional government and the Cabinet Office established mechanisms to deal with devolution, mirroring earlier exercises designed to obtain integration of European policy. Traditional mechanisms of coordination such as the Treasury and the Cabinet Office were reformed and reinforced. Above all, there was a concerted effort to strengthen the Prime Minister's Office and to make it (together with the Cabinet Office) a powerful engine of integration (see chapter 4). Whether what has been done is sufficient to counterbalance the tendencies towards fragmentation in the state remains to be seen. It is more likely that there is no final institutional solution to the problem of coordination and modern governments must reconcile themselves to developing imaginative techniques to control the Leviathan they have created. By the same token, it is now apparent that many of the traditional mechanisms of accountability are inappropriate or ineffective in the modern British state and that new techniques are required to supplement older instruments of control.

Key Questions

1 What factors have shaped the size of the state in the United Kingdom?
2 What mechanisms does British government have for intervention, and why does it sometimes choose one method rather than another?
3 Why has coordination become such a concern for recent British governments?

Further Reading

The growth of the state is well covered in G. Fry, *The Growth of Government: The Development of Ideas about the Role of the State and the Machinery and Functions of Government in Britain since 1780* (London: Frank Cass, 1979) and in W. H. Greenleaf's magisterial multi-volume study, *The British Political Tradition* (London: Methuen, 1983). D. Fraser, 'The post-war consensus debate', *Parliamentary Affairs*, 53: 2 (2000) covers the issues surrounding the post-war consensus. The debate about the role of government is considered in D. Helm (ed.), *The Economic Borders of the State* (Oxford: Oxford University Press, 1989). On regulation there is a wealth of interesting material, including a number of works by Hood. See, for example, C. Hood, O. James and C. Scott, 'Regulation of government: Has it increased, is it increasing, should it be diminished?', *Public Administration*, 8: 2 (2000). The machinery of government is examined from a historical perspective in Peter Hennessy's *Whitehall* (revised edn; London: Fontana, 1990). C. D. Foster and F. J. Plowden, *The State Under Stress: Can the Hollow State be Good Government?* (Buckingham: Open University Press, 1996) looks at changing state capacity.

Several articles provide useful information on joined-up government and modernization. See, for example, A. Gray and B. Jenkins, 'Government and administration', *Parliamentary Affairs*, 53: 2 (2000); C. Hays and D. Richards, 'The tangled webs of Westminster and Whitehall', *Public Administration*, 78: 1 (2000); D. Kavanagh and D. Richards, 'Departmentalism and joined-up government', *Parliamentary Affairs*, 54: 1 (2001); R. A. W. Rhodes, 'New Labour's civil service: Summing-up joining-up', *Political Quarterly*, 71: 2 (2000); R. A. W. Rhodes, 'The hollowing out of the state: The changing nature of the public service in Britain', *Political Quarterly*, 65 (1994); and A. Taylor, 'Hollowing out or filling in? Task-forces and the management of cross-cutting issues in British government', *British Journal of Politics and International Studies*, 2: 1 (2000).

 Websites

See also the list of general websites at the back of the book.

- www.ukonline.gov.uk – Portal into UK government sites

Government departments

- www.defra.gov.uk – Department for the Environment, Food and Rural Affairs
- www.dfes.gov.uk – Department for Education and Skills
- www.culture.gov.uk – Department of Culture, Media and Sport
- www.doh.gov.uk – Department of Health
- www.dfid.gov.uk – Department for International Development
- www.dwp.gov.uk – Department for Work and Pensions
- www.dti.gov.uk – Department of Trade and Industry
- www.odpm.gov.uk – Office of the Deputy Prime Minister
- www.fco.gov.uk – Foreign and Commonwealth Office
- www.hm-treasury.gov.uk – HM Treasury
- www.homeoffice.gov.uk – Home Office
- www.dca.gov.uk – Department for Constitutional Affairs
- www.mod.gov.uk – Ministry of Defence

Selected executive agencies

- www.csa.gov.uk/ – Child Support Agency
- www.foodstandards.gov.uk – Food Standards Agency
- www.hmce.gov.uk – HM Customs and Excise
- www.hmprisonservice.gov.uk – HM Prison Service
- www.passport.gov.uk – UK Passport Agency

Selected regulatory bodies

- www.ofcom.gov.uk – Office of Communication
- www.ofsted.gov.uk – Office for Standards in Education
- www.rail-reg.gov.uk – Office of the Rail Regulator
- www.ofwat.gov.uk – Office of Water Services

4 The Executive

In the previous chapter the many diverse functions of the modern state were examined. Discussion of the various functions of government highlighted the way in which the numerous tasks taken on by the state have become ever more complex. The growth of the state and its responsibilities has inevitably generated a need for coordination, which in recent years has been exacerbated by a new degree of fragmentation of state structures and a dispersal of political authority. In this chapter we examine the structure and powers of the British central executive from both a political and an administrative perspective and assess the manner in which politics and policy are integrated at the highest levels.

Constitutionally, the British system is one of cabinet government. In that system executive leadership and political direction are provided by a cabinet, consisting of a small group of senior ministers who head the major departments. The cabinet is chaired by a prime minister who, although without any formal powers, is in practice much more powerful than other ministers. Collective government means that the prime minister is there as the strong leader of a team and does not exercise power in his or her own right. The government is collectively responsible to Parliament for its decisions, which are in theory taken after extensive collegial discussion.

Although the United Kingdom has retained the form of cabinet government, in practice the way the system operates today is very different from what even the cabinet known by Harold Macmillan (1957–63) might suggest. Change is occurring on a number of levels. On a political level, the increased prominence of the prime minister inevitably creates an imbalance in the political relationships inside the cabinet. Full cabinet is less significant as a decision-making arena and work is devolved to a greater degree, not merely to lower-level cabinet committees and subcommittees but also to structures and mechanisms outside the formal cabinet system. New institutional arrangements have been put in place to bolster the central authority of the core executive, including political staff and special advisers whose presence has changed the system in a number of ways. In addition there have been several institutional innovations designed to improve the quality of policy making at the centre and the effectiveness of policy implementation.

The first part of the chapter will thus examine in some detail the changing pattern of relations between prime minister and cabinet as well as many other actors and institutions that are vital to the process of executive leadership. These institutions and actors include the Treasury and the Cabinet Office as well as the key cadres of senior civil servants and advisers responsible for taking strategic decisions within government. They are sometimes referred to as the 'core executive' to distinguish them from others whose concerns are more routine and managerial. In the second part of the chapter we examine the role of ministers and the relationship with the departments in order to provide a preliminary overview of the executive. This approach to the character of the executive in the United Kingdom thus involves placing familiar questions, such as the relative power of the prime minister and the cabinet, in the context of a much broader agenda of questions about the capacity of British central government.

The Constitutional Framework of Executive Power

As was seen in chapter 3, constitutional law finds the concept of the state alien and unfamiliar. Nor does it use the concept of the executive. Rather, the legal system recognizes the Crown and individual ministers in whom legal powers are vested. More surprisingly perhaps, neither the cabinet nor the prime minister receives much recognition in law, although of course both occupy central positions in the political system and are crucial actors in the core executive.

The formal legal position is worth remembering for two reasons. First, it is a reminder of the monarchical origins of the British political system and of the extent to which the machinery of central government emanates from the Crown. This monarchical legacy gives the executive in Britain a continuing degree of authority and autonomy in its day-to-day operations, although some aspects of the use of prerogative power are politically controversial. Secondly, the formal legal position underlines the constitutional importance of individual ministers and departments in the processes of government, a point that is sometimes overlooked against the backdrop of concern with prime ministerial power.

A web of conventions governs the operation of the British executive. Here the conventions of collective responsibility and individual ministerial responsibility play a crucial role, even if their meaning and effectiveness are contested. In addition, the executive operates to a great extent within a semi-formal framework of rules, notes of guidance and Cabinet Office directives. This framework includes the Ministerial Code (see box 4.2); but it also now encompasses a range of concordats with devolved governments and contracts with executive agencies. It is also worth noting that legal issues increasingly have to be taken into account as a result not just of the growing significance of administrative law but also of the new role of human rights concerns in decision making. Questions of legality, which used not to weigh heavily on administrators, now do, as the regular circulation and publication of the memorandum 'The judge over your shoulder' illustrates (see box 4.1).

The Historical Origins of Cabinet Government

The cabinet developed from the group of the monarch's most senior advisers who formed a small inner committee of the Privy Council. The position of the cabinet became increasingly institutionalized from the late seventeenth century as the monarch's powers were subordinated to Parliament. The Glorious Revolution of 1688 was

Box 4.1 'The judge over your shoulder'

Originally produced by the Cabinet Office, the third edition of this booklet appeared in March 2000, just as the Human Rights Act 1998 came into force in the United Kingdom as a whole. It sets out the legal context in which administrators operate and alerts decision makers to factors that might trigger judicial review. Although it has no formal legal status, it offers a non-technical guide to the principles of lawful decision making and underlines the extent to which ministers and civil servants must now incorporate the possibility of a legal challenge into their daily work. The full version can be found on the Treasury Solicitor's website: http://www.treasury-solicitor.gov.uk/

a major turning point on the road to the supremacy of Parliament in the political system. With the succession to the throne of George I (1714–27), cabinet became the dominant source of executive power. Gradually over the late eighteenth and nineteenth centuries the monarch lost power to this inner council or cabinet, which, under the leadership of the prime minister, took effective responsibility for the government of the country. Many of the features of cabinet government as it developed during this period were the product of a political system that was very different in kind from today's mass democracy and were fashioned for a government that had a much smaller role than is the case in the contemporary world.

When the outlines of the modern cabinet emerged in the eighteenth century, the cabinet's authority was derived from the monarch, not from Parliament. The continuation of a government in office at that time depended on the monarch's goodwill rather than on the government's being able to command a majority in the House of Commons. Slowly over the nineteenth century the monarch's political power was eroded, so that today almost all actions of the monarch are taken on the advice of her ministers and there is virtually no room for independent influence to be exercised by the sovereign.

The twentieth century witnessed further adaptation of the structure and form of cabinet government. Both world wars brought about major changes in the structure of the cabinet system to make it more efficient. The experience of the First World War necessitated substantial reform of the cabinet structure through the creation of a Cabinet Secretariat. The Second World War and its immediate aftermath prompted the extensive use of cabinet committees, which were institutionalized by Attlee when he became prime minister in 1945. The structure of cabinet government is thus an evolving one, adapting old forms to meet new political and administrative exigencies.

The British executive is distinctive among modern democracies for the extent of its constitutional powers. Perhaps the growth of government would by itself inevitably have created an imbalance between the powers of the executive and those of the legislature and between the government and the individual. In the United Kingdom, the control of Parliament through the discipline of party government and the weakness of constitutional checks created an executive with formidable powers. In addition the executive has continued to use the monarch's prerogative powers, which give it a substantial degree of autonomy in matters of routine business. These powers underline the fact that government is carried out in the Crown's name, although the monarch no longer exercises these powers personally and always relies on the advice of her elected ministers (see chapter 2).

The prerogative powers of the Crown are not all of the same type. As was noted in chapter 2, two of the monarch's most important prerogative powers – the power to appoint a prime minister and the power to dissolve Parliament – are *personal* prerogatives of the Crown. The exercise of these sensitive powers – which only becomes other than routine in unusual or crisis situations – has the potential to involve the sovereign in political controversy. In order to avoid embroiling the monarchy in political argument, much reliance is placed on the advice of the private secretary to the monarch, who will carry out soundings and consultations on her behalf in the event of a constitutional crisis (Hennessy, 1995).

There are in addition various prerogative powers that are exercised by ministers in the monarch's name. Thus, for example, although many of the legislative authorizations that ministers and departments require to carry out the routine tasks of government are derived from statutes, the executive carries out some of its functions by prerogative powers that give it a degree of inherent legislative power, which can be especially useful when speedy action needs to be taken. Prerogative powers enable the government to sign treaties without prior parliamentary approval or to declare a state of emergency. Reorganizations of governmental functions may be done by Orders in Council. Other areas of prerogative power are more specific. The Home Secretary (acting in the monarch's name) may pardon a convicted criminal or reduce a punishment imposed by the court. This prerogative of mercy, which derives from the theory that the monarch is the fount of all justice, is perhaps less significant now that the United Kingdom has abolished the death penalty, but it can be crucial in commuting severe sentences or where there is doubt about the soundness of evidence used at a trial.

Decisions implemented by invoking the prerogative powers of government need no formal legislative endorsement. This formal freedom of action is in fact constrained by political reality. Parliament will always be given the opportunity to debate major developments and no government would take significant foreign policy initiatives without keeping Parliament fully informed. In many cases also, the provisions of a treaty require subsequent parliamentary legislation before they can have effect. Ministers know that they will be held individually and collectively responsible to Parliament for the use of these powers.

The Privy Council itself has survived as the formal machinery through which the queen exercises her prerogative powers, including the important function of issuing prerogative orders (i.e., Orders in Council, discussed below). The nominal membership of the Privy Council is extensive, comprising all past and present cabinet ministers and a number of public figures to a total of about 500. However, the working character of the Privy Council in fact is that of a small body of government ministers who are called together to witness the monarch signing formal documents – the Orders in Council – which may be used to declare war, commit troops to action or issue a declaration of a civil emergency. There is thus an overlap between members of the cabinet and members of the Privy Council. Confidentiality, which is seen as essential to the effective operation of cabinet government, is imposed on the cabinet by virtue of the oath of secrecy that cabinet members swear as Privy Councillors.

The Privy Council has a number of important committees which the monarch does not attend. These committees carry out advisory functions in relation to such matters as the legislation from the Channel Islands and the Isle of Man and from the universities of Oxford and Cambridge. One very important committee of the Privy Council – the Judicial Committee (JCPC) – increased its role as a result of the 1997 Labour government's constitutional reform programme. It had long been the final court of appeal from a declining number of Commonwealth countries, from the Channel Islands, from some ecclesiastical courts and from some professional bodies such as the British Medical Council (BMC), which regulates the medical profession in the United Kingdom. As a result of devolution, disputes that are designated as devolution issues go to the JCPC. The reason for choosing this method of settling devolution issues was partly that the Privy Council had a history of resolving constitutional cases and partly that it avoided asking the House of Lords to resolve disputes that might involve the UK legislature of which it is a part. At the core of the JCPC at present are the 12 law lords of the United Kingdom, together with other senior judges who are Privy Councillors, including senior Scottish judges and judges from Commonwealth countries. Proposals for the creation of a single constitutional court, if they take effect, would bring together much of the jurisdiction of the House of Lords and the JCPC.

The Modern Workings of Cabinet Government

The routine workings of the cabinet and the position of the prime minister are governed by rules drawn from convention and usage, not from formal law. The cabinet has adapted its operation to take account of the increase in administrative workload and newer pressures arising from the media and the changed international context of government. Although formally at the apex of the British system of government and politics, the role of full cabinet as a decision-making body is now less significant than that of a number of other decision-making arenas, both inside the formal cabinet structure (such as cabinet committees) and outside it (such as bilateral meetings of ministers, working groups and task forces). Yet for all the agreement about the changed role of full cabinet as a decision-making body, it retains its *political* significance as an institution where the governing party's most senior figures meet regularly to discuss strategy. And even if full cabinet meetings have for the most part become increasingly marginal to the routine processes of government decision making, they remain potentially important as a forum of last resort for resolving administrative and political differences. Equally, the cabinet retains its authority as a body for legitimizing decisions taken elsewhere in the system.

In recent years many of the practices of cabinet government have been codified and published in the Ministerial Code (formerly Questions of Procedure for Minis-ters), which is a handbook or digest covering such issues as which matters should come to full cabinet and how ministers should avoid conflicts of interest (see box 4.2 for extracts). The Ministerial Code has no formal legal status and may be changed by the prime minister of the day. A new edition is issued after each general election and the 2001 edition had several amendments to cover the increased concern with sleaze and the determination to maintain a unified approach to the media.

Box 4.2   Extracts from the Ministerial Code

Ministers of the Crown are expected to behave according to the highest standards of constitutional and personal conduct in the performance of their duties.

This Code provides guidance to Ministers on how they should act and arrange their affairs in order to uphold these standards. It lists the principles which may apply in particular situations drawing on past precedent. It applies to all members of the Government (and covers Parliamentary Private Secretaries in section 4).

Ministers are personally responsible for deciding how to act and conduct themselves in the light of the Code and for justifying their actions and conduct in Parliament. The Code is not a rulebook, and it is not the role of the Secretary of the Cabinet or other officials to enforce it or to investigate Ministers, although they may provide Ministers with private advice on matters which it covers.

Ministers only remain in office for so long as they retain the confidence of the Prime Minister. He is the ultimate judge of the standards of behaviour expected of a Minister and the appropriate consequences of a breach of those standards, although he will not expect to comment on every allegation that is brought to his attention.

The Code should be read against the background of the overarching duty on Ministers to comply with the law, including international law and treaty obligations, to uphold the administration of justice and to protect the integrity of public life. They are expected to observe the Seven Principles of Public Life set out in the first report of the Nolan Committee, repeated in annex A, and the following principles of Ministerial conduct:

   i. Ministers must uphold the principle of collective responsibility;

  ii. Ministers have a duty to Parliament to account, and be held to account, for the policies, decisions and actions of their departments and 'next steps' agencies;

 iii. It is of paramount importance that Ministers give accurate and truthful information to Parliament, correcting any inadvertent error at the earliest opportunity. Ministers who knowingly mislead Parliament will be expected to offer their resignation to the Prime Minister;

 iv. Ministers should be as open as possible with Parliament and the public, refusing to provide information only when disclosure would not be in the public interest, which should be decided in accordance with the relevant statutes and the Government's Code of Practice on Access to Government Information;

  v. Ministers should similarly require civil servants who give evidence before Parliamentary Committees on their behalf and under their direction to be as helpful as possible in providing accurate, truthful and full information in accordance with the duties and responsibilities of civil servants as set out in the Civil Service Code;

 vi. Ministers must ensure that no conflict arises, or appears to arise, between their public duties and their private interests;

vii. Ministers should avoid accepting any gift or hospitality which might, or might reasonably appear to, compromise their judgement or place them under an improper obligation;

viii. Ministers in the House of Commons must keep separate their roles as Minister and constituency Member;

 ix. Ministers must not use government resources for Party political purposes. They must uphold the political impartiality of the Civil Service and not ask civil servants to act in any way which would conflict with the Civil Service Code.

Source: *Ministerial Code*, chapter 1, http://www.cabinet-office.gov.uk/central/2001/mcode/contents.htm

Recent practice has changed the operation of cabinet government in a number of important respects. The machinery of cabinet government has long been surrounded by a veil of secrecy, so much so that not until John Major's premiership (1990–7) was the full structure of cabinet committees made public. Secrecy is deemed essential in relation to the proceedings of the cabinet, both because of the inherent sensitivity of matters under discussion and because of the convention of collective responsibility, which requires that all members of the cabinet must defend the decisions of the government whether or not they agree with them or even (in today's highly fragmented system) knew about them. Clearly, if political positions taken in cabinet by individual ministers became known, the convention would be undermined. In contemporary Britain, however, the convention of collective responsibility has had to adjust to the practice of leaks to the media and a greater willingness of politicians to reveal in print the details of sensitive internal government conflicts. In practice, some of the regular breaches of confidentiality come from the government itself through the **lobby**, the inner group of political journalists who provide a special channel for the release of government information. During Margaret Thatcher's premiership (1979–90), the use made of the lobby by her press secretary Sir Bernard Ingham was a cause of great complaint by cabinet ministers, who felt that she was using the system to undermine individual ministers and to promote her own, rather than the collective, interest. Under Blair, concern with presentation and media control has gone even further, partly as a result of the position of Alastair Campbell as the prime minister's director of communications and strategy, and partly because of the increased perception that presentation of policy and news management had become heavily politicized. In addition, personal enmities within the Blair cabinet have also resulted in an increase in leaks.

In May 2002, changes were proposed to the lobby system which would allow the morning lobby briefing to be open to other journalists, including foreign reporters. Cabinet ministers, other ministers and officials were permitted to give briefings to the lobby. Most importantly, briefings would be on the record and their source could be quoted directly rather than referred to in coded language (see box 4.3).

lobby (1) Area in Parliament outside the chamber. (2) Collective name given to the press who are allowed into the Members' Lobby and who receive special briefings from the government.

Box 4.3 Changes to the lobby system

November 1997	The Mountfield Report on government communications recommended that the twice-daily lobby briefings be on the record. On-the-record briefings begin, attributable to the prime minister's official spokesperson (PMOS).
October 2002	Morning lobby briefings made open to all journalists, including foreign journalists and specialist correspondents, not just designated lobby members. Briefings were to be followed by televised ministerial press conferences. Blair was to appear monthly. Afternoon briefings continue to be restricted to lobby journalists.

The role of the prime minister

The position of the prime minister emerged in the early eighteenth century. Sir Robert Walpole (1676–1745) is generally acknowledged as the first of Britain's prime ministers, although he was not given that title. Formally, the prime minister is 'first among equals' in the cabinet; but that has always been something of a political fiction. The prime minister (who has the formal title of First Lord of the Treasury and Minister for the Civil Service), although possessing few statutory powers, has long enjoyed a degree of power and patronage quite different from that of other ministers. Today, the prime minister is the person who symbolizes the government and who is expected to provide leadership and coordination within the administration and the party.

Historically, the premiership was sometimes combined with another office. Lord Salisbury was prime minister and Foreign Secretary. Winston Churchill was prime minister and Minister of Defence. Such a combination would be difficult to imagine with today's prime ministerial and ministerial workload. Nevertheless, the prime minister traditionally exercises special responsibility in some subject areas (for example, intelligence and the security services as well as the civil service). And from time to time he may signal the importance of an issue by taking direct responsibility for it or making a working group or task force report directly to him.

The apparent growth in the power of the prime minister has attracted a good deal of polemical and academic attention. For some observers the prime minister's powers have transformed cabinet government into a constitutional fiction and created in Britain a quasi-presidential form of government. Indeed, in some ways a strong prime minister is potentially more powerful than a president because of the absence of checks and balances on the executive in the Westminster model. Critics of Tony Blair's and Margaret Thatcher's assertive version of prime ministerial power often focus on the way they used the media to project their personality. Mo Mowlam also explicitly criticized Blair for taking decisions without consulting other members of the cabinet (Mowlam, 2002). Margaret Thatcher was frequently accused of undermining her own cabinet and for being authoritarian.

One important version of the strong prime minister hypothesis argues that the experience of government, especially since Mrs Thatcher's premiership, has altered the contours of the political system so that strong personal leadership from the centre is now deemed essential.

Critics of the prime ministerial power hypothesis argue that the proponents of prime ministerial power place too much emphasis on personality at the expense of structure and oversimplify the relationships at the centre of British government by portraying the prime minister's relationship with the cabinet and with other actors in the core executive in terms of a zero-sum power game (M. Smith, 1999). Instead, the prime minister and other key actors should be seen as power-dependent: they have resources which they must exchange with other core executive actors to achieve their goals. Although the prime minister is endowed with more political resources than any other single actor is, he or she is constrained both by having to act within the structure of cabinet government and by the need to cooperate with other actors. The core executive on this theory is thus best understood as a complex process of personal and institutional interactions at the centre of government.

Leadership style

The opponents of the strong prime minister hypothesis are not, of course, denying the role of personality in the executive; they simply argue that it is only one factor in the account of the British executive. Clearly, individual prime ministers have brought very different personalities, political skills and administrative habits to the job. Thus in addition to the changes to the prime ministerial role that have occurred as a result of external factors, the incumbents themselves have reinterpreted it to fit their own leadership style. That reinterpretation may not be as drastic as in a presidential system like the American one; but it may have an impact on future understandings of the premiership. Clement Attlee (Labour's prime minister in the 1945–51 governments) exercised his authority in a way which was extremely low key by comparison with Churchill's flamboyant, even eccentric, behaviour. Harold Wilson was generally thought to have been a manipulator of his colleagues rather than a confrontational leader. Margaret Thatcher revelled in the role of visionary leader, frequently pitting herself against her own cabinet, in contrast to her successor John Major, who used a more collegial leadership style (a 'government of chums' as it was dubbed) in an effort to hold government and party together. Tony Blair based much of his reform of the Labour Party around a strengthened leadership and has embraced an intensely personal leadership style in office.

Cabinet formation

Much of the undoubted power of the prime minister over his party colleagues comes from the extensive patronage at his disposal. This patronage includes the range of government posts but extends to a large number of appointments beyond the government (for example, judicial and ecclesiastical appointments and peerages). Politically, the most significant powers the prime minister has are the power to select members of the government and the power to fire them.

The size of cabinets has fluctuated only slightly in the period since 1900. In that year the number of ministers in the cabinet was 19, a figure to which the Macmillan cabinet of 1960 still adhered. The Heath cabinet of 1970–4 had 21 members, despite the prime minister's efforts to streamline the government. The Thatcher cabinet of 1980 had 22 members, but the Blair government of 2003 had 23 members.

The most significant deviation from this size of cabinet has been in wartime, when prime ministers have found it more efficient to form small cabinets or cabinet committees to concentrate entirely on the war effort. Thus in the First World War Lloyd George established a cabinet of five, while in the Second World War Churchill operated with a cabinet of nine. During the Falklands conflict Margaret Thatcher handled the war through a cabinet committee, (OD) SA, and Major handled the first Gulf War through a similar committee, OD (G).

Prime ministers in peacetime have on occasion tried to cut the size of the cabinet, believing that a reduced cabinet would make it a more efficient forum for strategic decision making. On his return to power in 1951, Churchill experimented with

overlord system A system of organizing the cabinet used by Winston Churchill when he returned to government in 1951. Churchill wanted to reproduce for peacetime the style of government he had operated from 1940 to 1945. The idea was to have a small number of ministers (largely peers without constituency duties) overseeing several departments, but the system broke down in practice because of the difficulty of securing accountability and clear lines of control.

pay-roll vote Term used to refer to the large number of MPs who are either salaried members of the government or unpaid parliamentary private secretaries. These MPs may be expected automatically to vote for the government in the division lobbies rather than take an independent line.

smaller cabinets based on an **overlord system**, in which a small group of senior politicians, who were largely in the House of Lords, formed the cabinet. Such experiments have tended to fail, not least because they have required the exclusion of major departments and their ministers from the cabinet.

By contrast with the relative stability of cabinet size, the numbers involved in the government as a whole have grown dramatically since 1900 as a result of the steady expansion in the numbers of junior ministers – from 41 in 1900 to 89 in 2002 (see table 4.1). Although it could be argued that the growth in the business of government required an expansion of ministers, the size of the so-called **pay-roll vote** leads some to raise the issue of the independence of Parliament. Suggestions that the size of government should be cut have surfaced regularly in debates about the legislative–executive balance. In addition, there has been a growth of parliamentary private secretaries (PPSs), who are unpaid aides to ministers. These appointments are recognized as the first step on the road to office and, although without remuneration, their holders are expected to support the government or resign. Thus in 2003 there were 6 resignations from PPS positions as a result of internal disagreement of the government's handling of the conflict with Iraq.

The major departments of state are represented in the cabinet, although the Treasury now has two representatives there: the Chancellor of the Exchequer and the Chief Secretary. There are in addition to the holders of the substantive offices one or two offices where the departmental duties are light. Thus the three offices of Lord Privy Seal, Chancellor of the Duchy of Lancaster and Paymaster General have been used to bring into the cabinet ministers who are to have general governmental remits such as chairing cabinet committees or managing parliamentary business rather than a specific departmental portfolio. The Blair cabinet of 2003 contained one Minister without Portfolio who was also the Party Chair (Ian McCartney) and one minister (Peter Hain) who combined the duties of being Leader of the House of Commons, Lord Privy Seal and Secretary of State for Wales.

There are, however, some significant constraints on the power of the prime minister to dispose of governmental jobs. First, the freedom to allocate people to positions is limited by the overall need to ensure that the government works effectively and by the expectations of senior party colleagues. Some cabinet posts such as Chancellor of the Exchequer and Foreign Secretary have obvious seniority and will have to be allocated carefully. Given the power of the Treasury within Whitehall, the Chancellor of the Exchequer holds a strategically key position at the heart of government – but the need for economic expertise adds its own constraints as to who can be chosen for the post. Incoming prime ministers are also to some extent constrained by party considerations, including the need to balance party factions. When a party comes to power after a period in opposition, the experience of being the shadow spokesperson for a department will itself generate expectations of being appointed to a comparable post in government.

Table 4.1 Growth in size of government since 1900

	1900	1910	1920	1930	1940	1950	1960	1970	1980	1990	2002
Cabinet ministers	19	19	19	19	9	18	19	21	22	22	23
Non-cabinet ministers	41	43	62	39	65	63	63	81	85	81	89
MPs in paid government posts	33	43	58	50	58	68	65	85	86	80	88
(% of total MPs)	(5%)	(6%)	(8%)	(8%)	(9%)	(11%)	(10%)	(13%)	(14%)	(12%)	(13%)
Peers in paid government posts	27	19	23	8	16	13	17	17	21	22	24
(% of total peers)	(5%)	(3%)	(3%)	(1%)	(2%)	(2%)	(2%)	(2%)	(2%)	(2%)	(3%)
Total paid government posts	60	62	81	58	74	81	82	102	107	102	112
Parliamentary private secretaries in Commons	9	16	13	26	25	27	36	30	37	47	42
Total	69	78	94	84	99	108	118	132	144	149	154

Source: Adapted from Butler and Butler (2000), pp. 71, 224; Butler and Kavanagh (2002), p. 260; Cabinet Office, UK Ministers http://www.cabinet-office.gov.uk/central/2001/ministers.htm#whips

The political strength of individual cabinet ministers will be uneven. Political authority within a cabinet is not necessarily related to the office held, although some positions (notably Chancellor of the Exchequer, Foreign Secretary and Home Secretary) are always likely to give their holders substantial authority.

The role of Gordon Brown as Chancellor of the Exchequer under Blair is especially powerful. Brown chairs a number of the most significant cabinet committees, including one (Economic Affairs, Productivity and Competitiveness) usually chaired by the prime minister. Structural changes in the handling of public expenditure have given Brown new power over departmental policy and an especially influential role in welfare policy. Politically, Brown's position is highly unusual: he is widely seen as being the likely successor to Blair and, although the man whose support is crucial to success of the government, he is also a rival with a different set of policy preferences. The Blair–Brown relationship is considered by many as dividing government under Blair, producing two rival 'gangs' of supporters whose loyalty is to their patron rather than to the government as a whole (Naughtie, 2002).

In any cabinet there are also likely to be individuals who enjoy a special influence because of personal friendship or usefulness to the prime minister. In Blair's 1997–2001 government, Lord Irvine, the Lord Chancellor, and for a time Peter Mandelson enjoyed this special standing. The importance of managing intra-party relations may sometimes give enhanced status to an individual cabinet minister. Thus in the Blair government John Prescott's personal popularity amongst Labour's rank and file made him important in addition to the influence he wielded as deputy prime minister. William Whitelaw's seniority and popularity in the Conservative Party made him a crucial element of Margaret Thatcher's governments. There will also be a distinction between ministers on the way up (rising stars who may expect to be promoted in a reshuffle) and ministers whose career has peaked and who are on the way down.

Although the title of deputy prime minister is sometimes used, its significance varies. Sir Geoffrey Howe was given the title in 1989 but found that its value had been undermined by the prime minister. After John Major's re-election as party leader in 1995, Michael Heseltine was given a powerful role as deputy prime minister, with his own office and the chairmanship of a number of central cabinet committees. Under Tony Blair, the position of deputy prime minister has been changed again. After an experiment with using the deputy prime minister, John Prescott, as part of the team coordinating central business through the Cabinet Office, Prescott (whose position is simply listed as deputy prime minister) has been given his own central department separate from the Cabinet Office. This department now has extensive responsibilities in relation to a range of cross-cutting regional and local government issues. Prescott's department by 2003 covered the Social Exclusion Unit, the Regional Coordination Unit and the Government Office for the Regions and was expanded to include regional policy, local government and local finance, planning, housing, urban policy, the Neighbourhood Renewal Unit and the fire service. In addition to these subject-specific responsibilities, the deputy prime minister has a range of other duties, including deputizing for the prime minister and chairing seven cabinet committees and subcommittees.

The power to appoint to a cabinet position, to dismiss a cabinet minister and to move cabinet members between departments gives the prime minister enormous leverage over his colleagues. Put bluntly, the prime minister can make or break his colleagues' careers, although the prime minister will always need to be aware of the danger of creating enemies on the **backbenches** by dismissing or slighting a minister. On the other hand, the power to dismiss is crucial to the standing of the government. A prime minister must know when to remove ministers not capable of doing the job or ministers who have acted in a way damaging to the government.

The need to freshen the image of a government and the need to promote talented younger members and to discard tired or ineffective older ones requires regular reshuffles of the government. Such reshuffles are eagerly anticipated but must be handled with care if they are not to produce resentments on the government **frontbenches**. When Harold Macmillan radically reshuffled his government in 1962 in the night of the long knives, sacking one-third of his cabinet, it damaged his standing because it looked savage and panicky. Reshuffles that move opponents of the prime minister from the discipline of the cabinet may backfire if they provide a focus for opposition on the backbenches.

While cabinet appointments naturally attract the lion's share of press attention, appointments lower down the ladder are also significant as MPs are keen to get their feet on the first rung of the ladder or to move up it. Ministers in charge of departments rarely have any say over who their junior ministers are to be because the allocation of government jobs is very much a strategic issue for the prime minister and, at the lower levels of government appointments, the whips. However, in the Blair government, Brown was adept at ensuring his people were in key positions, even pressing for the reinstatement of one supporter, Michael Wills, who was given a job just a few days after losing his original position in the 2002 reshuffle.

backbencher Member of Parliament (or, by extension, of other legislative body such as the Scottish Parliament) who does not hold office in the government or have responsibility as an opposition spokesperson. At Westminster these MPs sit on the benches behind the frontbench spokespersons.

frontbencher Member of Parliament (or, by extension, of other legislative body such as the Scottish Parliament) who holds office in the government or has responsibility as an opposition spokesperson. At Westminster these MPs sit on the frontbenches.

The use of the cabinet

Prime ministers vary in their management of the cabinet and in their approach to the wider issues concerned with the machinery of government. The complexities of modern government have increasingly changed the role of full cabinet, making it unrealistic to think of it as the centre of government decision making. Full cabinet meets regularly but briefly; and the period since 1945 has seen a reduction both in the number and duration of meetings and in the the range of papers coming to cabinet. Clement Attlee, prime minister from 1945 to 1951, held cabinet meetings twice a week. From 1969 cabinet meetings have been held only once a week on a Thursday morning, and they rarely last more than an hour in length. Indeed, Tony Blair (whose preference for informal meetings is well known) has frequently kept his cabinet meetings to 30 minutes. Short cabinet meetings can be a sign of unity, longer ones a sign of internal disagreement. Thus James Callaghan and John Major both held longer than average meetings as they attempted to resolve differences over the IMF loan and Europe, respectively.

There have also been changes in the personnel attending cabinet meetings. In addition to the prime minister and members of the cabinet, one or two other ministers may be asked to attend. Thus Tony Blair's December 2003 cabinet list revealed that the chief whip in the Lords was also an attendee at cabinet (see box 4.4). In Blair's first cabinet (1997–2001), the press secretary Alastair Campbell was a regular attendee.

It is necessary to have civil servants present to take a record of proceedings. Traditionally, the Cabinet Secretary takes the minutes of the cabinet meetings. In recent years the number of private secretaries also in attendance has grown. Cabinets (and cabinet committees) may meet without civil servants if they are discussing entirely *party* political (as opposed to governmental) matters. Thus civil servants will not attend a cabinet in which the date of an election is going to be discussed. Substantial use of these so-called political cabinets was made by John Major, whose government was peculiarly torn by intra-party strife.

Box 4.4   Cabinet, December 2003

Prime Minister, First Lord of the Treasury and Minister for the Civil Service – The Rt Hon Tony Blair MP

Deputy Prime Minister and First Secretary of State – The Rt Hon John Prescott MP

Chancellor of the Exchequer – The Rt Hon Gordon Brown MP

Secretary of State for Foreign and Commonwealth Affairs – The Rt Hon Jack Straw MP

Secretary of State for the Home Department – The Rt Hon David Blunkett MP

Secretary of State for Environment, Food and Rural Affairs – The Rt Hon Margaret Beckett MP

Secretary of State for Transport and Secretary of State for Scotland – The Rt Hon Alistair Darling MP

Secretary of State for Health – The Rt Hon Dr John Reid MP

Secretary of State for Northern Ireland – The Rt Hon Paul Murphy MP

Secretary of State for Defence – The Rt Hon Geoff Hoon MP

Secretary of State for Work and Pensions – The Rt Hon Andrew Smith MP

Secretary of State for Trade and Industry and Minister for Women – The Rt Hon Patricia Hewitt MP

Secretary of State for Culture, Media and Sport – The Rt Hon Tessa Jowell MP

Parliamentary Secretary to the Treasury and Chief Whip – The Rt Hon Hilary Armstrong MP

Secretary of State for Education and Skills – The Rt Hon Charles Clarke MP

Chief Secretary to the Treasury – The Rt Hon Paul Boateng MP

Leader of the House of Commons, Lord Privy Seal and Secretary of State for Wales – The Rt Hon Peter Hain MP

Minister without Portfolio and Party Chair – The Rt Hon Ian McCartney MP

Leader of the House of Lords and Lord President of the Council – The Rt Hon Baroness Valerie Amos

Secretary of State for Constitutional Affairs and Lord Chancellor for the transitional period – The Rt Hon Lord Falconer of Thoroton QC

Secretary of State for International Development – The Rt Hon Hilary Benn MP

Also attending cabinet:

Lords Chief Whip and Captain of the Gentlemen-at-Arms – The Rt Hon The Lord Grocott

The prime minister chairs the cabinet proceedings and the style in which business is handled will reflect his or her personality. Attlee's style was terse and business-like, as was Edward Heath's. Harold Wilson's was much more discursive. Margaret Thatcher was notoriously unwilling to allow free-ranging discussion, leading with her preferred position and daring challenge. Tony Blair seems similarly unenthusiastic about encouraging discussion in full cabinet.

In terms of *what* is actually discussed in cabinet, there are some regular items on the agenda in addition to specific issues. Notice is given of forthcoming parliamentary business and this often serves as an opportunity for general discussion. There will be reports routinely from the Foreign Secretary on foreign affairs and, since Edward Heath's time, on European Community matters. (Heath also made Northern Ireland a matter for regular report to cabinet.) Most of these reports are oral and cabinet is increasingly conducted on the basis of brief discussions rather than written reports. Indeed, one change in the way full cabinet works is the decline in the number of papers coming to it.

It should also be noted that some topics rarely if ever come up for cabinet discussion. Thus issues of nuclear policy, and intelligence and security matters generally, are usually handled outside the cabinet. In addition, some highly significant issues are taken outside cabinet. The decision to transfer sole power over interest rates to the Bank of England in 1997 was never discussed in cabinet. Even if cabinet meets, decisions can be railroaded through: the decision to proceed with the Millennium Dome was taken despite the fact that the majority of ministers were thought to be against it.

Cabinet committees

Mention has already been made of the importance of cabinet committees in the British system of government. These committees, rather than the full cabinet, are where policies are formally hammered out and where decisions are effectively taken. Although it is now difficult to imagine the British cabinet operating without these committees, it was only in Clement Attlee's 1945–50 government that a permanent system of cabinet committees was created. The complete list of cabinet committees was not officially made public until John Major's premiership.

Until recently cabinet committees could be divided into two basic kinds, standing committees (which would survive from one Parliament to the next, although the membership would change if the government did) and ad hoc or miscellaneous committees. Such committees would be set up for some special purpose and would cease to exist at the end of a government. (During any administration a large number of such committees might be set up, but in practice many committees would have ceased to function long before the end of that administration.) Among the most important standing committees of the cabinet are EA, which deals with Economic Affairs, and DOP, which deals with Defence and Overseas Policy. Ad hoc committees (labelled MISC or GEN in alternative administrations) of the cabinet may be established to deal with crucial elements of government business. A large number of such committees will exist at any one time, though not all will be functioning. Thus Tony Blair's 1997–2001 administration established cabinet committees of an ad hoc

Star Chamber Name given to the cabinet committee (MISC 62) which was established to arbitrate on public spending disputes.

nature to deal with such topics as utility regulation (MISC 3), biotechnology and genetic modification (MISC 6) and better government (MISC 7).

The picture has, however, become further complicated by the existence of subcommittees, which tend to have a narrower remit than cabinet committees. There has also been a much greater use since 1997 of less formal policy coordination devices. These include working groups, task forces and ad hoc meetings. Unlike cabinet committees and subcommittees, which have the authority of the cabinet as a whole, these groups have no formal status and cannot make binding decisions.

The Labour government elected in 1997 introduced a further device – the consultative committee. Consultative committees have the advantage of being able to include members from outside. Thus for the early part of the first Blair administration there was a joint consultative committee with the Liberal Democrats dealing with issues of constitutional reform. Although this consultative committee was later abolished, it was a highly unusual device since it involved bringing members of an opposition party onto a formal cabinet committee. A second consultative committee, the joint ministerial committee (JMC), was established to provide a forum for coordinating issues with the devolved administrations. The JMC was active in the first year of devolution but has since been little employed.

The use made of cabinet committees can be controversial. Richard Crossman, among others, argued that the use of ad hoc committees (as opposed to regular standing committees) enhances prime ministerial power. The prime minister decides who shall serve on cabinet committees and, although the membership of standing committees tends to be structured by departmental interest, it is easier to manipulate the membership and terms of reference of ad hoc committees. The selection of the chairman of a cabinet committee is often an indication of who are the prime minister's most trusted allies within a cabinet as well as of political strength. When John Major published the list of his cabinet committees, it provided a new insight into which ministers enjoyed the prime minister's confidence. Within Tony Blair's 2001 cabinet, John Prescott, Lord Irvine, David Blunkett and Gordon Brown all chaired a significant number of committees. Table 4.2 gives a list of the standing ministerial committees and subcommittees of the cabinet and their chairs as of March 2003.

The cabinet system and its official underpinnings are organized to resolve policy conflicts between departments and ministers. Every effort will be made to settle disagreements within government as early in the process of decision making as possible. Before any policy proposal surfaces as a legislative measure, it must have collective cabinet agreement, which will focus on the nature and timing of the change. Governments will plan their legislative programme for a five-year Parliament and there is always competition between departments and ministers for legislative time. Public expenditure has in the past generated intense interdepartmental conflicts. The handling of public expenditure was transformed in 1982 by the use of an ad hoc cabinet committee (MISC 62), dubbed **Star Chamber**, to settle differences between ministers over the allocation of money to the various departments. From 1992 a new arrangement was devised, whereby a Ministerial Committee on Public Expenditure (EDX) provided collective advice to the cabinet on public expenditure

Table 4.2 Standing ministerial committees and subcommittees of the cabinet, December 2003

Committee	Subcommittee	Code	Chair
Economic and Domestic Secretariat			
Criminal Justice System		(CJS)	Secretary of State for the Home Department, David Blunkett
	Crime Reduction	(CJS (CR))	Secretary of State for the Home Department, David Blunkett
	Information Technology	(CJS (IT))	Minister for the Cabinet Office and Chancellor of the Duchy of Lancaster, Douglas Alexander
Domestic Affairs		(DA)	Deputy Prime Minister and First Secretary of State, John Prescott
	Adult Basic Skills	(DA (ABS))	Secretary of State for Education and Skills, Charles Clarke
	Active Communities and Community Cohesion	(DA (ACF))	Secretary of State for the Home Department, David Blunkett
	Drugs Policy	(DA (D))	Secretary of State for the Home Department, David Blunkett
	Equality	(DA (EQ))	Minister of State, Department of Trade and Industry and Deputy Minister for Women, Jacqui Smith
	Energy Policy	(DA (N))	Deputy Prime Minister and First Secretary of State, John Prescott
	Older People	(DA (OP))	Secretary of State for Work and Pensions, Andrew Smith
	Rural Renewal	(DA (RR))	Secretary of State for the Environment, Food and Rural Affairs, Margaret Beckett
	Social Exclusion and Regeneration	(DA (SER))	Deputy Prime Minister and First Secretary of State, John Prescott
Economic Affairs, Productivity and Competitiveness		(EAPC)	Chancellor of the Exchequer, Gordon Brown
	Employment	(EAPC (E))	Chancellor of the Exchequer, Gordon Brown

(Continues)

Table 4.2 *Continued*

Committee	Subcommittee	Code	Chair
Environment		(ENV)	Deputy Prime Minister and First Secretary of State, John Prescott
	Green Ministers	(ENV (G))	Minister of State, Department for Environment, Food and Rural Affairs, Elliot Morley
English Regional Policy		(ERP)	Deputy Prime Minister and First Secretary of State, John Prescott
European Union Strategy		(EUS)	Prime Minister, Tony Blair
Local Government		(GL)	Deputy Prime Minister and First Secretary of State, John Prescott
	Local Government Performance	(GL (P))	Minister for Local Government, Office of the Deputy Prime Minister, Nick Raynsford
Legislative Programme		(LP)	Leader of the House of Commons, Lord Privy Seal and Secretary of State for Wales, Peter Hain
Organized Crime		(OC)	Secretary of State for the Home Department, David Blunkett
Devolution Policy		(PD)	Secretary of State for Constitutional Affairs, Lord Falconer
Regulatory Accountability[a]		(PRA)	Minister for the Cabinet Office and Chancellor of the Duchy of Lancaster, Douglas Alexander
Public Services and Public Expenditure		(PSX)	Chancellor of the Exchequer, Gordon Brown
	Electronic Service Delivery	(PSX (E))	Chief Secretary to the Treasury, Paul Boateng
	Inspection	(PSX (I))	Chief Secretary to the Treasury, Paul Boateng
Science Policy		(SCI)	Secretary of State for Trade and Industry, Patricia Hewitt
	Biotechnology	(SCI (BIO))	Secretary of State for Foreign and Commonwealth Affairs, Jack Straw
Welfare Reform		(WR)	Prime Minister, Tony Blair
Children and Young People's Services[b]		(MISC 9)	Chancellor of the Exchequer, Gordon Brown

Committee	Code	Chair
Delivery of Services for Children, Young People and Families	(MISC 9 (D))	Secretary of State for Education and Skills, Charles Clarke
Animal Rights Activists[b]	(MISC 13)	Secretary of State for the Home Department, David Blunkett
Universal Banking Services	(MISC 19)	Secretary of State for Work and Pensions, Andrew Smith
Social and Economic Aspects of Migration	(MISC 20)	Secretary of State for the Home Department, David Blunkett
Government's response to the Parliamentary Modernization	(MISC 21)	Leader of the House of Commons, Lord Privy Seal and Secretary of State for Wales, Peter Hain
Thames Gateway	(MISC 22)	Prime Minister, Tony Blair
Illegal Imports	(MISC 23)	Secretary of State for Environment, Food and Rural Affairs, Margaret Beckett
Electoral Policy	(MISC 24)	Leader of the House of Commons, Lord Privy Seal and Secretary of State for Wales, Peter Hain
Olympic Games	(MISC 25)	Secretary of State for Foreign and Commonwealth Affairs, Jack Straw
Constitutional Reform Policy	(CRP)	Secretary of State for Constitutional Affairs, Lord Falconer
House of Lords Reform	(CRP (HL))	Secretary of State for Constitutional Affairs, Lord Falconer
Consultative Committee with the Liberal Democrats	(JCC)	Prime Minister, Tony Blair

Civil Contingencies Secretariat

Committee	Code	Chair
Civil Contingencies	(CCC)	Secretary of State for the Home Department, David Blunkett

Defence and Overseas Secretariat

Committee	Code	Chair
Defence and Overseas Policy	(DOP)	Prime Minister, Tony Blair
Conflict Prevention in Sub-Saharan Africa	(DOP (A))	Secretary of State for International Development, Hilary Benn
Conflict Prevention outside Sub-Saharan Africa	(DOP (OA))	Secretary of State for Foreign and Commonwealth Affairs, Jack Straw
International Terrorism	(DOP (IT))	Prime Minister, Tony Blair

(Continues)

Table 4.2 *Continued*

Committee	Subcommittee	Code	Chair
	Protective and Preventative Security	(DOP (IT)(T))	Secretary of State for the Home Department, David Blunkett
	Consequence Management and Resilience	(DOP (IT)(R))	Secretary of State for the Home Department, David Blunkett
	London Resilience	(DOP (IT)(R) (LR))	Minister of State, Office of the Deputy Prime Minister, Nick Raynsford
Northern Ireland		(IN)	Prime Minister, Tony Blair
Intelligence Services		(CSI)	Prime Minister, Tony Blair
Restructuring of the European Aerospace and Defence Industries[b]		(MISC 5)	Secretary of State for Trade and Industry, Patricia Hewitt
European Secretariat	European Policy	(EP)	Secretary of State for Foreign and Commonwealth Affairs, Jack Straw

[a] Ministerial panel rather than committee
[b] Ministerial groups rather than committees

Source: Cabinet Office, http://www.cabinet-office.gov.uk/cabsec/index/index.htm

issues. This committee allowed ministers to become involved in the whole process of expenditure planning at an earlier stage and in theory helped develop a consensual view. Under Tony Blair, the introduction of a three-year public expenditure agreement has to a large extent removed the need for special machinery to cope with the conflicting claims of departments, though it has also strengthened the Treasury at the expense of the departments.

Cabinet committees developing specific legislation for handling a new policy issue may contain ministers not in the cabinet. Subcommittees will regularly contain junior ministers, although such subcommittees are much more likely to be concerned with the coordination of policy rather than its initiation.

Cabinet committees are regularly shadowed by committees of civil servants. These committees of officials are usually constructed to take account of interdepartmental questions and will be chaired by an official from the Cabinet Office. The process of having official committees shadowing cabinet committees aids administrative efficiency, although they sometimes seem to limit political innovation. Richard Crossman, for example, thought many of the decisions of cabinet committees had been pre-cooked by civil servants.

Decisions of cabinet committees have the force and authority of decisions of the cabinet as a whole. Because so much of the work of the cabinet has to be done in committee, business settled in full cabinet has become increasingly difficult to reopen in full cabinet. Harold Wilson formalized the rule that issues settled in committee should not be reopened in cabinet without the consent of the committee chair or the prime minister. Although Edward Heath appeared to have no need of the procedural device between 1970 and 1974, successive cabinets saw the rule become firmly established. Whether an issue is discussed in full cabinet will depend on its sensitivity as well as on the judgement of both the prime minister and the principal protagonists. In expenditure battles the Chancellor of the Exchequer may reserve the right to make a case to full cabinet if he believes a cut in a programme is necessary.

Although cabinet committees exist to expedite business, prime ministers must be careful to ensure that minority views do not seem unfairly silenced. If a minister or group of ministers feel that an important case has been overridden, they may resign with damaging consequences for the government as a whole. Michael Heseltine's resignation over the Westland affair (see box 5.5, p. 186) was caused in part by his disagreement with a majority of the cabinet on the issue of how to rescue the Westland helicopter company; but it was also the product of Heseltine's objection to the whole style of Margaret Thatcher's management of the cabinet.

Even with the power that a prime minister has over the committee structure, it may be that a prime minister will prefer to bypass the formal structure of the cabinet and its committees altogether and instead make decisions in more informal groups of ministerial colleagues and advisers. Over her long premiership, Margaret Thatcher increasingly tended to take decisions in this way. Tony Blair made clear his preference for less structured decision making from the beginning of his period as prime minister. The use of task forces was an important innovation of the Blair government. Task forces were designed to improve the quality of decision making in government. They bring together officials from a number of different departments and outside experts to cover issues that do not easily fit within departmental boundaries. Between May 1997 and July 1998, about 30 such task forces had been set up on subjects as diverse as disability rights and football. Informal decision-making methods do, however, pose problems for cabinet government since it is unclear to what extent decisions made by the prime minister and perhaps one or two other ministers can bind the government as a whole.

Institutional Support for the Cabinet and Prime Minister

Despite the growth in the role of government, institutional support for the central institutions of cabinet and prime minister remained undeveloped until the early twentieth century. The crisis of the First World War prompted organizational reform, and from that period there dates the formal machinery of the Cabinet Office. Because constitutional theory emphasized the role of the cabinet rather than that of the prime minister personally, efforts to strengthen the support available to the prime minister occurred in a slow and ad hoc fashion, with individual prime ministers adapting the machinery to suit their needs. However, with Tony Blair's premiership there was a much more conscious effort to strengthen the centre of government and to bring greater capacity by integrating the Prime Minister's Office and the Cabinet Office more effectively. This reshaping of the centre has not yet stabilized institutionally and is likely to be subject to further revision. In order to understand the problems involved in strengthening the centre of British government, it is necessary first to examine separately the two elements of institutional support – the Cabinet Office and the Prime Minister's Office.

The Cabinet Office

The Cabinet Office has increasingly become the nerve centre of British central government, growing in size and significance and taking on a number of tasks that might have generated new institutional arrangements. Thus its staff (who are generally high-fliers seconded from other departments for a short period) increased from 1,709 in 1987 to 2,120 in 2002, a figure which includes Cabinet Office and the Office of the Deputy Prime Minister (ODPM). The Cabinet Office contains a number of crucial mechanisms for the central coordination of policy at the highest levels and for maintaining the efficiency of the governmental machine. Inevitably, given its position at the heart of government and the close relationship between the prime minister and the Cabinet Secretary, the Cabinet Office will be involved in sensitive questions of political strategy as well as management and administrative issues.

There are several different units in the Cabinet Office. The most important politically is the Cabinet Secretariat, which provides administrative support for the system of cabinet government by ensuring that the cabinet and its various committees operate smoothly. Until 1916 there was no formal machinery for producing cabinet agendas or for recording cabinet decisions or ensuring follow-up. Now there is a large secretariat consisting of around 200 people (with an inner core of 50), headed by the Cabinet Secretary. The Cabinet Secretariat has the task of briefing the prime minister and cabinet committee chairpersons in advance of meetings, producing the agenda and supporting papers for those meetings, and drawing up and circulating the minutes.

The work of the Cabinet Secretariat has become increasingly specialized on functional lines. The precise division of responsibilities changed as a result of a report by Sir Richard Wilson in 1998 into the work of the Cabinet Office. Its organization is now divided into five units – Central Secretariat, Civil Contingencies, Overseas and Defence, Economic and Domestic, and European – each of which is headed by a deputy secretary.

The Cabinet Secretary will prepare the agendas and take the minutes of the full cabinet and of committees chaired by the prime minister, delegating the servicing of other cabinet committees. The Cabinet Secretary's responsibility for the smooth running of the cabinet system has given him a major role in the interpretation of cabinet practices, rules and conventions. Thus he will be involved when delicate questions about secrecy and leaks occur, as they did for example during the Westland affair. The rules governing the conduct of cabinet business and the behaviour of ministers in such matters as outside interests are laid down in the Ministerial Code. The Cabinet Secretary has also acquired major functions in relation to national security and intelligence matters as a result of the cabinet taking over these functions from the Joint Chiefs of Staff in the 1950s. However, in 2002 it was announced that the incoming Cabinet Secretary, Sir Andrew Turnbull, would give up his routine responsibilities in relation to security and the honours system in order to be able to concentrate on turning the Cabinet Office into an effective instrument of policy reform and delivery. Sir David Omand was appointed to a new post as Security and Intelligence Coordinator, while responsibility for vetting honours was passed to the permanent secretary at the Lord Chancellor's Department (now the Department for Constitutional Affairs). Figure 4.1 shows the organization of the Cabinet Office as of December 2003.

Apart from the Cabinet Secretary's role in relation to the machinery of government, the prime minister will also rely on him to warn ministers of possible breaches of confidentiality, or of the Ministerial Code, or of conduct which may make a minister open to blackmail. Thus the Cabinet Secretary was involved in warning Alan Clark about his personal lifestyle and behaviour and in questioning Jonathan Aitken about his links with arms sales. Under Margaret Thatcher the Cabinet Secretary was involved in a rather long-drawn-out effort to stop the publication of *Spycatcher*, the memoirs of an MI5 officer (see box 4.5).

Concern with the ability of the Cabinet Secretary to undertake inquiries into ministerial conduct and breaches of the Ministerial Code was one factor leading the Public Administration Select Committee (PASC) to recommend that inquiries about breaches of the Ministerial Code could be undertaken by the Parliamentary Commissioner for Standards. It was also thought that other bodies might want to refer breaches of the code by ministers to such a body. However, the idea was rejected by the government, not least because it would undermine the prime minister's control of his administration.

The Cabinet Secretary now has the title Head of the Home Civil Service, which further augments his power over the machinery of government issues. The two roles have not always been combined and some critics now suggest that the functions should be separated, both because of the workload involved and because of the potential for a conflict of interest. During the Thatcher–Major years, a number of issues arose about defending the boundaries of the civil service role. As Head of the Home Civil Service, the Cabinet Secretary may issue guidelines on general questions

Douglas Alexander Esq MP
Minister for the Cabinet Office and
Chancellor of the Duchy of Lancaster

Sir Andrew Turnbull KCB CVO
Secretary of the Cabinet and Head of the Home Civil Service

Coordination and promoting standards

Sir David Omand KCB
Security and Intelligence Coordinator,
Accounting Officer for the Single
Intelligence Account

John Scarlett, Director, ISS

Susan Scholefield, Director, CCS

To be appointed
Permanent Secretary, Government
Communications

Sir Stephen Wall[2] KCMG
Head, European Secretariat

Sir Nigel Sheinwald[3] KCMG
Head, Overseas and Defence Secretariat

Paul Britton CB
Head, Economic and Domestic Secretariat

Gay Catto, Head, Ceremonial Secretariat

Sue Gray, Head, Propriety and Ethics

Building capacity

Alice Perkins CB
Director General,
Corporate Development Group

Geoff Mulgan[4]
Director, Strategy Unit

Michael Barber
Director, Delivery Unit

Andrew Pinder
e-Envoy

Wendy Thomson
Director, Office of Public Service Reform

Simon Virley
Director, Regulatory Impact Unit

Richard Gillingwater
Chief Executive, Shareholder Executive

Peter Gershon[1]
Chief Executive,
Office of Government Commerce
Head of Efficiency Review

Managing the Cabinet Office

Colin Balmer CB
Managing Director
Permanent Head of
the Department
and Accounting Officer

Léonie Austin
Communication Director

John Sweetman
Business Development Director

Jerry Page
Finance Director

Claudette Francis
HR Director

Eric Hepburn
Infrastructure Director

Peter Norris
Internal Audit Director

Attached to the Cabinet Office

Carol Tullo, Controller, Her Majesty's Stationery Office

Alan Bishop, Chief Executive, COI Communications

Rob Behrens, Secretary to the Committee on
Standards in Public Life

Andrew Makower, Government Whips Office,
House of Lords

Jim Barron, independent offices

Tessa Stirling, Head of Histories and Records

Nick Matheson, Chief Executive, Government Car
and Despatch Agency

Roy Stone, Government Whips Office,
House of Commons

Geoffrey Bowman, First Parliamentary Counsel
Parliamentary Counsel Office

Notes

Some units contribute to more than one area of work:
coordination; building capacity; promoting standards

[1] OGC is part of HMT, not CO, but is a part of the Cabinet
Secretary's Delivery and Reform Team

The Efficiency Review is being undertaken jointly with
HM Treasury

[2] Sir Stephen Wall is also the Prime Minister's European
Adviser

[3] Sir Nigel Sheinwald is also the Prime Minister's Foreign
Policy Adviser

[4] Geoff Mulgan is also Head of Policy at No.10 Downing
Street

Figure 4.1 Organization of the Cabinet Office. *Source*: Cabinet Office.

relating to the conduct of civil servants. For example, the way civil servants give evidence before select committees is encapsulated in the so-called Osmotherly rules, which are circulated in a note from the Cabinet Secretary. In the 1980s following Clive Ponting's prosecution for revealing information to Parliament about the sinking of the Argentinian ship the *General Belgrano* during the Falklands War, controversy arose about how civil servants should handle ministerial policy instructions which offended their conscience or which they thought improper because they

Box 4.5   Clark, Aitken, *Spycatcher*

Alan Clark was a minister in the Departments of Employment, Trade and Defence under Margaret Thatcher. He was regarded as a maverick, with outspoken views and a colourful private life. Revelations about his extra-marital affairs led to a warning from Cabinet Secretary Sir Robert Armstrong. After standing down from the Commons in 1992, he published his diaries, which with their confessions of marital infidelity and humorous insights into the Thatcher governments went on to become bestsellers.

As Chief Secretary to the Treasury in the mid-1990s, Jonathan Aitken was accused by the *Guardian* newspaper of accepting hospitality from Saudi Arabians involved in the arms trade. Aitken resigned from his job in order to pursue libel proceedings against the *Guardian*. The trial collapsed in 1997 when it emerged that Aitken had asked his daughter to commit perjury, and he was later jailed for this offence.

In 1987 former MI5 agent Peter Wright tried to publish *Spycatcher*, an account of his time in the service. Among the book's claims were that MI5 'bugged and burgled its way across London' and that the security services had attempted to bring down the Wilson government of 1974–6. The book was banned in the UK but published abroad. Sir Robert Armstrong, the Cabinet Secretary, was sent to Australia in a failed effort to prevent publication there.

reflected party rather than governmental objectives. The then Cabinet Secretary Sir Robert Armstrong, as Head of the Home Civil Service, issued a memorandum of guidance – the **Armstrong memorandum** – which dismayed civil service unions because it seemed to avoid important ethical dilemmas facing civil servants in a changing political climate (see chapter 5).

The Cabinet Secretary also has a major influence on the personnel of Whitehall and the machinery of government. Part of the Cabinet Secretary's power comes from the amount of close and regular contact he has with the prime minister. He will probably see the prime minister alone more often than any individual cabinet minister. As a result, the Cabinet Secretary may become a close confidante of the prime minister and may exert a powerful influence on strategic issues. Certainly, there was some feeling that William Armstrong had become a deputy prime minister to Edward Heath in all but name (see box 4.6 for a list of Cabinet Secretaries from 1916 to 2003). A Cabinet Secretary's power also comes from intimate knowledge of the machinery and processes of government – topics that rarely engage prime ministerial interest in a sustained manner.

Apart from the secretariat, the Cabinet Office has a number of other coordinating functions. Special units that reflect the government's priorities, especially if those priorities cut across departmental boundaries, may be located in the Cabinet Office. Thus under the 1970–4 Conservative government a special unit was established to handle Britain's application to join the European Economic Community and a new body, the Central Policy Review Staff, was set up to improve the policy-making capacity of government as a whole. Under the Labour government of 1974–9 a dedicated unit was based in the

Armstrong memorandum Memorandum issued by Sir Robert Armstrong, Cabinet Secretary and Head of the Home Civil Service from 1979 to 1988, in 1985 and revised in 1987. The memorandum was a response to the ethical problem faced by a civil servant who believed instructions given by a minister were improper or illegal. The memorandum reiterated that civil servants had no identity distinct from that of the government of the day and insisted that civil servants' first recourse in cases of conscience was to their departmental civil service superior.

Box 4.6   Cabinet Secretaries, 1916–2003

1916	Sir Maurice Hankey
1938	Sir Edward Bridges
1947	Sir Norman Brook
1963	Sir Burke Trend
1973	Sir John Hunt
1979	Sir Robert Armstrong
1988	Sir Robin Butler
1998	Sir Richard Wilson
2003	Sir Andrew Turnbull

Cabinet Office to handle its (ultimately unsuccessful) devolution plans. Various initiatives related to efficiency and management reform in government have been based in the Cabinet Office, although sometimes there has also been close involvement of the prime minister as well.

Under the first Blair administration, an increased concern with coordination, delivery and cross-cutting issues generated a number of special units. Many of these were housed in the Cabinet Office, although one – the Delivery Unit – was transferred to the Treasury in 2003. Among special units housed at one time in the Cabinet Office were the Social Exclusion Unit (which focused on social deprivation), the Performance and Innovation Unit (which was a source of policy analysis across Whitehall), the Women's Unit and the Drugs Control Unit. All of these units have been designed to enhance the ability of government to meet its objectives and deliver services effectively.

The Prime Minister's Office

The political and administrative support available to the prime minister individually has historically not been extensive, although it was of a very high quality and highly adaptable to the needs and styles of different prime ministers. Whereas Gladstone managed with two aides when prime minister, Edward Heath in 1970 had 71 (Kavanagh and Seldon, 1999). As already noted, the Cabinet Office, although theoretically organized to serve the cabinet as a whole, is highly responsive to prime ministerial direction. Within No. 10 Downing Street (the office and home of the prime minister), there is a range of resources available. Trends towards greater systematic provision of support for the prime minister were noted during the premierships of Margaret Thatcher and John Major.

Under Tony Blair, however, the Prime Minister's Office has been expanded and politicized in order to sharpen its capacity to support Blair's strong personal view of the premiership. The enhanced strategic role of the Prime Minister's Office has inevitably caused some commentators to dub it a 'prime minister's *department* in all but name' (Burch and Holliday, 1999). And there has necessarily been a shift in the relationship with the Cabinet Office, which Blair has attempted to integrate more closely with the Prime Minister's Office. The growth in size of the Prime Minister's Office has been dramatic even in the period since 1970. By the end of

Tony Blair's first period of office in 2001, the number of staff had doubled to 150. These staff work in different sections, some long established, some new, within the Prime Minister's Office (see figure 4.2).

Prime Minister's Office

Prime Minister and First Lord of the Treasury and Minister for the Civil Service
The Rt Hon Tony Blair MP

Chief of Staff
Jonathan Powell

Director of Communications and Strategy
David Hill

Government and Political Relations
Baroness Sally Morgan

Principal Private Secretary and Head of Policy Directorate
Jeremy Heywood

Adviser on EU Affairs and Head of the European Secretariat
Sir Stephen Wall

Adviser on Foreign Policy and Head of the Overseas and Defence Secretariat
Sir Nigel Sheinwald

Parliamentary Private Secretary
David Hanson MP

Policy Directorate: Head of Policy
Geoff Mulgan

Policy Directorate: Senior Policy Advisers
Simon Morys
Geoffrey Norris
Patrick Diamond
Matthew Elson
Dr Arnab Banerji
Carey Oppenheim
Derek Scott
Ed Richards
Sarah Hunter
Simon Stevens
Justin Russell
Martin Hurst
Clare Sumner
Alasdair MacGowan
Andrew Adonis

Senior Policy Advisers: Foreign Policy
Matthew Rycroft
David Hallam
Liz Lloyd
Roger Liddle

Head of the Delivery Unit
Michael Barber

Head of the Office of Public Services Reform
Wendy Thomson

Secretary for Appointments
William Chapman

Executive Secretary
Jay Jayasundara

Director of Political Operations
Pat McFadden

Director of Events and Visits
Fiona Millar

Personal Assistant to PM (Diary)
Katie Kay

Parliamentary Clerk
Nicholas Howard

Communications and Strategy

Prime Minister's Official Spokesman (PMOS)
Godric Smith
Tom Kelly

Strategic Communications Unit
Peter Hyman

Research and Information Unit
Phil Bassett
Corporate Communications

Figure 4.2 The Prime Minister's Office. *Source:* Adapted from *Civil Service Yearbook*, 40th edn, 2003.

At the core of the prime minister's communications network is the **private office**. The principal private secretary to the prime minister may claim to be the key civil service adviser to the prime minister. Jeremy Heywood, who occupied the position under Blair, effectively managed the Downing Street machine with Jonathan Powell as Chief of Staff. The principal private secretary works with several assistants who divide the work along functional lines, covering such areas as economic affairs, home affairs and parliamentary business. These assistants are all high-flying civil servants seconded from other departments to work for the prime minister for a short period of two to three years. (The Foreign Office usually provides the senior foreign affairs adviser, which can produce a suspicion of divided loyalties inside No. 10.) The private office staff are not chosen personally by the prime minister, although close relationships may subsequently develop. In 2001 Blair's reliance on Jeremy Heywood was such that Downing Street resisted an attempt by the Chancellor of the Exchequer to move him back to the Treasury. The task of the private office is to organize the prime minister's work, controlling the flow of documents and briefing the prime minister on the varied issues that come before him. The prime minister's private office is also a key link with the departments, each of which has a private office that is central to the exchange of information and the coordination of policy in Whitehall.

One highly sensitive aspect of the private office's role is the briefing of the prime minister for the weekly appearance at PMQs in the House of Commons, a task which has become all the more arduous since the advent of television. Even apparently unflappable prime ministers such as Harold Macmillan and Margaret Thatcher have suggested that this gladiatorial battle is frightening. Another crucial function of the private office is liaison with the monarch to ensure that the queen is kept fully informed about all government business. This is achieved through weekly private meetings with the queen at Buckingham Palace.

The prime minister's private office is thus an established part of the Downing Street organization. Despite the closeness of some working civil servants to the prime minister, the fact that private office staff are neutral civil servants creates a void which prime ministers have attempted to fill by importing close political aides and confidantes into the structure of No. 10 through the political office. This office represents an attempt to maintain a high-profile political presence inside Downing Street and to see that the party dimension of policy is not lost. The presence of party political staff in Downing Street was once controversial but has become much more accepted in recent years. There will usually be a political secretary in addition to two parliamentary private secretaries for the Commons and the Lords.

Separate from both the private office and the political office is the press office. There has been a press adviser to the prime minister since the 1930s and the growth of the mass media has vastly increased the importance of media relations in all modern democracies. Outsiders have regularly been used as press advisers – William Clark under Anthony Eden, Trevor Lloyd Hughes and Joe Haines under Harold Wilson. As the marketing of politics has increased in salience, so the role of media advice has become more crucial. Sir Bernard Ingham's period as press secretary to Margaret Thatcher was highly controversial, even though Ingham was not an outsider. The controversy arose because of the extent to which the lobby was briefed to present the prime ministerial as opposed to the collective cabinet view. The emphasis on spin and media relations in the Blair government elected in 1997 focused additional attention on the role of the press office, and the potential power of its members. Alastair Campbell in particular came in for extensive criticism, which reflected a general unease that the distinction between policy and presentation had been eroded and that Campbell had acquired an unprecedented amount of political power. Individual departments have their own press and information services, which at the beginning of the 1997 Blair government were subject to an unusual degree of politicization. In addition to the press office, Labour established a new unit in Downing Street, the Strategic Communications Unit, to deal with longer-term media and presentation issues. There has also been a tightening of central control over press releases from the individual departments, a change reflected in the Ministerial Code (see box 4.7).

Although the private office, political office and press office all provide briefings and support for the prime minister, none of these offices is designed to produce systematic policy advice. The Cabinet Office provides briefings for the prime minister and the chairs of cabinet committees, but prime ministers have also sought policy advice of their own. Sometimes this has been done by bringing in personal advisers. Neville Chamberlain, for example, brought in Horace Wilson as a special foreign policy emissary. Margaret Thatcher's use of special personal advisers was highly controversial and her retention of Alan Walters as an economic adviser caused the resignation of the Chancellor of the Exchequer, Nigel Lawson.

Since 1974 there has, however, been a more systematic provision of policy advice for the prime minister through the Prime Minister's Policy Unit. This unit was established under Harold Wilson, with Bernard Donoghue as its first head. Under Margaret Thatcher the Policy Unit became more visible, partisan and comprehensive and operated with some very different directors, including Sir John Hoskyns, Ferdinand Mount, John Redwood and Lord Griffiths. John Major appointed an economic journalist (Sarah Hogg) and a management consultant (Norman Blackwell) as successive heads of the unit. Under Blair the unit was enlarged, first under the direction of David Miliband and then under that of Andrew Adonis.

Box 4.7   Extract from the Ministerial Code on media relations

In order to ensure the effective presentation of government policy, all major interviews and media appearances, both print and broadcast, should be agreed with the No. 10 Press Office before any commitments are entered into. The policy content of all major speeches, press releases and new policy initiatives should be cleared in good time with the No. 10 Private Office. The timing and form of announcements should be cleared with the No. 10 Strategic Communications Unit.

Source: Cabinet Office, Ministerial Code, Section 8: Ministers and the Presentation of Policy, http://www.cabinet-office.gov.uk/central/2001/mcode/p08.htm

---

The purpose of the Downing Street Policy Unit is to develop and protect party policy as well as to ensure that the presentation of issues is hard-hitting. This role can be especially important in the mid-term of a government after the initial impetus from the election has begun to fade. Members of the Policy Unit will be policy experts drawn from outside government, although sometimes the unit may include a civil servant. During Blair's administration the unit has become an instrument of central direction as well as a think tank for generating new ideas and providing alternatives to the departmental perspective. The Policy Unit at the centre is complemented by special advisers to ministers in the departments, and under Blair the whole network of policy advisers has been integrated fully into routine departmental processes and participating in expenditure reviews.

One important innovation under Tony Blair was the creation of a Chief of Staff, Jonathan Powell, to manage the whole Downing Street operation. Equally important has been the effort to integrate the prime minister's operations with those of the Cabinet Office to ensure that the Prime Minister's Office retains strategic control. The assertion of political control over the regular machine was underlined by the unusual decision to give Jonathan Powell and Alastair Campbell formal powers to direct civil servants, something that had to be done by an Order in Council. In the past, party appointments and special advisers in Downing Street, as in the departments, often found themselves resented and sidelined by regular civil servants.

The growth in size of the Downing Street staff is a mark of how far party concerns have penetrated the central machinery of government, but it is also a reflection of the extent to which strategic policy making in government inevitably has both an administrative and a political dimension. The insertion of party appointments into Downing Street and the departments is now largely accepted, although concern also developed about the proliferation of political appointees in Whitehall. Two recent investigations – one by the Public Administration Committee and one by the Committee on Standards in Public Life (Public Administration Select Committee, 8th Report, 2002; Wicks Committee, 2003) – exposed the extent of anxiety about the long-term impact of political advisers on relationships between ministers and civil servants and the conduct of policy. Efforts to introduce a new Civil Service Act to cope with the problem were resisted by the government, partly pleading a lack of legislative time. It seems likely, however, that this issue will remain a live one.

Ministers and Departments

The concentration in the first part of the chapter was on the political apex of the British executive, namely, the cabinet and prime minister. These institutions are, however, only a small albeit highly sensitive part of the British executive. The cabinet is not merely the inner group of the most senior politicians in the governing party. It also brings together the heads of the major departments responsible for policy making and coordinating administration in the various policy sectors of central government. Although the constitutional theory of cabinet government assumes that the government is a single entity, the practice of government is highly

Box 4.8   Government departments, December 2003

Government department	Date created
Cabinet Office	1916
Culture, Media and Sport	1997 (formerly Department of National Heritage)
Defence	1964
Office of the Deputy Prime Minister	2002
Education and Skills	2001 (formerly Education and Employment)
Environment, Food and Rural Affairs	2001 (formerly Environment, Transport and the Regions; Agriculture, Fisheries and Food)
Foreign and Commonwealth Office	1968 (formerly two departments)
Health	1988 (formerly Health and Social Security)
Home Office	1900
International Development	1997
Department for Constitutional Affairs	2003
Northern Ireland Office	1972
Privy Council Office	1405
Scotland Office	1926
Trade and Industry	1998 (formerly Department of Trade)
Transport	2002 (formerly Transport, Local Government and the Regions)
Treasury	1900
Wales Office	1964
Work and Pensions	2001 (formerly Education and Employment; Social Security)

Source: Cabinet Office website, http://www.open.gov.uk; Butler and Butler (2000), p. 73.

pluralistic, involving a large number of individual ministers operating in distinct organizational structures with a substantial degree of autonomy. While much stress has been placed on the leadership provided by the prime minister, this leadership is necessarily selective: only a few areas will attract or can be given prime ministerial attention.

The departments are therefore the hub of public policy management (see box 4.8, which gives a list of government departments as of December 2003). Individual members of the cabinet and other ministers who have the regular and exhausting task of handling the conduct of policy making and implementation live separate lives inside their departmental empires. While the prime minister has few legal powers, ministers have extensive legal powers vested in them. Moreover, central government departments operate in many respects as self-contained universes with their own cultures and traditions.

Structure of departments

Defining a department is difficult. As was seen in chapter 3, there are no clear doctrines governing the allocation of functions to departmental structures and there has been considerable fluctuation in the way functions and programmes have been grouped together as well as in the size and complexity of departments. Employment, for example, although long seen as a responsibility of government, has sometimes been linked with education but also needs to be thought of in the broader context of pensions and social security. The span of a department's responsibilities can be extensive and some giant departments cover disparate policy areas that might once have been located in separate ministries. This means that there may be internal rivalries and pressures within the confines of a single department, as became familiar between the service interests within the Ministry of Defence. Some departments are very large; some small. Some are relatively compact while others are highly fragmented. In some departments, much of the work has been hived off into agencies and is geographically dispersed.

Although there are wide varieties between departments as a result of culture and history as well as subject matter, there are also important similarities. At the head of each department will be the cabinet minister supported by a number of junior ministers. All these ministers will be drawn from the governing party with seats in either the House of Commons or the House of Lords. These ministers will direct and answer to Parliament for the work of the civil servants that provide the permanent bureaucratic staff of the executive. In each department the permanent civil servants will be hierarchically organized and headed by a permanent secretary (or permanent under-secretary), who combines the dual function of chief administrative and accounting officer with the task of providing policy advice to the minister. Although there is now a much greater range of advice available to ministers, this official channel remains an extremely important if not the most important conduit of policy advice within the department.

Each department will be organized into a number of functional divisions and sections. Two features of this organization deserve mention at this point. First, each minister will have a private office, headed by an official known as a private secretary. This official is a civil servant (usually one destined for rapid promotion), who will head a team of assistants and be the link with the rest of the department. Secondly, within each department there will be a principal finance officer (PFO) responsible for finance and public expenditure. The PFO will work closely with the relevant Treasury officials to secure agreement on public expenditure.

The structure of central government was radically altered following the 1988 Efficiency Unit Report (the Ibbs Report), which recommended significant changes both to the organization of government departments and to the role and culture of the civil service (see box 3.4, p. 97). The Ibbs Report, which had the personal backing of the then prime minister, Margaret Thatcher, argued that many clearly defined areas of administration and service delivery could be transferred to newly constituted executive agencies (or Next Steps Agencies) that would enjoy a degree of autonomy from their parent departments, which would retain responsibility for policy.

Box 4.9   Selected list of executive agencies

Benefits Agency
Central Office of Information
Child Support Agency
Civil Service College
Companies House
Crown Prosecution Service
Driver and Vehicle Licensing Agency
Employment Service
Food Standards Agency
Highways Agency
HM Customs and Excise
HM Prison Service
HMSO (Her Majesty's Stationery Office)
Inland Revenue
Meteorological Office
Office of National Statistics
Patent Office
Royal Mint
Serious Fraud Office
UK Passport Agency

Source: Butler and Butler (2000), pp. 311–14.

This decentralization of the British administrative process was implemented over the period of Conservative government from 1988 to 1997. By 1998, 138 agencies had been established, employing nearly 300,000 civil servants (see box 4.9 for a selected list of agencies). Agencies remained under the overall policy control of the minister, but responsibility for day-to-day operations was placed in the hands of a chief executive. Each agency was governed by a specific framework document and chief executives were given greater operational freedom, at least in theory, in such matters as recruitment and pay regimes. The way the experiment has worked in practice has been much more varied than this blueprint might suggest. The distinction between policy matters and operational ones has not always been observed. In some agencies, ministers have continued to intervene in issues that might be thought the province of the chief executive. The managerial freedoms available to agencies have not been extensively used. And while there has been some reduction of the workload on ministers as a result of hiving off blocks of departmental administration to agencies, there has been an increase in the need for coordination.

The ministerial hierarchy

Each department will have a number of ministers, although usually only one – its head – will be in the cabinet. (The Cabinet Office under Blair briefly had two ministers in the cabinet.) The Treasury has regularly had two ministers in the cabinet since Harold Macmillan's 1961 reforms, designed to secure greater control of public expenditure. Then it was felt that the Chancellor of the Exchequer needed extra help at cabinet level and the post of Chief Secretary was created with the special responsibility for monitoring public expenditure.

The precise number of ministers within each department varies (see table 4.3). The titles given to ministers also differ in a manner that can be confusing. Historical titles associated with the older functions of government may be kept, so that sometimes the Secretary of State responsible for trade will use the title President of the Board of Trade, as Michael Heseltine did. The normal title for senior ministers who will represent the department in the cabinet is Secretary of State. Until 1782 there was only one Secretary of State, and in constitutional theory this is still the case, although the numbers of ministers with this title have in fact increased. This constitutional fiction means that any Secretary of State, if necessary, can formally act on behalf of any other Secretary of State. Box 4.10 shows levels of ministerial appointment under the Blair administration.

Cabinet ministers constitute only a small proportion of the total government personnel. Below the cabinet minister in the hierarchy are tiers of ministers within each department, with ministers of state taking precedence over parliamentary secretaries. Some ministers below cabinet rank in the Treasury (which enjoys a special position among the departments) have specific titles. Thus the positions of Financial Secretary (whose position is older than that of the Chief Secretary), of Economic Secretary and of Paymaster General do not carry cabinet membership. For the most part, however, ministers below cabinet rank are given either the formal title of Minister of State (at the Department of which they are a minister), or Parliamentary Under-Secretary (Parliamentary Secretary if the departmental head is not a Secretary of State, as at Agriculture).

Ministers of state and other junior ministers will normally be allotted specific areas of responsibility which, although informal, are indicated in the list of government members (Theakston, 1987). Thus in the Blair 2003 administration some ministers within departments had designated responsibilities – for example Denis McShane, Minister of State (Europe) within the FCO – while others did not. Ministers of state will also be available to share in the general work of the department or to take on ad hoc duties. Successive prime ministers, for example Attlee and Heath who focused on machinery of government issues, have attempted to ease the

Table 4.3 Government ministers, March 2003

	House of Commons	House of Lords	Total
Cabinet ministers	21	2	23
Other ministers	52	14	66[a]
Law officers	2	1	3
Whips	15	7	22
Total	90	24	114

[a] 4 ministers hold unpaid posts.

Source: Cabinet Office, UK Ministers, http://www.cabinet-office.gov.uk/central/2002/ministers.htm#whips

Box 4.10 Blair administration with levels of ministerial appointment

Prime Minister	1
Chancellor of the Exchequer	1
President of the Council (Leader of the House of Commons)	1
Lord Chancellor	1
Lord Privy Seal (Leader of the House of Lords)	1
Chancellor of the Duchy of Lancaster	1
Secretaries of State	15
Parliamentary Secretaries	6
Captain of the Gentlemen at Arms (Lords Chief Whip)	1
Chief Secretary (Treasury)	1
Paymaster General	1
Financial Secretary	1
Economic Secretary	1
Attorney General	1
Solicitor General	1
Lord Advocate for Scotland	1
Ministers of State	30
Parliamentary Under-Secretaries[*]	31
Treasurer of HM Household (Whip)	1
Comptroller of HM Household (Whip)	1
Vice-Chamberlain of HM Household (Whip)	1
Lord Commissioners of HM Treasury (Whips)	5
Assistant Whips	9

[*]Two Parliamentary Under-Secretaries are also whips.

burden of work on cabinet ministers and to reduce overload by encouraging **delegation** by cabinet ministers to their subordinate ministers. The success of such delegation within each department is very dependent on the relationships between the various ministers. In an ideal world, the cabinet minister heading the department would be able to treat all that department's ministers as a coherent team that could be deployed to support him or her in discharging the workload. In practice, differences of personality, experience and responsibility will create their own impediments to a successful corporate approach. The formal constitutional doctrine of ministerial responsibility also to some extent acts as a constraint on delegation since Parliament is likely to hold the Secretary of State responsible for decisions made within the department, whatever the internal delegation.

The existence of tiers of junior ministers is also important as a way of providing a form of apprenticeship for the job of being a minister (Theakston, 1987). Running a government department is an increasingly demanding and daunting job: the learning curve even for junior ministers is steep. Yet those who become ministers may have had little training in any remotely comparable career, especially if, as

delegation Process by which a superior official or authority allows lower-level authorities or individuals to take decisions on their behalf.

happened in 1997, the incoming government has been in opposition for an extensive time. Not surprisingly, after being out of power for so long, Labour took advantage in 1997 of a number of seminars and training courses designed to equip it for government. Even when there is a long period of government by the same party, and hence the possibility of a more effective ministerial apprenticeship, the practice of moving ministers frequently (and moving them across departments) severely reduces their capacity to become experts in the subject matter of their department.

In addition to the tiers of junior ministers, each Secretary of State will have an unpaid parliamentary private secretary or PPS (not to be confused with the minister's private secretary, who is a paid civil servant). The PPS, who is an MP, has the role of keeping the minister in touch with parliamentary and party opinion. Although unpaid, the job constitutes the first step on the path to office and is eagerly sought after by ambitious MPs. Parliamentary private secretaries are bound by collective responsibility and may be sacked if they fail to toe the party line. As a result, they may find the constraints of the job unacceptable and resign if promotion is not soon forthcoming.

Ministers are also able to appoint special advisers to give policy advice independently of the department. Although such advisers had been used in an intermittent and ad hoc way for much of the twentieth century, their extensive use dates back to Harold Wilson's 1974 administration, when there were 28. Wilson allowed ministers to appoint special advisers on a regular basis and their use became institutionalized under Margaret Thatcher and John Major. However, their number has grown. Thus whereas there were 38 special advisers in post before the 1997 general election, by March 2003 there were 81 at a cost of £5.1 million (Kavanagh and Seldon, 1999; Wicks Committee, 2003; see table 4.4). Theoretically, the number of advisers is limited to two per minister (and this is reflected in the Ministerial Code); but a number of ministers in the Blair governments appointed additional advisers.

Table 4.4 Special adviser numbers and pay since 1994/95

Financial year	Special adviser numbers			Special adviser pay (£ million)	% increase in pay year on year
	Total	No. 10	Departments		
1994/95	34	6	28	1.5	–
1995/96	38	8	30	1.5	0
1996/97	38	8	30	1.8	20
1997/98	70	18	52	2.6	44.4
1998/99	74	25	49	3.5	34.6
1999/00	78	26	52	4.0	14.2
2000/01	79	25	54	4.4	10
2001/02	81	26	55	5.1	15.9

As at 13 March 2003, there were 81 special advisers, 27 in No. 10 and 54 in departments.
Source: Committee on Standards in Public Life, Ninth Report, *Defining the Boundaries Within the Executive: Ministers, Special Advisers and the Permanent Civil Service*, http://www.public-standards.gov.uk/reports/9th%20 report/report/report.pdf

As noted earlier, special advisers have occasioned controversy for a variety of reasons and there is media suspicion of them. They bring an important extra-departmental perspective to the policy process but may sometimes impede close relations between ministers and their senior civil servants. Advisers are not subject to the same strict rules as civil servants on subsequent employment in the private sector. And the ability to appoint special advisers constitutes a new form of patronage, especially since such jobs are rarely advertised. The controversy over the roles of Jo Moore (see box 5.7, p. 190) and other special advisers in the Blair governments led to renewed efforts to regulate their conduct more effectively.

The ministerial role

The job of a minister is multi-faceted and extremely demanding (Headey, 1974). A minister has to juggle several different roles and activities frequently within the space of a single (sometimes very long) day (Kaufman, 1997; see box 4.11). The minister has a responsibility for the development of policy inside the department. Although the contribution that individual ministers make to policy process varies considerably, all ministers have the task of familiarizing themselves with the major policy issues of their department and, to the extent they can, contributing to the collective policy of their party in government. There is the executive function of managing the department and processing key decisions. Ministers have to act as departmental spokespersons, representing the departmental interest both in negotiations with other departments and agencies inside government, and in the wider policy universe where the department has to engage with other public sector bodies such as local authorities and pressure groups. Equally importantly, the minister has to be the spokesperson for the department in the media. Alongside all of this goes the parliamentary aspect of the job, which involves piloting legislation through Parliament and also providing answers and information to Parliament at question time or in select committees about the policies of the department. On top of all this, the minister is a key party figure in demand for television and radio appearances, conferences and constituency activities in addition to his or her own constituency party functions and casework, which do not disappear simply because an MP has become a minister.

Policy making

In theory the direction of departmental policy is set by ministers, but there are serious limitations on the extent to which they can be expected to affect more than a restricted number of policy areas. The scale of government business is vast, and ministers are unlikely to be specialists in the area of policy covered by the department. Indeed, given the complexity of modern government and the range of issues with which it has to deal, it is difficult to see how a minister could be familiar with more than a small section of the administration's agenda. Put another way, civil servants rather than ministers will take a large number of decisions within the department, including ones with a policy content, although they will usually be careful to refer politically sensitive issues to their political superiors. Indeed, one of

> ## Box 4.11 Gerald Kaufman on being a minister
>
> 'One of the most powerful networks in Whitehall is the private office grapevine.'
>
> 'If [officials] really want to help...[they]...can find ways not only round substantive difficulties but also round procedural problems.'
>
> 'If the Whitehall machine as a whole is a Daimler, stately and effective, the Cabinet Office is a Ferrari built for speed and action.'
>
> 'The question that civil servants ask themselves when required to advise in implementing polemical proposals is not "Do I agree with it?" but "Can it be made to work?"'
>
> 'Before the meeting [of the cabinet committee] you will receive the departmental briefing.... Your departmental briefings are works of art. They will analyse the issue and the papers concerned not from the standpoint of the government as a whole but purely from the departmental point of view. They will advise you of the "Line to Take" (a heading all on its own), the sentences beginning with masterly injunctions such as "The Minister will wish to say..."...They will even include speaking notes which the minister can read out without having taken the trouble to study the cabinet papers at all.'
>
> 'Though your officials would be perfectly happy for you to remain permanently in your department and totally in their thrall, fortunately for you (and in fact for them) you will have many duties to perform in the House of Commons. Indeed your department will have a parliamentary branch especially established to facilitate your dealings with both Houses.'
>
> *Source*: Kaufman (1997).

the most important skills required of a minister is knowing how to use the official and other help available.

Ministers in most departments are generalists who bring to the job qualities of good judgement rather than specialist policy knowledge. Some departments do, however, require specialist skills. Thus the Exchequer is generally thought to require some economic or financial training and legal qualifications are necessary for the Lord Chancellor and law officers. It also has to be remembered that the process of policy making and implementation involves various bodies outside the formal structure of the department. These include local government bodies, advisory committees, pressure groups and task forces.

The role of ministers in the policy process will vary according to the stage of the government and the character and personal skills of the minister. It will also vary according to the character of the issue. Policy ideas come from a number of sources, including think tanks and policy institutes. Policy proposals may have been fully worked out in opposition, although an opposition will be wise not to commit itself too publicly to priorities or policies until it does have the full facts available. After an election, it is likely that a minister will come to office with at least some radical policy commitments from the manifesto, although these may have to be modified once in government when the full information is at the minister's disposal. In the mid-term of a Parliament or in relation to many routine aspects of policy, the cabinet minister may well be selecting options from policies put forward by civil servants or even rubber-stamping a departmental consensus.

Where policy needs to be reviewed or there are especially intractable problems, the government sets up an internal departmental committee of inquiry or, much more rarely, a royal commission. When it came to power in 1997, Labour instituted some 500 policy reviews in its first year. Some of these reviews were conducted on the basis of internal departmental reviews, but a new direction was set by the extensive use of task forces, which involved a range of outside representatives in the review process. This across-the-board policy reappraisal reflected the long years in opposition and the desire to bring new groups and actors into the policy process. The scale of the process, however, inevitably made the pace of life more onerous for new ministers than it would have been under their predecessors.

Executive management

Policy development takes up only a small fraction of the ministerial day. In terms of routine responsibilities, a cabinet minister has several important duties in relation to the management of the department as a whole and the discharge of executive functions within it. The ability of the minister to manage the department is to some extent limited by the fact that he or she does not control the budget or departmental resource and staffing levels. Moreover, the minister has no power over who his or her immediate political deputies will be or who will occupy the senior civil service posts within the department. Ministers will want to try to establish their control of the departmental organization, however, both because a weak minister is unlikely to impress colleagues and because ministers themselves need to have confidence in the way issues are handled within the department.

The difficulty ministers have in implementing their own policies and asserting control of their departments (together with a certain suspicion of the civil service) produced a series of experiments with devices to enhance ministerial effectiveness. The most publicized of these experiments was MINIS, which Michael Heseltine introduced first at the DoE and then at Defence. MINIS (which was a system designed to identify precisely the costs and purposes of all the functions carried out by the government) enabled ministers both to be informed about and to understand the detailed decision making of their departments, including the crucial expenditure decisions that were being made.

The routine content of a minister's day is likely to involve a good deal of correspondence and paperwork, which will be handled initially by civil servants. Papers which ministers have to read are prepared on a daily basis by the civil servants and placed in red boxes, which constitute a kind of eternal homework even for junior ministers.

Departmental representation

One important aspect of the cabinet minister's role (and to a lesser extent that of junior ministers) is to defend the interests of the department within the government as a whole. Many decisions and policy initiatives impinge on the interests of another department and may involve complex efforts to secure agreements when departments view issues differently. Competition for resources between departments is intense, whether measured by budget or by legislative time.

There are a number of routine mechanisms for reconciling differences between departments, but sometimes final resolution is possible only at the cabinet committee or, in the last resort, cabinet level. Departments expect their minister to defend their interests vigorously in interdepartmental meetings and, if necessary, at cabinet committee or cabinet level.

One particularly important process where ministers were once expected to defend their department's interests was the annual public expenditure review, where ministers fought each other for a slice of the spending pie. However, increasingly the process has become depoliticized by the use of special cabinet committees to adjudicate departmental bids. Now the comprehensive spending review (CSR) fixes departmental spending on a three-year basis, which has to a large extent removed the uncertainty of the allocation and allowed a more rational approach to spending decisions. Nevertheless, it has, especially when combined with performance targets, given the Treasury enhanced power over the detail of policy.

Parliamentary activity

Ministers live a strangely schizophrenic existence. Most of their day is spent in the department running their particular section of the executive. But they also have to pay extensive attention to Parliament, both because of the formal requirements of parliamentary control and because of the less formal impact of parliamentary opinion on the status of the government as a whole and on their own political careers and reputations. Parliamentary skills are vital for the ambitious minister, which means knowing how to judge the mood of the House of Commons and how to defend policies effectively.

Ministers probably now spend less time informally in the House of Commons than they once did. Certainly, prime ministers devote less of their time to the House of Commons. Individual ministers have to be present in the House for debates that affect their departments and when they need to show solidarity with their colleagues. They must, of course, be present for their own departmental question time and to answer select committee inquiries. What has perhaps diminished, not least because of the better office facilities for MPs at Westminster and the shift away from late parliamentary sittings, is informal mixing in the House of Commons.

Party and media

A minister, unless he or she is in the House of Lords, remains a constituency MP and as such is expected to carry out the normal routine of casework for constituents and party meetings. (Peers are not excused party functions, however.) Indeed, becoming a minister increases the demand by raising the profile. Moreover, the increasing emphasis on the presentation of policy has placed additional demands on ministers to deal with the media. In order to cope with this growing demand, Downing Street has developed an electronic database – the Knowledge Network – to explain and promote the government's core message. It ensures that all ministers produce a common message and enables the government to dominate the handling of information by the press.

Conclusions

The period since 1979 has seen a marked strengthening of the office of the prime minister and subtle changes in the way the cabinet system operates. One element of this strengthening has been an expansion of the institutional support available to the prime minister and a refashioning of the role of the cabinet. In addition, central government has seen a series of experiments designed to make decision making more efficient and to overcome some of the endemic weaknesses of the British governmental system. Traditionally, these weaknesses have been poor coordination at the centre and a tendency towards departmentalism. Furthermore, the British system has been seen as one that was better at policy making than policy delivery. Finally, the system has frequently been criticized for its approach to (or rather neglect of) long-term strategic thinking, not least because of the extent to which ministers with their multiple roles are often overloaded. Labour's emphasis on joined-up government and on transforming the centre into a more integrated and proactive mechanism is designed to overcome these problems. Although, as has been seen, there have been significant changes in the structure and mission of the Prime Minister's Office and the Cabinet Office, these modifications carry dangers of personalized politics. Departmentalism has been addressed through the creation of more cross-cutting agencies to deal with the so-called 'wicked' issues of Whitehall, those that straddle departmental boundaries. Again, it is perhaps too early to tell how far this difference of approach has really altered departmental mindsets. Finally, more strategic thinking (and more concern with management and policy delivery) has been injected into Whitehall through the greater use of external advisers and specially constructed units such as the Performance and Innovation Unit (now the Strategy Unit). Ultimately, however, politicians are only a small part of the decision-making process: the quality of government depends to a very great extent on the quality of the permanent staff it recruits and, equally importantly, on how effectively ministers use their personnel resources. That is the subject of the next chapter.

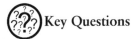 Key Questions

1   What factors make a prime minister more powerful than his cabinet colleagues?
2   Is the system of cabinet government an efficient one for running a modern state?
3   Is the policy-making process in the United Kingdom too centralized or too fragmented?

Further Reading

There is still much to be gained by reading John P. Mackintosh, *The British Cabinet* (3rd edn; London: Stevens, 1977) and Peter Hennessy's *Cabinet* (Oxford: Blackwell, 1986), but both should now be supplemented with Hennessy's *The Prime Minister: The Office and its Holders since 1945* (London: Penguin, 2001), which provides an excellent overview of the prime minister's office. Also good on the general issues of cabinet government are S. James, *British Cabinet Government* (London: Routledge, 1999) and Rod Rhodes and Patrick Dunleavy (eds), *Prime Minister, Cabinet and Core Executive* (Basingstoke: Macmillan, 1995). M. Smith, *The Core Executive in Britain* (Basingstoke: Macmillan, 1999) offers an interesting analysis of the debate. The role of prime minister is now better covered than it once was. In addition to Hennessy there is Anthony King (ed.), *The British Prime Minister* (2nd edn, London: Macmillan, 1985) – still worth reading, though obviously now somewhat dated. G. Thomas, *Prime Minister and Cabinet Today* (Manchester: Manchester University Press, 1998) offers a succinct account. R. Rose, *The Prime Minister in a Shrinking World* (Cambridge: Polity, 2001) is always thought provoking, not least because it places the British executive in a wider perspective. G. Kaufman, *How to be a Minister* (London: Faber, 1997) is a witty insider's view of the job of being a minister.

There are a number of stimulating accounts of the executive under Blair. Michael Foley, *The British Presidency: Tony Blair and the Politics of Public Leadership* (Manchester: Manchester University Press, 2000) focuses on leadership. Peter Hennessy, 'The Blair style and the requirements of twenty-first-century premiership', *Political Quarterly*, 7: 4 (2001) also looks at leadership style. Amy Baker, *Prime Ministers and the Rule Book* (London: Politicos, 2000) considers the formalization of executive management, while M. Burch and I. Holliday, 'The prime minister's and cabinet offices: An executive office in all but name', *Parliamentary Affairs*, 52: 1 (1999) investigates the changing organization of the cabinet and the prime minister's office.

The growing role of political advisers is examined in D. Kavanagh and A. Seldon, *The Powers Behind the Prime Minister* (London: HarperCollins, 1999). The concept of ministerial responsibility is explored in G. Marshall (ed.), *Ministerial Responsibility* (Oxford: Oxford University Press, 1989) and in a series of articles, for example V. Bogdanor, 'Ministerial accountability', *Parliamentary Affairs*, 50: 1 (1997); R. Scott, 'Ministerial accountability', *Public Law* (1996); and D. Woodhouse, 'Ministerial responsibility: Something old, something new', *Public Law* (1997). Adam Tomkins, *The Constitution After Scott: The Constitution Unwrapped* (Oxford: Oxford University Press, 1998) looks at a number of issues to do with executive power. B. Headey's discussion of cabinet ministers, *British Cabinet Ministers* (London: Allen and Unwin, 1974), remains a classic. Richard Rose, *Ministers and Ministries* (Oxford: Clarendon Press, 1987) is an important functional analysis. K. Theakston, 'New Labour, New Whitehall?', *Public Policy and Administration*, 13 (1997) covers the role of junior ministers. P. Thain and M. Wright, *The Treasury and Whitehall* (Oxford: Oxford University Press, 1993) is an excellent analysis of the power of the Treasury, as is Nicholas Deakin and Richard Parry's *The Treasury and Social Policy* (Basingstoke: Palgrave, 2000). T. Daintith and A. Page, *The Executive in the Constitution: Structure, Autonomy and Internal Control* (Oxford: Oxford University Press, 1999) provides an original analysis of the role of the executive.

 **Websites**

See also the list of general websites at the back of the book.

- www.number-10.gov.uk – No. 10 Downing Street
- www.cabinet-office.gov.uk – Cabinet Office

- www.privy-council.org.uk – Privy Council Office
- www.cabinet-office.gov.uk/central/2001/mcode/contents.htm – Ministerial Code
- www.ncl.ac.uk/geps/about/politics/whitehall/index.html – ESRC Whitehall Programme
- www.nuff.ox.ac.uk/Politics/whitehall/ – A history of the organization of government departments, 1964–92

5 The Civil Service

bureaucracy Government by administrative officers. Since the nineteenth century, the bureaucracy in the UK has been based on hierarchy and appointment on merit, an approach praised by Max Weber, who argued that this was the basis for rational administration. Weber, however, highlighted the potential for conflict between elected politicians and permanent civil servants. More recent critics of bureaucracy have criticized its wastefulness and tendency to pursue its own interests.

The role of the **bureaucracy** is an important element in understanding the character and efficiency of any political system. The discussion of the expanding role of the state in chapter 3 and of the character of the British executive in chapter 4 underlined the scope and scale of government in the United Kingdom. Both chapters also emphasized the complexity of policy and the extent of the public sector's responsibilities. Constitutional theory assumes that ministers direct the policy process and control the administration. In practice, however, ministers see only a limited amount of their own department's work – perhaps as little as 1 per cent – and a minister is by background usually a generalist rather than a policy specialist. Ministers are also likely to be moved from department to department, their average tenure in any position being about two and a half years. The quality of policy making and policy implementation therefore clearly depends to a very large extent on the continuing policy advice and administrative support given at the central level by officials who can provide greater expertise and who are employed on a more permanent basis than ministers. This chapter examines the specific qualities of that advice and support by analysing the organization and culture of the British civil service. It also considers the relationships between officials and ministers, focusing especially on the senior civil service (SCS), which comprises the 3,000 or so most significant policy advisers and managers. The chapter begins by looking at the problems generated by bureaucracy in all democratic political systems, and then provides a brief history of the way the British civil service evolved and its distinctive characteristics. It then discusses the series of civil service reforms that have occurred, particularly in the period since 1979, as a result of new thinking about the proper role of bureaucracy and the changing skills required as the role of government altered. Finally, it examines some of the key issues surrounding the future structure, role and management of the civil service.

The Problem of Bureaucracy

The role of the central bureaucracy in any democratic system is likely to generate controversy. Max Weber's writings about the character of the modern state highlighted the extent to which government would increasingly become a matter of rational administration requiring knowledge and expertise. In the modern state, the bureaucrat is therefore better placed to shape policy than the career politician. The process by which bureaucratic influence expands inevitably raises questions of democratic control and of the extent to which an elected government's policies may be modified or even subverted by the bureaucracy. Although hardly a novel insight into public adminis-tration, numerous analysts of bureaucracy, including public choice theorists, suggest that bureaucrats frequently use their position, especially their command of informa-tion, to pursue their own interest whether it be **budget maximization** or some other goal such as **bureau-shaping** (Dunleavy, 1991; Niskanen, 1971, 1973).

It is clear that bureaucrats do sometimes have their own agendas and distinctive strategies for advancing them, and that these agendas may exist independently of those of the elected government. Such conflicts are not limited to public sector organi-zations and may arise in any large enterprise, whether in the private or the public sector. Nevertheless, the problem of control looms large in the management and organization of a democratic polity where it is necessary to make bureaucrats respon-sive both to the directives of the elected government and to citizens, as well as to ensure that they do not become an isolated and insulated elite pursuing their own goals.

Promoting that responsiveness may involve a number of strategies and instru-ments. Recruitment processes and training are essential factors in shaping the personnel and norms of the bureaucracy as well as determining what skills are appropriate for the policy process at any time. Promotion and evaluation processes reward certain kinds of behaviour, while the expectations of polit-icians themselves will shape the roles played by bureaucrats. External instruments, whether political or legal, will monitor the efficiency and probity of the system. The wider political culture – especially the degree of freedom of information and the activism of the media – will promote or limit knowledge of how a bureaucracy functions.

One recurrent theme in much of the recent debate about the role of the bureaucracy has been that the balance between policy advice and management in the work of the civil service needs to be increasingly focused on management. Sometimes reformers have argued that politicians should set *policy* while bureaucrats should confine themselves to the tasks of *implementation, management* and *admin-istration*. This distinction between policy and administration, although initially appealing, is itself highly contentious. For some, it is a naive division given the value-laden nature of the whole policy process and the extent to which, in practice, politicians and civil servants play overlapping roles. For others it is a useful dividing line that helps to clarify the relationship between politicians and bureaucrats as well as allowing some areas of administration to be hived off organizationally, with accompanying managerial benefits.

budget maximization An alleged tendency on the part of bureaucrats to maximize the budget allotted to their bureau/department to ensure status and influence, leading to the overproduction of public goods and services. This critique of bureaucracy is associated with public choice theorists, particularly William Niskanen, Gordon Tullock and James Buchanan.

bureau-shaping An adapta-tion of the budget maximiza-tion critique of bureaucracy, the bureau-shaping approach argues that bureaucrats maxi-mize prestige and influence not through increasing the size of their budget but by reshaping their bureaux. This allows senior bureaucrats to separate off routine implementation functions and to increase con-trol over policy-making and managerial functions. The bureau-shaping model, de-veloped by Dunleavy (1991), could be used to explain the creation of executive agencies within the UK.

Problems of Definition

The focus of this chapter is primarily on those public sector officials employed as civil servants. Civil servants constitute approximately 10 per cent of the public sector workforce. The vast majority of employees in the public sector (for example, those who work in local government and the National Health Service) are not civil servants. There is thus no single state bureaucracy. What distinguishes the civil service from other public sector employment is that its members are servants of the Crown. Thus the Tomlin Commission in 1931 defined civil servants as servants of the Crown (other than holders of political or judicial offices) who are employed in a civil capacity and whose remuneration is paid wholly and directly out of monies voted by Parliament. Put more directly, the term 'civil servant' refers to an official who works for a central government department or agency or for the devolved government in Scotland or Wales (Northern Ireland has its own civil service).

The separation of the civil service from other parts of the public sector is no longer as marked as it once was. Transfer between different parts of the public sector is encouraged as a way of broadening expertise. Equally significantly, the growing concern with public service policy delivery means that central governments will seek increasingly to influence the way policies are administered by all agencies, not just by the civil service proper.

The Characteristics of the British Civil Service

The British civil service is in outline a product of the nineteenth century and owes its formation to the Northcote–Trevelyan Report of 1854. Before then, officials were appointed largely on the basis of patronage and without any consistent effort to control the quality of appointees. From 1854, however, a series of reforms was implemented (especially the creation of a Civil Service Commission in 1855 and the introduction of competitive examinations in 1870) which provided the framework for a profession recruited on merit (see box 5.1).

The British civil service has, of course, evolved considerably since the nineteenth century. For much of the twentieth century it retained features that were seen as integral to its identity and that distinguished it from the bureaucracies of many other states. Because some of these features are now being questioned, it is worth examining them in a little more detail.

Most important was the notion that the civil service was an independent and prestigious profession with its own intrinsic values and collective identity. Nineteenth-century reformers and later innovators such as Warren Fisher wanted to make the civil service at the highest levels an attractive career for university graduates, and they were keen to unify the civil service around common ideals and a sense of professionalism. For much of its history the internal norms of the civil service were informal and implicit, but they were given explicit recognition in the Civil Service Management Code (1993) and the Civil Service Code (1996), which were introduced to provide a statement of the roles and responsibilities of civil servants following a series of clashes between civil servants and the government. The codes underlined the fact that the civil service had no independent constitutional status. They emphasized the long-cherished traditions and values of

Box 5.1 Key stages of civil service evolution

1854 Northcote–Trevelyan Report calls for a civil service based on merit rather than patronage.

1855 Civil Service Commission created to oversee competitive examination for civil servants.

1968 Fulton Report calls for a more professional civil service based on a wider recruitment base and more effective management.

1968 Civil Service Department established to oversee personnel matters, including pay, which had previously been overseen by the Treasury.

1979 Thatcher sets up Efficiency Unit to review departmental performance.

1981 Thatcher abolishes Civil Service Department, seeing it as a block on efficiency reforms. Replaced by Office of Personnel and Management, with key control over pay and management transferred back to Treasury.

1982 Financial Management Initiative (FMI) launched, followed by Rayner scrutinies. Aimed to clarify responsibilities of managers and establish effective managerial and financial responsibility.

1987 Office of Personnel and Management abolished.

1988 Next Steps Report calls for creation of autonomous executive agencies, separating management off from policy. Agencies begin to be set up.

1991 Citizen's Charter initiative launched by John Major. Aims to make public services more responsive to their users. Citizen's Charter Unit created within the Cabinet Office.

1992 Office of Public Service and Science (OPSS) created, within Cabinet Office, with responsibility for most civil service functions.

1995 OPSS reorganized with science being detached, leaving a restructured Office of Public Service.

1998 *Modernizing Government* white paper sets out Labour's vision for civil service reform. It calls for 'joined-up' policy making and services that focus on users, not on providers. Increased focus on delivery targets.

2001 Prime Minister's Delivery Unit and Office of Public Services Reform set up to improve public service delivery as part of the *Modernizing Government* reform programme.

Rayner scrutinies Device used during Mrs Thatcher's premiership to bring private sector methods into government. Sir Derek Rayner was asked to establish an efficiency unit attached to the Prime Minister's Office. It conducted a series of ad hoc investigations of public sector practices and recommended a closer linkage between policy making, management and implementation.

Financial Management Initiative (FMI) The system established in 1982 partly as a result of Rayner's efforts to improve management and decision making in government. This improvement was to be achieved primarily by clarifying objectives and managerial lines of control.

the British civil service, which included integrity, honesty, impartiality and objectivity (see box 5.2).

Linked to this notion of professionalism is the key notion of **political neutrality**. Essentially, political neutrality means that civil servants have the duty to serve the elected government of the day whatever its political complexion. This capacity loyally to serve successive governments was frequently seen as one of the distinctive strengths of the British system, not least because it allowed the UK to avoid the kind of interregnum that marks transitions between administrations in the

political neutrality The duty of civil servants to serve the elected government of the day whatever its political complexion.

Box 5.2   Civil Service Code: Key points

1   The constitutional and practical role of the Civil Service is, with integrity, honesty, impartiality and objectivity, to assist the duly constituted Government of the United Kingdom, the Scottish Executive or the National Assembly for Wales constituted in accordance with the Scotland and Government of Wales Acts 1998, whatever their political complexion, in formulating their policies, carrying out decisions and in administering public services for which they are responsible.
2   Civil servants are servants of the Crown. Constitutionally, all the Administrations form part of the Crown and, subject to the provisions of this Code, civil servants owe their loyalty to the Administrations in which they serve.
3   Civil servants must recognize their accountability to ministers, and their duty to discharge public functions reasonably and according to the law.
4   Civil servants should conduct themselves with integrity, impartiality and honesty. They should give honest and impartial advice to the Minister or, as the case may be, to the Assembly Secretaries and the National Assembly as a body or to the office holder in charge of their department, without fear or favour, and make all information relevant to a decision available to them. They should not deceive or knowingly mislead Ministers, Parliament, the National Assembly or the public.
5   Civil servants should endeavour to ensure the proper, effective and efficient use of public money.
6   Civil servants should not without authority disclose official information which has been communicated in confidence within the Administration, or received in confidence from others.
7   Where a civil servant believes he or she is being required to act in a way which: is illegal, improper, or unethical; is in breach of constitutional convention or a professional code; may involve possible maladministration; or is otherwise inconsistent with the Code; he or she should report the matter in accordance with procedures laid down in the appropriate guidance or rules of conduct for their department or Administration.
8   Civil servants should continue to observe their duties of confidentiality after they have left Crown employment.

Source: The Civil Service Code, revised edition 1999, http://www.cabinet-office.gov.uk/central/1999/cscode.htm

United States. Thus long before a general election civil servants will have appraised the contents of the opposition's manifesto and its implications, drawn up an alternative **Queen's Speech** and have appropriate briefing notes for incoming ministers. Indeed, since the Douglas Home premiership (1963–4), the opposition has some access to civil servants prior to an election.

Queen's Speech Address by the queen to Parliament, in which she states the government's legislative programme for the new session. The speech takes place in November at the start of a new parliamentary session, or after a general election.

An important corollary of this political neutrality is that civil servants would be recruited on merit and could expect to retain their jobs even when the government changed hands. Moreover, civil servants could not be moved around by ministers. Thus the British civil service has traditionally been organized on the basis of its being a career for life. Entry to the civil service could be early – at the upper levels entrants were typically recruited straight from university (and in fact the reforms of the nineteenth century were designed to open it to Oxford and Cambridge graduates). It was assumed that such recruits would for the most part remain in the civil service until retirement rather than moving into the private sector or some other occupation. As will be seen later, this feature of civil service life has been progressively eroded in recent years, raising some of the ethical issues found in other systems where the transfer from public to private employment (the so-called 'revolving door') may create a conflict of interest. The recruitment process was administered by independent bodies.

Political neutrality also has a number of other important implications for the recruitment, deployment and roles of civil servants as well as for the activities that civil servants may undertake. For example, although drafting speeches for ministers is an important part of senior civil servants' work, they are not supposed to draft speeches for use in a purely party political context such as a party conference or constituency party meeting. At the same time, civil servants are not expected to be apolitical in the sense of not taking the political dimensions of policy into account. On the contrary, they are supposed to be intensely aware of the political repercussions of everything they do and of the impact of policy on government. At the highest levels, therefore, civil servants have to be slightly schizophrenic: seeing policy through the minister's eyes and taking account of its implications for the government yet retaining sufficient distance to be able to give an objective view.

Civil servants were traditionally anonymous in the sense that, although they might exercise significant amounts of influence in the policy-making process, their advice would be confidential and it was the political superior – the minister – who would take credit for success and shoulder the blame if things went wrong. The constitutional convention of ministerial responsibility and the need for trust between the minister and his or her advisers were mutually reinforcing. For this reason, select committees are not allowed to probe civil service advice to ministers, the freedom of information legislation excludes that advice, and one administration's papers may not be seen by its successor.

The British civil service was, at least from the 1930s, a unified service in that recruitment was to the civil service as a whole rather than to a department. The process of unification and the sense of a common service emerged gradually; but they were evident by the 1919–39 period, not least as a result of the Treasury's acquisition of a coordinating role for the civil service and of Warren Fisher's determined efforts to create unification. The merits of centralization (and the need for a homogeneous profession with a common ethos) are now much questioned and, as will be seen, one of the marked trends running through much of the civil service reform of recent years is that of decentralization. This decentralization has occurred as a result of both administrative change – especially the creation of agencies within departments – and devolution, where the establishment of new political bodies in the form of the Scottish Parliament and the Welsh and Northern Ireland Assemblies has placed further strain on the idea of an integrated civil service.

Promotion, like the recruitment process, was based on systemic criteria rather than on political or personal patronage. From the 1920s the Treasury took control of

line management The chain of command and accountability between managers and employees.

the classification and pay of civil servants and the promotion process was handled by senior civil servants, although from the 1920s the prime minister also had to approve appointments to the most senior departmental positions. Civil servants could not engage in party politics and were expected to resign if they wanted to stand as parliamentary candidates.

The civil service was traditionally organized hierarchically into a range of classes and grades. The hierarchy provided a clear structure of **line management** and reporting, thereby underpinning the convention of ministerial responsibility. The separate classes were organized on the basis of the category of work that was expected and the entry qualifications of the civil servants. Thus the main civil service classes were administrative, executive and clerical. Within each class there were grades. Although movement between classes was possible, it was expected that employment would generally be within a class. One feature of this system was that the administrative class was very much the dominant class and the one that stamped its values on the service as a whole. Another feature was that the technical and specialist staff were organized separately from the general classes. There was thus none of the emphasis on technological and scientific expertise found in the French civil service.

Finally the skills required of the civil service at its highest levels reflected both the character of British education and the role which the civil service was expected to play in the system. Within the administrative class there was a heavy emphasis on policy analysis and on drafting written submissions and relatively little emphasis on management. The qualifications that entrants brought to the job of being civil servants were those of the British higher education system, which was itself biased towards the arts. Formal training and specialist skills in the British civil service were acquired on the job.

Civil Service Reform

The British civil service was long seen as one which at the highest levels provided ministers with policy advice and administrative support of a very high quality. It was sometimes likened to a Rolls Royce in terms of the smoothness with which it handled policy problems and eased the transition into government of new ministers. It was also admired for its integrity and professionalism as well as its knowledge of the administrative machine. However, as was increasingly recognized, advice to ministers was only one part of the civil service role, and perhaps in the context of a highly complex welfare state, not the most important part.

Thus, although the British civil service continued to be admired for many of its distinctive qualities, in the period after 1960 it was also increasingly criticized. As a result there emerged a series of reform proposals, which aimed to alter many aspects of the way the bureaucracy worked in the United Kingdom. These criticisms came from various quarters and addressed several different aspects of the traditional civil service.

One criticism, which was especially popular on the left in the 1960s, was that the civil service (or at least its highest reaches) was elitist in composition and rigid in structure. The Labour governments of 1964–70 assumed an expanding public sector and there was concern that the higher grades of the civil service, those most responsible for policy advice, represented too narrow a stratum of society because of the dominance of Oxbridge arts graduates in the administrative class. There was disquiet about whether enough weight was given to specialist qualifications and expertise, especially in the areas of economics and science, as opposed to generalist administrative skills.

A second criticism was that the civil service was unresponsive to political direction. This argument was popular in the Labour Party in the 1960s, when it was feared that an inherently conservative civil service might prove a barrier to radical change. This argument was not, however, confined to the left and surfaced again in 1979 when the Conservative Party, and especially Margaret Thatcher, viewed the civil service as an impediment to its programme of radical reform.

A third criticism that was regularly encountered in the post-1960 period was that the British civil service did not have the right intellectual and managerial qualities for running a modern state. Clearly, the tasks which civil servants were required to perform had changed as the role of the state had changed (see chapter 3). Greater intervention by government in the economy and the growth of the welfare state placed a premium on economic expertise. At the same time, external pressure from Britain's competitors in an increasingly global economy raised questions about whether British civil servants were sufficiently entrepreneurial in their approach or sufficiently specialist in the skills they brought to the policy process.

The advent to power of Harold Wilson's 1964 Labour government put civil service reform on the political agenda. Wilson had himself been a civil servant and there was much emphasis on improving the quality of decision making in the public sector, especially by properly exploiting scientific advances. There was thus particular concern about whether the higher grades of the civil service (those most responsible for policy advice) were drawn from too narrow a section of society and whether enough weight was given in the system to specialist knowledge and training (e.g. in economics and the natural sciences) as opposed to general administrative skills. Was the civil service insufficiently geared to management functions as opposed to framing policy advice? Questions of this kind led Harold Wilson to establish the Fulton Committee, with a very general remit to examine the structure, recruitment, management and training of the civil service, though not the key issues of the relationship between civil servants and ministers and the machinery of government.

Although its recommendations were never fully implemented, the Fulton Report had the effect of producing some major changes in civil service structure and highlighted important themes (such as the need for better training, wider recruitment and more emphasis on management) that have continued to figure in debate about the future of the civil service. Box 5.3 shows the Fulton Report's main recommendations.

The Fulton Committee wanted to see a simplification of the complex grading system with its rather invidious and rigid divisions into classes and sub-groups, each with its own slightly different pay and grading structures. Instead of the tripartite division into an administrative, executive and clerical class, Fulton recommended a unified pay and grading system that could cover the whole of the non-industrial part of the civil service. This simplification, which was introduced, meant that the

Box 5.3 Fulton Report: Main recommendations

Recruitment

- Inquiry into methods of recruitment.
- Larger graduate entry.
- Preference for relevant degrees.
- Administrators to specialize in either economic administration or social administration.

Training

- Civil Service College to be established with research and management training functions.

Career structure

- Unified grading.
- Greater transfer between public and private sector.

Structure of government

- Civil Service Departments to be responsible for personnel and machinery of government questions.
- Promotion of accountable management.
- Hiving off of some government functions.
- Greater strategic control of policy through planning units headed by senior policy advisers.

Table 5.1 Composition of civil service by grade, April 2001 (full-time equivalents)

Grade	Total	Men	Women
Non-industrial	453,770	224,360	229,410
Senior Civil Service	3,840	3,030	810
Grades 6/7	21,120	15,590	5,530
Senior/Higher Executive Officer	71,550	48,100	23,450
Executive Officer	112,990	55,690	57,300
Administrative Officer/Assistant	228,780	90,310	138,470
Unknown	15,490	11,640	3,850
Industrial	28,920	24,950	3,970
Total	**482,690**	**249,310**	**233,380**

Source: Civil Service Statistics, 2001, http://www.civil-service.gov.uk/statistics/documents/pdf/css01.pdf

structure now runs from permanent secretary (which is grade 1) through to principal grade (grade 7) and there is then a unified administration group (see table 5.1).

The Fulton Committee had severely criticized the way the existing structure separated staff into vocational and technical specialists and administrative generalists. This division was thought increasingly anomalous and damaging for the policy process, especially as only generalists reached the very top posts of the service. As a result of the Fulton recommendations, the top grades of the civil service were opened to specialists as well as generalists through the so-called open structure. This change meant that whenever there was a vacancy within grades 1–7 (which has now been replaced by the senior civil service payband system), the way vacancies were handled encouraged consideration of people from beyond the ranks of generalists. (A more radical change occurred in 1994 as a result of the Efficiency Unit Review, which advocated the opening of all senior posts to open competition across the whole civil service.)

The Fulton Report was highly controversial. For some critics it was a superficial analysis of the civil service because it neglected the very significant changes that had been made to adapt to the demands of the modern state. For others it was a much-needed effort to make the British bureaucracy more efficient, effective and responsive. The civil service itself was highly sceptical of Fulton, and this fact, together with the decline of interest in the subject of civil service reform in cabinet, meant that its recommendations were only partially implemented (Crowther Hunt and Kellner, 1980).

The impact of Thatcherism

The period of Conservative government under Margaret Thatcher and John Major witnessed not merely a shift of emphasis in the debate but a quickening of the pace of civil service reform. Although it is doubtful that the government elected in 1979 started with a blueprint for restructuring the civil service, the combination of a powerful prime minister with a bias against the existing culture of the civil service, a strong preference for radical market solutions and political longevity provided a much greater opportunity for changing key aspects of the British civil service. Indeed, as will be seen, all of the key features of the traditional civil service as previously identified were either questioned directly or eroded during this period. The Thatcher–Major years thus constitute a turning point in the history of the British civil service, so much so that many critics would suggest its essential character was transformed.

Margaret Thatcher entered Downing Street as a profound critic of the role of post-war British civil service. Unlike many of her predecessors, she was no admirer of the smoothness of the civil service machine whose consensual policy advice she saw as being an important component in Britain's post-1945 policy failures. Her own experience as Secretary of State for Education had reinforced her hostility towards many of the senior civil service, including the most senior mandarins, the permanent secretaries who headed the official side of the various departments and who were the primary channel of policy advice to ministers. Indeed she had tried, albeit unsuccessfully, to get her own permanent secretary at the Department of Education and Science (DES), Sir William Pile, moved. As prime minister, with a special responsibility for the civil service, she took an active interest in promotions at the highest levels of the service, provoking charges that she was politicizing senior appointments.

Promotion at the highest levels is formally handled by a committee (the Senior Appointments Selection Committee or SASC), which was set up in 1968. This committee is chaired by the Cabinet Secretary as Head of the Home Civil Service and is composed largely of senior civil servants, although the first civil service commissioner (currently Baroness Prashar) also sits on SASC as a guarantee of the integrity of the system. (Civil service commissioners, who regulate the recruitment process, are appointed by Order in Council and are independent of the government.) When there is an impending vacancy, SASC decides whether it is to be filled by a managed move or from a promotions list or whether it is advertised either internally or externally. The committee then draws up a shortlist of names in rank order, bearing in mind both the requirements of the job and the implications of the appointment for the deployment of other senior staff. For the top two levels of the civil service (grades 1 and 2), the approval of the prime minister is required, but not the approval of the minister in whose department the appointment is to be made. It is an important feature of the British civil service as currently organized that ministers do not choose their own permanent secretaries or other senior officials, though they may choose their special political advisers. However, there are instances where ministers have succeeded in moving officials when the 'chemistry' was not right or when ministers were in an especially strong bargaining position. Thus Alistair Darling was allowed to take his former permanent secretary (Rachel Lomax) with him when he was moved to the Department of Transport following a restructuring of the Department of the Environment, Transport and the Regions (DETR) in 2002. More generally, some critics of the existing system of promotion have argued that ministers should be able to interview candidates for senior posts in their departments, thereby giving them greater input into the appointment of their civil servants.

This system of promotion in the senior ranks of the civil service has always attempted to balance a number of factors. From the civil service perspective, it is important that promotions should be seen to be fairly administered and structured to encourage the long-term efficiency of the service. From the government's perspective, however, the pressures are very different. Individual ministers want to work with senior civil servants whose personality and approach are compatible with their own. The permanent secretary will see the minister usually on a daily basis and, although the permanent secretary no longer enjoys the monopoly of influence he or she once had, this is a key relationship for the success of a department and a ministerial career. Ministers want civil servants who can reinforce their own strengths and help them make an impact within a short timeframe. If they are new to government or to a department within it (and it must be remembered that ministers change roughly every two and a half years), ministers may need, yet resent, substantial policy briefing that may include pointing out the weaknesses and problems with a minister's proposed course of action. From the prime minister's perspective, however, it is vital that civil service departments, individually and collectively, work effectively, which is why most prime ministers, although anxious to avoid real personality clashes, have been cautious in their handling of personnel issues and have been reluctant to accede to ministerial requests for any redeployment of senior civil servants.

There is little doubt that Margaret Thatcher's keen interest in civil service matters and the suspicion that her personal views were affecting promotions focused attention on the extent to which the system could be changed from the top. Whereas in the past the prime minister's approval for a SASC recommendation had generally been a formality, Thatcher used the opportunity to promote civil servants whose style and approach she could endorse, even if this meant bypassing more senior candidates in favour of younger ones. Thus the appointment in 1983 of Peter Middleton as permanent secretary to the Treasury, and, to a lesser extent, the appointment of Sir Clive Whitmore as permanent secretary at the Ministry of Defence at the age of 47, were seen as highly significant, both because these individuals seemed to epitomize a new style of civil servant and because their appointment circumvented the normal expectations about the age at which promotion to a permanent secretaryship would be achieved. Although initially it was suggested that these candidates had secured quick promotion because of political and policy compatibility, the consensus by the end of the Thatcher period was probably that their rapid advance had more to do with chemistry and personality, as well as a preference for younger candidates, than it had to do with ideology. And that was probably also true of the instances where Thatcher's intervention appears to have been used to block the promotion of those unfortunate individuals whom she had taken against, such as Donald Derx, who apparently displeased the prime minister by pointing out that she was not fully informed of the facts of an issue (Hennessy, 2001c). In many respects, personal likes and dislikes should not enter the calculations of a rational bureaucracy; but Whitehall is, as Heclo and Wildavsky underlined in their work on the Treasury, a village where ministers and civil servants work in close proximity (Heclo and Wildavsky, 1974). It is therefore essential that individual ministers and civil servants can work together effectively. In this sense, Mrs Thatcher's approach was not such a radical departure from previous practice, although she may have been seeking rather different qualities in her top appointments. Nevertheless, the perception that there had been a personalization of appointments had a number of significant consequences. It undermined civil service morale and introduced a certain randomness into the system, thereby, arguably, making the system less efficient because it encouraged civil servants who wished to be promoted to concentrate on telling politicians what they wanted to hear rather than giving a candid appraisal of policy. Apart from the risk of losing good people to the private sector, it also carried the danger that civil servants who had visibly flourished in one regime, however loyal and professional, would be less useful in the next. This was to some extent true even in the transition from Thatcher to Major as civil servants who had been promoted under Thatcher came into conflict with ministers. Thus Peter Kemp, one of the architects of the Next Steps proposals (which started with the Vehicle Inspectorate), was effectively sacked by William Waldegrave. Ironically, two permanent secretaries who had achieved rapid promotion under Mrs Thatcher (Clive Whitmore and Geoffrey Holland) resigned in circumstances that suggested their positions had been made untenable because of policy or personality clashes with their new ministers.

If Margaret Thatcher's intervention in senior civil service appointments generated controversy, so too did her use of civil servants as close personal advisers. In the case of two of them – Bernard Ingham, her press secretary, and Charles Powell, the civil servant in the private office at No. 10 responsible for advising her on defence and foreign policy – they became so identified with the prime minister personally that they lost all credibility as civil servants.

The size of the civil service

Margaret Thatcher's concern with the role of the senior civil service has to be placed against the background of her own ideological agenda. The Conservative government elected in 1979 was much less interested in strengthening the state's capacity to solve social problems (the Wilson/Callaghan concern) than in reducing the size of the public sector. Its promise to roll back the frontiers of the state put the civil service in the firing line as reductions in the number of public sector employees became an important yardstick of implementing the pledge to cut the size of government. Since the late 1970s the number of civil servants has fallen dramatically – from around 751,000 in 1978 to about 506,000 in 2001 – a decline in numbers of around one-third (see figure 5.1 and table 5.2).

Managing the civil service

One of the reforms resulting from the Fulton Committee Report had been the creation in 1968 of a separate Civil Service Department (CSD) to handle the pay

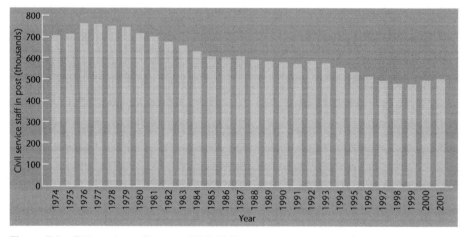

Figure 5.1 Civil service staff in post, 1974–2001.

Table 5.2 Civil service staff by function, 2001

Function	Percentage
Defence	20.4
Revenue	18.4
Social Security	17.0
Law and Order	17.1
Employment	7.8
Health	1.1
Other	18.3

Source: Civil Service Statistics, Key Figures, 2001, http://www.civil-service.gov.uk/statistics/documents/pdf/keyfigures.pdf

and management functions which had been controlled by the Treasury since the 1920s. The rationale for the change was that it would allow personnel matters to be considered independently of financial considerations. This argument became less convincing as the need to control public expenditure loomed larger in the public debate. Moreover, by the late 1970s and early 1980s the political climate was much less sympathetic to a department that appeared to be there primarily to defend the interests of the civil service, for example through inflation-proof pay rises. Margaret Thatcher abolished the CSD in 1981 and there then followed a series of adjustments of the functions formerly discharged by the department. The Treasury regained responsibility for civil service manpower. The recruitment aspects of the CSD's work that covered primarily personnel matters, but also the politically sensitive issue of efficiency, were transferred to a new ministry, the Office of Personnel and Management (OPM), which was based in the Cabinet Office. The Cabinet Secretary was (from 1983) designated Head of the Home Civil Service (HHCS), giving him responsibilities both for the efficient operation of the government and for its personnel. In 1987 OPM was abolished and further aspects of its work related to conditions of employment within the civil service were transferred to the Treasury, leaving a limited number of responsibilities for a minister for the civil service associated with the Cabinet Office. The situation was rationalized somewhat in 1992 when a new ministry, the Office of Public Service and Science (OPSS), was established. OPSS took over various functions in relation to the civil service but the Treasury retained its overall interest in management and pay aspects. In 1995 the office was again restructured, with the removal of science from its remit. The remaining civil service functions were grouped in an Office of Public Service (OPS).

The drive for efficiency and the application of market-inspired solutions

The Thatcher government was not interested simply in reducing the size of the civil service. It had its own radical neo-liberal agenda which involved two other strands: securing greater efficiency and value for money and enhancing ministerial control over departmental business. Margaret Thatcher became a vocal advocate of systematically reforming the civil service by importing private sector techniques into the public sector. Manpower controls were followed by the Financial Management Initiative (FMI) and the so-called Rayner scrutinies, which were designed to improve the efficiency of government. The series of radical initiatives in the management and organization of the civil service (and indeed of other elements of the public sector) led commentators to speak of a new public management (NPM). This NPM had several different elements, including the transfer of some functions to private sector delivery and a general decentralization or disaggregation of hitherto centralized civil service structures.

Next Steps Agencies

The most radical reform of the Thatcher years and one designed to have a major impact on British administration was the creation of executive agencies, the so-called Next Steps Agencies. This reform, which followed on from the FMI and was intended to separate policy-making functions from those of routine operation and service delivery, swiftly took root, so that now almost every department has a number of agencies within its organizational structure and a high proportion of civil servants work in agencies. As we have already seen in previous chapters, these agencies were intended to have a significant impact on the organization of government and on the way that public services were delivered. The agencies were also designed to bring about a major transformation in the culture of the civil service. Indeed, the Treasury and Civil Service Select Committee called the introduction of agencies the most important administrative reform of the twentieth century because of its implications for the organization and ethos of the British bureaucracy. In order to understand the impact of the Next Steps Agency initiative, it must be placed in the context of its authors' belief that the management of civil service work, as opposed to its policy-making aspects, should be emphasized.

The Next Steps initiative took as its starting point the idea that only a small amount of government work is related to policy – perhaps as little as 10 per cent according to a subsequent white paper on civil service reform, *Continuity and Change* (1994). Apart from this small policy component, the bulk of the civil service's work could be broadly described as managerial or oriented to the delivery of services. These tasks could be separated from the central policy functions of government and would be more effectively organized through specialist agencies.

The Next Steps initiative assumed a progressive transfer of government functions to agencies; and indeed the movement of civil service staff to agencies was dramatic. By 1999 the then Head of the Home Civil Service, Sir Richard Wilson, reported that three-quarters of all civil service staff were operating in agencies (Wilson, 1999; see table 5.3).

Agencies were welcomed as a means to a number of organizational and managerial improvements. They would, it was hoped, encourage a much greater focus on management rather than on policy among senior staff. Agencies clarified the goals of an organization by separating out identifiable blocks of responsibility. The burden on ministers would be lightened. Finally, efficiency savings and strategic freedom for managers were envisaged through the loosening of central control over such issues as pay and grading. Traditionally, pay and grading had been controlled by the Treasury and the Cabinet Office in a way which took little account of individual performance or local conditions but which also imposed a national scale regardless of local employment circumstances.

Table 5.3 Civil service staff in Next Steps Agencies, 2001

Next Steps Agency	Percentage
Social Security	22
Inland Revenue	17
Defence	16
Home Office	13
Education and Employment	9
Customs and Excise	6
Other	17

Source: Civil Service Statistics, Key Figures, 2001, http://www.civil-service.gov.uk/statistics/documents/pdf/keyfigures.pdf

Initially there was some suspicion that agencies were simply a staging post for privatization. Although some agencies have been privatized, the Conservative government in fact engaged in a systematic process of reviewing all options available for the delivery of a government function that was a candidate for agency status.

Margaret Thatcher's successor John Major continued the lines of reform, expanding the drive for efficiencies through such devices as **market testing**, privatization and contracting out work normally done by government as well as by the increased use of management techniques imported from outside the civil service. Much emphasis was also put on performance indicators and other tools for measuring individual job performance. Certainly, some success was claimed for these initiatives. By 1995 the Cabinet Office reckoned that £410 million had been saved as a result of these reforms (Cabinet Office, Next Steps Briefing Note, 1995).

The use of private sector methods in government received a slightly different emphasis when Major took over from Thatcher as prime minister. Successive governments have wanted to improve public accountability and service delivery as well as efficiency. Whereas Thatcher had primarily been keen to reduce the costs and size of government, Major was interested in the *quality* of public services and their responsiveness to consumers. He wanted greater monitoring of the standard of government services and a new emphasis on the consumer dimension of public services. Responsiveness to consumers was to be emphasized by the Citizen's Charter initiative launched in 1991 and which aimed to create a new climate in the delivery of public services (see box 5.4).

> **market testing** The process of measuring public services against equivalent private sector provision to evaluate their cost-effectiveness and indicate ways to improve efficiency. This may include contracting out the service to the private sector if savings cannot be made in-house.

Constitutional problems

Many of the debates about the role and structure of the civil service in the Thatcher–Major years were comparatively low key and attracted limited political attention. However, the same period also saw a succession of highly publicized

Box 5.4 The Citizen's Charter

The Citizen's Charter was introduced by the Major government in 1991. Described as Major's 'big idea', it was a ten-year programme designed to increase the responsiveness of public services to their users. It was intended in part to differentiate Major's approach to public service reform from that of Margaret Thatcher, by demonstrating his faith that public provision could be improved. The Charter initiative emphasized the publication of information and standards, with complaints and compensation procedures for users who received a substandard service. A special Cabinet Office Unit was set up to oversee the range of initiatives covered by the Charter. These included mini-charters for various service users, including a Patient's Charter, a Parent's Charter and a Passenger's Charter for rail users. There were an estimated 40 Charters in place by the 1997 election. The incoming Labour government in 1997 moved away from the language of Charters, renaming the Charter Unit the Service First Unit, although it retained a similar emphasis on responsiveness to public service 'customers'.

disputes which either exposed the workings of the civil service to unflattering public appraisal or pinpointed ethical issues that had gone unresolved.

One issue thrown into sharp relief by the 1985 Ponting case is the extent to which civil servants have a wider public duty than their duty to obey the government of the day. The Ponting controversy (which arose out of the Falklands War) involved the prosecution of a civil servant under the 1911 Official Secrets Act for revealing unauthorized information to Tam Dalyell, an opposition MP. The resulting trial and surprise acquittal provoked an adamant restatement of the duties and responsibilities of civil servants – the so-called Armstrong memorandum – but it left a number of questions unanswered. Did a civil servant have an obligation to obey every order given by a minister even if it was manifestly unethical, involving, for example, deceiving Parliament? What should be the procedure for a civil servant who could not in conscience follow a ministerial order? Even if a civil servant's duty was to the government of the day, what should be done if the civil servant thought the minister's actions were detrimental to the interests of the government as a whole?

In the Westland affair (see box 5.5) the actions of civil servants came under the microscope in a rather different way. The improper behaviour of civil servants (at the DTI) in this episode, which was in part authorized by their minister and by No. 10 Downing Street, led to their being named in the House of Commons and by a select committee. What caused concern was not merely the proactive role that civil servants appeared to have taken in a highly political and personal conflict between departmental ministers, but also the tension between the increasing visibility of civil servants and the fragility of the doctrine of ministerial accountability. In this instance the civil servants who were named were not protected by their minister, but neither were they able to defend themselves before the select committee.

One point that was frequently made in the wake of Westland was the difficulty of having the same person (then Sir Robert Armstrong) as Cabinet Secretary and Head

---

Box 5.5   The Westland affair

Cabinet discussions on the future of the Westland helicopter company at the end of 1985 came to illustrate the workings of two conventions of the British constitution: collective and individual ministerial responsibility. The Westland issue provoked conflict between the Defence Secretary Michael Heseltine and the Secretary of State for Trade and Industry Leon Brittan about the best options for Westland's future. Tensions deepened when the DTI leaked a letter from the Solicitor General criticizing Heseltine, which appeared to be a deliberate attempt to discredit the Defence Secretary. At a cabinet meeting in January 1986, Heseltine stated that he could not be bound by collective responsibility on the Westland issue because he felt that he was not being properly consulted. He announced his resignation from cabinet. An investigation into the leaked letter from the DTI revealed that it had been authorized by Leon Brittan and the prime minister's own press secretary. Coming under media and backbench pressure for his role in attempting to discredit Heseltine, Brittan announced his resignation two weeks after Heseltine. In resigning in response to criticism of conduct within his own department, Brittan was upholding individual ministerial responsibility.

of the Home Civil Service. Inevitably, it was suggested, he would be torn between his loyalty to the prime minister and his responsibility to provide a court of appeal when civil servants found themselves in ethically difficult situations. From this point the civil service unions and especially the First Division Association (FDA) argued strongly for new guidelines to protect their members.

It was not always the case, however, that civil servants were pressured into acting improperly by ministers. As the **Scott Report** revealed, it was possible for civil servants to become so identified with the policies of a minister or government that they either did not recognize or did not want to erect a barrier to morally questionable policy.

New Labour and the civil service

When it came to power in 1997, the Blair government accepted the broad thrust of the NPM approach. However, a modernizing agenda of its own emerged with the publication in 1999 of the white paper *Modernizing Government* (see box 5.6). Labour's policy priorities also had extensive implications for the civil service. Constitutional reform, for example, further increased the need for coordination at the centre. Devolution in particular had a major impact because of the extent to which it further fragmented the policy process and the civil service itself. The Blair government was also concerned to overcome the fragmentation in policy making and to find joined-up solutions to the more intractable policy problems (see also chapters 3 and 4). Part of the recipe for making the machine more responsive was to strengthen the centre of government, meaning No. 10 and the Cabinet Office. This entailed a further reshaping of the Cabinet Office role and the institutional arrangements for managing the civil service. OPS was merged with the Cabinet Office and new units were set up to promote service delivery and implementation.

New Labour's agenda and approach to government placed further strain on the traditional conception of the role of the civil service. When Tony Blair's government first took office in 1997, there were conflicts with the then Cabinet Secretary, Sir Robin Butler, over the number of special advisers Labour wanted to import and their role, particularly the dominant role Blair wanted to give to Jonathan Powell and Alastair Campbell. What was controversial about the Blair government's use of special advisers was their number and their overarching power. In 1997 the incoming government's concern to control the presentation of policy – indeed, to see presentation as an integral part of the policy process – strained traditional mechanisms for handling information inside Whitehall. Contrary to normal practice, a number of civil servants in the GICS were removed and in some cases no alternative job was found for them. These two issues – the proper role of political advisers and the question of information management – continued to generate political problems for the government, most notably in the drawn-out controversy surrounding Stephen Byers and his political adviser Jo Moore (see box 5.7). This scandal focused further attention on the expanding role of special advisers and the implications for relationships within departments.

Most importantly, Labour's emphasis on improving the quality of policy making and policy delivery generated a range of initiatives

Scott Report Report into the breaking of the embargo on the export of arms to Iraq, published in 1996. The report was highly critical of the government, accusing ministers and civil servants of misleading Parliament.

Box 5.6 *Modernizing Government* white paper, 1999, executive summary

Modernizing government is central to the Government's programme of renewal and reform.

- In line with the Government's overall programme of modernization, modernizing government is **modernization for a purpose – to make life better for people and businesses.**
- Modernizing government is a **long-term programme of improvement.**

This involves a **new package of reforms:**

- a commitment to ensure that public services are available **24 hours a day, 7 days a week** where there is a demand, for example **by the end of 2000** everyone being able to phone **NHS Direct at any time** for healthcare advice.
- **joined-up government in action** – including a clear commitment for people to be able to notify different parts of government of details such as a change of address **simply and electronically in one transaction.**
- a **new drive to remove unnecessary regulation**; and a requirement on departments preparing policies which impose new regulatory burdens to submit high-quality **Regulatory Impact Assessments**, and to consult the Cabinet Office in advance.
- a **new target** of all dealings with Government being **deliverable electronically by 2008.**
- new 'Learning Labs' to encourage new ways of front-line working **by suspending rules that stifle innovation.**
- taking a more creative approach to financial and other **incentives** for public service staff, including a commitment to explore the scope for **financial reward** for staff who identify financial savings or service improvements.
- within Whitehall, **a new focus on delivery**, asking every Permanent Secretary to ensure that their Department has the capacity to drive through achievement of the key Government targets and to take a personal responsibility for ensuring that this happens. Bringing **more people in from outside** and bringing able, younger people up the ladder more quickly.

To ensure that government is both inclusive and integrated, we have **three aims in modernizing government:**

- ensuring that policy making is more **joined up and strategic**
- making sure that **public service users**, not providers, are the focus, by matching services more closely to people's lives
- delivering public services that are **high quality and efficient**

(Continues)

Box 5.6   *Continued*

We are centring our programme on **five key commitments**:

1 **Policy making**: we will be **forward looking** in developing policies to deliver outcomes that matter, not simply reacting to short-term pressures. We will:
   - identify and spread best practice through the new Centre for Management and Policy Studies
   - bring in joint training of ministers and civil servants
   - introduce peer review of departments

2 **Responsive public services**: we will deliver public services to **meet the needs of citizens**, not the convenience of service providers
   - a big push on obstacles to joined-up working, through local partnerships, one-stop shops, and other means
   - a big effort to involve and meet the needs of all different groups in society

3 **Quality public services**: we will deliver efficient, high-quality public services and **will not tolerate mediocrity**. We will:
   - review all central and local government department services and activities over the next 5 years to identify the best supplier in each case
   - set new targets for all public bodies, focusing on real improvements in the quality and effectiveness of public services
   - monitor performance closely so that we strike the right balance between intervening where services are failing and giving successful organizations the freedom to manage

4 **Information-age government**: we will use **new technology** to meet the needs of citizens and business, and not trail behind technological developments
   - an IT strategy for Government will put in place cross-government coordination machinery and frameworks on such issues as use of digital signatures and smart cards, web sites and call centres; and
   - benchmark progress against targets for electronic services

5 **Public service**: we will **value public service**, not denigrate it. We will:
   - modernize the civil service, revise performance management arrangements, tackle under-representation of women, ethnic minorities and people with disabilities and build the capability for innovation
   - establish a public sector employment forum to bring together and develop key players across the public sector
   - This long-term programme of **modernization for a purpose** will move us towards our central objective in modernizing government:

Better government to make life better for people.

Source: *Modernizing Government* white paper, executive summary, http://www.cabinet-office.gov.uk/moderngov/download/execut.pdf

Box 5.7   Jo Moore and the resignation of Stephen Byers

Jo Moore was special adviser to the Secretary of State for Transport, Local Government and the Regions, Stephen Byers. On 11 September 2001, minutes after hijacked planes flew into the World Trade Centre and the Pentagon, Moore sent an email suggesting that it was 'a very good day to get out anything we want to bury' – such as increased allowances for local councillors. The email was leaked to the press and drew widespread condemnation. Byers stood by his special adviser, insisting that it was not 'a sacking offence'.

Moore continued in her position but controversy exploded again in February 2002 when a further email was leaked to the press implying that Moore had sought to use Princess Margaret's funeral as a cover for releasing bad news about the rail industry. Moore denied the story and it was suggested that Martin Sixsmith, the department's head of communications, and other civil servants in the department were deliberately trying to smear Moore.

Both Moore's and Sixsmith's resignations were announced by the permanent secretary of the Department of Transport, Local Government and the Regions on 15 February 2002. Sixsmith subsequently denied he had resigned and claimed he had been forced out to protect Byers's political reputation. As the circumstances of Sixsmith's departure continued to generate controversy, and Byers faced criticism for his handling of the transport brief, media pressure on Byers intensified. He resigned on 28 May, admitting, 'I have become a liability for the government'.

designed to modernize the civil service, to diversify its composition, to enhance its managerial ethos and to equip it with new skills, especially in the field of information technology (IT), which would enable services to be delivered electronically.

The Composition of the Civil Service

Efforts to modernize the British civil service have inevitably focused on its composition and the processes of recruitment and training. In the late nineteenth century the primary goals of reformers were the elimination of patronage and the improvement of the quality of entrants by the application of objective criteria to the process of recruitment. This concern led to the refinement of both the methods of recruitment and the structures of training, pay and promotion within the context of a highly regulated and hierarchical profession. The contemporary civil service, by contrast, has placed much greater emphasis on management within the civil service and has looked beyond comparisons with other bureaucracies to the private and the voluntary sectors for comparisons. Thus a report on civil service reform to the meeting of permanent heads of departments insisted that the way the civil service recruited, identified potential and developed careers had to be carried out against criteria that included the new values of the civil service. The civil service, it said, supported new ways of working and valued and made use of diversity in its employees. This shift of emphasis has inevitably changed the mechanisms of recruitment to the civil service as well as the approach to employment within it.

Recruitment to the civil service was traditionally governed by an independent body, the Civil Service Commission. The Commission, which was established in 1855, was a crucial part of the effort to eliminate patronage from government employment, so it was essential for it to be distanced from the government of the day. Although many senior civil service positions were recruited externally until well into the twentieth century, the role of the Civil Service Commission, which certified individuals deemed fit for government employment, was vital to the creation of a career bureaucracy. When the Civil Service Department was created as part of the Fulton reforms in 1968, the Commission was brought within its remit although its independence was preserved by the device of continuing to appoint individual members to the Commission by the Crown under the royal prerogative rather than by ministerial patronage. In 1978, responsibility for recruitment to junior grades below the level of executive officer was transferred to departments.

Over the 1980s thinking about recruitment changed radically and much emphasis came to be placed on flexibility. In 1982 the general delegation of clerical recruitment was reorganized by Order in Council and in 1991 responsibility for recruitment to all grades below grade 7 (the old principal grade) was transferred to departments and to the newly established executive agencies. Two separate organizations were established to manage recruitment in place of the Civil Service Commission. One, the Office of the Civil Service Commission, operates much like its predecessor, though its remit is restricted to a limited section of the civil service – broadly, the top echelons. The other organization, now privatized, the Recruitment and Assessment Services Agency, is designed to provide flexible job recruitment in a world where there is now a great variety of pay and conditions and much greater use of specially drafted contracts for individual employees.

Although the Civil Service Commission is no longer responsible for the bulk of civil service recruitment, it retains an important role in relation to senior appointments and by its ability to set and monitor standards for appointments throughout the service. Additionally, in 1995 it was given the responsibility for hearing appeals under the Civil Service Code. As of 2002, only four such appeals had been lodged, which in the view of the first civil service commissioner Baroness Prashar (speaking in the House of Lords, 1 May 2002) suggests that the process is too daunting and that civil servants may be reluctant to come forward. To this responsibility was added the role of hearing appeals from civil servants about the application of the Special Advisers Code.

Diversity

One perennial concern of critics of the civil service in the post-1945 period had been its composition and especially the extent to which at the higher levels it was dominated by graduates of Oxford and Cambridge. The composition of the civil service also incurred extensive criticism because of its failure to offer equal opportunities for women and ethnic minorities, especially at the highest levels.

The question of the civil service's ability to provide equality of opportunity for its female staff has become increasingly significant since the 1970s. It is worth remembering that the civil service for much of its history practised formal discrimination against women, who were expected to resign from the administrative class on marriage. The Cassells Report of 1983 pointed out that although almost half the civil service were women, women formed a much higher percentage of the junior grades than the senior ones. It was also noted how few of the very top posts were held by women. A decade later in 1994, an analysis conducted by the FDA compared the percentage of women in the top three grades in the civil service of the United States, Canada, Australia and Great Britain and found that Britain's percentage of 8.6 was the lowest compared to the United States (10.1 per cent), Australia (12.9 per cent) and Canada (16.1 per cent). Similarly, a 1991 Civil Service Commission report found that although the numbers of men and women entering the qualifying test for the civil service were roughly equal (1,250 : 1,065), the ratio of men to women in the final numbers passed by the selection board at the end of the process was very much more favourable to men. On the other hand, a 1992 report identified the civil service as having a good record of providing equal opportunities for women.

Since 1992 (when the civil service launched a campaign to secure greater equality for women), there have been considerable changes. Subsequently, the Blair government's modernizing agenda has produced other new initiatives designed to put greater emphasis on diversity in its own right as well as encouraging the proper use of talent. In order to maximize female opportunity within the civil service, this means a new emphasis on flexible attitudes to work.

How far has the new emphasis produced success? Statistically, there is evidence of a slight increase in the female percentage of the workforce from 47 per cent of full-time employees in 1997 to 51 per cent in 2001. And there is evidence that women have made a significant increase within the senior grades of the civil service. The civil service's target is for 25 per cent of the top 600 posts to be held by women by 2004/5. In 2001 the figure was 23 per cent, up from 14 per cent in 1999. However, there are still only a handful of women at the very highest levels of the service – at permanent secretary level or equivalents. Concern for ethnic diversity has acquired an increasingly high profile in the civil service in recent years. In 2002 Suma Chakraburti became the first ethnic minority permanent secretary (at the Department for International Development).

In addition to the issues of promoting equality for female and ethnic minority recruits, the civil service has also emphasized its commitment to promoting equality of opportunity for the disabled. According to the 2001 figures, 3.1 per cent of civil service staff are disabled compared with 11 per cent of those in employment generally. Disabled staff are more numerous in junior grades (around 3.6 per cent are in administrative and executive grades) than at senior levels. Some 2.4 per cent of staff at grade 6/7 and 1.8 per cent of senior civil service staff have a disability (see table 5.4).

Open competition

The emphasis on a career civil service meant that for much of the twentieth century it was comparatively rare to recruit personnel to the top jobs from outside. Desire to increase the diversity of the civil service and to expand the range of skills has led to a much greater use of open competition. The Blair government's *Modernizing*

Table 5.4 Composition of the civil service by gender, ethnicity and disability, October 2001

Composition	Home civil service	Senior civil service
Total	504,450	3,941
Men	245,660	3,052
Women	258,790 (51.3% of total)	889 (22.6% of total)
Ethnic minority	24,870 (4.9% of total)	29 (0.7% of total)
Disability	15,630 (3.1% of total)	69 (1.8% of total)

Sources: Home civil service staff in post, summary by gender – October 2001, http://www.civil-service.gov.uk/ statistics/documents/pdf/gender_oct01.pdf; Home civil service staff in post, summary by ethnic origin – October 2001, http://www.civil-service.gov.uk/statistics/documents/pdf/ethnic_oct01.pdf

Table 5.5 Senior civil service, levels of pay, 2001

Pay band	Range minimum (£)	Range maximum (recruitment and performance ceiling) (£)
I	51,250	107,625
IA	59,450	117,875
2	70,725	148,625
3	87,125	184,500
Perm Sec	115,000	245,000

Source: Civil Service Management Code, http://www.cabinet-office.gov.uk/civilservice/managementcode/ csmc.pdf

Government agenda envisages an increase in open competition. In 2001, there were 151 posts within SASC's remit and about 42 per cent were put to open competition. Table 5.5 shows levels of pay in the senior civil service as of 2001.

Temporary appointments and politicization

Historically, the elaborate machinery of the Civil Service Commission was designed to ensure that appointment was on the basis of merit rather than patronage and to contribute to the development of a profession with its own career structure. Nevertheless, the extent to which civil service regulars could claim a monopoly of senior advisers has varied. It was still quite common before 1914 for permanent secretaries to have had some experience outside the service; but with the consolidation of the civil service into a career bureaucracy between the two world wars, the number of external recruits declined. The last 40 years have, however, seen an erosion of the presumption that senior posts should be appointed from within the civil service. The Civil Service Code allows a few exceptions to the principle of appointment on the basis of open competition. Such appointments are of different kinds – short-term appointments; secondments; reappointment of former civil servants; and transfers into the service of people with special skills.

Training

One of the Fulton Committee's achievements was the establishment of a Civil Service College that could provide a variety of training courses and perhaps some research capacity for the civil service, and indeed for the public sector as a whole. Opened in 1970, the College was in part inspired by France's École Nationale d'Administration (ENA), although it never achieved the same status. In 1998, following a review of the Cabinet Office, a new unit, the Centre for Management and Policy Studies, was set up incorporating the Civil Service College. The revamping of civil service training has been part of a wider effort to enhance the role of management throughout the public sector generally and to place greater emphasis on service delivery. Indeed, Sir Andrew Turnbull, appointed as Cabinet Secretary in 2002, made delivery and reform his priorities and reorganized the role of the Cabinet Secretary to allow him to concentrate on those tasks.

Change or continuity?

The ethics of a country's civil service are of crucial concern. How far has the civil service culture changed? One explicit part of Margaret Thatcher's agenda was to change the culture of the existing civil service, a determination that gave rise to anxiety among those who thought this cultural shift might be at the expense of core values. During the 1980s and 1990s, as we have seen, a number of celebrated cases drew attention to the dilemmas that individual civil servants might encounter. More generally, there arose new questions of propriety as civil servants left government for the private sector. Business Appointment Rules govern what jobs former civil servants may take, and when, in order to try to prevent private sector hiring of recently employed civil servants who have inside knowledge of government thinking. However, it is not clear how effective this system of regulation is. There is a similar, albeit voluntary, code for ministers.

Conclusions

Surveying almost a quarter of a century of explicit reform of the organization and management of the British civil service prompts the question of how far its fundamental character has been transformed. In terms of the quality, professionalism and integrity of its members and its ability to serve governments of different parties loyally and effectively, the higher civil service is still recognizably the one that existed before 1979. On the other hand, many of the features of the older civil service have been seriously eroded. There is much less hierarchy than before. Neutrality in the sense of professionalism endures, although, as the Scott Report showed, civil servants may become dangerously identified with the policies of their ministers. The traditional anonymity of civil servants has been undermined by a succession of reforms and by a growing and informed interest in the civil service in the media and in academic circles. The career for life once offered by the civil service is not only no longer available but also, perhaps, not wanted by today's recruits. The unity of the civil service has been broken down by successive developments, notably agencies and devolution.

Does it matter if features of the civil service once regarded as sacrosanct disappear? Certainly, some senior civil servants such as the former Head of the Civil Service, Sir Richard Wilson, do think the identity and character of the service are vulnerable and that something precious could be lost in the urge to modernize (Wilson, 2002). Such arguments are hard to press against ministers who want a flexible bureaucracy that can produce results quickly. From the public perspective, the merits of a professional civil service are also hard to sell. What is clear is that the current emphases of civil service reform are unlikely to be abandoned and that the style and ethos of the British civil service are likely to bear an increasingly closer resemblance to those of private sector managers and administrators than to the profession portrayed by Sir Edward Bridges or caricatured by Lord Balogh as the 'apotheosis of the dilettante' (Bridges, 1950; Balogh, 1959).

There is now much pressure for a Civil Service Act that could clarify the roles of civil servants, enshrine the Civil Service Code of Conduct and place the civil service generally on a statutory basis rather than on the royal prerogative. There is also increasing pressure for greater clarification of the roles of special advisers within government (Committee on Standards in Public Life, 2003). Yet such formalization of the civil service can only go so far. Ultimately, its strength and durability lie in its ability to adapt to the changing needs of government and of government ministers and to perform a large number of overlapping roles within the political system.

 Key Questions

1 Is it still possible or desirable to have an independent and politically neutral civil service?
2 Why have ministers found the reform of the civil service so difficult?
3 What has been the impact of agencies on the organization and culture of the civil service?

 Further Reading

The historical evolution of the civil service is well covered in P. Hennessy, *Whitehall* (revised edn; London: Fontana, 2001) and G. Fry, *Statesmen in Disguise* (London: Macmillan, 1969). Good overviews of the contemporary civil service are offered in Peter Barberis (ed.), *The Civil Service in an Era of Change* (Aldershot: Dartmouth, 1997) and in K. Dowding, *The Civil Service* (London: Routledge, 1995). C. Campbell and G. Wilson, *The End of Whitehall* (Oxford: Blackwell, 1995) presents an interesting perspective on reform, as does V. Bogdanor, 'Civil service reform: A critique', *Political Quarterly*, 72: 3 (2001). The Next Steps reforms are examined in G. Drewry, 'Revolution in Whitehall: The next steps and beyond', in J. Jowell and D. Oliver (eds), *The Changing Constitution* (3rd edn; Oxford: Oxford University Press, 1994). R. Mountfield, 'The new senior civil service: Managing the paradox', *Public Administration*, 75 (1997) looks at the issue with the insight of an insider. D. Richards and M. Smith, 'The public service ethos and the role of the British civil service', *West European Politics*, 23: 3 (2000) and

F. F. Ridley, 'What are the duties and responsibilities of civil servants?', *Public Administration*, 65 (1987) both consider changing values in the civil service, as does R. A. Chapman (ed.), *Ethics in Public Service* (Edinburgh: Edinburgh University Press, 1993). Christopher Pollitt, *Managerialism and the Public Services* (Oxford: Blackwell, 1993) investigates the general issue of managerialism. Two articles by R. A. W. Rhodes focus on the relationship between the civil service and governance: 'The governance narrative: Key findings and lessons from the ESRC's Whitehall programme', *Public Administration*, 78: 2 (2000) and 'New Labour's civil service', *Political Quarterly*, 71: 2 (2000). K. Theakston, 'New Labour, New Whitehall?', *Public Policy and Administration*, 13 (1997) addresses the general issue of Labour's approach to the civil service.

 Websites

See also the list of general websites at the back of the book.

- www.civil-service.gov.uk – the civil service
- www.cabinet-office.gov.uk/cservice/index.asp – Cabinet Office civil service links
- www.cabinet-office.gov.uk/guidance – Guidance for civil servants
- www.cabinet-office.gov.uk/central/1999/cscode.htm – Civil Service Code
- www.fda.org.uk – First Division Association

6 Parliament

The last three chapters focused on aspects of the governing process – on what the government does and how the multiple responsibilities of central government are organized and given political direction. Government, however, takes place within a framework of democracy and, more specifically, parliamentary democracy. In this chapter we shall therefore examine the multiple functions of Parliament and evaluate how effectively its various roles and duties are performed.

Parliament is the source of constitutional legitimacy in the British political system. It is, as one report on the reform of Parliament put it, the essential and definitive link between government and citizens (Commission on Strengthening Parliament, 2000). Voters decide through the mechanism of a general election who will represent them in Parliament and which party will form the next government. A government continues in office by virtue of its capacity to command a majority in the House of Commons. The government is responsible to Parliament for its handling of policy and administration. Between general elections, Parliament provides a forum for the expression of opinion and the promotion of interests. In this way, the government of the United Kingdom is made both representative and responsible.

In addition to these basic democratic roles, Parliament performs a number of other essential functions in the British political system. It is the institution which must approve legislation and authorize public spending and the raising of revenue through taxation. Parliament is the source from which ministers in the government are drawn, so that members of the British government, whatever their other skills, will be socialized into the distinctive culture of Parliament. Parliament is also the institution that holds the government publicly accountable for its policies. This scrutiny of the government is both collective and individual, and the scrutiny process is exercised through a range of parliamentary procedures including parliamentary questions, debates and committee investigations. Although the official opposition (the second largest party in Parliament) will regularly criticize the general policies of the government, government backbenchers (members of the governing party who are not members of the government) and members of minor parties also have an important role to play in the process of securing accountability by detailed examinations of the administration. Parliament is thus engaged, at least in theory, in a continuous process of education of the electorate, both about key public policy issues and about the character and competence of the country's governing elites.

Despite the continued possession of these crucial political functions, and the undoubted importance of Parliament in the evolution of Britain's system of

Table 6.1 Majorities at general elections since 1945

Election	Majority party	Size of majority
1945	Labour	146
1950	Labour	5
1951	Conservative	17
1955	Conservative	58
1959	Conservative	100
1964	Labour	4
1966	Labour	96
1970	Conservative	30
1974 (Feb)	Labour	No majority
1974 (Oct)	Labour	3
1979	Conservative	43
1983	Conservative	144
1987	Conservative	101
1992	Conservative	21
1997	Labour	179
2001	Labour	166

Source: *Dod's Parliamentary Companion 1994*, p. 760; Butler and Kavanagh (2002), p. 260.

constitutional government, the contemporary position of Parliament is normally analysed in terms of weakness rather than strength. While the principle of parliamentary sovereignty is frequently invoked, the reality of British constitutional life today is that, once elected, a government can in normal circumstances control Parliament through its disciplined party majority. The support or confidence of the House of Commons is thus something which can usually be assumed, although the relatively recent experience of the Major government of 1992–7 underlines the extent to which party disunity may make a government's command of Parliament fragile. Major won re-election in 1992 with a majority of 21, but deaths, by-election defeats, defections and the withdrawal of the whip eroded that majority to a point where the government's survival and its ability to get legislation through were in doubt. While elections typically produce a government with a working majority, they do not always do so, as was shown in February 1974 (see table 6.1, which gives a list of government majorities since 1945). For the most part, however, a government with a working majority will result and will consequently expect to be able to survive until the next election. Indeed, its prime minister will expect to be able to choose the date of that election rather than be dismissed by a vote of the House of Commons.

To some extent, of course, this relationship is inherent in the Westminster model of democratic government. The legislature is not expected to govern, nor is it expected to take an independent view of legislation. Rather, it is expected to operate as a democratic counterweight to the executive by responding to policy initiatives coming from government; and through its proceedings, whether overtly or subtly, Parliament is expected to examine and scrutinize government thinking. This framework is thus one in which the role of the legislature is far more reactive and limited than in a separation of powers system such as the United States. Even so, for many critics the power of the executive in relation to the legislature in the UK is excessive. Moreover, recent developments both inside the United Kingdom and beyond it have also had the effect of marginalizing further Parliament's role in the political system. For example, the growth and complexity of the modern state (described in earlier chapters) makes Parliament's ability to scrutinize the executive increasingly difficult. Technological developments have deflected political and public attention away from Parliament and made the media powerful agenda setters in the political system. (There are frequent complaints from MPs that ministers pay more attention to the Radio 4 *Today* programme than to Parliament.) Constitutional reform has also created new centres of authority in Cardiff and Edinburgh and new political actors, despite the determination of politicians to believe that new constitutional structures and processes have no implications for parliamentary sovereignty. Above all, the expanding reach of the European Union presents a growing challenge to Parliament's ability to keep up with, let alone influence, the legislation that affects the lives of British citizens.

These arguments will be examined in more detail later in the chapter. Here it is sufficient to note that there is considerable concern that Parliament's role has become progressively weaker, although there is inevitably substantial disagreement about how this weakness should be remedied.

The Historical Legacy

Parliament's legislative role originated in the need of medieval monarchs to associate the great feudal lords and other representatives of the propertied classes with the process of law making. The monarch also required that the representatives of taxpaying groups should assent to the levying of taxes. The need for taxation occurred whenever some emergency, most often a war, made it impossible for the monarch to meet his expenses out of revenues from his own lands. From this function, known as supply, came Parliament's demands for the redress of grievances in exchange for the voting of taxation. Eventually it became accepted that ministers of the Crown must be able to command the support of the House of Commons, which had become all powerful in matters of finance.

Even today – despite the recent efforts both to reform the House of Lords and to modernize the proceedings of the House of Commons – the composition, structures and procedures of the two Houses of Parliament reflect their medieval origins and historical evolution. The great ceremonial occasions of Parliament also underline its long traditions. Thus in the state opening of Parliament there is a moment when the Commons closes its doors against Black Rod, the monarch's messenger, symbolizing the historical struggle between Crown and Parliament.

In the House of Lords the principle of hereditary membership survived in a very diluted form, despite a substantial decline in the power of the aristocracy and the removal of the right of all but a few hereditary peers to sit in the Upper House after 1999. Similarly, the presence in the House of Lords of bishops of the Church of England reflects the earlier religious unity of the country and the church's power within it. The presence of judges (known as law lords) and the Lord Chancellor in the legislature long reflected the historical overlap between the judicial and legislative work of Parliament. Just as there is doubt about whether the privileged position of the Church of England can be justified in the context of modern Britain, there was by the late 1990s intense debate about how far the presence of the law lords in the legislature was compatible with the independence of the judiciary. In 2003 the government radically reformed the office of the Lord Chancellor and announced plans to establish a separate Supreme Court whose members would not sit in the legislature (see chapter 13).

Like the House of Lords, the House of Commons reflects its medieval origins and long history. Representation in the Middle Ages was felt to be of communities rather than of individuals. The communities were the counties and the boroughs, which were also for a long time the principal units of local government and the administration of justice. Not all representation was territorial, however. Universities were represented in the House of Commons from the seventeenth century until 1950, a process that gave graduates a second vote until these seats were abolished.

The Composition of Parliament Today

The British Parliament remains a bicameral legislature consisting of the elected House of Commons and the non-elected House of Lords composed of life peers, bishops and (for the moment) law lords together with a small number of representatives of the hereditary peers. (For a discussion of the issues relating to House of Lords reform, see chapter 2.) The two chambers each play an important, though somewhat different, part in the legislative process. The House of Commons and the House of Lords have met separately since 1377 and never now meet together as a whole in working sessions. They do combine for ceremonial occasions – visiting heads of state can address 'joint' sessions, for example. For such formal occasions as the state opening of Parliament, MPs are summoned to the Lords. There are in addition some joint committees of the two Houses set up under **standing orders**, for example on human rights and statutory instruments. Joint committees may also be appointed to consider draft bills. In addition, ad hoc joint committees can be appointed. Thus the task of taking House of Lords reform further was given to a joint committee of the Lords and the Commons in 2002 (Evans, 2002).

The House of Commons

The House of Commons is the democratically elected part of the legislature and is much the more important of the two chambers. Each of the 659 members of the House of Commons is elected in a single-member constituency by the simple plurality or first past the post (FPTP) system (see chapter 7). The link with a single constituency is a very important one for MPs, and by tradition the first or maiden speech of an MP in the House will make reference to the special concerns of his or her constituency. Although a party label is not a legal requirement, independents normally stand virtually no hope of election. There have been two recent exceptions to this rule. In the 1997–2001 Parliament Martin Bell, a journalist running on an anti-sleaze ticket, became the first independent elected to Parliament since 1945. Bell was elected in

standing orders Rules for the conduct of business of a legislative or other body.

Tatton, the constituency previously held by Neil Hamilton, who had been accused of taking gifts from the owner of Harrods Mohammed Al-Fayed. Bell's victory could in part be explained by his celebrity status and the intense media coverage of the sleaze issue in the 1990s. Significantly, no Labour or Liberal Democrat candidate stood against Bell. In 2001 another independent MP, Richard Taylor – a doctor campaigning against local hospital closures – was elected in the Wyre Forest. He was also helped by the fact that the Liberal Democrats did not put up a candidate in that seat.

Party organization is crucial to the operation of the House of Commons and the two major parties – Labour and Conservative – expect to take the vast majority of parliamentary seats and, as government and official opposition, to dominate parliamentary proceedings. The culture of the House of Commons is adversarial – a feature that is reflected and reinforced by its shape, which ranges government and opposition against each other in the chamber (see figure 6.1). By comparison, most continental legislatures are semi-circular in shape. That said, a number of minor parties are represented in the House of Commons and may affect the calculations of parliamentary arithmetic in a vote and the organization of the House. The largest minor party currently is the Liberal Democrat Party, with 53 MPs (see table 6.2).

The extent to which the House of Commons is a microcosm of the wider society is limited. Efforts have been made by all parties to increase the number of female MPs. The use by Labour of all-women shortlists (AWS) in 1997 doubled the number of women MPs from 60 to 120, a figure that was only slightly reduced (to 118) in 2001.

Table 6.2 Minority parties in the House of Commons since 1945

Election	Total	Liberals[a]	Scottish National Party	Plaid Cymru	Irish Unionist Parties	Irish National Parties	Other
1945	34	12	–	–	1	3	18
1950	12	9	–	–	–	2	1
1951	9	6	–	–	–	3	–
1955	9	6	–	–	–	2	1
1959	7	6	–	–	–	–	1
1964	9	9	–	–	–	–	–
1966	14	12	–	–	–	1	1
1970	13	6	1	–	1	3	2
1974 (Feb)	38	14	7	2	11	1	3
1974 (Oct)	39	13	11	3	10	2	–
1979	27	11	2	2	10	2	–
1983	44	23	2	2	15	2	–
1987	45	22	3	3	14	3	–
1992	44	20	3	4	13	4	–
1997	74	46	6	4	12	5	1
2001	81	53	5	4	11	7	1

[a] Liberal Party: 1979; Liberal–SDP Alliance: 1983–7; Liberal Democrat Party: 1992–2001.

Source: Butler and Butler (2000); Dod's Online, http://www.politicallinks.co.uk/politics2/commons/Stateofthe Parties(Commons).asp

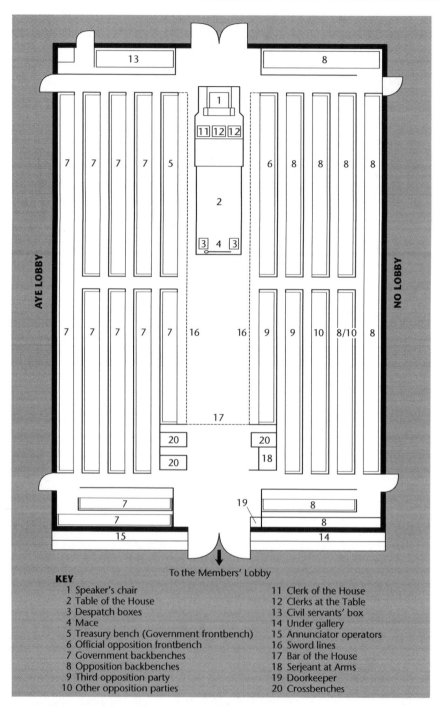

Figure 6.1(a) The Chamber of the House of Commons (floor level). *Source: Evans Handbook of House of Commons Procedure.*

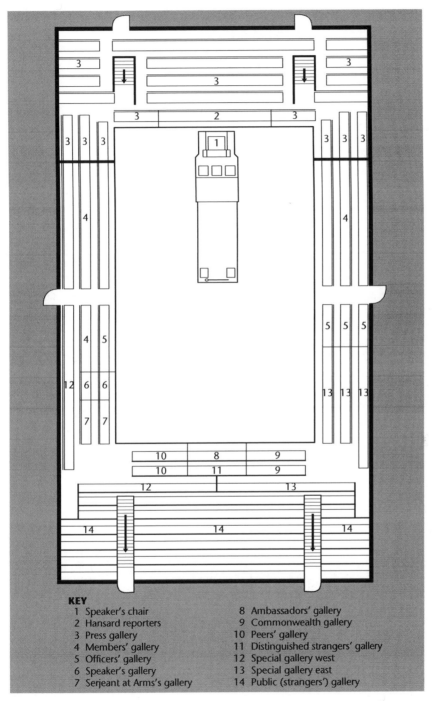

1 Speaker's chair
2 Hansard reporters
3 Press gallery
4 Members' gallery
5 Officers' gallery
6 Speaker's gallery
7 Serjeant at Arms's gallery
8 Ambassadors' gallery
9 Commonwealth gallery
10 Peers' gallery
11 Distinguished strangers' gallery
12 Special gallery west
13 Special gallery east
14 Public (strangers') gallery

Figure 6.1(b) The Chamber of the House of Commons (gallery level). *Source: Evans Handbook of House of Commons Procedure.*

Important though this dramatic progress was for the symbolic or descriptive representation of women, the method used to achieve it was controversial in Labour circles. The AWS device that had delivered much of the increase in the numbers of women MPs was declared illegal in 1995, but in the 2001 Queen's Speech legislation was announced to legalize affirmative action. Many of the women elected to the House of Commons found its male ethos highly uncongenial. One newly elected female MP (Tess Kingham) decided not to stand again as a result of disillusion with the culture of the House of Commons.

The increased salience of ethnicity in the United Kingdom has produced an expansion in the number of ethnic minority MPs (to 12 in 2001), all of them Labour MPs. Although this rise still left Britain's ethnic minorities under-represented, it reflected a growing interest among the ethnic minority communities in standing for Parliament and a greater willingness to select such candidates in winnable seats. Tables 6.3 and 6.4 show the gender and ethnic composition of the House since 1945.

Although the dimensions of gender and ethnicity create some variety within the House of Commons, there is a sense in which the parliamentary cohorts of the two major parties are becoming more homogeneous. As an analysis of the MPs and candidates at the 2001 election underlines, Labour has become the party of the public sector professional class, while the Conservatives are the party of the private sector professionals (Criddle, 2002; see table 6.5). A number of factors affect recruitment to Parliament, not least the pay and conditions of the job. MPs were first paid a salary in 1912. Until then a private income was necessary to support a

Table 6.3 Women in the House of Commons since 1945

Election	Total elected	% of all MPs	Lab	Con	Lib[a]	Other	Women candidates	% of total candidates
1945	24	3.8	21	1	1	1	87	5.2
1950	21	3.4	14	6	1	–	126	6.7
1951	17	2.7	11	6	–	–	74	5.4
1955	24	3.8	14	10	–	–	89	6.3
1959	25	4.0	13	12	–	–	81	5.2
1964	29	4.6	18	11	–	–	90	5.1
1966	26	4.1	19	7	–	–	80	4.7
1970	26	4.1	10	15	–	1	99	5.5
1974 (Feb)	23	3.6	13	9	–	1	143	6.7
1974 (Oct)	27	4.3	18	7	–	2	161	7.1
1979	19	3.0	11	8	–	–	210	8.2
1983	23	3.5	10	13	–	–	280	10.9
1987	41	6.3	21	17	2	1	329	14.2
1992	60	9.2	37	20	2	1	568	19.3
1997	120	18.2	102	13	3	2	672	18.0
2001	118	17.9	95	14	5	4	631	19.2

[a] Liberals: 1979; Liberal–SDP Alliance: 1983–7; Liberal Democrats: 1992–2001.

Source: Adapted from House of Commons Factsheet Member/Elections Series No. 4, *Women in the House of Commons*, http://www.parliament.uk/commons/lib/fs05.pdf, and Butler and Butler (2000).

Table 6.4 Ethnic minorities in the House of Commons since 1945

Election	Total elected	% of all MPs	Lab	Con	Lib[a]	Other
1945	–	–	–	–	–	–
1950	–	–	–	–	–	–
1951	–	–	–	–	–	–
1955	–	–	–	–	–	–
1959	–	–	–	–	–	–
1964	–	–	–	–	–	–
1966	–	–	–	–	–	–
1970	–	–	–	–	–	–
1974 (Feb)	–	–	–	–	–	–
1974 (Oct)	–	–	–	–	–	–
1979	–	–	–	–	–	–
1983	–	–	–	–	–	–
1987	4	0.6	4	0	0	0
1992	6	0.9	5	1	0	0
1997	9	1.4	9	0	0	0
2001	12	1.8	12	0	0	0

[a] Liberals: 1979; Liberal–SDP Alliance: 1983–7; Liberal Democrats: 1992–2001.
Source: Adapted from Butler and Butler (2000) and Rich (1998), p. 100.

parliamentary career, and even after 1912 salaries were so low that it was difficult for those without an independent income to survive financially. In order to aid the recruitment of working-class MPs early in the twentieth century, the trade unions took to sponsoring candidates, effectively paying them from their funds. Trade union sponsorship was abolished in 1995 (see chapter 8).

Even with salaries, it used to be common for MPs to combine membership of the House of Commons with other professional activity outside Parliament. However, this is now rare. The House of Commons has evolved into a much more professional body where membership is seen as a full-time occupation and where greater policy specialization is required. The demands of constituency work and the parties' expectations of their MPs have also increased markedly in recent years. At the same time, the growing intensity of many professions also makes the combination of politics with another career difficult. As a result, there are a number of MPs whose only career experience has been in active politics and politically related occupations (such as work in think tanks and policy units), a trend that has been encouraged by the willingness of constituency parties to select relatively young candidates (see table 6.6). Alongside the greater emphasis on professionalism has gone a demand for better pay and facilities within Westminster, and although the House of Commons still compares poorly in this respect with many other legislatures, the working environment for MPs has been significantly improved in recent years, not least in terms of the provision of secretarial support and offices in new blocks located around Westminster.

There has been debate about whether the rise of the so-called career politician is healthy for the overall political system. Opponents of the trend point to a narrowing of the experience of MPs and a consequent lack of expertise. (In this the House of

Table 6.5 Occupation of MPs elected in 2001

Occupation	Total	Lab	Con	Lib Dem
Professions				
Barrister	33	13	18	2
Solicitor	35	18	13	4
Doctor/dentist/optician	8	2	3	3
Architect/surveyor	6	1	4	1
Civil/chartered engineer	7	5	1	1
Accountant	6	2	3	1
Civil service/local govt	35	30	2	3
Armed services	12	1	11	–
Teachers: University	21	18	1	2
Polytech/coll.	32	31	–	1
School	64	49	6	9
Other consultancies	5	3	2	–
Scientific/research	6	6	–	–
TOTAL	270 (41%)	179 (43%)	64 (39%)	27 (52%)
Business				
Company director	29	5	18	6
Company executive	48	10	31	7
Commerce/insurance	8	2	6	–
Management/clerical	15	12	2	1
General business	7	4	3	–
TOTAL	107 (16%)	33 (8%)	60 (36%)	14 (27%)
Miscellaneous				
Misc. white collar	76	73	2	1
Politician/pol. organizer	66	44	18	4
Publisher/journalist	50	32	14	4
Farmer	6	–	5	1
Housewife	2	–	2	–
Student	–	–	–	–
TOTAL	200 (30%)	149 (36%)	41 (25%)	10 (19%)
Manual workers				
Miner	12	11	1	–
Skilled worker	38	37	–	1
Semi-skilled worker	3	3	–	–
TOTAL	53 (8%)	51 (12%)	1 (1%)	1 (2%)
GRAND TOTAL	630 (96%)	412 (63%)	166 (25%)	52 (8%)

Source: Butler and Kavanagh (2002), p. 204.

Commons stands in marked contrast with the House of Lords.) Secondly, it could be argued that the career politician is likely to be less independent of the party leadership. Thirdly, given that career politicians see themselves as professionals rather than amateurs, they are likely to try to improve the facilities and remuneration of the job. Against these arguments, it may be countered that parliamentary duties require an MP's full professional attention and that for too long facilities and pay at Westminster lagged behind those of many other legislatures.

Table 6.6 Age of candidates and MPs, 2001

Age	Total		Labour		Conservative		Liberal Democrat	
	elected	defeated	elected	defeated	elected	defeated	elected	defeated
20–29	5	172	4	29	1	79	–	64
30–39	78	418	39	84	25	195	14	139
40–49	230	361	152	65	64	118	14	178
50–59	245	264	165	46	57	69	23	149
60–69	63	68	44	4	18	13	1	51
70–79	9	6	8	–	1	–	–	6

Source: Adapted from Butler and Kavanagh (2002), p. 199.

Table 6.7 Salaries and allowances of MPs and peers

Salary/allowances	House of Commons	House of Lords
Member's parliamentary salary/Lords' expenses	£51,822	Day £60
		Overnight £120 (when House sitting)
Office costs allowance	£13,190	£50 per day the House sits
Staffing allowance	£45,000–£52,000	–
Incidental expenses allowance (IEP)	£13,500	–
IT equipment	£3,000	–
Pension provision for members' staff (max.)	10% of employee's gross salary	–
Supplementary London allowance	£1,507	–
Additional costs allowance (max.)	£18,009	–
Winding-up allowance (max.)	one-third of staffing provision + the IEP	–
Motor mileage allowance (per mile)	24.8p–53.7p	24.8p–53.7p
Bicycle allowance (per mile)	6.9p	6.9p

Source: House of Commons Library Research Paper, 01/87, *Parliamentary Pay and Allowances*, November 2001, http://www.parliament.uk/commons/lib/research/rp2001/rp01-087.pdf

The level of salaries and allowances for MPs became increasingly contentious in the 1990s because of public concern about the extent to which MPs were boosting their earnings by lobbying and other activities that opened them to allegations of corruption. In order to eliminate such practices, efforts were made to ensure that the regular salary and other allowances made to MPs kept pace with those of comparable professions. The current salary (2003) is £51,822. In addition, a range of allowances is payable (see table 6.7).

MPs divide their working week between their constituency and the House of Commons, a split which may require a good deal of travel if the constituency is far from London. Typically, an MP will be in London for the early part of the week and return to the constituency for the weekend.

The House of Lords

The second chamber of the British Parliament – the House of Lords – is composed of a mix of hereditary peers, life peers, 26 bishops of the Church of England and the law lords, who sit by virtue of their office. Since 1999, the balance has changed as a result of legislation passed to abolish all but 92 of the hereditary element of the House of Lords. The mix would change again if ever a formula for the stage of reform could be agreed. The layout of the House of Lords is shown in figure 6.2, while table 6.8 gives the composition of the House of Lords before and after reform.

Even before the removal of the automatic right of hereditary peers to sit in the House of Lords, membership of the second chamber had been modified considerably. Until 1958, a prime minister who wished to create new peers could do so only by giving a hereditary peerage – except in the case of law lords and bishops. The passage of the 1958 Life Peerages Act created much greater flexibility and was more in tune with the increasingly egalitarian sentiments of British society. It also made it easier for the Labour Party (which was generally hostile to the hereditary principle) to create new peers. From 1964 to 1983, no new hereditary peerages were created and, although Margaret Thatcher defiantly resumed the creation of hereditary peerages in 1983, only a few – 5 – have been created since then.

Other changes altered the role of the House of Lords in the wider political system. In 1963 a successful campaign by Tony Benn (then the second Viscount Stansgate) brought about a change in the law which enabled someone inheriting a peerage to disclaim it for his lifetime. The ability to disclaim a peerage was essential for anyone who had serious political ambitions since peers could not stand for election to the House of Commons. The legislation was used by Sir Alec Douglas Home to renounce his peerage and become prime minister in 1963; but it was also used by Quintin Hogg and Tony Benn to develop their political careers. With the removal of the hereditary element from the House of Lords, the way is open for more peers to stand for Parliament in their own right.

The creation of life peerages was intended to broaden the composition of the House of Lords, which had been overwhelmingly Conservative since the secession of Liberal Unionists from the Liberal Party in 1886. To some extent life peerages did indeed achieve this objective. However, because life peerages are given on the advice of the prime minister, they afford him or her a massive source of patronage. Thus while some peerages will be created in consultation with leaders of other parties, and although they are now subject to the review of a scrutiny committee (designed to prevent abuses, including the use of honours to reward party donors), successive prime ministers have been able to boost their own support in the Lords. Tony Blair in the period since entering office in 1997 created 280 life peers, of whom 112 were Labour supporters.

Even after the removal of most of the hereditary element, the total number of peers bears only a limited relationship to the effective working chamber, although the relationship is much closer than it was prior to 1999 (see table 6.9). Of those entitled to attend the House at any time, a small number – 13 in 2003 – will have applied for leave of absence permitting them to be away and, equally importantly, aiding the calculations of the whips in assessing the turnout for votes. Since 1958,

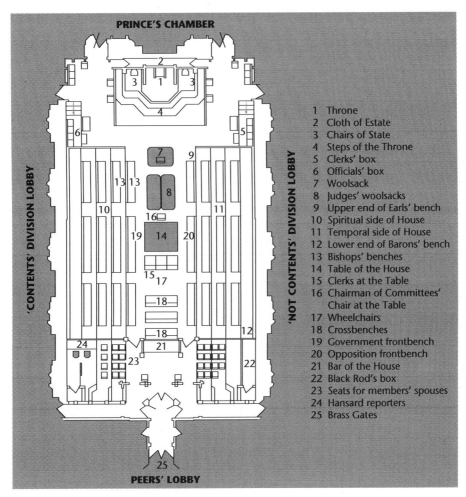

PRINCE'S CHAMBER

'CONTENTS' DIVISION LOBBY

'NOT CONTENTS' DIVISION LOBBY

1 Throne
2 Cloth of Estate
3 Chairs of State
4 Steps of the Throne
5 Clerks' box
6 Officials' box
7 Woolsack
8 Judges' woolsacks
9 Upper end of Earls' bench
10 Spiritual side of House
11 Temporal side of House
12 Lower end of Barons' bench
13 Bishops' benches
14 Table of the House
15 Clerks at the Table
16 Chairman of Committees'
     Chair at the Table
17 Wheelchairs
18 Crossbenches
19 Government frontbench
20 Opposition frontbench
21 Bar of the House
22 Black Rod's box
23 Seats for members' spouses
24 Hansard reporters
25 Brass Gates

PEERS' LOBBY

Figure 6.2 Diagram of the House of Lords.

peers have been encouraged to attend the Lords by the payment of expenses for travel, subsistence and secretarial help (see table 6.7).

Proceedings in the House of Lords differ from those in the Commons in a number of respects. The House of Lords makes less use of committees than does the Commons and there are fewer procedural restrictions than in the Lower House. Although the weight of government representation will be in the House of Commons, some members of the government must be in the House of Lords to answer questions and supervise the passage of legislation through that chamber. The current practice is that in addition to the Lord Chancellor (who acts as the House of Lords' presiding officer), one or two members of the cabinet should sit in the House of Lords. One of these ministers will act as leader of the House of Lords and it is a convention that every government department should have a spokesperson in the Lords (see table 6.10).

Table 6.8 Composition of the House of Lords before and after reform

Composition	January 1999	October 2001
Hereditary peers	636	0
Life peers	503	582
Life (hereditary given life peerage)	–	13
Elected hereditary	–	88
Archbishop/Bishop	26	26
Hereditary royal office holder	–	2
Total	1,165	711

Source: House of Commons Library Research Paper, 01/77, *House of Lords: Developments Since 1997*, http://www.parliament.uk/commons/lib/research/rp2001/rp01-077.pdf, and House of Commons Library Research Paper, 99/5, *House of Lords Bill: First Stage Issues*, http://www.parliament.uk/commons/lib/research/rp99/rp99-005.pdf

Table 6.9 Average daily attendance since the House of Lords Act 1999

Session	Average daily attendance	Percentage of eligible peers
1999–2000	352	51.9
2000–2001	340	50.1
2001–2002	370	54.6

The organization of political parties in the House of Lords is somewhat less rigid than in the House of Commons (see table 6.11). Whipping does exist, but there is much less obligation on peers to follow their leaders' advice or even to turn up for a vote. In addition there is an important element in the House of Lords – the so-called crossbenchers (see figure 6.2) – who, although organized, are not 'whipped' and act independently of the parties.

Overall, the House of Lords plays an important legislative and scrutiny role, not least in tidying up legislation which may have been passed in a rush by the Commons and which consequently may contain technical defects. It also has a crucial scrutiny function in relation to European legislation. Its debates benefit from a range of expertise and experience quite unlike those of the Commons.

The parliamentary timetable

Each Parliament (which may be of variable length but on average lasts four years) is divided into yearly sessions. In the early twentieth century Parliament sat for only about half the year, but now the burden of public business means that Parliament has many more sitting days annually. In a typical year, the session will open with the Queen's Speech in November and will sit (with recesses for public holidays) until the autumn (see box 6.1).

Table 6.10   Members of the government in the House of Lords, December 2003

Title	Department	Holder
Secretary of State for Constitutional Affairs and Lord Chancellor for the transition (cabinet member)	Department for Constitutional Affairs	Rt Hon The Lord Falconer of Thoroton QC
Lord President of the Council and Leader of the Lords (cabinet member)		Rt Hon Baroness Valerie Amos
Captain of the Honourable Corps of the Gentlemen-at-Arms (attends cabinet)	Lords Chief Whip	Lord Grocott
Minister of State (Housing and Planning)	Office of the Deputy Prime Minister	Rt Hon The Lord Rooker of Perry Barr
Minister of State	Culture, Media and Sport	Rt Hon Baroness Blackstone
Parliamentary Under-Secretary of State	Ministry of Defence	Lord Bach
Parliamentary Under-Secretary of State	Education and Skills	Baroness Ashton of Upholland
Parliamentary Under-Secretary of State	Environment, Food and Rural Affairs	Lord Whitty
Minister of State (Trade)	Foreign and Commonwealth Office	Rt Hon the Baroness Symons of Vernham Dean
Parliamentary Under-Secretary of State	Health	VACANT FOLLOWING RESIGNATION OF LORD HUNT
Parliamentary Under-Secretary of State	Home Office	Lord Filkin
Parliamentary Secretary	Lord Chancellor's Department	Rt Hon Baroness Scotland of Asthal QC
Parliamentary Under-Secretary of State	Trade and Industry	Lord Sainsbury of Turville
Parliamentary Under-Secretary of State	Work and Pensions	Baroness Hollis of Heigham
Attorney General	Law Officer	The Lord Goldsmith
Captain of The Queen's Bodyguard of the Yeomen of the Guard	Deputy Chief Whip	Rt Hon The Lord McIntosh of Haringey
Lords in Waiting	Whip	Lord Davies of Oldham
	Whip	Lord Bassam of Brighton
	Whip	Lord Evans of Temple Guiting
Baroness in Waiting	Whip	Baroness Farrington of Ribbleton
	Whip	Baroness Andrews
	Whip	Baroness Crawley

Table 6.11 Parties in the House of Lords, March 2003[a]

Party	Life peers	Hereditary elected by party	Hereditary elected office holders	Hereditary royal office holders	Bishops	Total
Conservative	164	41	8			213
Labour	184	2	2			188
Liberal Democrat	60	3	2			65
Crossbench	146	29	2	1		178
Archbishops and Bishops					26	26
Other[b]	7			1		8
Total	561	75	14	2	26	678

[a] Figures exclude 13 peers on leave of absence
[b] Independent and non-affiliated
Source: House of Lords Briefing, Analysis of Composition, 3 March 2003,
http://www.publications.parliament.uk/pa/ld/ldinfo/ldanal.htm

Much effort has recently been made to try to make the hours of Parliament less onerous, especially for MPs with families. The Labour government elected in 1997 followed its predecessors in trying to find ways of making more efficient use of parliamentary time, abolishing all-night sittings and injecting greater predictability

Box 6.1 Typical parliamentary session

	Usual time	*2002–2003 session*
State opening of Parliament	November	13 November
Christmas recess	Late Dec–early Jan, usually 2–3 weeks	20 December–7 January
Half-term recess	February, usually up to a week	14 February–24 February
Easter recess	Usually Good Friday and around one more week	11 April–28 April
Whit recess	Usually the week of the late spring bank holiday	23 May–3 June
Summer recess	Mid-July to early September	18 July–8 September
Conference recess	Mid-September to mid-October	19 September to 14 October
Prorogation	November	

Source: House of Commons Information Office, Factsheet P4, Sittings of the House of Commons, http://www.parliament.uk/commons/lib/p04.pdf

Box 6.2 The parliamentary day

11.30 a.m. Prayers – Read by the Speaker's Chaplain. The Speaker then takes the Chair.

Preliminary business, motions for new writs – For by-elections in vacant seats.

Unopposed private business – Private bills (no debate possible).

11.35 a.m. Questions to ministers – Oral answers are given.

12 noon Questions to the prime minister – Wednesdays only.

12.30 p.m. Private notice questions – Urgent questions allowed to be asked without the usual notice.

Business taken after questions

Ministerial statements – A minister explains the government's position on something important that has happened.

Requests for emergency debates – Requesting a debate on an urgent matter. If allowed by the Speaker it will normally take place the following day.

Public business

Introduction of public bills – First reading.

Government business motions – For example, to allow the House to sit beyond 7.30 p.m. that day to discuss important business.

Motion for leave to introduce bills – (Tuesday and Wednesday only). A type of private bill, known as a 'ten-minute-rule bill'.

Other public business – The majority of the day's business: later stages of bills, general debates, etc.

7.00 p.m. Public business ends – Can be later if the House agrees.

Presentation of public petitions – Motion for the adjournment of the House; the adjournment debate is held.

7.30 p.m. House adjourns

On some days extra items may be discussed, and not all of the items will take place every day.

Source: Adapted from House of Commons, Parliamentary Education Unit, Parliament Explained 2, http://www.explore.parliament.uk/teachers/pdfs/es02.pdf

into the timetable. Thus when its Modernization Committee looked at the issue of sitting hours of the House of Commons, it recommended reorganizing the week so that proceedings could start earlier on Tuesdays, Wednesdays and Thursdays and also end earlier. Question time was moved and the times for standing committees were altered to earlier in the day. All-night sittings were abolished in 2000.

As a result, Parliament now follows a somewhat irregular weekly working pattern (see box 6.2; figure 6.3 shows a typical working week). It sits on Mondays from 2.30 p.m. until the formal end of business at 10.30 p.m. On Tuesdays and Wednesdays proceedings begin at 11.30 a.m. and continue until 7.30 p.m. On Thursdays the house meets at 11.30 a.m. but rises at 6.30 p.m. On Fridays, traditionally a less heavy working day and one where private members' rather than government business can be conducted, business begins at 9.30 a.m. and ends at 3 p.m. (see box 6.3).

Despite these reforms, working hours still remain somewhat unpredictable. Although the most unsociable aspects of the hours have been removed, some critics argue that the reforms have reduced the excitement of the House and limited the ability of the House of Commons to scrutinize the executive, a trend exacerbated by

The Week Ahead: Monday 10 – 14 March 2003

Date	Commons Chamber	Standing Committees	Select Committees	Lords Chamber	Lords Select Committees
Mon 10 Mar	OPQ – Culture, Media and Sport; Church Commissioners; Public Accounts Commission; and Speaker's Committee on Electoral Commission Leg – Local Government Bill (RS) Adj – Post Offices in Sutton	2nd DLSC – Health Scrutiny Functions; Commission for Patient and Public Involvement in Health Regs	Education and Skills ODPM: Urban Affairs subcommittee	OPQ Leg – Community Care (Delayed Discharges) Bill (Rep) Unstarred Question – UK's treatment of children	None
Tues 11 Mar	Westminster Hall Private Members' Debates (9.30–11.30 & 2.00–4.30) OPQ – Scotland; Advocate General; Lord Chancellor's Department; President of the Council and House of Commons Commission TMR – Specialist Schools (Selection by Aptitude) Leg – Estimates; Foreign policy aspects of the war against terrorism Adj – Employee health in the workplace	SC D – Railways and Transport Safety Bill SC E – Police (NI) Bill 1st DLSC – Asylum (Designated States) 3rd DLSC – PACE 1984 4th DLSC – Apple and Pear Research Council; Horticultural Council	Culture, Media and Sport Health – Maternity Services Home Affairs International Development Lord Chancellor's Department (now Department for Constitutional Affairs) ODPM: Housing, Planning, Local Govt. and the Regions Regulatory Reform Trade and Industry Treasury	OPQ Leg – Licensing Bill [HL] (3R) Del Leg – Anti-Terrorism, Crime and Security Act; PACE Act 1984	Economic Affairs Science and Technology Subcommittee I Science and Technology Subcommittee II European Union Subcommittee A
Wed 12 Mar	Westminster Hall Private Members' Debates (9.30–11.30 & 2.00–4.30) OPQ – NI; Prime Minister TMR – Prevention of Driving under the Influence of Drugs (Road Traffic Amendment) Bill Leg – Consolidated Fund (No. 2) Bill Deb – Welsh Affairs Adj – Rail services to Hassocks	7th DLSC – Local Government Finance (Hackney) 8th DLSC – Education Regs	Education and Skills Environment, Food and Rural Affairs Public Accounts Transport	OPQ Deb – (i) Corporate Governance (ii) US Missile Defence Programme at Fylingdales Leg – Patients' Protection Bill [HL] (2R)	European Union Subcommittee F European Union Subcommittee E Constitution
Thurs 13 Mar	OPQ – Education and Skills; Solicitor General Deb – Flood and Coastal Defence Policy Adj – Water fluoridation **Westminster Hall 2.30–5.30** Financial regulation of public limited companies	SC A – Industrial Development (Financial Assistance) 5th DLSC – Medicines for Human Use (Kava-Kava) 6th DLSC – GLA Regs 9th DLSC – Rehabilitation of Offenders Act 1974 10th DLSC – Employment Rights Act 1996	Environmental Audit: Education for sustainable development Public Administration Trade and Industry	Leg – Regional Assemblies (Preparations) Bill (Comm 1st day); European Parliament (Representation) Bill (Grand Comm) Unstarred question – North Korea	European Subcommittee C Science and Technology Subcommittee I Science and Technology Subcommittee II
Fri 14 Mar	Private Members' Bills Adj – Ciproxin trials at Southampton General Hospital	None	None	Deb – Report (i) Chips for Everything; (ii) Environmental Regulation and Agriculture Leg – Equality Bill [HL] (Comm)	None

Figure 6.3 Typical House of Commons week.

Box 6.3 The new House of Commons working hours

Monday	2.30 p.m.–10.30 p.m.
Tuesday	11.30 a.m.–7.30 p.m.
Wednesday	11.30 a.m.–7.30 p.m.
Thursday	11.30 a.m.–6.30 p.m.
Friday	9.30 a.m.–3.00 p.m.

The finish times for business are the 'normal' time set down. The House may sit beyond these hours (or occasionally finish earlier). From January 2003, the House only sits on the Fridays where private members' bills are to be discussed.

Source: House of Commons Information Office, Factsheet P4, Sittings of the House, http://www.parliament.uk/commons/lib/p04.pdf

the replacement of the twice-weekly – short – prime minister's question time with a single – although longer – Wednesday slot.

The House of Lords has slightly fewer sittings than the House of Commons and the sittings are shorter. Peers sit for about 7 hours each sitting day but the pressure of work is very unevenly spread. Most politically controversial bills begin their life in the House of Commons, although about half of all bills are introduced first into the Lords. This means that sometimes bills from the Commons tend to arrive in the Lords towards the end of the session. Then the power that the Lords exert is the threat to delay passage. This delaying power may be weakened, however, now that bills can be carried over to the next session.

Managing the British Parliament

The formal proceedings of the House of Commons are presided over by the **Speaker**, who (since 2000) is Michael Martin. The office is filled by election from the ranks of MPs. When the Speakership became vacant in 2000, the election process and the outcome were both highly contentious because, in the view of some critics, Labour loyalists had supported a less suitable candidate of their own party against the wishes of their own frontbench and in defiance of a convention that the Speakership alternates between the two main parties. On attaining office, the Speaker will become a non-partisan figure and at each general election will stand as the Speaker without a party label. The task of the Speaker is to keep order in debates, to ensure fairness between the parties in calling participants and to guarantee a fair hearing for minority perspectives. The style of the Speaker can have an important impact on proceedings. For example, he sets the pace of debate in question time and determines how to treat points of order (procedural points) from MPs. He also has the power to discipline members whose behaviour has breached a parliamentary rule or convention. If there is a tie in a debate, the Speaker's casting vote is by convention cast with the government.

Speaker The impartial officer who presides over the House of Commons.

215

usual channels Informal system by which the whips of the two major parties in Parliament arrange parliamentary business.

Parliament and its committees are staffed by a special group of officials known as clerks, whose primary responsibility is to interpret the standing orders and procedural rules of the House and to advise MPs. The staff and resources of the House of Commons are relatively few, especially by comparison with those available to members of the US Congress. Some 270 clerks in the House of Commons and a smaller number in the Lords provide advice on and keep a record of procedure. They are servants of their respective chambers, not civil servants, and together with the 200 or so staff of the Library they also provide a certain amount of research support.

Despite the fact that the standing orders of the House of Commons make no mention of party, the distinction between government and opposition is the primary factor in the organization of proceedings in both the House of Commons and the House of Lords. The key to understanding the dynamics of the British Parliament is thus the extent to which it is organized on party lines and the cohesive nature of the parties there. Party permeates every aspect of life in the House of Commons. It is also an important though less dominant feature of the work of the House of Lords.

Responsibility for managing the parliamentary agenda belongs to the Leader of each House. Thus they have a responsibility both for getting the business of the government through and for general issues related to the organization of Parliament. The early period of Blair's second term saw both chambers with leaders (Robin Cook and Lord Williams) who favoured making reforms designed to strengthen the independence of Parliament. However, Cook's resignation in opposition to the war on Iraq changed the situation and it became unlikely after 2003 (when another executive-oriented figure, John Reid, was appointed Leader of the House) that very many new initiatives would be forthcoming in relation to reform. In fact, in another reshuffle in 2003, Reid was replaced by Peter Hain, but by that stage it seemed the movement for reform of the Commons had lost momentum.

The main way in which the party element of parliamentary routine is managed is through the whip's office. The whips of the major parties informally negotiate with each other a broad (and non-public) series of understandings about the programme of legislative business for the parliamentary session. This process of securing cross-party agreement between the whips of the two major parties is referred to as the **usual channels**. (The government whips meet separately with the Conservatives and the Liberal Democrats to negotiate business: there are no trilateral meetings.) Equally important, the whips are the people responsible for ensuring that each party's members know the order of business and that the maximum vote for each party is obtained when there is a division. The notice of each week's parliamentary business is also known as the party whip. It tells the order of proceedings and which ones will have the party whip applied. This is done by underlining the item on the order according to how essential it is to attend and vote with the party. A three-line whip is the most significant (see figure 6.4). Only very occasionally is a division a free vote in which the party whips do not give a directive as to how to vote. Such free votes are usually on matters of conscience, where opinion in each party is divided, or on procedural change, where the whips may be active behind the scenes even on an ostensibly free vote.

PRIVATE & CONFIDENTIAL   PARLIAMENTARY LABOUR PARTY

MONDAY, 2nd MARCH 1998   The House will meet at 2.30 p.m.

1. Home Office Questions.   Tabling for Culture, Media and Sport, Millennium Experience, Church Commissioners and Public Accounts Commission.

2. GOVERNMENT OF WALES BILL: (Rt. Hon. Ron Davies and team).   COMPLETION OF CONSIDERATION IN COMMITTEE.

YOUR ATTENDANCE FOR A RUNNING WHIP FROM 3.30 PM AND UNTIL THE BUSINESS IS CONCLUDED AT 11.00 PM IS ESSENTIAL.

PROVISION WILL BE MADE FOR THE TEN O'CLOCK RULE TO BE SUSPENDED.

FRIDAY, 6th MARCH   The House will meet at 9.30 a.m.

PRIVATE MEMBERS' BILLS.

1. Wild Mammals (Hunting with Dogs) Bill: Report Stage   – Michael Foster.

2. Private Hire Vehicles (London) Bill: Committee Stage   – Sir George Young.

3. Welfare of Pigs Bill: Second Reading   – Chris Mullin.

YOUR ATTENDANCE IS REQUESTED

Figure 6.4 The Whip.

The whips in each party thus perform two distinct and mutually complementary roles. First, they are the principal assistants of the party leadership in organizing debates and ensuring turnout in votes. Equally importantly, they are also the means through which the leadership's views are conveyed to backbenchers and backbenchers' views to the leadership. It is for this reason that the government chief whip normally attends cabinet and those cabinet committees that plan the parliamentary timetable.

The whips are thus at the heart of the power struggle between the parties. Their task will obviously vary according to such factors as whether the government has a large majority or a small one. It also matters significantly whether there are issues on the political agenda that threaten to divide the parties. Whips maintain their control by a number of methods, ranging from appeals to party loyalty to threatening recalcitrant MPs with **deselection** by their parties. (Local parties are not always sympathetic to attempts to discipline MPs and are often likely to encourage their MP to take an independent line.) Whips have a significant amount of influence in relation to the careers of backbench MPs. This influence can be either negative, in the sense that whips can sometimes veto appointments to office, or positive, in that they can identify talented newcomers who deserve promotion.

deselection Process by which a constituency party removes a sitting MP. Deselection became controversial in the Labour Party during the 1970s and 1980s when it was systematically used to ensure that MPs adhered to their local parties' policy preferences rather than their own preferences or those of the leadership.

pairing The practice of agreeing with a member of a different political party to be absent from Parliament, with the two absent votes cancelling each other out.

By convention the whips are silent in debates and operate very much behind the scenes. Although there is a strong element of gamesmanship in their behaviour, they also know that they must cooperate with one another across the party divide to manage the business of Parliament. While it is true that a government with a majority could impose its will unilaterally, organizing some aspects of the timetable by mutual consent makes life much more comfortable for all MPs. It allows, for example, the practice of **pairing**, the arrangement whereby members on opposite sides of the House can agree to absent themselves from a division without affecting the government's majority. These informal arrangements are organized through the whips' offices, where a whip is designated as the pairing whip.

In extreme political circumstances, the 'usual channels' may cease to work. Thus the opposition may feel that the government is trampling on its rights and may withhold cooperation in protest. An example of this occurred in July 1990, when Labour MPs claimed that the then Conservative government was springing statements on the House without agreement in order to exploit television coverage. Sometimes organizational agreements between the parties can completely break down and the opposition institutes a period of non-cooperation involving the withdrawal of pairing arrangements.

Although the party leadership will normally be able to call on the total loyalty of its members, the degree of party cohesion in Parliament has fluctuated in the period since 1945 (Cowley, 2001b). MPs' willingness and their incentive to dissent from the official party line change with the political circumstances. Thus although the outcome of the vast majority of divisions in the House of Commons is predictable, party managers cannot afford to be complacent and the whips have to be engaged in a constant process of consultation and persuasion. In 2003, for example, it was reported that concessions to legislation on foundation hospitals had been secured to make it more palatable to backbench Labour MPs. The Labour government elected in 1997 introduced new disciplinary rules for the parliamentary party in order to avoid public displays of dissension. In addition, the availability of pagers allowed the whips to keep in permanent contact with MPs in a way which was wholly new, and which some MPs like Tony Benn found offensive. As a result, the 1997–2001 Parliament saw relatively little dissent (see table 6.12). But there were a few dramatic episodes in which Labour MPs did not vote the party line. In the 2003 Parliament there were some further spectacular rebellions with high numbers of Labour MPs voting against their own government on the war with Iraq and on the issue of foundation hospitals.

For the most part, then, the organization of the House assumes a party system, and indeed much of it is arranged on the basis of the interests of the government and the largest opposition party. Reformers may wish that party considerations were less dominant in the organization of parliamentary business, but the reality at present is that party concerns are paramount in virtually every aspect of House of Commons life. And it is also a fact of life that government defeats in the House of Commons are very rare (see table 6.13).

The basic framework of debate takes the form of a dialogue, not between the executive and the legislature, as in a separation of powers system, but between the government and the largest opposition party. The special position of the major opposition party is recognized and specific facilities in debate and resources are

Table 6.12 Dissent in the House of Commons, 1997–2003[a]

Issue	Total number of MPs voting against their whip (excluding abstensions)
Social Security Bill (1997)	47
Competition Bill (1998)	25
Criminal Justice (Terrorism and Conspiracy) Bill (1998)	37
Teaching and Higher Education Bill (1998)	34
Iraq (1998)	22
Access to Justice Bill (1999)	21
House of Lords Bill (1999)	35
Welfare Reform and Pensions Bill (1999)	74
Child Support, Pensions and Social Security Bill (2000)	41
Criminal Justice (Mode of Trial) Bill (2000)	37
Freedom of Information Bill (2000)	41
Transport Bill (2000)	65
Iraq (2003)	139

[a] Rebellions in which 20 or more Labour MPs voted against their party whips.
Source: Cowley (2001a), p. 821.

Table 6.13 Government defeats on the floor of the House of Commons, 1970–2001

Session	Number of defeats
1970–4	6
1974	17
1974–9	42
1979–83	1
1983–7	2
1987–92	1
1992–7	9
1997–2001	0

Source: Adapted from Butler and Butler (2000), p. 201; House of Commons Information Service.

accorded to that party. The pervasiveness of the conflict between government and opposition in the UK's political life has been labelled adversarial politics and it creates a distinctive style at Westminster. It should be noted that this style is less marked in the Scottish Parliament in Edinburgh and the Welsh Assembly in Cardiff, both of which have made efforts to create a more consensual legislative chamber and have coalition governments.

The Legislative Process

Legislation is divided into two broad kinds, **public legislation** and **private legislation**. (There is a third kind – **hybrid legislation** – which has elements of both public and private legislation, but it is relatively

public legislation Legislation which applies generally rather than to some specific person or groups of people.

private legislation Legislative proposals which apply not to the whole country but to a section of it.

hybrid legislation Used to refer to a bill which is part private and part public.

private member's bill (PMB)/private member's legislation Private members' bills are public bills introduced into Parliament by backbench MPs. A ballot process is used to decide which MPs will be allowed to introduce PMBs in a particular session. Few PMBs make it into the statute books to become legislation and die at the end of the session in a process colloquially known as the 'massacre of the innocents'.

rare.) Public legislation, which is by far the most important in terms of volume and character, is usually introduced by the government. However, it may be introduced by backbench MPs through what are known as **private members' bills** (not to be confused with private legislation). These private members' bills (PMBs) usually only stand a chance of becoming law if the government decides to make time available for them or to assist them in some way (see box 6.4). Thus the Labour government elected in 2001 provided time to assist the passage of legislation banning foxhunting.

Private legislation (sometimes known as local and personal legislation) deals with matters affecting the interests of local bodies or named individuals. In the nineteenth century such private Acts of Parliament were very common and were often used to secure a divorce, for which general statutes did not provide until 1857. Today most of these issues can be dealt with under the provision of general statutes. However, private legislation is still used when a local authority wishes to acquire a new function that is not covered by

Box 6.4 Examples of successful private members' bills, 1995–2002

Session	Title	Member
1995–6	Marriage Ceremony (Prescribed Words)	Mr Julian Brazier
	Offensive Weapons	Lady Olga Maitland
1996–7	Telecommunications (Fraud)	Mr Ian Bruce
	Road Traffic Reduction (National Targets)	Cynog Dafis
1997–8	Community Care (Residential Accommodation)	Marsha Singh
	Employment Rights (Dispute Resolution)	Lord Archer of Sandwell [John Healey]
1998–9	Breeding and Sale of Dogs (Welfare)	James Clappison
	Football (Offences and Disorder)	Simon Burns
1999–2000	Warm Homes and Energy Conservation	David Amess
	Census (Amendment)	Lord Weatherill [Jonathan Sayeed]
2000–1	No private members' bills received royal assent during this session, which was short due to the calling of the election in May 2001	
2001–2	Private Hire Vehicles (Carriage of Guide Dogs etc.)	Mr Neil Gerrard
	Employee Share Schemes	Mr Mark Lazarowicz

Source: House of Commons Information Office, Factsheet L3, http://www.parliament.uk/commons/lib/l03.pdf

existing powers or when a local authority or other public body needs to acquire land by compulsory purchase. The procedure that private bills must follow is more akin to judicial proceedings and very different from the adversarial method used in passing public legislation. A private bill must clear a number of preliminary hurdles designed to allow objections to a measure to be heard, and these procedures may involve public inquiries, a town poll or a town meeting. Only after the completion of this expensive and time-consuming process can the first formal stage (or first **reading**) of the bill be taken. If the bill is unopposed, progress will be rapid; but an opposed bill after second reading has to go to a private bill committee of MPs, which again operates more like a court than an ordinary standing committee in that the proponents and the opponents of the bill are represented by legal counsel and call witnesses to give evidence on their behalf. The private bill committee can deal with both the desirability of the bill itself and its details. If it rejects the measure, the rejection is taken as final; if approval is given, the subsequent procedure is similar to the normal procedure for a public bill. Private bills must go through both Houses of Parliament according to the same procedures.

Public legislation forms by far the most important category of legislation in the United Kingdom. The government dominates all stages of the preparation and passage of the vast majority of public bills. The legislation itself will be drafted on departmental instructions by one or more parliamentary draftsmen in the parliamentary counsel's office (which is part of the Cabinet Office) following a long process of policy making, which may include the publication of a **green paper** and/or a white paper signalling the issues involved and the government's thinking on them. All important bills will be presented in Parliament by the appropriate minister who, aided by his or her civil servants and draftsmen, will pilot the bill through its various stages of parliamentary scrutiny. The minister's aim will be to secure the safe passage of the bill onto the statute book, either in its original form or with only such amendments as are acceptable to the government. The government will usually be able to ensure such an outcome because it has a majority in the House of Commons and can thus control all legislative proceedings. The overall majority in the House of Commons is reflected in the party composition of the standing committees that examine the details of legislation, so that the government will expect to determine both the principles and the specific wording of a bill. Box 6.5 gives an overview of the legislative process.

One continuing concern in relation to the legislative process is the lack of simplicity and clarity of statutes. Different explanations for the poor technical quality of legislation have been put forward at various times, including the volume of legislation, the pressures of parliamentary draftsmen and weaknesses in the parliamentary scrutiny of bills. Of course, incoherent or ambiguous legislation can be tidied up later by the judiciary, but the interpretation given to a measure by the judges may vary from what was originally intended. Recent developments in government practice and parliamentary procedure mean that more explanatory material is available to Parliament as it considers a bill. There have also been experiments that enable more extensive consideration of legislative proposals. Following the 1997 report of the Select Committee on the

readings (of legislation) Stages at which legislative proposals are considered.

green paper Statement of government thinking on issues raised by a public policy problem. Such a paper invites consultation and discussion. By comparison with a white paper it is used when government thinking is still at an early stage.

Box 6.5 The legislative process

House of Commons

First reading: Bill introduced into the Commons. Clerk reads out the title of the bill. No debate or vote at this stage, so bill automatically goes through.

Second reading: Minister in charge of the bill explains its main purpose and answers general questions about the bill. Bill must be passed by voice or division.

Committee stage: It is here that a bill will be examined in detail for the first time. Most government bills are considered in standing committees of between 15 and 50 MPs, with membership roughly in proportion to each party's strength in the Commons. At least one minister from the sponsoring department will be on the committee, as will a frontbench spokesperson from each of the main opposition parties. Amendments to the bill can be tabled, which are voted on by voice or division. Bills with constitutional significance or those that require very rapid passage will be heard by a committee of the whole House.

Report stage: MPs consider the revised bill and may table further amendments.

Third reading: House considers the bill as a whole, but cannot change it considerably at this stage. It must be accepted or rejected. Often bills pass their report and third reading stages at the same time.

House of Lords

After passage in the Commons, a bill will be carried to the Lords for consideration. A sizeable proportion of bills start in the Lords and so will go through the Lords before reaching the Commons.

First reading
Second reading
Committee stage
Report stage
Third reading

These processes are broadly the same as in the Commons, except that the committee stage will usually be considered by a committee of the whole House.

Reconciliation between Commons and Lords

Bills have to be agreed in the same form by both Houses, so if amendments have been passed in one House the bill must go to the other House for approval. If the Lords has passed amendments with which the Commons does not agree, the Commons will send a note to the Lords explaining the reasons. This ping-pong process will continue until an agreement is reached. If they fail to agree, the Commons can invoke the Parliament Act and introduce the bill in the next parliamentary session with no scope for the Lords to reject it.

Royal assent

Rather than signing bills herself, the queen signs letters patent or royal commissions which authorize the Speakers of the two Houses or certain Lords known as royal commissioners to announce that royal assent has been given.

Modernization of the House of Commons dealing with the legislative process, it was suggested that draft bills should be employed more frequently and that greater use should be made of the facility to send bills to a select committee for pre-legislative scrutiny. Four bills were sent to a select committee for pre-legislative scrutiny in 2000, but only two were so handled in 2001. The government is, however, committed to using the pre-legislative scrutiny mechanism more extensively.

Another important issue for the government is the management of parliamentary time. Keeping control of the legislative timetable is always a major government concern because legislation may be lost if the schedule is disrupted. Maintaining the legislative timetable is not, however, something that is always in the interests of the opposition. Thus while some parts of the legislative timetable can be agreed through the usual channels, on certain issues the opposition will feel so strongly that it will use any strategy it can find to derail legislation and other government business. Sometimes it is not so much the official opposition but a determined minority out of sympathy with both frontbenches that seeks to sabotage the government's ability to get its measures through. In these circumstances the government has one important weapon at its disposal: an allocation of time order or guillotine by which the government uses its majority to curtail debate.

The guillotine in the House of Commons was introduced in the late nineteenth century to counter the wrecking tactics and filibustering of the Irish nationalists. (It was first used on the Criminal Law (Amendment) Bill of 1897.) Each guillotine order is specific to the legislation being debated and effectively sets a time limit for debate on one or several stages of the bill. In fact the guillotine is not often used since the government will always prefer to proceed by agreement through the usual channels, if possible.

In the 1997–8 Parliament a new procedure was used to introduce predictability into parliamentary business. This was the so-called programme motion. By contrast with the guillotine (which is a weapon deployed by government to force its measures through), the programme motion proceeds on the basis of agreement between the government and the opposition. Each bill is given its own timetable, which allocates a set amount of time to each stage. It is thus more formal than the usual channels but more flexible than the guillotine. The device was used for the first time in the debates on the Scotland Bill of 1997–8.

The parliamentary stages of the legislative process are known as readings. The first reading is a purely formal process in which the title of the bill is put down on the **order paper**. The second reading provides an opportunity for the general principles of a proposed measure to be debated on the floor of the House of Commons. (At present a few non-controversial bills will be considered not by the House as a whole but in a second reading committee.) For most bills, however, it is the second reading debate that marks the point at which the United Kingdom's parliamentary proceedings are the most theatrical. The outcome of this second reading debate can usually be predicted because the vote on second reading will almost always reflect the government's majority in the House of Commons. Just occasionally, however, the government may lose a vote on second reading, as happened with the Shops Bill of 1986. The fact that the vote on second reading will typically be a foregone

royal assent The final stage before a bill becomes law; the queen must signal her authorization of the bill before it can pass.

order paper The name given to the daily publication which gives the agenda of parliamentary proceedings for each sitting day.

conclusion means that the debate takes the form of an argument about the merits of the bill between the government and the opposition on the basis of their rival philosophies. It is at this stage that the adversarial style of British politics is most obvious as both sides seek to score points and influence public opinion. The result of the vote on second reading will determine whether a bill is to proceed. If the vote is positive the bill will go to its committee stage, which involves a clause-by-clause, and perhaps a line-by-line, discussion. (Clauses in a bill eventually become sections in the Act.)

At the committee stage, although the intent is to examine the bill in detail, the style in which this is done is still adversarial. In the House of Commons (though not the House of Lords), the committee stage will normally take place in a standing committee. Only bills of unusual constitutional importance, such as the European Communities Bill of 1972 or the House of Lords Bill of 1998/9, together with bills that require a quick passage are dealt with at the committee stage by the whole House, or on the floor, as the procedure is known. However, the main provisions of finance bills are dealt with in this way.

Standing committees in the British Parliament were first used in the 1880s and had become a regular part of the legislative process by the early twentieth century. They are not committees already in existence with a defined membership or subject specialization. Rather, standing committees are newly appointed for each bill and there will be perhaps nine in being at any one time. (One will be reserved for private members' bills.) The precise membership of a standing committee depends upon the particular bill under discussion. Membership is usually about 18, but for large and complicated bills the number of members required to serve can be as many as 50. Formal nomination to these committees is carried out by the Committee on Selection, which will have to take into account the need for party composition to reflect the House as a whole and is heavily influenced by the whips. A primary concern of the whips who suggest MPs to staff these standing committees is the maintenance of the government's timetable for the passage of the bill. This priority may, in turn, encourage the whips to prefer docile to informed MPs. The essential requirement of each committee is that the balance of votes should reflect party strength in the House as a whole. Thus except where there is no overall majority in the House (as was the case from 1976 to 1979) or where the governing party's majority is fragile (as was the case towards the end of John Major's 1992–7 government), the government can nearly always rely on being able to defeat any amendment to which it takes exception. The minister responsible for taking a bill through the committee stage also has the advantage of having civil servants on hand to brief him or her about the implications of any proposed amendment. Sometimes an amendment will be produced that raises new issues, perhaps as a result of a government backbencher's intervention rather than from the opposition. In theory, committee amendments must be in harmony with the overall purpose of the bill. In practice, successful committee amendments will be those supported by the government.

The weaknesses of this part of the legislative procedure are readily apparent. Consideration of the detail of legislation is handled by committees whose membership has no specialist background in the subject matter of the bill and where there is little opportunity to examine the bill's provisions in depth. As a result, ill-constructed bills often emerge unamended from the committee stage. One remedy for these defects is to make use of the facility to send a bill for its committee stage to a select committee or a special standing committee. Special standing committees can adopt a less rushed, less adversarial and more consultative approach to a bill and may be used in relation to complex legislation of a technical and non-partisan kind. Such a special standing committee was used in 2002 to consider the Adoption of Children Bill.

After the committee stage comes the **report** (or **consideration**) **stage** when the bill, as amended in committee, is reported back to the House. This stage gives the government a further opportunity to put forward its own amendments to a bill, to reverse amendments made in committee, or to endorse the treatment accorded to a bill by the standing committee or committee of the whole House. As at the committee stage, the introduction of government amendments here may reflect party or interest group representations made between the formal introduction of the bill into Parliament and its detailed consideration. Equally, government amendments may reflect changed circumstances that make alterations to the bill desirable.

The final stage of the House of Commons' consideration of a bill is the third reading. This stage involves the discussion of the bill's principles again, although this time taking account of any amendments made during the committee and report stages. However, no amendments are allowed to a bill at this point. It is possible that the government may encounter new difficulties with the bill at this stage, especially if there is opposition within the governing party to some aspect of the measure. The outcome of the debate and the subsequent vote, like that at second reading, is usually predictable, however, since it will be controlled by the government's majority.

Once a bill has passed through all its stages in one House it must be considered by the other chamber. The legislative process in the House of Lords differs slightly, notably because the committee stage is usually taken by the whole House rather than in committee. Also, there are no guillotines in the House of Lords and amendments are possible at third reading stage. The House of Lords may make changes to bills that have passed through the House of Commons, though the House of Commons has the power to reject such amendments and often does so.

Once a bill has passed through both Houses it is ready for the royal assent. The monarch's assent to legislation is now taken as automatic and no monarch has refused this assent since 1707. The fact that legislation is on the statute book does not necessarily mean it will immediately come into effect. Both the Human Rights Act of 1998 and the Freedom of Information Act of 2000 had their coming into effect delayed because both Acts were thought to require substantial administrative preparation.

The effectiveness of the legislative process

The total impact of the House of Commons on the detail of legislation is very slight in proportion to the amount of time devoted by MPs to legislative matters. Well over 90 per cent of all bills are introduced by the government and pass in the form the government wants. This fact, together with frequently heard criticisms of the

report stage The stage in a bill's passage when, following committee consideration, it is reported back to the House together with the committee's recommendations, which may be approved or rejected. The report stage may see the introduction of new amendments to the bill. Also called consideration stage.

quality of legislation, makes the legislative process a favourite target of reformers. The Labour government elected in 1997 made the legislative process one of the first items on the agenda of the new Select Committee on the Modernization of the House of Commons. This produced some useful reforms, although critics argue that many of them have helped the executive get its legislation through as much as they have strengthened Parliament. Among its recommendations were the greater use of programme motions, the possibility that bills might be carried over from one session to another, and the more streamlined scrutiny of European legislation. It also recommended earlier sittings on Thursday and a general modernization of some of the more archaic procedures of the House of Commons.

Delegated legislation

Thus far we have considered the effectiveness of the way Parliament handles primary legislation. However, Parliament also finds it difficult to deal with the extensive volume of secondary or delegated legislation that is passed every year. Secondary, delegated or subordinate legislation is legislation made by the executive by virtue of powers conferred by statute on departments or individual ministers. The most common form used is the **statutory instrument,** known as an SI (see box 6.6 for some examples). Statutory instruments are published serially by the year and most are governed by the Statutory Instruments Act of 1946. Delegated legislation is used to cover a number of circumstances where it is not feasible to pass new primary legislation. So, for example, benefit payments may be varied by delegated legislation, as may traffic regulations. The use of secondary legislation to vary tax rates is, however,

statutory instrument (SI)
The most important form of secondary or delegated legislation in the United Kingdom.

Box 6.6   Examples of statutory instruments

- The Revenue Support Grant (Specified Bodies) (Amendment) (England) Regulations 2003
- M62 Motorway (Junction 10) (Temporary Prohibition of Traffic) Order 2003
- The Friendly Societies (Modification of the Corporation Tax Acts) (Amendment) Regulations 2003
- The Value Added Tax (Health and Welfare) Order 2003
- The Prohibition of Keeping or Release of Live Fish (Specified Species) (Amendment) (England) Order 2003
- The National Health Service (Out of Hours Provision of Personal Medical Services and Miscellaneous Amendments) (England) Regulations 2003
- The Sheep and Goats Identification and Movement (Interim Measures) (England) (No. 2) (Amendment) Order 2003
- The Access to the Countryside (Provisional and Conclusive Maps) (England) (Amendment) Regulations 2003
- The Supply of Beer (Loan Ties, Licensed Premises and Wholesale Prices) (Revocation) Order 2003
- The Environmental Protection (Duty of Care) (England) (Amendment) Regulations 2003

extremely sensitive given the House of Commons' traditional authority in relation to tax (see also below, p. 228). Other types of subordinate legislation include rules made by local authorities and other public bodies, as well as some Orders in Council, i.e., legislation made under the royal prerogative. Sometimes delegated legislation can be extremely controversial; changes to the weights and measures regulations led to the 'metric martyr' case and the banning of the sale of beef on the bone was done by delegated legislation. Keeping delegated legislation under review is, however, a massive task: there were 3,412 statutory instruments passed by Parliament in 2000, a rise of about a third from the 1960s.

Formal parliamentary control over delegated legislation is maintained by two basic procedures that date from the Statutory Instruments Act of 1946, although Parliament has varied its own machinery for monitoring subordinate legislation. The two basic procedures are the negative and the affirmative procedure. Under the negative procedure, the parent legislation will provide that a statutory instrument will become law after a given time (usually 40 days) unless a negative resolution (in the form of a motion for its annulment) has in the meantime been passed by either House. In the case of some statutory instruments an affirmative resolution is required. Where an affirmative procedure is used, a motion approving the order has to be passed by both Houses within a period specified in the legislation, which may be 28 or 40 days. The affirmative procedure, which is obviously more time-consuming and requires more parliamentary scrutiny, applies to all statutory instruments of constitutional significance and those concerned with the implementation of major aspects of the parent legislation.

Parliament is somewhat weakened in the process of scrutinizing delegated legislation by the fact that statutory instruments cannot be amended by either House: they can only be accepted or rejected. Nevertheless, the affirmative procedure in particular means that a minister may have to defend before Parliament the substance of a piece of delegated legislation. The negative resolution procedure, on the other hand, is only a limited protection against arbitrary and unwise governmental action. The sheer volume of delegated legislation makes it difficult for Parliament to consider each and every item of delegated legislation, especially European legislation. Ultimately, the executive can use its majority to secure the desired delegated legislation whether the affirmative or negative procedure is used.

Serious concerns about Parliament's weapons for scrutinizing delegated legislation have been voiced from a number of quarters in recent years. In a report in 1992, the Hansard Society thought that legislation which gave broad powers to ministers to change the law with little or no parliamentary supervision was highly undesirable (Hansard Society, 1992). The then Conservative government's application of such powers in the Deregulation and Contracting Out Act of 1994 provoked a further storm of controversy. The use in that Act of so-called Henry VIII clauses (which empower ministers to use secondary legislation to amend or repeal primary legislation) was especially contentious. Yet such clauses continue to be used by the executive, for example in the Local Government Acts of 1999 and 2000.

Parliament has established special committees in order to keep delegated legislation under review. Since 1973 the technical consideration of statutory instruments has been the responsibility of a joint committee of both Houses of Parliament, a device which, as noted earlier, is used rather infrequently in the British system. The joint committee does not look at the merits but considers the form and legality of all statutory instruments, except in matters of financial legislation, which is deemed to be the prerogative of the House of Commons. In the House of Commons, statutory instruments may be referred to a standing committee that is entitled to consider the merits of the proposed instrument and may actually debate it, especially if it is of the type that requires ratification by the affirmative procedure. (These standing committees on delegated legislation usually have about 17 core voting members, although any MP may attend.) The instruments then go to the House of Commons for formal approval. The opposition can, and sometimes does, object to a statutory instrument's being dealt with in committee and can insist on its being debated on the floor of the House.

The increased use of delegated legislation in the modern state means that Parliament is continually searching for ways of improving its oversight. Among the recent suggestions for reform are the use of a single committee to sift all statutory instruments and an extension of the time during which Parliament could annul a statutory instrument. It is also worth noting here that the courts have an important role to play in relation to secondary legislation, since they can review the use made by a minister of powers given under legislation.

Parliament and Finance

Parliament's role in financial matters is by tradition an extremely important one. Indeed, in constitutional theory parliamentary power derives from its authority over financial matters, especially taxation. As **Erskine May** puts it, 'the Crown demands money, the Commons grants it, and the Lords assent to the grant' (19th edn, p. 695). Traditionally, Parliament maintains a formal and strict distinction between what May calls 'functions of initiation and administration' on the one hand and the function of control on the other. Yet, as with so much else in the life of Parliament, it is the executive that is dominant in the handling of financial business. Although processes connected with public spending and revenue raising, as well as with financial accountability, absorb a good deal of parliamentary time, the ability of Parliament to influence the executive in financial matters, as in so much else, is limited. Nevertheless, the mechanisms and procedures concerned with expenditure and taxation retain their significance, not least as broad political rather than narrowly financial instruments for holding the executive to account for its policies.

The first point to notice about Parliament's role in finance is that it is an area that is the preserve of the House of Commons rather than Parliament as a whole. This point was reinforced following the constitutional crisis of 1909–11. Since that time, if the Speaker certifies a bill to be a **money bill**, it can be delayed by the House of Lords for no more than one month.

Three aspects of the House of Commons' role in relation to financial matters need to be considered here. First, there is the general question of the government's expenditure plans (the annual granting

Erskine May Erskine May (1815–86) was clerk of the House of Commons between 1871 and 1886. His *Treatise upon the Law, Privileges and Usage of Parliament* (1844) effectively became the procedural bible of Parliament and is now in its 28th edition.

money bill A bill which involves the authorization of expenditure from government funds or seeks to raise money from taxes. Since the 1911 Parliament Act, money bills may not be amended by the House of Lords.

of supply), which detail the money that will be demanded by the government. These plans will be debated in the context of the executive's general assessment of the economy and sanctioned by Parliament. Secondly, there is the question of providing funding for those plans through taxation and other revenue-raising methods. Finally, there is the issue of monitoring how public funds have been spent.

The House of Commons has long operated on the theory that it would first consider what the government needed to spend in the coming financial year and then make provision for such expenditure through taxation. In the autumn of each year, the Chancellor of the Exchequer makes a statement giving details of public expenditure plans across the various spending departments. In the spring of each year, the Chancellor of the Exchequer presents to Parliament in the form of the budget detailed changes in the tax system to pay for that spending. These proposals are then followed by a series of budget resolutions and a finance bill to give effect to them. Obviously, these two points of financial decision making themselves mark the end of a long and complex process of deliberation inside government departments, including of course the Treasury.

It may seem illogical to separate spending decisions from the process of determining how those spending decisions will be funded. Indeed, for a brief period (between 1993 and 1996), the two processes were brought together as a unified budget so that spending and taxation changes could be presented to Parliament in a single end-of-year statement in December. However, the Labour government elected in 1997 discontinued this experiment and the two processes are again separated by a period of nearly four months. An overview of the financial calendar is shown in box 6.7.

Although consideration of departmental estimates remains an important part of the work of the House, it began to be recognized from the late nineteenth century that the debates on **supply days**, as they were then known, focused on general policy rather than on detailed expenditure and these days were increasingly available for the opposition to criticize government policy. Important though these 20 days were in the life of the House of Commons, this erosion of discussion on the government's expenditure plans left a gap in the machinery of financial control. This gap has been acknowledged by a series of changes in the machinery for considering estimates as well as proposals for future change from the procedure committee.

Part of the problem for the House of Commons as it attempts to participate in a meaningful way in these financial procedures is that it cannot hope to match the expertise of the executive. It is also increasingly difficult for Parliament to exert real influence on an annual basis over a decision-making process that is often based on a 3-, 5- or 10-year cycle. To some extent the work of the departmental select committee dealing with Treasury matters has given certain MPs a degree of expertise and has altered parliamentary thinking about financial issues, but the general problem remains.

In some ways the House of Commons' ability to monitor expenditure after it has occurred is greater than its ability to influence public spending and taxing decisions, where the reality of modern government has concentrated power increasingly inside the Treasury. Parliament's instruments of control, especially the Public Accounts Committee, which is backed by the Comptroller and Auditor General and his staff, are designed to check in detail that money has been spent only

supply days Now called opposition days. These are the 20 days set aside in each session when the opposition selects the topics for parliamentary debate.

Box 6.7 The financial calendar

Month	Budget cycle	Estimates cycle	Reporting cycle
October/ November	Pre-Budget Report or 'Green Budget'	Winter Supplementary Estimates (for current financial year) presented	Resource Accounts (for previous financial year) presented
December		Consolidated Fund Bill (Consolidated Fund [No. 2] Act) passed	Departmental Performance Reports (for previous financial year) published
February		Spring Supplementary Estimates (for current financial year) and Excess votes (for earlier years) presented	
March	Budget Statement and Debate	Main Estimates (for next financial year) presented Consolidated Fund (No. 2) Bill (Consolidated Fund Act) passed	

Start of	The New	Financial	Year
April	Finance Bill published and given second reading		Departmental spending plans and reports (for current financial year plus the next two years) published
May	Finance Bill in Committee	Summer Supplementary Estimates and Revised Estimates (for current financial year) presented	
June			
July	Finance Bill Third Reading in House of Commons and pro-forma consideration by House of Lords (Finance Act)	Consolidated Fund No. 3 Bill (the Appropriation Act) passed	

Source: Derived from the *Handbook of House of Commons Procedure*, 3rd edn (London: Vacher Dod Publishing, 2002).

on the purposes for which it was voted by Parliament. The Public Accounts Committee is thus seen as a protection against corruption and government overspending. Transformations in the structure of the British state in recent years, together with changes in the approach to public expenditure, have brought important new developments to expenditure control – for example, the expanding role of the National Audit Office – in the field of financial accountability.

Scrutiny and Select Committees

The extent to which the government will in normal circumstances dominate Parliament should already be apparent. The independent influence of individual MPs and peers, and indeed of the House of Commons and the House of Lords as a whole, is inevitably limited by the subordination of most legislative activity to the dynamics of party politics and the control which the government can exert over Parliament through its disciplined party majority. Although this subordination is one in which MPs have largely been willing collaborators, successive reform efforts over the years have tried to find ways of strengthening Parliament's independence. From the 1960s onwards one strategy of reformers centred on enhancing the role of select committees in the work of the House of Commons. By sharpening the scrutiny functions of Parliament, it was hoped that backbenchers could develop a more independent role than was open to them in legislative proceedings where inevitably party concerns dominated.

Select committees had a long history as devices for conducting special inquiries, not least because select committees have the power to take both written and oral evidence. In the 1966–70 Parliament Richard Crossman initiated an experiment with specialist select committees, and in the 1970s the Expenditure Committee conducted wide-ranging inquiries through subject-organized subcommittees. In 1979 proponents of reform succeeded in establishing a comprehensive new system of subject select committees, which is the basis of the contemporary system of departmental select committees. These departmental select committees provide coverage of the whole range of government activities. They last for the life of a Parliament, although a committee's precise membership may alter during the course of a Parliament. Each committee is composed of about 11 members (some are larger) and will meet weekly while Parliament is sitting.

Initially, 12 departmental select committees were set up together with two more general committees concerned with Scottish and Welsh affairs. Inevitably, the number and remit of the committees have had to be adjusted to reflect alterations in the organization of the government departments being monitored by the committees. Thus the significant changes in Whitehall that followed the 2001 election resulted in a major reorganization of the departmental select committees. And in 2003 the growth in responsibilities of the Lord Chancellor's Department prompted the establishment of a select committee to monitor its work. Today there are 18 departmental committees (see box 6.8). Since 2001 all departmental committees have the power to establish subcommittees, and two (Environment, Food and Rural Affairs and Transport, Local Government and the Regions) can set up two subcommittees.

Box 6.8   Select committees of the House of Commons

Departmental

- Culture, Media and Sport Committee
- Defence Committee
- Education and Skills Committee
- Environment, Food and Rural Affairs Committee
- Foreign Affairs Committee
- Health Committee
- Home Affairs Committee
- International Development Committee
- Constitutional Affairs Committee
- Northern Ireland Affairs Committee
- Office of the Deputy Prime Minister (Housing, Planning, Local Government and the Regions)
- Scottish Affairs Committee
- Science and Technology Committee
- Trade and Industry Committee
- Transport Committee
- Treasury Committee
- Welsh Affairs Committee
- Work and Pensions Committee

Non-departmental

- Accommodation and Works Committee
- Administration Committee
- Broadcasting Committee
- Catering Committee
- Environmental Audit Committee
- European Scrutiny Committee
- Finance and Services Committee
- Information Committee
- Liaison Committee
- Modernization of the House of Commons (Select Committee on the Modernization of the House of Commons)
- Procedure Committee
- Public Accounts Committee
- Public Administration Select Committee
- Regulatory Reform Committee
- Standards and Privileges Committee
- Statutory Instruments (Select Committee on Statutory Instruments)

In addition there is a Liaison Committee, consisting of the chairs of the departmental select committees, which considers issues related to all departmental select committees. In the 1997–2001 Parliament the Liaison Committee became a protagonist for strengthening the independence of the departmental committees by reducing the whips' role in selecting members to serve on these committees. Membership of the various departmental select committees is managed by the Committee of Selection, which is, in theory if not in practice, an impartial body responsible for recommending members of select and standing committees to the House of Commons as a whole. In reality, it is dominated by the whips and by the majority party. The recommendation to give the process of selecting members greater autonomy from the whips, although initially rejected by the government, was subsequently taken up again by the Modernization Committee in its 2002 report on select committees. (Similar proposals for securing greater independence for select committees had been put forward also by the Hansard Society and the Norton Report.) Somewhat surprisingly on an allegedly free vote, though one where the whips may have exercised influence, the House rejected the idea of a new and independent Committee of Nomination. The House did, however, accept some other elements of the Modernization Committee's suggestions, including enhanced resources for committees and additional payments for select committee chairs. (Staffing of select committees is by the clerks, but select committees may also employ part-time advisers with special knowledge of the subject.)

Membership of departmental select committees reflects the party composition of the House as a whole, so that on a typical departmental committee of 11 members in the current Parliament elected in 2001 there would be seven Labour members, three Conservatives and a representative of a minor party. The criteria used for appointing departmental select committee members excludes ministers and opposition frontbench spokespersons. However, there is competition among backbenchers for membership of select committees, so that at the moment the whips can use membership as a form of patronage to their own side. The opportunity for influence by the whips exists not only when a committee is formed after each general election but also when an MP resigns from the committee, as a result of becoming a minister, for example.

In theory the chairmanship of these committees is determined by each committee, with a fair distribution between the parties. In practice there has been not a little inter-party wrangling and interference from the whips over the allocation of chairmanships between the parties and the identity of the chair. (Apart from having a casting vote, the chair of a select committee can shape the direction of an inquiry.) Both parties have been guilty when in government of appearing to undermine the independence of select committees by exerting pressure to remove chairs of committees. In 1992 Nicholas Winterton was removed from his chairmanship of the Select Committee on Health when Conservative whips discovered a so-called 'three-term rule', which set a limit of the parliamentary terms for an MP to hold the chairmanship of a select committee. In 2001 there was an attempt to dislodge Gwyneth Dunwoody and Donald Anderson as Labour chairs of the Transport and Foreign Affairs select committees, respectively. This interference occasioned a rebellion by backbench Labour MPs and the two chairs were reinstated.

What sort of topics a select committee takes on depends very much on the individual committee. Opinions differ as to the kind of inquiry best suited to departmental select committees. In some cases a short, incisive report on a topical subject can be highly effective; in other cases there is much to be said for in-depth investigation or a panoramic study of a subject such as organized crime in Britain. Box 6.9 gives some examples of inquiries by departmental select committees.

Box 6.9 Major select committee reports, 1997–2001

- **Culture, Media and Sport Committee**
  1999–2000 First Report, The Operation of the National Lottery
- **Defence Committee**
  1998–9 Fourteenth Report, Lessons of Kosovo
- **Education and Employment Committee**
  1998–9 Fourth Report, The Role of OFSTED
  2000–1 Fifth Report, The New Deal: An Evaluation
- **Environment, Transport and Regional Affairs Committee**
  2000–1 Sixth Report, Rail Investment: Renewal, Maintenance and Development of the National Rail Network
  1999–2000 Fourteenth Report, Funding of London Underground
  1998–9 Third Report, The Future of National Air Transport Services
- **Foreign Affairs Committee**
  1998–9 First Report, Foreign Policy and Human Resources
  1997–8 First Report, Treaty of Amsterdam
- **Health Committee**
  1998–9 Fourth Report, Long-term Care of the Elderly
- **Home Affairs Committee**
  1999–2000 Second Report, Control over Firearms
  1998–9 Third Report, Accountability of the Security Service
- **Liaison Committee**
  1999–2000 First Report, Shifting the Balance: Select Committees and the Executive
- **Modernization Committee**
  1997–8 First Report, The Legislative Process
  1997–8 Seventh Report, The Scrutiny of European Business
- **Public Accounts Committee**
  2000–1 Fifteenth Report, The Strategic Rail Authority: Action to Improve Passenger Rail Services
  1999–2000 Twenty-Fourth Report, The Passport Delays of Summer 1999
  1998–9 Thirty-Fourth Report, BSE: The Cost of a Crisis
- **Public Administration Select Committee**
  1997–8 Third Report, Your Right to Know: The Government's Proposals for a Freedom of Information Act
  2000–1 Third Report, The Ministerial Code: Improving the Rule Book (HC 235); Fourth Report, Special Advisers, Boon or Bane? (HC 293)
- **Treasury Select Committee**
  1999–2000 Eighth Report, Economic and Monetary Union
  1997–8 First Report, Accountability of the Bank of England

Rossi doctrine Doctrine associated with Sir Hugh Rossi MP, who when chair of the Environment Committee in the 1980s argued that in order to maximize their effectiveness, select committees should only investigate topics outside the mainstream of partisan debate. In this way, Rossi thought the select committees would avoid dividing on partisan lines. The logic of the Rossi doctrine was to confine select committees to non-controversial topics, and support for the doctrine has accordingly eroded.

Initially, one school of thought argued strongly that because a select committee would exert most influence if it could produce a united report, it would be better to avoid matters of intense party controversy. This view – known as the **Rossi doctrine** – is less widely held than it once was. Furthermore, select committees have become much more assertive in their questioning of witnesses.

Select committees have the power to send for individuals and for papers, but the relationship between select committees and the government they are investigating is not always smooth. Although all governments will pledge cooperation with committees, in practice select committees can meet resistance when they try to question ministers, special advisers and civil servants. Cabinet Secretary Robert Armstrong, for example, and junior minister Edwina Currie were both extremely recalcitrant witnesses before select committees. Such conflicts are not perhaps typical: for the most part, government ministers and civil servants are happy to cooperate in explaining departmental policies. In an effort to improve his relationship with the House, Blair agreed in 2002 to appear before the Liaison Committee twice a year.

The impact of select committee reports is difficult to assess. In the past it was argued that too many of them were simply ignored, both by government and by the House of Commons itself. However, since 1999 the creation of a second separate debating chamber in the **Grand Committee** room off Westminster Hall means that more select committee reports can be debated, and indeed the Modernization Committee recommended that any report which had not received a government response within 60 days should be automatically put down for a short debate in Westminster Hall (see figure 6.5). But debates by themselves do not provide evidence of the influence of departmental select committees. What is telling is the extent to which these committees have become not merely an accepted element of Westminster's structures of scrutiny but an institutionalized component of its fabric and, in the eyes of many observers, the key to effective reform of Parliament.

Other Instruments of Parliamentary Scrutiny

Select committee activity is only one aspect of Parliament's traditional role as a watchdog over the executive. This role means that MPs and peers will try to expose broad errors of government policy, administrative failings and mistakes that have harmed individuals. The fact that Parliament is so dominated by party obviously constrains the airing of general grievances and the increasing complexity of the state makes it correspondingly difficult for MPs by themselves to investigate claims of **maladministration** in government. Nevertheless, the traditional procedures for scrutinizing government action may still be powerful instruments in the hands of an MP, and in some areas (notably through the National Audit Office and the Parliamentary Commissioner for Administration) there have been improvements and innovations in the machinery supporting parliamentary scrutiny.

Parliamentary questions

The most direct instrument that MPs can use to probe government policy is the parliamentary question. Three kinds of question can be put down for answer: an oral question, a written question and a private notice question. Oral questions are the most searching.

Grand Committees Committees of the House of Commons consisting of all MPs with constituencies in a defined area, sometimes supplemented by other members to make the composition of the House as a whole. A Scottish Grand Committee was set up in 1907, the Welsh Grand Committee in 1960 and the Northern Irish in 1994. During the period immediately prior to devolution, the Grand Committees were given powers to handle an extensive amount of parliamentary business affecting their area.

maladministration Term used especially in relation to the jurisdiction of the Parliamentary Commissioner for Administration or Ombudsman. It was defined in 1967 by government minister Richard Crossman as 'bias, neglect, inattention, delay, incompetence, ineptitude, perversity, turpitude, arbitrariness and so on', but later interpretations have broadened it. Essentially, the term refers to errors in the process of decision making rather than in the substance of policy.

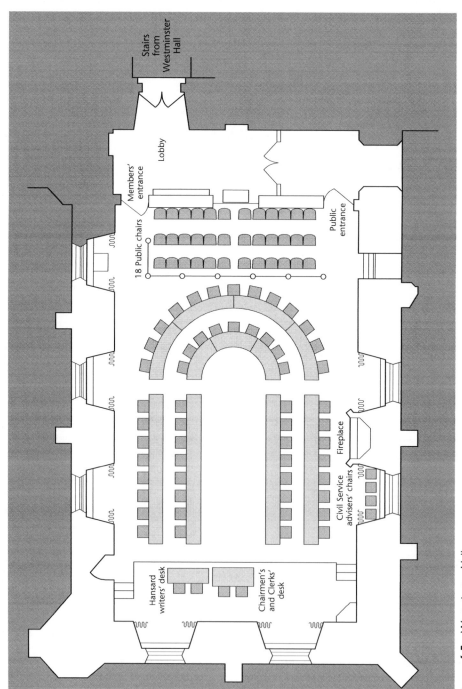

Figure 6.5 Westminster Hall.

Departmental spokespersons answer questions by rota. Long a part of the dramatic ritual of Parliament, question time acquired greater impact with the advent of television. An MP puts a question down by handing it into the Table Office; but because the question has to be put down in advance, the minister will have some opportunity to prepare an answer. However, the real test of a minister lies in his or her ability to answer supplementary questions which may be difficult to anticipate.

In addition to the questioning of departmental ministers there is each week on Wednesdays a half-hour slot for prime minister's questions (PMQs). This occasion (which was initiated in 1961) used to take place twice a week for 15 minutes on Tuesdays and Thursdays but was changed into a single half-hour slot by Blair in 1997. In theory the change was part of the more general modernization of the House of Commons and was designed to make PMQs more effective. In reality critics suspected Blair (not a natural parliamentary performer) of seeking to avoid the parliamentary jousting that question time entails. The fact that the change had been made without consultation reinforced the impression that it had little to do with improving the workings of Parliament. The result is generally seen as disappointing to those who value the opportunity PMQs offers for a high-profile clash between party leaders. Certainly, many journalists regarded the new arrangements as less exciting than the old ones; and from the perspective of the leader of the opposition, they reduced the opportunity to create good headlines by scoring hits against the prime minister. (The leader of the opposition is allowed three or four supplementary questions in succession in addition to his initial question, so that he has an extended opportunity to harry the prime minister.) The Liberal Democrat leader also is allowed a regular question.

Initially, the purpose of question time was to gain information or to press for action. In reality question time – especially PMQs – has become a central element of the party battle at Westminster. As a result, much of its forensic quality has been lost and the process, so far from being spontaneous, is manipulated by party managers and conducted in a raucous atmosphere. Question time has other weaknesses – not least the fact that coverage of the administration is patchy and not all questions will be reached in a given session. Some questions are blocked because they fall outside the remit of the department. Recent reforms have tried to give additional spontaneity by reducing the time needed for notice to raise a question from 10 days to three.

Written questions are a useful way of extracting information. Sometimes the answers are published; occasionally a minister writes to the MP who has asked the question and places the answer in the Library. Although questions are answered in the minister's name, the creation of executive agencies saw a change in the procedure for answering written questions. Ministers devolve replies to written questions to the chief executive of the agency and the reply is published in *Hansard*. Most replies, however, still come from ministers.

Other opportunities for debate exist. An MP may put down a private notice question. MPs may also sign **early day motions**, which although of no formal significance are useful mechanisms for conveying the opinion of backbenchers.

Hansard The official report of the proceedings in the House of Commons and the House of Lords. (Luke Hansard was a Commons printer who first published reports in 1812.)

early day motions Motions for debate put down by backbenchers in the House of Commons. There is no time allotted for the motions and their value is primarily as a way of expressing opinion on a controversial issue.

Parliament's Role in the Wider Political System

Parliament and the European Union

It has already been argued that British membership of the European Union has profound implications for Parliament's constitutional role. From the very beginning of the period of Britain's membership of the European Communities, it was evident that Parliament would have to develop special procedures and machinery to give it any ability even notionally to influence the European Community legislative process (described in further detail in chapter 15). Both the House of Commons and the House of Lords established committees designed to draw the attention of their respective Houses to European issues of major significance where it was thought crucial for Parliament to have an opportunity to express a view before the Commission took a decision. Parliament has passed resolutions stating that ministers should not agree to any proposal in the Council of Ministers unless Parliament has had an opportunity to debate it (this is known as the scrutiny reserve). The increasing volume of European legislation and the passage of the Single European Act in 1987 led Parliament to review its own procedures for scrutinizing European issues. In 1989 the Select Committee on Procedure issued a report that led to the establishment of two special standing committees in the House of Commons to monitor the flow of documents and legislative proposals from Europe. (The House of Lords, in contrast, from an early point established a much more specialized committee to monitor European policy.)

Several weaknesses in the system of scrutiny became apparent and demand for further reform became more vocal as the range and scale of European Union activity increased following Maastricht. In 1998 the Select Committee on the Modernization of the House of Commons issued a report on the scrutiny of European business and its recommendations were implemented later that year. Among its concrete recommendations were the passage of a new scrutiny reserve resolution, an increase in the number of standing committees to scrutinize European legislation and the establishment of a European Legislation Committee to scrutinize European documents. In addition, the Modernization Committee report recommended the development of better informal links between the British national Parliament and its members and the European Parliament and wanted to see individual select committees take a closer interest in the European dimension of their work.

The constituency dimension

What happens at Westminster is, of course, only one facet of the lives of Members of Parliament. MPs also have constituencies that they must represent. The relationship between an MP and his or her constituency is one which in turn has many aspects. Arguably, it has also become more demanding and important in recent years (Norton and Wood, 1995).

The tasks performed by any individual MP vary, but an MP will always be expected to champion the special interests of his or her community, be they farming or a particular industry. In addition, he or she will be expected to help constituents with any complaints they may have about public services or other problems, ranging from welfare to immigration. This aspect of an MP's duties means that MPs typically spend a substantial part of their working time answering their postbag, meeting constituents – usually in a regular surgery – and dealing with a heavy caseload of problems. During the 1960s it became apparent, however, that the facilities available to individual MPs for investigating complex cases were inadequate and reforms based on the Scandinavian ombudsmen system were introduced in 1967 when a Parliamentary Commissioner for Administration (PCA) was established. This reform was initially constrained by the requirement that members of the public who wanted to pursue a complaint had to refer it initially to their MP, who would if necessary refer it to the PCA. Although direct access to the PCA was frequently advocated, it was long resisted by MPs who feared an erosion of their role as champions of their constituents. Recently, however, there has been a significant shift in opinion in relation to both the organization and jurisdiction of the ombudsman and the role of MPs within the system (see chapter 14 for a more detailed discussion of the ombudsman's role). It now seems likely that there will soon be legislation to reconstitute the system of public sector ombudsmen and in the process allow direct access by the public. Whether this will significantly affect the caseload of MPs remains to be seen.

Parliament and the media

Any analysis of Parliament's role in the wider political system has to take into account its sensitive relationship with the media. The relationship is double-edged because, on the one hand, Parliament is often jealous of what it sees as media usurpation of its prerogatives – for example, by ministers unveiling policy initiatives on radio or television programmes before they have announced them in the House of Commons. On the other hand, MPs as politicians know the extent to which they rely on journalists to take their message to a wider public and understand the significance of the media's role in modern politics.

Until 1978 neither direct radio nor television broadcasting of parliamentary proceedings was permitted. In 1978 radio was allowed to broadcast debates, and television cameras were allowed first into the House of Lords and then into the House of Commons in 1989. In addition, there is now a dedicated Parliament channel on satellite television.

The impact of televising parliamentary proceedings was much debated at first – largely in terms of the extent to which it had altered the atmosphere of Parliament. Some thought that the introduction of television had created a new dynamic inside the House of Commons by shaping new opportunities for individual MPs to gain publicity and had made point scoring in debates more important. Increasingly, however, it became apparent that debates inside Parliament attracted very little attention, either from journalists or from the public. And in so far as the public did watch parliamentary proceedings, they were often unimpressed. Ministers, especially the prime minister, increasingly regard Whitehall, not Westminster, as the real hub of their political world and even

advocacy rule Rule which prevents MPs and peers from raising a subject in Parliament in which they have a material interest. It was formulated after the 1995 Nolan Report but builds on resolutions of the House of Commons that have been in place since the late nineteenth century.

backbench MPs are finding that much of the parliamentary action is occurring outside the chamber in committees. Newspapers and radio have cut back their detailed coverage of Parliament. (It is also worth asking whether the improvement in parliamentary office space has contributed to a dispersal of activity away from the chamber.) How to make itself interesting and relevant to the wider electorate thus remains a crucial problem for Parliament, one that is likely to be exacerbated by greater pluralism in the structure of the media.

Parliamentary ethics

In any parliamentary system delicate questions of political ethics and conflict of interest will arise. Until the 1990s MPs had maintained their regime of self-regulation, although a register of members' interests had been introduced in 1974. However, the 1990s witnessed the disclosure of numerous incidents of MPs taking cash for questions and of dubious relationships between MPs and lobbying firms. This spate of episodes led the government to establish the Committee on Standards in Public Life (the Nolan Committee), which issued a series of reports designed to change the culture of various public bodies, including Parliament, by promoting changes in the rules and standards to be applied.

New machinery for complaining about the conduct of an MP, the mechanisms for investigating an allegation and the process of adjudication have all been revised since 1994. A new register of interests was put in place to provide more information on MPs' outside earnings and associations. There is an **advocacy rule** which prevents MPs from initiating parliamentary proceedings on a matter in which they have an interest or from approaching members of the government on behalf of anyone with whom they have a financial relationship. A new Committee of Standards and Privileges was established in 1995, and in the same year an independent Parliamentary Commissioner for Standards was instituted with the power to investigate complaints. Once a complaint has been investigated, the Committee on Standards reaches a judgement and may apply a punishment, which can vary from a reprimand to a suspension. There is a degree of tension between the two bodies and one Commissioner (Elizabeth Filkin) found that her position was undermined by MPs who regarded her work as over-zealous.

Opinions differ as to how well the new, slightly more stringent regime is working. For some the system is still too informal and lacks enough independence to command support. For others, the new machinery is too cumbersome and out of proportion to the scale of the problem. Analysis by the Select Committee on Standards and Privileges in 2002/3 suggested that the regime needed to be more flexible. The most extensive problems in relation to MPs' behaviour now seem to stem not so much from their relationship with lobbyists as from their exploitation of the system of allowances.

Conclusions

The debate about how far Parliament has been marginalized in the British political system and what to do about it has been going on for a long time – at least since the 1950s. But recent developments in the British political system – especially devolution and the growing importance of the European Union – have given the debate a new urgency. Blair's government promised to address the issue, and certainly there has been an extensive raft of changes in the way the House of Commons does its business. However, any reform that strengthens Parliament inevitably makes life difficult for the executive, and it is hardly surprising that the modernization pro-gramme put forward for the House of Commons after 1997 has been seen by many observers as unimaginative and timid. That is probably inevitable, unless and until the majority of MPs decide they want to assert their powers against the executive. In the meantime, some of the reforms that have been introduced and some of the issues that have been raised may incrementally stimulate further thought about what role Parliament wishes to play in the twenty-first century.

 Key Questions

1 What are the chief weaknesses of the House of Commons as a legislative body?
2 What has been the impact of the Blair modernization agenda on the House of Commons?
3 What reforms might be suggested to improve the efficiency of the House of Commons?

 Further Reading

There are good general overviews in Andrew Adonis, *Parliament Today* (Manchester: Man-chester University Press, 1993); P. Norton, *Does Parliament Matter?* (London: Harvester Wheatsheaf, 1993); and P. Silk and R. Walters, *How Parliament Works* (4th edn; Harlow: Longman, 1998). R. Blackburn and A. Kennon (eds), *Griffith and Ryle on Parliament: Functions, Practice and Procedures* (London: Sweet and Maxwell, 2003) is an authoritative survey. Reference should also be made to the publications of the Hansard Society, including *Making the Law: Report of the Hansard Society Commission on the Legislative Process* (London: Hansard Society, 1992), and to N. Johnson, 'Opposition in the British political system', *Government and Opposition*, 32: 4 (1997).

The modernization debate is well covered in J. Seaton and B. K. Winetrobe, 'Modernising the Commons', *Political Quarterly*, 70: 2 (1999) and in P. Cowley and M. Stuart, 'Mostly continuity, but more change than you'd think', *Parliamentary Affairs*, 55: 2 (2002) as well as in P. Riddell, *Parliament Under Blair* (London: Politicos, 2000).

Executive scrutiny is addressed in a number of important works and pamphlets. Gavin Drewry, *The New Select Committees* (Oxford: Clarendon Press, 1989) is extremely thorough and insightful, as is P. Giddings, *Parliamentary Accountability: A Study of Parliament and Executive Agencies* (Basingstoke: Macmillan, 1995). The Hansard Society Commission on

Parliamentary Scrutiny's *The Challenge for Parliament: Making Government Accountable* (London: Hansard Society, 2001) argues the case for reform. The Norton Commission is also valuable in this respect. M. Flinders, 'Shifting the balance: Parliament, the executive and the British constitution', *Political Studies*, 50: 1 (2002) provides recent information on the effort to make Parliament more independent of the executive.

The House of Lords is covered in D. Shell, *The House of Lords at Work* (Oxford: Clarendon Press, 1993), which can be brought up to date with a number of articles, including V. Bogdanor, 'Reform of the House of Lords: A sceptical view', *Political Quarterly*, 70: 4 (1999); I. McLean, 'Mr Asquith's unfinished business', *Political Quarterly*, 70: 4 (1999); M. Russell, 'What are second chambers for?', *Parliamentary Affairs*, 54: 3 (2001); D. Shell, 'Labour and Lords reform', *Parliamentary Affairs*, 53: 2 (2000) and 'The future of the second chamber', *Political Quarterly*, 70: 4 (1999); D. E. Smith, 'A House for the future: Second chamber reform in the UK', *Government and Opposition*, 35: 3 (2000); and Lord Wakeham, 'The Lords: Building a House for the future', *Political Quarterly*, 71: 3 (2000).

Parliamentary ethics are examined in F. F. Ridley and A. Doig (eds), *Sleaze: Politicians, Private Interests and Public Reaction* (Oxford: Oxford University Press, 1995) and in M. Rush (ed.), *Parliament and Pressure Politics* (Oxford: Clarendon Press, 1990). A. Doig, 'Sleaze fatigue in the house of ill-repute', *Parliamentary Affairs*, 55: 2 (2002) and D. Woodhouse, 'The Parliamentary Commissioner for Standards: Lessons from the "Cash for Questions" Enquiry', *Parliamentary Affairs*, 51: 1. (1998) are useful for their discussion of the new machinery of regulation. *Standards in Public Life: First Report of the Committee on Standards in Public Life (the Nolan Committee)*, Cmnd 2850-1 (London: HMSO, 1995) is an essential starting point for understanding the new approach to regulating Parliament.

The relationship between MPs and their constituencies is well covered in Philip Norton and David Wood, *Back from Westminster* (Lexington: University of Kentucky Press, 1995), and also in Donald Searing, *Westminster's World: Understanding MPs' Roles* (Cambridge, MA: Harvard University Press, 1994).

Parliament's relationship with the media is explored in S. Coleman, *Electronic Media, Parliament and the People: Making Democracy Visible* (London: Hansard Society, 2000) and in S. Coleman, J. Taylor and W. Van De Donk, *Parliament in the Age of the Internet* (Oxford: Oxford University Press, 1999). Paul Flynn, *Commons Knowledge: How to be a Backbencher* (Bridgend: Seren, 1997) provides an irreverent and witty interpretation of the reality of life in the House of Commons.

 Websites

See also the list of general websites at the back of the book.

- www.parliament.uk – Parliament
- www.explore.parliament.uk – Explore Parliament
- www.parliament.uk/commons/lib/fact.htm – Parliamentary Information Office, factsheets on the parliamentary system
- www.parliament.uk/parliament/edunit.htm – Parliamentary Education Unit
- www.hmso.gov.uk/acts.htm – Acts of Parliament
- www.publications.parliament.uk/pa/ld/ldreg.htm – Register of Lords' Interests

- www.parliament.the-stationery-office.co.uk/pa/cm200203/cmregmem/ memi02.htm – Register of Members' Interests
- www.public-standards.gov.uk – Committee on Standards in Public Life
- www.hansard-society.org.uk – Hansard Society

7 The Electoral System

Democratic government necessarily involves competitive elections. The way those elections are conducted powerfully affects the quality of a polity's civic culture and the effectiveness of its system of representative government. The level of participation in the democratic process may be affected by a number of factors, including the political awareness and interest of the electorate, the ideological distance between the parties and voters' belief in their ability to affect the result. Participation in the electoral process may also be affected by mechanical factors related to the administrative methods used for elections and how easy or difficult those methods make the process of voting. This chapter examines the UK's electoral system and assesses its impact on the wider pattern of political participation and party competition. It raises such questions as how far the electoral system encourages or discourages participation and to what extent it provides a level playing field between the different parties. This discussion will focus both on the machinery of electoral administration – the seemingly dry but nonetheless crucial institutions and rules covering such issues as electoral registration, constituency redistribution and campaign spending – and on the constitutionally controversial question of the existing method of translating votes into seats – the so-called simple plurality system or first past the post (FPTP).

Two general points should be made before moving to the more detailed analysis of the British electoral system. First, although it is relatively easy to identify the general criteria by which an electoral system should be judged, the variety of electoral practice even among advanced democracies shows that there is no consensus about how to translate these values into practice. Different political systems have produced enormous variation in the detail of their electoral laws and their own distinctive formulas for creating a good electoral system. Such central questions as who should have the right to vote, whether voting should be compulsory, whether the state should take responsibility for the electoral register, and how far the state should regulate the campaigning and party-funding processes receive very different answers in otherwise comparable democracies.

Similarly, while many democracies use a form of proportional representation to translate the votes cast by electors into seats, there are various electoral formulae in use in modern democracies across the world. These reflect different political traditions and different preferences about representation.

Secondly, although we speak of the UK's electoral 'system', we should more properly be speaking of electoral 'systems'. There are now several different electoral systems operating within the confines of the United Kingdom itself, largely as a result of the various constitutional reforms introduced since 1997 (see box 7.1).

Box 7.1   Different electoral systems in the UK

First past the post (Westminster elections, local elections)

The candidate receiving the highest number of votes in a constituency is elected. There is no requirement to obtain a majority over all the other candidates combined, or to obtain a given proportion of the total vote; the successful candidate must simply obtain more votes than the next placed candidates. (The system is sometimes also referred to as a simple plurality system.)

Additional member system (Scottish Parliament, Welsh Assembly, Greater London Assembly)

Under this system, some proportion of the seats in the legislature are single-member constituency seats, directly elected on a first past the post basis; the remaining seats are allocated to parties on a regional list basis so as to achieve as nearly as possible a proportional result overall. The individual elector has two votes, one for the candidate and one for the party. It is the latter which counts in determining the overall representation, since individual constituency results are then topped up by members from respective party lists in proportion to the number required to ensure overall proportional representation. In London, there is a threshold requirement of 5 per cent of the votes for parties to obtain 'additional member' list representation. This system may also be referred to as 'mixed member system'.

Supplementary vote (London mayor)

Under this system, instead of voting for one candidate in a single-member constituency, the voter lists his or her first and second preferences between candidates. Any candidate securing 50 per cent of first preferences is elected. If no candidate does so, then all but the first two candidates are eliminated. Second preferences for the remaining candidates are then added to their first preference votes; and the candidate with the most votes is elected. This system is a variant of the alternative vote system, in which voters list all candidates in order of preference rather than being restricted to two. As under the supplementary vote, the lowest-placed candidate drops out and his or her second preferences are transferred to the remaining candidates. This process continues until one candidate achieves an overall majority.

Single transferable vote (Northern Irish Assembly)

This requires multi-member constituencies. The system and methods of calculation involved are complex; but, put simply, voters have to list candidates in order of preference, and a candidate must reach a quota in order to be elected; any votes for that candidate in 'excess' of the quota are redistributed according to second preferences. If no candidate reaches the quota, the lowest-placed candidate then drops out and his or her second preferences are transferred. This process continues down the order until the required number of candidates has been elected – bringing in third, fourth and possibly even fifth preferences, if necessary. The more seats per constituency, the more proportional the overall result is likely to be.

(Continues)

Box 7.1   *Continued*

List system (European Parliament)

These systems involve large multi-member constituencies (or regions), in which the elector votes not for an individual candidate but for a party list of candidates. Seats in the constituencies are divided between the parties, according to the proportion of the vote each has gained in the constituency. The seats are allocated to individuals according to their position on the party list. For European parliamentary elections, a closed system is used, meaning that voters are not able to alter the position of individuals on the list. Alternative variants of the list system use an open list, which allows voters to vote for individuals rather than for blocs of parties.

Source: Adapted from *The Plant Report*, Appendix 2.

Thus in addition to the use of the FPTP system for Westminster and local government elections, the UK has the alternative member system (AMS, sometimes called mixed member system) for the Scottish Parliament and Welsh Assembly elections as well as for the Greater London Assembly. The London mayor is elected by the supplementary vote (SV) method. Direct elections to the European Parliament now use a system of proportional representation based on a closed party list, except in Northern Ireland, which elects its three members of the European Parliament by the single transferable vote (STV). The need for cross-community consensus in Northern Ireland means that the STV has been adopted for the Northern Ireland Assembly and local elections. STV ensures that minority opinion will be represented. (Northern Ireland election law differs in many respects from that of the mainland, so that, for example, there are stricter residency requirements before a voter can get onto the electoral register.)

In addition to these varied electoral systems, it should be noted that the United Kingdom has now gained experience of referendums at the national, regional and local levels on such topics as membership of the European Community, devolution and the decision to have directly elected mayors. The government's decision to create optional regional assemblies for England necessitated legislation in 2003 to allow consultations and referendums on the subject.

Debate about the desirability of further electoral reform continues not just in relation to Westminster but also in relation to local government, where concern about modernizing and reviving local democracy has led to important changes in the machinery of electoral administration and to significant amendments to the rules governing election funding and campaign expenditure, as well as to pressure for proportional representation.

Speaker's Conference All-party conference called to discuss matters which it is thought should be handled in a non-partisan way. Such conferences have frequently been used to deal with issues of electoral reform. The advent of the Electoral Commission in 2000 may make them less necessary.

Discontent with aspects of the electoral system – including the FPTP method of translating votes into seats – is not of course new. In fact, it has been on the political agenda for much of the period since the late nineteenth century (Butler, 1963; Hart, 1992). At several points the existing system came very close to being changed. Indeed, in 1917 an all-party **Speaker's Conference** unanimously recommended a switch from FPTP, and in 1931 a bill to introduce the alternative vote (AV) was passed through the House of Commons but was rejected by the House of Lords.

Given the inevitable relationship between party advantage and the electoral system, debates about electoral reform can never wholly revolve around such abstract issues as electoral fairness or the most effective system of securing representation or accountability. The choice of electoral system cuts to the heart of party self-interest. Not surprisingly, therefore, the minor parties such as the Liberal Democrats have been most in favour of reform. The Conservatives have most consistently opposed it, although they may need to reconsider that opposition if their support slips further. Although the movement for electoral reform gained political salience in the 1990s, Labour was deeply divided over the issue. Despite a promise in its 1997 manifesto for a referendum on electoral reform, Blair side-stepped the question, setting up the Jenkins Commission as a way of buying time (see chapter 2). Furthermore, the Jenkins Commission, which recommended a switch to a mixed system known as 'AV plus', was ignored.

Experience of the impact of a different system in Wales and in Scotland has, if anything, made the local Labour parties deeply suspicious of it, since it so clearly strengthens third parties at Labour's expense. At present, enemies of electoral reform, including such powerful figures as John Prescott, almost certainly outnumber its advocates in the Labour Party. Thus, although the last decade has seen a good deal of debate swirling around the British electoral system as well as a number of important innovations, the familiar FPTP system retains support where it most matters – with the major parties.

The Evolution of the Electoral System

The United Kingdom's electoral system was not rationally planned or comprehensively designed. It evolved slowly as changes occurred in political values, as abuses generated demands for reform, and as partisan governments seized the opportunity to adjust the electoral machinery in ways they thought would favour them (see box 7.2 for a list of major changes since 1832). The extension of the **franchise**, the introduction of the secret ballot in 1872, the setting up of regular machinery for constituency redistribution, and the development of rules governing campaign spending and broadcasting all occurred incrementally. Given the ad hoc character of reform, rules governing the British electoral system have to be gleaned from a range of statutes and common law precedents. Inevitably, the system displayed anomalies and in many respects failed to keep pace with the reality of modern methods of campaigning and increasingly competitive elections. The whole area of party funding and campaign spending, for example, was governed by rules which, until the passage of new legislation in 2000, controlled constituency expenditure but not the hugely more extensive spending by the national parties.

Until the 1990s the administration of the electoral system was relatively uncontroversial, although much of the detail dated from 1918 and was widely seen as in need of overhaul. The administration of the rules governing registration provoked little discussion and there was limited scope for corruption or electoral malpractice. During the 1990s, however, a series of interrelated concerns about electoral administration surfaced, prompting a reconsideration of

franchise The right to vote. The franchise was gradually extended throughout the nineteenth and twentieth centuries, and by 1969 all those aged over 18, with a few exceptions, had the right to vote.

Box 7.2   Major changes to the British electoral system since 1832

1832	Representation of the People Act (known as the First Reform Act): Modest reform of electoral law, extension of the franchise and redistribution of seats.
1867	Representation of the People Act (sometimes known as the Second Reform Act): Extension of the franchise and redistribution of seats.
1868	Parliamentary Elections Act: Removed the trial of election petitions from a House of Commons committee to the courts.
1872	Ballot Act: Introduced voting by secret ballot.
1883	Corrupt and Illegal Practices Prevention Act: Placed a maximum limit on election expenses incurred by candidates.
1884	Representation of the People Act (sometimes called the Third Reform Act): Extension of the franchise and redistribution of seats.
1918	Representation of the People Act: Abolition of property qualifications for voting gave universal male suffrage. Women enfranchised at the age of 30 and over. Charges of returning officers no longer to be paid by candidates. All polls at general elections to be held on the same day. Postal and proxy voting introduced for servicemen. Candidates required to lodge £150 deposit on nomination, which was forfeited if they failed to poll more than one-eighth of the total votes cast. Candidates entitled to free postage on their election addresses or leaflets. Redistribution of seats.
1922	Irish Free State (Agreement) Act: No further writs to be issued for constituencies in Ireland other than Northern Ireland.
1924	First use of radio for broadcasts by the party leaders during a general election campaign.
1926	Re-election of Ministers Act (1919) Amendment Act: Removed the necessity for ministers of the Crown to seek re-election on accepting office.
1928	Representation of the People (Equal Franchise) Act: Women enfranchised at age 21 and over. Male and female suffrage achieved.
1948	Representation of the People Act: All plural voting and university constituencies abolished. Extension of postal voting to civilians. Limit on the number of cars which candidates could use on polling day. Redistribution of seats.
1949	Electoral Registers Act: Persons coming of age between November and June each year to be included in the electoral register, marked by the symbol 'Y' and eligible to vote at any election from October onwards.
1951	First use of television for broadcasts by the party leaders during the general election campaign.
1958	Representation of the People (Amendment) Act: Removal of the restriction on the number of cars which candidates could use on polling day.
1963	Peerage Act: Peers allowed to disclaim peerages for life and thus become eligible for membership of the House of Commons.
1969	Representation of the People Act: Extension of the franchise to persons at age 18 and over. Close of poll extended from 9.00 p.m. to 10.00 p.m.
1981	Representation of the People Act: Disqualified convicted persons serving sentences of more than 12 months from nomination to or membership of the House of Commons.

(Continues)

Box 7.2 *Continued*

1985 Representation of the People Act: Extended the franchise to British citizens who are residents outside the UK to qualify as 'overseas electors' in the constituency for which they were last registered for a period of 5 years. Extended absent voting to holidaymakers and raised the deposit to £500 but reduced the threshold to one-twentieth of the total votes cast.

1992 Maastricht Treaty: Provides for equal voting rights for citizens of the European Union in country of residence regardless of nationality.

1998 Registration of Political Parties Act: Established a register of political parties. All parties wishing to contest elections must be listed on the register.

1999 European Parliamentary Elections Act: Enabled the 1999 and subsequent European parliamentary elections in Great Britain to be conducted using a regional list electoral system.

2000 Representation of the People Act: Changes electoral procedures in relation to electoral registration and absent voting and allows for experiments involving innovative electoral procedures.

2000 Political Parties, Elections and Referendums Act: Establishes the Electoral Commission. Requires registered parties to maintain accounts of their income and expenditure and to submit annual statements of accounts to the Electoral Commission. Applies restrictions on campaign expenditure incurred by political parties in respect of Westminster parliamentary elections, European parliamentary elections and elections to the devolved legislatures. Limits also placed on 'third-party' spending. Imposes restrictions on the sources of donations so as to prohibit foreign and anonymous donations to political parties.

Source: Adapted from Craig (1989), Appendix 2, p. 179 and other sources.

British practice. Declining turnout at successive general elections raised the question of whether the process of voting should be made easier, especially in relation to absentee and proxy voters, as well as deeper questions about political education and citizenship. Doubt was cast on whether local authorities were doing enough to maintain as accurate an electoral register as possible. Technological developments opened up new possibilities for making the whole system more efficient. Two enquiries (Chataway and Plant) argued the case for extensive changes to the system of electoral administration. Following the general election of 1997, a comprehensive review of electoral law was set in train by the Home Office, and the Home Affairs Select Committee also looked at the topic of electoral administration. As a result, significant alterations have been made to the way Britain handles the related issues of electoral registration, exclusion from the register and the methods of voting. Further innovations, especially at the local level, may be expected as pilot studies of reforms are encouraged by the Lord Chancellor's Department (LCD), which took over responsibility for substantial elements of electoral law from the Home Office in 2001. The LCD took over responsibility for policy relating to electoral administration from the former Department of Transport, Local Government and the Regions in 2002, and the new Department of Constitutional Affairs (DCA) has a division covering electoral issues. That division (within the Constitutional

Directorate of the DCA's Policy Group) works closely with the Office of the Deputy Prime Minister and the Office of the e-Envoy.

Three pieces of legislation – the Registration of Parties Act 1998, the Representation of the People Act 2000 and the Political Parties, Elections and Referendums Act 2000 – have together produced a much more comprehensive regulatory regime for elections and referendums. The need for a register of parties arose from the shift to the use of a party list system for European parliamentary elections. Until that point also the Conservative Party had no formal legal existence. The new registration requirements prevent the kind of confusion that could ensue from maverick candidates standing with a name very similar to that of another party. The most blatant example of this was a candidate – Richard Huggett – who stood as a Literal Democrat in the 1994 European elections and secured 10,203 votes in the process. After the 1998 legislation candidates who had not registered as a party had to stand as independents.

The Representation of the People Act (RPA) 2000 was a response to the widespread belief that new technology should make the process of voting easier. As such, the Act was an unusually comprehensive effort to modernize and reinvigorate the electoral process. Previous RPAs had generally made small or single amendments to the law. RPA 2000 (which followed a Home Office working party chaired by George Howarth) revised many elements of the machinery for administering elections – especially registration – and introduced some new devices designed to bolster turnout and participation. It sent a signal that further experiment at the local level with such tools as electronic counting and all-postal voting would be welcome.

The Political Parties, Elections and Referendums Act (PPERA) 2000 was similarly innovative and extremely wide-ranging. It has been described as the most radical legislation on election funding since the 1883 Corrupt and Illegal Practices Act (Fisher, 2002). PPERA followed widespread unease about the major parties' methods of raising money, and fear that their spending in elections had escalated into 'an arms race'. The legislation adopted much of the Neill Committee's approach to party funding, especially the need for stricter controls on donations (5th Report of the Committee on Standards in Public Life). The 1990s had seen extensive concern about the corrupting effects of escalating campaign costs which forced parties into an increasingly intense search for funding from private donors.

PPERA was significant not just for its attempt to get to grips with a range of issues that had been neglected for much of the twentieth century. It was highly important also because it introduced a new and independent body – the Electoral Commission – to monitor electoral administration. Such a body had been urged by the Jenkins Commission and the Neill Committee, as well as by other experts and academics, including the Hansard Society. Its establishment appears to be part of a growing trend to give greater autonomy to bodies regulating elections (Elkit and Reynolds, 2001). It has both supervisory and administrative powers and will cover such questions as boundary reviews, campaign spending, party fundraising and election broadcasts. The Commission at present consists of five members (only one of whom – the chair – is full time) and reports to a committee chaired by the Speaker. The Electoral Commission is now a major source of ideas and information about the British electoral system and a catalyst for electoral reform.

The Right to Vote

Although constitutional debate now focuses primarily on the merits of the FPTP system, what principally concerned nineteenth- and early twentieth-century reformers was the right to vote itself. Each successive change in the franchise was a matter of party controversy as well as a stimulus to debate about the foundations of the constitution. Walter Bagehot described the Second Reform Act of 1867 as the 'most silent of revolutions', but he realized that the expansion of the franchise had shifted power within the United Kingdom, moving the country closer to a mass democracy.

The right to vote in Britain was initially connected to property and was extended very slowly. Despite the successive reforms of the nineteenth century, only a small proportion of the population could vote before 1918. Compromise and tolerance of anomalies ensured that even when the principle of full adult male suffrage was implemented in 1918, vestiges of older theories of representation lingered on. Corporate or group representation in the House of Commons survived in the form of 12 university constituencies, four of which were multi-member seats elected by STV. These university seats survived until 1950 when, despite a contrary recommendation in 1944 by a unanimous all-party Speaker's Conference, they were abolished along with provisions for additional voting on the basis of occupation of business premises.

Women achieved the vote only in 1918. Even then the fear that they would be a numerical majority in the electorate induced Parliament to differentiate between the sexes over the voting age: men were given the vote at 21, but initially women had to wait until they were 30 for the right to vote. The Representation of the People Act of 1928 abolished this anomaly, but the change then was deeply divisive and many Conservative politicians wrongly thought that this so-called 'flapper vote' had lost them the general election of 1929.

The most recent alterations in the franchise have related to the voting age, to the rights of overseas residents and to voting rights of hereditary peers. In 1969 the voting age was lowered from 21 to 18, following the report of the Latey Committee on the Age of Majority and the passage of the Family Law Reform Act 1969. (A Speaker's Conference that had suggested lowering the age to 20 was ignored.) The fact that the change came at the end of a decade of student unrest was symbolically significant. Young people, like women half a century earlier, were incorporated into the political system. The extension of the vote to 18- to 21-year-olds may have been a contributory factor in decreasing the proportion of the electorate that actually votes, since young people have a greater tendency to be non-voters.

A different sort of change in the franchise occurred in 1985 when a Representation of the People Act gave British citizens living abroad the right to vote in parliamentary and European elections. Residence in a constituency is ordinarily a necessary condition for being able to vote, although a few exceptions have always been made, for example for voters in the services. This new provision (which benefited some 3 million overseas residents) was subject to criticism, not least because many of these expatriate voters had moved abroad to avoid British tax. Initially, the legislation limited this privilege to persons who had been living abroad for a period of up to 5 years. This privilege was extended to 20 years in 1989, a

disfranchisement Removal of the right to vote.

development which, while not opposed by the then Labour opposition frontbench, was heavily criticized on the Labour left because the expatriate vote was thought likely to benefit the Conservatives. In 2000 the passage of PPERA meant that the law was again changed to reduce to 15 years the length of time expatriates could live abroad but still retain their right to vote in UK elections (Child, 2001). In 2001, of the 44,545,654 on the register, 11,506 (or 0.03 per cent of the electorate) were overseas voters.

Members of the House of Lords may not vote in general elections. Hereditary peers (apart from the 92 members of the peerage elected to the transitional House) who until recently could not vote at general elections because they had direct representation in the House of Lords were given the right to vote in parliamentary elections when their automatic right to sit in the Lords was removed in 1999.

Some people are excluded from voting in the United Kingdom. Convicts serving a prison sentence may not vote, although prisoners held on remand, given non-custodial sentences or imprisoned for contempt of court are not thereby **disfranchised**. Persons who are convicted of corrupt or illegal electoral practices in the United Kingdom are disfranchised for a period of 5 years, although in the case of illegal practices (which are effectively technical breaches of election law, as opposed to the more serious corrupt practices), disfranchisement relates only to the constituency in which the offence occurred.

Disfranchisement also applied until 1982 to all persons in a mental hospital, but disquiet arose when it became evident that some 50,000 voluntary patients in mental hospitals and psychiatric clinics were deprived of the vote. In 1982 the Mental Health (Amendment) Act provided a mechanism by which voluntary patients could vote. Involuntary patients held in mental hospitals are not eligible to vote.

Aliens may not vote. Who counts as an alien is, however, peculiarly defined in the United Kingdom. Eligibility to vote in British elections still reflects Britain's imperial past in that it is exercised by all British subjects and citizens of other Commonwealth countries resident in Britain as defined under the British Nationality Act of 1981. This Act was specifically declared not to affect the question of voting rights. There are about 1.5 million Commonwealth subjects entitled to vote in the UK (Blackburn, 1995). Another legacy of Britain's imperial past is that citizens of the Republic of Ireland who live in Britain (about 400,000) can vote at all elections. This right is based on section 32 (1) of the British Nationality Act of 1948, which states that Irish citizens are not aliens. Part of the reason for retaining this arrangement for Irish citizens was the extensive freedom of movement between Britain and Ireland.

The extension of freedom of movement within the European Union has also brought reciprocal voting rights. Since the 1992 Maastricht Treaty citizens of all EU countries have had the right to vote at local and European elections in their country of residence.

Under the European Parliamentary Elections Act 1999, the right to vote in a European Parliament election is one that the European Court on Human Rights has said must be extended to 17,000 citizens of Gibraltar. As a result of that ruling, the British government in 2001 enfranchised Gibraltarian electors for European elections, making it part of a combined region.

To summarize, the right to vote in the United Kingdom at parliamentary elections may be exercised by anyone who is a British, Commonwealth or Irish citizen who is resident in a constituency and whose name is on the electoral register. Generous provision is made for overseas voters who live abroad, but members of the House of Lords (which now for the most part means life peers) may not vote at parliamentary elections.

Registration

The role of the electoral register is crucial to the electoral process, as it is necessary to be on the electoral register to vote. Since 1918, compiling the register had been the responsibility of local authorities, whose electoral registration officers (EROs) supervise all aspects of the system. This process was traditionally based on annual October house-to-house canvassing to create a list of those entitled to vote. In Britain, while voting is not compulsory, there is a legal obligation on the householder to submit a return for registration purposes and the process is publicly funded and managed (the annual cost of maintaining the register in 1997 was £50 million). As the Houghton Committee on financial aid to political parties recognized in 1976, this is an enormous advantage for parties, who do not have to spend money themselves on the process of registering their supporters.

By 1997 it had become increasingly anomalous in a highly mobile society to construct a register on an annual basis. It is estimated that an annual register has an initial 8 per cent inaccuracy (Ballinger, 2002). RPA 2000 (which came into effect in 2001) introduced a rolling register, which means that people can register voluntarily or change their details at any time of the year. The register is updated monthly. The 2000 legislation also attempted to solve the problem of homeless people and others without a settled residence who were among the groups least likely to be registered. By introducing the concept of a notional residence, it enabled them to register if they could show a strong link with a locality.

One change that may occur in the near future as the result of the increase in postal voting and the fear of fraud is the move from household registration (where the head of the household fills in a form for all its members) to individual registration, which can be backed by better methods of validating the identity of voters. It is also anticipated that there might be a national electronic register rather than a local database (Electoral Commission, 2003).

The Voting Process

Several aspects of the traditional electoral system were criticized in the 1990s because of the extent to which they appeared to make voting more difficult than it need be. Accordingly, the Labour government's review of election law recommended that the government should have greater flexibility to experiment with the voting process itself. Thus it wanted to see pilot studies done of such reforms as electronic voting, extended voting hours, early voting and mobile voting (see box 7.3).

Box 7.3   New ways of voting

Pilot schemes introduced following RPA 2000:

All-postal ballots
Longer voting hours
Weekend voting
Mobile polling booths
Voting in supermarkets or post offices
Online voting
Text messaging
Touch-screen voting

One reform, which was introduced in time for the 2001 elections, concerns access to a postal or proxy vote. Until RPA 2000, anything other than voting in person was difficult and in 1997 a mere 2.3 per cent of the total vote was cast by post (House of Commons Research Paper 01/37). RPA 2000 made the process of obtaining a postal or proxy vote much easier. Now a postal vote can be obtained on demand without giving a reason. In 2001 the number of postal votes was significantly up on the two previous elections and represented 5.3 per cent of all voters (Ballinger, 2002). The problem with extensive postal voting is that it can make fraud easier. The 2001 general election was the first held under the new regime put in place by RPA 2000 and PPERA 2002. The unusually low turnout at that election (59.4 per cent) suggested that, while improvements in the methods of registration and voting might be desirable (see box 7.4), they would not by themselves produce greater voter participation. However, all-postal voting seems likely to become increasingly popular for local elections. In 2003 it was suggested that the government was considering it for European elections, although the Electoral Commission in fact decided not to proceed with this initiative.

The Constituencies

Voting at parliamentary (Westminster) elections in the United Kingdom is now done entirely through single-member constituencies. Many defenders of the FPTP system see the unique link between a geographically well-defined constituency and its MP as one of the great merits of Britain's electoral machinery. The introduction of multi-member and mixed systems has thrown up some evidence of changed patterns of interaction between representatives and their constituents (Lundberg, 2002). In the case of the Scottish Parliament, signs emerged of tension between MSPs elected in a constituency and ones elected from the list.

Nevertheless, the United Kingdom's attachment to the single-member constituency in national elections is not perhaps as established as is sometimes thought. Until 1885 double-member constituencies were the norm, and some of them survived until the general election of 1950. In part, some double-member constituencies were retained because cities were reluctant to see their separate identity disappear, even when the growth in population justified the creation of additional seats. What the

Box 7.4 Experiments to increase turnout in local government elections

	No. of councils	
	May 2002	May 2003
All-postal voting	14	33
E-voting and counting	13	5
Weekend voting/extended polling hours	2	3
Council-funded leaflets from each candidate	1	0
Watermark on ballot paper	0	2
Automated issue of postal ballots	0	1
Mobile voting	0	2
Internet voting and touch-tone telephone	0	9
Text messaging and digital TV	0	9

Source: Electoral Commission, http://www.electoralcommission.gov.uk/elections/
modernising.cfm

mystique of the constituency link underlines is the strength in the British tradition of thinking about representation of the territorial unit and the relative weakness of thinking about representation in terms of abstract formulae.

The British electoral system's remoteness from the idea of representation of individual voters may be traced back to the earliest Parliaments. These Parliaments were summonses from the monarch to representatives of the counties and the boroughs as well as to the peers of the realm to attend at Westminster; thus the idea of representing a town or a shire goes back to the Middle Ages. Democratic ideas about securing equal representation of individuals have, in a sense, been grafted onto these earlier approaches to representation.

The principle of equality of representation in the electoral process is now increasingly thought to demand that each constituency should, as far as possible, contain the same number of voters. In Britain this goal has not been applied rigidly and constituency size does vary considerably. Across the United Kingdom the largest constituency, the Isle of Wight, has 104,000 electors, while the smallest, the Western Isles, has 21,900 (Parliamentary Information Office, http://www.parliament.uk/works/elections.cfm#constits).

As with the arguments surrounding the simple plurality system, the problem of revising constituencies to create greater equality historically was approached in a spirit that tolerated anomalies and sought rough-and-ready fairness rather than attempting to impose electoral equality by slide rule. There was no permanent mechanism for redrawing constituency boundaries in the United Kingdom until 1944. In the nineteenth and early twentieth centuries, boundaries were revised by Act of Parliament following each extension of the franchise. These redistributions of seats in 1832, 1868, 1885 and 1918 sought to bring parliamentary representation more into line with the reality of Britain's population and to eliminate the worst anomalies. (Criticism of the pre-1832 system had highlighted the fact that that system gave parliamentary representation to depopulated ancient boroughs while denying any representation to the new centres of population created by the industrial revolution.) In 1944 the House of Commons (Redistribution of Seats) Act, which followed a Speaker's Conference, established four Boundary Commissions, one each for England, Scotland, Wales and Northern Ireland. These Commissions are now constituted under the Parliamentary Constituencies Act of 1986 as amended by the Boundary Commissions Act of 1992. Responsibility for boundary reviews is now being transferred to the Electoral Commission.

In order to determine how many electors an average constituency should have, the number of seats available for the area is divided into the population on the electoral register at the start of a boundary review. The process of conducting and implementing a comprehensive review of constituency boundaries was always slow. It was also intensely partisan. At the local level, it frequently involved local inquiries as the various parties tried to defend or attack proposals on the basis of their own interests. At the national level, the parties would inevitably try to calculate how far the process would aid their cause and might intervene to delay or promote redistribution. Thus in 1969 the then Labour government refused to implement boundary recommendations – a move which meant that the general election of 1970 was fought on boundaries that had not been changed since 1954. After the 1992 general election the then Conservative government (anticipating that a review would aid its cause) devoted extra resources to help the Boundary Commission complete its work prior to the next general election.

Redistributions are not popular with MPs or political parties. An MP may find that his or her constituency is transformed by boundary changes or even written out of existence. Political parties are organized around constituencies at the local level and may have to reconstitute themselves after a boundary review. Not all reviews are equally wide-ranging, but the one that occurred just before the 1983 general election left only a small number of constituencies unchanged.

Both Scotland and Wales are currently over-represented in proportion to population. This over-representation can be traced to the 1944 Redistribution Act, which not only created four separate Boundary Commissions, rather than one single one, for the whole of the UK, but also set a minimum number of seats for Scotland and Wales. Scotland could not under this provision fall below 71 seats and Wales could not have fewer than 35 seats. The increase in population in England has therefore been coped with by adding extra seats for England rather than redistributing seats – a process that has led to the House of Commons becoming ever larger.

Although this situation was criticized prior to 1997, it became especially contentious after the Government of Scotland Act 1998 gave Scotland its own Parliament but retained the same level of Scottish representation at Westminster. The Scotland Act itself required the Boundary Commission to disregard the 1944 statutory minimum requirement in the next boundary review, thereby opening the way to a reduction in the number of Scottish seats. In 2002 the Boundary Commission provisionally recommended that the number of Scottish seats at Westminster be cut from 72 to 59. This change will not occur, however, until the next general boundary review in 2005. Although it was originally envisaged that the number of seats in the Edinburgh Parliament would also be reduced, it was announced in 2003 that the Scottish Parliament seats would stay the same at 129.

The Timing of Elections

A general election can be called at any date of the prime minister's choosing subject to the statutory framework of a maximum five-year Parliament. For many critics this degree of discretion puts too much power into the hands of the governing party, which may call an election at a moment most favourable to itself or even engineer a pre-election boom to produce a climate conducive to re-election. Certainly, some European countries (such as Norway and Switzerland) have fixed-term Parliaments; and legislative terms are fixed in the United States. On the other hand, fixed-term legislatures do suffer from some disadvantages. They can be inflexible because they preclude the ability to seek a fresh **mandate** in a crisis situation, such as occurred when Edward Heath (unsuccessfully as it turned out) sought electoral endorsement in his fight with the miners in February 1974. Fixed-term Parliaments could also force an executive to continue in office despite the loss of legislative support.

By contrast with general elections, European Parliament elections, local elections and elections to the Scottish Parliament and Welsh Assembly are fixed by statute. European Parliament elections take place every five years. Elections to the Scottish Parliament and Welsh Assembly take place every four years. Elections to local authorities vary with the type of authority, so that some councils – notably the English counties – are elected as a whole for a four-year term while the English unitary authorities are elected in staggered elections, one-third at a time, with each third serving for four years. Although it is rare for the government to alter the dates of fixed elections in peacetime, in 2001 the outbreak of foot and mouth disease caused the government to postpone the local elections due to take place in May and to hold them instead in June, on the same day as a general election. In wartime the executive has enormous discretion about whether to postpone general and local elections. No general election was held in Britain between 1935 and 1945 because of the outbreak of war in 1939, and in 1939 all local elections were suspended for the duration of the war by legislation which had to be renewed annually.

By-elections

Some parliamentary seats fall vacant between general elections as a result of the death or resignation of the sitting MP. Under the British system, these vacancies are filled by holding special elections, or by-elections, to fill the seat. By-elections differ from general elections in a number of important ways. First, the unique circumstances of a by-election may witness very different voting patterns from the previous general election. Lower turnout, protest voting, local personality and local issues all shape by-elections in a way that does not occur at national elections. Many of the seats currently held by the Liberal Democrats were first won at by-elections. Secondly, intense concentration of publicity may

mandate Endorsement of a party's policy platform gained through electoral success. Winning parties usually claim a mandate to govern, even though voters may not be well informed about their specific policy proposals.

encourage candidates with a particular agenda to stand, as well as an assortment of protest candidates and parties. The by-elections held between 1997 and 2001 saw several party splinter groups (such as Pro-Euro Conservatives) putting themselves forward as well as candidates representing the Pro-Life Alliance and the Legalize Cannabis Alliance. At the Kensington and Chelsea by-election of 25 November 1999 (which enabled Michael Portillo to return to Parliament), 15 other candidates stood and achieved together 12.2 per cent of the vote. Thirdly, by-elections may be interpreted as indicative of general – national – political opinion.

By comparison with the Major government of 1992–7, whose already small majority was eroded through by-election defeats, the Blair government of 1997–2001 did not lose a single seat in 17 by-elections held in the period. It is necessary to go back to the 1951–5 government to find a party in office faring so well. Indeed, in only two of the 1997–2001 by-elections did a seat change hands. In Romsey the Liberal Democrats took the seat from the Conservatives after the death of the MP, and in South Antrim the Democratic Unionist Party (DUP) took the seat from the Ulster Unionists (UUP) (see table 7.1).

National and Local Dimensions of Elections

The contest at a general election has both national and local dimensions. Increasingly, general elections are seen as a national contest between the political parties rather than as a local race in the constituencies, although the intensity of campaigning at the local level as well as local factors can have a major impact on the results. Because marginal seats are likely to be the most important in determining an outcome, the campaign will be concentrated there. Certainly, Blair in 1997 focused Labour's strategy on a series of target seats that might change hands rather than on safe or hopeless constituencies for the party.

The 2001 general election underlined the extent to which electoral contests had everywhere become at least three-party races where **tactical voting** might make a difference. Although the strategic considerations in each constituency are distinct, the trend has been for campaigns increasingly to be set from the centre. In contrast to the position in the United States and France, local issues play only a limited part in UK general election campaigns. However, the pattern of politics in Scotland and Wales is becoming more differentiated from that of England. Northern Ireland's politics revolve around a completely different set of issues from those on the mainland (see chapter 12).

tactical voting Voting in which the elector casts his or her vote in a way which does not reflect his or her preferred option but which takes into account the candidates' relative strength. Thus a Labour supporter in a seat where the Liberal Democrats were the most effective challenger to the Conservatives might vote tactically for the Liberal Democrats.

National issues usually predominate in the candidates' election addresses, although in 2001, Wyre Forest elected an independent campaigning on a highly local issue – hospital closure. In England at least, the geographical origins of a candidate are relatively unimportant. Candidates do not, for example, have to fulfil any formal residence requirements, although they will have to comply with the informal pressures and expectations generated by party activists and voters about having a home in the constituency. Equally, if a constituency does have distinctive characteristics – if, for example, fishing or farming play a significant role – then

Table 7.1 By-elections in the 1992–7 and 1997–2001 Parliaments

Constituency	Reason for by-election	Date of election	Result	New member
Newbury	Death (Judith Chaplin)	6 May 1993	Lib Dem gain from Con	D. Rendel
Christchurch	Death (Robert Adley)	29 Jul 1993	Lib Dem gain from Con	D. Maddock
Rotherham	Death (Jimmy Boyce)	5 May 1994	Lab hold	D. MacShane
Barking	Death (Jo Richardson)	9 Jun 1994	Lab hold	M. Hodge
Bradford South	Death (Bob Cryer)	9 Jun 1994	Lab hold	G. Sutcliffe
Dagenham	Resignation (Bryan Gould)	9 Jun 1994	Lab hold	J. Church
Eastleigh	Death (Stephen Milligan)	9 Jun 1994	Lib Dem gain from Con	D. Chidgey
Newham North East	Death (Ron Leighton)	9 Jun 1994	Lab hold	S. Timms
Monklands East	Death (John Smith)	30 Jun 1994	Lab hold	H. Liddell
Dudley West	Death (Dr John Blackburn)	15 Dec 1994	Lab gain from Con	I. Pearson
Islwyn	Resignation (Neil Kinnock)	16 Feb 1995	Lab hold	D. Touhig
Perth & Kinross	Death (Sir Nicholas Fairbairn)	25 May 1995	SNP gain from Con	R. Cunningham
North Down	Death (Sir James Kilfedder)	15 June 1995	UKU gain from UUP	R. McCartney
Littleborough and Saddleworth	Death (Geoffrey Dickens)	27 Jul 1995	Lib Dem gain from Con	C. Davies
Hemsworth	Death (Derek Enright)	1 Feb 1996	Lab hold	J. Trickett
Staffordshire S.E.	Death (Sir David Lightbown)	11 Apr 1996	Lab gain from Con	B. Jenkins
Barnsley East	Death (Terry Patchett)	12 Dec 1996	Lab hold	J. Ennis
Wirral South	Death (Barry Porter)	27 Feb 1997	Lab gain from Con	B. Chapman
Uxbridge	Death (Sir Michael Shersby)	31 Jul 1997	Con hold	J. Randall
Paisley South	Death (Gordon McMaster)	6 Nov 1997	Lab hold	D. Alexander

(Continues)

Table 7.1 (Continued)

Constituency	Reason for by-election	Date of election	Result	New member
Beckenham	Resignation (Piers Merchant)	20 Nov 1997	Con hold	J. Lait
Winchester	General election result challenged	20 Nov 1997	Lib Dem win	M. Oaten
Leeds Central	Death (Derek Fatchett)	10 Jun 1999	Lab hold	H. Benn
Eddisbury	Resignation (Sir Alastair Goodlad)	22 Jul 1999	Con hold	S. O'Brien
Hamilton South	Elevation to peerage of George Robertson	23 Sep 1999	Lab hold	B. Tynan
Wigan	Death (Roger Stott)	23 Sep 1999	Lab hold	N. Turner
Kensington and Chelsea	Death (Alan Clark)	25 Nov 1999	Con hold	M. Portillo
Ceredigion	Resignation (Cynog Dafis)	3 Feb 2000	PC hold	S. Thomas
Romsey	Death (Sir Michael Colvin)	4 May 2000	Lib Dem gain from Con	S. Gidley
Tottenham	Death (Bernie Grant)	22 Jun 2000	Lab hold	D. Lammy
South Antrim	Death (Clifford Forsythe)	21 Sep 2000	DUP gain from UUP	W. McCrea
Glasgow, Anniesland	Death (Donald Dewar)	23 Nov 2000	Lab hold	J. Robertson
Preston	Death (Audrey Wise)	23 Nov 2000	Lab hold	M. Hendrick
West Bromwich West	Resignation (Betty Boothroyd)	23 Nov 2000	Lab gain from Oth	A. Bayley
Falkirk West	Resignation (Dennis Canavan)	21 Dec 2000	Lab hold	E. Joyce
Ipswich	Death (James Cann)	22 Nov 2001	Lab hold	C. Mole
Mid Glamorgan, Ogmore	Death (Sir Raymond Powell)	14 Feb 2002	Lab hold	H. Irranca-Davies
Brent East	Death (Paul Daisley)	18 Sep 2003	Lib Dem gain from Lab	S. Teather

Con Conservative; Lab Labour; Lib Dem Liberal Democrat; SNP Scottish National Party; PC Plaid Cymru; DUP Democratic Unionist Party; UKU United Kingdom Unionist Party; UUP Ulster Unionist Party; Oth Other

candidates will be well advised to familiarize themselves with these policy areas. Often the constituency for which a candidate stands will be the product of chance – or parachuting – rather than because there are any local links or matching of interests between the area and the would-be MP. Thus Shaun Woodward, formerly Conservative MP for Witney, was found a safe Labour seat in St Helens when he defected to New Labour before the 2001 election.

Parties normally will have chosen their candidates well in advance of the election and will hope to have a well-oiled machine ready to swing into action as soon as the date of the poll is announced. (The selection of candidates is discussed in chapter 8.) Once a candidate has been chosen by a party, he or she must be formally nominated by 10 electors and pay a deposit, which was set at £500 by the Representation of the People Act of 1985. The deposit is returned if the candidate gets 5 per cent of the votes cast. (The size of the deposit is larger at European elections – £5,000 for each list per constituency – and is returned if the party gets one-fortieth of the vote.) The obligation to furnish a deposit was introduced in 1918 and is meant to be a deterrent to frivolous candidates. How far it really serves this purpose is a moot point. For some smaller parties the prospect of losing a number of deposits may be discouraging. On the other hand, the amount spent on lost deposits may well be worth the gain in publicity, especially for a small party or pressure group such as the Green Party or the Right to Life Alliance. The number of lost deposits between 1918 and 2001 is shown in table 7.2.

The rules governing standing for Parliament are different from those that govern taking up the seat. Certain categories of person are banned from sitting in the House of Commons, notably people serving prison sentences or in detention under the Mental Health Act of 1959. (Bobby Sands was elected to Parliament in 1981 but could not take his seat because he was serving a prison sentence.)

It used to be the case that ordained clergy of the Church of England and Roman Catholic priests (including ex-priests) could not sit in the House of Commons, but recent legislation – the House of Commons (Removal of Clergy Disqualifications) Act 2001 – abolished the disqualification. This reform allowed David Cairns, a former Roman Catholic priest, to take his seat as MP for Greenock. Bishops may not sit in the House of Commons because they are directly represented in the House of Lords. Until very recently, hereditary peers other than Irish peers could not sit in the Commons; but the 1999 reform of the House of Lords means that all but the representative 92 members of the hereditary peerage may sit in the House of Commons if elected, and one – Viscount Thurso – was elected in 2001.

The holders of certain offices of profit under the Crown are also debarred from sitting in the Commons. The House of Commons (Disqualification) Act of 1975 lists those offices that are deemed incompatible with membership of the House. Judges, serving members of the armed forces and civil servants are thus all precluded from being an MP. These restrictions were thought necessary to secure the independence from party politics of the profession concerned and to ensure that the House of Commons was not dominated by persons in the pay of the Crown. The goal of an independent House of Commons is now more obviously threatened by the so-called pay-roll vote, the large number of MPs on the government side who either hold paid office (as members of the government) or act as unpaid parliamentary private secretaries.

Table 7.2 Number of lost deposits, 1918–2001

Year	Con	Lab	Lib/Alliance	Other	Total	% of all candidates
1918	3	6	44	108	161	9.9
1922	1	7	31	13	52	3.6
1923	–	17	8	2	27	1.9
1924	1	28	30	9	68	4.7
1929	18	35	5	35	113	6.5
1931	–	21	6	58	85	6.6
1935	1	16	40	24	81	6.0
1945	5	2	76	99	182	10.8
1950	5	–	319	137	461	24.6
1951	3	1	66	26	96	7.0
1955	3	1	60	36	100	7.1
1959	2	1	55	58	116	7.6
1964	5	8	52	121	186	10.6
1966	9	3	104	121	237	13.9
1970	10	6	184	208	408	22.2
1974 (Feb)	8	25	23	265	321	15.0
1974 (Oct)	28	13	125	276	442	19.6
1979	3	22	303	673	1001	38.1
1983	5	119	10	605	739	28.7
1987	–	–	1	307	289	12.4
1992	3	1	11	888	903	30.6
1997	7	–	10	1576	1593	42.8
2001	2	0	1	1282	1285	38.7
Deposits lost in general elections						
1918–2001	122	332	1,584	5,351	7,389	17.7

Source: Adapted from Butler and Butler (2000), p. 261 and Butler and Kavanagh (2002).

Campaign Spending

The rules governing campaign spending are crucial to the integrity of any democratic system. If there are no rules, the system will be vulnerable to distortion and corruption; if the rules are too strict or inappropriate, they may hinder the effective operation of the parties or impede freedom of communication and may weaken rather than strengthen the democratic process. Rules that do not command respect may be flouted. In the United Kingdom, limits were placed on campaign spending in the late nineteenth century when the 1883 Corrupt and Illegal Practices Act was passed. At that point elections were assumed to be primarily local events consisting of constituency contests between candidates. Accordingly, limits were placed on candidates, who were given expenditure ceilings that were calculated on the basis of the number of electors in the constituency and varied between urban and rural constituencies.

This approach to campaign spending survived until PPERA 2000, based on the Neill Committee's recommendations, was passed. A succession of party-funding scandals under the Conservatives had highlighted the extent to which the major parties were vulnerable to corruption because of their reliance on donations from wealthy individuals, firms and interest groups. Donations from abroad were a particular cause of concern. Although the 1997 Blair government had condemned the Conservatives' methods of raising money, New Labour itself became suspect as it tried to raise funds to make itself independent of the unions. The Bernie Ecclestone affair led Blair to ask the Neill Committee to consider the whole question of party funding and campaign spending.

The problem with the traditional approach to campaign expenditure was that it regulated only the amount spent by candidates in a constituency during the formal election campaign, i.e., the period from the dissolution of Parliament until election day. It did not regulate the increasingly large sums spent by the parties at national level outside of the campaign period.

The trend of party spending was thought by the Neill Committee to be damaging to the quality of British democracy because it meant that smaller, poorer parties, including the Liberal Democrats, could not compete and because it created a potentially corrupting fundraising imperative. PPERA 2000 creates a new regime for electoral expenditure by placing a cap on expenditure at the national level and introducing new reporting requirements. The limits on how much a candidate may spend locally remain in place. In 2001, these limits were about £9,000 per constituency based on a formula of £5,483 plus 6.2p per voter in a county constituency and 4.6p per voter in a borough constituency. National party spending was capped for the first time. In the year up to an election, parties were limited to an expenditure of just under £20 million divided between the component parts of the UK, as shown in table 7.3.

One further change to the rules of campaign spending should be noted. In the past, pressure groups (third parties) who had wanted to intervene in an election campaign had been severely restricted. In 1998, a case concerning the fairness of these restrictions was taken to the ECJ (*Bowman* v. *UK*). PPERA 2000 raised the amount that could be spent by a pressure group in an election from £5 to £500. However, by registering as a third party, higher spending limits could be applied. Under PPERA 2000, it is an offence for a third party to incur expenditure of more than £10,000 in England (£5,000 in each of Scotland, Wales and Northern Ireland) during election campaigns for the UK and European Parliaments and for the devolved legislatures. Controlled expenditure is incurred only during regulated periods, i.e., during the 365 days ending with the date of the poll in the case of a UK parliamentary election, and the four months ending with the date of the poll in all other cases.

Table 7.3 Election spending restrictions post-PPERA 2000

Country	No. of parliamentary seats	Maximum expenditure limit (£ 000s)
England	529	15,870
Scotland	72	2,160
Wales	40	1,200
TOTAL Great Britain	641	19,230
Northern Ireland	18	540
TOTAL United Kingdom	659	19,770

Source: Political Parties, Elections and Referendums Act 2000, Explanatory Notes, http:// www.legislation.hmso.gov.uk/acts/en/00en41-c.htm

The 2000 legislation also changed the method of enforcement. Prior to the new legislation, all authorized expenditure had to be made through a candidate's agent, who would at the end of the process certify compliance with the limits. Although legal challenges could be mounted, the major parties often colluded in excess spending. Under the new legislation, the whole gamut of campaign spending has to be reported regularly and is monitored by the Election Commission, which has the power to investigate complaints and scrutinize accounts.

The Media and the Electoral Process

The role of the mass media in politics has become increasingly influential in election campaigns. The parties vie with one another to set the agenda for debate in an election period, and in this battle the press and television are crucial.

Unlike in the United States, there is a ban on paid television advertising in the UK, although the parties may place advertisements in the press. Each party is instead given a certain amount of free television advertising, **party political broadcast** which it uses for **party political broadcasts**. These short slots have **(PPB)** A 3- to 5-minute tele- come to seem less significant to the parties than ordinary news vision slot in which a political coverage, where internal rules require that programmes display a party can present its message rough balance between the parties. The press does not have to be to voters. Only major parties neutral.
are eligible for PPBs.

Counting the Votes

The voter is presented with a list of names, which now have party labels attached to those candidates who are not independents. (Until 1969, only the names of candidates, not their party label, appeared on the ballot paper.) The 1998 Registration of Political Parties Act introduced for European elections was intended to prevent deception and confusion of voters by outlawing misleading descriptions on the ballot and running candidates with the same name as a major candidate.

The simple plurality system or FPTP allocates each constituency to the candidate who, in that constituency, gained the most votes. All the parties have representatives at the count and closely scrutinize both the process as a whole and the small number of votes (about 0.3 per cent of the total) that are deemed to have been spoiled. If the result looks like being very close, a recount may be demanded. After the vote, a result may be challenged in legal proceedings. Such challenges are rare but have occurred. Thus after the 1997 general election in Winchester, a legal challenge was mounted by the Conservative who lost to the Liberal Democrat by 2 votes. The Literal Democrat Richard Huggett also stood in Winchester in 1997, polling 59 votes. The challenge resulted in an order for the election to be re-run, but on that occasion the Liberal Democrat increased his majority to 21,556 and indeed kept the seat at the 2001 general election.

Assessing the British National Electoral System

The contemporary British electoral system is thus now more complex and more contentious than it once was. In assessing the way it operates and its consequences, it is important to remember that no electoral system is neutral. The selection of a new electoral system for Westminster elections would thus change the balance of political forces and very probably transform many other elements of the British political system.

The first argument in favour of the existing system is that it is easy to use and readily comprehensible. Voters need only to place a cross by their preferred candidate. Although voters now have experience of using other systems, there is some evidence to suggest that electors are not entirely clear about the mechanisms used in the AMS system for translating votes into seats. The counting (which occurs immediately after the polls have closed) is straightforward and relatively quick. Indeed, in each general election there is a well-publicized race to be the first constituency to return a result, with the quickest being able to make an announcement within 45 minutes of the close of the poll.

A second advantage of FPTP, for national elections at least, is that it has on most occasions since 1918 delivered a government with an overall majority in the House of Commons (although many governments have had to operate with very small majorities; see table 6.1, p. 198). Thus proponents of the system usually argue that it produces strong government and one that can be easily removed. A more proportional system would be almost certain to require some kind of coalition.

A third advantage alleged for the FPTP system is that, by creating a powerful bond between an MP and a constituency, it encourages a high degree of constituency service. AMS and proportional systems create different incentives, sometimes making it more likely that the candidate will seek to please party bosses rather than constituents.

Against these advantages, however, there must be weighed some very serious disadvantages and distortions. The FPTP system rewards larger parties and disadvantages parties that are not spatially concentrated. The big losers in the British system since 1918 have been the Liberal/Liberal Democrat Party, which has regularly won a smaller proportion of parliamentary seats than its share of the popular vote would command in a proportional system. The revival of the Liberal Democrats in the 1997 and 2001 general elections suggests that some of this disadvantage may have been overcome. But although the Liberal Democrats' tally of 52 seats in 2001 was the best since 1945, it is still lower than its share of the vote would deliver in a more proportional system.

It should be noted that FPTP is not so disadvantageous for nationalist parties, such as the Scottish National Party (SNP) and Plaid Cymru (PC), which concentrate their vote. Even so, many think the SNP has fared less well under FPTP than it would have done under a more proportional system. The FPTP system is also one that exaggerates small movements of opinion. In addition it wastes votes, piling them up in safe seats, and by the same token it creates electoral deserts for parties in areas where they are not strong enough to take a seat.

hung Parliament Parliament in which no one party has sufficient support to form an administration by itself. Minority government or coalition government may follow from the election of a hung Parliament. Both have been rare at the national level, but Labour took office as a minority government in 1924 and 1929. The first Welsh Assembly elections created an Assembly (1999–2003) in which there was first a minority administration, then a formal coalition.

Individual constituencies may be won on a minority of the vote. It has also been the case that the party with the largest share of the votes has not gained the largest share of the seats. This has happened on two occasions since 1945 – in 1951, when Labour polled more votes than the Conservatives but won 26 fewer seats, and in February 1974, when the Conservatives polled 180,000 more than Labour but gained four fewer seats (see table 7.4).

The operation of the system according to some observers has been made more capricious as a result of changes in electoral behaviour (Bogdanor, 2003). Certainly, increased electoral volatility and the rise of tactical voting have had an impact on electoral competition. FPTP is also thought by some observers to restrict the ability of minority groups and women from gaining representation. Although the number of women in the House of Commons increased dramatically to 120 after 1997, there is still under-representation of women in the Conservative ranks and only a small number of ethnic minority MPs (see tables 6.3 and 6.4, pp. 204 and 205). A more proportional system – especially a list system – would enable parties to create a more balanced ticket. Indeed, the European Parliament, Scottish Parliament and Welsh Assembly offer some evidence of how a list system may be used to produce more balanced representation than a constituency system provides.

Finally, the use of FPTP for Westminster is linked to a style of politics that some observers see as too adversarial and party-dominated. A shift to another electoral system might encourage a more inclusive and consensual style of politics.

However cogent these arguments are against FPTP, the likelihood is that it will remain for Westminster. It is improbable that Labour would dare to reform it while it continues to deliver majorities for the party. Indeed, it is the Conservatives who now find themselves at a systemic disadvantage under FPTP. What could trigger a change? A series of **hung Parliaments** might, although there is always a tendency to see an individual election as anomalous. So could a realignment in which the Liberal Democrats replaced the Conservatives as the second major party. Short of that happening, the existing system seems likely to survive.

Conclusions

Debate continues to swirl around the British electoral system. Reforms since 1997 have produced improvements in many aspects of the electoral machinery in an attempt to make elections fairer and easier. However, the central feature of the British electoral system – the FPTP method of translating votes into seats – has not been changed and probably will not be unless and until the system ceases to deliver single-party governments with working majorities. The British electoral system is in many ways extremely unfair, and the failure to address the issue of electoral reform at the national level looks all the more anomalous given the use of other systems for subordinate elections. However, it is also a system which has yielded highly stable and responsive government in the past, and it may be that, in this respect at least, those who benefit from the system are rightly reluctant to dismiss its concrete advantages too quickly, however appealing the abstract arguments against it.

Table 7.4 Relationship between votes and seats under FPTP, 1945–2001

Year	Conservative		Labour		Liberal/Alliance		PC/SNP		Communist, 1945–79; Greens 1979–2001		Others (mainly NI)	
	Votes %	Seats %	Votes %	Seats %	Votes %	Seats %	Votes %	Seats %	Votes %	Seats %	Votes %	Seats %
1945	39.8	33.3	48.3	61.4	9.1	1.9	0.2	0	0.4	0.3	2.1	3.1
1950	43.5	47.8	46.1	50.4	9.1	1.4	0.1	0	0.3	0	0.9	0.3
1951	48	51.3	48.8	47.2	2.5	1.0	0.1	0	0.1	0	0.5	0.5
1955	49.7	54.8	46.4	44	2.7	1.0	0.2	0	0.1	0	0.8	0.3
1959	49.4	57.9	43.8	41	5.9	1.0	0.4	0	0.1	0	0.5	0.2
1964	43.4	48.3	44.1	50.3	11.2	1.4	0.5	0	0.2	0	0.6	0
1966	41.9	40.2	47.9	57.6	8.5	1.9	0.7	0	0.2	0	0.7	0.3
1970	46.4	52.4	43	45.7	7.5	1.0	1.3	0.2	0.1	0	1.7	0.8
1974 (Feb)	37.8	46.8	37.1	47.4	19.3	2.2	2.6	1.4	0.1	0	3.1	2.2
1974 (Oct)	35.8	43.6	39.2	50.2	18.3	2.0	3.5	2.6	0.1	0	3.1	1.9
1979	43.9	53.3	37	42.3	13.8	1.7	2	0.6	0.1	0	3.2	1.9
1983	42.4	61.0	27.6	32.2	25.4	3.5	1.5	0.6	0.2	0	2.9	2.6
1987	42.3	57.8	30.8	35.2	22.6	3.4	1.7	0.9	0.3	0	2.3	2.6
1992	41.9	51.6	34.4	41.6	17.8	3.1	2.3	1.1	0.5	0	3	2.6
1997	30.7	25.0	43.2	63.4	16.8	7.0	2.5	1.5	0.2	0	6.6	3.0
2001	31.7	25.2	40.7	62.5	18.3	7.9	2.5	1.4	0.6	0	6.2	3.0

Source: Adapted from Butler and Kavanagh (2002), pp. 260–1.

Key Questions

1 Can the retention of FPTP for Westminster be justified?
2 Why should campaign spending be controlled in a democracy?
3 Is it logical to have so many different electoral methods in use at the same time in the United Kingdom?

 Further Reading

General elections each receive scholarly treatment in the Nuffield series, of which the most recent is D. Butler and D. Kavanagh (eds), *The British General Election of 2001* (Basingstoke: Palgrave, 2002). See also earlier editions on previous elections since 1945.

Pippa Norris (ed.), *Britain Votes 1997* and *Britain Votes 2001* (Oxford: Oxford University Press, 1997, 2001) are valuable collections, as are D. Denver, G. Hands and S. Henig (eds), *British Elections and Parties Review. Volume 8: The 1997 General Election* and *Volume 12: The 2001 General Election* (London: Frank Cass, 1998, 2001). The electoral system as a whole is examined in R. Blackburn, *The Electoral System in Britain* (London: Macmillan, 1995), though it now badly needs updating. J. Curtice, 'The electoral system: Biased to Blair', *Parliamentary Affairs*, 54: 3 (2001) looks at the effects of the system. D. Farrell, *Comparing Electoral Systems* (London: Prentice-Hall, 1997) offers a comparative perspective.

The issues surrounding electoral reform are discussed in M. Dummet, *Principles of Electoral Reform* (Oxford: Oxford University Press, 1997) and in the *Report of the Independent Commission on the Voting System (Jenkins Report)*, Cmnd 4090 (London: HMSO, 1998). P. Dunleavy et al., 'Mixed electoral systems in Britain and the Jenkins Commission on Electoral Reform', *British Journal of Politics and International Relations*, 1: 1 (1999) and I. McLean, 'The Jenkins Commission and the implications of electoral reform for the UK constitution', *Government and Opposition*, 34: 2 (1999) present stimulating arguments about reform.

 **Websites**

See also the list of general websites at the back of the book.

- www.club.demon.co.uk/Politics/elect.html – British politics, elections
- www.election.demon.co.uk/ – UK election results
- www.ukelect.co.uk – UK elections site
- www.essex.ac.uk/bes – British Election Study
- www.electoralcommission.gov.uk – Electoral Commission
- www.electoral-reform.org.uk/ – Electoral Reform Society
- www.makevotescount.org.uk – Make Votes Count

8 Parties and the Party System

In the last chapter we examined the rules of the electoral game in the United Kingdom and in the various subsystems of the country. In this chapter we consider the players in that game – the political parties – who compete for power. Contemporary British parties present us with something of a paradox. Clearly, British government is suffused with party and, as seen in chapter 6, party considerations explain many of its institutional features. For example, much of the executive's strength and the lack of independence of the legislature is the product of party cohesion in the House of Commons. Parties provide a crucial linkage between government and the citizen and simplify electoral choice. Indeed, for many observers, the two-party system is the decisive element underpinning the whole Westminster model of democracy.

On the other hand, in many respects parties appear to be increasingly marginal to the democratic life of the United Kingdom. Recent trends in party organization suggest that in the search for electoral success, there has been a shift of power towards the professionals of politics – the media advisers, pollsters and campaign managers – and away from the voluntary and grassroots party structures, which have correspondingly declined. Undoubtedly, political parties now appear to excite little interest in the public: membership of political parties in the United Kingdom has declined so that fewer than 2 per cent of the population now belong to a political party (Seyd and Whitely, 1992, 2002; Seyd, Whitely and Parry, 1996; Seyd, Whitely and Richardson, 1994; Whitely and Seyd, 2002). Party finances, both centrally and at the grassroots, appear to be in a constant state of crisis, raising the issue of whether parties should be financed from public funds as an alternative to voluntary donations. And, as will be explored more fully in the next chapter, the parties' hold on the loyalty of their voters has weakened. For example, the percentage of people saying that they have a strong attachment to a political party, which in 1964 stood at 42 per cent of the population, had declined to 16 per cent in 1997. Butler and Kavanagh (2002) note that, 'On key questions such as keeping promises, understanding the problems facing Britain and representing all classes, the parties have been in a downward spiral between 1992 and 1997, and 1997 and 2001'. Disenchantment with the role of parties is further underlined by other opinion poll findings. Thus in 1992, 38 per cent of respondents said that the Conservative Party 'understands the problems facing Britain'. In 1997, this figure was down to 20 per cent and had fallen again to 18 per cent by 2001. The equivalent figures for Labour were 40 per cent in 1992, 37 per cent in 1997 and 18 per cent in 2001. In the

2001 election, according to a MORI poll for the Electoral Commission, fewer people than ever cared who won (Electoral Commission/MORI, 2001). At the time of the 1987 and 1992 elections, over 80 per cent of voters said that they cared which party won. In 1997 this proportion had fallen to 69 per cent, and it fell again in 2001 to 66 per cent.

This detachment of the voters from parties creates a more fluid environment of party competition and inevitably requires a greater emphasis on professional campaigning, media influence and policy presentation. The importation of greater professionalism into campaigns can itself have an effect on parties, making traditional party organization redundant and, as in the United States, reducing candidate dependence on party (Blumenthal, 1982). Increasingly sophisticated marketing strategies are now an essential tool not just of election campaigns but of all aspects of government policy making and presentation.

In examining contemporary British parties, therefore, we not only have to be aware of their continuing significance as institutions that perform a range of crucial functions, not least those of aggregating policy, simplifying electoral choice and linking government and the electorate. We also need to bear in mind that they operate in an environment where many of their traditional functions seem redundant and where the public appear largely indifferent to them.

Sources of Party Change

Political parties are by definition institutions that must adapt to changing circumstances. Failure to adapt to shifts in the policy agenda, to variations of electoral mood or to new technology may doom a party. Even so, the recent past has seen an unusually concentrated period of pressure on British parties. Some of it has been generated externally – for example, by the Labour government's 2000 legislation to reform the system of party funding and campaign spending, the Political Parties, Elections and Referendums Act (PPERA), which was discussed in chapter 7. This new regulatory regime not merely has the effect of providing us with greater information about who funds the parties; it also changes the climate in which parties compete. The machinery of regulation is impartial, but the impact of the reform initially appears likely to eliminate the advantage traditionally enjoyed by the Conservative Party in terms of fundraising and campaign spending.

Many internal party changes have been initiated in response to electoral defeats. The determination of successive Labour leaders after 1983 to reinvent their party and make it electorally competitive had enormous implications for its organizational and institutional relationships as well as for its ideology and policies. As we will see throughout this chapter, 'New Labour' both in opposition and in government has had a radical and controversial impact on the traditional structures and ideological orientation of the Labour Party. The Conservative Party under William Hague's leadership (1997–2001) embarked on a similar process of organizational reform in response to the massive defeat of 1997 (Peele, 1998). Although it is not clear how stable these reforms will prove, much less whether they will deliver electoral success, they changed many fundamental relationships inside the Conservative Party.

Two other sources of contemporary party change stand out. First, constitutional reform – devolution for Scotland and Wales – has created new arenas of competition for the parties, ones which different electoral rules make more open to effective challenge from smaller parties such as the Liberal Democrats and the nationalists. The logic of decentralization is also likely to make its mark on party structures, pushing them further towards a quasi-federal system. Secondly, new technology – especially email, the Internet and the Web – have transformed campaigning and the ability of parties to communicate with their supporters.

The Party Systems of the UK

Political parties do not operate in isolation from each other. Their strategies and behaviour are shaped by the wider party system. The questions that are generally asked of a party system (as opposed to an individual party) tend to focus on the number of parties, their ideological distance and coalition potential as well as the stability of the parties and their relationship to social and economic cleavages.

The number of parties represented in the UK Parliament is currently nine. However, the vast majority of seats are in the hands of the Labour and Conservative parties. The Liberal Democrat Party is the third largest party in the UK and (as of 2003) has 53 MPs, including Paul Marsden, who defected from Labour to the Liberal Democrats in December 2001. Britain is not a multi-party system; but it is not a two-party system, either. At the electoral level, although the two larger parties still dominate the system, the percentage of the vote that they together command has declined markedly since 1945. There are no longer straight two-party fights in any constituencies. As was emphasized earlier, devolution has created new political arenas with their own party systems in Scotland and Wales. (Northern Ireland's party system is also distinct.) In these subsystems we see a different constellation of parties (see table 8.1). It should also be noted that parties may be successful at the local level while failing to make a national impact, although as the Liberal Democrats have demonstrated, a strong showing locally can provide a springboard for a better national performance.

Coalition at the national level has been rare in the United Kingdom, although coalitions were formed in the First and Second World Wars, and to cope with the economic crisis of 1931. Sometimes the parliamentary arithmetic requires governments without a good working majority to enter informal understandings or, more rarely, formal pacts, with smaller parties (see table 8.2). The Liberals (later Liberal Democrats) are obviously a key block, to which both major parties have in the past looked for support in coalition formation. However, it has become clear in recent years that the Liberal Democrats are very much closer ideologically to Labour than to the Conservatives. In the Scottish Parliament and Welsh Assembly, some kind of coalition arrangement appears essential because no single party has an overall majority at present. In searching for coalition partners in the devolved systems of Scotland and Wales, the only viable coalition at the moment is Labour–Liberal Democrat, although after the 2003 elections in Wales Labour opted to govern alone. In Northern Ireland the organization of politics around the fundamental cleavage between loyalists and nationalists creates a totally different pattern of

Table 8.1 The party systems in the regions

		Share of votes cast 2001 (%)				
	Turnout	Con	Lab	Lib Dem	Nationalists	Others
England	59.1	35.2	41.4	19.4	–	3.9
South	60.3	38.4	34.6	22.8	–	4.2
Midlands	60.3	37.1	43.2	15.8	–	3.9
North	56.3	28.2	51.5	16.9	–	3.4
Wales	61.6	21.0	48.6	13.8	14.3	2.3
Scotland	58.2	15.6	43.9	16.4	20.1	4.0
Great Britain	59.2	32.7	42.0	18.8	2.6	3.9
Northern Ireland	67.8	0.3	–	–	–	99.7
United Kingdom	59.4	31.7	40.7	18.3	2.5	6.8

Source: Butler and Kavanagh (2001).

Table 8.2 Coalitions and minority governments, 1900–2001

Year	Coalition arrangements
1916–22	A faction of Liberals form a wartime coalition with the Conservatives, under the leadership of the Liberal Lloyd George.
1918–22	Coalition Liberals and Conservatives stand under a united banner in the 1918 election and win. Remain in coalition under leadership of Lloyd George until 1922.
1923	Minority Labour government elected, led by Ramsay MacDonald. Survives in office for 10 months with the support of the Liberals.
1929–31	Liberals give support to a minority Labour government, led by MacDonald.
1931–45	Coalition of Labour, Conservatives and Liberals set up 'National government' in response to economic depression. Some Labour and Liberals refuse to join the Conservative-dominated coalition. Coalition leader Ramsay MacDonald is expelled from the Labour Party. Conservative Neville Chamberlain heads the coalition from 1937 to 1940, and is replaced by Churchill.
1974 Feb–Oct	Minority Labour government led by Harold Wilson.
1977–8	By-election results deny Labour an overall majority. Supported by Liberals in a Lib–Lab pact from 1977 to 1978. Labour continue in office as a minority government from October 1978 to the election in May 1979.
1995–7	By-election results and withdrawal of whip from 'Euro rebels' erode the Conservative's overall majority, leaving them reliant on support of the Ulster Unionist parties.

party competition; and although there were once strong links between the Ulster Unionists and the Conservatives, these were severed in the 1970s.

The Parties

The position of a party within the wider party system needs to be borne in mind in examining its distinctive features. Parties are competitive institutions. However rooted a party may be to its own ideology and policies and to its own organizational structures, it may be forced to adjust and adapt by a threat to its position from another party. Equally, innovation by an opponent, for example in election campaigning or fundraising, is likely to be imitated. There is also some transnational fertilization of domestic approaches to campaigning and organization. For example, New Labour's post-1992 campaign strategy was in part influenced by Bill Clinton's successful Democratic campaign of that year.

Parties are fragmented, not monolithic, institutions. There will be frequent internal divisions and differences of perspective between the parliamentary elite and conflicts over priorities between a party's parliamentary element, its voluntary wing and its professional bureaucracy. There may also be intense disputes over the control and content of policy, reflecting deep ideological disagreements. Or there may be personality conflicts and rivalries. How well a party manages these differences will determine how effectively it can respond to electoral demands and how far it will remain competitive. To put the matter slightly differently, political leaders must always bear in mind two constituencies that may not be in alignment – the party organization and the wider electorate.

In examining the individual parties, we will look first at the party's broad ideology – meaning the set of ideas and core values that unite a party and create its identity. Ideology is in a sense the glue that provides coherence for disparate policy platforms and the broad framework within which appeals to electors are made. Party ideology in a modern democratic system is unlikely to be rigid or fixed. Parties can emphasize one or other elements in their ideological heritage depending on their appraisal of the electorate's attitude or their analysis of policy needs; and they can reinterpret familiar doctrines to meet a changing political context. The period since Margaret Thatcher's leadership of the Conservative Party saw the neo-liberal free-market tendency within the party (where it had previously been a minority) become much more assertive. Under Tony Blair Labour's policies have been refashioned to erase elements that no longer seemed relevant to contemporary policy arguments or to appeal to voters. New Labour under Blair thus embraced globalization and market capitalism and explicitly removed its traditional commitment to public ownership, to trade union rights, and to high taxation and the redistribution of wealth. Thatcher's radical revision of Conservative policy and Blair's reinvention of Labour policies inevitably created internal divisions and accusations that they had distorted the 'true' character of their respective parties. Certainly, there continues to be a lively debate around the character of both New Labour and Thatcherism and their relationship to their respective party traditions.

The brief examination of ideology is followed by a review of the role of the leadership and of the various facets of party organization, both inside and outside Parliament. Although the different histories of the parties have given them distinct formal structures as well as different internal relationships and cultures, there are important points of comparison across the parties. Such crucial functions as candidate selection and fundraising demand the attention of all parties. Moreover, all parties have to address such issues as the role of leadership, the extent to which they wish to promote intra-party democracy, and the degree of centralization within the party structure. At the end of the chapter, we underline some organizational trends that appear to be common to both major parties in the twenty-first century.

The Conservative Party

The Conservative Party, officially titled the Conservative and Unionist Party but colloquially referred to as the Tory Party, is the oldest of the political parties in the United Kingdom (see box 8.1 for a brief history of its evolution). The intellectual origins of the modern party can be traced to the debates occasioned by the French Revolution of 1789, or even to the Restoration period of the 1660s when the word 'Tory' was first used. Most historians prefer to locate the formation of the Conserva-

---

Box 8.1 Historical evolution of the Conservative Party

1820s	Tories, led by Duke of Wellington, appear to be in decline as pressures to increase the franchise threaten their support base.
1830s	Following 1832 Reform Act, Robert Peel leads the Tories to a new revival based on the values of tradition and stability. Party is renamed the Conservative Party.
1840s	Party splits over the Corn Laws. Free traders leave to join the Whigs (Liberals). Disraeli leads the Conservative Party to renewed electoral strength based on a 'one-nation' vision of social unity.
1870s	Primrose League founded to spread Conservative principles and increase party membership, particularly among the working classes.
1886	Conservatives take office as part of Liberal Unionist coalition. Remain in power for next 20 years.
1905	Conservatives and Liberal Unionists lose general election to Lloyd George's Liberals.
1922	Break-up of Conservative and Liberal Unionist coalition. Conservatives elected to government under Bonar Law.
1926	General strike broken by Conservative government.
1931	Financial crisis leads to Conservative-dominated National government.
1940–5	Wartime coalition.
1945	Conservatives under Churchill lose to Labour in a surprise defeat.
1951	Conservatives win the election and remain in office until 1964. Accept much of Labour's programme of nationalization and the welfare state. Heralds a period of relative consensus between the two parties.
1964	Out of office, the party begins to move to the right under Edward Heath.
1970	Heath elected on a programme of reduced state spending and trade union reform, but in office fails to enact substantial change.
1973–4	Industrial unrest, particularly from miners, leads to three-day week and a general election on the question 'Who governs Britain?'. Labour lose the election in February by a small margin, and lose again in October by a larger majority.
1975	In a surprise result, Thatcher wins leadership of the party.
1979–90	Thatcher wins three general elections on a programme of reduced state spending, financial orthodoxy, privatization and trade union reform. Wins the Falklands War in 1983.
1990	With Thatcher's popularity in decline, she is challenged for the leadership. Failing to win a decisive victory, she stands down and the subsequent leadership ballot is won by John Major.
1992	Major wins the general election with a small majority.

(Continues)

Box 8.1 *Continued*

1992–7	Following withdrawal from the ERM in September 1992, the Conservatives slump in the polls and continue to languish for the next five years. Financial and sexual scandals force the resignation of a series of ministers, and Major's authority is challenged by Eurosceptics in his own party. Major resigns as leader in 1995 and stands for re-election. Wins but without the decisive backing of his MPs.
1997	Conservatives defeated at the general election by a record margin, losing over half their MPs. William Hague becomes leader of the party and undertakes a succession of internal reforms to pass power to local constituencies.
2001	Conservatives lose by a similar margin as in 1997. Hague resigns and is replaced by anti-European Iain Duncan Smith, who takes the party further to the right and struggles to establish his credibility with the press and the public. A new split between traditionalists and modernizers emerges within the party.
2003	Iain Duncan Smith loses vote of no confidence. Michael Howard unanimously elected leader.

tive Party in the period of Sir Robert Peel's ascendancy between 1834 and 1846. It was then that there emerged an identifiable group of supporters united by loyalty to a common leader and broadly attached to common policies. The policy of the Conservative Party in the early part of the nineteenth century was to support established interests – Crown and aristocracy, landowners, agriculture and the church. It supported the existing constitutional order and was hostile to reform or democratization. Its strength was rooted in the counties and small boroughs rather than in larger cities and it was also firmly based in the southern part of England. The significance of Peel's leadership was that the wider electorate created by the expansion of the franchise in 1832 made it necessary to broaden the party's appeal, and indeed the Tamworth Manifesto of 1834 is sometimes seen as the beginning of modern party competition. Peel's dilemma as leader was how to reconcile the party's need for a national electoral appeal with its vested sectoral interests, especially the farming interest. Put more generally, the Conservative Party had to accommodate the interests of supporters with the demands of a changing electorate. Peel's repeal of the Corn Laws in 1846, against the evident interests of his agricultural supporters, split the parliamentary party so that the cohesion which he had introduced was short-lived.

The further extension of the electorate in 1867 made it essential for the Conservative Party to maintain unity in the House of Commons and stimulated the formation of extra-parliamentary machinery to mobilize the new voters. By the time of the third great reform of the franchise in 1884, the skeleton of the twentieth-century Conservative Party was clearly visible. There was an increasingly cohesive group of MPs in the House of Commons, an organization (the National Union) linking the constituency associations of members together in a federal structure, and a professional party bureaucracy at Conservative Central Office to deal with electoral arrangements.

The major opponent of the Conservative Party from 1867 to 1918 was the Liberal Party. At the general election of 1918, the relatively young Labour Party became the principal opposition party, and for much of the rest of the twentieth century party

one-nation Toryism Style of Conservatism which dates from the 1950s and which emphasizes the importance of progressive social legislation in order to avoid class conflict. Its reformist stance looks to Disraeli for inspiration. Although it was to some extent eclipsed by Thatcherism within the Conservative Party, the tradition of 'one-nation' politics was provocatively claimed by Blair for New Labour.

competition at the national level was dominated by the contest between Labour and the Conservatives. The Liberal Party did not disappear, however, and indeed its revival in the 1990s significantly changed the dynamics of party conflict and weakened the Conservatives' position.

The advent of a mass electorate with the 1918 Representation of the People Act forced the Conservatives to appeal to a wider spectrum of society than ever before. It also obliged them to develop new techniques of electioneering. Taken together, the willingness to adjust its message to what the electors wanted and not be bound by ideology and the professional exploitation of new campaigning techniques made the Conservative Party enormously successful at the national level. When it did lose elections, it was usually able to draw lessons from the defeat and make suitable reforms. This was notably so in 1945, when the Conservatives revamped both their policies and their party machinery. So successful was the party's electoral record over the twentieth century that it came to think of itself as the natural party of government. Although its position changed after 1997, its capacity to adapt to a changing electoral environment and to fashion a party with national appeal has been impressive.

The Conservative success in surviving the challenge of socialism for so long stemmed primarily from its ability to capture what was seen as the centre ground in politics in each generation. It also managed to display a general competence in government. This meant that it had to adapt to new national needs and concerns. Despite its identification with some of the country's most established (and reactionary) groups and classes, it had to be sufficiently pragmatic to meet the expectations of new electors, such as women after 1918. Conservative leaders tended to deny the sectional or class aspects of their policies, emphasizing their concern with the *national* interest. They also tended to promote themselves as the party of patriotism and loyalty, stressing also (when it was relevant) the advantages of the Empire and a strong international role for the UK. Above all, Conservative leaders eschewed dogma and ideology, seeing in the party's flexibility the key to its success.

In the 1970s, however, many of these assumptions collapsed. The period associated with Margaret Thatcher's leadership saw a marked change in the culture of the Conservative Party. For much of the twentieth century, domestic party competition revolved around the issues of national economic management, the distribution of wealth, and inequality. Labour had set the agenda and the Conservatives had for the most part merely responded to or modified it. By the mid-1970s, Margaret Thatcher and a small group of neo-liberal Conservatives began to express their deep opposition to the direction of post-1945 consensus politics. When Thatcher gained the leadership of the Conservative Party in 1975, and, much more, when she became prime minister in 1979, a new synthesis of conservatism was expounded. Thatcherism emphasized free-market values, low taxation and enterprise and was sceptical about efforts to manage the economy on Keynesian lines. It was a robust message expressed with clarity and conviction. This new formulation was in many ways more appropriate to the changed world economic order of the 1970s than the more state-centric approaches of **one-nation Toryism** and Butskellism. Yet, although the Conservative Party from 1979 to 1997 enjoyed a series of spectacular electoral successes at the national level, it is not clear that the voters really endorsed

Thatcher's philosophy of reducing public sector involvement. Nevertheless, her long period in power allowed her governments to implement a succession of major changes in public policy, including such important initiatives as privatization and the restructuring of industrial relations.

One crucial element in the Conservative Party's success in the 1979–92 period was the weakness and internal division of Labour as the main opposition party. Once Labour rebuilt itself, however, the Conservative Party was extremely vulnerable. The scale of the Conservative Party's defeat at the 1997 election was dramatic. It was especially difficult for the Conservatives to counter the appeal of Tony Blair and New Labour because Labour had accepted so much of the new political framework set by the Conservatives.

Factionalism in the Conservative Party

For the most part, the Conservatives' lack of interest in ideology and their intense concern with winning elections limited the extent to which the party was willing to sacrifice unity in ideological or policy battles. Factionalism has generally not been a major feature of the Conservative Party, although there have always been subtle differences within the party based on political outlook. In each generation a self-consciously progressive group of Conservatives can be identified as a catalyst for the development of new ideas. Ideological conflict has not been entirely absent from the Conservative Party, however: there have been some spectacular and damaging rows about policy issues including free trade, India and foreign policy. Nevertheless, these divisions (which have often been characterized as 'tendencies' rather than factions to denote their looser and less-organized features) have generally faded.

The advent of Thatcherism starkly emphasized the importance of ideas in the Conservative Party. Divisions within the party over economic and social policy and over neo-liberalism versus a more pragmatic Toryism became more apparent. The Thatcherite style of conviction politics was anathema to many Conservatives such as Sir Ian Gilmour, who identified with one-nation conservatism (Gilmour, 1993). This division – which became stereotyped as a division between so-called 'wets' and 'dries' or between Thatcherites and others – created new antagonisms in the party. However, it was the issue of Europe that was to shatter the party's image as a unified party and create such tension that it became very difficult to lead. Opposition to the Maastricht Treaty in 1993 almost brought down the Conservative government and the issue led to an unprecedented withdrawal of the whip from a small group of regular rebels. So damaged was Major's authority by 1995 that he resigned the party leadership and successfully stood for re-election in order to re-establish that he had sufficient support in the party to continue.

The seriousness of the Tory split over Europe was on one level puzzling. After all, the Conservatives had taken Britain into Europe in the early 1970s. However, the quickening pace of integration, the adoption of a more social and political agenda by the European Union and the realization that British control in many policy areas was being eroded changed the party's attitude. Debate about the European Union exposed divisions in the party and produced a new mood of nationalism. Even after the Conservatives lost power, the European issue continued to destabilize the party and certainly weakened the appeal of Kenneth Clarke – a senior but pro-European figure – in his 1997 and 2001 bids for the leadership.

By early 2003 other divisions had appeared within the party, including a fundamental cleavage between those who wanted to modernize its doctrine and those who wanted the party to adhere to traditional Conservative values, especially on moral and social issues. In addition, there are numerous so-called fringe groups and recognized organizations such as the Conservative Christian Fellowship, the Conservative Medical Society and the Tory Reform Group that cater for particular sectional interests within the party or exist to push a particular policy approach.

The leader and the parliamentary party

Historically, one of the most conspicuous aspects of the internal politics of the Conservative Party has been the amount of autonomy and discretion allowed to the leader. This autonomy reflected both a party structure that was hierarchical in form and attitude and the fact that the Conservative Party developed as a parliamentary force long before it began to build an extensive extra-parliamentary organization. Although a highly efficient mass organization was created to mobilize the voters after the expansion of the franchise, there was no pretence that the organization was internally democratic. At times indeed, the leadership seemed to treat the party organizationally as the personal vehicle of the incumbent leader (McKenzie, 1964).

The traditional Conservative Party has also frequently celebrated strong leadership, creating icons of Winston Churchill, Harold Macmillan and Margaret Thatcher. Conservative leaders have generally been allowed a dominant role in the policy-making process and given virtually unlimited powers to appoint cabinet colleagues when the party is in power and **shadow cabinet** members when the party is in opposition. The leader was also given a good deal of freedom to set the policy direction and to appoint key members of the party organization, including the party chairman and the party treasurer. The emphasis on strong leadership chimed well with the increasing emphasis on personality in politics.

The emphasis given to leadership within the Conservative Party places a premium on electoral success. The Conservative Party is likely to be ruthless about removing leaders who seem unable to deliver it. There were several instances in the twentieth century of leaders who were forced out, including Arthur Balfour, Edward Heath and Margaret Thatcher. Electoral defeat in 1997 and 2001 caused John Major and William Hague to resign the leadership immediately, as both knew that defeat had destroyed their authority. Following a period of intense criticism of his leadership and the loss of a vote of no confidence, Iain Duncan Smith resigned in 2003.

The Conservative Party (like Labour) has in recent years made substantial changes to its system for choosing a leader. Until 1965 there was no formal procedure for electing a leader at all. The fact that the Conservative Party had been in government for much of the twentieth century meant that an election could be avoided by the simple expedient of taking as leader whoever the monarch invited to form an administration.

shadow cabinet The front-bench spokespersons of the major opposition party.

The involvement of the monarch only arose if a Conservative prime minister died or resigned in office so that a new prime minister had to be found. If there was a vacancy in the leadership while the party was in opposition, the party had to choose a leader by election. In fact, this situation rarely arose in the twentieth century since the Conservatives were in opposition only for short periods and there was usually a former prime minister available to act as leader. It did occur, however, in 1911, when the party was deeply divided over tariff reform. Then Andrew Bonar Law was elected unopposed because it was known that neither of the two more established candidates, Austen Chamberlain and Walter Long, would be able to command a decisive majority and unite the party afterwards. In the process of nominating Bonar Law, Long emphasized what degradation it would be for the party to have to elect a leader by competitive ballot (Ramsden, 1978).

If the party was in power, the monarch relied for advice on an inner group (known as 'the magic circle') of senior Conservatives who would themselves have taken soundings about who was likely to be acceptable to the party as a whole (Punnett, 1992). The advantage of such a procedure was twofold. It avoided the rather pedestrian and divisive processes of election. Secondly, it allowed party elders to prevent an individual from becoming leader simply on the basis of a narrow majority in the parliamentary party. The appearance of monarchical selection had the added benefit in a deferential party of cloaking the new leader in the mystique of monarchy and making it difficult publicly to oppose the new incumbent.

The dangers of the method were that it could look like a conspiracy and was increasingly anomalous in a democratic age. It also risked bringing the monarch into political controversy. Too much depended on the judgement of a small group of party grandees – senior (and elderly) Conservatives – who might themselves be remote from sentiment inside the Commons and the electorate.

The decision to move to an election for the leadership, even if the party was in power, stemmed from the controversy surrounding the selection of the Earl of Home (Sir Alec Douglas Home as he became) as prime minister in 1963. Lord Home's selection as successor to Harold Macmillan was highly unusual because at the time he was a peer. And there was a more obvious candidate in the Commons in the person of R. A. Butler. After the Conservatives lost the 1964 election under Sir Alec Douglas Home's leadership, a formal election procedure was devised and Sir Alec Douglas Home's successor, Edward Heath, was chosen by this method in 1965.

Conservative leaders have been elected, although the procedure has changed substantially, since 1965 (see box 8.2). An early concern was to build a degree of consensus into the process. Therefore it contained multiple ballots with a requirement that, at least at the early stages, no one could win without a commanding lead over an opponent. Initially it was intended for use only when the leadership was vacant, but a review of the election by the 1922 Committee (the representative body of Conservative backbench MPs) made it possible to challenge an incumbent leader. It was that system which allowed Margaret Thatcher to oust Edward Heath.

The current method of selecting is a radical departure from previous Tory practice. Changes in the method of electing the leader were clearly on the agenda after the calamitous 1997 election defeat, for which many members of the **mass party** blamed MPs, not least because of their public wrangling over Europe. Although Hague was elected under a system in which only Conservative MPs could vote, reforms introduced in 1998 give the final decision about who should be leader

mass membership party
A form of political party which places emphasis on an extensive party membership for mobilizing votes and policy making. In mass membership parties there is usually a strong expectation that the members will play a significant role in the life of the party and not be subordinated to the parliamentary party.

Box 8.2 Different leadership mechanisms in the Conservative Party since 1965

1965–1991

Formal election machinery adopted in the party for the first time. Leadership to be chosen by vote of all Conservative MPs. To be elected on the first ballot, a candidate must win an overall majority plus 15 per cent of those eligible to vote. If no candidate achieves this on the first ballot, there is a second ballot, in which new candidates may stand and in which only an overall majority is necessary for victory. If there is still no winner, a third ballot is held; only the candidates with the three highest votes may stand. MPs rank candidates in order of preference and the winner is determined by adding the number of first preferences to the redistributed second preferences on the papers of the third candidate. This system was used to elect Heath in 1965, Thatcher in 1975 and Major in 1990.

1991–1998

The above system was modified to allow a fourth ballot in the event of a tie between the two candidates. This system was used to elect William Hague in 1997.

Since 1998

New system introduced to give the final decision to party members. MPs vote on candidates, and the top two go through to a vote of the party membership. This was the system used to elect Iain Duncan Smith in 2001. In 2003, however, Iain Duncan Smith's resignation was followed by the selection of a new leader, Michael Howard, without a contest.

to party members. A leadership contest is thus at present formally still a two-stage encounter involving a primary election among MPs and a final vote of the grassroots party membership (Alderman, 1999). But it is perhaps a matter of time before the rules are again revised.

Several features of the new system mark a radical break with traditional Conservative practice. First, this empowerment of ordinary members adds a further dimension of **plebiscitary democracy** to Conservative politics. In the past MPs had been expected to consult with their constituency members (usually the chairman), but there was no provision for a formal vote, and MPs were free to disregard the advice of their constituency chairmen. During William Hague's leadership a number of membership ballots were taken in an effort to bolster support for his policy stance on Europe and his organizational reforms. Such ballots could not have taken place without national membership lists and they were calculated to provide support for the leader's position rather than offering a genuine choice of policy. These experiments with membership consultation and the involvement of the membership in the leadership selection process have occurred, ironically, at a time when the level and age of the voluntary membership are themselves a major cause of organizational weakness. Thus the choice of leader may have been thrown to a group which is itself highly

plebiscitary democracy Form of democracy in which key issues are frequently put to a referendum rather than relying on representative institutions. While referendums may augment representative democracy, they may also be manipulated and used to enhance the power of individual leaders.

unrepresentative of the electorate. In the election, 328,271 ballot papers were issued but a mere 256,797 votes were cast.

Secondly, the new system is much more transparent than previous ones; candidates must be declared at the start of the process and there is no provision for new candidates to come forward at a later stage. In earlier electoral systems used by the Conservative Party, it was possible for new candidates to emerge once the authority of the existing leader had been dented (Alderman, 1999).

How far the introduction of elective leadership has altered the basis of the leader's authority in the party is a difficult question. What can be said is that exercising leadership in the Conservative Party has become more arduous as the party demands both strong *and* responsive leadership. In opposition, a leader does not have the patronage or other resources of a prime minister and it is difficult to stamp authority on the party. Even in power the appearance of deep ideological divisions, especially, but not exclusively, over Europe, in the recent past have made the party harder to lead.

The backbench Conservative parliamentary party is formally organized through the 1922 Committee (Goodhart, 1973). In government the patronage that leaders and whips have will usually be sufficient to induce backbenchers to obey the party line; but occasionally – as Major found out between 1990 and 1997 – a party with a small majority has little available to persuade doubters. In opposition backbenchers are more difficult to lead; they may absent themselves from parliamentary business or devise their own tactics for harrying the government, as some groups such as that around Eric Forth did in the 1997–2001 Parliament (Cowley, 2001b).

The Conservative frontbench

Conservative leaders have enormous power to advance (or restrict) the careers of their parliamentary supporters. When the Conservative Party is in opposition the leader will appoint a number of frontbench spokespersons to assist in the parliamentary work of the party. They are the personal choice of the leader, in contrast to Labour shadow cabinets, which are elected by their fellow MPs in opposition. Traditionally, Conservative leaders have tried to create a shadow cabinet that reflects opinion in the party. Michael Howard departed from usual practice by making his frontbench team small in number.

Party bureaucracy

Conservative Central Office was founded by Disraeli in 1870 to support the drive to win votes from an expanded electorate. The post of party chairman, the key officer in the party bureaucracy, has existed since 1911 and the choice of party chairman is the leader's.

Historically, there was a division between the party bureaucracy (Central Office) and the National Union and the constituency parties. The party had no formal constitution, did not exist in law and had a culture that eschewed formal rules. In 1998, however, as the starting point of Hague's effort to reform both the organization and the culture of the Conservative Party, the hitherto deliberately self-contained elements of the party (the parliamentary party, the voluntary wing and the professional bureaucracy) were merged into a single organization with a constitution and common rules. Power was centred in a 15-member Board of Management, of whom only a minority were appointed by the leader. In addition, there was an executive director who was responsible for the day-to-day operation of the party organization (Peele, 1998).

The reforms were publicly discussed in terms of principles of unity, openness, decentralization, democracy, involvement and integrity, but many critics noted that centralization and administrative efficiency were equally powerful principles guiding the reforms. Long-term internal critics of the style of Conservative organization (such as the Charter Movement and the Campaign for Conservative Democracy) quickly dismissed much of the reform as cosmetic. Such critics pointed to the failure to make either the party chairman or the treasurer elective offices, despite the importance of the posts to the mass membership.

A different line of criticism emerged in 2003 when Iain Duncan Smith dismissed a number of key Central Office staff and appointed his own choice of director (Barry Legg) in an effort to root out opposition to his leadership. The action was not merely politically controversial, signalling a determination to rid the party of key modernizers; it was also arguably unconstitutional under the party's new organizational structure, which stipulated that the board appoint the director. Ultimately, Iain Duncan Smith was forced to dismiss the director.

Membership

For much of the twentieth century the Conservative party claimed a genuine mass membership, unlike Labour, which was a mass party only by virtue of its affiliated union members. The Conservative Party long insisted that it did not have membership figures, although individual constituencies had them. Indeed, vying with each other over membership growth and fundraising was a favourite sport of constituency parties at conference. There is now a central database, which was used to send out ballots in the 2001 leadership election.

In 1953 the Conservative Party claimed a membership of 2,805,832. Recent studies suggest, however, that membership of the Conservative Party is declining precipitously. From a position of about 1 million in the early 1980s, estimates suggest that numbers had fallen over the 1990s to about 250,000 in 2001. One expert survey of constituency associations in 1997 found that even in the strongest associations, membership had dropped by two-fifths in the previous three years (Pinto-Duschinsky, 1997). Equally seriously for the future health of the party, there was concern that the remaining membership was ageing and unrepresentative of the multi-racial, multi-cultural society that Britain had become. There had also been dramatic drops in the membership of various youth movements, though there were reports in 2003 that membership had picked up again (see table 8.3).

The decline of Conservative constituency associations had severe implications for campaigning, for fundraising and for morale. Hague's 1998 remedy was to try to rebuild the party's mass membership through a coordinated recruitment drive. The Hague membership blitz, which aimed to achieve a million members by the millennium and was always extremely ambitious, was quietly dropped.

Table 8.3 Conservative Party membership

Year	Membership (000s)
1953	2,806
1969–70	1,120–1,340
1975	1,120
1984	c.1,200
1997	250
2000	318
2002	330

Source: Party membership figures prior to 2000 are an approximation, as there was no national list of members. The figures cited are those identified by Butler and Butler (2000), pp. 141–2 as giving the best indication of party membership at that time. Figures for 2000 and 2002 are official, cited on the *Guardian* website, http://politics.guardian.co.uk/specialreports/tables/0,9071,641234,00.html

Candidate selection

The right to select a parliamentary candidate is one that has been traditionally guarded by the Conservative constituency parties, despite the obvious impact that these candidates have on the image and electoral appeal of the party nationally. One of the significant changes of the post-1945 reform of the party was to ensure that candidates were not precluded from standing for a constituency because of their inability to contribute their own money to it. A series of other reforms gradually allowed Central Office to participate in the process, primarily by ensuring that parties choose their candidate from a national list, by professionally screening would-be candidates and by exercising a right of veto over unsuitable candidates. The National Union's control of the candidates' list is now delegated to a subcommittee of the Board of Management. Constituencies seeking a candidate draw up a shortlist and at the final selection stage there is a panel interview.

During the 1990s the Conservative Party became very sensitive to the need for greater diversity among its candidates. It was especially aware of the dearth of women candidates, especially as Labour was taking highly effective steps to get more women adopted in safe seats through the use of all-women shortlists (AWS). Although a 1993 review and the Hague reforms emphasized the need for more women to be adopted, the party was adamantly opposed to using quotas, AWS or any other formal device to increase the number of women. Not surprisingly, therefore, the number of women fielded by the Conservatives was low by comparison with Labour in both 1997 and 2001 and the number of women elected as Conservative MPs negligible; while Labour returned a record 101 women MPs in 1997 and 95 in 2001, the Conservatives elected just 13 women MPs in 1997 and 14 in 2001.

Deselection

Before the traumatic fights over Europe, Conservative candidates rarely faced deselection. Constituency parties were more likely to try to oust a sitting MP or candidate on the grounds of personal misconduct, feuds with constituency activists or age than for reasons of policy difference. (Thus John Browne in Winchester was deselected in 1992, as was Nicholas Scott in Kensington and Chelsea in 1996, because of constituency disapproval of the MP's personal conduct.) However, constituency parties have sometimes attempted to remove an MP whose policy stance offends the local party. The classic example of this happening is Nigel Nicolson over Suez in 1956. Sir Anthony Meyer was deselected by Clywd NW in January 1990 following his 'stalking horse' challenge to Margaret Thatcher's leadership (Meyer, 1990). Other MPs publicly supportive of Michael Heseltine's 1990 challenge to Thatcher encountered difficulty in their constituencies, though most managed to resist it. In the 1992–7 Parliament certain of the more vocal Eurosceptics met constituency pressure, some of which was allegedly orchestrated through Central Office. After 1997, it was often strong Europeanists who experienced difficulties (Criddle, 1997, 2002).

Agents

Another prerogative that used to be jealously guarded by constituency parties was the right to employ their own agents – constituency organizers who are responsible for both election management and campaigning and generating party activity between elections. Central Office frequently wanted to control the deployment of agents so that the best could be sent to marginal seats rather than be located in safer Tory constituencies. Such a move was bitterly resisted by the constituency parties, who saw the local employment of an agent as crucial to a local party's ability to raise its own funds. MPs also feared that centrally employed agents might become an instrument for putting pressure on them in any policy dispute with the leadership. The general decay of Conservative Party organization and the pressures on party finance have shifted the terms of the debate. Now the issue is not so much how far Central Office can control the deployment of agents but to what extent either the centre or the constituencies can maintain an expansive professional organization. The drop in the actual number of agents is a measure of the decline. In 1966 there were 421 full-time agents. By 1980 this figure had dropped to 330, and by 1997 it was 148. By 2003 the number of agents working for the Conservative Party was said to be about 160, but many of these were part-time and operating out of Central Office rather than working full-time in the constituencies.

Conference

Traditionally, policy making was for most of the nineteenth and twentieth centuries seen as the preserve of the party elite. The annual party conference, to which all constituencies were entitled to send representatives, has generally been regarded as powerless, certainly by comparison with the traditional Labour conference, which was a forceful policy-making body and is still in theory the sovereign organization within the Labour Party. Debates at Conservative conferences were generally anodyne. The stage-managed appearance of the proceedings and resolutions that were not binding infuriated those who wanted meaningful political debate. The development in the Thatcher period of a ritualistic and noisy reception of the leader's speech (accompanied by boisterous singing of 'Land of Hope and Glory') gave conference the quality of a rally rather than a deliberative or policy-making arena. Although some observers suggested that the system of specialist conferences across a year had more influence than was realized, the general role of the annual conference was seen as marginal (Kelly, 1989).

Since the party lost power in 1997, the conference has experimented with its format, moving from the traditional arrangement of formal set-piece debates to shorter and more informal sessions. However, these changes have not remedied the overall impotence of conference. It is still very much geared towards the presentation of policy and the party and its agenda is still very much controlled by the platform. Indeed, if anything it is more stage-managed and the opportunities for genuine political debate are more limited (Kelly, 2001). That said, conference has in the post-1997 period displayed far less deference towards the parliamentary party and it was clear in the aftermath of the 1997 election defeat that many activists blamed the parliamentary party for the party's decline. The Hague reforms of the party structure have also changed the pattern of party meetings that take place in addition to the annual conference. The spring convention (which replaced the spring council) has been the target of criticism because of its restricted opportunities for debate.

The Labour Party

The Labour Party dates from the formation in 1900 of the Labour Representation Committee (LRC), which was designed to promote the interests of the working class by electing its representatives to Parliament. A number of different interests and forces in British politics came together in this project, but the most important element in the new alliance was the trade union movement. The trade unions – and their representative body the Trades Union Congress (TUC) – had been promoting parliamentary representation of working-class interests for over a quarter of a century and it was as a direct result of a resolution passed at the congress of the TUC in 1899 that the move to form a new party occurred. Although the late twentieth century witnessed a deliberate weakening of the ties between the Labour Party and the unions, the relationship between Labour and the unions shaped the party's history and gave its ideology, structure and policies their distinctive character (Minkin, 1992). (See box 8.3 for a brief history of the Labour Party's evolution.)

Another element in the alliance forged in 1900 was a diverse group of small socialist societies. While the unions were concerned primarily with improving the standard of living of their members within the capitalist system, many of these socialist groups were more radical and ideological in character. They included the Independent Labour Party (ILP), which had also played an active role in bringing the new alliance into being, and the cooperative movement.

The ILP had been founded in 1893 by Keir Hardie and others and was an explicitly socialist party. Although it was not initially aligned with the trade unions, the ILP realized that the small socialist societies needed the financial and membership strength of the trade unions in order to be able to compete with the Conservative and Liberal parties. This pragmatic compromise between groups inspired by

Box 8.3   Historical evolution of the Labour Party

1900	Labour Representation Committee (LRC) set up, with affiliated organizations including trade unions and socialist parties such as the Independent Labour Party (ILP). Two LRC MPs elected in 1900, including leader Keir Hardie.
1906–14	Labour MPs support the incumbent Liberal Party, passing legislation such as the 1906 Trade Disputes Act.
1918	Labour Party agrees a new constitution, including Clause 4, its commitment to public ownership of the means of production, distribution and exchange.
1923–4	Minority Labour government elected. Holds office for a few months under Ramsay MacDonald.
1929–31	Labour government in office, dependent on Liberal support.
1931	Ramsay MacDonald forms a National government with the Conservatives and Liberals. Is seen to have betrayed Labour and is expelled from the party.
1940–5	Labour plays significant role in wartime coalition, dominating the home ministries.
1945	Labour government elected, led by Clement Attlee. Institutes welfare state, including National Health Service, and nationalizes basic industries.
1951–64	Party out of office. Internally divided between left and right wings.
1964–70	Wins general elections of 1964 and 1966 under leadership of Harold Wilson. Financial credibility undermined by devaluing of sterling in 1967. Attempts at trade union reform fail. Labour loses the 1970 general election.
1974–9	Labour in power again, led first by Wilson (1974–6) and then by James Callaghan (1976–9). Party divided between left and right on Europe and economic reform. Dwindling majority leave them dependent on Liberal support by 1977.
1979–92	Labour loses 1979 general election after a period of industrial unrest – the so-called 'winter of discontent'. Party moves to the left under leadership of Michael Foot; right wing breaks away to form the Social Democratic Party in 1981. With a socialist manifesto in 1983, the party loses very heavily. Kinnock becomes leader in 1983; begins a long period of reform, bringing the party back towards the centre.
1992	Despite predictions to the contrary, Labour loses for the fourth time in a row in the 1992 general election. Kinnock resigns as leader and is replaced by John Smith. Smith continues internal party reform.
1994	John Smith dies and is replaced by Tony Blair. Blair institutes rapid process of modernization, abandoning the party's commitment to nationalization and embracing much of the Thatcherite consensus on management of the economy.
1997	Labour wins a landslide victory. Institutes a constitutional reform programme, removing hereditary peers from the House of Lords, devolving power to Scotland, Wales and Northern Ireland, and incorporating the European Convention on Human Rights into British law.
2001	Labour elected to a second term in office with a barely diminished majority.

varieties of socialist theory and the essentially defensive and pragmatic trade union movement created a fertile source of controversy and conflict. The ILP separated itself from the Labour Party in the 1930s.

In addition to the ILP, two other organizations deserve special mention as indications of the breadth and diversity of political activity tapped by the LRC in 1900. The Fabian Society, which had been founded in 1884, was to have an enormous impact on Labour's future, not least because of the influence of early Fabian intellectuals such as Beatrice and Sidney Webb, who left their mark on the constitution and ethos of the party. It was not a mass membership organization – indeed, it claimed only 861 members in 1900 – but was a powerful source of progressive ideas. (The Fabian Society has survived and after the Second World War became strongly associated with the revisionist philosophy of **social democracy** associated with Anthony Crosland.) The Social Democratic Foundation, led by H. M. Hyndman, was Marxist and claimed about 9,000 members in 1900 compared with the 13,000 then claimed by the ILP.

The peculiar circumstances of its founding and diversity of the Labour coalition affected its subsequent history in a number of ways. First, within the confederation formed in 1900 the trade unions enjoyed numerical and organizational strength and became the dominant influence in Labour's internal politics. Although the divergent nature of the trade union movement itself meant that its influence was not necessarily a systematic or uniform one, this close alliance between the unions and the Labour Party made the British left both more pragmatic and less ideological than many of its European counterparts. 'Labourism', not socialism, much less Marxism, was the dominant creed. Labour's internal politics as a result became intricately entwined with those of the trade union movement and with the leadership skills and political balance of some of the individual unions.

Secondly, the party's structures were cumbersome and its internal processes awkward. The Labour Party as established in 1900 was a federation of affiliated organizations and it only became a national organization in 1918 when a new constitution was adopted. Even then Labour's structures were devised to represent its different interests, so that Labour needed to rely to a much larger extent than the Conservatives or the Liberals on written rules, standing orders and its constitution.

Thirdly, Labour's internal structures were opaque and often undemocratic. Several features of Labour organization were anomalous from its early years. It accorded little attention to its individual members. Despite the recent emphasis on empowering individual members, at its original formation in 1900 the Labour Party made no provision for individual membership of the party. Individuals would join by virtue of being a member of an affiliated organization, usually a trade union. Although Labour's revised 1918 constitution introduced individual membership, many commentators have noted the paradox that Labour has, over its history, been relatively neglectful of its mass membership (McKibbin, 1974). Indeed, in many respects until the 1990s it had less claim to be a mass party than the Conservatives. Votes taken at conference were dominated by the unions, but the union leaders would cast those votes on the basis of

social democracy Political doctrine originally associated with Marxism but which has come to be associated with revisions of socialism that emphasize the possibility of gradual change rather than revolution. In Britain, the social democratic wing of the Labour Party explicitly criticized public ownership. In 1981 a split within the Labour Party brought about the creation of a separate Social Democratic Party, which later merged with the Liberals to form the Liberal Democrat Party.

287

block vote Method of allocating votes at conference and in other Labour selection processes in which union delegates could cast the whole of their affiliated vote behind a proposal. It was the source of enormous power over Labour policy for a few trade union leaders, whose support would therefore be courted behind the scenes at conference.

no prior consultation with their membership. Moreover, it was traditionally the case that each union's vote would be cast as a whole – the so-called **block vote**. The impact of this was that even where a union leader was aware of internal division on an issue, the whole of a union's vote would be cast as one rather than proportionally divided to represent opinion within its executive or membership.

Finally, Labour acquired a diverse and colourful intellectual heritage: trade unionism, Christian and ethical socialism, Fabianism and Marxism. Additionally, Liberal recruits to the party from the early twentieth century onwards brought their own distinct ideological outlook to it.

From the beginning, therefore, Labour was a broad movement as much as it was a party, a confederation of distinct groups sometimes with conflicting loyalties. This diversity, together with a strong tradition of internal democracy, created tensions and made Labour a more difficult party to manage than the Tories.

One of the features of the British electoral system that was noted in the last chapter is that it has proved hard for new parties to gain access to the system. In 1900 Labour won just two parliamentary seats; but as a result of a secret electoral pact in 1903 with Herbert Gladstone, the Liberal chief whip, Labour was given a straight fight with the Conservatives in a number of seats. Thirty Labour MPs were returned in 1906 and the LRC was formally renamed the Labour Party. Once the entire male working class was given the vote in 1918, Labour soon displaced the Liberals (who had been deeply divided over the First World War) as the Conservatives' main challenger. In 1922, Labour (with 142 seats) became the official opposition. In 1924 and 1929, Labour took office briefly and controversially as a minority government. In 1940, it entered Winston Churchill's wartime coalition government. When Labour finally won a majority in its own right in 1945, its victory then enabled it to implement a range of welfare reforms. Labour enjoyed office again from 1964 to 1970 and from 1974 until 1979; but over that period it encountered extensive difficulty over economic policy and trade union militancy. The collapse of James Callaghan's minority government in 1979 and Margaret Thatcher's electoral victory in 1979 ushered in a period of intense internal conflict in the Labour Party, which remained out of power until 1997.

New Labour

The defeats of 1979 and 1983 caused Labour to begin a long process of internal rebuilding, and indeed to change many aspects of its ideology, organization and image. The process was initiated under the leadership of Neil Kinnock (1983–92) and John Smith (1992–4) but advanced dramatically under Tony Blair (1994–). Blair persuaded Labour to abandon the commitment to socialism by repealing Clause 4 of its constitution, which pledged the party to public ownership. Previous leaders such as Hugh Gaitskell in the late 1950s had tried in vain to change this clause, but Blair succeeded in winning a ballot to remove Clause 4, substituting a modern statement of aims and values. Blair did more than remove archaic symbolism and persuade Labour to moderate its ideological rhetoric. Under his leadership,

Labour also accepted much of the Thatcherite framework of public policy. Blair himself argued for a 'third way' in politics, a new course between the neo-liberal and socialist ideological poles. New Labour policy embraced capitalism and the imperatives of a newly globalized economic environment, placing great emphasis on providing skills to compete in that milieu. Its approach to welfare emphasized obligations as much as rights.

Much of the novelty of New Labour was organizational. Labour became a much more leadership-dominated party, one where the old sources of power – the unions, the conference and National Executive Committee (NEC) – were severely weakened. In that process, as we shall see, the role of individual members was strengthened in a bid to counterbalance the role of unions and traditional party activists. Campaigning became central to the New Labour Party and the presentation of the party and its image became increasingly professionalized. This was a trend that Neil Kinnock had started when he set up the Shadow Communications Agency (SCA) under Peter Mandelson in 1985, but it was taken much further under Blair.

Factionalism and dissent

Not surprisingly given Labour's diverse ideological tradition and its constitutional complexity, its politics have always been prone to factionalism and in-fighting. The issues that occasioned internal division and factionalism have, of course, varied over the party's history, but in any Parliament there can usually be found a number of organized groups within Labour ranks, many of them dedicated to pushing the party towards the left and reasserting party adherence to socialism. Almost inevitably, this factionalism has spread beyond the Parliamentary Labour Party (PLP) to the unions and the constituency parties. Until it dissociated itself from Labour, the ILP operated as a left-of-centre faction within the PLP. The *Tribune* newspaper founded in 1937 became a focus of left-wing dissent, as did the Victory for Socialism group founded in 1944. In the post-1945 period there was a Keep Left group, which articulated an alternative agenda to the leader's on domestic and foreign policy and was associated with Aneurin Bevan. More recent left-of-centre groups have included the Tribune group (which was founded as an organization in 1966), the Campaign group, the Rank and File Mobilizing Committee and the Campaign for Labour Party Democracy (CLPD) (Seyd, 1987). Factionalism on the right has generally been viewed with less suspicion by the leadership and during the 1950s and early 1960s the Gaitskellites organized behind the then leader Hugh Gaitskell to promote a social democratic agenda and resist the tactics of the party's left-wing factions.

Bevanites Adherents of a loose left-wing group which formed around Aneurin Bevan (1897–1960) after his resignation as Secretary of State for Health in 1951. The group attacked the Labour leadership on domestic policy and on foreign policy, where it advocated unilateral nuclear disarmament. It had sufficient strength in the Labour Party to gain substantial representation on the NEC but ceased to be effective when Bevan himself abandoned the policy of unilateralism in 1957.

The attitude of the party as a whole to factionalism has varied. Different periods have seen different answers to the question of how far dissent on grounds of conscience could be tolerated in a party that relied for its impact on solidarity. Sometimes, as in the 1940s and 1950s, the party leadership has made strenuous efforts to contain factionalism, expelling left-wingers such as Konni Zilliacus and Leslie Soley from the party in 1949 and withdrawing the whip from the **Bevanites**, the left-of-centre group

289

organized behind Aneurin Bevan in 1951. Sections of the party that appeared to have become too left wing were liable to be disbanded – a fate that befell the Labour League of Youth. From its early days both the Labour Party leadership and the trade unions were fearful of far-left and Communist infiltration. Efforts to prevent such infiltration in the party's early years led to a list of proscribed organizations, although this was abandoned in 1973. This list was reinstated in 1982 in an effort to cleanse the party of a new generation of ultra-left infiltration from the Militant Tendency and other far-left groups (Crick, 1986). The balance between allowing intellectual diversity to flourish and leaving the party vulnerable to colonization has been a difficult one to maintain.

Maintaining unity within the PLP has similarly presented party leaders with a problem. When the Labour Party is in government it has tried to create a linking structure (known by various names such as the Liaison Committee) that aims to smooth relations between the frontbench and backbenches. The election of a Labour government with a massive majority in 1997 presented party managers with a serious dilemma: how to maintain discipline in circumstances where backbenchers might feel that the very size of the majority rendered rebellion acceptable. In fact Tony Blair, conscious of what loose discipline had done both to his predecessor as prime minister, John Major, and to earlier Labour governments, has tried to impose a tight disciplinary regime on the PLP since 1997. He appointed a party chairman with a seat in cabinet in an attempt to keep the lines of communication with the party open. Blair departed from normal opposition practice by selecting the chief whip himself. PLP standing orders were amended to make clear the obligations of MPs to the party line. In government, pagers were introduced to keep MPs aware of their voting and attendance obligations and to remind them of the party stand – to keep them 'on message'. This new approach to discipline was scornfully derided by independent-minded backbenchers such as Tony Benn. Where MPs did take an independent line, the traditional weapons of the whip's armoury were deployed. Written reprimands were issued and copies sent to constituency parties, though this tactic often backfired (Cowley and Stuart, 2003). Yet even in these circumstances of tighter control, some Labour MPs were willing to defy the leadership in the 1997–2001 Parliament. Despite the absence of widespread dissent, there were some serious rebellions over the issues of disability benefits and lone-parent benefits. In the 2003 Parliament the leadership experienced severe opposition over the war with Iraq. Not only did one senior minister, Robin Cook, resign over the issue, but substantial numbers of Labour MPs voted against their own government. There were also rebellions over the issue of public–private partnerships, which were seen as undermining public services.

Party organization

Enough has already been said to indicate that Labour's internal relationships have always been very much more complicated and formal than those of the Conservative Party. Different elements of the party (the leader, the parliamentary party, the unions and the constituency parties as well as the NEC) all vie for influence over party policy and management. Conflicts over ideology and policy were fought out in the different arenas of the Labour Party, but most publicly in the party's annual conference. Although the traditional dynamics of Labour Party politics have been substantially altered in the period since Blair's leadership, the magnitude of that transformation cannot be appreciated without setting it against an outline of the party's organization prior to Blair's leadership.

Constitutionally, power in the Labour Party has always resided with conference, which was (and still is, theoretically) the party's sovereign body (Minkin, 1978). Between elections decision-making power rested with the NEC, which was elected annually at conference and itself reflected the different elements of the party. Initially it consisted of seven trade unionists and five socialist society members, but in 1918 the NEC was expanded to 23 seats, giving formal representation to the constituency Labour parties (five seats) and to women (four seats). However, at that time trade union representation was increased to 13 seats and socialist organization representation was reduced to one, so that the unions had the dominant influence. This influence was even more pronounced because, until 1937, voting for the various representatives took place in conference as a whole, not in separate sections. As a result, the unions (whose members overwhelmingly dominated conference) could control the outcome of the elections in the constituency and women's sections. After 1937 voting was in separate sections, but the unions still dominated the composition of the NEC because, in addition to their own seats, the vote for the treasurer, an ex officio member, was by conference as a whole.

The NEC determined policy between conferences. Conference had the final say on what was official party policy. Motions adopted by a two-thirds majority became official party policy. When Labour was in power, conference and the NEC would generally be subordinated to the prime minister and cabinet in the policy-making process, though Labour leaders recognized the electoral damage and embarrassment that policy divisions inside the party could cause. For example, conference in 1968 voted overwhelmingly against a statutory incomes policy and a decade later, in 1978, voted against the government's 5 per cent wage increase guideline. In opposition, however, a real struggle for control of policy would frequently occur. Hugh Gaitskell in 1960 was confronted with a vote in favour of unilateral nuclear disarmament which he was able to reverse the next year. The NEC would frequently fall into the hands of the left and provide opposition to the party leader, whether the party was in government or not. Thus the authority of the leader of the PLP, and indeed of a Labour prime minister, has sometimes been challenged by officials of the NEC who have tried to hold the leader accountable to party policy. Harold Laski, for example, tried unsuccessfully to use his position as chairman of the Labour Party to direct Attlee's handling of foreign policy in 1945. In the 1970s Tony Benn, when chairman of the backbench PLP and then of the NEC home policy committee, regularly crossed swords with Wilson and Callaghan over their fidelity to official Labour party policy.

Under Blair the NEC was restructured and the unions lost their majority. More importantly, the creation of a wholly new policy process – the National Policy Forum – effectively sidelined the NEC's role.

electoral college A body
which is given the responsibility of electing to an office.
The members of an electoral
college will usually be
selected to represent different parts of a wider constituency or they may be elected.
This form of indirect election
has been extensively used in
the Labour Party for its leadership elections.

The leader and the parliamentary party

Historically, the Labour Party did not place as much emphasis on leadership as the Conservatives. Labour's extra-parliamentary origins, its own traditions of internal democracy and its cumbersome federal structure meant that at the beginning of its life the party did not accord the leader of the PLP much deference.

From its beginning as a parliamentary party, however, the PLP elected its own chairman, who increasingly came to be leader of the PLP. A deputy chairman was also elected. In opposition elections were annual. The leader began to be regarded informally as the leader of the party as a whole. (Not until Kinnock was the leader given the title Leader of the Labour Party.) The PLP also appointed whips and devised written rules for itself. A Labour leader is constrained in opposition by the fact that his or her immediate colleagues – the shadow cabinet spokespersons – are elected by the PLP as a whole. They may thus reflect an individual's party popularity rather than parliamentary or potential administrative ability and they may constitute a very differently balanced team from that which a leader would pick if prime minister.

Despite electing members of the shadow cabinet in opposition, Labour leaders have assumed from the time Labour first took office in 1924 that a Labour prime minister would be free to choose his cabinet, rather than be subject to election. That said, the fact that the shadow cabinet is elected means that an incoming Labour prime minister is more constrained than an incoming Conservative prime minister would be. Historically, most Labour prime ministers have felt the need also to balance the different wings of the party in government. Blair, however, appointed to his government very few who were outside the ideological ambit of New Labour.

From the 1920s until the 1970s it was accepted that it was for Labour MPs alone to choose the leader, and more recently the deputy leader as well. The question of changing this assumption became a staple item of debate as the conflict between the PLP and the rank and file intensified in the 1970s. From 1972 to 1981, the issue of the leadership selection mechanism appeared on every conference agenda in some form. The point was that by changing the leadership method, it was hoped to lock the leadership more effectively into what was then a left-of-centre agenda. The project was deftly promoted by CLPD, which used model resolutions to push this and two other items of constitutional reform – automatic reselection of MPs and greater control for the NEC over the party manifesto (Kogan and Kogan, 1983).

In fact, CLPD was successful in securing a change in the rules for election to the leadership. Following a special conference at Wembley in 1981, it was decided that there would be an **electoral college** in which the unions, the constituency Labour parties (CLPs) and the MPs were each given a share of the vote in the proportion 40 : 30 : 30. The outcome quickened the departure of a group of senior right-of-centre Labour MPs, including Shirley Williams, David Owen and Bill Rogers, who together with Roy Jenkins formed the Social Democratic Party. They issued their Limehouse declaration (which signalled the break with Labour) the day after Labour's special conference on revising the method of leadership election.

Although Neil Kinnock was the first Labour leader elected under the new rules, he realized that he had to reassert the autonomy and authority of the leadership if Labour were ever to regain electoral credibility. In addition to a wide-ranging policy review, Kinnock established new institutions that would enable him to bypass the traditional party structures and develop the power of the leader's office. The rules for the leadership election were also subsequently modified to make them more open and democratic. Significantly, the percentage distribution within the electoral college was changed so that the unions no longer had a numerical advantage. At the 1993 conference the rules were further amended to give the unions, MPs and MEPs, and CLPs each 33 per cent of the vote. Unions were also obliged to consult their members by ballot, just as CLPs had to consult their members by ballot. Thirdly, a new method of aggregating the vote was announced. The winner-take-all rule was abandoned and union votes were distributed in proportion to members' preferences. The total impact of these changes was to reduce union power and strengthen individual members. In July 1994, Tony Blair was elected leader under this revised system.

Blair's conception of how to lead the Labour Party was heavily conditioned both by the success of Margaret Thatcher and by his perception that Labour had to devise policies that would appeal to the voters rather than the party. The systematic strengthening of the Labour leadership had in fact been started by Kinnock, who developed the infrastructure of the leadership within the party and played a much more interventionist role in the policy process. (He also marketed himself more directly than his predecessors had done and waged a determined war against far-left infiltration of the party.)

Blair, however, took the centralization of the party and the strengthening of the leadership much further than did either Kinnock or Smith. Although Smith put his leadership on the line to push through one member one vote (OMOV) reforms, he was less convinced of the arguments for organizational modernization than either Kinnock or Blair (see box 8.4). Blair's reforms have had an impact at all levels of the party, but especially on the roles of the unions and the membership, and on Labour's traditional policy-making bodies – conference and the NEC. Candidate selection has also been heavily influenced by Blair's reforms, though in some instances the desire to ensure that only New Labour candidates are selected has backfired badly – as it did for the first Welsh leadership election, the first Scottish Parliament elections and in relation to the first London mayoralty race.

The trade unions

The unions were always a major force in the Labour Party, not least because of their financial clout. Although approximately only one-third of its money now comes from the unions (see table 8.4), the estimated percentage in the past has been much higher. The unions provided Labour with its income in a number of ways. One was through affiliation fees. Once a union had affiliated to the Labour Party, it paid the party a political levy for each member it affiliated. This system, which was introduced in 1903, was an important source of income for the Labour Party, yet it was one which the unions controlled. A union did not need to affiliate all its members, and a union could under-affiliate if it wished. As of 2002, there were 22 unions affiliated to the Labour Party.

Box 8.4   Labour modernization by leader

Neil Kinnock

- Expelled Militant Tendency from the party.
- Set up a new Campaigns and Communications directorate under Peter Mandelson. Used volunteers from advertising, marketing and polling to modernize Labour's image for the 1992 election.
- Changed the party emblem from red flag to red rose.
- Undertook a policy review, which ended Labour's commitment to unilateral nuclear disarmament, high taxation and old-style nationalization.
- Reduced the dominance of the trade unions in the electoral college for candidate and leadership selection.
- National Policy Forum set up to increase the role of the leadership and parliamentary party in policy making.

John Smith

- Moved to one member one vote for candidate and leadership selection, removing direct union representation in parliamentary selections.
- Voting power of trade unions at the annual conference reduced.

Tony Blair

- Reformed Clause 4 of the party's constitution to end its commitment to nationalization of the major industries.
- Campaigning and communications became increasingly professionalized.
- National Parliamentary Panel set up to vet potential parliamentary candidates.
- Voting power of trade unions at the annual conference further reduced.
- 'Partnership into Power' reforms created a two-year rolling programme for policy making headed by a Joint Policy Committee, further weakening the scope for delegates at the annual conference to make policy unilaterally.

Another device that provided the party with financial help and reinforced a close relationship between a union and an MP was sponsorship. For much of Labour's history, candidates who might be sponsored by unions brought advantages to constituency parties in terms of additional money and organizational support. Unions would also dip into their pockets to find extra money for Labour at election time and they also provided the party with a number of in-kind subsidies. The unions were an equally powerful force in the constituencies and at conference, where they controlled 87 per cent of the vote as late as 1992 and 13 out of 24 seats on the NEC.

How the unions exercised this widespread influence varied over time depending on such factors as the issue agenda and the leadership of individual unions. Although the unions were not always at one with the parliamentary leadership, for much of the period up to the 1960s they could be relied on for support on matters that did not threaten union interests. However, this pattern changed when wage restraint and industrial relations reform policies became a staple part of the country's political agenda. Moreover, the volatility of the unions' own internal politics created

Table 8.4 Biggest Labour union affiliates

Labour Party affiliates	Annual donation, 2002 (£)
Unison	986,758
GMB (General and Municipal Boilerworkers)	891,400
TGWU (Transport and General Workers Union)	880,284
Amicus–AEEU (Amalgamated Engineering and Electrical Union)	691,986
CWU (Communication Workers Union)	526,425
USDAW (Union of Shop, Distributive and Allied Workers)	495,992
Amicus–MSF (Manufacturing, Science, Finance)	295,981
Amicus	217,625
GPMU (Graphical, Paper and Media Union)	144,050
UCATT (Union of Construction, Allied Trades and Technicians)	111,426
The Community Union (steel and metal workers)	103,092
RMT (Rail, Maritime, Transport)	62,550
TSSA (Transport Salaried Staff Association)	60,426
FBU (Fire Brigades Union)	44,692
CATU (Ceramics and Allied Trades Union)	33,631
National Union of Knitwear, Footwear and Apparel Trades	33,282
ASLEF (Associated Society of Locomotive Engineers and Firemen)	33,151
MU (Musicians Union)	23,337
BECTU (Broadcasting, Entertainment, Cinema and Theatre Union)	23,300
NUM (National Union of Mineworkers)	5,451

Source: Electoral Commission, Donations Register.

instability in the balance within the wider Labour Party. A shift in position of one or two of the largest trade unions at conference such as the Transport and General Workers Union (TGWU), the General and Municipal Boilerworkers (GMB) or the Amalgamated Engineering and Electrical Union (AEEU) could be decisive in a policy vote or election. Not surprisingly, Labour leaders always felt it essential to try to maximize their support with union leaders and Labour conferences were marked by behind-the-scenes bargaining to try to gain the support of individual unions in key votes.

The link between the unions and the Labour Party became a crucial item on the agenda of party reform in the period immediately following the loss of the 1983 election, when three successive leaders – Neil Kinnock, John Smith and Tony Blair – embarked on a crusade of modernization. Crucial to this reform was the bid to shift many of Labour's election mechanisms to a one-member-one-vote basis, a move which was at first strenuously resisted by the unions. The trade union proportion of the votes at conference was cut from 87 per cent to 70 per cent in 1992 and to 50 per cent (co-equal with the constituency section) in 1995. Sponsorship of candidates was abolished in 1995. An effort was made to replace Labour's dependence on trade union money with donations from other sources – a task that was made much easier by Labour's accession to power in 1997. Most importantly, Blair in opposition and in power made it very clear that while unions could expect to have their views taken into account, they could expect no special favours. Despite these changes, the trade unions are still extremely important in the Labour Party as a source of members and money and because of the long-standing identity of interest.

Membership

Individual membership of the Labour Party, as we have noted, was not given much emphasis in the party's early years, even after individual membership was introduced in 1918. Rather, the influential players in the party were the corporate members – especially the unions – who were more numerous than the individual members and more influential. In the post-war period, the level of individual membership has ebbed and flowed (see table 8.5). Some of the loss of membership was artificial, as in the 1980s when the rule that specified a minimum number of members for affiliation was repealed and parties returned their real membership rather than artificially inflated numbers. Other membership gains and losses reflect fluctuations in party fortune and more general social factors such as the declining appeal of joining a political party.

From the period of the Kinnock leadership in 1983, determined efforts were made to increase the level of the individual membership and its role in the party. Individual members were seen as important to the wider process of rebuilding the Labour organization and making its policies more marketable to the electorate as a whole. It should be emphasized that Labour leaders were *not* attempting to enhance the powers of the activists who had contributed to the party's leftward shift in the late 1970s and early 1980s. Instead, they wanted to broaden the base of membership and bring into the party new members who were in tune with ordinary voters. Empowering such individual members would, it was hoped, constrain the power both of the unions and of the unrepresentative activists who had gained power through their ability to capture moribund constituency parties. Thus the expansion of individual membership was crucial to changing the internal power structure of the Labour Party. Reinforcing the role of individual members also strengthened the leadership because it was assumed that ordinary Labour members (like Conservative ones) would be responsive to the leadership and would endorse its candidates, policies and strategies.

Table 8.5 Labour Party membership

Year	Membership (000s)
1945	487
1950	908
1955	843
1960	790
1965	817
1970	680
1975	675
1980	348
1985	313
1990	365
1996	400
2000	311
2002	280

Source: Figures are individual party members and do not include membership of affiliated organizations such as trade unions and cooperative societies. Figures up to 1996 are taken from Butler and Butler (2000), pp. 158–9; those for 2000 and 2002 are official figures cited on the *Guardian* website, http://politics.guardian.co.uk/specialreports/tables/0,9071,641234,00.html

The drive to increase membership in the 1990s was initially highly successful and the campaign introduced important innovations such as centralized membership. The build-up to the 1997 election saw Labour's individual membership overtake that of the Conservatives. Once in power, however, Labour's ability to attract new members fell back. In 2002 the party announced that it had lost 40,000 members the previous year.

Efforts to cede more power to individual Labour members transformed a number of the party's internal processes. Individual members had been given a role in the leadership election process in 1981. In 1993 the rules of candidate selection and of the leadership selection were changed to replace voting in sections by OMOV. Conference was reformed to reduce the power of the unions within it and, at the same time, much of the power of conference was reduced by the establishment of alternative policy-making processes controlled by the leadership.

The new power balance within the Labour Party has not gone unchallenged. In the summer of 2003, it was reported for example that a broad left movement aiming to 'reclaim the party' had secured the support of four major unions in a bid to challenge the leadership on key policies at the 2003 conference. Although unlikely to shake the government's position, the initiative was indicative that opposition to the leadership within Labour ranks was still a threat to unity.

Policy making

It is important to remember that Labour's constitution gave power not to the parliamentary party but to conference and to the NEC. Neither of these bodies was composed in a way which automatically provided a reliable block of support for the parliamentary leader. Historically, the party leadership kept control of party policy by making alliances with union leaders to dominate conference votes. Party leaders also maintained the right to select which elements of party policy would appear in the manifesto and would be emphasized in an election campaign. However, the ability of the party leadership to control conference in this way was very dependent on the attitudes of individual unions and the issue agenda. Even if the leadership succeeded in winning a policy battle at conference, this victory would come at a price. Conference would often involve damaging fights over the content of the policy and allegations of behind-the-scenes manoeuvring to fix alliances between unions and the leadership and to bypass the alleged will of the party. Party activists frequently resented the ability of the leadership to ignore official party policy, and in the 1970s and early 1980s CLPD made the right to control the manifesto an important item on its agenda.

Kinnock, Smith and Blair all sought to move the policy-making process away from the conference and the NEC and to create new institutions that would be under their control. Kinnock introduced the Campaign Strategy Committee and generated a policy review which was masterminded from the leader's office. In 1990 a National Policy Forum (NPF) was introduced which ensured that the parliamentary party – especially the leader and shadow cabinet – had a much greater role in the policy process. Not least, the NPF allowed the parliamentary party and leadership to set the agenda rather than forcing them to respond to conference and NEC motions.

Leadership drafts formed the basis of discussion. The NPF meets in private, thereby avoiding the embarrassment of public wrangles over policy and enabling deals to be done.

In the run-up to the 1997 election, Blair further modified the system. 'Partnership in Power' introduced a series of reforms that were endorsed by conference. A new body – the Joint Policy Committee – took over responsibility for promoting policy debates. The idea appears to be that forward policy making will now take place over a two-year cycle involving a good deal of consultation with all sections of the party, an enhanced role for the leadership and a final vote by conference. By placing the policy framework in the context of a two-year cycle, the leadership hopes to have devised a mechanism for creating consensus rather than conflict and avoiding the need to negotiate policy in front of the media at conference. Policy issues can be considered in the round and over a longer time period away from the rather feverish atmosphere of conference; and the leader and his team, not the party, are in the driving seat (Heffernan, 2000; Webb, 2000).

Candidate selection

Candidate selection in the Labour Party became a highly contentious issue in the 1970s. The traditional system allowed constituency parties seeking a candidate to select from one of four lists. These were the 'A' list, which contained trade union-sponsored candidates; the 'B' list, which contained a rather larger number of constituency-nominated candidates; and the 'C' list, which contained applicants sponsored by the Cooperative Society, an organization affiliated to the Labour Party. In 1989 a separate list of women candidates (the 'W' list) was introduced. The system favoured the affiliated organizations, especially the unions, by making it clear which candidates had union sponsorship and hence would be less costly for the constituency party seeking to select a candidate. Although there were some mechanisms to allow the centre to veto candidates deemed unsuitable, it was a system that left substantial power in the hands of the local constituency parties and the local activists. Indeed, the national party usually only became involved in constituency selection if the contest was a by-election or if it looked as though the party might not be able to find a suitable candidate. The centre might also become involved if there was an allegation of procedural impropriety in the selection process. A feature of local selection processes prior to the 1990s was that they were often controlled by small, unrepresentative cliques of activists, or were dominated by the unions, who might also be to the left of the electorate as a whole. The campaign in the 1970s and 1980s to select MPs responsive to their constituency parties thus threatened to produce a bloc of candidates whose ideologies were far out of alignment with the median voter. In order to break this system, the method of selection had to be changed and greater power to decide who could be a candidate had to be transferred to the centre. The introduction of OMOV in 1992 diluted the power of the activists and was much more transparent, but it did not by itself yield greater power to the centre to influence the kind of candidate who would be selected. In 1997 the Labour Party created a single national list – the National Parliamentary Panel – which provided for better screening of candidates. This creation of a more professional mechanism of national control over candidates was naturally viewed with suspicion on the left as another method for promoting leadership control. The new methods, it was alleged, would produce a homogeneous party of docile New Labour footsoldiers. In fact, as was noted earlier, the 1997–2001 Parliament and the Parliament elected in 2001 have witnessed some serious backbench rebellion within Labour ranks, but there is a powerful sense that the balance in the party has swung too far to the centre and right in relation to candidate selection.

One feature of selection contests in the run-up to the 1997 election was the determination to secure a greater diversity of candidates, and especially better representation of women through the use of AWS. Although these shortlists were sometimes controversial, they secured the aim of radically increasing the selection of women in safe seats and, in 1997, the number of women in Parliament. All-women shortlists have now been replaced by 50–50 selection lists, in which there will be an equal balance of men and women. This raises the issue of whether there has been a genuine change of Labour culture or whether 1997 should be seen as an isolated exercise in securing gender equality. Union officials still seem skilled at getting candidates into safe seats. Indeed, one-fifth of the admittedly small number of new MPs in 2001 were ex-union officials (Criddle, 2002).

The leadership's effort to influence selection procedures was not by any means a universal success. Although it was able to secure safe seats for some leadership-promoted candidates just before the 2001 election, the attempt to control selection procedures generated a good deal of resentment and opposition. This was especially marked in the London, Welsh Assembly and Scottish Parliament elections, where the London leadership exerted enormous efforts to exclude or disadvantage candidates who were seen as being out of step with the New Labour agenda.

Deselection

One of the most bitter periods of recent Labour history occurred in the 1970s and 1980s as left-of-centre constituency parties exercised their right to remove an MP with whose policy stances they disagreed. This fate befell such prominent figures as Dick Taverne and Bob Mellish. In 1980 following mobilization from CLPD, a system of mandatory selection for MPs was introduced. This meant that all Labour MPs, instead of being able to assume reselection, had to go through a new selection process in each Parliament. Between 1981 and 1986, 14 MPs were deselected and, in addition to those who were actually rejected, there were a number who opted for retirement rather than face a long battle with their local party. Some MPs who might have been rejected by their local party pre-empted the fight by leaving Labour and joining the breakaway SDP in the 1980s.

When Kinnock became leader he tried to modify the power of CLPs to deselect by broadening numbers who participated in the selection process. Although he failed to modify the deselection rules prior to 1987, the 1987 conference agreed to establish an electoral college for candidate selection, a method which allowed the unions to retain some power in the process. When John Smith became leader he achieved a switch to a system in which each party member had one vote in the selection process.

affirmative nomination
New selection process designed to give some security of tenure to sitting Labour MPs and to prevent constituency Labour parties removing MPs on ideological grounds.

Now a new selection process can only occur if there is a 50 per cent vote among the members to call for it. The new system is called **affirmative nomination** and again gives MPs security of tenure. To a large extent, the threat to sitting MPs had in any case diminished during the 1990s as members became more concerned with gaining and keeping office than with ideological in-fighting (Criddle, 2002). However, Labour MPs have always been somewhat closer to the delegate theory of representation than to the trustee theory and there is no guarantee that divisions between constituency parties and the national leadership will not surface again (Cowley and Stuart, 2003).

The Liberal Democrats

The Liberal Democrat Party is a relatively young party formed from an alliance of the old Liberal Party and the Social Democratic Party (SDP), which had been formed in 1981 as a result of a split within the Labour Party (see box 8.5 for a brief history of the party's evolution). Historically, the Liberal Party had been extremely successful during the late nineteenth and early twentieth centuries, drawing its support especially from the areas of religious non-conformity, the towns and industrial areas of the country, and the periphery. However, the rise of Labour and the mobilization of party conflict around class-based issues after the First World War effectively weakened the party. Its seats in Parliament declined and in the immediate aftermath of the Second World War it nearly disappeared altogether as a national party. The 1951 election saw it gain only 2.5 per cent of the national vote. However, it was never totally obliterated from Parliament and the post-1955 period saw periodic Liberal revivals in the polls and sporadic by-election victories. Although the Liberal Party did not participate in any national government after the coalition of 1940–5, it remained an important force in local government where its emphasis on community politics gave it a special appeal. The SDP, by contrast, was formed by senior figures from the Labour Party with extensive governmental experience. Their opposition to Labour's leftward drift in the 1970s and 1980s inevitably created a certain suspicion of grassroots activism, although they recognized that their new party would have to build a strong individual membership base. These two centre parties had developed a working relationship as the Alliance in the general election of 1983 and had come close to overtaking Labour. However, there was a marked personality clash between their then leaders, David Steel and David Owen.

Formal merger of the Liberal Party and SDP occurred in 1988. Although a majority in both parties voted for merger, there were some groups on both sides who resented the move. As a result, the early years of the Liberal Democrats, as the new party became after a postal ballot of members in 1989, did not produce a major surge in support. Nevertheless, the new party was clearly ideologically broader than either of its component parts and better placed than either had been to challenge the two larger parties. The merger between the Liberals and the SDP brought to the old Liberal organization (which had been marked by increasing tension between the parliamentary party and the more radical extra-parliamentary party) a new drive for efficiency and modernization. The SDP had been formed from the top down and

Box 8.5   Historical evolution of the Liberal/Liberal Democrat Party

1859	Liberal Party established through coalition of the Whigs with free-trade Conservatives and new Radicals. Lead by Gladstone, the party dominates government for the next half-century.
1886	Gladstone's First Home Rule Bill for Ireland splits the party.
1906	Liberals win a landslide victory under leadership of Lloyd George. Introduce programme of social reform, bringing in pensions and unemployment relief. Clash with the Lords over the budget in 1911 leads to Parliament Act limiting the power of Lords to a delaying power. Pass a number of bills on Home Rule for Ireland.
1905–22	Splits in the party and the expansion of the franchise increase Labour's support at the expense of the Liberals.
1916	Liberals split over the conduct of the war. Lloyd George replaces Asquith as prime minister. Liberals remain split between the 'Lloyd George' and 'Asquith' Liberals until 1923.
1922	Liberals pushed into third place in the election, where they remain for the rest of the century.
1923	Liberals support a minority Labour government for ten months.
1931	Party split again between National Liberals (who eventually merged with the Conservatives) and the Liberals.
1945–70	Liberals squeezed by two major parties, netting less than 3 per cent of the vote in the 1951 and 1955 elections.
1974	Surge in the Liberal vote to 19 per cent in February election and 18 per cent in October.
1981	The formation of the Social Democratic Party (SDP) from dissatisfied Labour moderates creates a challenger for the centrist vote.
1983	Liberals and SDP form an Alliance and net 25 per cent of the vote. The distortions of the electoral system give the Alliance only 23 seats (4 per cent) in Parliament.
1988	Liberals and SDP merge to form the Social and Liberal Democrats, shortened a year later to the Liberal Democrats, led by Paddy Ashdown.
1994–7	Close links between Ashdown and Labour leader Blair, signalled by increased Labour support for electoral reform.
1997	The Liberal Democrats show signs of converting their votes into seats more efficiently, gaining 46 seats (7 per cent) from 17 per cent of the vote. Labour manifesto promises a referendum on electoral reform and Blair gives Liberal Democrats seats on a Cabinet Committee on Constitutional Reform.
1999	Charles Kennedy becomes leader of the party. With no evidence that the government intends to move on electoral reform, Kennedy begins to distance the party from Labour. With support for the Conservatives falling, Kennedy talks of the Liberals breaking through to become Britain's second party.
2001	Liberals increase their parliamentary representation to 52, but their vote share increases by only 1 per cent to 18 per cent – not the predicted breakthrough.

placed a great emphasis on new methods of campaigning through the media, whereas the grassroots of the Liberals had come to exercise increasing influence. The merger provided the opportunity to create a new constitution, which could avoid some of the perceived organizational weaknesses of the old Liberal Party without losing its emphasis on individual membership participation.

Liberal Democrat ideology draws on the intellectual traditions of two very different parties and its early years were marked by conflict over which of these two traditions should be dominant. The old Liberal Party drew its ideas from a rich ideological tradition stretching back at least as far as Gladstone. It placed great importance on individualism, on rationalism and on freedom as well as on morality in the domestic and international sphere. As a party its style has been to emphasize participation and community politics as well as decentralization. The SDP, by contrast, drew on the revisionist strand of Labour Party thinking that emphasized pragmatic adjustment to capitalism and that rejected doctrinaire socialism. The SDP's origins made it very aware of the significance of the media and of professional campaigning as well as of the need for adequate funding.

The Liberal Democrats in recent years have stressed their commitment to constitutional reform, to high-quality public services, to internationalism and to environmentalism. As the lines of continuity between New Labour's and the Conservative government's approach to public spending and taxation became clearer after 1997, Liberal Democrats have stressed their commitment to additional public spending on such items as welfare, the National Health Service and education, even though that commitment might entail a rise in direct taxation. Its emphasis on civil liberties, constitutionalism and public spending thus puts the Liberal Democrats in some ways to the left of New Labour. In 2003, the Liberal Democrat leader Charles Kennedy publicly opposed the Iraq war.

The accent on public spending underlines one of the Liberal Democrats' strategic problems: how to differentiate themselves in the party system. The party has long been seen as a centre party – midway between Labour and the Conservatives. Increasingly, however, it has moved closer to the Labour Party, formally abandoning the position of 'equidistance' between the parties in 1995 and cooperating (under Paddy Ashdown) with the development of Labour's constitutional reform agenda, including briefly sitting on a cabinet committee with Labour ministers. This policy stance of 'constructive opposition' was not always popular with the Liberal Democrat rank and file. Cooperation with Labour over constitutional reform has been much less marked under Charles Kennedy's leadership, but the two parties continue to collaborate informally at the electoral level; and it appears that their voters were prepared to vote tactically against the Conservatives in 1997 and 2001.

Organizationally, the Liberal Democrats are a federal party with autonomous parties in England, Scotland and Wales as well as a federal party covering the whole of the United Kingdom. There is a strong commitment to decentralization, which entails a regional structure in England and separate parties in Scotland and Wales. The emphasis on decentralization sometimes conflicts with the demands of effective leadership and the perspective of party headquarters. The whole party membership elects its leader on the basis of OMOV. The president of the party (a two-year post) is also elected and is responsible for the management of the organization. Parliamentary candidates are elected by postal ballot. Policy is made in an exhaustive process which is initiated at the grassroots through policy working groups and is debated and endorsed at conference, after consideration by the Federal Policy Committee (FPC). The party has approximately 76,000 members who may join as individuals or as members of associated organizations or special associated organizations. The Liberal Democrats are weakened by the absence of regular corporate donors, so that their funding always appears fragile. The new register of donations showed that the party had received no gifts over £250,000 in the period since the register was established. Clearly, the Liberal Democrats would benefit from a greater degree of public funding than exists at present (Electoral Commission, 2003).

In the 1997 general election the Liberal Democrats obtained 46 MPs, their best result since 1929. That number increased to 52 at the 2001 election and was 53 in 2003. Liberal Democrats have made significant advances at the local government level, challenging both the Conservatives and Labour. They have representation in the European Parliament, where they form part of the European Liberal, Democrat and Reform Group. And they have shared power as part of a coalition in the Scottish and Welsh executives.

Smaller Parties

The British electoral system used at the national level (FPTP) clearly disadvantages smaller parties. Other aspects of the British electoral system, such as the requirement that candidates pay a deposit, also disadvantages minor parties if they do not have strong financial backing. Although the advent of new political arenas that do not use FPTP has clearly improved the chances of some of the smaller parties – such as the Scottish National Party (SNP) in Scotland, Plaid Cymru (PC) in Wales and the Green Party in London – these smaller parties have little chance of forming a national government and may seem marginal to the battle for power between the major parties. There are, however, important reasons for taking note of some of them. Small political parties may organize to give expression to a single interest such as a demand for national independence or hostility to abortion. They may reflect splits in the established parties. Or they may enjoy a regional rather than a national appeal. Among the smaller parties with representation in the House of Commons, mention should be made of the two nationalist parties, the SNP and PC. Both parties obviously have a greater impact because of devolution and are discussed in greater depth in chapter 12. The important point to note here is the extent to which they have grown from tiny political organizations that made relatively little impact even in their own areas to become a significant electoral force. Alongside electoral success have come better organizational provision, membership growth and financial viability. Chapter 12 also examines the political parties of Northern Ireland, where party competition revolves around quite different issues from those on the mainland.

Other smaller parties can have an impact from time to time, although generally not at the parliamentary level where the FPTP electoral system operates against them. Concern with environmental issues has created a fluctuating constituency for the Green Party, although the environmental movement has a much broader influence than the vote for that party might suggest. Although the Green Party (which is the successor to the Ecology Party) has suffered from financial difficulties, internal splits and organizational weakness, it has secured representation at the local level. More dramatically, the use of the list system of proportional representation has given it seats in the European Parliament. In the first Greater London Assembly elections it won three seats and one of its members – Darren Johnson – was appointed to be Ken Livingstone's environmental adviser. Scotland and Northern Ireland have their own Green Party organizations.

There are a range of small left-wing parties that sometimes field candidates, though their vote is negligible. Parties of the far right, especially the British National Party, have recently caused concern because of their capacity to exploit and exacerbate racial tensions in such centres as Oldham.

Two parties that emerged in the 1990s as a result of debate about Britain's role in Europe – the Referendum Party and the UK Independence Party – gained an unusual amount of media coverage. The Referendum Party was the creation of James Goldsmith and may have had an electoral impact at the margins, primarily taking votes from the Conservatives. In 1997 it contested 547 seats and gained some 3 per cent of the vote. The UK Independence Party in 1997 contested 194 seats and gained 1.1 per cent of the vote. The use of a party list system of proportional representation for the European elections in 1999 helped the UK Independence Party, which has three MEPs.

Party Finance

Running a political party is an expensive activity. Parties need money to maintain their organizations between elections and to provide a variety of membership services, publicity material and policy research. They also need money to campaign in elections and while British elections are relatively low cost by comparison with those in the United States, for example, developments in campaign technology and increasingly competitive elections have caused the cost of elections to shoot up. The fact that there are now more elections further adds to the parties' burdens. Both major parties in the recent past have experienced extreme financial embarrassment. It was reported in 2003 that Labour was £6 million overdrawn, while the Conservatives after the 1997 election were £4 million overdrawn and found their bank refusing to extend the overdraft.

Membership fees alone would not fund the expenses of any modern political party. The *Guardian* reckoned in 2002 that only 8 per cent of Labour's costs come from member subscriptions. Traditionally, the parties have found their money from different corporate sources: Conservatives have been dependent on business and Labour has been heavily reliant on trade unions. Although the unions are still very generous donors to Labour, recent years have seen a deliberate move away from reliance on union money by the leadership, which feared that such a close association with the unions had become electorally unpopular. For their part, the unions displayed marked resistance to supplying cash to a Labour Party that was pursuing policies the unions disliked. As a result, Labour has had to cultivate alternative sources of finance. Indeed, the *Guardian* reckoned the unions' share of party expenditure had fallen from 66 per cent in 1992, to 40 per cent in 1997, and to about 33 per cent in 2001. Another article in 2003 maintained that 27 per cent of Labour's costs were met by union money, with the bulk coming from donations. Individual donors such as Lord Sainsbury (who from 1999 to 2003 gave £8.5 million to Labour), Sir Gulam Noon and Lady Hamlyn have also been extremely important on the Labour side; while Paul Getty, Stuart Wheeler and Michael Ashcroft in the recent past have given large sums to the Conservatives, who raise approximately 90 per cent of their funding from donations. Although the issue of state funding of parties has been on the political agenda at least since the mid-1970s, there is no consensus about moving towards greater state involvement in that area. At present, therefore, the financial regime under which parties operate involves a small number of subsidies for parties in elections (e.g., use of school halls for meetings, free party political broadcasts and free mailshots), plus a subsidy designed to help parties discharge their parliamentary duties (known as **Short money** in the House of Commons, and as **Cranleigh money** in the House of Lords).

The introduction of PPERA 2000 also saw the creation of a new source of state money through the introduction of a Policy Development Fund, which was capped at £2 million per annum (Fisher, 2002). This fund was initiated to aid the parties in policy development.

PPERA was intended to promote greater transparency in party funding and to eliminate funding practices that might expose a political party, especially one in government, to the possibility of corruption. Not surprisingly, those who give money expect some return, even if it is only the prospect of an invitation to a small party at which a minister will be present for privileged access rather than an explicit concession over policy or an honour. PPERA achieved its aims by requiring parties to publish annual accounts, mandating that all donations over £200 be recorded and national donations over £5,000 be reported. It also banned foreign donations.

To some extent PPERA made the lives of the parties in a competitive age much more difficult, not merely by restricting access to funds but also by imposing a series of bureaucratic requirements (quarterly returns and recorded election expenses within a set period) which fall especially heavily on smaller parties but which also burden large party organizations. On the other hand, PPERA in theory placed a restriction on the escalating cost of election campaigns by setting limits on what the parties could spend nationally in an election. This cap amounted to about £15.36 million per party in 2001. The Electoral Commission in 2002 set in motion a review of the legislation that could lead to a regime with a lighter touch.

Underlying the PPERA review is the argument for an extension of state aid. In addition to the arguments on principle that surround state aid, there are deep disagreements about how such aid should be distributed. One frequently canvassed method which links money to votes at the previous election is open to the powerful objection that it is unfair to small parties and replicates past strength. Another method would be to calculate the sums to be distributed on the basis of party membership. Both schemes would be likely to face great unpopularity, especially if it were thought that this use of taxation would be at the expense of other public services.

Short money A subsidy designed to help parties discharge their parliamentary duties. Known as Cranleigh money in the House of Lords.

Conclusions

Britain's major political parties have very distinct histories and ideological and organizational traditions. Nevertheless, the last few years have witnessed the development of a number of common patterns and trends. Leaders have sought to focus their appeal to the electorate and to marginalize the role of their traditional activists when these have seemed to interfere with electoral success. At the same time the parties, conscious that they do need members, have experimented with other mechanisms for including members in key activities of policy making, leadership and candidate selection. This trend has often been presented as a move to enhance internal democracy. However, much of it has been cosmetic, balancing enhanced leadership control with a semblance of membership participation. Greater internal democracy in the 1990s was thus calculated to be a tool for allowing greater control for the leadership rather than a method of membership empowerment. As such, it must be placed in the context of a series of other developments – especially the move towards greater emphasis on professionalization and marketing – which have also strengthened the central party and the leadership. That movement towards greater professionalism in the search for votes itself reflects profound changes in voting behaviour and participation and a loosening of the ties between voter and parties. Those changes are the subject of the next chapter.

 **Key Questions**

1 Can a party survive without a strong mass membership?
2 Would public funding make parties stronger?
3 Is internal party democracy necessarily healthy for the democratic system as a whole?

 Further Reading

Good general overviews of the contemporary party system can be found in Paul Webb, *The Modern British Party System* (London: Sage, 2000) and in his 'Parties and party systems: More continuity than change', *Parliamentary Affairs*, 54: 2 (2002). The shorter work by R. Garner and R. Kelly, *British Political Parties Today* (Manchester: Manchester University Press, 1998) is also valuable. Policy making is addressed in R. Kelly, 'Farewell conference, hello forum: The making of Labour and Tory policy', *Political Quarterly*, 72: 3 (2001), while Paul Whitely and Patrick Seyd, 'The dynamics of party activism in Britain: A spiral of demobilization', *British Journal of Political Science*, 28: 1 (1998) considers the issue of activism. Participation is examined at greater length in Whitely and Seyd's *High-intensity Participation: The Dynamics of Party Activism in Britain* (Ann Arbor: University of Michigan Press, 2002).

The Conservatives are covered in A. Seldon and S. Ball (eds), *Conservative Century: The Conservative Century since 1900* (Oxford: Oxford University Press, 1994) and in R. Blake, *Conservative Party from Peel to Thatcher* (London: Fontana, 1985). G. Evans, 'Economics and politics revisited: Exploring the decline in Conservative support, 1992–95', *Political Studies*, 47: 1 (1999) and, more generally, I. Gilmour, *Whatever Happened to the Tories?*

(London: Fourth Estate, 1997) look at aspects of Tory decline. K. Alderman, 'Revision of leadership election procedures in the Conservative Party', *Parliamentary Affairs*, 52: 2 (1999) examines the leadership rules, while there is a variety of articles on Conservative organization reform: D. Collings and A. Seldon, 'Conservatives in opposition', *Parliamentary Affairs*, 54: 4 (2001); R. Kelly, 'Democratising the Tory Party', *Talking Politics*, 11: 1 (1998); and Gillian Peele, 'Towards "New Conservatives"? Organisational reform and the Conservative Party', *Political Quarterly*, 69: 2 (1998). The organization reforms are set out in the Conservative Party, *The Fresh Future: The Conservative Party Renewed* (London: CCO Publications, 1998).

The Labour Party's historical evolution is discussed in K. Jeffrys, *The Labour Party since 1945* (Basingstoke: Macmillan, 1993) and in Henry Pelling, *A Short History of the Labour Party* (Basingstoke: Macmillan, 1996). M. Smith and J. Spear, *The Changing Labour Party* (London: Routledge, 1992) is also valuable. Reference should also be made to the party's own publication, *21st-Century Party* (London: The Labour Party, 1999). The background to New Labour is discussed in P. Anderson and N. Mann, *Safety First: The Making of New Labour* (London: Granta, 1997) and in P. Gould, *The Unfinished Revolution* (London: Little, Brown, 1999). Anthony Giddens, *The Third Way* (Cambridge: Polity, 1998) provides an authoritative account of New Labour ideology.

The most recent study on the Liberal Democrats is C. Cook, *A Short History of the Liberal Party, 1900-2001* (6th edn; London: Macmillan, 2002), which should be supplemented with J. Stevenson, *Third Party Politics since 1945* (Oxford: Blackwell, 1993). The SDP is well covered in I. Crewe and A. King, *SDP: The Life, Birth and Death of the Social Democratic Party* (Oxford: Oxford University Press, 1995).

Models of party organization are discussed in M. Duverger, *Political Parties: Their Organization and Activity in the Modern State* (London: Methuen, 1954) and O. Kirchheimer, 'The transformation of western European party systems', in J. LaPalombara and M. Weiner (eds), *Political Parties and Political Development* (Princeton, NJ: Princeton University Press, 1966). A. Panebianco, *Political Parties: Organization and Power* (Cambridge: Cambridge University Press, 1988) is important for his discussion of electoral professional parties, while a general discussion may be found in R. S. Katz and P. Mair, 'Changing models of party organization and party democracy: The emergence of the cartel party', *Party Politics*, 1 (1995).

Two recent helpful works on party funding are J. Fisher, 'Next step: State funding for the political parties?', *Political Quarterly*, 73: 4 (2002) and K. D. Ewing, *Trade Unions, the Labour Party and Political Funding* (London: Catalyst Forum, 2002).

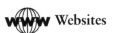 Websites

See also the list of general websites at the back of the book.

- www.party-register.gov.uk/framesregister.html – Register of political parties
- www.conservatives.com – Conservative Party
- www.labour.org.uk – Labour Party
- www.libdems.org.uk – Liberal Democrats
- www.snp.org.uk – Scottish National Party
- www.plaidcymru.org – Plaid Cymru
- www.uup.org – Ulster Unionist Party
- www.dup.org.uk – Democratic Unionist Party

- www.sdlp.ie – SDLP
- www.sinnfein.ie – Sinn Fein
- bubl.ac.uk/uk/parties.htm – Links to other political parties

9 Voting Behaviour, Public Opinion and the Mobilization of the Electorate

The previous two chapters analysed the electoral rules that govern competition between the parties and outlined some of the parties' ideological and organizational features. In this chapter we examine different dimensions of the electoral and party systems by looking at the changing patterns of voting behaviour and political opinion in the United Kingdom. This means shifting the focus to the changing basis and distribution of party support. It also means looking in outline at some of the principal models used by academic analysts to explain why people vote for one party rather than another, and at the various factors which shape the public's electoral behaviour. The chapter also discusses the strategies and tactics used by the parties as well as their increasingly sophisticated efforts to market themselves, not simply for the short period of an election campaign but over the much longer period of a Parliament.

We noted in the last chapter that many analysts of political parties see common trends across modern parties. They point to the rise of a model of party in which power is increasingly centralized and resources are directed towards the electoral arena in the struggle for votes. In this process, a new class of professionals has appeared – the pollsters, media consultants and analysts – who manage what has been called 'designer politics' (Scammell, 1995). New Labour's triumphs of 1997 and 2001 – which many hailed as **critical elections**, signalling a new pattern of party alignment – were in large part built on the successful adoption of an electoral strategy that took full advantage of the new campaign professionalism. But they were also underpinned by a series of profound changes in British voting behaviour and in the interpretation of those trends and their incorporation into Labour's approach to policy, party organization and campaign management. Thus, although Labour's landslide 1997 election victory and its consolidation in 2001 were based on the party's capacity to transform itself into a catch-all party, that successful appeal was in large part the product of a sophisticated industry of political consultants. Crafting New Labour's image and message, handling the media and campaigning were all grounded in a highly professional approach to understanding the dynamics of electoral opinion and selling the party in the light of that knowledge.

critical elections A series of elections in which there are major long-term changes in voting behaviour and party alignment.

The 1997 general election was one in which the relationship between politicians and their professional advisers and the media appeared to undergo a qualitative change. It was also an election that inflicted a massive defeat on the Conservative Party and ended 18 years of Conservative government. So great was the political transformation that commentators in 1997 described it as an 'earthquake' or an 'explosion'. Labour, rebranded as New Labour, won a landslide majority and the United Kingdom moved further in the direction of becoming a multi-party rather than a two-party system. The 2001 general election, though much less exciting than that of 1997, underlined the reversal of fortune that had occurred in 1997 and seemingly confirmed a pattern of party competition in which Labour was the dominant party. Certainly, Labour's second landslide gave the government a flexibility to plan policy for the longer term and was widely interpreted as a triumph for Tony Blair's strategy of party modernization. Yet dramatic though Labour's 1997 and 2001 electoral victories were, they raised a number of key questions about the future of party competition in the United Kingdom and the changing habits of the British electorate. Such questions included the extent to which New Labour had forged a new and durable coalition of support, the prospects for revival, if any, of the Conservative Party, and the likely impact of constitutional change on voting behaviour. They also included the question of whether the new style of media management, and indeed the whole professionalization of campaigns, would backfire on politicians, creating a more cynical and apathetic electorate.

In this chapter we look first at some key features of the 2001 general election and identify numerous ways in which electoral behaviour has changed since the 1960s. We then examine some of the major theoretical explanations for those changes and discuss their implications for the future of party competition. Finally, we consider the way in which political communications affect the character of party competition and electoral choice.

A New Electoral Apathy?

The most marked feature of the 2001 general election was the drop in turnout everywhere except in Northern Ireland. (The rise in turnout in Northern Ireland – from 67.1 per cent to 68 per cent – pointed to the continued intensity of political division there.) Politicians and journalists reacted with shock to a turnout figure of 59.4 per cent, which was the lowest since 1918 (Jones, 2001). Academics underlined the extent to which this 'apathetic landslide' reduced the legitimacy of Labour's mandate (Geddes and Tonge, 2002; Norris, 2001). The Electoral Commission, in its first major report on a general election, noted that there appeared to be 'a growing disconnection between the electorate and the electoral process' (Electoral Commission, 2001). It pointed up the need for better information, campaigns which engaged more effectively with the voters and more extensive voter education. (The Electoral Commission assumed responsibility for voter education after July 2001.)

The decline in turnout in 2001 occurred despite a series of reforms of the electoral machinery designed to make voting easier (see chapter 7 for a discussion of these). This drop in turnout at a general election was not entirely novel: successive general elections since 1950 (where turnout had peaked) had witnessed a decline in the percentage of voters who chose to participate in the central process of British democracy. To some extent it mirrored developments in comparable democracies elsewhere, but, as the Electoral Commission pointed out, the stark drop of 12 full percentage points (equivalent to some 5 million individuals) since 1997 was startling (see table 1.10, p. 21).

The low level of participation in the 2001 general election has prompted extensive discussion of its causes and of measures that might revive the electorate's apparently flagging interest in politics – including the suggestion that voting should be made compulsory. Participation in general elections is only one element of the total picture of civic involvement and participation in the United Kingdom. There are many other elections in the United Kingdom – local, European and regional – as well as occasional by-elections and referendums. Unfortunately, turnout in these elections has also shown a marked decline in recent years. While some of these other elections may be regarded as **second-order elections** and generally excite less interest than a general election, the comparative drop gives cause for concern. The UK's turnout for European elections is now the lowest in Europe, falling from 36.5 per cent in 1994 to 24 per cent in 1999. Even in the first elections for the Scottish Parliament and the Welsh Assembly, disappointingly low participation rates occurred, averaging 58 per cent in Scotland and 46 per cent in Wales. In the second round of Scottish Parliament and Welsh National Assembly elections held in 2003, turnout fell dramatically: the Scottish Parliament saw a fall in average turnout of 9 per cent (49 per cent across the constituencies and regions as opposed to 58 per cent) and Wales saw a fall of 8 per cent to hit a low of 38.2 per cent (House of Commons Research Papers, 2003). The dismal levels of voting for directly elected mayors, a device that many hoped would renew interest in local government, was one factor contributing to the election of a number of independent and maverick candidates in those races (see table 9.1).

second-order election An election other than a major national election (effectively, a general election in the UK). For example, in the UK, a local, regional or European election would all be second-order elections. First-order elections have the most salience with voters and are likely to affect the pattern of voting at second-order elections. Thus, voters in European and local elections may be casting their vote on the basis of national issues and personalities rather than European and local ones.

Table 9.1 Turnout in mayoral elections

Date	Location	Turnout (%)	Winning candidate	Party
May 2002	Doncaster	27.1	Martin Winter	Labour
May 2002	Hartlepool	28.8	Stuart Drummond	Independent
May 2002	Lewisham	24.8	Steve Bullock	Labour
May 2002	Middlesbrough	41.3	Ray Mallon	Independent
May 2002	Newham	25.5	Sir Robin Wales	Labour
May 2002	North Tyneside	42.3	Chris Morgan	Conservative
May 2002	Watford	36.1	Dorothy Thornhill	Liberal Democrat
Oct 2002	Bedford	25.4	Frank Branston	Independent
Oct 2002	Hackney	26.4	Jules Pipe	Labour
Oct 2002	Mansfield	18.5	Tony Egginton	Independent
Oct 2002	Stoke-on-Trent	24.0	Mike Wolfe	Mayor 4 Stoke

Source: Adapted from New Local Government Network, http://www.nlgn.org.uk/nlgn.php

It could be argued that voting in elections is not a reliable guide to political interest and that other measures of political activism should be used. Yet here too we find evidence of disengagement. Clearly, membership of political parties has been declining in the UK, suggesting what some authors have called a spiral of demobilization. Membership of some single-issue groups, on the other hand, appears to be on the increase, suggesting a preference for new styles of activism and political involvement (see chapter 10). Social movements and single-issue group demonstrations such as the Countryside Alliance marches, demonstrations against capitalism and the 2003 marches against the war with Iraq attracted very large numbers of adherents, including people from the younger age groups where voting in 2001 seemed disproportionately low. It is difficult to know, therefore, whether 2001 represented a general political disengagement or a retreat from conventional party politics.

The low turnout in 2001 was explained by a number of factors specific to that election. The changes to the election machinery, while likely to make registration and voting easier in the long run, appear to have been too late to make a significant difference to participation in 2001. Postal voting was up but it was not possible to take advantage of the rolling register in time for the general election (Butler and Kavanagh, 2002). The relatively short time between the passage of the Political Parties, Elections and Referendums Act (PPERA) 2000 and the 2001 election caused some confusion and appears to have reduced the level of trade union mobilization for fear of contravening the new legislation (Fisher, 2002). Opponents of FPTP inevitably also pointed the finger at the electoral system and the distorting effects of its method of translating votes into seats. Although this may have been a factor, it does not explain why there should have been such a sudden drop in 2001. Nor can it be said that the use of alternative electoral systems in Scotland and Wales has greatly increased participation.

There were other factors specific to the 2001 election which may explain the drop in turnout. The run-up to the election was unusually long because the anticipated date of 3 May had to be postponed for a month as a result of the disruption caused by the foot and mouth epidemic that occurred in the early part of 2001. Party war machines geared for a May election had to be put on hold, despite extensive preparations. The public therefore had an even more protracted period than normal to grow weary of electioneering. The campaign itself was generally seen as unexciting, not least because the result was taken as a foregone conclusion. The perception, created by the government's sustained lead in the polls, was that Labour was bound to win, thereby removing the 'horse-race element' as well as an incentive to vote. (Unusually for an incumbent government, Labour had stayed ahead in the polls for the whole period since the 1997 election apart from a brief interval during the fuel crisis of the autumn of 2000.) Labour's defensive electoral strategy in 2001 reflected its confidence of victory by emphasizing the need to get its own voters out rather than any need to fend off a Conservative challenge.

The security of Labour's position in 2001 anaesthetized the electorate. So too, it is argued, did the convergence of the parties towards the centre ground of British politics. Having persuaded middle England that it was safe to vote Labour in 1997, Tony Blair (aided by his chancellor's prudent economic policies) had apparently established Labour as the competent natural party of government. There were few issues and no real challenger. In one way, therefore, non-voting was a rational response to a non-election (Evans, 2003).

Consideration of the turnout in 2001 had the effect of highlighting other features of the changing electoral sociology of the country. It reminded analysts that some groups are regularly less likely to vote than others – the younger age groups, the poor, and some, but not all, ethnic minorities. In 2001 these groups all proved less likely to vote than older, more affluent and white citizens. There was also considerable variation in turnout between constituencies. Voters in safe Labour seats were more likely than average to abstain in 2001. Turnout was highest in seats where there was an above-average proportion of the well educated or elderly. And turnout was also high where there was a significant third-party intervention.

The 2001 election was another disaster for the Conservative Party, despite William Hague's extensive attempt to rebuild party organization. There was virtually no improvement on the shattering defeat of 1997. As a result, the Conservative Party found itself thrown back on its rural southern heartland and a small group of affluent commuter suburbs (see map 9.1). Even in these seats, however, it found itself increasingly squeezed in a political system where the Liberal Democrats as well as Labour had made serious inroads on Conservative support. Many observers pointed to the Herculean task that any leader of the Conservatives faced in winning the next general election or even bringing the Tories within sight of a subsequent victory. To win with a majority of one seat (hardly a comfortable outcome) would require a massive **swing** of 9.7 per cent (Henig and Baston, 2002).

Looking at the distribution of support in 2001, Labour continued its cross-class appeal to middle England established in 1997. As Tony King noted, Blair's strategy in the run-up to 1997 was calculated to win the support of non-Labour voters, not to mobilize the traditional Labour support because these voters by themselves could not yield victory. Labour in 2001 was preferred to the Conservatives in every social group except the middle class (AB) group, and even here its position in relation to the Conservatives improved slightly over 1997 (see table 9.2, which gives the social characteristics of the vote in 2001). As one commentator put it, 'Blair made further inroads into the leafy suburbs of Brent North, Enfield Southgate, Wimbledon and Bristol West' (Norris, 2001). This advance by Labour into constituencies that would hitherto have been deemed very unpromising territory built on Labour's capture of such formerly rock-solid Conservative seats as Hove on the south coast. Indeed, after the 2001 election there was much speculation about the extent to which any Conservative seat could be considered 'safe' and about the vulnerability of leading Tory figures (including the then party chairman Theresa May in Maidenhead) to electoral defeat.

What seems to have been happening over the period 1992 to 2001 is a continuing dissociation of class and voting preference and an erosion of support for the Conservatives where once they had been strongest (see table 9.3). The implications of the erosion of the class cleavage for electoral behaviour will be discussed at length later; but for the moment it is important to note that it had an impact on the Conservatives' electoral base as well as on Labour's.

swing Summary measure used to calculate movement between elections. In its classical form, Butler or two-party swing measures the support for parties by calculating the average of the gain in the winning party's share of the vote between two elections and the losing party's deficit. Swing is a difficult measure to apply in multi-party situations and many analysts now prefer to use other measures to chart the flow of the vote.

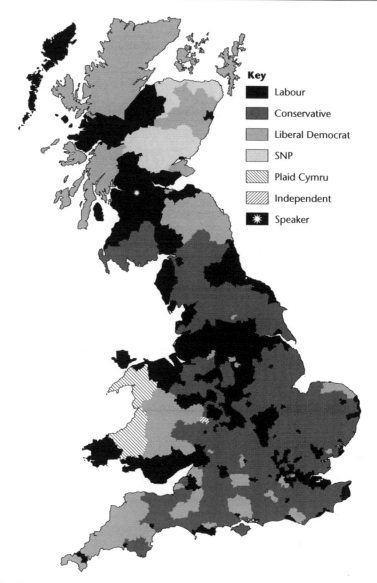

Map 9.1 The political complexion of the UK, 2001. *Source: Independent.*

We have already noted the extent to which it is the youngest age cohort (18–24) that is least likely to vote. According to MORI research for the Electoral Commission, 39 per cent of 18- to 24-year-olds did not vote in 2001. However, although there appeared to be little difference between this group and their elders in seeing the vote as important, there was a marked difference in party preference. People in the 18–24 age group were much less likely than their elders to see the Conservatives as an option and much more likely to see the Liberal Democrats as a real choice. There

Table 9.2 Social characteristics of the vote in 2001

	Con	Lab	Lib Dem	Other	Turnout
Total	**33**	**42**	**19**	**6**	**59**
Gender					
Men	32	42	18	8	61
Women	33	42	19	6	58
Age					
18–24	27	41	24	8	39
25–34	24	51	19	6	46
35–44	28	45	19	8	59
45–54	32	41	20	7	65
55–64	39	37	17	7	69
65+	40	39	17	4	70
Social class					
AB	39	30	25	6	68
C1	36	38	20	6	60
C2	29	49	15	7	56
DE	24	55	13	8	53
Work status					
Full-time	30	43	20	7	57
Part-time	29	43	21	7	56
Not working	36	41	18	5	63
Unemployed	23	54	11	12	44
Self-employed	39	32	18	11	60
Housing tenure					
Owner	43	32	6	6	68
Mortgage	31	42	7	7	59
Council/Housing Assoc.	18	60	8	8	52
Private renting	28	40	7	7	46

Source: MORI, http://www.mori.com/polls/2001/election.shtml

Table 9.3 Party support by class, 2001

Social class	2001 (change since 1997) %		
	Con	Lab	Lib Dem
AB	39 (−2)	30 (−1)	25 (3)
C1	36 (−1)	38 (1)	20 (12)
C2	29 (2)	49 (−1)	15 (−1)
DE	24 (3)	55 (−4)	13 (0)

Source: MORI Aggregate Campaign Polls, cited in P. Norris, 'Apathetic landslide: The 2001 British general election', in Norris (2001), p. 15.

was for a long time a gender gap in British politics. Women, except in the youngest age groups, tended to be more likely to vote Conservative than men. Because women form a slight majority of the population and have a higher propensity to vote, this advantage to the Conservatives was often significant. The late 1990s saw Labour making a special appeal to women. The record number of women elected to Parliament in 1997 and 2001 underlined the party's commitment to gender equality. What impact this had on voting behaviour is difficult to assess, but by 1997 there was no gender gap by comparison with an overall gap of 6 per cent in 1992. Analysis of the role of gender in the 1997 and 2001 elections suggests that there are still some differences between the genders in voting preference, but that these are also related to generation. Older women are more likely than older men to be Conservative. Younger women are more likely than younger men to be Labour supporters.

British voting behaviour has, of course, long displayed sharp regional variations. Scotland and Wales have traditionally been more supportive of Labour and more to the left ideologically than England (Sanders, 1999). There has also long been a north–south divide and a contrast between the voting patterns of the large towns and the suburbs and rural areas. The north–south divide became particularly marked after 1979 and regional variation intensified. Although the Conservatives won four general elections in a row between 1979 and 1992, it was evident that the party's appeal was increasingly concentrated in the southern part of England and that it was losing support in northern cities, in Scotland and in Wales. In 1997 the Conservatives failed to win a single seat in either Wales or Scotland. Although the Conservatives won one seat in Wales in 2001, they remained unrepresented in Scotland at the Westminster level.

Ethnicity and race are factors shaping voting behaviour in a number of different ways. As the United Kingdom's black and ethnic minority population has grown, so ethnic identity has become an increasingly important factor in voting behaviour. Black and ethnic minority groups now constitute over 8 per cent of the population. There is, however, considerable variation within that black and minority ethnic (BME) population. Research for the Electoral Commission after the 2001 election found that, although non-voting is a marked feature of Caribbean and some South Asian groups, people of Indian heritage are actually more inclined to vote than white citizens. Black and minority ethnic citizens tend to be concentrated in a small number of constituencies. Despite the efforts of all major parties to woo the BME vote through the selection of candidates from BME backgrounds, it is overwhelmingly a Labour vote. Indeed, research on the 1997 general election suggested that only 11.5 per cent of all votes cast by Caribbean and Asian voters went to the Conservative Party (British Election Study, quoted in Saggar, 1998).

Religion had been thought to have only a limited impact on the politics of mainland Britain outside cities such as Liverpool and Glasgow, where there are still vestiges of Roman Catholic versus Protestant rivalry. (It is, of course, a major factor in Northern Ireland.) However, there is some association between religion and political preference. The Roman Catholic vote has tended towards Labour, partly because much of that vote is Irish in origin and had working-class associations. Nonconformist associations with the old Liberal Party translated into support for the Liberal Democrats and church-going Anglicans have tended to be Conservative.

However, these associations are very weak and under the Conservative governments of 1979–97 church leaders were increasingly critical of social policy. As table 9.4 shows, within each religious denominational group there is a majority for Labour but the gap between Conservative and Labour scores is highest for Roman Catholics and lowest for Anglicans.

Identifying political preferences among different groups of a highly heterogeneous population is, of course, a necessary step towards understanding contemporary voting behaviour. However, it is not in itself enough because we need to know much more about how stable these patterns of allegiance are and the nature of the link between, for example, belonging to an ethnic minority and voting Labour. Underlying the 1997 and 2001 general election results there was a long period of change in British electoral behaviour and the way voters relate to parties. Of course, no period of politics is completely static: issues and political leaders come and go and demographic change alters the composition of the electorate. But most observers seem agreed that a series of profound shifts has occurred in British voting behaviour in the period since the mid-1960s, although there is much less agreement about the cause or nature of these changes. The concept that is frequently employed to explain what has happened to voting behaviour during this period is **dealignment**. What this means can be best illustrated by comparing the current pattern of party support with that of the electorate 40 years ago.

A snapshot taken of the British electorate in the mid-1960s would have shown a stable system of two-party competition based on a clearly aligned electorate (Denver, 2003; Sarlvik and Crewe, 1983). Today, however, the dominance of the two major parties is much less secure: only 74.7 per cent of those who voted in 2001 voted for the two major parties compared with 89.8 per cent in 1950 and 87.7 per cent in 1964. There is greater **volatility** among voters, that is, voters' willingness to desert their normal party and switch to another; indeed one commentator suggested that the 1997 election recorded the highest level of volatility since the 1930s (Sanders, 1999). Opinion polls and survey data record fluidity in the opinions of voters between elections. Parties can rely much less surely than they once could on the loyalty of their supporters. These developments, along with other crucial social and cultural changes including declining party membership, have created a new environment for party competition (Denver, 2003).

dealignment Concept used to explain the decline of group identities, especially those based on social class, and the loosening of ties between political parties and distinct social groupings.

volatility Electoral movement between elections which may involve a shift in support between parties and between voting and abstention.

Table 9.4 Voting by religious denomination

	All	Roman Catholic	Church of England	Church of Scotland	Free Church	Other Protestant	Other	None
Con	27	19	33	20	24	29	12	22
Lab	52	60	50	53	48	33	63	52
Lib Dem	16	16	14	6	24	12	22	21
SNP/PC	3	1	0	21	1	27	2	3
Other	3	5	2	0	3	0	1	3

Source: MORI, May 2001, http://www.mori.com/polls/trends/religion/index.shtml

Several other features of the changes in voting behaviour deserve to be mentioned. From roughly 1940 to 1970, when the two major political parties (Conservative and Labour) dominated the competition for votes, political choice was primarily seen as an automatic assertion of identity, not a considered preference for a particular party's policies or candidates. Electors were overwhelmingly loyal partisans, aligned into two groups with strong Labour or strong Conservative party associations. The two parties advanced programmes designed to appeal to and reinforce the preferences of their particular constituencies, which were largely defined on the basis of social location or class. Labour was predominantly the voice of the less advantaged and of trade unionism in British society, while the Conservatives advanced a more individualistic, patriotic and nationalist appeal which denied the relevance of the class struggle but which also fitted well with the interest of the middle classes. There were few floating voters and there was little room for other parties. The two major parties together took the overwhelming share of the vote and the overwhelming majority of parliamentary seats. Attachment to one or other of the Labour and Conservative parties thus appeared entrenched in the behaviour of the British electorate, as table 9.5 shows. Electoral patterns and party politics in the quarter-century after the Second World War were, as Ivor Crewe put it, typically depicted as '[a] neat and tidy binary structure of two classes, two ideologies and two parties bound together and reinforced by the single member, simple plurality electoral system. This dovetailing of class, ideological and party allegiance formed the framework for an exceptionally stable, evenly balanced and nationally uniform two-party dominance over the electorate and within Parliament' (Crewe and King, 1995). Few voters in the United Kingdom switched parties and most voters' loyalties hardened as they aged.

Table 9.5 Changing two-party share of the vote, 1945–2001

Year	Percentage of votes cast		Total of the two
	Conservative[a]	Labour	
1945[b]	39.8	48.3	88.1
1950	43.5	46.1	89.6
1951	48.0	48.8	96.8
1955	49.7	46.4	96.1
1959	49.4	43.8	93.2
1964	43.4	44.1	87.5
1966	41.9	47.9	89.8
1970	46.4	43.0	89.4
1974 (Feb)	37.8	37.1	74.9
1974 (Oct)	35.8	39.2	75.0
1979	43.9	37.0	80.9
1983	42.4	27.6	70.0
1987	42.3	30.8	73.1
1992	41.9	34.4	76.3
1997	30.7	43.2	73.9
2001	31.7	40.7	72.4

[a] Includes Ulster Unionists 1945–70.

[b] The 1945 figures exclude university seats and are adjusted for double voting in the 15 two-member seats.

Source: Adapted from Butler and Kavanagh (2002).

The geographical uniformity of the vote in the period 1945–70 was also very marked. This is not to say that party strength was distributed uniformly across the country, since the Conservative Party's support was always greater in the southern half of England and rural areas than in northern and urban England, Scotland or Wales. Rather, the net movement of support between the major parties (sometimes expressed as the swing between the parties) tended to be uniform across the country. For this reason, analysis of the results in a small number of constituencies early on election night enabled commentators to predict with confidence the outcome of most general elections. The fragmentation of the party system and increased voter volatility after 1974 has made swing a more difficult measure to use, although there have been efforts to adapt it to a multi-party context. Instead, many analysts prefer to focus simply on the changes in each party's share of the vote (Denver, 2003). See tables 9.6 and 9.7.

A Dealigning Electorate?

Party alignments are not necessarily permanent and the tidy binary structure identified by Crewe and others appeared to break down in the 1970s. Instead of a strongly entrenched two-party system reflecting a fundamental class cleavage between the middle and the working classes, there appeared a multi-party system (at the electoral if not at the parliamentary level) and a much more fragmented electorate. The precise point at which significant shifts in voting patterns became clearly visible was the February 1974 general election called by Edward Heath in an effort to defeat the miners' strike. The election saw a massive increase in voter volatility.

Table 9.6 Swing at elections, 1945–2001

Election	Total-vote swing since previous election[a]
1950	3.0
1951	3.1
1955	2.1
1959	1.5
1964	3.2
1966	2.7
1970	4.7
1974 (Feb)	7.3
1974 (Oct)	2.1
1979	5.2
1983	5.5
1987	1.7
1992	2
1997	10.3
2001	1.8

[a] Total-vote swing is the average of the change in the Conservative share of the vote and the Labour share of the vote.
Source: 1997 figure, Butler and Kavanagh (1997), p. 297; 2001 figure, Butler and Kavanagh (2002), p. 305; all other figures calculated using above method, taking raw figures from Butler and Kavanagh (2002), pp. 260–1.

Table 9.7 Parties' share of seats and votes, 1945–2001

Election	Conservative		Labour		Liberal/Alliance		PC/SNP		Comm, 1945–79; Greens, 1979–2001		Others (mainly NI)	
	Votes %	Seats	Votes %	Seats	Votes %	Seats	Votes %	Seats	Votes %	Seats	Votes %	Seats
1945	39.8	213	48.3	393	9.1	12	0.2	0	0.4	2	2.1	20
1950	43.5	299	46.1	315	9.1	9	0.1	0	0.3	0	0.9	2
1951	48	321	48.8	295	2.5	6	0.1	0	0.1	0	0.5	3
1955	49.7	345	46.4	277	2.7	6	0.2	0	0.1	0	0.8	2
1959	49.4	365	43.8	258	5.9	6	0.4	0	0.1	0	0.5	1
1964	43.4	304	44.1	317	11.2	9	0.5	0	0.2	0	0.6	0
1966	41.9	253	47.9	363	8.5	12	0.7	0	0.2	0	0.7	2
1970	46.4	330	43	288	7.5	6	1.3	1	0.1	0	1.7	5
1974 (Feb)	37.8	297	37.1	301	19.3	14	2.6	9	0.1	0	3.1	14
1974 (Oct)	35.8	277	39.2	319	18.3	13	3.5	14	0.1	0	3.1	12
1979	43.9	339	37	269	13.8	11	2	4	0.1	0	3.2	21
1983	42.4	397	27.6	209	25.4	23	1.5	4	0.2	0	2.9	17
1987	42.3	376	30.8	229	22.6	22	1.7	6	0.3	0	2.3	17
1992	41.9	336	34.4	271	17.8	20	2.3	7	0.5	0	3	17
1997	30.7	165	43.2	418	16.8	46	2.5	10	0.2	0	6.6	20
2001	31.7	166	40.7	412	18.3	52	2.5	9	0.6	0	6.2	20

Source: Butler and Kavanagh (2002), pp. 260–1.

Some of these changes inevitably cancelled one another out; but it was the restlessness of the electorate in 1974 that was novel. The February 1974 election was also important because it witnessed the emergence of marked regional variations in voting behaviour. Although, as we have noted, the movement of electoral opinion had normally been remarkably similar across the country, in February 1974 there was more geographical variation than before. The causes of these regional and local variations, which have persisted, are not entirely clear. To some extent they are a reflection of differences in economic circumstances, especially differences in employment prospects. To some extent also they may reflect the demographic composition of the area, for example the ethnic and age mix. But it seems that these marked geographical effects cannot be reduced entirely to economic conditions or demography. The regional, local or constituency environment appears to be exerting an increasingly independent influence. Although there is still much debate, the causal mechanism involved would seem to suggest that simply being in an area where one party is strong may have an impact on voters who might in other circumstances have voted differently. Thus from 1974, what seems to have been emerging is a culture of place, which has acted as an independent variable on voting behaviour.

The most obvious regional variations from 1974 onwards were in Scotland and Wales, where significant nationalist parties emerged. In these areas the Conservative Party was increasingly marginalized, although Labour remained strong. The advent of devolved assemblies as a result of Labour's constitutional reforms has since created new political arenas and semi-autonomous party subsystems within the United Kingdom. From the 1970s also the party system of Northern Ireland was severed from that of the mainland. Party competition in Northern Ireland revolves around the conflict between the loyalist/Protestant and nationalist/Catholic division. The renewed violence of the late 1960s prompted restructuring of the party system as the Unionist Party divided over its attitude to reform and as new parties (such as the Social and Democratic Labour Party and the Democratic Unionist Party) were formed to take account of a changing political context (see chapter 12).

Within England important regional differences emerged, especially in the pattern of Liberal Party strength. In the south-west of England and in the home counties, the Liberal Party (and later the Liberal Democrats) became increasingly strong and the more effective challenger to Conservative hegemony in those areas. Indeed, the south-west to some extent became the Liberal Democrat heartlands (see map 9.1). At the constituency level also there appeared a willingness to engage in tactical voting, where voters would opt for a party other than their own first preference to keep out their least preferred party. Studies suggest that the amount of such tactical voting has risen slightly in recent years to about 10 per cent of voters. Tactical voting was seen as a factor explaining a number of Liberal Democrat and Labour gains from the Conservatives in 1997 and the ability to keep those seats in 2001.

The February 1974 general election was initially interpreted as an abnormality, the product of the peculiar circumstances in which it was called. In fact, a second general election in 1974 confirmed some of the changes in British electoral behaviour identified earlier in the year. Volatility remained a feature of electoral behaviour. Patterns of electoral behaviour had been broken, although the electoral system with its use of FPTP masked the impact of the major parties' loss of support for some time.

Initially, the 1979 election looked like a return to 'normal' two-party politics in that it produced a government with a working majority. It should be noted, however, that the Conservative victories of 1979, 1983, 1987 and 1992 were won on a stable fraction of the vote but were in large part the product of a divided opposition. The 1979 election also saw a marked sharpening of the north–south divide, with Labour doing well in Scotland and the north of England, while the Conservatives polled strongly in the south and midlands. But by-elections soon revealed that electoral volatility was still a major feature of British politics (Norris, 1990). The formation of the SDP in 1981 and its subsequent alliance and merger with the Liberals to form the Liberal Democrat Party produced a marked but erratic third-party vote. The general election of 1992 – which many had not expected the Conservatives to win – saw the Tories returned for a fourth successive victory on roughly 42 per cent of the vote.

The 1992 result was a huge disappointment for Labour, not least because it had been fought in an economic recession that might have been expected to damage the Conservative government and help Labour. Labour's 1992 defeat paradoxically ushered in a period of unprecedented Conservative unpopularity and a new phase of Labour modernization and revival. In particular, the Conservatives' image over this period changed and they became associated with sleaze and internal disunity. Most significant of all, in some ways, was the destruction of their reputation as the party of economic competence by their handling of Britain's departure from the exchange rate mechanism (ERM) in September 1992. By contrast, the Labour Party over the 1992 to 1997 period rebuilt its image by further modernization and policy reform and the acquisition in 1994 of an attractive younger leader in Tony Blair.

Two Approaches to Understanding Voting Behaviour

The general elections of 1997 and 2001 suggested strongly that a new pattern of voting behaviour was emerging in the United Kingdom. What was not so clear was how long-lasting this pattern would prove. Was the shift of loyalties likely to provide the basis for a realignment, or were these changes the manifestation of broader transformations in the relationship between voters and parties? At this stage we must examine briefly the models that analysts use to understand voting behaviour and to predict changes in electoral behaviour.

There are broadly two approaches to understanding voting behaviour that may be found in the academic literature. Each approach makes different assumptions about the way voters reach their decision about which party to support, and each approach adopts a different model of how voting is linked to the wider social structure. As we shall see too, there are variants of these approaches. It should perhaps also be noted here that neither of these broad approaches to voting behaviour is particularly flattering to democratic government.

The first approach emphasizes the process of structural factors, social location and socialization as the keys to political attitudes and hence to party choice. This approach (which is traditionally associated with theorists such as Seymour Martin Lipset and Stein Rokkan) stresses the significance of social cleavages in shaping political identity. In the British case the most important social cleavage in the twenti-eth century was social class, although religion played a major role in shaping nineteenth-century political preferences because the nonconformist vote was so strongly identified with the old Liberal Party. How far social inequality continues to shape political identity and voter choice is intensely debated. Some analysts have sought to keep class inequality at the centre of their explanations of voting behaviour, although they have reformulated the conceptualization of social inequality to take account of changes in British society. Other analysts have argued that social class is no longer the overwhelming determinant of political attitudes and point to the greater role of other factors (such as region, gender and ethnicity) or even consumption patterns in shaping social identity (Dunleavy and Husbands, 1985; Franklin, 1985).

The second approach, by contrast to the socially determined approach of the first model, explains voting in individual and psychological terms. It sees the voter as a rational actor and the vote as a calculated and deliberate act taken on the basis of information about the likely impact of an election on the individual's life and well-being (Himmelweit, Humphreys, Jaeger and Ktaz, 1981). Voters are thus like consumers, who will compare products before buying them. While the first approach to voting behaviour emphasizes long-term factors in explaining voting behaviour, the rational choice approach emphasizes medium- and short-term factors such as a party's record in government, the issues involved in an election, and the personal popularity and style of party leaders. One version of this more consumerist approach especially emphasizes the extent to which the state of the economy and the voter's sense of well-being are powerful predictors of voter choice (Sanders, 1991, 1996). This approach to voting behaviour inevitably places a heavy stress on selling the party, linking policy issues and party image in the voters' minds to create support. It accordingly allows a major role for the management and manipulation of the media and for campaigning as well as for exploiting the perceived strengths of the party leader.

It is worth noting that the first approach assumes relatively limited knowledge of political issues. Voters acquire a political loyalty that helps them interpret political controversies and provides cues for voting. The second approach, by contrast, while not requiring detailed knowledge, assumes a minimal level of familiarity with party positions or images. It is of course somewhat artificial to see these two approaches as competing rather than overlapping explanations. A total explanation of British electoral behaviour must take both the socialization and the rational choice elements of voting into account.

In looking at electoral behaviour in modern Britain, we therefore have to bear in mind that voters will be affected by a number of different influences. There are *long-term* group associations and identities that include patterns of family partisanship, ethnic identity, religious affiliation, neighbourhood identity, educational background, occupation, trade union membership and social status. Together, these long-term influences mould a distinctive social identity that in turn is reflected in party allegiance and voting behaviour. The circumstances of social life in modern Britain have altered the way many of these influences operate in the early twenty-first century compared with earlier years. For example, the decline of heavy industry and blue-collar work and the rise of the service sector and self-employment have created a new employment pattern. Trade union membership has not only declined in absolute terms; as was seen in chapter 8, there has also been a weakening of many of the formal links between the trade union movement and the Labour Party. Home ownership has increased steadily since 1945 and council (i.e., public) housing has declined – a trend that has weakened

Labour subcultures on housing estates. Indeed, to some extent these trends were encouraged by Conservative government policy as they sought to strengthen the support for values associated with property ownership. Other divisions such as ethnicity, national identity and neighbourhood may have become more significant politically than they once were, creating new politically relevant identities.

In addition to these long-term influences there are *medium-term* influences on British voters. These influences may come from the images created by the parties themselves, or they may be the result of the media's assessment of a party or its leaders. Politics is as much about symbolism as it is about substantive policies; and it is therefore likely that voting decisions will be as powerfully affected by the images and sometimes subconscious message projected by parties and their leaders as by their manifestos. Such symbolism may be positive or negative. Labour's old association with the trade union movement and the manual working class, while a source of strength for the early part of the twentieth century, became negative images in the 1980s. The rebuilt Labour Party – with the brand image of New Labour – acquired a classless, modern appeal that greatly aided its decisive victories in 1997 and 2001.

Short-term electoral factors are also highly significant in shaping electoral outcomes. Each election campaign is dominated by a unique set of issues and competing personalities. The interplay of policy, leader and image will structure an electoral contest. Although the weight that can be assigned to each of these factors will vary from campaign to campaign, policy and personality appear increasingly important. The result of a general election will therefore be determined by the short-term factors of issues and public perceptions of the party leaders as well as by the public's comparative assessments of the parties (see table 9.8).

Socialization and Class

For those who emphasize socialization as the key to voting, party attachments are habitual and traditional. In the British context commitment to a party would be built

Table 9.8 Influences on voting behaviour
Please tell me how much influence, if any, each had on your decision about what you would do on election day.

	% saying 'a great deal'	
	Voters	Non-voters
Election coverage on TV	12	17
Coverage in newspapers	7	10
Party election broadcasts on TV	5	8
Views of friends or family	5	6
Election coverage on radio	5	5
Leaflets/letters from parties	4	4
Opinion polls	2	3
Political ads on billboards	2	3
Personal calls from parties	2	1
Coverage on Internet	–	1

Source: MORI/Electoral Commission, 2001, http://www.mori.com/pubinfo/pdf/rmm-res2001.pdf

up over a lifetime, as David Butler and Donald Stokes argued in their influential study of partisanship, *Political Change in Britain* (1970). This work, which still provides an excellent introduction to the socialization approach, demonstrated how family background and schooling in youth and church membership, workplace and other influences affected political behaviour by creating a party identification. Following the model of voting behaviour developed at **Michigan**, Butler and Stokes discussed individual socialization and systemic change in terms of an electoral life cycle. Political opinions, attitudes and attachments were relatively plastic in youth but became more firmly rooted as voters aged. Thus only a very small proportion of the electorate would shift its vote between elections. Although these so-called floating voters could be significant in determining the outcome of a single election (and hence would be assiduously courted by the parties), scholarly interest was directed not so much at these shifts as at the factors shaping partisanship in the long term. Such factors included social class, income, trade union membership and education. Crucially, they also included the major political issues and contests of the voters' early years. Thus age as such was not seen by Butler and Stokes as a key determinant of voting behaviour. What was crucial was *when* the voter's political consciousness was shaped. Occasionally there would be critical or defining political events such as a recession or war; or leaders who polarized opinion within a generation. For the most part, however, the process of political consciousness-building or socialization occurred slowly and incrementally. Significant systemic change in the Butler–Stokes model is primarily the product of changes in the composition of the electorate. Thus much attention is paid to political differences between age cohorts within the electorate and to the process of cohort replacement, whereby new voters come onto the register and replace those who have died.

Social class has generally been seen as the most important structural factor shaping British political identity. Indeed, for a long period analysts discounted other factors in explaining British voting patterns. This orthodoxy is nicely captured in Peter Pulzer's much-quoted comment that class was the basis of British party politics and all else was 'embellishment and detail' (Pulzer, 1967).

Pulzer's statement was a very positive affirmation of the way in which voter loyalties were primarily the product of a dichotomous social alignment. It was also a denial of the relevance of cleavages that are often politically significant in other societies: religion, national identity, ethnicity, neighbourhood, gender and age. Pulzer was writing in the mid-1960s in the period of stable two-party politics. Forty years later, some of those cleavages, such as national identity and ethnicity, have acquired political salience in British politics.

The growing awareness that there are a number of social divisions that shape voting behaviour does not, of course, mean that class has ceased to be relevant to contemporary British politics. Indeed, as already noted, several analysts of British voting behaviour remain convinced that social inequality is the most important clue to the electoral sociology of the UK, although there is intense controversy both about the way that division influences voting behaviour and, more technically, about how it should be measured. Thus, although it is not always easy to operationalize the concept of class, it is in many

Michigan model A model of voting behaviour developed at the University of Michigan's Survey Research Center in the 1950s which used survey data to test voters' attachments to political parties. The Michigan model placed considerable stress on the explanatory role of partisan identifications, arguing that attachments to one or other of the major parties were strong, predisposing electors to vote for the party with which they identified. This partisan identification was in turn the product of long-term political socialization.

ways the starting point for mapping contemporary political allegiance. It therefore merits further examination.

What is social class?

Social class is a widely used and multi-faceted idea. It is also a difficult one to define. At its simplest it refers to the structure of stratification in a society. In the United Kingdom, a person's position in the class structure is usually determined on the basis of occupation. Classes can be categorized in a number of different ways and used for very different purposes. Thus market researchers may wish to divide the population very differently from researchers whose primary interest is the study of voting behaviour. Moreover, the distinctions used by researchers, whether academic or commercial, are not necessarily identical to the perceptions of class found in the population.

In Britain the strong link between class and party support was highlighted by Butler and Stokes in the first edition of *Political Change in Britain*, which appeared in 1963. Thus Butler and Stokes found that occupation was for most people the key variable associated with class. Class identity at that time had a sufficiently strong meaning that almost all of the population could put themselves into one or other class. Politically, the most relevant class division was between the middle and the working classes, which roughly corresponded at that time to the division between manual and non-manual workers. The marked disjuncture of political alignment between the classes can be seen in table 9.9.

The class-based model of partisanship which Butler and Stokes put forward suggested that the self-ascribed members of the manual working class (mainly manual workers) would overwhelmingly identify with the Labour Party and that, conversely, self-ascribed members of the middle class would identify with the Conservative Party.

The explanation of so much of British voting in terms of a structural class cleavage left several questions unanswered even in the 1950s and 1960s. The Liberal vote, albeit small for much of the twentieth century, was difficult to explain in class terms. There was also an increasingly large group of voters whose class was objectively difficult to categorize. Some classification problems were caused by the existence of occupations that fell outside the stark manual–non-manual divide. With the decline of manufacturing – especially of heavy industry – and the rise of the service sector, these problems multiplied (see table 9.10). But they were always there. Additionally, there were methodological problems about how to code women who might be ascribed a class on the basis of the husband or male head of household's occupation rather than on their own status. Indeed, some analysts have argued that the use of social class as a classificatory tool is inherently biased and fails to be sensitive to the female half of the population.

The model of class–party alignment (at least in the rather stark form of a two-class/two-party model) never completely described electoral reality in Britain since there were always significant sections of both the working and middle classes who were deviants in the sense that they voted against their 'natural' party. Disraeli in the nineteenth century noted the existence of a substantial working-class Conservative vote – the so-called 'angels in marble' (McKenzie and Silver, 1968). Much

Table 9.9 Voting by middle and working classes, 1945–2001

Party	Average 1945–70		1979 election		1983 election		1987 election		1992 election		1997 election		2001 election	
	Non-manual	Manual	Non-manual	Manual	Non-manual	Manual	Non-manual	Manual	Non-manual	Manual	Non-manual	Manual	Non-manual	Manual
Con	65	30	55	36	51	35	49	37	49	35	39	29	38	27
Lab	24	62	26	46	18	37	20	40	26	45	33	45	34	53
Lib	10	8	19	17	31	28	31	23	25	20	25	14	23	14

Source: 1945–92 figures taken from Crewe (1993), p. 99, based on Harris/ITN exit polls (3 May 1979; 9 June 1983; 11 June 1987; 9 April 1992); 1997 and 2001 figures adapted from Butler and Kavanagh (2002), p. 257.

Table 9.10   Objective and subjective measures of class
(a) Objective measures

Social class	Total GB population	
	000s	%
A	1,511	3.2
B	9,670	20.5
C1	13,053	27.7
C2	9,865	20.9
D	8,302	17.6
E	4,712	10

Source: National Readership Survey, 2003.

(b) Subjective measures

A survey of 1,000 members of the AB social group found that over half considered themselves to be working class or 'C2DE'.

Source: RSGB Taylor Nelson consultancy survey of 1,000 'ABs', April 2000, cited on MORI website, http://www.mori.com/digest/2000/pd000505.shtml#hal)

Conservative strategy over the twentieth century – including the formation of organizations such as the Primrose League – was geared to building up support among the working class and, of course, the Conservatives could never have enjoyed such electoral success over the late nineteenth and early twentieth centuries without the support of a substantial number of working-class voters. Middle-class radicals were also an important feature of British politics, providing leadership for pressure groups and increasingly dominating the parliamentary Labour Party. To that extent, while class was clearly an important factor in shaping voter alignments, it was never a totally polarizing one. Yet class remained the dominant factor in explaining British voting behaviour until the 1970s.

From the 1970s the role of class in shaping electoral behaviour appeared to change markedly. This change was most dramatically revealed by a rise in cross-class voting, that is, voting for a party which is not the 'natural' choice. Ivor Crewe, for example, charted political change in the 1970s in terms of what he called a dealignment of the electorate. This dealignment involved a weakening of both class identity and party loyalties. Whereas in the period 1945–70 nearly two-thirds of the electorate voted for their 'natural' class party, from February 1974 that link 'slowly and fitfully' weakened and after 1983 the majority of electors voted for parties that were either the class enemy or for third parties whose appeal was not based on class issues (Crewe, 1993; Crewe and King, 1985; Sarlvik and Crewe, 1983). Other changes in relation to class have been noted since the 1970s. One important factor that has to be taken into account, regardless of any change in voting behaviour within the classes, is the changing relative size of the classes. The middle class has become larger and the working class smaller in terms of the percentage each represents in the population. Thus in 1961 manual workers constituted 61 per cent of the electorate but by 1991 that figure had declined to 42 per cent. Yet oddly, as table 9.10 shows, over half of a sample of 1,000 members of the AB category considered themselves working class, pointing up the differences between subjective and objective measures of class.

The middle class has also become much more mixed in composition, involving both public sector and private sector workers. Some authors see the division between private and public sector employment and consumption as highly significant divisions within both the middle class and the working class (Dunleavy and Husbands, 1985). Others draw more complex distinctions on the basis of whether an occupation involves managerial authority or cultural expertise (Heath et al., 1991).

The perception that class had ceased to have such a prominent impact on British voting behaviour spawned a range of theories about the new motors of electoral choice. Some authors have emphasized the extent to which voters' evaluations of the personalities of party leaders have become increasingly important in shaping electoral choice, especially since 1987 (Mughan, 2000). Issue voting is also seen by some authors as crucial to electoral choice. Voters will thus opt for the party whose stance on the major issues of a campaign corresponds most closely to their own, although voters are not always fully aware of changes in parties' issue positions (Anderson, Heath and Sinnott, 2002). Of particular importance here is the issue of the management of the economy and which party has the greater credibility in relation to delivering prosperity (Sanders, 1991, 1996; Sanders, Clarke, Stewart and Whitely, 2001).

The debate about the changing role of class obviously has profound implications for party strategies. If class identity no longer shapes party allegiance as clearly as it once did, the parties find themselves in a position where they must reach beyond their core vote, if indeed they still have one. Labour was the party that first took note of this message, recognizing the need to broaden its appeal far beyond its traditional base and to draw in the middle-class vote. This strategy was essentially the one adopted by Blair for New Labour on the advice of analysts such as Philip Gould. On the other hand, it is a strategy which the Conservatives must equally take note of, as the decline of class identity also erases their base. From 1997 to 2001 the Conservatives seemed to recognize this to some extent, but appeared uncertain as to how to cope with adapting their policies to the new environment.

Political Communications and the Political Campaign

We have emphasized throughout the discussion that there have been profound changes in the way politicians interact with the electorate and that modern electioneering is very different from what it was even in the 1960s. Campaigns became increasingly centralized and professional. They also became more costly, leading observers to speak of an arms race between the major parties. Changes in the nature of political communications have indeed been seen as important explanations of broader electoral change in their own right (Norris, 2002; Scammell, 1999). The media – television, radio and the newspapers – have become crucial players, not just in the process of winning elections but in the much longer-term battle to shape favourable party images in the minds of the voters and indeed to convey accurate information about their issue positions to the public.

There has also been a widespread change in the way in which politicians and their electorates interact. Technological innovations have produced increasingly sophisticated methods for interpreting public opinion and selling policies and leaders to the voters. Campaigning tactics and strategies have been transformed into highly professional, expensive and centralized operations quite different in character from the amateur, face-to-face and local exercises of earlier periods. Increasingly, the parties' use of polling and marketing techniques has become an integral part of the policy-making process itself. During election campaigns the parties' pollsters play a central role in developing strategies; but their importance is not confined to an election period. Polls and focus groups will be organized daily to pick up shifts in the voter mood. There are regular meetings between Downing Street and Philip Gould, Blair's polling guru. It may be that the parties are listening to voters more than ever before, although, paradoxically, the parties are also using the mass media more than before to carry their message back to the voters. Every day of the campaign will be carefully planned in advance in the hope of maximizing media coverage. Parties may appear to be more responsive to voters than in the past, but only to some voters – those in marginal constituencies who are likely to switch their vote. It is on these voters that parties concentrate their resources. Ascertaining how the electorate will respond to an issue and the linked efforts to manage the media, not merely during a campaign but in the day-to-day routine of political debate, have transformed political life. The new limits on campaign spending at the national level will restrict the amount parties can spend on these techniques and force them to prioritize between them.

The Changing Structure of the Media

The mass media are not simply there to pander to politicians. They provide news and political commentary as part of a service to their audience. In an increasingly complex, crowded and competitive environment, they must maintain their audience by providing stories that are both newsworthy and entertaining.

Television has long been the most important source of political information, but over a series of campaigns there has been evidence that viewers are bored by election material. The strict rules that govern balance and the allocation of party broadcasts on television are in a sense becoming redundant because of the changes in the structure of television and the advent of new technology. Thus not only do cable and satellite television offer much more choice to the viewer, but linked developments such as the existence of 24-hour news programmes have altered the significance of regular news and commentary programmes. The greater availability of additional channels and the spread of cable and satellite and the Internet mean that viewers can take advantage of many different sources of political commentary, but they can also avoid political material if they wish.

Despite the apparent variety of a large number of titles, the ownership of the press in Britain is heavily concentrated. By 2003 the pattern revealed several highly individualistic newspaper magnates such as Rupert Murdoch (who owns *The Times*, the *Sun*, the *Sunday Times* and the *News of the World*), Conrad Black (who owns the *Daily* and *Sunday Telegraph* and the *Spectator*) and Lord Hollick (who owns the *Express*). Amongst the tabloids, the *Sun* and the *Daily Mail* enjoy a substantial advantage, with a circulation of about 3.4 million and 2.3 million respectively. Table 9.11 shows the circulation of the major British newspapers plus their political affiliation.

The concentrated ownership of the British press does not automatically produce a homogeneous political outlook. Unlike the requirement of political neutrality that is imposed on television, there are no such strictures for newspapers to be politically neutral. Editors therefore have complete freedom to align their papers and offer what advice they choose on political issues. Increasingly, however, national newspapers shifted from an alignment based on party to one which is more issues-based. Certainly, the Murdoch group has made its papers' opposition to closer European integration very clear.

Cultivating the press had been an important goal of New Labour in opposition. In 1995 only one paper – the *Daily Mirror* – was an explicit supporter of Labour, although at least two of the quality dailies were critical of the Conservatives. But disillusion with the Conservatives' record and the careful cultivation of the press by Blair altered this picture. The *Sun*, which had trumpeted its contribution to earlier Conservative victories in the 1980s, switched to supporting Blair, and indeed for a time was viewed by some journalists as the official noticeboard of No. 10 to some extent after Blair became prime minister (Jones, 2001).

Table 9.11 UK national newspapers

Newspaper (date of foundation)	Owned by	Circulation figures[a]
Dailies		
Popular		
Daily Mirror (1903)	Trinity Mirror	2,150,711
Daily Star (1978)	Northern and Shell	676,671
Sun (1964)	News International	3,497,402
Mid-market		
Daily Mail (1896)	Daily Mail and General Trust	2,381,154
Express (1900)	Northern and Shell	906,539
Qualities		
Financial Times (1888)	Pearson	461,095
Daily Telegraph (1855)	Telegraph Group	968,926
Guardian (1821)	Guardian Media Group	390,278
Independent (1986)	Independent Newspapers	196,089
The Times (1785)	News International	666,576
Sundays		
Popular		
News of the World (1843)	News International	3,971,478
Sunday Mirror (1963)	Trinity Mirror	1,809,691
People (1881)	Trinity Mirror	1,385,859
Mid-market		
Mail on Sunday (1982)	Daily Mail and General Trust	2,309,008
Express on Sunday (1918)	Northern and Shell	876,755
Qualities		
Sunday Telegraph (1961)	Telegraph Group	769,370
Independent on Sunday (1990)	Independent Newspapers	216,055
Observer (1791)	Guardian Media Group	419,724
Sunday Times (1822)	News International	1,353,900

[a] 2001 figures.

New Labour in government developed an increasingly systematic and professional approach to media management, establishing a dedicated unit (the Strategic Communications Unit) inside No. 10 for the purpose. This determination to control the news – the ubiquity of spin and spin doctors – may have been a contributory factor in the cynicism displayed towards politicians in 2001.

For all the efforts devoted to control the media, however, it is not clear what impact either the press or television has on voting behaviour (see table 9.12). Politicians clearly believe they have a lot of influence and there is unlikely to be a return to a situation where less strenuous efforts were made to manage the media. For their part, voters in 2001 complained that there was too much campaign coverage in the media and the election viewing figures were down (though not so dramatically as in 1997). According to the Britain Votes 2001 survey, while the weekly soap operas continued to attract viewing figures of about 13 million, the BBC 6 o'clock news dropped from a peak of 5.4 million in the first week of the campaign to 4.8 million in the fourth week, while the ITN *News at Ten* moved from a peak of 5.9 million to 5.4 million in the same period. The BBC's *Question Time*, in which the party leaders were open to challenge, attracted fewer than 3 million viewers. The average viewing figures for party election broadcasts were also down. According to the Electoral Commission, only slightly more than half (55 per cent) of respondents to a MORI poll say they saw any of the party election broadcasts on television, down from 73 per cent in 1992 (MORI poll, http://www.mori.com/pubinfo/pdf/rmm-res2001.pdf).

There is a tendency for the media to report on the political process and the horse-race element rather than on the issues. As in 1997, in 2001 the media reported on the parties' strategies and tactics as much as they did on the issues, and where issues

Table 9.12 Who do voters trust?

For each category, who do you generally trust to tell the truth or not?

Category	% Trust	% Don't trust
Doctors	87	9
Teachers	85	10
Clergymen/priests	78	16
Professors	76	11
Judges	77	15
TV newsreaders	73	18
Scientists	60	25
The police	60	33
Man/woman in the street	52	34
Pollsters	46	35
Civil servants	47	40
Trade union officials	38	47
Business leaders	28	60
Government ministers	21	72
Politicians generally	20	74
Journalists	15	78

Source: MORI/Electoral Commission, 2001, http://www.mori.com/pubinfo/pdf/rmm-res2001.pdf

were covered they were likely to be low-salience topics such as Europe. About half of the political coverage in the press and on television referred to the process and conduct of the campaign. Issues such as Europe and the health service were dealt with in less than 10 per cent of the coverage; agriculture received only 2 per cent of media attention despite the foot and mouth crisis. This was actually an improvement on the 1997 election, where the media devoted two-thirds of their coverage to the conduct of the campaign and to the party leaders rather than to the issues (Deacon, Golding and Billig, 2001).

Conclusions

British voting behaviour is now clearly different from what it was in the 1960s. A two-party system based around a fundamental class cleavage has given way to a more fragmented (and competitive) party system where the personality of party leaders, issue voting, campaigning strategy and new social identities all play a role in shaping electoral choice. In this environment of dealigned politics, the media and political communications have acquired enhanced significance. Here a paradox emerges. Politicians spend more money and time than ever before attempting to ascertain the mood of the public and to sell policies to the electorate. Yet far from appreciating this attention, the public appears to be increasingly apathetic about traditional party politics and suspicious of the message that is being marketed. In the short run, such cynicism is probably not going to inflict long-term damage on the legitimacy of the political system. But it is difficult to reconcile with New Labour's vision of democratic renewal and a revived democracy.

 Key Questions

1 What are the most important factors in explaining how people vote?
2 Why is the media so important in elections?
3 What could and should be done to make people more interested in electoral politics?

 Further Reading

There is an enormous literature on voting behaviour. David Butler and Donald Stokes, *Political Change in Britain* (Basingstoke: Macmillan, 1970, 1974) is still a classic which repays careful reading. B. Sarlvik and I. Crewe, *Decade of Dealignment* (Cambridge: Cambridge University Press, 1983) examines the 1970s.

Good contemporary general overviews are provided in D. Denver, 'The British electorate in the 1990s', *West European Politics*, 21: 1 (1998) as well as in G. Evans and P. Norris (eds), *Critical Elections: British Parties and Voters in Long-term Perspective* (London: Sage, 1999). G. Evans (ed.), *The End of Class Politics?* (Oxford: Oxford University Press, 2001) places the decline of class voting in Britain in comparative perspective.

Three works by A. Heath, R. Jowell and J. Curtice – *How Britain Votes* (London: Pergamon, 1985), *Labour's Last Chance* (Aldershot: Dartmouth, 1994) and *The Rise of New Labour* (Oxford: Oxford University Press, 2001) – all provide important statements about the changing basis of voting behaviour.

D. Sanders, 'The dynamics of party preference change in Britain, 1991–96', *Political Studies*, 47: 2 (1999) offers a different interpretation of voting behaviour. G. Evans, 'Economics and politics revisited: Exploring the decline in Conservative support, 1992–95', *Political Studies*, 47: 1 (1999) is a stimulating interpretation of Conservative decline. The relationship between the media, political strategy and voting behaviour is explored in P. Norris, *Virtuous Circle: Political Communications in Postindustrial Societies* (Cambridge: Cambridge University Press, 2002), which presents a comparative perspective, and in N. Gavin, 'The impact of television news on public perceptions of the economy and government, 1993–94', *Elections and Parties Yearbook 1996* (London: Frank Cass, 1996).

The political marketing approach is explored in N. Jones, *Sultans of Spin: The Media and the New Labour Government* (London: Gollancz, 1999) and in D. Kavanagh, *Election Campaigning: The New Marketing of Politics* (Oxford: Blackwell, 1995). J. Lees-Marshment, *Political Marketing and British Political Parties* (Manchester: Manchester University Press, 2001) and P. Norris, J. Curtice, O. Saunders and M. Scammell, *On Message* (London: Sage, 1999) offer important accounts, as does M. Scammell, *Designer Politics* (London: Macmillan, 1995). Reference may also be made to Scammell's more recent article, 'Political marketing: Lessons for political science', *Political Studies*, 47 (1999).

 Websites

See also the list of general websites at the back of the book.

- www.crest.ox.ac.uk – Centre for Research into Elections and Social Trends
- www.obv.ogr.uk – Operation Black Vote
- www.yougov.com – Online voting and polling site
- www.mori.com – MORI opinion research
- www.nopworld.com – NOP opinion research
- www.icmresearch.co.uk – ICM

10 Pressure Groups and Participation

In the previous three chapters we analysed the United Kingdom's institutions of representative democracy through a discussion of the role of the electoral system, political parties and voting behaviour. Much of that discussion assumed that the primary way in which governments are linked to popular opinion is through the mechanisms of elections and the mobilization of support by parties. Yet one of the most marked recent developments in Britain's politics is the extent to which interest in what might be called orthodox politics has atrophied. Whether measured by turnout or by more stringent tests such as membership of a political party, participation in the public life of the country appears to have declined. This decline has occurred despite governmental attempts to make the process of voting easier and strenuous efforts by the parties to recruit new members.

Voting and party membership do not, however, constitute the only form of political participation. Between elections individuals may engage in a diverse array of political activity, ranging from writing a letter to a newspaper or signing a petition or joining a pressure group or **lobbying** organization (see table 10.1). Individuals may also engage in some form of non-violent **direct action** by going on a march or demonstration. In this chapter attention is focused on these broader dimensions of participation. We assess the range of interest groups and **non-governmental organizations** (NGOs) which aim to influence the policy-making process between elections, and we attempt to identify trends and currents in the pattern of contemporary pressure group organization and social movement activism. The style and extent of this participation are extremely important elements in the political life of the country.

There is no uncontested way to describe these groups, any more than there is agreement about how best to categorize them. Various terms have been used at different times. Pressure groups, interest groups, lobbying groups, advocacy groups and NGOs are all terms that will be encountered in this chapter. The term most often used in this chapter is pressure group, although the concept is sometimes seen as carrying negative connotations. Its advantage is that it is broader than either interest group or lobbying group. Generally, however, we may define a pressure group as an organization that seeks to influence the decision-making process without itself aiming towards government. Not only do pressure groups provide

lobbying group Group of people representing a particular political interest, e.g. the environmental lobby.

direct action The use of tactics, which may be violent or non-violent, that bypass the normal institutions of representative government. Typically, these tactics involve some form of public protest such as a demonstration or march to publicize a cause. Direct action is associated especially with the emergence of radical social movements.

non-governmental organization (NGO) A term usually applied to voluntary sector bodies and pressure groups to signal that, although they may provide public services and seek to shape government policy, they are formally separate from the state.

Table 10.1 Participation between elections

Which, if any, have you done in the last 2 or 3 years?	1972	1999
Voted in the last general election	74	73
Helped on fundraising drive	22	29
Made speech to organized group	11	17
Urged someone to vote	18	17
Urged someone to contact MP/councillor	14	16
Been officer of organization/club	14	14
Presented views to MP/councillor	11	15
Written letter to editor	6	8
Played active part in a political campaign	4	3

Source: Jessica Elgood and Roger Mortimer, 'What can the general election tell us about consumers?', MORI, 2001, http://www.mori.com/pubinfo/pdf/rmm-res2001.pdf

an additional outlet for political expression; they also channel preferences into the policy process. In recent years a good deal of attention has been paid to the role of networks in the governmental process, especially in the context of arguments about the changing character of the British policy process (Marsh, Richards and Smith, 2001; Marsh and Rhodes, 2001). The network approach focuses not on small groups of decision makers (ministers and civil servants) but on a series of networks, which may vary from tight policy communities to much more open issue networks. Public policy making on this view is best understood as the product of interchanges and exchanges between members of these networks. Pressure groups, interest groups, voluntary organizations and professional representatives may all participate in these networks. The concept of networks nicely captures many features of the complex relationships between interest groups and government and underlines the variety that occurs between policy sectors and over time. Network theory also captures well the way in which many of the lines of communication between the public and private sectors and between governmental and non-governmental actors have also become much less clear-cut in recent years. That said, however, there is no consensus about the utility of the term, much less over how the network model relates to the distribution of power in society or the democratic control of policy. Networks may be seen as spreading power extensively across the political system or they may be seen as concentrating it in a small number of closed policy communities.

The Diversity of Group Activity

Pressure groups have, of course, long been present in the United Kingdom. Thus, for example, the anti-slavery society and the railway interest were familiar features of nineteenth-century political life. For much of the second half of the twentieth century, government was absorbed in the task of trying to orchestrate agreement over economic policy between trade unions and employers in a process that gave both groups enhanced political status. In the early twenty-first century, however, several changes in pressure group activity and in the relationships between groups and government can be detected. Although many of the interactions between groups and government are highly institutionalized, changes in the structure of central government, in patterns of consultation and in the issue agenda of government have created subtle alterations of organization and influence since the period of Conservative government since 1997. In addition, the style and tactics of many pressure groups have been transformed. Moreover, the increased salience of single-issue groups that has been noted in recent years – and the greater willingness of some groups and movements to use direct action – raise important questions about the political culture. The chapter therefore has a dual focus. It attempts to assess the effect of the rich universe of non-governmental groups and associations that constitute civil society in the United Kingdom, and it endeavours to gauge the impact of these groups on the policy-making process and the power structure of the country.

The United Kingdom, in common with other advanced democracies, displays a very wide range of pressure groups formed for different purposes. Many of them have a long history. Thus two very popular mass membership groups – the Royal Society for the Protection of Birds (RSPB) and the National Trust – date from the late nineteenth century. Others, such as Greenpeace and Friends of the Earth, are of relatively recent foundation (see table 10.2). Their numbers are extensive and some pressure groups such as the National Trust and the RSPB have a membership that exceeds all the combined totals of Britain's three major political parties. On a quite different level, numerous professional groups, employers' organizations and trade associations seek to influence government on behalf of their sectors. Sometimes these groups have a mass membership. Sometimes they simply have highly professional staff and little mass membership.

Such groups may be organized to defend the interests of different sections of the economy and those of their own members, whether they be producers (such as farmers, motor manufacturers or retailers) or workers who are members of a trade union or professional association. Such groups aim to be well informed about matters affecting their industry and to communicate their point of view. The preferred style of interest group activity by producer groups is usually one that cultivates decision makers behind the scenes in an effort to shape policy. Trade unions, by contrast, have employed a variety of tactics, including consultation and negotiation when those methods are available; but trade unions have also been willing in the last resort to use their distinct form of direct action – a strike.

Some groups are formed not so much around sectional interests as around causes. Such groups may have a single-issue focus, such as the reform of the abortion laws or the abolition of fox hunting; or they may have a broad-based agenda, such as the prevention of child poverty or the promotion of constitutional reform.

In addition to the array of explicit campaigning and defensive groups are several voluntary organizations – over 500,000 of them within the United Kingdom. Not all have charitable status, although some 190,000 do (such as the Sunshine Home for Blind Babies, the Royal National Institute for the Deaf and Dr Barnardo's). Why some voluntary organizations qualify for charitable status and others do not is now a matter of controversy. Some groups fail to qualify because their objectives are not sufficiently broad. Others fail because they are thought to be too political. For some groups, such as Oxfam and Shelter, there is a tension between their agenda, which requires political activism and campaigning, and their charitable status, which is not available to explicitly political organizations. Indeed, some groups

Table 10.2 Membership of selected environmental voluntary organizations in the UK, 1997

Group	Membership (000s)	Foundation	Purpose
National Trust	2,488	1895	Acts as a guardian for the nation in the acquisition and protection of threatened coastline, countryside and buildings.
Royal Society for the Protection of Birds	1,007	1889	Seeks to encourage the conservation of wild birds and their habitats.
Civic Trust	330	1957	Fosters high standards of planning and architecture in towns and cities.
The Wildlife Trusts	310	1912	Nationwide network of 46 local charities working to protect wildlife in the towns and countryside.
World Wide Fund for Nature	241	1961	Seeks to preserve the world's biological diversity and promote sustainable development.
National Trust for Scotland	228	1931	Protects and promotes Scotland's natural and cultural heritage.
Greenpeace	215	1977	Seeks to expose global environmental problems and their causes, and research the solutions and alternatives.
Woodland Trust	195	1986	Protects the UK's native woodland heritage.
Ramblers Association	123	1967	Exists to promote walking outdoors, increase access to land and promote respect for the life of the countryside.
Friends of the Earth	110	1981	Seeks to expand education about ecological issues and promote conservation of natural resources.
Council for the Protection of Rural England	45	1964	Promotes the preservation of the English countryside and educates the public on conservation issues.

Source: Adapted from Office for National Statistics, *Britain 1999.*

such as the Family Planning Association and Oxfam have had their charitable status threatened by opponents. There is thus a grey area about the extent to which a group may engage in political campaigning while retaining charitable status as well as a difficult borderline for charities that engage in commercial activity. As a result, there is currently a demand from a number of charities for a thorough review of the law in this area as well as efforts by the Charities Commission and the Cabinet Office to modernize the regulation of voluntary activity.

By mobilizing support for their various interests and causes, pressure groups communicate opinion and expertise to government. Like political parties, they also form an important part of civil society and serve as another bridge between the market and formal institutions of the state. As such there has been a determined effort by both national and local government to strengthen the role of such groups as well as an enhanced interest by the European Commission in developing their role.

On a practical level, interest groups and voluntary organizations may try to influence government policy and legislation and they may be consulted by government about changes in policy, perhaps even to the extent of being asked to help write or implement it. But government also needs these groups in the policy process for their expertise and to legitimize decisions taken in the various policy arenas where a group may have special standing or knowledge. Pressure group leaders may be asked to serve on a range of representative institutions or appointed bodies at local and national level.

Why people join pressure groups may pose a puzzle for some observers. After all, it could be argued that an individual's membership of a group is not likely to have an impact on its efficiency, and from the individual's perspective it may be irrational if the goals of the group are public goods. One important examination of why individuals join pressure groups, Mancur Olson's *Logic of Collective Action* (1965), emphasizes the role of **selective benefits** (benefits which only they receive) as an incentive to individuals to join interest groups. Frequently, pressure groups provide such selective benefits as discounts on insurance or information about a trade sector in an attempt to broaden their membership and their ability to speak for a sector or cause.

The fact is, however, that in modern Britain there has been a vast increase in the number of organized groups and many pressure groups can claim very large memberships. Thus the National Trust in 1999 claimed 2,488,000 members and Greenpeace claimed 215,000 members. Of course, many of these members may be doing little more than paying a subscription. Assessing the political effect of such activity is more difficult than charting it. Nevertheless, the strength of these voluntary groups' membership affects the fabric of society and the political culture. Some authorities see the vitality of the country's network of associative groups as crucial to the health of democracy (Putnam, 2000, 2002). In this context, even if the armchair membership of a group falls far short of active participation, a pressure group's membership may form an important resource in a policy battle.

For some critics, however, pressure group activity is a threat to democracy since it distorts the public policy process in the interests of unrepresentative sections of society. How the state interacts with

selective benefit A term used by Olson (1965) to describe a benefit provided to interest group members which is limited to members of that group, such as cheap insurance. Selective benefits can be contrasted with collective benefits, such as a cleaner environment, which are enjoyed by all members of society and cannot be restricted to group members.

different social groups and what interests have access to the policy process are thus key questions in any political system, but especially in a system that claims to be a democracy.

Social Movements

Sectional interest groups and pressure groups usually display a substantial degree of formal organization. They are often elitist and hierarchical (Lent, 2001). There are, however, also important social movements that are more amorphous and have a less clearly defined membership than orthodox pressure groups. Such movements are usually more radical in purpose and in campaigning style than established pressure groups, although frequently social movements will tap the support of a variety of sympathetic individual groups and organizations. These social movements may be an expression of a pent-up demand for social reform (for example, through the movement for homosexual equality or the women's movement) or moral change (through the peace movement); or they may be reactionary and seek to restore a social order that has been changed. (An example of a reactionary movement in the United Kingdom is the National Viewers and Listeners Association, which the late Mary Whitehouse formed in an attempt to 'clean up' British television and radio; in 2001 it was reformed as Mediawatch-UK.)

Often social movements represent the mobilization of distinct sections of the population – women, gays, ethnic minorities and the disabled – whose consciousness of shared interests and identities has formed slowly. Important social movements have also formed around the issues of environmentalism and consumerism. Such movements tend to cover rather different issues from those advanced by more traditional groups and will be organized more responsively than regular pressure groups. Thus while many traditional pressure groups such as trade unions and business groups are hierarchically organized, social movements have a flatter organizational structure and are more internally democratic.

Social movements can have an impact on the political system not least because of their ability to mobilize large numbers of people. They are also able to exploit links with other sympathetic pressure groups. Many of these movements have also been able to conduct shrewd and hard-hitting campaigns and to use various forms of direct action ingeniously. The Countryside Alliance March of 1998 saw the participation of over 300,000 people, and the same number also joined in a similar march in September 2002. The London march against the war with Iraq in February 2003 claimed over a million participants, with smaller demonstrations in other cities.

It should also be noted here that contemporary social movements are not confined to the national arena. Indeed, the movement against global capitalism that gathered pace in the 1990s saw demonstrations orchestrated against the World Trade Organization (WTO) in Seattle in 1999 and in Washington, DC, against the World Bank, as well as at the EU 2001 summit in Gothenburg. On May Day 2001, there were anti-capitalist demonstrations around the world, including in London, linked to the group Reclaim the Streets (RTS) and the umbrella group People's Global Action. Although these demonstrations were large and often resulted in violence, they seemed to be allied to no obvious political party, although some sympathetic organizations of the left did join in. These protests were also much aided by the Internet, which allowed notice of demonstrations to be spread quickly and efficiently and which needed little prior organization (*Guardian*, 30 April 2003).

The Changing Context of Pressure Group Activity

Social movements provide an important example of new patterns of mobilization within and beyond British society. Even when we turn back to the more institutionalized world of sectional interest groups and more orthodox causal groups, it is evident that the world in which they operate is not static. Clearly, the universe of pressure groups itself is very fluid. As the country's political agenda changes over time, new opportunities for mobilization appear and may generate group formation. New groups can easily be formed around new causes since the start-up costs of an organization are relatively low, especially compared to political parties, where the national electoral system provides high barriers to entry. Some groups lose membership and are either wound up or become inactive.

There is always competition between groups within a given area of public policy as well as realignments and reorganizations. The largest representative body of industry, the Confederation of British Industry (CBI), acquired a corporatist image as a result of its role in tripartite policy making between business, unions and government over the 1960s and 1970s. Its claim to speak for business was challenged by the formation of the Institute of Directors (IOD), with a free-market orientation. During the Thatcher years it was the IOD rather than the CBI that had greater access to government. The British trade union movement has always experienced conflicts as individual unions have competed with one another for membership. Recent years have witnessed an extensive amount of reorganization and merger within British trade unions. Established cause groups can find their dominant role threatened. During the 1980s the Howard League for Penal Reform was challenged on the left by more radical groups, such as Radical Alternatives to Prison (RAP). Today the Howard League faces rather different competition in the sense that, while it does not take government funding, several groups involved in research in the area of penal policy are funded by government. The Penal Research Consortium operates as an umbrella organization for various small groups conducting research in the field. Professional groups such as the Bar and the Law Society have faced competition since the 1980s. This competition occurred over their response to changes in the structure of the profession, where there was demand from groups like Campaign for the Bar for more radical action. It also occurred over the content of legal policy generally, where groups like the Legal Action Group have challenged the profession's claim to speak for lawyers. Organizational divisions have also appeared in the last few years within the farming industry, where a new group called Farm has challenged the National Farmers Union (NFU). Farm's objections to the NFU are that it is too close to government and the agricultural business sector and insufficiently geared to campaigning and lobbying. Farm is also hostile to the EU subsidy system (*Guardian*, 5 November 2002).

Sometimes change and competition within the world of pressure groups occurs when a new leadership challenges an established elite or when an organization adopts a more radical strategy than before. Thus changes at the top of individual trade unions can signal a change of tactics and political stance. Such leadership changes are inevitably watched closely by government as they can herald a more militant strategy. Thus when Derek Simpson was elected to lead Amicus in 2002, there was fear that he might turn the union in a more radical direction. Similarly, when Kevin Curran replaced John Edmonds as leader of the GMB in 2003, there was concern about both his stance on the issue of financing public services through public–private partnerships and his call for a review of the union's link with the Labour Party.

International developments may affect the world of pressure groups. Controversial international issues – the Vietnam war in the 1960s, the war against Iraq in 2003, the cause of Palestine or even globalization itself – may become the focus of campaigns in their own right. But pressure groups must also take account of international developments to a much greater degree than ever before. Obviously, the international economic climate will have an effect on the position of all sectors of the British economy, but some sectors such as energy may find their position radically affected by international developments. The growing role of the EU in some policy sectors entails the need for some groups to pay as much if not more attention to policy issues at that level. The trade union movement, for example, has become increasingly supportive of European integration and is much more willing to participate in European-level activities, despite a long period of outright opposition to the European venture. Change within the pressure group universe can also occur as a result of technological innovations. Advances in communications (especially the ability to reach members by websites, email and text messaging) have had a major impact on the capacity of groups to organize and campaign as well as on the government's ability to consult with the public. Even the organization of a rally or demonstration has been made easier by the use of websites, emails and the mobile phone. From the government's perspective, the new technology allows extensive new opportunities for consultation and policy testing through the use of focus groups, citizens' and people's panels (see table 10.3). New technologies have thus made the government's job both harder and easier. It is harder in the sense that groups can organize direct action and other forms of protest more easily by exploiting the Internet; but it is easier in that government itself can contact the public using new technological opportunities. How effective or genuine these new pathways of consultation are is a matter of debate; but they at least raise the possibility that a government could bypass groups claiming to represent specific sections of the population in the process of policy making, as well as bypass Parliament.

Changes in Governmental Structure

In addition to changes in the number and type of pressure groups, the way they operate is affected by changes in the organization, operating style and ideology of government. The organizational focus of pressure groups will reflect the decision-making processes of government and groups will have to respond to constitutional and other changes that affect those processes. Earlier in the book we discussed the extent to which the UK was becoming a multi-layered polity as a result of such

Table 10.3 Methods of consultation

Method	Description
Complaints/suggestion schemes	Ongoing opportunities for citizens to respond to service experiences and to report needs.
Service satisfaction surveys	Surveys of specific services or overall service provision. May be postal, face-to-face, over the telephone or by email.
Other opinion polls	Surveys which gain views on non-service-specific issues.
Deliberative opinion polls	Use survey methods but allow citizens to discuss issues and take evidence before giving views.
Interactive websites	Invite email messages from citizens on service or policy matters.
Referendums	Votes on policy or service options, which may be binding or advisory.
Community plan/needs analysis	Reviews of the needs of local communities through discussion with residents, public meetings, etc.
Citizens' panel	Ongoing panels made up of statistically representative sample of citizens whose views are sought several times a year.
Co-option/committee work	Citizens from a particular community or interest group sitting on committees in advisory or decision-making capacity.
Question and answer sessions	Held at the end of meetings to allow citizens to question decision makers.
Consultation documents	Allow public consideration of and response to policy proposals prior to decision making.
Public meetings	Bring decision makers and interested members of the public together to present and debate issues.
Citizens' juries	Small group of broadly representative citizens brought together to consider a particular issue over several days. Can question witnesses and take evidence.
Consensus conferences	Operate like a citizens' jury but seek to achieve consensus on a particular issue and map out common ground on which policy can be developed.
Focus groups	Small discussion groups, recruited on the basis of interest or locality, asked to report their needs or experiences.
Visioning exercises	Range of methods used to allow citizens to present their preferred vision for a locality or service issue.
Planning for Real exercises	Allow citizens to plan area development through use of 3D models and other visual techniques.
Forums	Ongoing bodies with regular meetings that focus on a particular issue, citizen group or locality.
User management of services	Citizens given direct control over the management of local services and resources.

Source: Adapted from Lowndes et al. (1998).

constitutional changes as devolution and regionalism. This shift means that there are important new arenas of decision making where pressure groups must attempt to promote their case. And indeed, we find that groups in Scotland and Wales are looking towards their devolved governments rather than to London. The strengthening of the regional dimension within England may also be expected to lead to a refocusing of some pressure group activity. Local government is also a focus of group attention in its own right. Recent shifts in the approach to local government which emphasize the significance of the voluntary sector in the government of the community have also been important in enhancing the legitimacy of a host of philanthropic and voluntary organizations at the local level. There is a much greater tendency to see the role of the local authority as enabling and orchestrating services for the community rather than directly providing those services. Decision making is much more likely than in the past to involve a range of non-governmental actors – voluntary groups, churches, ethnic group representatives and others.

Multi-level decision making is a product not only of efforts to devolve power but also of the Europeanization of many policy sectors. Lobbying at the EU level has been essential for many groups since the UK entered the European Community in 1973. Although the extent to which European decision making impinges on pressure group strategy will vary from sector to sector, the European dimension of all policy affecting the UK is growing and is especially important in such sectors as agriculture, consumer affairs and the environment. The quickening pace of European integration is also forcing many pressure groups to adjust their tactics. As a result of the Maastricht and Amsterdam treaties, groups must pay rather more attention than before to the European Parliament, which has strengthened its role in the legislative process (see chapter 15).

It is not only the radical changes of government structure entailed by devolution and regionalization that can affect the way pressure groups work and their ability to influence policy. At the central level of government, departmental reorganization may have an impact on relationships between pressure groups and government. Thus it has been noted that a substantial change occurred when the Department of Energy was abolished and its functions merged into the Department of Trade and Industry and the Department of the Environment. The old Department of Energy was organized in divisions that were highly responsive to their producer interests. Privatization and departmental reorganization disrupted these established relationships and it was found that the issue of energy efficiency was handled quite differently at the Department of the Environment from the way it had been handled at the Department of Energy (Marsh, Richards and Smith, 2001).

The discussion of how the context of group activities can be changed by government reorganization underlines the extent to which the relationship between a group and a department or section of government can become so close that the governmental actor is colonized or captured. It then acts like a pressure group on behalf of its interests or groups. This is not, of course, a new development. There have always been spending departments at the central level of government that have acted as powerful pressure groups; and policy communities such as defence or education have frequently battled for their clients rather than taking a collective governmental view. Some departments became so closely identified with an interest that they risked reorganization or outright abolition. The Civil Service Department incurred prime ministerial hostility in the 1980s because it was thought to be defending the special privileges of civil servants. The old Ministry of Agriculture, Fisheries and Food (now the Department for the Environment, Food and Rural Affairs) was dominated for most of its existence by the NFU, which from its foundation in 1908 enjoyed enormous clout as the leading voice of British agriculture. Quangos such as the Arts Council (and newer bodies involved in such policy areas as urban development) inevitably act as pressure groups. What is new is the extent to which governmental organizations at one level – for example, a local authority – may find it necessary to maintain representation at other levels of the system – for example, in Europe.

Other changes in the character of the British state outlined earlier – especially privatization and the creation of agencies as well as new forms of regulation – have altered the range of bodies with which decision makers and special interests must deal. Regulation and law have become salient features of the modern British state in the twenty-first century. The enhanced role of law in the modern British state is a product of many developments, not least the growing role of the European Union and the passage of the 1998 Human Rights Act. As a result, many pressure groups have to pay considerably more attention to legal issues than in the past. For some pressure groups – notably British trade unions – fighting legal cases has become an important strategy in securing workers' rights.

The additional complexity of the state has placed a greater premium on understanding the intricacies of decision-making processes, thereby creating greater space for public affairs specialists within large firms. These specialized units handle a range of public relations and communications functions, presenting the firm's case to the outside world but also harmonizing strategy within the firm. They may also make contact with specialist political consultants whose task is to advise the firm on how best to present its case to government.

Ideological changes can also affect the context of pressure group activity. The replacement of a neo-liberal Conservative government by a Labour one in 1997 changed the approach to consultation by government and the kinds of groups it consulted on a regular basis. The 1979–97 Conservative governments were hostile to the style of corporatist politics embraced by governments of both parties between 1961 and 1979. The importance of consultation with pressure groups was de-emphasized in the drive to alter the direction of policy making and to reduce the role of the state. The advent of Labour to power in 1997 saw renewed stress on consultation, both as a means of building legitimacy and as a way of exploiting expertise.

Sleaze and the Regulation of Parliamentary Lobbying

One final transformation that has taken place in the past decade in the environment within which groups work relates to the regulation of group activity. The traditional dominance of the executive in the British system of government meant that sectional groups would generally concentrate their lobbying efforts on the departments rather than the legislature. During the Thatcher and Major years, however, Parliament gained importance as a forum of pressure group activity. This was partly because the radical programmes espoused by the Thatcher government were often adopted without the extensive pre-legislative consultation that had been normal in earlier years, thus prompting groups to mobilize and conduct public campaigns. Parliament had always been significant as an arena for gaining publicity for issues because of the opportunities afforded by early day motions, parliamentary questions and private members' bills as well as the opportunity for backbenchers to move amendments to legislation. Groups recognize of course that publicity is not always a good thing, and the most successful groups will often be those that work quietly behind the scenes. For such groups, publicity is a last resort to be used when other tactics have failed.

Parliamentary lobbying may involve both the House of Commons and the House of Lords. Indeed, with its looser party discipline and greater freedom to discuss issues outside the mainstream of partisan debate, the House of Lords has always provided an important forum for pressure group activity, especially by groups such as academics, farmers, landowners and lawyers. The House of Commons also became much more friendly to lobbying activities during the 1980s. In particular, deregulation and privatization created new opportunities for financial gain. There developed a new style of lobbying in which commercial multi-client lobbyists (such as Ian Greer Associates) recruited MPs to assist their clients in pressing their case.

A series of scandals in the Major years (including the discovery that MPs were being paid to put down parliamentary questions) led Major in 1994 to set up a Committee on Standards in Public Life under Lord Nolan. The impact of the Nolan Committee was a revision of the rules governing the relationship between MPs and peers on the one hand, and lobbyists on the other. Although the regime of self-regulation for the most part still held, it was reinforced by new elements. A new Committee of Standards and Privileges was introduced to regulate MPs' conduct. A Code of Conduct for MPs was introduced along with a Standards Commissioner (currently Sir Philip Mawer), who was also given an investigative role. One element of the Code of Conduct was an increasingly restrictive attitude to any promotion of a cause by an MP in return for payment. Thus the advocacy rule prohibited an MP from introducing or raising any issue in return for payment, and this was later extended to prohibit an MP from introducing a delegation to a minister or civil servant. Greater attention was paid to the register of members' interests and a range of specialized registers was established for parliamentary journalists, staff and all-party and parliamentary groups.

Industry, Business and Finance

Now that we have highlighted some of the factors that have changed the way pressure groups operate in the United Kingdom in recent years, it is possible to look very briefly at two or three important areas of pressure group activity before considering the resources that pressure groups have at their disposal. In any modern political system, business broadly defined will be a key pressure group, though it rarely speaks with a single voice. In the United Kingdom the organization of business and financial interests has been heavily conditioned by historical factors, including the country's position as an international trading centre. As a result, there are marked differences of outlook between the financial and manufacturing sectors and within industry as a whole (especially between larger firms and smaller ones).

The lobbying behaviour of financial institutions and the City of London has always exerted pressure on British governments, especially through the Department of Trade. The style of this pressure changed markedly in the 1980s with deregulation and the exposure to a much harsher climate of competitiveness. The gentlemanly and discreet style employed by City of London merchant banks and stockbroking institutions gave way to more aggressive methods as British financial organizations fought to capture lucrative new markets and exploit the new emphasis on enterprise.

The effects of deregulation ('big bang' as it was popularly known) were compounded by other Conservative policies which created myriad financial opportunities and an economic climate that encouraged mergers and takeover bids. In these circumstances, financial institutions extended their lobbying techniques from behind-the-scenes contacts to more overt methods. These tactics included the use of commercial lobbyists and the establishment of commercial or public affairs departments within firms to coordinate strategy and communications. These new activities became commonplace even in traditional firms such as merchant banks. The financial sector thus acquired a much higher profile as a lobbying group after 1979.

British industry is represented by a range of organizations and relations between interest groups and government varies by policy sector. In the nineteenth and early twentieth centuries, business had tended to be represented on an industry-by-industry basis rather than through any broad organization, although the Association of British Chambers of Commerce (ABCC) was founded in 1860 to represent small firms. While the peak business group – the CBI – represents over 150,000 businesses, it is vulnerable to claims that it does not speak for all sections of industry. Division between large manufacturing industries and medium and small firms is reflected in the existence of a Smaller Businesses Association, which was set up in 1971, as well as a special organization for small businesses within the CBI, the Small Business Group. Retail as opposed to manufacturing tends to be represented through the Retail Consortium and there are other specialist organizations. The perception that the CBI is not vigorous enough has also led to the establishment of independent new bodies such as the Institute of Directors and, within the CBI, the National Manufacturing Council. The total membership of employer organizations is currently 272,930 (Annual Report of the Certification Officer, 2001–2).

One feature of the pattern of industrial representation as it developed over the twentieth century was the way in which government itself prompted and encouraged the formation and reorganization of representative bodies in industry. The formation of the Federation of British Industry in 1916 was a response to wartime controls on industry; and the creation of the CBI in 1965 reflected the desire of government to have a body with which to deal in determining industrial policy. As head of the newly created Department of Economic Affairs (DEA), George Brown in 1965 wanted a single employers' group to aid economic planning and growth. Michael Heseltine in the 1980s encouraged reform of the trade associations to promote the efficient representation of industry.

The formation of the CBI from a merger of a number of smaller organizations expanded its membership and allowed it to extend its activities. The amalgamation also spurred the CBI into a more overtly political role than any of its three

tripartism Approach to economic policy making in the 1970s which emphasized the need for consensual agreements between the government, employers and unions.

component parts had hitherto played. This higher public profile was prompted initially by a Labour government, which had placed the management of the economy firmly on the agenda and needed the cooperation of the employers in the regulation of prices and incomes. This approach marked British economic policy making for the period 1964–79 and entailed an increasing incorporation of business into many aspects of policy making and implementation.

The rejection of **tripartism** or corporatism as a strategy for managing economic policy by the Conservative governments of 1979–97 saw a certain distancing of the CBI from the inner counsels of government. New Labour, by contrast, made it clear that it wished to gain the confidence of business and since 1997 the CBI has enjoyed enhanced access to Whitehall.

In addition to the representations that firms make through the CBI, some businesses will have fostered their own contacts with government. Such firms – especially large ones such as British Aerospace, ICI and Rolls Royce – increasingly bypass the CBI and negotiate directly with the appropriate government department; and some will have their own direct contact with ministers. However, even the largest firms will also use the CBI for general promotion of business interests. Smaller businesses, which by contrast have too few resources to put independent pressure on the government, value their membership of the CBI both for its advocacy of their cause and for the selective benefits it brings. The decision as to whether to press the case of a business directly when legislation is being drafted will depend on the sensitivity of the issue.

Trade Unions

The power of the trade union movement has always been a highly contentious issue in British politics. Trade unionism started as a movement to protect the exploited and economically weak, but as the movement grew in strength it has frequently been accused of threatening the national interest. Political organization was an important aspect of trade union strategy and it first allied with the Liberal Party to promote reform. In 1900 the Trades Union Congress (which had been founded as the representative organization of trade unions in 1868) helped to bring the Labour Party into being. Over the first half of the twentieth century unions in alliance with Labour secured improvements in the rights of workers and in material conditions. The participation of the unions in the Second World War and the election of a Labour government in 1945 saw trade unions gain a new legitimacy. In the 1960s and 1970s, however, the trade union role in the political and economic system became increasingly identified as a major policy problem and there developed a consensus that the movement had become far too powerful. Partly this concern arose from the absence of any legal framework to regulate industrial actions by unions; partly it was the product of the power that unions wielded as a result of their ability to influence public policy, to promote pay claims and to shape policy inside the Labour Party.

Since the 1980s the power of the organized trade union movement has declined. A number of factors have contributed to that process, but here three should be mentioned. First, the period of the Thatcher–Major years witnessed a determined effort to reform trade union law and practice. As a result, a new framework of law regulates the scope of lawful industrial action, controls the way in which unions raise and distribute money for political purposes and provides new rights for employers.

Secondly, there have been marked changes in the labour market over the period since 1979. These changes reflect broader economic shifts, especially the decline of manufacturing industry and the rise of the service sector, which is less heavily unionized. (There is no real distinction between membership of manual and non-manual unions or of unions catering to production or service workers and both have approximately 30 per cent density of membership. However, there is an interesting distinction between the public sector, where approximately 60 per cent of the workforce is unionized, and the private sector, where only 20 per cent are members of a union.) One consequence of these changes was a decline in union membership, which dropped from a high of 12.3 million in 1976 to 7.7 million in 2001–2 (Annual Report of the Certification Officer, 2001–2; see tables 1.6, p. 10, and 10.4). Changes in the economy together with changes in the framework of industrial law produced a marked reduction in the number of strikes and industrial disputes. The days lost by strikes dropped from 4,266,000 in 1981 to 499,000 in 2000 (table 10.5).

Thirdly, the unions' relationship with its major political ally, Labour, has weakened. Although not all unions are affiliated to the Labour Party, Labour is traditionally seen as the party of the unions. As was noted in chapter 8, New Labour in opposition was determined to distance itself from the trade union movement, fearing that a strong association with the trade unions could be electorally damaging. The Labour Party changed a number of its institutional links with the unions, revising its sponsorship arrangements, the representation of the unions at conference

Table 10.4 Union density by sector, 2001

Industry	All	Private sector	Public sector
Agriculture, forestry and fishing	9	6	a
Mining and quarrying	25	25	a
Manufacturing	27	27	61
Energy and water	53	53	a
Construction	19	14	69
Wholesale and retail trade	12	12	a
Hotels and restaurants	5	4	32
Transport and communication	42	37	75
Financial intermediation	27	27	a
Real estate and business services	11	8	54
Public administration	59	33	61
Education	53	29	57
Health	45	16	62
Other activities	22	11	49
All employees	29	19	59

[a] Sample size too small for a reliable estimate.

Table 10.5 Days lost through strikes, 1901–2000

Year	Days lost (000s)
1901	4,130
1906	3,019
1911	10,155
1916	2,446
1921	85,872
1926	162,233
1931	6,983
1936	1,829
1941	1,079
1946	2,158
1951	1,694
1956	2,083
1961	3,046
1966	2,398
1971	13,551
1976	3,284
1981	4,266
1986	1,920
1991	761
1996	1,303
2000	499

Source: Office for National Statistics, *Social Trends 30* and *Annual Abstract of Statistics 2002*.

and the role of the unions in the candidate selection process. Currently there are 199 trade unions, 22 of which are affiliated to the Labour Party.

The advent of a Labour government in 1997 confirmed a distancing of the party from the unions, although there were some pro-union changes after 1997, for example on workplace ballots. Industrial relations became more militant. By July 2002, *The Times* was heralding a new era of union militancy as the biggest single union walkout since 1979 occurred. At the same time, union leadership seemed to be shifting away from support for New Labour and towards the left. In July 2002 the government lost one of its key allies, Sir Ken Jackson, who was defeated in the election for general secretary of Amicus by a left-winger, Derek Simpson.

Other unions replaced moderate leaders with more left-leaning ones. The cut in funding for New Labour MPs and for the Labour Party created a cash crisis for Labour. A new generation of left-of-centre trade union leaders presents a potential threat for a Labour government since it risks raising the union issue again if there is a resurgence of strike activity, especially in the public sector, or any significant push for substantial change in the employment law framework put in place under the Conservatives between 1979 and 1997.

In these circumstances, the trade union movement has had to develop new tactics. One feature of its new approach has been to reach out beyond the UK to make alliances with other unions in the European Union and, more generally, to seek to influence policy there. This embrace of the EU is in marked contrast with earlier opposition to Europe. A linked union tactic has been the use of legal mechanisms to secure workers' rights by taking advantage of both the expanding role of European law and the passage of the Human Rights Act.

Environmental Activism

Environmental groups have always been strong in Britain but the environmental lobby has become increasingly significant in British politics since the 1980s, developing into a powerful social movement as well as a set of discrete pressure groups. The environmental lobby itself is extremely diverse and ranges from traditional and established interests such as the RSPB, the Council for the Preservation of Rural England, the National Trust and the Green Alliance to more radical groups such as Greenpeace, Earth First and Friends of the Earth. In addition to these groups there are numerous campaigns and local action groups with very different degrees of organizational resources as well as some self-proclaimed anarchist and libertarian groups such as Leeds Earth First. What is remarkable about these groups is their rapid growth in size, resources and prominence, the increased awareness of environmental issues among the public, and the closer working relationship that many of these groups now have with government.

The environmental movement's issue agenda has broadened considerably since the 1980s and now takes in a variety of topics ranging from the preservation of biodiversity and habitats to waste management and pollution control as well as the more general goal of sustainable development. Although the traditional parts of the environmental lobby always had a degree of what Grant has called 'insider status' (Grant, 2000) and have been consulted on policy in the area, the increased salience of environmental issues from the 1980s and shrewd lobbying by environmentalists has brought the lobby into a much closer working relationship with government. Thus the Green Alliance (which was formed in 1978) claimed in its 2001/2002 report that it had been responsible for the adoption by the Treasury of a systematic environmental audit of departmental spending bids in that year's spending round. It also claimed that it contributed to DEFRA's sustainable development strategy.

In addition to the enhanced political access since the 1980s there has also been an increased sophistication in the use of the media and a much greater use of coordinated campaigning between groups. Not all of the environmental lobby enjoys access to government in this way. Some groups on the fringes of the orthodox environmental lobby, such as animal rights groups, prefer direct action – demonstrations, sit-ins and boycotts – to advance their cause.

The environmental lobby is a good example of one where changes in the structure of decision making require it to maintain a presence at different levels of the system – in Europe, at regional and local levels as well as at the level of central government and the various environmental agencies. Environmental groups have also made good use of new opportunities in Parliament, especially through the select committees, to advance their cause.

Resources, Tactics and Strategies

The extent to which a pressure group can influence policy depends very much on the resources it has at its disposal as well as on the strategies and tactics it can deploy to press its case. It may be able to call on extensive *funds*, as many business groups or trade unions can. For example, 58 per cent of trade union members belong to a union with a political fund and the political funds of unions raised £16 million between April 2001 and March 2002 (Annual Report of the Certification Officer, 2001–2). It may have a large *membership*, although the sheer weight of numbers is not by itself an advantage in getting a case across. The quality and commitment of a group's membership are important, as is the saturation or density of the membership pool, that is, the extent to which it can claim the group really speaks for a particular section of society. *Expertise* is an all-important resource that can compensate for size. Indeed, sometimes it is a distinct advantage to have a relatively small group whose members can be easily mobilized. Some environmental pressure groups have not found their low levels of members by comparison with other such groups to be a disadvantage in their efforts to influence the government. Thus two relatively small groups, the Civic Trust and the Wildfowl and Wetlands Trust, have proved helpful to government in drafting legislation. For example, the Civic Trust was associated with the drafting of the Civic Amenities Act 1967, which gave statutory expression to the idea of conservation areas. Later the Trust was asked by the government to provide the secretariat for European Heritage Year 1975. Similarly Shelter, the organization that campaigns on homelessness issues, had a significant impact on the Homelessness Act 2002, which was in part drafted by Shelter's legal team.

Leadership

Leadership is also an extremely important resource. Pressure group leaders need a clear cause, a strong intellectual case and the ability to communicate the group's agenda to decision makers and the wider public. The difference made by an individual to the style of a pressure group and its success can be enormous. Understanding the media and a flair for publicity can be crucial to getting a group's case across. Groups such as Child Poverty Action Group and Shelter benefited greatly from having two charismatic figures – Frank Field and Des Wilson, respectively – as their chairmen, while Jonathan Porritt and David Bellamy have provided distinctive leadership within the environmental movement. More controversially, Peter Tatchell has played a prominent part in developing the tactics of OutRage within the movement for homosexual equality.

Access

Access is itself an important resource. One crucial distinction is that between *insider* groups and *outsider* groups. Insider groups are ones that are regarded by government as legitimate and regularly consulted by it. Such groups are generally seen as having superior access to the policy process (Grant, 1995, 2000, 2001). Insider groups for their part adopt a strategy of discreet consultation and abide by the rules of the game. Outsider groups are ones whose legitimacy is questioned by government and who do not wish to be compromised by discussions with government. Such groups necessarily use a more public and campaigning strategy.

Grant's basic but important distinction can be refined further by distinguishing between 'prisoner' groups (those which find it hard to break out of their close relationship with government because of dependence on it for support, for example in terms of funding) and low-profile or high-profile groups, depending on the group's relationship with the public and the media. Here Grant contrasts the CBI, which has a very high profile in terms of its activities, with the British Employers Confederation, a low-profile group.

Outsider groups can be subdivided into whether they are potential insiders (perhaps new groups that have not gained acceptance), groups that are outsiders of necessity because their cause does not fit with the prevailing orthodoxy, and ideological groups with wide-ranging agendas. Whether a group is an insider or an outsider depends on a number of factors, including the party in power, the government's approach to consultation and the issue agenda. Thus trade unions have generally enjoyed better access to Labour governments and business has found its access enhanced under the Conservatives. That said, New Labour's relationship with the unions has become cooler in the period since 1997 as a result of both New Labour's general distancing from the unions and differences over specific issues such as the Private Finance Initiative (PFI). Thus former 'insider' groups may lose their privileged position and as a result may change their tactics.

Pressure groups have become increasingly adept at exploiting the mass media. Issues that have the potential to arouse public indignation make good copy and the press and television have given extensive coverage to campaigns such as the movement to prevent the export of live animals, the movement to ban genetically modified (GM) foods and the marches of the Countryside Alliance, the fuel protesters and the anti-Iraq war demonstrators.

Direct action

In striking contrast to the insider tactics of many groups, there is the use of direct action. This is not of course a new tactic. Trade unions' use of strikes is a long-established form of direct action. So too is the boycott of goods. Other forms of direct action include marches and demonstrations. Such forms of direct action are usually legal in themselves but may produce illegal action if, for example, a march becomes violent or results in damage to property, as both the poll tax riots of 1989 and 1990 and the more recent anti-globalization demonstrations did.

Direct action may be used as a last resort by the powerless; but it can also be an extremely powerful publicity tool as well as a means of creating solidarity amongst supporters. Campaigners against the poll tax, against cuts in student grants and against the transport of live animals have all used forms of direct action to promote their causes. The petrol crisis of 2001 was another example of the potential for direct action.

The use of direct action by pressure groups became more frequent in the 1990s. Some of that protest was deliberately violent: for example, action by the animal rights movement and by the movement against GM crops. Other forms of direct action simply involved the peaceful assembly of large groups of protesters and others in a public display of support.

Why should there be a greater use of direct action in the late twentieth and early twenty-first century? One reason may be the rise of causes and movements with a broad general appeal – such as environmentalism, which put the emphasis on the expressive function of pressure groups. The period of Conservative government from 1979 to 1997 was also one in which long-standing patterns of consultations were broken. It was also a period of consciousness-raising and one in which new social movements emerged. Unlike the older social movements of the 1970s and 1980s, which had an affinity with Marxist ideologies, these newer social movements were more oriented to environmentalism and libertarianism (Lent, 2001). Technological change has also made an impact. The World Wide Web and email technology have made it easy to publicize demonstrations. And, as noted earlier, journalists are often in sympathy with some causes and willing to publicize issues.

Conclusions

The role of pressure groups in the British system of government raises significant theoretical issues both for the quality of British democracy and for the analysis of policy making. As far as the democratic process is concerned, pressure groups complement the electoral and party system by providing ways in which minorities can express intensely held preferences and promote separate and distinct interests. As such, pressure groups are a highly visible and important part of the British political process and it is difficult to imagine a democracy in which pressure groups did not operate freely. Pressure groups together with the whole range of voluntary organizations and representative bodies constitute a necessary part of civil society.

On the other hand, pressure groups present a number of problems for democratic theory. The first relates to inequality within the system. Although all groups are free to organize, some causes and groups enjoy better resources and access than others. Business groups for example, in the United Kingdom as elsewhere, are better funded than groups that represent welfare claimants. Professional groups such as the Association of Chief Police Officers (ACPO) are always well placed to exert influence on the Home Office because the Home Office needs ACPO's support in devising and delivering policy (Marsh, Richards and Smith, 2001). Other groups enjoy only intermittent access. How far this imbalance siphons some interests and groups out of public debate and gives undue influence to others is an open question. But it would be naive to assume that the increasingly large number of groups operating within the United Kingdom can automatically be translated into a greater pluralism and more equal distribution of power within the society.

Secondly, pressure groups raise suspicions about the democratic process by seeming to encourage secret understandings and pacts. Sometimes, of course, they may appear to contribute to the corruption of the political process if they attempt to bribe politicians. But even when groups adopt tactics that exploit their superior access, they in a sense undermine the democratic process. The decline of liberal corporatism after 1979 forced many groups to change their tactics during the Thatcher–Major years and perhaps made some groups much more willing to give greater emphasis to open campaigning than to behind-the-scenes accommodation with government. Pressure groups have themselves become increasingly sophisticated in their campaigning skills and strategies; and they have shown themselves more eager to build coalitions behind their causes. More recently, the introduction of tough conflict of interest and standards regimes, together with greater emphasis on freedom of information, have forced groups to abide by more stringent standards and removed much of the temptation for politicians to develop unhealthily close links with groups. Ethical questions will doubtless continue to circulate around the relationship between decision makers and special interest groups, in the United Kingdom as elsewhere. The vital requirement for the quality of democracy in the UK is perhaps not so much the imposition of restrictions on lobbying as the continuing effort to subject the world of pressure group activity to public scrutiny.

As far as attempting to monitor how far pressure groups affect the process of policy making in government is concerned, three points should be made. First, to the extent that the structures of government in the United Kingdom are becoming more fragmented, there are more opportunities for outside interests to influence policy. Secondly, while some groups are undoubtedly more institutionalized than others in their relations with central departments, there is a good deal of change, fluidity and unevenness in the system. Finally, the approach of the post-1997 Labour government, while its pattern of consultation has limitations, is much more committed to participation than its predecessor was. To that extent, models of governance that emphasize the role of pressure groups in policy formation shift the focus of concern to the question of how far the groups themselves are sufficiently representative to provide legitimacy.

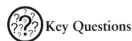 Key Questions

1   How do pressure groups affect the policy process?
2   In what ways might pressure groups undermine the democratic system?
3   Why would people join a pressure group rather than a political party?

 Further Reading

Good overviews can be found in W. Grant, *Pressure Groups and British Politics* (Basingstoke: Macmillan, 2000) and in the same author's *Pressure Groups, Politics and Democracy in Britain* (London: Phillip Allan, 1995). Grant's 'Pressure politics: From "insider" politics to direct action', *Parliamentary Affairs*, 54: 2 (2001) is a valuable updating. E. C. Page, 'The insider/outsider distinction: An empirical investigation', *British Journal of Politics and International Relations*, 1: 2 (1999), G. Wilson, *Interest Groups* (Oxford:

Blackwell, 1990) and Wilson's study *Business and Politics: A Comparative Introduction* (Basingstoke: Palgrave/Macmillan, 2003) discuss a range of different debates about interest groups. Grant Jordan and Jeremy Richardson, *Governing Under Pressure* (Oxford: Blackwell, 1997) is another very stimulating text. P. Byrne, *Social Movements in Britain* (London: Routledge, 1997) is a judicious study, while F. F. Ridley and G. Jordan, *Protest Politics: Cause, Groups and Campaigns* (Oxford: Oxford University Press, 1998) provides an illuminating insight into the new environment. Adam Lent, *British Social Movements since 1945: Sex, Colour, Peace and Power* (Basingstoke: Palgrave, 2001) is an excellent overview. A. Denham and M. Garnett, 'Influence without responsibility? Think tanks in Britain', *Parliamentary Affairs*, 52: 1 (1999) looks at the role of think tanks in the policy process. The policy impact of groups is considered in J. J. Richardson, 'Government, interest groups and policy change', *Political Studies*, 48: 5 (2000). B. Doherty, 'Paving the way: The rise of direct action against road-building and the changing character of British environmentalism', *Political Studies*, 47 (1999) examines new tactics in the world of pressure groups, while Peter Hall, 'Social capital in Britain', *British Journal of Political Science*, 29: 3 (1999) is a useful account of civic culture. Grant Jordan, 'Politics without parties', *Parliamentary Affairs*, 51: 3 (1998) explores pressure group activism from an original perspective.

 Websites

See also the list of general websites at the back of the book.

- www.appc.org.uk – Association of Professional Political Consultants, regulatory body for lobbyists

Selected pressure groups

- www.amnesty.org.uk – Amnesty International
- www.countryside-alliance.org.uk – Countryside Alliance
- www.foe.org.uk – Friends of the Earth
- www.greenpeace.org – Greenpeace
- www.nspcc.org.uk – National Society for the Prevention of Cruelty to Children
- www.rspb.org.uk – Royal Society for the Protection of Birds
- www.shelter.org.uk – Shelter
- www.stonewall.org.uk – Stonewall

Selected trade associations

- www.britishchambers.org.uk – British Chambers of Commerce
- www.bma.org.uk – British Medical Association
- www.cbi.org.uk – CBI
- www.fsb.org.uk – Federation of Small Businesses
- www.iod.co.uk – Institute of Directors
- www.lawsoc.org.uk – Law Society
- www.nfu.org.uk – National Farmers Union

Selected trade unions

- www.tuc.org.uk – Trades Union Congress
- www.aeeu.org.uk – Amicus-Amalgamated Engineering and Electrical Union
- www.cwu.org – Communication Workers Union
- www.nus.org.uk – National Union of Students
- www.unison.org.uk – UNISON
- www.tgwu.org.uk – Transport and General Workers Union

11 Government on the Ground: The Local Dimension

One of the themes running through this book is the extent to which the United Kingdom has become a multi-level polity. This multi-level polity is in part the product of constitutional reforms that have decentralized and devolved powers, creating new political arenas and fragmenting the policy process. It is also the product of the strengthened impact of the European Union on the United Kingdom. In one sense, of course, the United Kingdom has always been a multi-level polity because there has always been a *local* dimension to politics and administration. Indeed, as was noted in chapter 3, before the twentieth century many governmental services and activities were delivered by local bodies, not least because of the weakness of the national administrative infrastructure. Today many essential governmental functions, including such key services as education and personal social services, refuse collection, leisure and planning, fire and police, are directly or indirectly provided by local government. Spending by local government is an extremely important part of the national public expenditure. Estimates vary, but in 2000–1 local government accounted for roughly £76.8 billion of public spending. Local government is also a major employer, with over 2 million people working in this part of the public sector. Equally importantly, local government provides a distinct arena of democratic politics.

There are in England and Wales 410 local authorities of different types and over 2,000 elected councillors (see table 11.1). Their task is to represent their local constituents and to set policy for their localities. The administration of local authority responsibilities is supported by a range of professional and permanent staff who constitute a distinct bureaucratic cadre.

Although much of the focus of the chapter will be on the most familiar and visible element of local government – elected local authorities – it is important to remember that elected local government is only one dimension of the total world of politics and policy making at the local level. There are, for example, a number of appointed rather than elected bodies operating locally, as well as voluntary and business organizations that may be operating in a contractual relationship to supply services to the community. The proliferation of appointed special authorities, voluntary agencies and private sector actors working in partnership with or alongside elective local government has changed the contours of the British local government system. These developments raise important questions about patronage, democracy and accountability at the local level.

Table 11.1 Local authorities in England and Wales

Local authorities	No.
County councils (inc. Greater London Assembly)	35
County boroughs	36
Non-county boroughs	47
Urban district councils	238
Rural district councils	22
London boroughs and City of London	33

Source: Adapted from Butler and Butler (2000), p. 473.

In this chapter we focus on the system of local government in the United Kingdom by looking at the structure of elective local authorities, their powers and funding and their relationships with other levels of the system, especially central government. The main emphasis in the chapter will be on local government in England, though some mention will be made of Wales, Scotland and Northern Ireland. Local government outside England receives further coverage in chapter 12.

Before examining the various aspects of local government in more detail, two important general points about the position of local government in the contemporary British political system should be borne in mind. The first is that local government is inevitably affected by changes at other levels of the system. Movements towards an enhanced regional dimension and devolution affect the context in which local government operates. Changes at the European level can also have an important impact on local politics. However, local authorities are not necessarily the passive victims of developments elsewhere. So far from being the lowest point in the structural and constitutional food chain, they can use the opportunities presented by multi-level government to exert more leverage and press for their preferred policies.

The second general point also relates to the context in which British local government operates. Although local government is logically distinct from national government, there are very few, if any, policy areas in which local government has complete autonomy. Policy responsibilities within local government are to a very large extent set by national legislation. Moreover, local government is powerfully affected by the politics of Whitehall. London's priorities and management style create the environment in which local government must operate. Fundamental changes of direction at the centre will produce effects throughout the system of local government. Thus the period of Conservative government from 1979 to 1997 had a massive impact on local government. Although local government gained some functions, especially in relation to the personal social services, its role in education (where schools were encouraged to acquire direct management responsibilities) and housing (where councils were forced to make their homes available for sale to sitting tenants) was reduced. Equally important was the Conservatives' promotion of new public management (NPM), reflecting their vision that market competition and private sector techniques would yield greater efficiency in service provision. Between 1979 and 1997 councils were forced to put their services out to tender (contracting out) and were encouraged to explore ways of engaging with the private sector. Rather than provide a range of services itself, the local authority came to be seen as the purchaser of services provided indirectly by third parties. Thus the role of the local authority was subtly altered to one that was much more strategic (or enabling) than in the past.

When it came to power in 1997, Labour expressed a much more positive view of local government, emphasizing its desire to give local authorities greater freedom, to develop partnerships and to ease some of the controls put in place between 1979 and 1997. There was talk of a 'new localism' and a series of initiatives generated by John Prescott from the increasingly powerful Office of the Deputy Prime Minister (ODPM). Labour committed itself to strengthening local democracy and reforming the internal processes of local government. But Labour's emphasis on public service delivery and performance, and its own distinctive approach to public sector management, placed other constraints on local government. Thus Labour, while encouraging a greater role for local authorities as partners of central government, made it very clear that the framework of that partnership would reflect central values and that greater local authority autonomy would depend on achieving nationally set performance targets. Labour also introduced its own new techniques for improving efficiency in local government – the Best Value framework (introduced in 1999) and the comprehensive performance assessment (CPA), which ranked local authorities in terms of overall efficiency in an exercise that many authorities found time-consuming and demoralizing. Contracting out was abandoned but the Private Finance Initiative (PFI) encouraged private–public partnerships as a way of injecting new capital into local government.

Labour had of course inherited a system of local government that had been extensively altered by Conservative policies. The enabling authority which increasingly replaced the traditional local authority could be seen as a way of shrinking the role of local government in the community. Labour, by contrast, wanted to heighten the local authority role as the focus of the neighbourhood or community, giving local government a new leadership mission. Labour's 1998 white paper, *Modern Local Government: In Touch with the People*, outlined a new role for local authorities that would make them outward-looking and responsive in relation to their local communities. Thus in addition to the familiar debates surrounding the internal and external structures, policies and funding of local government, recent years have seen a fundamental questioning of the very purpose of local government in Britain. At its most extreme, that debate polarized between those who saw local government as an unnecessary structure whose functions would wither away and those who saw it as an essential part of democratic politics. Although some of this questioning reflected profound policy disagreements between the parties, it also reflected a long-standing tension within the British system about the role of local government.

Why Local Government?

Democratic political systems generally value the local dimension for the contribution it can make to the overall health of the political system. Local democracy provides an important opportunity to make public policy and decision makers responsive to local communities. It is also often argued that local government has an educative effect on those who participate in the process. Writers such as John Stuart Mill in the nineteenth century emphasized the representative aspect of local government, which made it an inherently valuable institution. Such writers also saw local self-government as a useful protection against even enlightened despotism. A division of powers between the different levels of government could thus prevent the dangers of centralized government. Arguments that emphasize the benefit of diversity and a division of powers have generally not been accorded great weight in the British political system, which has been marked by centralization and parliamentary sovereignty. Even today when devolution and regionalism seem designed to promote different constitutional values from those that marked the British state for much of the twentieth century, the balance of the political system seems heavily tilted towards the centre.

In stark contrast to those who emphasize the democratic qualities of local government is the perspective that emphasizes local government's role in service delivery. This approach to public services has deep roots in the British political tradition, so that in the nineteenth century reformers such as Edwin Chadwick placed a much greater value on efficiency than on local self-government. The emphasis in this approach to local administration was not so much on the process of decision making or self-government as on the contribution that local government could make to the administration of an efficient system of schools, social services, refuse collection or public health. Those who placed a high premium on the efficient delivery of services would expect an administrative structure calculated to promote that aim regardless of its correspondence to local identities. Those who valued equality would be unlikely to tolerate substantial diversity in the provision of key services because of local authority variations in resources, political complexion or administrative efficiency. New Labour's emphasis on national standards and efficient service delivery is inherently difficult to reconcile with extensive local autonomy.

It is also important to ask whether the existing structures of local government correspond to public perceptions of its role. The low level of interest in local government as measured by turnout at local elections (which rarely exceeds 40 per cent and in 1998 was down to as low as 10 per cent in some wards) suggests that something is wrong with the existing system and needs to be addressed. Low turnout weakens the legitimacy of local government; but it also makes it less effective as an instrument of policy making. An important part of Labour's agenda for local government is to expand the level of democratic participation both by reforms to the electoral process itself and by changes that will give local government greater salience. In addition, local authorities are themselves taking initiatives to consult their citizens on policy issues through such mechanisms as citizens' juries, advisory referendums, focus groups and opinion polling.

The Constitutional Position of Local Government

In the absence of a written constitution, local government in the United Kingdom has no constitutionally secured powers. Although many boroughs and counties have a long historical pedigree, all local authorities are now the creation of statute. Central government may change local boundaries and remove functions from local government. Central government can if it wishes abolish a tier of local government, as occurred with the abolition of the Greater London Council (GLC) and other

ultra vires Doctrine which states that acts of a public authority must be within its legal powers. This means that there must be legal authority to perform a substantive function (e.g. operate a school) and that the local authority must comply with the procedural standards of administrative law. If the actions of a local authority are found to be ultra vires (beyond its powers), they are legally void. The doctrine has been seen as placing a brake on local authority enterprise.

surcharge Legal procedure by which elected councillors could be fined for excessive spending by their authorities.

statute law The law which is contained in Acts of Parliament and secondary legislation, in contrast to the law which is contained in judicial opinions.

metropolitan counties in 1985. Indeed, central government could abolish the whole local government system, an outcome that some observers thought might occur under the Conservative governments of 1979–97 (Chisholm, 2000).

Traditionally, local government has been limited in other ways. Its power has been closely constrained so that local authorities have lawfully been able to engage only in activities for which they have express statutory authority, either as a result of a statutory requirement or a discretionary power. If a local authority engaged in activities for which no statutory authorization existed, it risked legal challenge and could be struck down as **ultra vires**. If a local authority incurred expenditure in pursuit of an activity that was beyond its legal powers, it risked having that expenditure declared illegal and the councillors who had incurred it might find themselves **surcharged** by the auditor. Although the Local Government Act 2000 abolished the weapon of surcharge in favour of a broader regime of accountability, these constraints on local government had the effect of making local authorities extremely cautious about innovation and generally created a climate that avoided enterprise.

These tight controls on local government have often been highly controversial, not least because they seemed to limit local government's ability to initiate policies for the well-being of their communities. They also forced the courts to resolve policy differences between a local authority and its critics. Thus in the celebrated 'Fare's fair' case the London borough of Bromley successfully brought suit to prevent the GLC from pursuing a policy of free public transport that would have to be paid for by other boroughs. The case was especially controversial because the House of Lords appeared to restate the nineteenth-century assumption that a local authority owed a greater duty to its taxpayers than to either the users of its service or its voters (see box 11.1).

The emphasis on grounding local authority action in an express statutory grant of power had the effect of compartmentalizing local government's responsibilities and reducing the ability of local authorities to intervene for the benefit of their communities. Labour's approach to local government emphasized the leadership role of local government in the community, and accordingly the Local Government Act 2000 gave local councils a new and broad general power to promote the economic, social and environmental well-being of their areas. However, the power was subject to some restrictions; it cannot be used to expand their money-raising powers and any specific use of it can be overridden by the Secretary of State. The exercise of the power must also conform with existing **statute law** and be exercised in a way that conforms with administrative law.

The Structure of Local Government

There has long been a tension in local government between the creation of units that will be administratively efficient and the creation of units that reflect the communities with which people identify. The debate about the relative value to be placed on local

Box 11.1   GLC 'Fare's fair' case (*Bromley LBC* v. *GLC* 1982)

This case concerned the now defunct Great London Council (GLC) but it raised a number of issues both in relation to local government and about the role of the courts in reviewing decisions of elected authorities, especially when those decisions are politically controversial.

Following an election pledge by Labour to cut the cost of public transport in London by 25 per cent, the GLC made a grant to the London Transport Executive (LTE) to budget for a deficit, even though the Transport (London) Act of 1969 seemed to preclude deficit budgeting (requiring that transport be 'integrated, efficient and economic') and even though the decision had financially damaging consequences. Funding the subsidy was achieved by imposing a **precept** on the London boroughs, pushing up their spending and taxing. Under the 1980 Government and Land Act the individual boroughs had to finance the grant. (The 1980 legislation identified local authorities who were 'overspenders' and reduced central grant accordingly.) One of the boroughs that stood to lose and did not benefit directly from the imposed GLC subsidy of transport was the outer London borough of Bromley, which was Conservative-controlled. Bromley applied for judicial review to quash the imposition of the GLC precept. Bromley lost in the High Court but won on appeal in the Court of Appeal and again in the House of Lords.

Controversial aspects of the case included:

- the extent to which courts can take account of manifesto commitments;
- the nature of the fiduciary duty owed to ratepayers;
- the reasonableness of the GLC's policy;
- the role of the courts in controlling the decisions of elective local authorities.

The Court recognized that a local authority had discretion in a wide range of policies. Even if it had been elected on a manifesto that committed it to a specific policy, a local authority could not be totally bound by that commitment. In exercising the discretion it had, the local authority had to act *reasonably*, which meant taking into account all the categories of people to whom it owed a duty, including ratepayers as well as transport users. If it did not exercise that discretion reasonably, the local authority would be acting ultra vires (outside its powers). Moreover, when considering legislation that used words like 'economic', the term must be taken to mean at least cost-effective or operating on business lines.

This decision clearly pitted the courts' assessment of the proper balance between the interests involved in the case against the GLC's view. It was thus a controversy of how the courts can review decisions by political bodies on grounds of legality. It also had the dimension of pitting different political values (with strong party connotations) against each other.

---

government's functions of representation and service delivery is thus reflected in debates about the proper structure of local government. And of course the terms in which the debate is conducted are themselves contested. For example, there is no straightforward answer to the question of what counts as an 'efficient' size for administrative purposes. Sometimes large authorities are favoured since they are thought to bring economies of scale. Sometimes smaller ones are seen as more responsive to the needs of their areas. Nor is it entirely clear who constitutes the local government community

precept The method by which a non-billing authority obtains income to cover its expenditure.

rates Local tax on property.   or how patterns of work and residence relate to each other. Reforms of local government structure have been partly driven by changing attitudes to the administration–representation trade-off, although as we shall see, they have also been driven by other more political factors.

The growth of English local government in the nineteenth century was triggered by the need to meet the challenges of industrialization and urbanization. The system that emerged in the nineteenth century was very much a patchwork containing multi-purpose authorities and boards and other agencies created for special purposes such as sanitation and education. The first major reform of the local government system affected the larger boroughs through the Municipal Corporations Act of 1835. The counties, however, were left undisturbed and continued to be governed as they had been since Tudor times, by the justices of the peace (JPs) assembled in quarter sessions. It was not until Lord Salisbury's unenthusiastic acceptance of the need to introduce the elective principle into the administration of the counties in the late 1880s that there was democratically elected local government across the whole country. The right to vote continued to be based on the payment of **rates** and remained so linked until 1945. Indeed, the short-lived and unpopular poll tax of the Thatcher years (which substituted a personal tax for the rates) was justified by some as an attempt to re-establish the bond between taxation and representation.

The system of elective local government established between 1888 and 1894 lasted until the reforms of the 1972–4 period. The structure of local government had, however, become increasingly unstable over the twentieth century and many would argue that the system was flawed from its inception. The problem of matching administrative jurisdiction to community identity was as perplexing as in the late nineteenth century and as it was to become by the early twenty-first century. The 1888 Act, which covered the whole of England and Wales (Scotland was covered in separate legislation), made the county council the major unit of local administration. Yet even when the legislation was passed, the fierce sense of municipal pride of the larger boroughs made it politically necessary to exclude these towns from the county's jurisdiction. Therefore, 61 boroughs were made into all-purpose authorities and given a degree of autonomy *within* the counties and a status similar to that of the county councils.

The provision for county boroughs immediately set up competition within the local government system. Not only could other towns apply for county borough status; existing county boroughs could also apply to have their territorial jurisdiction extended, a process that would naturally be resisted by the county council, which would fear the loss of area and income. Thus, although superficially the system established in 1888–94 appeared rational and stable, the search for county borough status was disruptive. It was also relevant that traditionally the counties and the boroughs had very different styles of politics. Although the organization of local politics on party lines is now virtually universal, party organization and competitive elections developed earlier in the boroughs than in the counties. In the towns, local politics were from the nineteenth century much more organized. Party played a greater role and in some cities such as Birmingham and Liverpool political machines emerged. In the counties uncontested and non-partisan elections lasted much longer, except in counties such as Glamorgan and Durham, where there was an early culture of radical politics.

One other feature of the 1888–94 system deserves comment because of its legacy to subsequent debate about local government structure. Although the 1888 legislation established a series of elected county authorities, subsequent legislation in 1894 set up a structure of lower-level authorities – district councils – to handle some local government functions. These smaller authorities (known as urban or rural districts) were devised to administer functions at a level closer to the local community than the widely drawn county council. The merits and demerits of a two-tier system of local government, and the proper allocation of functions between them, remains controversial today.

The first comprehensive review of local government structure thus came late in the nineteenth century; government intervention in a range of policy areas had occurred in piecemeal fashion long before then. Before the reform of the local administrative structure, new governmental functions tended to be allocated to specially created or ad hoc authorities. The utilitarians, inspired by **Benthamism,** were anxious to impose their ideas of rationality on English institutions and they were not great admirers of localism. They saw in local government only an irrational set of authorities inimical to the efficient provision of services. Not surprisingly, they wanted to establish functional authorities with expertise and they wanted authorities designed to fit their purpose. The special needs of poor law administration were taken into account when the Poor Law Amendment Act of 1834 grouped parishes together on functional principles that took little notice of historical boundaries. The poor law unions later became the administrative units for a number of other functions, including the registration of births, deaths and marriages. When public health authorities were established in the 1850s following the widespread concern about cholera, the pattern imposed on them was that of the earlier poor law unit. The advantages of these functional structures over traditional units of local government were uniformity and adaptability. For example, sanitary authorities could be constructed over the whole drainage area of a town regardless of formal local boundaries. Above all, technical efficiency and professionalism, enforced by central inspection, could be promoted much more easily in a functional authority than in traditional local government.

The reform of local government in 1888 removed some of the weaknesses of the system of elective local government but did not automatically ensure that the responsibilities of these special authorities were immediately transferred to the counties and county boroughs. There was some movement in this direction when education was transferred to elected councils from the school boards in 1902. But not until 1929 were the poor law guardians abolished and their functions transferred to local government, a move which greatly enhanced the role of local government in the administration of welfare.

Yet the suspicion remained that local government lacked expertise. Not merely were important functions transferred from local government to special authorities over the course of the twentieth century; it was also noticeable that when crucial new functions were undertaken by government (as in the immediate post-1945 period when the National Health Service was set up), there was a determination to exclude local government control.

Benthamism Moral and political doctrine developed by Jeremy Bentham (1748–1832) and the utilitarians which advocated that institutions should be judged on whether they advanced the greatest happiness of the greatest number. The doctrine was used to advocate reform of many aspects of British life in the nineteenth century and to justify the growth of governmental intervention in a number of areas.

unitary authority Local authorities which exercise all local powers, as opposed to authorities which split them between different tiers.

Redcliffe Maud and after

The nineteenth-century structure survived until the early 1970s despite the series of criticisms that were increasingly levelled at local government after 1945. Some of these criticisms related directly to structure, especially the argument that the units of local government related poorly to the pattern of contemporary British life. Often, however, the criticism related to the conduct of local government more generally. For example, the finances of local government appeared increasingly weak and dependent on central government grants. Despite the creation of an elaborate welfare state in the 1945–51 period, Labour in those years made no major reform to local government except to its franchise. (Universal suffrage at the local level became the rule after 1948.) The Conservatives on their return to power in 1951 made a succession of minor reforms to local government but effected no wholesale changes, with the notable exception of the reform of London government in 1963 when the old London County Council was replaced by a Greater London Council in order to take account of the growth of the capital. This reform was radically changed again in the mid-1980s when, following successive policy clashes between the GLC and the central government, the Conservatives abolished the GLC and the other metropolitan counties. More recently, as will be discussed later, Labour reintroduced a Greater London Assembly and a directly elected mayor.

The expansion of the welfare state in the second half of the twentieth century highlighted some of the importance of local government in relation to service delivery. Inevitably, when Labour returned to power in 1964 local government reform was on the agenda. Responsibility for shaping that reform was given to a Royal Commission headed by Sir John Maud (later Lord Redcliffe Maud). Unfortunately, the Commission had problems from the beginning. The terms of the inquiry excluded finance, which made it unlikely that local government could be reformed in a way that would genuinely strengthen it. The Commission also had built into its membership some of local government's endemic conflicts over jurisdiction because it included representatives of the different local government tiers (the counties and the boroughs), each determined to protect their immediate interest. (Until 1996 different bodies represented different types of authority, so that there was an Association of District Councils, an Association of County Councils and an Association of Metropolitan Authorities. Since 1996 they have been merged in a single pressure group, the Local Government Association.) These organizations were sectional and partisan, making it difficult to approach the problem of structural reform from a dispassionate viewpoint.

The Redcliffe Maud Commission's analysis identified the structure of local government as it then existed as flawed and argued that the jungle of local government jurisdictions no longer reflected the living patterns of the population. The fragmentation of England at that point into 45 counties and 79 county boroughs made the provision of some services, notably transport and planning, difficult. The Commission also criticized the division within counties into a two-tier structure of counties and district councils. It wanted to see more coordination across local authorities and saw logic in **unitary multi-purpose authorities** that could deliver all the services for a given area. The recommendations of the majority report were to scrap the counties (outside the large metropolitan areas) and replace them with 58 unitary authorities.

The Labour government broadly accepted the Redcliffe Maud recommendations. But the proposals did not command universal support, not least because of strong lobbying from the county council representatives. When the Conservatives replaced Labour in 1970, they abandoned the idea of unitary authorities and imposed instead a uniform two-tier system of local government on England and Wales. The new set of local government areas was implemented in the Local Government Act of 1972. The top tier of the new structure (the 39 county authorities) was given major local government functions, including the key functions of education and social services. The majority of these counties were based on the old shire counties to retain historical linkages. In three areas (Avon, Cleveland and Humberside) new counties were established, destroying historic links and subordinating community identity to administrative convenience. The small counties of Herefordshire, Rutland and Westmoreland were abolished to produce county areas that conformed to the population norm. (Another small county, Middlesex, had been abolished as part of the London government reorganization of 1963.) In addition to these basic changes there were a number of minor boundary changes so that, as far as possible, local boundaries coincided with natural social and economic areas and retained meaning for their inhabitants. The restructuring in the 1990s saw another reorganization of the counties and the abolition of Avon, Berkshire, Cleveland and Humberside as well as a redrawing of the boundaries of Hereford and Worcestershire.

The 1972 legislation thus created a two-tier system, against the thrust of the Redcliffe Maud proposals It subdivided the 39 counties into 296 subunits known as districts, which were given a range of local functions such as refuse collection and leisure as well as housing. Although clearly smaller than the counties, they were larger than the old pre-1972 urban and rural districts had been. Nevertheless, the perpetuation of a two-tier system continued confusion about responsibilities and blurred accountability. The two-tier system also blurred accountability by obscuring the relationship between income collecting and spending authorities. The county council, like some other authorities such as police authorities, does not itself collect local income but issues a precept to the local authorities it serves for the cost of the function. The collecting authority (which in a two-tier authority is the lower-level authority) collects the money and transfers it.

Three other aspects of the 1970s reforms should be noted. First, the 1972 legislation introduced different structures for the large metropolitan regions. The heavily populated regions of Merseyside, Greater Manchester, the West Midlands, West Yorkshire, South Yorkshire and Tyne and Wear presented different problems from those encountered by the majority of counties and a different pattern of authorities was set up in which the lower-level authorities – the 36 metropolitan districts – were given functions such as education and social services which elsewhere were deemed county-level functions (see table 11.2).

A second structural feature of the 1972 legislation was the establishment of smaller local units known as parish councils. The Redcliffe Maud Commission had proposed a system of parish councils to act as the voice of local communities and this was enacted by the 1972 legislation. The need for parishes was twofold in the government's view: parishes could transmit community feeling upwards within

Table 11.2 Tiers of government and powers

	Metropolitan/London authorities				Shire/Unitary authorities	
	Joint authorities	Metropolitan councils	London boroughs	District councils	Unitary authorities (England and Wales)	County councils
Education		•	•		•	•
Housing		•	•	•	•	
Planning applications		•	•	•	•	
Strategic planning		•	•		•	•
Transport planning		•			•	•
Passenger transport	•				•	•
Highways		•	•		•	•
Fire	•				•[a]	•
Social services		•	•		•	•
Libraries		•	•		•	•
Leisure and recreation		•	•	•	•	
Waste collection	•	•	•	•	•	
Waste disposal		•	•		•	•
Environmental health		•	•	•	•	
Revenue collection		•	•	•	•	

[a] Joint fire authorities operate in counties with unitary authorities in them. These are combined fire authorities. There are three combined fire authorities for Wales.

Source: Local Government Association Factsheet, http://www.lga.gov.uk/Category.asp?lsection=120

the local government system and they could play a practical part in the working of small-scale administration. Rural areas were automatically divided into parishes; but the provision of small-scale units was not confined to rural or semi-rural areas. The district councils of urban areas were allowed to seek successor parish status and some did so. The problem in urban areas was to identify the community (usually of some 10,000 to 20,000 people) on which the 'parish council' could be based. In urban areas, neighbourhood councils – which unlike parish councils are non-statutory bodies – constitute an alternative form of organization. These neighbourhood councils are extremely diverse in scope and by no means all of them are elected. They have proved useful in conveying local sentiment, especially on planning and development issues. Both parish councils (of which there are over 8,000) and neighbourhood councils provide arenas in which local residents and neighbourhood groups, as well as more general pressure groups such as those concerned with homelessness, can promote activity on a small scale. They also made a contribution to campaigning activities on environmental matters – for example, the long campaign to oppose the building of the motorway through Twyford Down in the early 1990s.

The role of parishes has recently been increased and their number expanded. There are 80 new parishes in England alone and they have been given new powers in relation to key community issues, including traffic calming, community transport and crime prevention. Parish councils can raise up to £5 per elector per annum for their own purposes and the sum is collected through the council tax.

The third feature of structural reform in the 1970s that should be noted was the tentative consideration of regional authorities above the level of the county. Redcliffe Maud had suggested that regional authorities might exercise responsibility for a range of strategic planning functions which demanded larger areas than the unitary authorities he recommended would have covered. The 1972 legislation took regional authorities no further. By the early 1990s, however, regionalism was again an issue. The Conservatives introduced a regional dimension into the organization of central government departments and when Labour returned to power in 1997 the deputy prime minister John Prescott became a powerful advocate of a strengthened regional dimension.

This rewriting of the map of local government in the early 1970s seemed extremely arbitrary. It had been imposed by central government and it had been done in a way which contradicted the recommendations of the Redcliffe Maud Commission. Many historic boroughs lost their independent existence and some counties were abolished or had their names altered. The retention of a two-tier system meant that a costly and disruptive reform did little to improve the transparency or accountability of decision making.

The new local government system established in 1972–4 was born in a period of increasing political conflict over local government issues. Even in the period before the election of the Conservatives on a radical platform in 1979, the need to control public expenditure occasioned clashes between central and local government. After 1979 intense partisan conflict erupted as Labour-controlled local authorities resisted national initiatives on such issues as the sale of council houses. Some Labour authorities attempted to make local government a base for promoting their own agenda of urban socialism. The far-left Militant Tendency made inroads into the political organization of some local authorities, including Liverpool (Crick, 1986).

Although much of the controversy of the 1980s centred on funding and policy issues (and especially the community charge or poll tax) rather than on the structure of local government, there were demands for further reform of the distribution of powers between types of authority. Within the local government community itself, the Association of District Councils (ADC) argued for a greater devolution of power to the lower-level districts. Significant think tanks such as the Adam Smith Institute (ASI) thought that accountability would be aided by the abolition of the counties and their replacement by unitary authorities on the lines of the 32 London boroughs that had replaced the GLC. Both major parties saw merits in reform, the Conservatives because they wanted to remove layers of bureaucracy and Labour because the counties had traditionally been bulwarks of conservatism.

When, following the fall of Margaret Thatcher, Michael Heseltine was given the brief to kill the poll tax, he initiated a wide-ranging review of many aspects of local government. On structure he set up the Local Government Commission under Sir John Banham as part of a comprehensive review of local government in England. (In Wales and Scotland unitary authorities were imposed in 1996.)

The Local Government Commission for England was given the task of reviewing the structure, boundaries and electoral arrangements of all local authorities in England. As part of that review it considered whether unitary authorities might replace the two-tier structure. Although it was thought that the Conservative government was pushing the Banham review to promote unitary authorities, the

Banham consultations persuaded it to prefer a modified version of the status quo – a continued division between county and district authorities. The approach of the Commission and its final recommendations led the Secretary of State for the Environment to sack Banham and his team and to order some of the work done for the Commission in the early 1990s to be repeated. There were, however, reorganizations in 25 counties creating a new set of 46 unitary authorities and consequent readjustments to the counties.

From 2002 the Electoral Commission has taken over the work of conducting local government boundary reviews, thereby making the process more independent of the government of the day.

Labour and Local Government Structure

When Labour came to power in 1997, it therefore inherited a local government structure that had been significantly amended even since the implementation of the 1972 legislation (see map 11.1).

For the most part Labour had little direct interest in further reforming the structure of local government, preferring instead to concentrate on the related issues of democratic renewal, community leadership and internal management as well as the question of how to improve service delivery. However, Labour's constitutional agenda inevitably had implications for local government structure.

Regionalism

Regional government in Britain had generally been developed for reasons of administrative convenience and economic incentive rather than democratic control or territorial management (see map 11.2). Labour pledged in its 1997 manifesto to develop the regional tier in England and it established regional development agencies when it came to power; but it was clear that this was only a first step towards a more ambitious regional policy. Following the 2001 election the government published a white paper, *Your Region, Your Choice: Revitalising the UK*, which envisaged giving regions of the UK the power to set up regional assemblies if there was popular demand. Any decision to set up such an assembly would require a referendum to approve it (see box 11.2).

Labour's enthusiasm for regional assemblies presented three problems. First, there was bound to be an impact on the local government structure. Widespread adoption of democratically elected regional authorities in England would inevitably prompt a reorganization of the two-tier local government structure and the replacement of the counties and districts by unitary authorities below the regional authority. Secondly, the voluntary nature of the elective assemblies seemed destined to produce further asymmetrical government. Although campaigns for regional assemblies have been launched in a number of areas, it is in the north-east that the movement for regional government seems most likely to succeed in the short term. Thirdly, it was not at all clear what power the regional authorities would have.

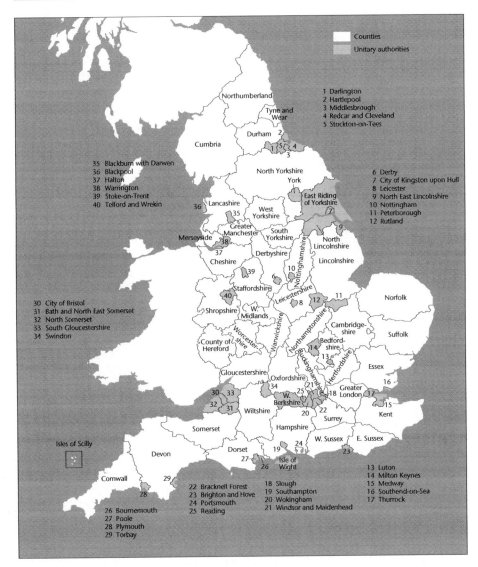

Counties

Unitary authorities

Northumberland

Tyne and Wear

Durham 2

Cumbria

North Yorkshire

York

East Riding of Yorkshire

Lancashire

West Yorkshire

Greater Manchester

Merseyside

South Yorkshire

Derbyshire

Cheshire

Staffordshire

Shropshire

W. Midlands

County of Hereford

Worcestershire

Warwickshire

Gloucestershire

Oxfordshire

Wiltshire

W. Berkshire

Somerset

Hampshire

Devon

Dorset

Isle of Wight

Cornwall

Isles of Scilly

Lincolnshire

North Lincolnshire

Leicestershire

Nottinghamshire

Norfolk

Northamptonshire

Cambridge-shire

Bedford-shire

Buckinghamshire

Hertfordshire

Greater London

Surrey

W. Sussex

E. Sussex

Suffolk

Essex

Kent

1 Darlington
2 Hartlepool
3 Middlesbrough
4 Redcar and Cleveland
5 Stockton-on-Tees

6 Derby
7 City of Kingston upon Hull
8 Leicester
9 North East Lincolnshire
10 Nottingham
11 Peterborough
12 Rutland

35 Blackburn with Darwen
36 Blackpool
37 Halton
38 Warrington
39 Stoke-on-Trent
40 Telford and Wrekin

30 City of Bristol
31 Bath and North East Somerset
32 North Somerset
33 South Gloucestershire
34 Swindon

26 Bournemouth
27 Poole
28 Plymouth
29 Torbay

22 Bracknell Forest
23 Brighton and Hove
24 Portsmouth
25 Reading

18 Slough
19 Southampton
20 Wokingham
21 Windsor and Maidenhead

13 Luton
14 Milton Keynes
15 Medway
16 Southend-on-Sea
17 Thurrock

Map 11.1   England: Counties and unitary authorities.

London

One of Labour's most significant moves in relation to local government was the reintroduction of an authority for the whole of London and a directly elected mayor. The creation of a new strategic authority for London, the Greater London Authority (GLA), was an important element of Labour's constitutional reform agenda, but the new institutions were in many ways anomalous. First, they had

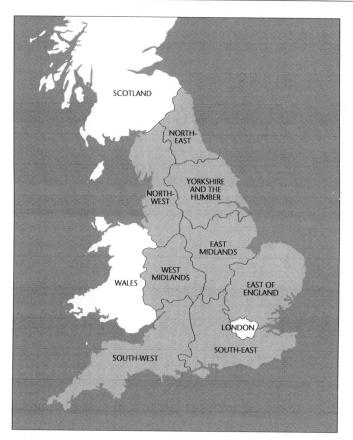

Map 11.2 The English regions.

to be superimposed upon the existing 32 London boroughs, which had since the abolition of the GLC in the mid-1980s become increasingly self-confident and assertive. These boroughs delivered most of the basic services at the local government level, while the newly created mayor and GLA were expected to devise strategies for cross-cutting services such as transport. Secondly, the directly elected mayor of London and the GLA were intended to create a new style of politics that was less partisan and more responsive to local needs. Although the election of Ken Livingstone as an independent as the first directly elected mayor was a departure from the normal pattern of party competition, his response to the situation in which he found himself was to put together a personal coalition rather than to attempt to build a cross-party coalition. Finally, there was a tension in the relationship between the mayor and the GLA on the one hand, and between the mayor and central government on the other. In key policy areas such as transport, extreme conflict emerged between the central government and the mayor. More generally, there was a perception that the mayor was not consulting as widely as he should and that the process of scrutiny had broken down.

Box 11.2   Regional activity in England, 1996–2003

England has eight administrative regions plus London. A very large amount of the work of government departments and agencies has a regional dimension. Each region has a Government Office plus a Regional Director. There is also a Regional Coordination Unit.

1996	Regional Policy Commission publishes *Renewing the Regions*.
1997 May	Labour wins the election with a commitment to strengthening the regional dimension. Queen's Speech promises regional development agencies (RDAs) but delays commitment on elected assemblies.
1997 November	Publication of *Declaration of the North*.
1997 December	Publication of white paper on RDAs.
1998	Legislation to establish RDAs passed.
1998 April	North-east Constitutional Convention set up.
1998 April	Campaign for Yorkshire set up.
1999 March	Campaign for the English regions launched.
1999 April	RDAs vested with powers.
1999 May–July	Designation of chambers or assemblies.
1999 July	North-west Constitution Convention set up.
1999 September	Production of regional economic strategies.
2000 February	Cabinet Office PIU Report, *Reaching Out*.
2000 May	LGA Report, *Regional Variations*, published.
2000 November	Gordon Brown announces new financial autonomy for RDAs.
2001 March	Gordon Brown and John Prescott announce new financial regime and possible resources for regions.
2001 May	Labour wins general election on a manifesto that promises to establish regional assemblies if there is demand for them.
2001 June	Major reorganization of Whitehall departments. Office of Deputy Prime Minister set up within the Cabinet Office; responsibility for RDAs transferred to DTI. Reorganized Department of Transport, Local Government and the Regions given constitutional responsibility for regional assemblies.
2002 May	White paper, *Your Region, Your Choice: Revitalising the English Regions*, published. Promises regional assemblies.
2002 November	Queen's Speech announces referendums to be held on the establishment of regional assemblies.
2002	Regional Assemblies (Preparations) Bill introduced.
2003 January	Regional Assemblies (Preparations) Bill completes House of Commons stages.
2003 May	Local elections.
2003 June	Government announces three referendums to be held in the North-East, North-West and Yorkshire, probably in 2004.

Source: Derived from Hazell (2000), Trench (2001) and Constitution Unit websites.

Local Councils and Local Democracy

One theme running through much of the reform of structure in the 1970s was the notion that the creation of larger and better-resourced authorities would generate new public interest in local government. Reforms designed to improve local councils as agents of service delivery were thus also calculated to stimulate democratic participation and renewal. The years 1979–97 saw much greater emphasis placed on efficient service delivery and the use of market mechanisms than on democratic participation and accountability at the local level. There was a slump in local government morale and a sharp decline in turnout at local elections. Thus by the time Labour returned to power in 1997, it was evident that a new strategy was required to strengthen the institutions of local democracy and to engage the attention of local communities.

One problem that has always faced the local government system has been its ability to recruit able people willing to give up substantial amounts of time to serve their local communities as councillors. Why do people become councillors? How far are those who do become local councillors genuinely representative of their local communities? How responsive are they to their local constituencies? What sorts of skills and expertise do they have? These questions are of course intricately entwined with the question of the role of political parties in local government, since clearly one motive for becoming a councillor might be the hope that it would lead to a national political career. A strong role for political parties in local government has the effect of heightening interest in elections and giving coherence to council policy making. Yet it can also undermine local government by subordinating it to national party concerns.

How representative?

In democratic theory, elected representatives may be expected to reflect their constituents in a number of ways. They may simply be expected to reflect their party preferences or they may be expected to reflect key sociological characteristics such as gender, ethnicity and age (see table 11.3). Those who argue that representatives ought to mirror their constituents are not simply seeking a statistical match; rather, they are suggesting that such shared characteristics add legitimacy and facilitate the ability to express the views of different segments of the community. Councillors are elected to serve their communities, but how do local councillors in fact perceive their role? And how far do they reflect the sociological characteristics of their constituents?

One of the most comprehensive surveys of the 21,000 or so councillors taken in 2001 showed that councillors in office in May 2001 were predominantly male (71.3 per cent) – a figure that was very similar to that in 1997, when 72.6 per cent of councillors were men. Representation of female councillors was highest in the Liberal Democrat Party (34.4 per cent), with Plaid Cymru scoring the lowest percentage of female representation. Female councillors were more evident in shire districts, London boroughs and unitary authorities. Representation of female councillors was highest in the south-east, south-west and north-west.

Table 11.3 Profile of councillors

Profile	2001	1997 (where available)
Gender		
Men	71.3%	72.6%
Women	27.9%	
Ethnicity		
White	97.4%	
Ethnic minority	2.5%	3%
Disability		
Non-disabled	86.9%	
Disabled	13.1%	10.8%
Age		
Below 25	0.1%	
25–34	3.2%	
35–44	10.9%	
45–54	24.3%	
55–64	34.5%	
65–74	22.9%	
75+	4.1%	
Average age	57	55

Source: Improvement and Development Agency, *National Census of Local Authority Councillors in England and Wales, 2001*, http://www.idea.gov.uk/member/census2001.pdf

The vast majority of councillors in 1997 were aged over 45 (86 per cent), with an average age of 55 years, lower than the 2001 average of 57. Councillors from the shire counties and Wales tended to be slightly older than average; those from London boroughs and the metropolitan districts slightly younger than average.

A mere 2.5 per cent of Britain's councillors were of ethnic minority background in 2001, a decline from 1997. Labour had the highest proportion of ethnic minority councillors (5.6 per cent) and representation of ethnic minority councillors was highest in London and the south-east (4.2 per cent).

The employment status of councillors was atypical of the population as a whole. Only 36.2 per cent of councillors were employees either full-time (26.8 per cent) or part-time (9.4 per cent). Self-employed councillors constituted 15.9 per cent of the total. A greater percentage of councillors were retired (37.5 per cent) than were in full-time employment. And there were significant differences between councillors on different types of authority, with only 17.4 per cent of councillors in the shire counties being in full-time employment compared to 40.2 per cent of councillors in the London boroughs. Among the 52 per cent of all councillors in employment, the majority (61 per cent) were in the private sector and over half (65 per cent) were in managerial, professional, technical or executive jobs.

Thus, the picture of the typical councillor had not changed greatly in 2001 since the previous census of this kind in 1997, except that councillors had become slightly older, more likely to have a disability and to be a full-time councillor. Conservative representation had also risen.

The role of party politics

Local democracy does not operate in a vacuum but is closely related to the national framework of party competition. Although it was not always so, local politics are now overwhelmingly organized on party lines. Local councillors thus have a dual role: they are the elected representatives of their local areas, but they are also standard bearers for their national parties. National parties generally pay great attention to the opinions of their local government wing and certainly see control of local councils as an essential goal. Local politics is important to national parties because of the important policy role that councils have and because local government provides a platform for the expression of party values.

Although experience of local government is not necessary for success in national politics, all parties value service at the local level as a background to parliamentary politics. But long service at the local level is difficult to combine with a successful political career in the House of Commons. Joseph Chamberlain and Neville Chamberlain in Birmingham and Herbert Morrison in London to some extent stood out as exceptions to a pattern in which local government offered a lifetime career of its own. More recently, there is evidence of individuals using local government as a stepping stone to national politics. Thus several members of the Blair administration, such as David Blunkett (a former leader of Sheffield Council) and Margaret Hodge (a former leader of Islington Council), successfully made the transition to national office. A slightly different career path (which may become more common in future if greater attention is paid to devolved and regional politics) is the recruitment into the Upper House of politicians with long records of leadership at the local level. In the Conservative governments of 1979–97 Janet Young and Emily Blatch were given ministerial office after many years in local government in Oxfordshire and Cambridgeshire, respectively. Labour similarly appointed to the Upper House Baroness (Josephine) Farrington, who had been prominent in local government in Lancashire.

Party has not always been so dominant a feature of local government. Many local authorities until the 1970s were devoid of intense partisan conflict and many elections, especially in rural areas, were not organized on party lines. In the pre-1972 system many seats were uncontested. Lack of party organization tended to be associated with remoteness from London and with relatively low levels of industrialization, for example in the west of England and parts of Wales.

The reorganization of local government that occurred between 1972 and 1974 accelerated the trend towards politicization. The distinction between the ethos of local politics in urban and rural areas was eroded in the new units created by the reforms and all parties vigorously fought for control of the new authorities. Labour was especially keen to improve its position in the new counties, which had acquired the crucial administrative functions of education and social services. Although there are still expressions of regret that local government is organized on party lines rather than on local issues or good government lines, it is difficult to imagine modern local government without party.

Although local government now operates largely on party lines, local politics are distinct from national party politics in a number of ways. First, there is room in local

Table 11.4 Political parties in local government, 2002

Party	Councillors	Councils
Conservative	7,067	109
Labour	7,576	122
Liberal Democrat	4,223	27
Independent	2,064	17
Plaid Cymru	207	3
No overall control	–	132

Total: 21,137 councillors in England and Wales; 410 councils in England and Wales.
Source: Local Government Association Factsheet, http://www.lga.gov.uk/Category.asp?lsection=120

politics for third parties and independents to make an impact. Liberal Democrats have become an extremely important force in British local government, and now control a number of councils. Overall (as of May 2002), there were 21,137 councillors of whom the majority (35.8 per cent) were Labour and 33.4 per cent were Conservative. However, 19.9 per cent were Liberal Democrat and 9.8 per cent were independents (see table 11.4).

There are also scatterings of minor party and independent representation at local council level. The Green Party claimed 53 councillors in 2003. Independents can sometimes make an impact. Thus in 2002 the Independent Kidderminster Hospital and Health Concern took Wyre Forest where an independent MP had been elected in 2001. An independent residents group also took control of Elmbridge. (In both cases, these groups took control in a council where previously no party had had overall control.) Such diversity is for the most part a welcome change from the pattern of Westminster politics, although local contests can also allow extremist parties to gain a foothold. Thus the right-wing and nationalist British National Party (BNP) fielded 68 candidates in 2002. Three BNP candidates were returned in Burnley, one in Blackburn and one in Halifax. In 2003 the BNP renewed its challenge, fielding a record number of candidates (over 200) across the country and winning 11 seats.

Local politics may also diverge from national politics if the local party adopts a distinctive ideological or policy stance, or if it disagrees with the national party on a particular issue. During the 1980s some Labour local authorities adopted programmes that were much more radical and left wing than those of the national party. Many cities, for example Manchester, declared themselves nuclear-free zones. Although the variation between Conservative policies at national and local level has been less marked, there were differences over the poll tax. In West Oxfordshire a group of Conservatives resigned the whip over the issue.

Local elections are often described as second-order elections in the sense that they more frequently revolve around national issues than local ones. Clearly, for much of the 1979–97 period local politics to a large extent were shaped by national issues. This feature of local politics is less evident but still marked in 2003.

There are a number of different election cycles in local government. Thus in 2002 there were:

- elections for the whole council in 46 shire districts[*]
- elections for one-third of the council in 42 shire districts

- elections for one-third of the council in 32 metropolitan boroughs
- elections for all of the councils in 32 London boroughs
- elections for all of the councils in 6 unitary authorities[*]
- elections for one-third of the council in 12 other unitary authorities

[*]reverts to elections by thirds in 2003

Sadly, the most marked feature of local elections in contemporary Britain is the lack of interest shown in them. Turnout levels have plummeted (see table 2.5, p. 66) and although the English local elections of 2002 registered an average turnout of 32.8 per cent, in many contests the turnout was much lower. Low turnouts have allowed extremist candidates to gain seats in some areas and in the elections for directly elected mayors were one factor contributing to the success of independents.

Labour had initially suggested that annual elections might add a stronger dimension of democracy and accountability to local government, but this idea was not implemented. Instead, the Electoral Commission was given the task of examining the electoral cycle in local government.

In addition there has been much encouragement of pilot schemes at the local level designed to make voting easier (see box 7.4, p. 255). Thus the 2002 elections saw experiments with electronic voting, Internet voting, all-postal voting, electronic counting and on-line registration. Of these experiments, only all-postal voting seemed to have a significant impact. Nevertheless, there were further experiments in 2003.

The explanation of the popular alienation from local democracy probably has much more to do with the perception that local government is relatively powerless and a lack of information about what the different tiers of local government actually do. Research by MORI for the Electoral Commission in 2002 found that 60 per cent of the public said they would be encouraged to vote if local government had more independent decision-making power and control of taxing and spending.

Leadership and Internal Management

Labour's post-1997 agenda for local government placed great emphasis on leadership and reform of the internal structure of local government. Traditionally, local government in the United Kingdom had operated on a committee-based system. Policy was made in a set of committees containing members of all parties in proportion to their strength on the council as a whole. The process was slow and cumbersome. Although the proceedings in open committees of the council were the formal locus of decision making, in many instances the effective decisions would be taken beforehand in closed group meetings of the governing party. As a result, council committees lacked transparency.

Labour saw a clear separation of the executive and legislative roles of local government as the key to reform of its internal structure. A smaller group of councillors would be responsible for decision making; the rest would be able to strengthen their representative roles. In this way, the leadership of local authorities would be sharpened. To achieve this change the government required a major reorganization of local authority constitutions and decision-making processes. The

Local Government Act 2000 mandated that every council undertake a consultation exercise to ascertain which of three models was preferred by that area. These three models were a council leader and cabinet; an elected mayor and cabinet; or an elected mayor and council manager. Some small district councils were allowed to adopt 'alternative arrangements', which were in effect a modified form of the old committee system. All of the other models were novel in the British setting. A council leader and cabinet was the model that was closest to the existing practice because the leader would be selected from the ranks of the ruling party rather than (as in the directly elected mayor models) have an independent mandate.

Directly elected mayors had been urged for local government since the early 1990s and were the preferred choice of modernizers in the Labour Party and local government community. However, they were viewed with suspicion by many councillors and by sections of the Labour Party, including John Prescott. Two slightly different forms of the elected mayor model were put forward, one the elected mayor and cabinet model and the other the elected mayor and council manager model (see box 11.3).

By 2003 all local authorities had gone through elaborate processes of consultation with their publics. In those cases where it seemed a directly elected mayor was the appropriate new format there had to be a referendum. A referendum could also be

Box 11.3   Options for reform in local government

A directly elected mayor with a cabinet

The mayor is elected by the whole electorate. The mayor once elected selects a cabinet from among the councillors. The cabinet can be drawn from a single party or a coalition. These cabinet members have portfolios for which they take executive decisions acting alone. The mayor is the political leader for the community, proposing policy for approval by the council and steering implementation by the cabinet through council officers. The chief executive and chief officers are appointed by the full council. The chief executive has particular responsibility for ensuring that both executive and backbench councillors receive all the facilities and officer support necessary to fulfil their respective roles. The office of directly elected mayor is separate from the traditional ceremonial mayor.

Leader and cabinet

Under this option a leader is elected by the council and the cabinet is made up of councillors, either appointed by the leader or elected by the council. As with a directly elected mayor model above, the cabinet can be drawn from a single party or a coalition. The model is very similar to the mayor and cabinet system except that the leader relies on the support of members of the council rather than the electorate for his or her authority and can be replaced by the council. While the leader could have similar executive powers to a directly elected mayor, in practice the leader's powers are less likely to be as broad as there is no direct mandate from the electorate for the leader's programme.

(Continues)

Box 11.3 *Continued*

Mayor and council manager

The mayor is directly elected to give a political lead to an officer or 'manager' to whom both strategic policy and day-to-day decision making are delegated. The mayor's role is primarily one of influence, guidance and leadership rather than direct decision taking. Using a private sector analogy, the mayor might resemble a non-executive chairman of a company and the council manager its powerful chief executive. Again, this can be separate from the traditional ceremonial mayor.

There is also a fourth option that can be chosen by those authorities with a population under 85,000 or which have had a referendum for a mayor that has been rejected by the local electorate. This is:

Alternative arrangements

The full council has an enhanced policy-making role under alternative arrangements with all councillors acting together as the full council. The local authority will be able to delegate implementation of its policy to streamlined committees. Under alternative arrangements councillors will have the following roles:

- Adopting the new constitution and any subsequent changes to it.
- Adopting the local authority's code of conduct.
- Agreeing the local authority's policy framework and budget.
- Making appointments to committees.
- Making or confirming appointment of the chief executive.

Alternative arrangements must involve effective overview and scrutiny.

Source: Local Government Association Factsheet, http://www.lga.gov.uk/
Category.asp?lsection=120

forced on a reluctant council where there was a demand for a directly elected mayor. However, as of February 2003, only 11 local authorities had opted for a directly elected mayor. The overwhelming majority opted for the leader and cabinet model (see box 11.4).

One of the reasons why traditionalists feared a directly elected mayor was the concern that the local politics would revolve around personality rather than issues and party. In part that was what some advocates of the idea thought was needed to inject more interest into local government. In those areas that did opt for a directly elected mayor, there was certainly a break with conventional party politics. Five of the directly elected mayors had no conventional party affiliation. But whereas the proponents of the idea had seen the new-style position of mayor attracting prominent local figures, some of those who were elected were mavericks or populists whose anti-establishment platforms raised questions about their ability to work with their local councils. In May 2002 a former police chief, Raymond Mallon (Robocop), was elected in Middlesbrough on an anti-crime ticket, while in nearby North Tyneside a Conservative (Chris Morgan) was elected to head an overwhelmingly Labour local authority. (Morgan resigned in 2003 and was succeeded by another Conservative,

Box 11.4 New council structures

Structure	No. of councils
Leader and cabinet	316
Mayor and cabinet	10
Mayor and council manager	1
Alternative arrangements	59

Source: Local Government Association Factsheet, http://www.lga.gov.uk/
Category.asp? lsection=120

Linda Arkley.) Most bizarrely of all, in Hartlepool Stuart Drummond won the race for mayor after campaigning as a local football team mascot (H'Angus the Monkey) promising free bananas. Independents fared well in Bedford, Mansfield and Stoke, while in Watford, where Labour's Vincent Muspratt had long advocated the idea of a directly elected mayor, the Liberal Democrat won the office.

These independent mayors obviously had to calculate how they would work with their local authorities. But these early experiments with directly elected mayors seem unlikely to win further converts for the cause. For the vast majority of councils that adopted the leader and cabinet model, the experience of reform was not so extreme. Supporters found that there was a more structured sense of decision making. Critics identified a sense of exclusion among those not in leadership roles. Clearly, these new structures have yet to become established. The select committee when it reviewed the operations of the 2002 Act commented that much of the internal reform had been a distraction from the new management agenda.

The elected members of local authorities are served by professional officers. The relationship between professional and elected officers was a cause for concern in the 1980s when there were allegations that councillors were intervening in officers' work. The Widdicome Commission was established in an attempt to regulate the role of party in local government. Labour's 2002 white paper, *Strong Local Leadership*, emphasized the need to support and enhance the quality of member and officer training by such innovations as joint member and officer training, joint training for central and local officials across the public sector and a greater use of new technology. Clearly, the shift to an executive inside councils has created a new scenario for both council leaders and professional managers. In a sense, both now occupy complementary roles but compete for control of strategic decision making and it may take a little time before the new tensions in that relationship sort themselves out.

Local Government Finance

Much of the controversy surrounding local government in the Thatcher–Major years was generated by local government spending and the ill-judged effort to introduce a new tax to replace the rates. Even before the Conservatives came to power under Margaret Thatcher in 1979, central government and a Labour Secretary of State

(Anthony Crosland) had attempted to exert greater control over global spending totals by local government. The years of Conservative government from 1979 to 1997 saw clashes over expenditure which touched all aspects of the local government financial process. Two features of those years stood out: first, a determination by central government to impose its values on how the increasingly large central government grant was spent; and second, a resolve to deny local authorities the right to raise their own money. Under the Conservatives there were initiatives to limit the amount that could be raised by the rates and a reform of the system of local government finance. There was also a systematic weakening of local government's role in relation to education and housing.

Although Labour in opposition was harshly critical of Conservative initiatives on local government finance, in government after 1997 it was cautious about restoring local government powers in the financial arena.

The nature of local expenditure

Local authority expenditure is of two kinds: capital and current. Capital expenditure is expenditure on some asset of long-term benefit to the community, such as school buildings or the improvement of roads or libraries. Capital expenditure can be financed in a number of ways, including:

- borrowing;
- selling or leasing assets such as land;
- using contributions from revenue;
- agreements with other local authorities;
- special grants from central government or the European Union, e.g. for inner-city development;
- entering a public–private partnership or through the PFI.

Borrowing is by far the most important way for local authorities to fund their capital spending but such borrowing must be approved by central government. Under the Conservative administrations of 1979–97, controls on local borrowing were tightened by the Housing and Local Government Act of 1989. The tightening of controls was achieved by imposing a maximum annual capital expenditure (the annual capital guideline or ACG), which was imposed on individual authorities. It was announced as part of the government's local expenditure plans. The government would calculate how much a local authority should get from the sale of assets and the difference between that figure and the ACG was the borrowing limit or basic credit approval (BCA). Although the figure could be supplemented by additional borrowing, it effectively placed a limit on most local authority borrowing. Central government also tightened the amount of capital expenditure that could be funded from capital receipts. Only 25 per cent of housing sale receipts and 50 per cent of receipts from other sales could be ploughed back into capital expenditure. The remainder had to be devoted to paying off other debt. Other capital spending could be funded by special grants, which might come from central government or the EU. As a result of these restrictions, capital spending by local authorities fell significantly from the mid-1980s.

Labour when it returned to power in 1997 was pressed to relax some of these controls over borrowing. However, not until the Local Government Act 2003 was there any significant effort to change the rules governing capital expenditure. Instead of the detailed controls that had existed since 1989, the bill sets out a prudential regime designed to allow councils more freedom to manage their own capital expenditure. However, it does not abolish all central control of borrowing and indeed puts in place new powers for ministers to set the reserves a council must have and to monitor local authorities by requiring finance officers to report on the robustness of the budget and the adequacy of the reserves.

The income for revenue expenditure comes from three sources, although the balance between them has fluctuated noticeably in the post-1945 period. Today approximately 80 per cent of local government spending comes from central government grants rather than local sources – a figure that inevitably gives central government enormous influence over local authority decisions (see figures 11.1, 11.2 and 11.3).

The first source of income (though not now the most important) is money levied directly by local authorities on their own inhabitants. Traditionally, the method of raising income from local sources was the tax known as the rates, which were levied on property. Taxes could be levied both on householders (domestic rates) and on businesses, factories, shops, offices and other buildings (non-domestic or business rates). Agriculture has been exempt from rates since 1929.

Local rates had funded the expansion of welfare services from the early seventeenth century when the Poor Law of 1601 introduced rates in each parish for the relief of poverty. Through the nineteenth and early twentieth centuries the rates evolved into a general tax on property at the local level based on a coherent national system for assessing rateable values. However, with the expansion of local government provision, this form of funding had inevitably to be supplemented by central government grants. It is difficult to say why a tax that had existed for so long became

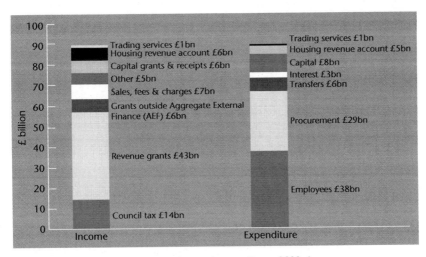

Figure 11.1 Local authority gross income and expenditure, 2000–1.
Source: http://www.local.dtlr.gov.uk/finance/stats/lgfs/2002/keyfacts.pdf

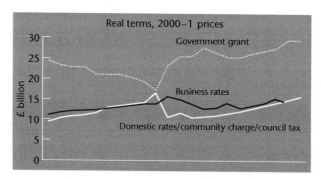

Figure 11.2 Sources of revenue funding, 1981–2 to 2002–3. *Source:* http://www.local.dtlr.gov.uk/finance/stats/lgfs/2002/keyfacts.pdf

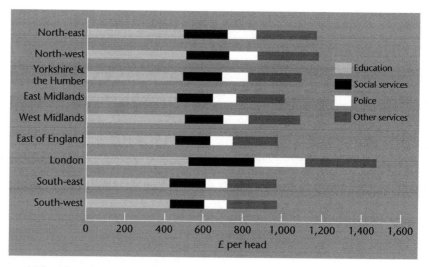

Figure 11.3 Net current expenditure on services per head by region, 2001–2. *Source:* http://www.local.dtlr.gov.uk/finance/stats/lgfs/2002/keyfacts.pdf

increasingly unpopular, but by the late 1970s the rates were extensively disliked. One reason for the unpopularity of domestic rates was that they were unrelated to the ability to pay. The occupation of property by itself was no guarantee of income. Although this disadvantage of the rates was to some extent ameliorated by the introduction of a wide range of rebates, this aspect of the rates made them politically sensitive. The rates were criticized on other grounds in the 1970s. It was argued that they blurred accountability. In the nineteenth and early twentieth centuries only ratepayers could vote at local elections, but the gradual extension of the franchise and changing views of democracy eroded the distinction between ratepayers and non-ratepayers at the local level. During the 1980s the argument that there ought to be a link between paying for local expenditure and voting at local elections resurfaced. Only householders paid rates directly, so that in theory electors who were not householders (such as students, adults living in rented accommodation and council house tenants) could vote for costly policies for which they would not have to pay. In fact, this argument was greatly exaggerated because such 'non-payers' usually had some element calculated into their rents to cover their landlords' expenditure on rates. However, the idea that there was a pool of financially irresponsible electors was one important factor in shaping the search for a substitute tax, a search that gave rise to the highly inflammatory poll tax.

Several alternatives to the rates had been discussed in official examinations of local government, including the extensive examination by the Layfield Committee in 1976. The rates survived in the absence of any consensus on an alternative until the introduction of the community charge or poll tax in 1988. The poll tax differed from the rates in a number of significant respects. First, all people who appeared on the register were required to pay the tax, unlike the domestic rates, which fell only on householders. More people were therefore liable to pay the poll tax, although this extension involved problems for administration and collection of the tax.

Secondly, the poll tax was a uniform tax unrelated to income or wealth. Thus everyone within any given local authority would pay the same amount, although there were variations for second homes and boarding houses. The amount charged could vary between local authorities. Indeed, it was intended that such variations should send powerful signals to the electors about the degree to which a local authority was being efficiently managed.

Finally, there were very few exemptions from the tax. Those with below-average incomes such as students and those on income support could be given a rebate up to 80 per cent of the total charge; but it was an important point of principle that as many people as possible should pay *something* towards their local expenditure.

These features of the new community charge pleased those who thought taxation should fall on individuals rather than on households and wanted to strengthen the accountability of local government to those who had to pay for it. Yet despite the seeming logic of the reform, it was from the outset deeply unpopular in principle and proved harder to collect. Although the community charge was supposed to clarify responsibility for service provision, the existence of two-tier authorities and central government intervention blurred this. There was widespread evasion of the tax and direct action that resulted in rioting in London. A series of by-election defeats in hitherto safe Conservative seats between 1987 and 1990 was widely attributed to the unpopularity of the community charge and in turn contributed to Margaret Thatcher's weakened leadership of the Conservative Party. When John Major replaced Thatcher in November 1990, the government pledged to replace the poll tax. In 1991 a community charge reduction scheme and then the Local Government Finance Act of 1992 abolished the community charge altogether, replacing it with the **council tax**, which is the current method used by local authorities to raise revenue from their inhabitants.

The council tax

The replacement for the poll tax was another new tax called the council tax, which came into effect in April 1993. It was primarily based on property but, unlike the rates, was based on the capital

council tax Local tax on property which was introduced to replace the community charge or poll tax.

value of property rather than the nominal rental value. It was also designed to be a fairer tax, which could take into account the circumstances of those who paid it. That flexibility was achieved in two ways. First, it was graduated – or banded – so that those with larger properties would pay more than those with smaller ones. (The top band was set at roughly three times the bottom one.) Every year the council calculates the level of council tax for their authority by calculating the charge payable by those in Band D. Those in other bands are charged according to a multiplier of that band (see table 11.5). Secondly, the council tax assumed that each household would have at least two adults. There were rebates of 25 per cent for single-person households and there were also exemptions for groups such as students and those on income support. Unlike the poll tax, it was possible to obtain a full 100 per cent rebate on the council tax.

Although the council tax has not been subjected to the same kind of objections as the poll tax, it is perceived to have some flaws. Much of the criticism has focused on the regressive nature of the tax, which means that lower-income families pay a larger amount of their disposable income in council tax. (Council tax has recently been rising faster than inflation and earnings with an average annual rise of 6.4 per cent.) The council tax has also lacked flexibility, at least in England. (Scotland can alter the system of local finance completely and can alter bands and multipliers. Wales can alter bands and multipliers through secondary legislation. In Northern Ireland the old rating system has been retained.) The council tax also encountered the problems of any tax based on property – that property values may change between the assessment of the tax and its imposition. Normally such changes would be marginal, but from the early 1990s there have been major fluctuations in property prices. As a result, the banding process has generated a large number of appeals.

On the other hand, the council tax has a number of strong points. It is relatively simple to understand and broadly fair. It is also relatively easy to collect. Thus although there is a campaign against the council tax, it is likely to remain as the major source of local authorities' own income. However, some adaptation and adjustment also seem likely. In 2001 the government announced changes to the banding structure and signalled that councils were to have some freedom to alter the

Table 11.5   Council tax bands

Band	Value of home (estimated at April 1991)	Proportion of the tax due for a Band D property [a]
A	Under £40,000	66.7%
B	£40,001–£52,000	77.8%
C	£52,001–£68,000	88.9%
D	£68,001–£88,000	100.0%
E	£88,001–£120,000	122.2%
F	£120,001–£160,000	144.4%
G	£160,001–£320,000	166.7%
H	Over £320,000	200.0%

[a] Band D is used as a basis for calculating the tax base.

Source: Office of the Deputy Prime Minister, 'News Release: Council Taxes in England, 2003–04', http://www.odpm.gov.uk/news/0303/ct1.htm

system of discounts. There is to be a revaluation in 2005–7 and a ten-year cycle of revaluations was announced in 2001.

The replacement of the poll tax by the council tax did not mean that central government gave up its powers to cap the level of spending. Labour ended universal capping but gave itself more selective reserve powers in the 1999 Local Government Act. In 2003 John Prescott announced that he would use the power to cap excessive local authority council tax increases.

Business rates

The 1988 legislation that abolished domestic rates and introduced the controversial community charge also changed the basis of non-domestic or business rates. Prior to 1988 local authorities could vary the rate levied on their non-domestic ratepayers. By the 1988 legislation the levying of non-domestic rates was transferred from local to central government, which sets a standard rate although it is collected locally. The non-domestic rate is now known formally as the national non-domestic rate (NNDR) or uniform business rate (UBR). The proceeds of this UBR are redistributed on a population per capita basis to local authorities. Although this reform removed the possibility that local authorities might tax their business communities heavily to raise income, the nationalization of the non-domestic rates has separated the business community from local government. It also incurred great unpopularity as a revaluation of property sent business rates soaring at a time when business was not able to meet the increased costs. Five-yearly revaluations occur.

Charging for local services

A second source of local authority income is money derived from trading and service provision – for example, payments for school meals, council house rents and the use of leisure facilities. Money collected for penalties – such as parking fines – also comes under this heading. Fees, penalties and charges represent about 11 per cent of local authority income from all sources – about £6 billion. They became increasingly controversial over the 1980s as central government sought to force councils to impose its view of charges that were 'realistic'. Thus the Transport Act of 1985 curtailed the powers of local authorities to subsidize local transport in their areas. However, the Labour government since 1997 has encouraged local authorities to charge for its discretionary (as opposed to statutory) services. (Some statutory services may be charged for, but the government sets the charge.) Indeed, the government's framework of comparative assessment of efficiency is designed to promote high-performing authorities delivering services to weaker councils.

Government grants

The third and most important source of income is money transferred from central government in the form of grants. These transfers from central government to local authorities are crucial to the operation of local government. There are different kinds of grant. Some are specific, special or ring-fenced grants which allow the central government to pay a percentage towards the cost of a service. Thus central government routinely pays to local police authorities a 51 per cent grant towards the costs of providing a police service. The ring-fenced grant gives central government greater leverage over the way a service is delivered. It is increasing as a percentage of total grant, having risen from a mere 5 per cent in 1997 to a projected 15 per cent in 2003/4. Not surprisingly, the features of ring-fenced grant that make it attractive to central government cause concern among local authorities. Central government has promised to keep this kind of grant under review. In addition to these special grants there may be targeted grants that may be paid only to selected authorities rather than to all authorities. These grants also aid central control because they will often have conditions attached.

The most important central grant to local authorities comes in the form of a block or general grant, now known as the general revenue grant. In 2002 the government allocated £40 billion between 432 authorities. In theory this grant is supposed to meet the shortfall between the money raised from a local authority's own resources and the total local authority expenditure income. In practice it has become the sharpest instrument available for shaping local authority spending and policies.

The method used for calculating this grant (called at various stages a general grant, a block grant and the rate support grant) has varied considerably even since 1970. The current formula dates from the early 1990s. It uses a complex calculation designed to take into account such factors as the different needs and resources of each local authority. Central government calculates the spending total for local authorities. It then calculates each local authority's allocation of grant by making a standard spending assessment (SSA) for each authority. The amount of grant is then calculated by deducting from that SSA the amount of revenue that will be achieved from a standard council tax and from the non-domestic rates. After 1979 there was much more emphasis on central government's judgment of local authority needs, which was often very different from the local authority's own assessment of its requirements. Confidence in the way the system works declined in the 1980s and 1990s. The whole concept of 'spending need' is ambiguous and the operation of the formula was seen as unpredictable and lacking in transparency. From 2003 there is a new grant formula to calculate SSA (see box 11.5).

The balance between the different sources of funding for local authorities fluctuated over the post-1945 period. As central government laid more obligations on local authorities, it felt bound to finance a higher proportion of the cost of local authority services. Changes in the structure of local government finance (for example the nationalization of the business rate) also made a significant difference. Whereas up until 1990 local taxes accounted for over 50 per cent of local authority revenue, after 1990 that proportion fell to 25 per cent.

Central–Local Relationships

Finance is one of the key levels for exerting central control over local government decisions. Under the Conservatives between 1979 and 1997, increasing mechanisms

Box 11.5 Allocation of standard spending assessment

When working out standard spending assessments, the government takes account of the population, social structure and other characteristics of each authority. The government (in consultation with local government) has developed separate formulas covering the following major service areas.

- Education
- Personal social services
- Police
- Fire
- Highway maintenance
- Environmental, protective and cultural services
- Capital financing

The formula for primary education, for example, is calculated as follows:

(a) **PUPILS AGED 5–10** *multiplied by* the result of:
    £1,965.89; *plus*
    £261.88 *multiplied by* **ADDITIONAL NEEDS**; *plus*
    £107.31 *multiplied by* **WARD SPARSITY**; *plus*
    £282.59 *multiplied by* **FREE MEALS**;

(b) The result of (a) is *multiplied by* **BOUNDARY CHANGE FACTOR I**;

(c) **RESIDENT PUPILS AGED 5–10** *multiplied by* the result of:
    £144.62; *plus*
    £145.35 *multiplied by* **ADDITIONAL NEEDS**; *plus*
    £108.98 *multiplied by* **WARD SPARSITY**;

(d) The result of (c) is *multiplied by* **BOUNDARY CHANGE FACTOR IV**;

(e) The results of (b) and (d) are added together and *multiplied by* **AREA COST ADJUSTMENT FOR EDUCATION**;

(f) The result of (e) is then *multiplied by* the scaling factor for the Primary Education sub-block.

Source: Office of the Deputy Prime Minister, *The Local Government Finance Report (England) 2002/03*, Section 4, http://www.local.dtlr.gov.uk/finance/ssa/0203/lgfrs/chap4.pdf and Office of the Deputy Prime Minister, *A Plain English Guide to the Local Government Finance Settlement* (3rd edn), http://www.local.dtlr.gov.uk/finance/ssa/0001/data/plaineng.doc

were put in place to allow central government to determine local spending and taxing levels. Under Labour from 1997 the initiatives have been designed to give Whitehall greater control of council efficiency and the way public services are delivered. Labour has quite explicitly set about trying to change the culture of local government and bring it into line with its own thinking about management and administrative reform. Specifically, the focus on leadership and responsiveness are part of a wider strategy to make local government more customer-oriented. (Local authorities have themselves also promoted greater customer orientation through the widespread use of consultation; see table 11.6.)

The reforms of the post-1997 period have created demanding new regimes of inspection and audit. Although government has recognized that for some smaller authorities a lighter touch is essential, the structure seems unlikely to be greatly altered for larger authorities. The systems instituted by Labour are important

Table 11.6 Consultation methods used by local authorities, 1997

Type of participation	Percentage of authorities using the method
Complaints/suggestion schemes	92
Service satisfaction surveys	88
Other opinion polls	46
Interactive websites	24
Referendums	4
Community plan/needs analysis	45
Citizens' panels	18
Co-option/committee work	61
Question and answer sessions	47
Consultation documents	85
Public meetings	85
Citizens' juries	5
Focus groups	47
Visioning exercises	26
Service user forums	65
Issue forums	50
Shared interest forums	40
Area/neighbourhood forums	61
User management of services	23

Source: Lowndes et al. (1998), p. 26.

because they allow central government to impose its values not just on the quality of a particular service but also on the internal processes of local authorities. In order to enhance accountability the Best Value system was introduced in the Local Government Act of 1999, replacing contracting out. Best Value required local authorities to develop a corporate strategy and to monitor their own performance for all functions over a five-year period. Local authorities were required to publish their own targets and plans for improvement in relation to individual services (see box 11.6). Detailed inspection supported by the Audit Commission (which now assumes a full role in the monitoring of local authorities) was crucial to this new regime. Central government was given the power to intervene where local authorities were failing to deliver adequate services to their areas.

In 2002 a new framework of assessment, the comprehensive performance assessment, was introduced. Local authorities were externally assessed on all their services and all single-tier and unitary authorities were ranked in a league table, using five categories of excellent, good, fair, weak and poor. These were published at the end of 2002 (see box 11.7). It is important to note here that these rankings went far beyond the capacity of a local authority to deliver core services such as education. They addressed such issues as financial management and leadership. The results of these rankings are to form the basis of the degree of freedom an authority will subsequently enjoy. An excellent authority may expect fewer inspections and greater financial autonomy, especially in relation to grant and borrowing. A weak authority may expect intervention perhaps to outsource a function. Applying a formula of this sort has advantages and disadvantages. On the plus side, it can highlight problems and point up underperforming authorities. On the minus side, the methodology is

Box 11.6 Best Value targets

There are 179 Best Value indicators. They include:

- Number of complaints to Ombudsman classified as maladministration (BV5)
- % turnout for local elections (BV6)
- % of council tax collected (BV8)
- % of senior management posts filled by women (BV11)
- % of economically active disabled people in local authority area (BV 16b)
- % of pupils achieving 5 or more GCSEs at grades A*–C or equivalent (BV38)
- % of homelessness applications decided within 33 working days (BV67)
- % of all respondents satisfied with service in benefit office (BV80 (ii)a)
- Household waste – percentage recycled (BV82a)
- Number of road accident casualties per 100,000: pedestrians killed/seriously injured (BV99a)
- % of new homes built on previously developed land (BV106)
- School pupil visits to museums (BV113)
- Burglaries: number per 1,000 households (BV126a)
- Number of recorded racial incidents per 100,000 population (BV174)
- % of total length of footpaths/other rights of way which are easy to use (BV178)

Source: Office of the Deputy Prime Minister, Best Value Performance Indicators, http://www.bvpi.gov.uk

Box 11.7 Comprehensive performance assessment

The comprehensive performance assessment is designed to supplement the Best Value indicators, assessing overall performance and gauging ability to improve. There are five categories from 'excellent' to 'poor'. Councils are assessed on a rating of one to four in eight service areas, from education to social care, housing, libraries and their ability to manage finance and staff. These are then combined into an overall 'score'. Results from 2003 found 22 excellent councils, 54 good, 39 fair, 22 weak and 13 poor.

Councils rated excellent

Bexley LBC
Blackburn with Darwen Borough Council
Camden LBC
Cheshire County Council
Cornwall County Council
Corporation of London
Derbyshire County Council
Dorset County Council
Gateshead Metropolitan Borough Council
Hammersmith & Fulham LBC
Hampshire County Council
Hartlepool Borough Council
Hertfordshire County Council
Kensington & Chelsea LBC

(*Continues*)

Box 11.7 *Continued*

Kent County Council
Kingston upon Thames LBC
Kirklees Metropolitan Borough Council
Sunderland City Council
Wandsworth LBC
West Sussex County Council
Westminster LBC (City)
Wigan Metropolitan Borough Council

Councils rated poor

Bedfordshire County Council
Coventry City Council
Hackney LBC
Islington LBC
Kingston upon Hull (City & County of)
Lambeth LBC
North-East Lincolnshire Borough Council
North Tyneside Metropolitan Borough Council
Swindon Borough Council
Torbay Council
Wakefield Metropolitan District Council (City of)
Walsall Metropolitan Borough Council
Waltham Forest LB

Source: Audit Commission, http://www.audit-commission.gov.uk/cpa/index.asp

crude and the public labelling of an authority as weak or failing does not always correspond to the reality of provision. Inevitably, such labelling gives political ammunition to the opposition and may demotivate staff.

Standards in Local Government

Just as the integrity of national government came under the searchlight of public scrutiny in the 1990s, so too did that of local government. Local government had traditionally seemed more vulnerable to corruption than national government. One reason for this was that local government offered multiple opportunities for financial gain because of its control of such matters as planning permission. Elected councillors are unpaid but allowances have existed since 1972. They were introduced in part to make it possible for individuals from all sections of society to become councillors, but it was also thought that allowances might reduce the likelihood of petty corruption. However, with the large increases that have been made in these allowances and the lack of national monitoring, these allowances are now open to criticism. Individual authorities were often controlled for long periods of time by a single party and less visible to the kind of scrutiny directed at national level by television and the press.

When the Nolan Committee examined local government, it pointed out that the general picture was one of honesty and integrity. Local government contained over 2,000 councillors and more than 2 million workers, but in 1995/6 there were only 1,475 proven cases of fraud and 21 cases of corruption. Nevertheless, such episodes as the Westminster council housing scandal show that there is no cause for complacency.

A statutory framework governing codes of conduct for councillors and conflicts of interest was revised in the Local Government Act 2000. This legislation meant that all local authorities must adopt one of four constitutions. All new councillors must say they have understood the register of interests, which entails declaring any interest and withdrawing from any proceedings where it might be an issue. There is also a code of ethics for council officers (see box 11.8). The application of the code of ethics to parish councillors has been highly controversial as many local councillors feel that the invasion of privacy entailed by the code of ethics and the register of interests is out of proportion to the scale of their spending powers. It was reported that the whole six-member parish council of West Ilsey in Berkshire had resigned in protest at the imposition of these rules and that perhaps as many as 100 other councillors had resigned (*Guardian*, 7 March 2003).

Box 11.8 New code of ethics for local councillors

Section 51 of the Local Government Act 2000 requires all relevant authorities to adopt a members' code of conduct. Each authority's code must incorporate the mandatory conditions contained in a model code of conduct issued by the Secretary of State and approved by Parliament.

The model codes contain mandatory provisions covering:

- the respect owed to people, including council employees;
- non-discrimination;
- access to information;
- impartiality, objectivity and integrity;
- stewardship of resources;
- accountability; and
- confidential reporting.

The codes also provide:

- that members should record their personal interests, and any gifts or hospitality that they receive as a consequence of their duties, in public registers to be maintained by the authority's monitoring officer;
- rules about when members should declare personal interests before participating in council business; and
- the circumstances in which they should take no part in council business because their interests could be considered to be 'prejudicial'.

Source: Office of the Deputy Prime Minister, *New Ethical Framework Members' Code of Conduct*, http://www.local-regions.odpm.gov.uk/ethical/members/index.htm

Grievance procedures in local government

The machinery through which individuals could challenge decisions made by a local authority was significantly improved in 1974 with the establishment of a network of local ombudsmen under the direction of a collegiate Commission for Local Administration in England and a Commission for Local Administration in Wales. The Commission's jurisdiction at present covers local authorities, police authorities and any joint boards of which local authorities are a constituent part. The Commission may examine any complaint made on behalf of a citizen who alleges 'injustice' in consequence of maladministration. Thus the local ombudsman, like his or her national counterpart, is primarily concerned with procedural irregularities rather than with the merits of a decision (see also chapter 14). There was initially restricted access requiring complaints to be made via a councillor, but this restriction has been removed. There have been other reforms of the Local Government Association's jurisdiction and powers. In 1978 local authorities were empowered to pay compensation to individuals found to have suffered injustice at the hands of a local authority. Although local authorities were sometimes slow to accept the verdict of the Local Government Association, the office has added an important dimension to the scrutiny of local government.

Conclusions

Local government in the early twenty-first century is in an ambiguous situation. On the one hand, the advent of a Labour government committed to greater decentralization has created a very different climate from that of the 1980s and early 1990s when local government's very existence seemed under threat. The emphasis on the local authority's leadership role in the community has energized a number of local authorities to think creatively about the part they play in the political system. On the other hand, the new localism of New Labour entails its own centralizing dynamic as a result of central government's concern with policy delivery. Given that the general population probably places more importance on the quality of services than local control, there is a logic to the framework for local government. It is likely that some local authorities, but not all, will flourish within that framework, though it is not evident that it will have a beneficial effect on the middle ranks of local authorities. By the same token, initiatives that further erode local independence and autonomy seem likely to reinforce the impression in voters' minds that local government is neither important nor interesting and that involvement in local politics – even at the minimal level of voting – is a waste of time. It may be that a strong regional initiative could allow local government to break out of this syndrome of decline, but it is not clear how much genuine appetite there is for it either in Whitehall or amidst the public at large.

 Key Questions

1 Why is local government so weak in the United Kingdom? What could be done to strengthen it?

2 What powers to vary services should local authorities have and what taxing and spending powers?

3 Does party have a role in local government?

Further Reading

Excellent introductory studies are to be found in D. Wilson and C. Game, *Local Government in the United Kingdom* (Basingstoke: Palgrave/Macmillan, 2002) and in R. Leach and J. Percy Smith, *Local Governance in Britain* (Basingstoke: Palgrave, 2001). J. A. Chandler, *Local Government Today* (3rd edn; Manchester: Manchester University Press, 2001) and D. Wilson, 'Local government: Balancing diversity and uniformity', *Parliamentary Affairs*, 54: 2 (2001) are also pertinent. Vernon Bogdanor, 'Local government and the constitution', in his *Politics and the Constitution: Essays on British Government* (Aldershot: Dartmouth, 1996) offers thoughtful reflections on the position of local government in the UK, as does Martin Loughlin, 'The restructuring of central–local government relations', in J. Jowell and D. Oliver (eds), *The Changing Constitution* (3rd edn; Oxford: Oxford University Press, 1994). Desmond King and Gerry Stoker, *Rethinking Local Democracy* (Basingstoke: Macmillan, 1996) contains a series of insightful and provocative essays. D. E. Butler et al., *Failure in British Government: The Politics of the Poll Tax* (Oxford: Oxford University Press, 1994) examines the poll tax issue in detail. Steve Leach, 'Introducing cabinets into British local government', *Parliamentary Affairs*, 52: 1 (1999) looks at executive restructuring in the wake of the 2000 Local Government Act. C. Rallings et al., 'An audit of local democracy in Britain: The evidence from local elections', *Parliamentary Affairs*, 52: 1 (1999) examines aspects of local democracy, while N. Rao, *Reviving Local Democracy: New Labour, New Politics?* (Bristol: Policy, 2000) considers local democracy more broadly.

 Websites

See also the list of general websites at the back of the book.

- www.local-regions.odpm.gov.uk/index.htm – Office of the Deputy Prime Minister, local government pages
- www.lgcnet.com – Local Government Chronicle, local elections site
- www.lga.gov.uk – Local Government Association
- www.idea.gov.uk – Improvement and Development Agency for Local Government
- www.info4local.gov.uk – Information for Local Government
- www.lgiu.gov.uk – Local Government Information Unit
- www.nlgn.org.uk – New Local Government Network
- www.london.gov.uk – Greater London Assembly and mayor
- www.regions.odpm.gov.uk/chambers/index.htm – links to regional development agencies
- www.cfy.org.uk – Campaign for a Regional Assembly for Yorkshire
- www.northeastassembly.gov.uk – Campaign for a North-east Regional Assembly

12 The Diversity of the UK: Governing after Devolution

One of the 1997 Labour government's most significant constitutional reforms was the introduction of devolved government for Scotland and Wales. The legislation was introduced partly to remedy the highly centralized structure of government in the United Kingdom and partly to respond to claims that these areas had distinct political identities that should be accommodated by radical changes in the system of government. Devolution in Northern Ireland had altogether different roots. Northern Ireland's position within the United Kingdom is bitterly contested by a substantial proportion of the population, which would prefer to see the statelet absorbed into a united Ireland. The fragile arrangements for devolved government were part of the complex peace process hammered out in the Belfast (Good Friday) Agreement of 1998. Northern Ireland had operated devolved government within the United Kingdom from 1921 until 1972, but that system's failure to accommodate the needs of the minority nationalist and Catholic community caused London to dismantle it. The new structures that were established in Northern Ireland after 1998 were deliberately designed to be inclusive of both the unionist Protestant population and the nationalist Catholic communities and were built on theories of **consociational** rather than **majoritarian democracy**. The arrangements for Northern Ireland's devolved government were thus very different from those of Scotland or Wales, not least because of their somewhat cumbersome requirements for cross-community **power sharing**.

While the devolved systems of government for Scotland and Wales were established with relative ease, the bitter sectarian divisions and the background of violence in Northern Ireland made devolution there altogether more difficult to operate. The Northern Ireland executive and Assembly experienced a series of crises as a result of the fundamental lack of trust between the parties and personalities who had to work the institutions. The Assembly and devolved government was suspended four times between 1998 and 2002. Not until 2003 was there sufficient evidence of renewed commitment to the peace process, allowing Assembly elections to be held in November. Thus, although the most recent arrangements for devolved government in Northern Ireland are fully discussed here, at the time of writing these institutions have been suspended and direct rule from London reimposed.

The outline of the new devolution settlements and the impact of devolution on the constitutional arrangements of the United Kingdom as a whole were addressed in chapter 2. In this chapter we examine the distinctive political characteristics of Scotland, Wales and Northern Ireland in more detail and analyse how the introduction of new institutions has changed their government and politics.

Scotland

Unlike Wales, which was subdued by conquest in the thirteenth century, Scotland was never permanently incorporated into the UK by force of arms. In 1603 the

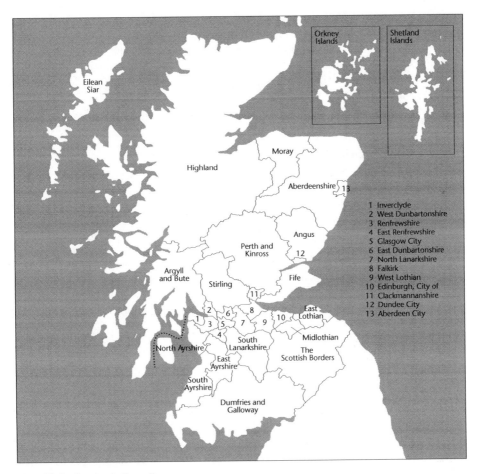

Map 12.1 Scotland: Council areas.

succession of James VI of Scotland to the throne of England as James I united the crowns of the two countries. The union was only a personal one, however, and Scotland retained its own political and legal system and its own church. The establishment of a common Parliament occurred as a result of the Treaty of Union of 1707. Although the separate Scottish Parliament was abolished, the Scots were given guarantees that certain features of their system would remain inviolate. The Church of Scotland (which is Presbyterian) was protected as the national church, and Scotland's separate legal system was preserved. (The Scottish legal system is very different from the English system, reflecting principles of continental jurisprudence derived from Roman law rather than common law.)

Scottish national institutions were thus constitutionally protected and, although the Scots retained a distinct sense of cultural identity, Scottish nationalism rarely appeared threatening to London after the suppression of the Jacobite uprising of 1745. Immediately after the Act of Union of 1707, Scotland had a Secretary of State to supervise its affairs and represent its interests in Parliament. But this arrangement was abandoned after the abortive rebellion of 1745 so that for much of the period from 1745 until 1885, Scottish issues were largely the responsibility of the Lord Advocate, a law officer. The nineteenth-century expansion of government necessitated the separation of administrative from legal functions and in 1885 it was decided that the Lord Advocate should concentrate on his responsibilities for legal matters. Administrative responsibilities thereafter were given to a Secretary for Scotland and a separate Scottish Office.

The revival of the office of Scottish Secretary in the late nineteenth century was one of the first steps along the road to administrative devolution. During the nineteenth century also, the growth of government intervention precipitated the formation of a range of new boards and ad hoc authorities at the local level to meet Scottish needs. The Scottish Secretary has been a regular member of peacetime cabinets since 1892 and the status of the Scottish Office was enhanced in 1929 when the Secretary for Scotland was made a full Secretary of State.

The Scottish Office itself moved to St Andrew's House in Edinburgh in 1939, although a small London office was retained. Several refinements of the organization of the Scottish executive occurred in the period between 1939 and 1998, but the important point to note is that, even before the devolution legislation of 1998, a very large part of Scottish government was administered from Edinburgh through the Scottish Office and its functional departments.

Separate parliamentary machinery for handling Scottish issues has existed for much of the twentieth century. A Scottish Grand Committee (consisting of all MPs with Scottish constituencies) has existed since 1907. Between 1994 and 1997 the Conservatives, in an attempt to meet demands for greater self-government without formal devolution, expanded the role of the Scottish Grand Committee to give it increased powers. After the creation of a separate Scottish Parliament in 1999, the legislative function of the Scottish Grand Committee has inevitably declined. There is also a departmental select committee covering Scotland – the Scottish Affairs Committee – which keeps the work of the Scottish Office under review and monitors relations between the Westminster and Edinburgh Parliaments as well as all aspects of Scottish affairs for which Westminster remains responsible.

Table 12.1 Support for the SNP at general elections, 1970–2001

Election	Candidates	Seats	% of Scottish vote
1970	65	1	11.4
1974 (Feb)	70	7	21.9
1974 (Oct)	71	11	30.4
1979	71	2	17.3
1983	72	2	11.8
1987	71	3	14.0
1992	72	3	21.5
1997	72	6	22.1
2001	71	4	20.1

Sources: Butler and Butler (2000), p. 181; Butler and Kavanagh (2002), p. 262; Electoral Commission, http://www.electoralcommission.gov.uk/elections/resultsandtimetables.cfm

Despite experiments with special arrangements for governing Scotland, demands for a more comprehensive form of self-government were frequently made in Scotland and the question of Scotland's distinct needs was never entirely off the twentieth-century political agenda. There were at least three factors keeping the Scottish issue alive in British politics. First, the Scottish National Party (SNP) – an explicitly nationalist party seeking Scottish independence – generated publicity for the cause. Founded in 1934, the SNP had relatively little impact until the late 1960s. In 1967, however, the SNP won the Hamilton by-election and thereafter it cleverly used salient political issues such as the discovery of North Sea oil and disenchantment with the established parties to build support (see table 12.1). Labour, as the dominant party in Scotland, was especially threatened by the growth of the SNP. A second factor keeping the Scottish issue alive was the reservoir of support and sympathy for Scottish claims in the Labour and Liberal (later Liberal Democrat) parties. Both parties had contained elements sympathetic to the case for a measure of home rule for Scotland; and Labour had a distinctive radical Scottish tradition. Many of the contemporary Labour Party's leading figures are Scots who have long supported the cause of devolution. John Smith as leader between 1992 and 1994 committed Labour to devolution, and such senior Labour figures as Gordon Brown, Robin Cook and the former Lord Chancellor, Lord Irvine, come from a background of Scottish politics.

Finally, the distinctive cultural institutions of Scotland – notably its education system and vigorous media (where in addition to Scottish editions of national newspapers there were several journals such as the *Scotsman* unique to Scotland) – created a political subsystem that was very different from that of England.

The demand for self-government

The rise of the SNP in the late 1960s was one factor that contributed to Labour's movement towards a radical policy of devolution for Scotland as part of a strategy to pre-empt the more extreme option of independence. The first attempt to introduce a separate Parliament for Scotland failed with the loss of the 1978 referendum, an event which indirectly led to the fall of James Callaghan's Labour government in

1979 and the election of the Conservatives under Margaret Thatcher. The years of Conservative government between 1979 and 1997 fuelled the demand for devolution and ensured that it spread much more widely across Scottish society than ever before. Mrs Thatcher's free-market policies alienated Scottish opinion and, as the Conservative vote in Scotland collapsed, Scotland's politics seemed to diverge more sharply from the politics of the United Kingdom as a whole.

In 1989 a broad coalition of groups established the Scottish Constitutional Convention, with the twin goals of broadening support for devolution and developing agreement about how a Scottish Parliament would work (Lynch, 2001). The work of the Scottish Convention, which was boycotted by the Tories and treated gingerly by the nationalists, over the period 1989–95 placed the restoration of a Scottish Parliament firmly on the political agenda. By clarifying much of the detail of how a devolved government could operate, it provided an effective blueprint for reform. The Convention also brought together not just the key political parties in favour of devolution but a wide range of Scottish civic and voluntary groups. On its return to power in 1997, Labour was committed to legislation offering Scotland a devolution package with a strong Scottish Parliament. In a referendum in which two questions were put to the population – whether there should be a separate Parliament and whether it should have tax-varying powers – the Scottish electorate answered 'yes' to both (see table 2.1, p. 58). The devolution package (contained in the Scotland Act 1998) was endorsed overwhelmingly. The first elections to the new Scottish Parliament took place on 6 May 1999 and the new Parliament was opened by the Queen in July 1999.

New institutions and new politics?

The 129-member Scottish Parliament (like the Welsh Assembly) is elected for a fixed term of four years. The electoral system employed is not first past the post (FPTP) but the additional member system (AMS), a form of proportional representation. The electoral system's use of AMS (which is fully described in chapter 7; see box 7.1, p. 245) involved electing 73 MSPs in constituencies by FPTP and 56 MSPs by a list system based on regions which could create proportionality. The choice of electoral system for the new Scottish Parliament was influenced by the need to make it difficult for the SNP to win an overall majority. Although it was recognized that this electoral system would weaken Labour's chance of securing an overall majority in its own right, this was thought preferable to risking the possibility that a small shift of electoral opinion could give the SNP a working majority which it could then use to demand full independence for Scotland.

The result in the first Scottish Parliament elections (on a 60.2 per cent turnout) was that no single party had an overall majority (see table 2.2, p. 58). Instead, six parties gained representation within the new Parliament. The bulk of the seats were divided between the four main political parties in Scotland: Labour, the Liberal Democrats, the SNP and the Conservatives. There was also some representation for two smaller parties, the Greens and the Scottish Socialists. Thus Labour's traditional grip on Scottish politics was broken, a development which made some Labour activists less than enthusiastic about devolution. (Since 1959 Labour has won the majority of Scottish seats and in 2001, 56 of Westminster's 72 Scottish constituencies

Table 12.2 Scottish Parliament elections, 2003

Party	2003	1999	Change
Labour	50	56	−6
Conservatives	18	18	0
Liberal Democrats	17	17	0
Green Party	7	1	+6
SNP	27	35	−8
Scottish Socialists	6	1	+5
Independents	4	1	+3

were held by Labour.) Since no single party had an overall majority, it was necessary to form a coalition with the Liberal Democrats to govern. This coalition is really the only viable one for Labour and the process of coalition formation was greatly eased by the experience the two parties had of working together during the Scottish Convention. Nevertheless, coalition rather than single-party government inevitably injected an element of instability into the executive and meant that the style of government would be different from that of London. The need to accommodate the policy demands of the Liberal Democrats meant that there was a greater likelihood that Scotland's policy priorities would diverge from London's, as quickly became apparent over the issue of university charges and later the cost of care for the elderly. Moreover, because the Liberal Democrats were themselves divided over some policy issues, their cohesion in the Scottish Parliament could not be guaranteed. The SNP (which was increasingly presenting itself as 'Scotland's party') became the official opposition.

The arrival of multi-party politics and coalition government suggested that in some ways Scotland would inevitably diverge from the pattern of London government, although it was not clear to what extent it would develop a radically new pattern of politics. In 2003 the second set of elections for Scotland's Parliament confirmed the trend towards party fragmentation and minor party gains at the expense of the major parties (see table 12.2). Although turnout did not confirm the worst fears of those who thought it would drop dramatically, it only just topped 50 per cent and in Glasgow only two out of five electors actually voted, making it difficult to interpret the results. Labour lost six seats while Tommy Sheridan's Scottish Socialist Party and the Greens made significant gains. In addition, an independent MSP, Jean Turner, campaigning on the issue of hospital provision, took a seat from Labour in Strathkelvin and Bearsden. The poor performance of the SNP in 2003 resulted in a concerted effort to remove the leader, John Swinney, as well as a resumption of the factionalism and in-fighting between those (like Swinney) who favoured gradualism and accommodation and those who wanted to move the SNP to a much more radical, pro-independence stance.

Constitutional powers

The form in which the 1998 Scotland Act divided powers was much more generous to Scotland than envisaged in the devolution debates and legislation of the 1970s. In

federalism A system of government in which power is divided constitutionally between a central authority and subordinate units such as states. It differs from devolution in that sovereignty is shared and the division of powers is symmetrical across the subnational units. Contemporary discussion of federalism within the UK centres on two issues: the future shape of the relationship between London and the devolved systems and the future shape of the relationship between the EU and the member states.

Sewel convention/Sewel motion Procedural device named after Lord Sewel (a minister at the Foreign Office) which allows the Scottish Parliament to permit Westminster to make policy in an area devolved to the Scottish Parliament. When devolution was introduced, it was recognized that Westminster retained sovereignty so could in theory legislate for areas that were devolved. But the spirit of the devolution scheme meant that Westminster would rarely use this power unilaterally. However, it was also recognized that there might be occasions when Edinburgh would want Westminster to legislate on a topic that had been devolved. In that case, the device of a Sewel motion would apply in order to provide a legitimizing mechanism for Westminster's intervention.

the 1998 Scotland Act powers reserved to Westminster were specifically listed; everything else was deemed to fall within the competence of the Scottish Parliament. The powers that were reserved to Westminster related to fiscal and monetary policy, foreign and defence policy, social security and employment. Edinburgh was thus accorded wide-ranging powers over virtually all other matters. As noted in chapter 2, disputes about legal competence were classified as 'devolution disputes', which would be decided by the Judicial Committee of the Privy Council (JCPC). The main forum for resolving political disagreements between the government of Scotland and the UK government was to be the joint ministerial committee, a body set up to integrate policy between the devolved areas and the centre. In fact, the relationship between London and Edinburgh thus far has not really needed this formal mechanism, although it could be important if the political complexion of the government in London were to change, for example if a Conservative government were to be re-elected.

Although the division of powers in the legislation superficially resembled that in a **federal** system, Westminster retains sovereignty. (The entrenchment clauses suggested by the Scottish Convention were not implemented.) Westminster therefore reserved the right in theory to legislate in any area of policy, whether reserved or not. However, both London and Edinburgh have recognized the **Sewel convention**, which assumes that London would not normally legislate in an area devolved to the Scottish Parliament but could do so in exceptional circumstances such as the need to legislate quickly for the whole of the United Kingdom. In those cases, Sewel motions would be brought forward to justify the unusual use of Westminster's sovereign powers. To clarify further the relationships between London and Edinburgh, formal memorandums of understanding and concordats were published in October 1999. Inevitably, however, the early years of devolution involved a good deal of pragmatic adjustment as both sides felt their way towards the establishment of working intergovernmental relationships. The situation was made more complex by the creation of the Department for Constitutional Affairs in 2003. The Scotland and Wales Offices were brought under the umbrella of this new department and those Offices continued to report to the Secretaries of State for Scotland and Wales. Although there is some evidence that the personal relationship between successive Secretaries of State for Scotland and Scottish ministers has not always been easy, real conflict has been avoided thus far.

In practice, the establishment of separate spheres of policy control is likely to be undermined by the inevitable tendency of policy problems to overlap, so that informal working arrangements between different levels of government are likely to be at least as significant as formal demarcations of responsibility. There is a danger that this pragmatic approach to conflict will not necessarily always work so smoothly, which is why the Committee on the Constitution argued for greater institutionalization of the machinery of liaison and coordination (Constitution

Committee, 2003). However, while a Labour government is in power at Westminster and remains the majority in a coalition in Edinburgh, relationships will probably remain harmonious.

Government formation

The first coalition agreed between Labour and the Liberal Democrats was enshrined in a document, *Partnership for Scotland*, which provided a joint policy agenda for the two parties. Donald Dewar became first minister in 1999. Labour as the major partner took the greater share of the cabinet positions. Jim Wallace, the Liberal Democrat leader, became Dewar's deputy. In fact, the succession of first ministers – from Donald Dewar to Henry McLeish and then to Jack McConnell – meant that there was a good deal of turnover in the cabinet membership on the Labour side, especially in the transfer of power from McLeish to McConnell. Scotland's executive is organized on cabinet lines, with a first minister, deputy first minister and cabinet, and was divided into nine departments reflecting the main responsibilities of the Scottish government (see box 12.1).

The fact that since devolution Scotland has operated coalition government makes the management of cabinet government in Edinburgh itself rather different from the mode of cabinet government in London. On one level, Edinburgh's style of cabinet government looked more like the textbook model in that less business is devolved to committees or taken outside the formal coalition structures. On the other hand, intra-party divisions and the pressures of running a coalition impose their own constraints. Although the formal rules of collective cabinet responsibility appear to apply (and indeed were published in two documents, *A Guide to Collective Decision-making* and the *Scottish Ministerial Code*), the interpretation of collective responsibility is malleable. Internal differences became public knowledge quite quickly in the life of the Scottish executive. There were a number of causes for internal disagreement. One was over tuition fees, where the Liberal Democrats wanted to implement the 1999 Cubie Committee's report but Labour was more hesitant on the issue. (The Cubie Committee's review of student finance had been established with the partnership agreement between Liberal Democrats and Labour in May 1999.) In 2001, Tavish Scott, a Liberal Democrat member of the cabinet, resigned because he could not support the Scottish executive's fisheries policy. In late 2002, culture minister Mike Watson flouted the conventions of collective responsibility by publicly attacking the executive's hospital reorganization plan relating to his Glasgow constituency. It is difficult to decide from these cases what 'rule', if any, is governing cabinet proceedings, although the case of Clare Short (who remained in Labour's cabinet for a period in 2003 despite her public criticisms of the prime minister and the Iraq war) also underlines how flexible the UK cabinet's interpretation of the convention of collective cabinet responsibility has become.

Keeping the coalition together inevitably meant that in some policy areas Edinburgh had to be prepared to diverge from London. Policy divergence is, of course, inherent in the idea of devolution, but the experience of policy difference in practice can be an uncomfortable one. The role of the first minister in keeping relations between London and Edinburgh harmonious was significant. Donald Dewar, first

Box 12.1 The Scottish executive 2003

(These portfolios are inevitably likely to change)

First minister

Jack McConnell: Head of the Scottish executive (SE), responsible for development, implementation and presentation of SE policies.

Deputy first minister and justice minister

Jim Wallace QC: With first minister, responsible for development, implementation and presentation of SE policies, including external relations. As justice minister, responsible for home affairs, including civil law and criminal justice, criminal justice social work services, police, fire, prisons and courts, law reform and freedom of information.
Deputy justice minister: Hugh Henry

Education and young people

Cathy Jamieson: Preschool and school education, children and young people.
Deputy: Nicol Stephen, with specific responsibility for teachers and schools.

Enterprise, transport and lifelong learning

Iain Gray: Economy, transport, business and industry including Scottish Enterprise, Highlands and Islands Enterprise, trade and inward investment, energy, further and higher education, public transport, roads, lifeline air and ferry services, lifelong learning and training, science.
Deputy: Lewis Macdonald, with specific responsibility for transport.

Environment and rural development

Ross Finnie: Environment and natural heritage, renewable energy, land reform, water, sustainable development, agriculture, fisheries, rural development including aquaculture and forestry.
Deputy: Allan Wilson

Tourism, culture and sport

Mike Watson: Tourism, culture and the arts, sport, built heritage, architecture, Historic Scotland, lottery funding and Gaelic.
Deputy: Elaine Murray, with specific responsibility for arts and culture.

Social justice

Margaret Curran: Social inclusion, housing and area regeneration including promotion of sustainable urban development, cities, the land-use planning system and building standards, equality issues and the voluntary sector.
Deputy: Des McNulty

Finance and public services

Andy Kerr: The Scottish budget, public service delivery, modernizing government including civil service reform, local government and European structural funds. Also responsible for strategic communications.

(Continues)

Box 12.1 *Continued*

Deputy: Peter Peacock, with specific responsibility for budgetary monitoring and control.

Health and community care

Malcolm Chisholm: The National Health Service, community care, and food safety.
Deputy: Frank McAveety
Deputy: Mary Mulligan

Parliamentary business

Patricia Ferguson: Parliamentary affairs and the management of executive business in the Parliament.
Deputy: Euan Robson, with particular responsibility for parliamentary handling of legislative programme. Also responsible for strategic communications.

Law officers

Colin Boyd QC: Lord Advocate
Elish Angiolini: Solicitor General

Source: The Scottish Parliament.

minister from 1999 to 2000, was widely seen as a steady pair of hands. His death in October 2000 produced a subtle change as his successor, Henry McLeish, who was more obviously responsive to Scottish sentiment than to London thinking, had, unlike Dewar, no experience of London government. McLeish was also seen as a modernizer, but his handling of the leadership soon irritated London. McLeish initially tried to make his style of government more distinctively 'Scottish' than had Dewar and he paid more attention than his austere predecessor to political advisers and media management. But if this suggested a new modernizing approach to government, sleaze and corruption demonstrated that an older style of Scottish politics had survived the transition to devolution. A scandal about the letting of parliamentary offices – dubbed 'Officegate' – forced McLeish to stand down as first secretary in the autumn of 2001. Jack McConnell, a former leader of Stirling Council who had previously run against McLeish for the leadership, was elected first secretary in his place. Although there were allegations of misuse of expenses in his case also, McConnell survived in the leadership. His style was more that of a machine politician than McLeish's had been and he brought a new group of personal supporters into cabinet office.

Finance

The money for services provided by the Scottish executive comes primarily from a block grant from the Treasury, which is fixed for a three-year period. In addition, under the Scotland Act the Scottish Parliament was given power to vary taxes, upwards or downwards, by the equivalent of 3p in the pound. This power was not, however, one which the Scottish Parliament would be able to use lightly, and indeed Labour pledged itself not to use it in the first four years of devolution. The Scottish Parliament has limited scope for borrowing and no control over monetary or fiscal policy, which remains with the Bank of England and the Treasury, respectively. There is, however, the possibility of additional money from the European Union.

The size of the block grant is controversial. It is calculated according to the Barnett formula, which was introduced in 1978. (The formula itself represented a revision of the earlier Goschen formula of 1888.) Under the formula, which is non-statutory and determines the percentage of public expenditure to be allocated to the component parts of the United Kingdom, Scotland gets roughly 10 per cent of total UK expenditure. The problem from Scotland's point of view is that the formula – which applies also to Wales and Northern Ireland – is based on population, not need. Scotland could argue that a needs-based formula would be fairer because it could take into account the special features of the Scottish economy and society.

The employment of a block grant formula means that London priorities may not necessarily be followed in Edinburgh. Thus substantial increases given by the UK Treasury for education and health do not have to be translated into additional spending on these services in Scotland. Nor at present have the public service agreements (PSAs) that the Treasury has imposed alongside the spending increases been replicated in Scotland. The allocation of money between services is thus a Scottish Parliament responsibility. In fact, over its short life the Scottish Parliament has acquired a range of additional commitments. Thus the implementation of the Cubie Committee's report on student finance added substantially to the education bill, while the Scottish Parliament acquired extra spending commitments on teachers' pay, care of the elderly and NHS salaries.

The Scottish Parliament has developed a relatively open budget consultation process and a timetable that involves draft budget enactment early in the year (see box 12.2). The executive has published an economic framework document, and there are now well-developed institutions of audit and financial scrutiny.

A New Model Parliament

The Parliament established under the Scotland Act was not intended to operate as a miniature copy of Westminster. From the period of the Scottish Convention it was evident that the model of parliamentary democracy envisaged for Edinburgh was much less adversarial and executive-dominated than Westminster's. The work of the Parliament was to be discharged through a strong committee system rather than revolve around the floor of the chamber. Sixteen strong committees were created to exercise legislative responsibilities and scrutiny functions (see box 12.3). Prior to the opening of the Parliament in 1999, a central steering group was charged with making detailed arrangements and standing orders for the new body. The steering group enunciated four guiding principles in its recommendations for how the Parliament should operate – power sharing, accountability, equal opportunities and participation – and these have combined to give the Edinburgh Parliament a different character from that of Westminster.

Box 12.2   The financial timetable 2002–2003

Other elements		Stage 1 (March–June 2002)
	2 April: Publication of Annual Expenditure Report	The Annual Expenditure Report (AER) is published and comprises a detailed breakdown of the executive's spending plans and priorities. Each chapter will cover the expenditure of particular portfolios. The relevant subject committees will be responsible for commenting on the relationship between expenditure plans and policy priorities in the spending area (this may also involve consultation with outside bodies and interested individuals)
Spring: UK Budget	⇩	
	Finance Committee oversees consultation process with subject committees	
	⇩	
End Year Flexibility Announce- ment (before or after summer recess)	April/May: Subject committees examine relevant chapter. Send reports to Finance Committee	
	⇩	These responses will be coordinated by the Finance Committee, which will report to the Parliament. The Report will be debated by the Parliament before summer recess. In the light of the Parliament's input (and comment from other interested bodies), the executive will prepare firmer plans.
	June: Finance Committee reports to Parliament. Parliament debates this Report	
UK Spending Review	20 September: Executive publishes draft budget and spending plans	Stage 2 (September–December 2002) This year's firmer spending plans will be published in September 2002. Again, each subject committee may report to the Finance Committee on relevant parts of the package, to identify whether the Parliament's Stage 1 recommendations have been acted upon by the executive.
	⇩	
	Subject committees examine and send reports to Finance Committee	
October: Autumn revisions	⇩	
	Finance Committee considers the draft budget and may propose alternative	At this stage the Finance Committee has the option of putting forward an alternative budget with the proviso that this must keep within the overall spending limit set by the executive's draft budget. In any event, the Finance Committee will produce a Report by December 2002 which will then be debated by the Parliament before Christmas recess.
Nov: UK Pre-Budget Report	⇩	
	December: Finance Committee Report; mid-Dec.: Parliament debates Report	
February: Spring revisions	January: Executive produces proposals (having considered Parliament's recommendations)	Stage 3 (January–February 2003) The formal parliamentary process of enacting the Budget Bill. The Budget (Scotland) Bill will be introduced in January 2003. Only a member of the executive may move amendments. Parliament has a vote to accept or reject it. If accepted, it will authorize expenditure for financial year 2003/4.
	⇩	
	Parliament debates Budget Bill	
	⇩	
	Executive amendments and parliamentary vote	

Box 12.3   Legislative committees of the Scottish Parliament

Committees are crucial to the working of the Scottish Parliament. Some are mandatory – required by standing orders – while others can be set up to deal with particular problems.

Mandatory committees

- Procedures Committee
- Standards Committee
- Finance Committee
- Audit Committee
- European Committee
- Public Petitions Committee
- Equal Opportunities Committee
- Subordinate Legislation Committee

Subject committees

- Education and Sport Committee
- Enterprise and Lifelong Learning Committee
- Health and Community Care Committee
- Justice 1 Committee
- Justice 2 Committee
- Local Government Committee
- Rural Development Committee
- Social Justice Committee
- Transport and Environment Committee

Source: The Scottish Parliament.

Accountability

The mechanisms of accountability operating in the Scottish Parliament appear to have real clout. There is a willingness to put down questions and these can be received even when the Parliament itself is in recess. However, there are gaps in the extent to which Scottish MSPs can investigate policy. For example, UK ministers have treated it as a matter of discretion as to whether they would appear before Scottish parliamentary committees.

Equal opportunities

In one respect the Scottish Parliament was very different from its Westminster equivalent. During the period of the Convention there had been sustained pressure for enhanced representation for women in any new legislature. The Women's Co-ordination Group spearheaded this pressure, which in turn led to an electoral agreement that for the first Parliament equal numbers of men and women would be fielded in winnable seats. The recruitment of a very large number of female candidates by Labour was achieved through a formal **twinning** mechanism and the SNP's recruitment of

twinning Device of pairing constituencies and requiring that, in at least one of the two, a woman candidate be selected.

a high percentage (43 per cent) of female candidates meant that the number of female legislators in the 1999 Parliament was very high. However, there were no ethnic minority members. In the Scottish Parliament elected in 2003, there was again a strong female contingent but no ethnic minority representation.

Participation and public access

From its inception the Scottish Parliament wished to be more accessible and innovative in the way it interacted with the public. It promoted this goal partly by an imaginative use of new technology, and partly by encouraging a more welcoming approach to visitors.

The legislative process itself is shorter than that at Westminster and involves three stages (see box 12.4). Although it was intended that the Parliament should avoid the executive dominance of Westminster, in practice the legislative agenda was very much controlled by the government. Individual MSPs have seemed reluctant to promote their own legislation, despite their power to lodge two private members' bills each per session. There have been some examples of robust MSP initiative, including Scottish Socialist MSP Tommy Sheridan's bill to reform debt recovery and Green MSP Robin Harper's organic farming bill.

The bureaucracy

The organization of the Home Civil Service remains integrated for England, Scotland and Wales and was made a reserved matter in the 1998 Scotland Act. As such, the UK prime minister, not the first minister of Scotland, formally exercises power over senior appointments to serve the Scottish executive. In practice, the informal situation allows the system to be responsive to Scotland's needs and there is as yet no evidence of real tension in the arrangement. Nevertheless, pressure has developed for the Scottish executive to have greater say over these senior appointments and to devolve the organization of the civil service in Scotland to Edinburgh. Although this has not yet happened, demands for an organizational separation of the Scottish civil service seem likely to increase.

A new Scottish agenda?

Opinion differs as to how far Scotland has developed its own new political agenda. In many respects Scottish politics since devolution has been remarkably routine, although on a few issues such as student finance and care for the elderly there has been a willingness to depart from the London line. There was also a very different campaign over the abolition of fox hunting and on the question of repealing the ban on discussion of homosexuality in schools.

Greater proximity to the Scottish population has undoubtedly made the Scottish Parliament more responsive to public opinion than Westminster can be. There is enhanced scope for pressure group activity, especially since the legislative process involves pre-legislative scrutiny. Pressure groups themselves, already often organized separately in Scotland, have adapted to the transfer of power to Edinburgh by

Box 12.4   The legislative process in Scotland

Most bills follow the three-stage process described below.

Stage 1

Initially, a bill is referred to the relevant subject committee (known as 'the lead committee') and, if it includes provision to make subordinate legislation, to the Subordinate Legislation Committee for consideration. The lead committee may take evidence at this stage. Other committees may be involved, such as Equal Opportunities or Finance, plus any other subject committee with an interest. These feed back into the lead committee and their views are included in the report.

Once the lead committee has reported on the bill, the Parliament itself considers the general principles as well. Then the Parliament decides whether these principles are agreed to. This decision is taken in light of the lead committee's report.

The bill may be referred back to the lead committee for a further report on the principles of all, or any part, of the bill before the Parliament makes its decision. More evidence may be taken at this stage.

If the Parliament does agree to the general principles, then the bill proceeds to stage 2. If Parliament does not agree, the bill falls and ceases to progress at this stage.

Stage 2

In this stage the bill receives more detailed 'line-by-line' consideration, either

- entirely by the lead committee, or
- entirely by a committee of the whole Parliament, or
- entirely by a parliamentary committee or committees other than the lead committee, or
- partly by the lead committee and partly by
  - a committee of the whole Parliament or
  - a parliamentary committee or committees other than the lead committee.

Each schedule, long title to and section of the bill is considered separately in stage 2, when amendments may be proposed and made.

Amendments may be made that would insert or substantially alter any provisions to confer powers to make delegated legislation. If that is the case, then the amended bill is referred to the Subordinate Legislation Committee for its consideration and report.

Stage 3

The amended bill is then considered by the Parliament, which can further consider and make amendments to its provisions. The Parliament then debates and decides whether the bill, in this final form, should be passed. At least a quarter of all MSPs must vote (whether 'for', 'against' or 'abstain').

At this point, up to half the sections of the bill may be referred back for further stage 2 consideration by the relevant committee or committees. On the bill's return to the Parliament after this, further amendments may be made only to its referred-back provisions.

The Parliament then considers and decides whether to approve the bill.

Once a bill has been passed or approved, it is then submitted by the presiding officer to the sovereign for royal assent. On receiving royal assent a bill becomes an Act of the Scottish Parliament.

Source: Scottish Parliament FactFile, http://www.scottish.parliament.uk/welcoming_you/ff3.htm#bill

directing additional resources there. Clearly also, many of the innovations of the Scottish Parliament, including its use of the Internet and information technology, are designed to make citizens feel closer to their political institutions. Indeed, analysts of the new Scottish Parliament have suggested that it has much to teach the Westminster Parliament. How far these institutions have gained legitimacy in the eyes of the Scottish public is a more difficult question to answer. Opinion polls suggest a degree of cynicism about the Scottish Parliament, but at the same time there is little support for a return to the pre-1999 position. On the other hand, the 2003 elections with their low turnout underlined the extent to which Edinburgh's politicians would have to struggle to maintain popular enthusiasm for the devolution project.

The elections of 2003 marked a new stage in the evolution of Scotland's devolved system of government and exposed difficult inter-party divisions. Although Labour and the Liberal Democrats remained the key partners in the coalition process, it took nine days to reach an agreement. In the partnership agreement for the 2003–7 Parliament, Labour conceded that proportional representation for local elections would be introduced by 2007, a highly unpalatable change for Labour which is likely to result in further erosion of its political strength in Scotland. The Liberal Democrats in turn accepted Labour's ideas for coping with youth crime. Scotland's politics will, it seems, continue increasingly to diverge from those of the rest of the United Kingdom.

Wales

Wales was first annexed to England in 1282, when Edward I conquered the country. The formal consolidation of that conquest was the work of the early Tudors, Henry VII and Henry VIII. The integration of Wales into the Tudor state was consolidated by two major Acts of 1536 and 1542 – measures which also marked the beginning of a long conflict between the English and the Welsh cultures. The assertion of English superiority was enshrined in the provision in these Acts that forbade the use of the Welsh language in administration.

Between the Tudor period and the onset of the industrial revolution in the nineteenth century, the relationship between Wales and England was relatively harmonious. The subordination of the principality was accepted and it was only with the changes engendered by industrial development that there emerged a new sense of Welsh identity. Yet the industrial revolution, while it forged a new Welsh consciousness, created other divisions in Welsh society. The divisions – which turned on cultural and linguistic issues – created an ambiguity about Welsh nationalism and identity that lasted into the twenty-first century and made devolution for Wales much more problematic than devolution for Scotland.

From the nineteenth century there can be seen two distinct patterns of politics and two traditions in Wales. On the one hand there was the radical and nonconformist Wales, which was for so long a bastion of the old Liberal Party. Its adherents became increasingly protective of the distinctive Welsh identity as expressed above all in the survival of the Welsh language, which was still the mother tongue of a substantial portion of the country. (The 1911 census recorded that roughly half the population of Wales was Welsh speaking.) On the other hand, industrialization had encouraged

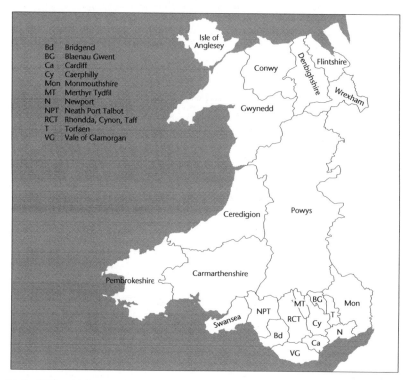

Bd   Bridgend
BG   Blaenau Gwent
Ca   Cardiff
Cy   Caerphilly
Mon   Monmouthshire
MT   Merthyr Tydfil
N   Newport
NPT   Neath Port Talbot
RCT   Rhondda, Cynon, Taff
T   Torfaen
VG   Vale of Glamorgan

Map 12.2   Wales: Unitary authorities.

emigration from England to Wales, where the coal mines and the factories needed workers. Here the bonds of class were more important than cultural ties and this section of Welsh society after 1900 became the preserve of the Labour Party. While the distinctiveness of these traditions should not be exaggerated, there is a difference between south Wales and the lower-lying coastal areas (where most of Welsh industry was concentrated) and the more rural areas of west and north Wales. Less populous and more likely to be Welsh speaking, it is west and north Wales that has traditionally been the more supportive of nationalism.

One important strand in Welsh nationalism has been the concern to protect the distinctive Welsh culture and language. When education was made compulsory in 1870, English was established as the medium for teaching in all state schools and it was only in 1889 that Welsh was allowed to be taught, even as a foreign language, so detrimental was it thought to be to educational achievement. The threat to the survival of the Welsh language mobilized supporters, however, and in 1885 the Welsh Language Society was formed. With the return of a sympathetic Liberal government in 1906, the Board of Education recognized the cultural autonomy of Wales by the formation of a separate Welsh department within it, with an official who had direct access to the minister. In 1907 charters were granted to the National Library of Wales and the National Museum of Wales, which together with the University of Wales have made major contributions to the preservation of the Welsh cultural heritage.

Since the Welsh Language Act 1967, Welsh has enjoyed equality with English in legal proceedings. A Welsh-language board was established in 1988 to advise on the promotion of Welsh and further legislative measures have since been taken to protect the language. Its powers were strengthened under the Welsh Language Act of 1993. The position of the Welsh language today appears to be relatively buoyant. Although between 1911 and 1991 the percentage of the population able to speak Welsh decreased from roughly 50 per cent to roughly 18.5 per cent, observers believe that the decline in the Welsh language has been arrested. It is significant that the 1991 census recorded a growth in the numbers and percentage of young people able to speak Welsh, and it is expected that this figure will increase as one-third of all primary school children now receive their education in Welsh-only or bilingual schools. The distribution of Welsh speaking is also apparently changing, with Welsh being spoken much more evenly across Wales. It was estimated from the 1991 census that over 10 per cent of all Welsh speakers lived within a 25-mile radius of the capital, Cardiff. The 2001 census revealed that 20.5 per cent of the population could speak Welsh and more than 28 per cent were able to understand it (see table 12.3).

Devolution for Wales

The close integration of the administration of Wales and England meant that far fewer separate arrangements were made for the government of Wales than were

Table 12.3   The distribution of Welsh speakers by unitary authority

Authority	Number	Percentage
Blaenau Gwent	1,523	2.5
Bridgend	10,159	10.3
Caerphilly	9,714	6.9
Cardiff	18,080	6.7
Carmarthenshire	89,213	54.3
Ceredigion	36,026	52.5
Conwy	31,443	29.6
Denbighshire	23,294	26.9
Flint	18,399	14.1
Gwynedd	78,733	67.3
Isle of Anglesey	41,240	62.3
Merthyr Tydfil	4,237	9.3
Monmouthshire	1,631	2.3
Neath Port Talbot	23,711	19.3
Newport	2,874	2.4
Pembrokeshire	19,759	18.4
Powys	23,590	20.9
Rhondda, Cynon, Taff	20,042	10.5
Swansea	28,557	13.9
Torfaen	2,128	2.7
Wrexham	15,990	14.5
Vale of Glamorgan	7,755	7.7

Source: Office for National Statistics, 1991 census, www.statistics.gov.uk

made for Scotland prior to devolution. Winston Churchill appointed a Minister for Welsh Affairs in 1955, but it was not until 1964 that a Secretary of State for Wales was created with a seat in the cabinet. Even then Richard Crossman described it as an 'idiotic creation'. There is also a Welsh Grand Committee and a departmental select committee – the Welsh Affairs Committee – which monitors the Welsh Office and relations between it and the Welsh Assembly.

Wales has its own nationalist party. Plaid Cymru (PC), the Welsh National Party, was founded in 1925 from two existing movements, Mudiad Cymreig (the Welsh Movement) and Byddin Ymreolwyr Cymr (the Welsh Home Rule Army) (McAllister, 2001). Although formed primarily as an instrument of cultural promotion, PC became an explicitly political organization in 1932 when it adopted a policy of self-government for Wales. Its impact was small until the 1960s, when a by-election victory in 1966 gave PC its first MP, Gwynfor Evans. Thereafter it gradually gained strength and developed its role as an explicitly nationalist left-of-centre alternative to Labour in Wales. The advent of devolution in 1999 saw PC expand from its base into Labour's heartlands to become the major opposition to a Labour–Liberal Democrat alliance. By 2001 it had 206 council seats, including control of three councils, and a small group of MPs and MEPs. Organizationally, its voluntary membership had grown to 16,000 and its paid staff numbered about 60 (McAllister, 2001). However, in the 2003 elections for the Welsh Assembly, PC's performance weakened and much of the advance it had made into Labour heartlands seemed to have stalled (see tables 12.4 and 12.5).

Table 12.4 Support for Plaid Cymru at general elections, 1970–2001

Election	Candidates	Seats	% of Welsh vote
1970	36	–	11.5
1974 (Feb)	36	2	10.7
1974 (Oct)	36	3	10.8
1979	36	2	8.1
1983	38	2	7.8
1987	38	3	7.3
1992	38	4	8.8
1997	40	4	9.9
2001	40	4	14.3

Source: Butler and Butler (2000), p. 181; Butler and Kavanagh (2002), p. 262; Electoral Commission, http://www.electoralcommission.gov.uk/elections/resultsandtimetables.cfm

Table 12.5 Welsh Assembly elections, 2003

Party	2003	1999	Change
Labour	30	28	+2
Conservatives	11	9	+2
Liberal Democrats	6	6	0
PC	12	17	−5
Independent	1	0	+2
Total	60	60	

Part of PC's dilemma had been how to develop its support beyond the areas of traditional support of Welsh-speaking Wales. This dilemma underlined a wider problem for Welsh nationalism, since its cultural dimension often had the effect of limiting its appeal to those who could not speak Welsh. English speakers in Wales feared they could become second-class citizens if Wales were given greater autonomy. This fear partly explains the massive rejection of the Welsh devolution proposals in 1978 and the tightness of the margin by which the more recent 1998 proposals for Wales were endorsed (see table 2.1, p. 58). The divisive potential of Welsh nationalism has long concerned observers. Even in the post-1945 period, Welsh nationalism has been associated with advocacy of direct action, including campaigns against English home owners in Wales. The advent of devolution initiated a series of inflammatory debates about the Welsh language and immigration into Welsh-speaking areas. In an attempt to circumvent the issue of cultural nationalism, the Assembly has committed itself to a bilingual Wales.

Constitutional powers

The form of devolution given to Wales was much less far-reaching than that devised for Scotland. Whereas Scotland was given a Parliament with primary law-making powers, Wales was given an Assembly with powers over secondary legislation. Moreover, the Welsh National Assembly was established as a corporate body rather than as one in which executive and legislative powers were separated. In theory, the Welsh National Assembly had powers to adapt secondary legislation to Welsh needs and to exercise scrutiny over Welsh administration, but in practice these opportunities remained very dependent on London. Yet developments since 1998 in Wales underline the extent to which the structures and powers accorded in the devolution framework are likely to evolve. The Welsh Assembly has squeezed more influence from the devolution settlement – for example by appointing its own representative in Brussels – and has urged a rethinking of the powers given to the Welsh Assembly by establishing review bodies. The Welsh Assembly has also transformed the conception of Welsh devolution by clarifying the distinct roles of the executive and the legislature and by adopting names which sound more powerful than the ones originally used. For example, the executive now refers to itself as the government of Wales.

The electoral system used for the Welsh Assembly, like that for Scotland, was the alternative member system. In the run-up to the first Assembly elections the position of the Labour Party in Wales was severely undermined by efforts from London to influence (some, such as MP Paul Flynn, would say 'stitch up') the selection of the leader. Partly as a result of this intervention, the first Assembly elections saw Labour emerge as the largest party but without a majority (see table 2.2, p. 58). The formation of a minority government under Alun Michael made the first year of the new executive highly unstable and when Michael's leadership collapsed in January 2000, this was seen not so much as a failure for devolution as the end of an interim stage of a process that had been sidetracked by the London Labour leadership's efforts to control it. Michael was replaced by Rhodri Morgan as first minister, following a no-confidence vote in January 2000. Morgan was seen as very much more independent of the Labour leadership and more responsive to Welsh sentiment than Michael had been. Instead of a minority Labour leadership, Morgan entered a partnership agreement with the

Liberal Democrats in October 2000, an arrangement that had the advantage of providing greater security in relation to the Assembly. As in Scotland, coalition created its own tensions as a result of inter-party differences on policy, though arguably Labour in Wales was more suspicious of the Liberal Democrat agenda, especially its desire for proportional representation, than in Scotland.

Formal coalition meant that, as in Scotland, the administration in Wales was more likely to develop its own distinctive policy agenda, which risked conflict with White-hall. Indeed, one example of a major policy clash between Cardiff and Whitehall came in mid-2002 when the Welsh Assembly unanimously voted to follow the Scottish example and fund free personal care for the elderly out of taxation. Other conflicts and divergences occurred over the Welsh Assembly's decision to abandon key stage one educational tests for 7-year-olds, over the introduction of foundation hospitals and over PFI. Not surprisingly, relations between Cardiff and the Welsh Office have not been particularly warm in the period since Alun Michael was removed from office.

The coalition agreement between Labour and the Liberal Democrats in Wales was obtained by a commitment to two reviews of the Assembly's powers (one internal, one external) and by an examination by the Sunderland Commission of the local government electoral system in Wales.

The internal review was chaired by Lord Elis-Thomas. The independent review of powers was established under the chairmanship of Lord Richards of Ammanford and, although not due to report until 2003, has clearly placed the whole operation of the Welsh system of devolution on the political agenda. Specifically, it is expected that the Welsh Assembly's lack of primary law-making powers and tax-varying authority will be re-examined in a way which exposes the fragility of the argument for denying Cardiff what has been given to Edinburgh.

The problems with the Sunderland Commission (which reported on the local government electoral system in July 2002) relate more directly to party self-interest since Labour fears electoral reform at the local level will further damage its position. The Commission took a broad view of its mandate to examine the working of local democracy. It was especially concerned about the high number of uncontested local elections in Wales, which meant that in 1999, 13 per cent of the Welsh population had no opportunity to vote at all. The Commission also found low levels of interest in, and information about, local government in Wales. To cure this situation, a majority of the Commission recommended changes to the electoral system, including lowering the voting age to 16 and a switch from FPTP to STV in time for the local elections of 2008.

Any recommendation for a switch to proportional representation at the local level is bound to be highly controversial because it further threatens Labour's crumbling hegemony in Wales. The Labour spring conference in 2002 unanimously adopted a report rejecting any change to the local government electoral system. Rhodri Morgan himself incurred hostility from his Labour supporters in the Assembly by even proceeding with consultations on the Sunderland Report.

Even without formal changes to the powers of the Welsh National Assembly, Cardiff has been learning how to squeeze power for itself. The Welsh Assembly's determined exploitation of its powers illustrates how the framework of devolution can be adapted and how it may operate in a manner different from what was originally envisaged. Of course, part of the push to claim more powers for the Assembly is a response to claims from PC that the whole scheme is flawed. Thus PC's leader Iuean

Wyn Jones (who replaced Dafydd Wigley) frequently argues that devolution as devised for Wales is inadequate for its needs. He branded the Assembly a failure and attacked Labour for trying to run Wales like a county council (*Guardian*, 20 September 2002). Jones demanded enhanced powers for the Assembly by the time of the 2007 election. Indeed, in October 2002, Rhodri Morgan himself admitted that many voters were still cynical about the Assembly and that it was hard to sell its achievements to the public (*Guardian*, 14 October 2002). Interestingly, given the tiny margin of support for the Assembly in the referendum, Wales appears to have warmed to the institution. Thus a poll taken in late 2002 suggested that support for the Assembly had strengthened since devolution, with support for direct rule falling from 40 per cent to 23 per cent over the five years since 1997. At the same time, however, the poll found low levels of knowledge about the National Assembly and a continuing scepticism about its importance as a political body (*Guardian*, 18 December 2002). These findings suggest that, although there is not strong enthusiasm for the Assembly, it – like its Scottish equivalent – is unlikely to be dismantled.

The 2003 elections saw, as mentioned earlier, a weakening of the position of PC and a determination by Rhodri Morgan to lead Labour in a government by itself, even though its overall majority was only one. Although this course is likely to provide difficulties in places, the decision to govern alone was made easier by the election of a leading PC member as President of the Assembly and by the retirement of some dissident Labour MWAs. The decision also avoided incurring the wrath of Morgan's own party as a result of compromise with the Liberal Democrats, along the lines of the Scottish coalition agreement, to move towards proportional representation at the local level.

Northern Ireland

Northern Ireland presented the greatest problem for the government's devolution strategy in the late 1990s, not least because of the deep social and political divisions and the persistence of armed conflict in the province. Northern Ireland had indeed provided a model for Scottish and Welsh devolution since for much of the twentieth century, following the partition of Ireland and the Government of Ireland Act of 1920, it operated an extensive form of self-government within the United Kingdom. However, although that earlier legislation was part of an attempt by the British government to solve the problem of Ireland's clashing identities and conflict-ridden politics, as a strategy it did not work because the devolution empowered only one of Northern Ireland's two warring communities. The 1920 legislation (which established a 26-member Senate and a 52-member House of Commons) thus failed to address the problem of the minority nationalist community, which would have preferred to belong to a united Ireland.

Enduring community conflict

Northern Ireland's bitter tensions have a long history. Although Ireland had been governed as part of the UK since 1800, the population of Ireland by the end of the

Map 12.3 Northern Ireland: Districts.

nineteenth century consisted of three distinct cultural groups. The first was a native population marked by its adherence to Roman Catholicism and a Gaelic cultural heritage. The attitude of this community towards the other elements of the population was one of alienation and hostility, since it regarded the settlers as colonists, the machinery of rule from Westminster as illegitimate, and the goal of true Irish men and women as independence. This group provided the backbone of the Irish nationalist movement, though not by any means all of its leaders.

The second significant group within Ireland at the turn of the nineteenth century was the Anglo-Irish component, which had settled in Ireland from the sixteenth century and taken over its estates. This group was culturally distinct both from the native Irish and from the mainland population. Although it was Protestant by religion, many members of the Anglo-Irish community identified more with Ireland than with England. The Anglo-Irish community was responsible for much of the flowering of intellectual activity in late nineteenth-century Ireland and was a source of agitation for home rule. Not surprisingly, many of this community remained even after the Treaty of 1921 had established an independent Irish state. The distinctive features of this community slowly eroded with independence.

The final cultural entity in Ireland's triangle of conflict was the group that had settled primarily in Ulster, the north-east corner of the country. Although Protestant by religion, this group had Scottish origins and adhered to the Presbyterian faith rather than the Church of Ireland (the Anglican church in Ireland). This group developed and was rooted in the industrialized parts of the country, which depended upon shipbuilding, textiles and tobacco. Irish nationalism and the demand for home rule posed a massive threat to the cultural identity, political sentiments and economic status of this group.

There was little sympathy or interaction between these three groups. Religion was the badge of their distinctiveness, but there were cultural cleavages that went far beyond confessional differences. Indeed, it is worth underlining that, although the contemporary divisions in Northern Ireland are sometimes seen as religious in origin, the conflicting political identities reflect a range of loyalties. Thus while 'Protestant' and 'Catholic' may be useful shorthand for capturing one dimension of the communal conflicts, **loyalist** and **republican** or unionist and nationalist are in many ways more apposite labels for distinguishing between the communities.

Two further complications to the communal conflict in Ireland should be noted. First, there was the question of relations with mainland Britain and the attitude of the British government itself to the different groups in Northern Ireland. Just as the three communities within Ireland as a whole were isolated from each other, so there was a comparable distance, both intellectual and social, between Ireland's inhabitants and the rest of the UK. Some links existed between landed families of England and Ireland and there were institutional links between Ulster Unionism and the Conservative Party until 1974. Yet Irish society and, within it, Northern Ireland society remained tangibly different from the rest of the UK. As the British government has adopted a role as a neutral player in the peace process, all groups in Northern Ireland have become distanced from London. And popular sentiment within Britain has become less supportive of Northern Ireland's place in the UK.

By 2001 a MORI poll found that two-fifths (41 per cent) of Britons believed that Northern Ireland should be joined with the Irish Republic, while only a quarter (26 per cent) said it should continue as part of the United Kingdom. The same poll also found that while 3 per cent of Britons blamed the unionists for the current problems in the Northern Ireland peace process and 5 per cent blamed the Republicans, the vast majority (64 per cent) blamed both sides equally. Such findings underline a long-term shift in British opinion towards Irish unity, as well as an alienation from the affairs of Northern Ireland on the part of the mainland.

A second complicating factor in the Northern Irish situation has been the fragmentation of the political parties claiming to represent the loyalist and nationalist communities. Although the division between nationalist and loyalist is still the major cleavage in Northern Ireland, there is now significant political fragmentation *within* the two communities. The splintering of unionist political organization is especially marked and reflects profound differences over tactics and strategies. Unionist control of Northern Ireland politics for much of the twentieth century was based on the solidarity of the Protestant population's support for the Ulster Unionist Party (UUP). From the 1970s that solidarity has eroded and the more fundamentalist and uncompromising Democratic Unionist Party (DUP) under Reverend Ian Paisley's leadership has gained at its expense. In addition, the UUP has experienced a series of smaller splits and factions in its ranks (see box 12.5).

loyalist Term used of those within the Northern Ireland population (essentially the Protestant population) who wish the province to remain part of the United Kingdom and who are loyal to the Crown.

republican Term used of those within Northern Ireland who want the province to cease being an integral part of the United Kingdom and become part of a united Ireland. While most Republicans are Roman Catholics, by no means all Roman Catholics in Northern Ireland are Republicans.

Box 12.5   The political parties of Northern Ireland

General

Political competition in Northern Ireland revolves around the division between the unionist and nationalist blocs, although there are a number of parties that try to appeal across the two communities. An equally important dynamic in contemporary Northern Ireland politics, however, is the competition *within* the two communities.

On the unionist side the more fundamentalist DUP under Rev. Ian Paisley's leadership has eaten into the UUP vote. In addition, smaller unionist parties have formed to express their own version of unionism. On the nationalist side the SDLP, which is a constitutional nationalist party, is in competition with Sinn Fein, the more radical republican grouping, which has a long association with armed conflict and violence in Northern Ireland. The competition *within* communities underlines the differences of ideology and political tactics in Northern Ireland.

The table is a simplified guide to the parties currently active in Northern Ireland politics. It shows the 2001 general election vote and the 2003 Assembly election vote. FPTP is used in general elections, while Assembly elections use STV.

Party	Share of vote in 2001 general election (%)	Share of vote in 2003 Assembly election (%)
Unionist Parties		
ULSTER UNIONIST PARTY (UUP) (1905–)		
Major unionist grouping formed to resist home rule. Operated in alliance with the Conservative Party until the imposition of direct rule in 1972. Cohesive but moderate group defending the position of Northern Ireland in the United Kingdom. Differences of style, tactics and policy – especially over power sharing – caused the party's support to fragment from the 1970s. Led by David Trimble.	26.8	22.7
DEMOCRATIC UNIONIST PARTY (DUP) (1970–)		
Paisley's more fundamentalist, anti-Catholic party firmly opposed to any deals with nationalists. Strongly opposed to Belfast Agreement.	22.5	25.7
UKUP (1995)		
Small unionist party founded and led by Robert McCartney. Opposed to the Belfast Agreement.	2	1

Box 12.5 *Continued*

Party	Share of vote in 2001 general election (%)	Share of vote in 2003 Assembly election (%)
PROGRESSIVE UNIONIST PARTY (PUP) (1977–)		
Party established to mobilize working-class loyalist vote and often linked to paramilitary organizations such as the Ulster Volunteer Force (UVF).	0.6	1
NORTHERN IRELAND UNIONIST PARTY (NIUP) (1999–)		
Group formed by four of five UKUP MLAs. Believes in principled unionism. Opposes Belfast Agreement. Led by Cedric Wilson.	0.2	n/a
UNITED UNIONIST ASSEMBLY PARTY (1998–)		
Founded as an anti-Belfast Agreement party by the three members of the new Assembly elected as Independent Unionists in 1998 on an anti-Agreement ticket. Leader is Denis Watson MLA.	0.3	n/a
Nationalist Parties		
SINN FEIN (1905–)		
Major Republican grouping founded to achieve an independent Ireland and frequently linked to the Irish Republican Army (IRA). Since 2001 the larger nationalist party. Led by Gerry Adams since the 1980s.	21.7	23.5
SOCIAL AND DEMOCRATIC LABOUR PARTY (SDLP) (1969–)		
Party formed 1969 to provide a new vehicle for the mobilization of the Catholic/nationalist vote. Employs constitutional methods and rejects violence. Formerly largest nationalist party but now overtaken by Sinn Fein.	21	17.0
WORKERS PARTY		
Party with origins and ties to old IRA. Known as 'Republican Clubs' for a long time.	0.5	n/a

(Continues)

Box 12.5 *Continued*

Party	Share of vote in 2001 general election (%)	Share of vote in 2003 Assembly election (%)
Cross-confessional/Non-sectarian Parties		
ALLIANCE PARTY OF NORTHERN IRELAND (APN) (1970–)		
Largest 'cross-community' party in Northern Ireland. Led since October 2001 by David Ford.	3.6	3.7
CONSERVATIVE PARTY OF NORTHERN IRELAND (1989–)		
Although the major British parties do not formally organize in Northern Ireland, in 1989 popular pressure urged the establishment of a Conservative Party there. A split over the Belfast Agreement saw the national party supporting it and the grassroots opposing it.	0.3	< 1
NORTHERN IRELAND WOMEN'S COALITION (1996–)		
Fields only women candidates.	0.4	1
GREEN PARTY OF NORTHERN IRELAND (1990–)		
Small party with origins in the former Ecology Party. Environmental politics, linked closely with the Green Party/ Comhaontas Glas in the Republic, who have 2 MEPs and 6 TDs, and also less closely with the Green parties in Scotland, England and Wales.	n/a	< 1

In the nationalist camp there is a split between the Social Democratic Labour Party (SDLP), which was formed in 1969 to provide a new political voice for constitutional nationalists and Catholics within Northern Ireland, and the more radical Sinn Fein. It absorbed much of the support of the nationalist party, which had been paralysed by the border issue (Mulholland, 2002). The SDLP was able to develop a more forward-looking agenda for Northern Ireland as well as new leadership, first under Gerry Fitt and later under the charismatic John Hume. The SDLP adherence to constitutional methods to achieve nationalist objectives pits it against militant nationalist groups (notably Sinn Fein), which have used violence to achieve their goals. Although to some extent that division has been blurred by the latest peace process, the distinction remains highly significant for the respective parties' appeal. It also explains why many unionists find the incorporation of Sinn Fein into government ethically unacceptable.

The government of Ireland from 1800 to 1921

Between the Act of Union of 1800 and the Irish Treaty of 1921, the whole of Ireland was an integral part of the United Kingdom, although the colonization of Ireland had begun long before 1800. By the 1800 Act of Union Irish MPs sat in the House of Commons and representatives of the Irish peerage sat in the House of Lords. The Act of Union with Ireland was modelled in large part on the 1707 Act of Union with Scotland, although Ireland was never accorded the respect and equality granted to Scotland. Indeed, in many ways Ireland was treated very much like a colony. From 1800 to 1921 the formal head of the Irish administration was the Lord Lieutenant, who was responsible to the Home Secretary, who was the official channel of communication with the Crown. The routine administration of Ireland was the responsibility of the Chief Secretary for Ireland, who sat in the House of Commons.

The difficulty of governing Ireland in the nineteenth and early twentieth centuries arose in part from its cultural and political conflicts and the increasingly eloquent and well-organized (and militant) nationalist movement that kept the issue of home rule on the political agenda. Violence then, as now, gave the Irish issue a bloody salience in British politics. There was constant agitation over land, and the emergence of new forms of protest and terrorism (Townshend, 1983). The murder of the newly appointed Chief Secretary for Ireland, Lord Frederick Cavendish, in Dublin in 1882, while repudiated by many nationalists, highlighted the determination of some Irish nationalists to secure independence, whatever the cost. The Irish issue spilled over into Westminster politics, not least because of this threat of violence and because of the disruptive presence there of a large block of Irish National Party MPs. (Their obstructive tactics were one of the reasons for introducing procedural devices such as the guillotine into the House of Commons.)

The spread of Irish nationalism in the later nineteenth century led Liberal British governments to consider home rule for Ireland. From the 1880s the threat of home rule stimulated the Protestants of Ulster to resist any settlement in which they might be left a small minority – no more than 27 per cent – in a country where Catholics were the majority. In 1905 the UUP was formed and in 1912 Ulster's Protestants signed a Solemn League and Covenant in which they pledged to maintain their status within the UK, by force if necessary. Although legislation to introduce home rule was passed by Asquith's Liberal government, it was suspended for the duration of the First World War. By the end of the war, it was clear that only some form of partition offered any hope of a peaceful solution. In 1920 Parliament passed the Government of Ireland Act, which delivered home rule not to a united Ireland but to two separate entities. Northern Ireland was given its own bicameral Parliament in Belfast (**Stormont**). The remaining 26 counties of Ireland were given their own Parliament in Dublin. The borders of Northern Ireland were drawn to maximize its territory, although this entailed bringing into Northern Ireland a population that was not exclusively Protestant. The six counties brought within Northern Ireland were Antrim, Tyrone, Down, Fermanagh, Armagh and Londonderry. Within Northern Ireland itself there was a marked division between the more Protestant east of the country and relatively more Catholic west.

Stormont Site of the devolved Northern Ireland Parliament and administrative offices of the Northern Ireland government.

Although the 1920 legislation was acceptable to the majority Protestant population in Northern Ireland, it was insufficient to meet Irish nationalist demands. Elections to Dublin's first post-1920 Parliament returned a virtually Sinn Fein Republican legislature and those representatives refused to take their seats in a subordinate institution. The southern part of Ireland was then granted independence within the Empire as the Irish Free State. Instead of two comparable devolved Parliaments, there emerged two very different legislatures: one the effective Parliament of a free state, the other a devolved Parliament within the United Kingdom.

The Anglo-Irish Treaty of 1921 occasioned a civil war in Ireland between the pro-treaty faction and the Republicans who refused to accept either partition or dominion status. That civil war raged from 1922 to 1923. In 1949 the Irish Free State became an independent republic outside the Commonwealth. Meanwhile, Northern Ireland had continued to operate the devolved institutions conferred on it by the 1920 Act. The aspiration for a united Ireland was not abandoned by nationalists and by the 1937 revision of its constitution the Irish Republic claimed sovereignty for the whole national territory, by which it meant the whole island of Ireland. This claim enraged Northern Ireland unionists. The Republic of Ireland revoked its constitutional claim to the North as part of the peace process of the late 1990s.

Devolved government in Northern Ireland, 1920–1972

From 1921 until 1972 Northern Ireland operated devolved government. The Northern Ireland Parliament which sat at Stormont and the Northern Ireland government exercised power over a wide range of matters devolved to Northern Ireland under the Government of Ireland Act of 1920. Westminster remained the superior legislature, responsible for all reserved and excepted matters – especially defence, foreign policy and economic policy. Although the broad guidelines of British legislation would usually be paralleled in Northern Ireland, some variations occurred. This arrangement worked relatively smoothly while London was content to ignore the internal politics of Northern Ireland.

The 1920 legislation had attempted to protect the minority community in Northern Ireland by incorporating into it guarantees of equal treatment before the law for both Catholics and Protestants. Specifically, the Act prohibited Stormont from giving any preference, privilege or advantage to or imposing any disability or disadvantage on account of religious belief or religious or ecclesiastical status. Such a prohibition was largely ineffective given the sense of insecurity that many commentators observed in the loyalist community's psychology. What has been called an institutionalized caste system developed in which the Protestant majority acquired a religious, political and cultural dominance in Northern Ireland. That dominance was expressed in symbolism – especially the use of the Union Jack – and in ceremonial and ritual – especially marches and parades – which came to play an important if confrontational role in Ulster's folk culture. Political dominance was maintained by ensuring that the UUP kept a firm and exclusively Protestant grip on political power, including within the Parliament and in the crucial arena of local government which allocated council housing.

The UUP was intricately tied to the structures of Protestant dominance in Northern Ireland, not least because of its close links with the Orange Order, a society founded in 1795 to preserve and promote Protestant culture. The UUP's political advantage was secured by such devices as constituency gerrymandering and the abolition of proportional representation, which had originally been provided for in the 1920 legislation. The Protestant community also enjoyed significant advantages in terms of municipal and private jobs and housing. Indeed, it was seen as a mark of loyalty for Protestant employers to give preference to their own community.

Not surprisingly in these circumstances, much of the nationalist minority denied the legitimacy of the state and its institutions, especially the law-enforcement agencies. The police were overwhelmingly Protestant in composition and they, along with the courts and the magistracy, were viewed by many nationalists as intrinsically biased against them. There thus emerged a pattern of government which would not have been tolerated on the mainland. The virtual insulation of the political system of Northern Ireland from Westminster scrutiny was eloquent testimony to the mainland's weariness with Irish affairs. Ulster MPs who came to Westminster were overwhelmingly unionist and until 1974 they were in formal alliance with the Conservative Party. Few questions were ever asked about the internal affairs of Northern Ireland between 1920 and 1966. Indeed, it was a convention that Northern Irish affairs were not a proper subject of debate in Westminster: from 1923 the Speaker refused to allow parliamentary questions dealing with matters devolved to Stormont. The other aspect of the convention was that Ulster MPs tended to keep a low profile at Westminster, especially since those with substantial political ambitions would pursue them at Stormont rather than at Westminster.

During these years, the fate of Ulster's Catholic minority was thus virtually ignored by London and the nationalist community was politically powerless. Although the Irish Republican Army (IRA) engaged in sporadic terrorist campaigns over the period, its operations were generally contained and had little impact. In the late 1960s, however, new movements began to appear in Ulster's rather stagnant politics. A new form of political campaign emerged, drawing lessons from the civil rights movement in the United States. In demanding greater equality for Catholics in Ulster, this civil rights movement (NICRA) transformed the landscape of Northern Ireland and publicized the issue of discrimination against the nationalist community. It also sparked a new period of intercommunal violence (known as 'the troubles'). The conflict this time was not confined to Northern Ireland but spread onto the mainland of Britain, which after 1968 experienced a series of terrorist attacks on both military and civilian targets.

British troops were sent into Northern Ireland in 1969 in an effort to calm the escalating violence. Although they were initially welcomed by the Catholic community, the army's handling of the situation soon alienated much of the population and created a new support for the **paramilitaries**. At the end of 1969, the IRA split into the Provisional and Official IRA, with the Provisional IRA taking charge of the militant campaign against the British presence in Ulster. On the Protestant side there was a resurgence of paramilitary activity through such groups as the Ulster Defence Force (UDF), Vanguard and the Ulster Volunteer Army (UVA). The presence of British troops

paramilitary groups Umbrella term given to armed groups who regularly engage in terrorist activity. Most widely used in Northern Ireland to refer to the activities of, on the nationalist side, the IRA and its splinter groups and the Irish National Liberation Army (INLA), and, on the loyalist side, a number of groups such as the Ulster Volunteer Force (UVF), which dates from 1912, and the Ulster Defence Association (UDA), which dates from the 1970s.

in Northern Ireland meant that London could not distance itself from Northern Ireland affairs. London's involvement meant that pressure was put on Northern Ireland's government to introduce wide-ranging reforms, although it quickly became apparent that Ulster Unionist politicians could not easily satisfy both the London demand for reform and their own grassroots opinion. By 1972 the British government had become reluctant to allow security policy to be controlled by Stormont when British troops were so heavily involved. The British government's demand that it have sole responsibility for security matters was something that the Northern Ireland government could not accept and the then prime minister of Northern Ireland, Brian Faulkner, resigned. The Stormont Parliament was suspended and direct rule was imposed, thereby ending Northern Ireland's first experiment with devolved government.

Direct rule and the search for a settlement, 1972–1998

The suspension of Stormont marked a turning point in the military and political character of the Northern Ireland problem. The Heath government (1970–4) assumed that direct rule would only be a temporary measure and began the long search for new political institutions that could command the assent of both communities in Northern Ireland. Essentially what this meant was that the new system of devolved government would have to involve the participation of the minority community as well as the majority. It would have to be based in effect on power sharing, not just in the Parliament but also in government. A brief experiment with an ambitious new structure of government for Northern Ireland showed how difficult it would be to find enough agreement to re-establish self-rule.

The 1973 Constitution Act set up a new Northern Irish Assembly based on proportional representation rather than FPTP in a bid to strengthen moderate opinion. The executive was given many domestic but no security functions, and was to be based on power sharing rather than on majority rule. In other words, the executive had to include members of the minority nationalist community. Most controversially of all, the agreement for the future government of Northern Ireland reached at Sunningdale in 1973 provided for a Council of Ireland to take account of the Irish dimension and to facilitate discussion between Dublin, Belfast and London. Provision for a Council of Ireland had been written into the legislation of 1920 as a way of transcending partition; but it had rapidly become a dead letter as partition assumed a permanent rather than a temporary status. Successive Irish governments had always displayed an intense interest in what was happening across the border, but they were themselves divided about how to respond to the resurgence of violence in the North in the late 1960s. UK governments had hitherto resisted the suggestion that Northern Ireland was anything other than a matter of internal British politics. Naturally, Ulster's loyalist community viewed with suspicion any device designed to legitimize the Irish Republic's direct involvement in Northern Ireland politics.

The Sunningdale proposals enacted in the Constitution Act of 1973 split the loyalist Unionist Party. Elections to the new Assembly showed that Brian Faulkner's moderate and pro-power-sharing unionists had won only a slightly smaller portion of the vote – 26.5 per cent – than had the hardline coalition of loyalists, who took 35.4 per cent. The latter group wanted a return to the old-style Stormont. Although the moderate unionists were able to take power in coalition with a group of other parties, pressure from his own party forced Faulkner to resign the leadership of the UUP. Nevertheless, despite its tiny majority of one in the Assembly, it survived for four months before being brought down by a loyalist strike.

After the collapse of the Sunningdale Agreement successive initiatives were explored. However, it was not until the 1985 Anglo-Irish Agreement that real movement in the handling of Northern Irish policy occurred. In a tacit admission of the stalemate that had been reached by trying to advance policy within a purely British framework, the agreement established a new set of institutions that engaged the Republic of Ireland in the process of seeking a solution to Northern Ireland's problems. These institutions – a joint ministerial conference and a secretariat – offered a forum in which the governments of the UK and the Republic of Ireland could discuss Northern Irish and other issues. Although there was no derogation of sovereignty over Northern Ireland and the prime ministers of the two countries accepted that change would only come about with the consent of the majority in Northern Ireland, the involvement of the Republic outraged unionists. There were widespread demonstrations and in December 1985 all 15 MPs at Westminster resigned their seats in protest to provoke a series of by-elections that they hoped would demonstrate constituent opposition to the treaty. All the unionists retained seats except in Newry and Armagh, where Seamus Mallon, an SDLP candidate, was elected.

The operation of the intergovernmental conference (IGC) varied, reflecting the changing mood of Anglo-Irish relations generally. In 1989 a review of the agreement emphasized the need to find some formula for devolved government. Initially this seemed as far away as ever. For nationalists, anything that would allow the majority to dominate the minority was unacceptable. For unionists, anything other than majoritarian democracy was viewed with implacable hostility.

Several factors, however, operated to shift the situation. First, the sickening level of violence against civilians in Northern Ireland and the mainland created unfavourable publicity for the IRA throughout Ireland (see table 12.6). Secondly, although the IRA had not explicitly lost the military campaign, it became apparent that this was a war it could not win. There was renewed pressure from the European Union and, after 1992, from the United States, which encouraged the Sinn Fein leadership to think positively about what might be gained from a renunciation of violence and participation in the political process. And there was growing evidence from 1993 of an understanding between the Sinn Fein leader Gerry Adams and SDLP leader John Hume. There was also some evidence of movement in the unionist camp in the early 1990s as the official UUP displayed more flexibility over power sharing and the Irish dimension. Finally, the Irish government (which had from the 1960s assumed that unification would be too costly an option) had become far more interested in promoting Ireland's new economic achievements than in defending what looked like outdated nationalism. Both the UK and the Irish governments thus could make common cause over the Northern Irish issue to the extent of jointly imposing a new approach.

In 1993 John Major and Albert Reynolds seized the initiative and issued the so-called 'Downing Street Declaration'. The declaration was notable for two reasons. First, it reaffirmed the determination of the British and Irish prime ministers to work together for peace in Northern Ireland. Secondly, it declared that the British government had no 'selfish or strategic' reason for staying in Northern Ireland.

Table 12.6 Deaths in the conflict in Northern Ireland, 1969–2001

Year	Republican	Loyalist	British	Others	Total
1969	3	3	10	0	16
1970	17	2	5	2	26
1971	98	21	45	7	171
1972	267	112	86	14	479
1973	132	86	32	3	253
1974	147	124	19	4	294
1975	125	121	8	6	260
1976	154	116	16	9	295
1977	75	27	8	1	111
1978	61	10	10	0	81
1979	102	17	2	0	121
1980	51	14	9	6	80
1981	70	12	18	13	113
1982	83	14	12	1	110
1983	61	10	12	2	85
1984	48	7	12	2	69
1985	48	4	5	0	57
1986	40	15	5	1	61
1987	71	15	10	2	98
1988	70	23	11	0	104
1989	54	18	3	0	75
1990	52	19	10	0	81
1991	50	40	6	0	96
1992	40	38	10	1	89
1993	38	49	0	1	88
1994	25	37	1	1	64
1995	7	2	0	0	9
1996	13	3	1	1	18
1997	5	15	1	0	21
1998	36	17	1	1	55
1999	4	3	0	1	8
2000	4	14	0	1	19
2001	3	12	0	1	16
Total	**2,054**	**1,020**	**368**[a]	**81**	**3,523**

[a] Includes 5 killings by Irish Republic's forces.

Source: Malcolm Sutton, An Index of Deaths from the Conflict in Ireland, http://cain.ulst.ac.uk/sutton/book/index.html

The Downing Street Declaration appeared to offer Sinn Fein a place in any negotiations about Northern Ireland's future so long as there was a complete renunciation of violence and evidence that the IRA had moved to place its weapons beyond use. Although warmly welcomed by Ireland and many other countries, the declaration was treated with caution by Sinn Fein, which kept asking for clarification of its meaning. Finally, in July 1994, the Downing Street Declaration was rejected by Sinn Fein. However, intervention by an American delegation seemed to put the peace process back on track, though with a number of question marks hanging in the air. In August 1994 the IRA made what it claimed was a permanent renunciation of violence, a move that was followed in October by a similar renunciation of violence by the Combined Loyalist Military Command.

The period between August 1994 and May 1997 saw the momentum for a settlement building, although it was always uncertain how far Sinn Fein would cooperate in the process, or indeed how far it would be trusted by the unionists. Two framework documents published in 1995 provided the impetus for further discussions about decommissioning and about all-party talks to see if a basis for devolved government could be found. In 1996 elections were held to produce representatives for the Forum for Peace and Reconciliation. These elections underlined the fragmented nature of Ulster politics. The unionists were divided between the UUP's 30 seats and the DUP's 24 seats. On the nationalist side, the SDLP gained 21 seats while Sinn Fein polled strongly with 17 seats. Smaller parties were also represented. The cross-community APNI gained 7 seats and the UKUP gained 3 seats (Mulholland, 2002).

The elections to the Peace Forum had taken place against the background of renewed violence, both in Northern Ireland and on the mainland. Little had been achieved to convince unionists of the IRA's intention to disarm and disband. Accordingly, when the talks opened in June 1996, Sinn Fein as the political wing of the IRA was excluded. Yet understandable as this exclusion was, it limited the prospect for a comprehensive settlement. A new turning point occurred with the Labour election victory of 1997. Multi-party talks were resumed and included Sinn Fein, even though there was no prior commitment to the decommissioning of weapons by the IRA. After a series of intensive talks, a breakthrough agreement was finally reached in 1998.

The Belfast/Good Friday Agreement

The agreement reached by the various parties in Northern Ireland was a complex and balanced package which had three strands. Strand one related to new institutional structures of devolved government in Northern Ireland, specifically the establishment of a 108-member Northern Ireland Assembly elected by proportional representation and an executive. Strand two established a council between Britain and Ireland. Strand three established a 'Council of the Isles', which was intended to bring together the several parts of the United Kingdom with the Irish Republic. An essential part of the package was the decommissioning of all weapons in paramilitary hands, which was to be effected by May 2000. To create support for these initiatives, efforts were made to meet long-standing grievances of the nationalist community. Some political prisoners were released and controversial reforms of the policing and legal system were set in motion. The new agreement was endorsed by referendums on both sides of the border in May 1998, with 71.1 per cent voting 'yes' in Northern Ireland (see table 2.3, p. 60) and 94.4 per cent approving in the Republic, which had been given the opportunity to register its view on the package.

Although there was initially support from both communities within Northern Ireland for the agreement, the unionist community viewed many aspects of it as threatening. It particularly objected to the release of prisoners whom it regarded as convicted murderers, and many resented the dismantling of the Royal Ulster Constabulary and the creation of the Police Service of Northern Ireland following the Patten Report. Not surprisingly, unionist support for the Belfast Agreement has ebbed as the IRA has failed to deliver on decommissioning. By 2002, support among unionists for the agreement had dropped to a mere one in three.

Elections to the Northern Ireland Assembly

Communal registration of the members was a requirement because many legislative measures needed cross-community agreement. The executive was also cross-community and was constructed by nominates from the four largest Assembly parties in turn using the d'Hondt method, which is a method of allocating seats in proportional electoral systems using party lists. As a result, the make-up of the executive included not merely Ulster Unionist and SDLP members but also Sinn Fein members. This was the first time Sinn Fein had served in government within Northern Ireland and two members of the executive, Martin McGuinness and Gerry Adams, controversially took the education and health portfolios. The DUP, which had rejected the Good Friday Agreement, abstained. As a result of the process of executive nomination, David Trimble of the UUP and Seamus Mallon of the SDLP became first minister and deputy first minister designate, respectively. In addition there were six unionist ministers and six nationalist ones.

Although power was transferred in December 1999, David Trimble's position remained extremely fragile. As noted earlier, the cohesion of Ulster Unionism had been eroding since the 1970s. Although Ulster Unionism has always contained a number of disparate strands, self-interest and most of all awareness of what it was against had kept the party together. The rise of Paisleyism and the formation of the DUP in 1970 created political competition at the heart of unionism. The DUP is more extreme than the UUP, and its vehement anti-Catholic and anti-ecumenical stance strongly appeals to more fundamentalist Protestants.

The background of sectarian violence and political conflict, as well as the very different structures of devolved government in Northern Ireland, have inevitably had an impact on what devolved government could deliver. The impression that (with the possible exception of transport and education) neither the Assembly nor the executive were ready to get to grips with the substantive problems of Northern Ireland, while in some respects inevitable, did not enhance the authority of the devolved system. As a result, public support for the new institutions was lukewarm. The suspension of devolved government at the end of 2002 was not greatly regretted by unionists, although it is recognized that direct rule is not ideal as a long-term solution. In the Assembly elections of 2003, the DUP polled more votes than the UUP.

The wider society

Northern Ireland remains a deeply divided society and one that has endured a degree of personal injury and violence. Even if that violence ends tomorrow, the society will have to live with its legacy of intercommunity distrust. The relationship between the unionist and nationalist communities has in some ways become more tense since the 1980s. Although there has been some demographic movement so that the balance between Protestants and Catholics is closer now than it was in 1991 (the 2001 census reported 737,412 Catholics to 895,377 Protestants out of a total population of 1,685,264), there is no evidence to support the view that Catholics will soon become a majority in Northern Ireland. Of course, even if they did, that would not by itself resolve the problem. Poll data suggest that approximately 20 per cent of the Catholic community would not wish to join the Republic if that were an immediate option, a figure that underlines both the complexity of opinion within the two communities and the volatility of political preferences between possible political solutions. The Good Friday Agreement broke a long stalemate and ushered in a period of rapid political change, forcing at least a partial reassessment of its future. Yet that process has by no means been completed, and managing the delicate situation in Northern Ireland is likely to remain on the British government's agenda for a long time to come.

Conclusions

The period since 1997 has seen the establishment of two distinct sub-governmental systems in Scotland and Wales. Although Scotland's is certainly more developed and powerful than that of Wales, it is doubtful if the discrepancy between the two will long survive. All the pressures within Wales point towards greater responsibility for the Assembly. Northern Ireland, on the other hand, remains a contested part of the British state and one where effective long-term solutions are difficult to envisage. Perhaps the only short-term solution is, as it has so often been, direct rule from London. In the meantime, Edinburgh and Cardiff have to some extent shown Ulster's politicians the prize that can be theirs if they can reach agreement. On a more general level, the structures of the British state have been decentralized and London has to live with a more fragmented and divergent policy system.

How far the devolved institutions have succeeded in establishing support for themselves and legitimacy among their own populations is a matter of debate. Part of the purpose of establishing devolved systems of government was of course to head off the challenge from separatist nationalist parties in Scotland and Wales, the SNP and PC. The second set of elections to the devolved Parliament and Assembly in 2003 did indeed see a decline in support for the nationalist parties, and in the SNP the emergence of bitter controversy over John Swinney's strategy. Yet the combination of low turnout and indications from other poll data suggests that the working of devolution thus far has earned only faint praise and interest. On the other hand, any suggestion that there should be a return to the status quo ante 1998 receives little support. The 2003 elections pointed up one further feature of the systems of devolution, which is the fluidity inherent in the system. Thus while Labour and the Liberal Democrats could put together a working partnership in both Scotland and Wales on the basis of the 1999 elections, there is no guarantee that such a coalition will always be wanted or possible. Devolved politics entail accepting different patterns in different arenas at different times. To that extent, devolution is bound to change the culture of the British political system as well as its institutional structures.

Key Questions

1 How stable is the devolution settlement?
2 What impact have the devolved governments had on their own societies?
3 Has devolution solved the problem of nationalism within the British Isles?

 Further Reading

Valuable general works on devolution include V. Bogdanor, *Devolution in the United Kingdom* (Oxford: Oxford University Press, 2001) and H. Elcock and M. Keating, *Remaking the Union: Devolution and British Politics in the 1990s* (London: Frank Cass, 1998). Reference may also be made to T. Nairn, *After Britain* (London: Granta, 2000) and to Arthur Aughey, *Nationalism, Devolution and the Challenge to the United Kingdom State* (London: Pluto, 2001). V. Bogdanor, 'Devolution: Decentralisation or disintegration?', *Political Quarterly*, 70: 2 (1999) provides an acute analysis, while general issues connected with devolution are also covered in J. Bradbury and J. Mitchell, 'Devolution and territorial politics, stability, uncertainty and crisis', *Parliamentary Affairs*, 55: 2 (2002).

There are two lively accounts of Scottish politics by Brian Taylor, *The Road to the Scottish Parliament* and *Scotland's Parliament: Triumph and Disaster* (Edinburgh: Edinburgh University Press, 2002). (University of Edinburgh Press coverage of Scottish devolution can also be found in Year Zero.) See also N. Bonney, 'Scottish devolution: What lies beneath?', *Political Quarterly*, 73: 2 (2002).

There are excellent historical studies of Wales, including K. O. Morgan's *Rebirth of a Nation: Wales 1880–1980* (Oxford: Oxford University Press, 1981) and D. Wigley's *Working for Wales* (Caernarfon: Welsh Academic Press, 2001). The referendum is covered in L. Andrews, *Wales Says Yes: The Inside Story of the Yes for Wales Referendum* (Bridgend, Wales: Seren, 1999). Gwynfor Evans, *For the Sake of Wales: Memoirs of Gwynfor Evans* (Caernarfon: Welsh Academic Press, 2001) provides a fascinating insider account. Laura McAllister, *Plaid Cymru: The Emergence of a Political Party* (Glasgow: Seren, 2001) is a full-length study of PC. See also her 'Changing the landscape? The wider political lessons from recent elections in Wales', *Political Quarterly*, 71: 2 (2000). M. Laffin, A. Thomas and A. Webb, 'Intergovernmental relations after devolution: The National Assembly for Wales', *Political Quarterly*, 71: 2 (2000) and D. Griffiths, 'Writings on the margins: Welsh politics', *British Journal of Politics and International Studies*, 2: 1 (2000) present valuable analyses.

There is an enormously rich literature on Northern Ireland. John Whyte's *Interpreting Northern Ireland* (Oxford: Oxford University Press, 1990) is an excellent starting point and should be supplemented with John McGarry and Brendan O'Leary, *Explaining Northern Ireland* (Oxford: Oxford University Press, 1995). Roy Foster, *Modern Ireland: 1600–1972* (Harmondsworth: Penguin, 1989) is highly stimulating, as is the same author's *The Oxford Illustrated History of Ireland* (Oxford: Oxford University Press, 2000). Marc Mulholland's *Northern Ireland: A Very Short Introduction* (Oxford: Oxford University Press, 2002) is a shorter but incisive recent overview.

Other useful accounts on Northern Ireland include P. Dixon, *Northern Ireland: The Politics of War and Peace* (Basingstoke: Palgrave, 2001) and Paul Arthur, *Special Relationships: Britain, Ireland and the Northern Ireland Problem* (Belfast: Blackstaff, 2000). There are detailed studies of Unionism in David Hume, *The Ulster Unionist Party 1972–1992* (Lurgan: Ulster Society, 1996) and in James Loughlin, *Ulster Unionism and British National Identity since 1885* (London: Pinter, 1995). Steve Bruce, *The Red Hand: Protestant Paramilitaries in Northern Ireland* (Oxford: Oxford University Press, 1992) examines loyalism, while his *God*

Save Ulster: The Religion and Politics of Paisleyism (Oxford: Oxford University Press, 1986) considers Paisleyism.

There are only a few studies of the SDLP. Ian McAllister's *The Northern Ireland Social and Democratic Unionist Party: Political Opposition in a Divided Society* (Basingstoke: Macmillan, 1977) is still worth reading, however, and may be supplemented with Paul Routledge, *John Hume: A Biography* (London: HarperCollins, 1998).

The IRA is covered in Henry Patterson, *The Politics of Illusion* (London: Lawrence and Wishart, 1997). Journalistic accounts include D. McKittrick, *Endgame: The Search for Peace in Northern Ireland* (Belfast: Blackstaff, 1994). Mike Morrissey and Marie Smyth, *Northern Ireland After the Good Friday Agreement: Victims' Grievance and Blame* (London: Pluto, 2002) looks at the legacy of the troubles in a broad social perspective. Shorter articles which are invaluable include G. Evans and B. O'Leary, 'Northern Irish voters and the British–Irish Agreement', *Political Quarterly*, 71: 1 (2000).

Finally, anyone with an interest in devolution is indebted to the Constitution Unit's monitoring of devolution in the different jurisdictions. Surveys of the results are contained in R. Hazell (ed.), *The State of the Nations: The First Year of Devolution in the United Kingdom* (Thorverton, Devon: Imprint Academic, 2000) and in two subsequent volumes, *The State of the Nations 2001*, edited by A. Trench (2001), and *The State of the Nations*, edited by R. Hazell (2003).

 Websites

See also the list of general websites at the back of the book.

Scotland

- www.scottishsecretary.gov.uk – Scotland Office
- www.scottish.parliament.uk – Scottish Parliament
- www.scotland.gov.uk – Scotland Executive
- www.scotland.gov.uk/digitalscotland – Digital Scotland
- www.bbc.co.uk/scotland – BBC Scotland
- www.guardian.co.uk/scotland – Guardian Scotland
- www.scottishtories.org.uk – Scottish Conservative Party
- www.scottishlabour.org.uk – Scottish Labour Party
- www.scotlibdems.org.uk – Scottish Liberal Democrats
- www.snp.gov.uk – Scottish National Party
- www.scotsocialistparty.org – Scottish Socialist Party
- www.scottishgreens.org.uk – Scottish Green Party

Wales

- www.assembly.wales.org.uk – National Assembly for Wales
- www.ossw.wales.gov.uk – Wales Office
- www.bbc.co.uk/wales – BBC Wales
- www.guardian.co.uk/wales – Guardian Wales
- www.iwa.org.uk – Institute of Wales Affairs
- www.plaidcymru.org – Plaid Cymru

- www.wda.co.uk – Welsh Development Agency
- www.walesgreenparty.org.uk – Welsh Green Party
- www.waleslabourparty.org.uk – Welsh Labour Party
- www.libdemwales.org.uk – Welsh Liberal Democrats

Northern Ireland

- www.nio.gov.uk – Northern Ireland Office
- www.ni-assembly.gov.uk – Northern Ireland Assembly
- www.nics.gov.uk – Northern Ireland Executive
- www.bloody-sunday-inquiry.org.uk – Bloody Sunday Inquiry
- www.dup.org.uk – Democratic Unionist Party
- www.irishnews.com – Irish News
- www.irishnews.com/mitchell.html – Mitchell Report
- www.nisra.gov.uk – Northern Ireland Statistics and Research
- www.paradescommision.org – Parades Commission
- www.sdlp.ie – SDLP
- www.sinnfein.ie – Sinn Fein
- www.uup.org – Ulster Unionist Party

England

- www.englishpm.demon.co.uk – Campaign for an English Parliament
- www.english-independence.co.uk – Campaign for English Independence

13 The Courts and the Administration of Justice

A country's legal institutions play an essential role in shaping its political system at a number of different levels. The values of the legal system inevitably have an impact on the political culture, promoting such ideas as procedural due process, **natural justice** and limited government. The efficiency and effectiveness of the legal system affects the security and prosperity of society as a whole and of the individual citizen. Legal rules and processes, and the character of the professional legal elite, have a profound direct and indirect influence on governmental policy making.

In the United Kingdom the courts and the judiciary, and indeed legal processes generally, were traditionally assumed to have only a limited role in the governmental process and to be insulated from political controversy (Stevens, 2002). The last two decades, however, have seen several domestic and international developments which have heightened the significance of law and legal issues in the political process and expanded the role of the judiciary. It seems inevitable that these trends will continue. It is necessary to examine the changing political context of the United Kingdom's legal system before examining the structure of the courts and the role of its law-enforcement agencies. (It should be noted that the discussion in this chapter is based primarily on the legal system that operates in England and Wales.)

The Changed Context of Legal Administration

Four interrelated factors have altered the intellectual and political climate in which the British legal system now works. First, recent constitutional reforms, especially the introduction of devolution and the passage of the Human Rights Act 1998 (HRA), have transformed the position of the judiciary and the agenda of the courts. Devolution (apart from sharpening the distinctions between the legal systems of Scotland, Northern Ireland and England and Wales) will inevitably generate a range of new disputes about the validity or vires of legislation and about the law-making powers of the devolved bodies. The HRA, which incorporates much of the European Convention on Human Rights (ECHR) into British law, creates new protections for individuals and imposes new obligations on public authorities.

natural justice Rules of fair play which must be followed in a range of judicial and administrative circumstances. Key principles of natural justice include the rule against bias – that no one should be judge in his or her own cause – and that both parties in an argument should be heard. These rules have been adapted and elaborated by the courts and applied in administrative law.

The HRA's emphasis on the right to a fair trial makes it especially relevant to the system of criminal justice and the operation of law-enforcement agencies. Indeed, the HRA has already generated a number of challenges to existing practice. (The 1998 HRA came into effect immediately in Scotland, Wales and Northern Ireland, but not until 2000 in England.) Thus in 1999 a Scottish case challenging the appointment of part-time judges caused the Lord Chancellor to abandon such appointments (*Starrs* v. *Procurator Fiscal*; Judicial Appointments Annual Report, 1999–2000). The HRA also placed a question mark over the historic institutions of the office of the Lord Chancellor because of its apparently incongruous combination of judicial, executive and legislative roles and the tensions inherent in its wide-ranging powers (Woodhouse, 2001). More generally, the HRA is likely to change the role of the judiciary, not least because it requires the judges to interpret a charter framed in terms of broad principle rather than tightly drafted law. The kinds of dispute that arise under the HRA are also inherently likely to raise issues of moral, political and social significance. Although it is as yet too early to say how the judges will develop human rights doctrine in a British context, it is important to note that the role they will play in interpreting the devolution legislation and the HRA has been given by legislation. By contrast with the judicial determination to develop a coherent system of administrative law from the 1960s onwards (which incurred extensive political criticism from governments of both parties), an extension of the judicial role into areas that will inevitably prove politically controversial has been legitimized, indeed mandated, by Parliament. (Administrative law is discussed further in chapter 14.)

The second change to the context of British legal procedures stems from the expanding role of the European Union. As was pointed out in chapter 6, which discussed the impact of British membership of the European Union on the doctrine of parliamentary sovereignty, conflicts between European Community law and national law are regarded as a matter of law to be decided in the courts. The supremacy of European Community law was underlined in the 1990 *Factortame* case, which not merely asserted rights in Community law over rights derived from statute but also forced the British courts to provide a remedy for the breach of European law. The reach of European Community law has grown broader and will inevitably continue to spread across a range of policy areas and legal specialisms. Not only does this incoming tide of Community law create complexity, it also forces the judges to familiarize themselves with doctrines and concepts derived not from the English common law but from other jurisdictions. As a result, the English common law system is inevitably open to new intellectual influences and pressures. (The role of the European Court of Justice is discussed in more detail in chapter 15.)

The third contextual change affecting the contemporary legal system is that the traditional insulation of legal policy and administration from the routine priorities of government has largely disappeared. Partly this change has occurred because many aspects of legal policy – especially the efficiency of the courts, access to justice, the cost of legal aid and the prosecution of crime – have become important elements of political controversy and administrative concern. The demand for joined-up government affected the administration and delivery of legal services as much as other elements of public policy. Indeed, the fragmentation of the various elements of legal administration came to seem increasingly anomalous, especially given the general shift of emphasis towards consumerism and away from the acceptance of restrictive practices in the professions. Accordingly, the elements of a strong management culture, with an emphasis on value for money, effective service delivery and customer satisfaction, became as significant in relation to legal matters as to other public policy areas. Quantifiable targets (for example, successful convictions and reduced backlogs) featured more prominently in departmental thinking. On one level this normalization of legal administration may seem entirely justified in a democracy. On the other hand, the imposition of bureaucratic values, including the priorities of the Treasury and the National Audit Office, may seem to impinge on the independence and integrity of the legal system.

The division of responsibility for legal and judicial matters has been substantially and radically reorganized in recent years, not least because of the increased salience of constitutional issues and the promotion of a major agenda of modernization of the legal system. Although the Home Office has retained important responsibilities for some courts (notably coroners' courts), its primary law-enforcement responsibilities are now concentrated in the field of penal policy, especially the administration of the prison service and the police. Responsibility for the court system and for constitutional and legal issues was increasingly consolidated within the Lord Chancellor's Department (LCD). Until 1998, the LCD always had a lawyer as its permanent secretary. Most of its key staff were also lawyers, reflecting the department's concentration on issues relating to the judiciary. After 1997 it became not merely a more typical department (with its ministers submitting to parliamentary questioning) but also an expanding one (see figure 3.4). Following a review of the department in 2002, the LCD acquired a new structure in the form of a corporate board under the permanent secretary in an attempt to promote clear lines of responsibility and joint working across the department as well as a better focus on customer satisfaction and service delivery for court users.

The role of the LCD thus increased notably under the Blair administrations. By early 1993 the LCD employed about 12,000 people, some 10,000 of whom worked in the Court Service, an executive agency set up in 1995 which manages the courts in England and Wales. The LCD had gradually taken over some responsibilities previously located in the Home Office – in particular constitutional matters such as House of Lords reform and, from 2002, electoral law administration, freedom of information and human rights as well as data protection responsibilities and party funding. It was also scheduled to take over responsibility for all tribunals in England and Wales, following the reorganization of the tribunal system recommended in the 2001 Leggatt Report, as well as for magistrates' court staff. The projected expansion of the LCD inevitably entailed an expansion of staff, whose numbers were predicted to reach 12,600 by 2005–6 (LCD Annual Report, 2002–3).

This expansion of the LCD's responsibilities was balanced by a greater degree of political scrutiny of the legal process by Parliament, and by the production of more information in the form of reports on the work of the LCD and of the law officers (the Attorney General and Solicitor General) as well as from the Crown Prosecution Service and such recently created bodies as the Commission for Judicial Appointments. Parliamentary control of the work of the LCD used to be fragmented; and until Lord Mackay it was rare for the Lord Chancellor to appear before MPs. The whole situation was transformed by the creation of a Select Committee on Justice

Kilmuir rules Guidelines established by the Lord Chancellor, Lord Kilmuir, in 1955 restricting the freedom of judges to speak to the press. The restrictions were lifted in 1987 by the then Lord Chancellor, Lord McKay, and since then some judges have used the press to criticize government penal policy.

and Constitutional Affairs, echoing the Department's changing remit as a Department for Justice, Rights and the Constitution and the explicit acknowledgement in the annual departmental report that the Lord Chancellor had become 'in effect, the principal minister of justice in England and Wales' (LCD Annual Report, 2002–3). In June 2003, the LCD formally became the Department for Constitutional Affairs.

The fourth contextual change is the growing willingness of the British judiciary to criticize government. Indeed, one feature of the period after 1979 was the succession of disputes between ministers and judges, such as Lord Taylor of Gosforth, Lord Browne-Wilkinson and, more recently, Lord Woolf, about legal issues. Sentencing policy generates intense conflict between judges and successive home secretaries, but there have also been very heated exchanges over natural justice, retrospective legislation and the availability of legal aid. On one level these public disputes can be seen as a healthy debate about legal issues. Yet they point up the very different perspectives which judges and politicians have on matters of legal policy (see box 13.1).

Judicial participation in public debate was facilitated by a change of policy on the part of the Conservative Lord Chancellor, Lord Mackay, in 1987. Until then, judges had been bound by the 1955 **Kilmuir rules**, which had precluded the contributions of judges to media debate. As a result of the liberalization, individual judges have

---

Box 13.1 Politicians and judges

Brian Mawhinney, Conservative Party Chairman: 'Magistrates and judges are good people, but they do not act in a vacuum. So praise them when you agree with them and let them know if you are dissatisfied, always remembering that, of course, they have heard all the evidence. The expression of the public's view on sentencing does have an effect.'
(A. Leathley, 'Criticism of court decisions urged', *The Times*, 11 October 1995)

Lord Donaldson: 'In recent months we have seen an entirely new development. This is an attack by politicians on the judiciary as a whole. This is without precedent in my professional lifetime and raises very serious constitutional issues ... It is one thing to be governed by the rule of law. It is quite another to be governed by a despotic, albeit no doubt benevolent, government. And any government which seeks to make itself immune to an independent review of whether its actions are lawful or unlawful is potentially despotic.'
(Lord Donaldson, 'Beware this abuse', *Guardian*, 1 December 1995)

David Blunkett, March 2003, after judges struck down part of the Nationality, Immigration and Asylum Act: 'Frankly, I'm fed up with having to deal with a situation where Parliament debates issues and the judges then overturn them ... Parliament did debate this, we were aware of the circumstances, we did mean what we said and, on behalf of the British people, we are going to implement it.'
(F. Gibb, 'Blunkett v. the Bench', *The Times*, 4 March 2003)

become better known to the public and have become more regular and robust participants in policy discussions.

The Characteristics of the English Legal System

Every legal system, as the 1994 Royal Commission on Criminal Justice noted, is the product of its distinctive history and culture. Despite the contemporary concern with modernization and reform, many substantive and procedural features of the law in England and Wales can only be explained by reference to history rather than logic. The elements of the English legal system that have produced its distinctive patterns and ethos are its use of common law reasoning; the relative neglect of public law; the dominance of adversarial proceedings; the maintenance of a divided legal profession; and the homogeneity of the judiciary.

The common law tradition

The English legal system is based on the common law, by contrast with the Scottish legal system and the systems used by many continental European countries, which are codified systems based on Roman law.

The most familiar image of the English common law system is of a body of rules that are developed incrementally (Hart, 1972). The task of the judge on this model is normally to scrutinize **precedents** to find and apply the appropriate rule to a legal problem, developing existing principles rather than making new law. Although few judges believe that this model of the judicial function is entirely accurate, it is one that has exercised a powerful influence on English thinking about the judicial role and the extent to which judicial discretion and policy making are limited.

The common law tradition inevitably emphasizes precedent but the approach of the English judiciary to precedent itself changed in the late twentieth century. In 1966 the House of Lords decided to modify its approach to precedent. Prior to 1966 it was thought that where the House of Lords had already considered a legal point, even if a long time previously, it had to follow the earlier precedent. In 1966 the House of Lords announced in a practice statement that it would feel free to depart from its own earlier decisions in exceptional instances. In fact, that freedom has been relatively little used. One area where it was used, however, was again in relation to the process of judicial interpretation. In *Pepper* v. *Hart* (1993), the House of Lords changed the rule that excluded consideration of parliamentary proceedings from the interpretation of the meaning of legislation. Whereas previously judges would look only at the words on the statute book, they may now in limited circumstances take into account such parliamentary evidence as ministerial statements about the purpose of a clause. Although some senior judges such as Lord Steyn think the change gives too much power to the executive, other observers have welcomed the flexibility given by *Pepper* v. *Hart*.

precedent Used in the legal system to indicate a rule laid down in one case which binds similar cases in future.

The reliance on precedent in the common law tradition carries the danger that the substance of the law may not reflect contemporary social needs. Although recent Lord Chancellors have been keen to promote wide-ranging reform of the law and the courts, the process of keeping the law up to date is a daunting one. Reform of the law in the English system is facilitated by the Law Commission, which has the task of keeping the different aspects of law under review. In addition, government departments and parliamentary select committees will monitor aspects of the law relevant to their subject areas. And the judges themselves may be powerful advocates of change and instruments of reform. Usually judicial innovation is incremental, but sometimes a trend may be detected in the opinions of a court or an individual judge. Thus Lord Denning as Master of the Rolls from 1962 to 1982 contributed to the reform of the law in a number of areas, although his approach to precedent was seen as highly unorthodox at the time. Similarly, the refinement and expansion of administrative law in the 1960s and 1970s owed much to the innovative approach of the House of Lords.

The change in judicial role should not be exaggerated. Judicial attitudes have not been transformed overnight and the English judiciary is still very sensitive to its constitutional subordination to Parliament and its adherence to precedent. But there is a detectable shift of emphasis which suggests that deference to Parliament and the executive is being replaced by a new concern for individual rights and a determination to assert the judicial view on legal issues.

Taken together, these developments have produced new pressure on the legal system and generated an expectation of further reform. This dynamic can be seen operating in relation to three distinctive aspects of the English legal system.

Public and private law

One traditional feature of the English legal system that was especially relevant for those interested in the political and governmental role of law was that until the 1960s public and administrative law issues were neglected. From the 1960s onwards, however, judges devoted considerable attention to developing administrative law doctrines and remedies, so much so that applications for judicial review rose dramatically, becoming, in the words of the introduction to 'The judge over your shoulder' (the Cabinet Office pamphlet on the subject), 'a growth industry'. Thus whereas there were a mere 160 applications for permission for judicial review in 1974, in 2001 there were 4,732, the vast majority in the field of immigration (see figure 14.2, p. 479). The growing public law caseload and the prospect that the implementation of the HRA might produce further pressure caused the Lord Chancellor in 1999 to commission a review of the Crown Office list. This review (the Bowman Review) recommended among other things that there should be greater specialization by judges in the field of administrative law, procedural simplification and the creation of a dedicated Administrative Court to deal with applications for judicial review, statutory appeals and extradition matters. A separate Administrative Court was created in October 2000, marking a further stage in an increasingly systematic process of creating an integrated body of administrative law within the United Kingdom.

The adversarial character of legal proceedings

One feature of the English legal system that distinguishes it from many continental systems, though not from American and Commonwealth common law ones, is its use of adversarial (as opposed to inquisitorial) proceedings in all but a handful of courts. Legal procedures, both civil and criminal, thus normally involve two parties who put forward claim and counterclaim to establish the facts. The role of the judge in adversarial proceedings is that of referee and ringmaster; he or she does not take a part in the establishment of facts.

The use of adversarial proceedings has many strengths. It also has some weaknesses. As scholars of the American judicial system have pointed out, the adversarial method is less than ideal in cases with a high policy content because the factual basis on which the decision will be made is limited by the evidence the two parties choose to put before the courts (Horowitz, 1977). Of more tangible significance is the extent to which the adversarial mode of conducting legal proceedings is both intimidating and costly. As a result, some courts in England and Wales, such as coroners' courts and small claims courts, do not use adversarial methods.

Tribunals, which developed as a way of providing an appeal mechanism largely in disputes between the citizen and the state over such matters as the administration of welfare benefits and taxation, also represented an effort to avoid the full adversarial method of resolving disputes. They have now become more common arenas for dispute resolution than the courts. This extensive network of tribunals in effect disposes of conflicts in more informal settings than ordinary courts and in a way which is much less expensive, not least because legal representation is often neither required nor allowed. Apart from recent reforms designed to streamline and integrate tribunals under the Lord Chancellor's jurisdiction, it seems likely that there will be further initiatives to promote alternative dispute-resolution mechanisms – and these will not always use adversarial procedures. (Tribunals are further discussed in chapter 14.)

Thus the pressure on the court system, especially on the civil side, has stimulated further interest in expanding the role of informal methods of dispute resolution that provide an alternative to the familiar adversarial style of the courts.

The maintenance of a divided profession

Perhaps the most familiar feature of the English legal system that is now under pressure is the organization of the legal profession, with its division into barristers and solicitors. This division creates two categories of lawyers whose skills are in theory distinct and complementary but which in practice overlap. Solicitors are the lawyers who deal with the public directly; they perform routine non-litigious legal tasks (such as conveyancing and drawing up wills) and prepare the background information when litigation is necessary. They form the most numerous branch of a rapidly growing profession. In 2003 there were about 85,000 solicitors and about 10,000 barristers in private practice. The growth in the legal profession has been fuelled by a number of factors, including the expansion in higher education, the provision of legal aid and the spread of home ownership. Solicitors (unlike barristers) may form partnerships with members of related professions such as accountants and may advertise their services. The spectrum in terms of size runs from the small country practice to large London firms. There has recently been a trend towards the creation of multinational giants in order to cope with the increasingly global nature of much legal work.

The senior and smaller branch of the profession – barristers – effectively provides a specialist legal advice service. Traditionally, solicitors were not allowed to appear in cases in any of the higher courts, where barristers alone had rights of audience. Since 1986, however, solicitors have been allowed to appear in the High Court in formal and uncontested cases and recent changes have granted them rights of access to all courts. The barristers' long monopoly on audience in the higher courts had the effect of increasing the cost of going to law. It was also the case that senior judges tended to be drawn exclusively from the ranks of barristers. In the last few years solicitors have been eligible to become judges, although, as table 13.1 shows, few have in fact done so.

Table 13.1 Composition of the British judiciary as of 1 March 2003

		Former barristers	Former solicitors	Total	% Women
Lords of Appeal in Ordinary	Women	–	–	–	–
	Men	12	–	12	–
	Total	12	–	12	–
	% Women	–	–	–	0
Heads of Division	Women	1	–	1	–
	Men	4	–	4	–
	Total	5	–	5	–
	% Women	–	–	–	20
Lord Justices of Appeal	Women	3	–	3	–
	Men	33	–	33	–
	Total	36	–	36	–
	% Women	–	–	–	8
High Court Judges	Women	6	–	6	–
	Men	99	2	101	–
	Total	105	2	107	–
	% Women	–	–	–	6
Circuit Judges[a]	Women	50	10	60	–
	Men	483	78	561	–
	Total	533	88	621	–
	% Women	–	–	–	10
Recorders	Women	143	28	171	–
	Men	1,074	111	1,185	–
	Total	1,217	139	1,356	–
	% Women	–	–	–	13
Recorders in Training	Women	7	2	9	–
	Men	46	3	49	–
	Total	53	5	58	–
	% Women	–	–	–	16

Table 13.1 *Continued*

		Former barristers	Former solicitors	Total	% Women
District Judges[b]	Women	10	69	79	–
	Men	16	331	347	–
	Total	26	400	426	–
	% Women	–	–	–	19
Deputy District Judges[b]	Women	32	129	161	–
	Men	58	566	624	–
	Total	90	695	785	–
	% Women	–	–	–	21
District Judges (Magistrates' Courts)[c]	Women	11	11	22	–
	Men	24	59	83	–
	Total	35	70	105	–
	% Women	–	–	–	21
Deputy District Judges (Magistrates' Courts)[d]	Women	9	19	28	–
	Men	43	79	122	–
	Total	52	98	150	–
	% Women	–	–	–	19

[a] Includes judges of the Court of Technology and Construction.   [b] Including the Family Division.
[c] As at 31 August 2000 all stipendiary magistrates became district judges (magistrates' courts).
[d] As at 31 August 2000 all deputy stipendiary magistrates became deputy district judges (magistrates' courts).
Source: Lord Chancellor's Department.

Pressures for change in the organization of the legal profession and in the delivery of legal services mounted in the 1980s. These pressures arose partly because of the Law Society's determined campaign to protect its members' interests when solicitors found their monopolies threatened by other professions. (The bar also became much more active in its campaigning.) Importantly, there was also a government thrust to remove restrictive practices from the law, as from other professions, in the interests of the consumer. The appointment of Lord Mackay of Clashfern as Lord Chancellor in the Thatcher government brought to the office a Scot who was more sympathetic to the need for reform of the legal profession than an English barrister might have been. Mackay's radical reforms (which were designed to open up the profession and eliminate restrictive practices) met fierce opposition from the bar and others who feared the erosion of professional independence. Nevertheless, the Courts and Legal Services Act of 1990 initiated important changes, including giving both solicitors and barristers the right of audience in all courts provided they had been granted a certificate of advocacy.

The Labour government of 1997 encountered much opposition from the bar in particular over the introduction of a new system of legal aid. Following the Middleton Report, which criticized many features of the existing legal aid system but especially the difficulty of controlling costs, the government passed the Access to Justice Act 1999. That legislation established a new Legal Services Commission, which operates two schemes – a Criminal Defence Service and the Community Legal

Service. The legal profession objected both to the strong emphasis given to cost-cutting in these schemes and to the effective creation of a cadre of state-employed lawyers to deliver legal services to those on legal aid.

Whether or not the division of the legal profession remains in the public interest is a debatable question. In 2000 the Office of Fair Trading made further suggestions for change, many of which were resisted by barristers. Although still fiercely opposed by the bar, the barriers between the branches are breaking down rapidly and it is likely that in the long run there will be a fused legal profession.

Homogeneity of the judiciary

One of the most significant effects of the division of the legal profession has been to restrict the pool of potential judges to barristers, as table 13.1 shows. At least two distinctive aspects of the restriction of judicial nominees to barrister should be noted here. First, the monopoly – or near monopoly – of barristers on judicial appointments means that Britain's judges are the product of a single professional background with its own distinctive culture. The appointments process, including the point at which barristers apply to become Queen's Counsel (QC) – senior barristers – is therefore highly sensitive to charges that it operates on the basis of an inner club or old boys' network. Equally worrying is the fact that access to, and success at, the bar has been dependent upon having an independent income in the early years. Although the composition of the judiciary was perhaps less controversial while judges exercised a limited role in the British political system, recent years have again focused attention both on the social representativeness of the judicial elite and on who appoints them.

The composition of the British judiciary has been censured on a number of grounds. As public concern with questions of equality of opportunity and diversity has risen, the judiciary's lack of women and ethnic minorities at the highest levels has invited criticism. The large number of judges with a public school background and the overwhelming dominance of Oxbridge education are also marked features of the judiciary. Labour Research, which runs regular surveys of the composition of the judiciary, pointed out in 2003 that it is still made up of the usual suspects – privileged white elderly men – despite the promise of change with the election of a young and fresh New Labour government in 1997. Such criticisms are difficult to rebut. Yet the continuities in socio-economic profile are not necessarily a good guide, or indeed any guide at all, to judicial attitude.

The process of appointing judges is open to objection on the grounds of its secrecy. It is formally the responsibility of the Lord Chancellor, who is solely responsible for all judicial appointments below the level of the Court of Appeal. Appointments to the two highest levels of the judiciary, the Court of Appeal and the House of Lords, are made by the prime minister, who may take advice from the Lord Chancellor but is not bound by it. The degree of political influence involved in the judicial selection process is unclear, but it has always been assumed that some degree of political intervention occurs when judges are chosen.

There has long been an effort to make the judicial appointment process more transparent. Lord Mackay introduced a number of reforms to the appointments process, for example by introducing advertisement and open competition for circuit judgeships. On entering office, Labour made further attempts to improve the process by inviting applications for High Court appointments, providing more information about the appointment criteria and extending the consultation process. Although the Lord Chancellor was initially opposed to a Judicial Appointments Commission, one was established in 2001 following the Peach Report (see box 13.2) on judicial appointments. The Judicial Appointments Commission effectively has the task of auditing appointments procedures for the judiciary and for QCs and of handling complaints.

The Court Structure

The administration of the network of civil and criminal courts in England and Wales is a major undertaking that is now the responsibility of the Court Service, an executive agency within the LCD. (The LCD does not, however, control the Judicial Committee of the House of Lords, which is run by a separate office.) Criminal and civil law procedures are very different. In criminal cases the state prosecutes when an offence has been committed and the accused, if found guilty, is punished. In civil cases a private party brings an action for a remedy – usually damages – for some loss that has been suffered. The structure of the criminal and civil courts in England and Wales is set out in figure 13.1.

In England and Wales, as in many other countries, there is increasing concern about the courts' capacity to operate effectively. The principal causes of that concern are the long delays that mark both civil and criminal proceedings, the high costs of litigation, which are a deterrent to using the civil courts, and the sense that many

Box 13.2   The Peach Report

In July 1999 the Lord Chancellor asked Sir Leonard Peach, formerly the Commissioner for Public Appointments, to examine appointments procedures for the judiciary and to recommend improvements. The Peach Report, published in December 1999, found that the consultation process currently in place for appointing the senior judiciary – sometimes known as taking 'soundings' – was controversial but worked well. Peach wrote: 'as an experienced selector, my conclusion is that to abandon the consultation process would be a neglect of valuable input as one part of the assessment'.

He concluded that the procedures and their execution were as good as any he had seen in the public sector. However, he made 26 recommendations for further developments to the procedures, including two major ones – setting up a Judicial Appointments Commission and a pilot scheme for a one-day assessment centre. The Lord Chancellor broadly welcomed the recommendations and a number of them have already been implemented.

Source: Lord Chancellor's Department, Peach Report, http://www.lcd.gov.uk/judicial/peach/peachrec.htm

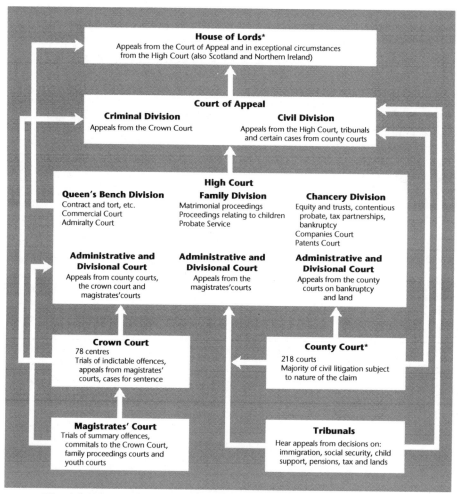

House of Lords*
Appeals from the Court of Appeal and in exceptional circumstances from the High Court (also Scotland and Northern Ireland)

Court of Appeal

Criminal Division
Appeals from the Crown Court

Civil Division
Appeals from the High Court, tribunals and certain cases from county courts

High Court

Queen's Bench Division
Contract and tort, etc.
Commercial Court
Admiralty Court

Family Division
Matrimonial proceedings
Proceedings relating to children
Probate Service

Chancery Division
Equity and trusts, contentious probate, tax partnerships, bankruptcy
Companies Court
Patents Court

Administrative and Divisional Court
Appeals from county courts, the crown court and magistrates' courts

Administrative and Divisional Court
Appeals from the magistrates' courts

Administrative and Divisional Court
Appeals from the county courts on bankruptcy and land

Crown Court
78 centres
Trials of indictable offences, appeals from magistrates' courts, cases for sentence

County Court*
218 courts
Majority of civil litigation subject to nature of the claim

Magistrates' Court
Trials of summary offences, committals to the Crown Court, family proceedings courts and youth courts

Tribunals
Hear appeals from decisions on: immigration, social security, child support, pensions, tax and lands

*Although the House of Lords and the magistrates' courts form part of the structure within England and Wales, the Court Service does not administer them. This diagram is necessarily much simplified and should not be taken as a comprehensive statement on the jurisdiction of any specific court.

Figure 13.1 The structure of criminal and civil courts in England and Wales.

procedures are unduly complex and time-consuming. Over the last decade a number of important enquiries into the operation of the legal system have taken place – notably Lord Woolf's civil justice review in 1996, Sir Peter Middleton's report in 1997, and Sir Jeffrey Bowman's review of the role of the Court of Appeal's Civil Division and his separate review of the Crown List. The Auld Report in 2001 recommended wide-ranging changes to the structure of criminal law courts. The Access to Justice Act 1999 introduced several reforms calculated to streamline the system of legal aid. The Leggatt Report on Tribunals suggested a rationalization and modernization of the system that would make tribunals better able to respond to the needs of their users.

Several common themes run through these reports. There was a desire for efficiency, especially in the time management of cases and the administration of the courts. Central to Lord Woolf's review of the civil courts, for example, was the idea that cases could be distinguished on the basis of how complicated they were and different procedures should apply according to the complexity of the case. Thus there is an attempt to ensure that the amount of time and money spent on a case is commensurate with its importance. There is also a new emphasis on those who use the courts, not just litigants but also witnesses and jurors. There is a desire to make proceedings more comprehensible, for example by anglicizing the names of legal procedures, writs and orders. Lord Woolf and others have been keen to harness the benefits of new technology to make the courts more efficient. As a result, such innovations as 'Moneyclaim Online' and 'Just Ask' have been created as websites for the public. And there has been concern to rebuild confidence in the courts, 'selling the product', as the jargon has it. This emphasis on consumer confidence is seen as especially important among groups such as ethnic minorities, whose experience of the judicial process has been shaped by such incidents as the Stephen Lawrence affair (see box 13.3, p. 457).

The civil courts

Leaving aside for the moment the rather special small claims court, the majority of civil actions in England and Wales are handled by the 218 county courts. County courts were first established in 1846. These courts are regionally organized and now have a wide-ranging jurisdiction including all cases in tort, contract and the recovery of land and a range of family law matters. They also handle some bankruptcy matters. Each county court will be staffed by two different levels of judge – a circuit court judge, who will hear the most complex and the most serious cases, and a district judge (formerly known as a registrar), who will hear disputes of a more straightforward kind, those involving small sums of money and uncontested cases. The district judge may also deal with some pre-trial matters.

Above the county court is the High Court, which has three specialized divisions: the Queen's Bench Division (QBD), which includes the Commercial Court, the Admiralty Court and the Administrative Court, the Chancery Division and the Family Division. The QBD is headed by the Lord Chief Justice and cases are heard by him and 73 High Court judges. The QBD has original jurisdiction in civil matters, including applications for judicial review of administrative action. Claims may be started in the High Court rather than in the county court, even if they relate to a relatively small sum of money, and a claimant may choose to go directly to the High Court if the case involves establishing a legal principle or testing the law in a way which has implications for other claims.

The QBD has an important supervisory jurisdiction in relation to lower courts and the wide range of tribunals that decide disputes in such areas as employment, social security benefits and tax. The High Court exercises this control over subordinate jurisdictions through its ability to issue prerogative writs and orders.

The High Court is also an appellate court which hears appeals from magistrates' courts and tribunals on points of law. (In criminal matters it also hears appeals from the crown courts.) When hearing appeals the QBD normally sits in panels of three, though occasionally as many as five judges may hear a case. If, however, a statute provides for an appeal on a point of law from a tribunal to the QBD, a single judge will normally hear the case.

The Chancery Division of the High Court originated in the distinct set of legal processes and remedies known as equity, which developed to supplement the inflexible procedures of the common law. These two aspects of English law, common law and equity, have now been merged almost entirely, so that claimants no longer have to choose whether to bring a case in the common law or the equity courts. The distinctive feature of the Chancery Division is still the type of case it handles: trusts, land, taxation, company law and bankruptcy as well as contentious probate and succession matters. The Lord Chancellor is the nominal head of the Chancery Division, but in practice its 17 judges are presided over by a Vice-Chancellor.

The Family Division of the High Court was created in 1971 when the old Probate, Divorce and Admiralty Division ('wills, wives and wrecks' as it used to be dubbed) was abolished and its functions redistributed among other courts. The Family Division is headed by a president and has 17 judges. Its jurisdiction covers matters such as the breakdown of marriage, the disposition of family property and the custody of children.

Above the level of the High Court is the Court of Appeal, which has two divisions, one for civil and one for criminal matters. The Court of Appeal was established in the late nineteenth century under the Judicature Acts of 1873–5 to hear civil appeals. It takes appeals on civil matters from both the county courts and the civil divisions of the High Court. The Court of Appeal as a whole is presided over by the Lord Chief Justice and the Master of the Rolls and is staffed by 35 Lords Justices of Appeal. On the civil side the judges traditionally sat together in courts of three, but recent reforms have allowed the Master of the Rolls to exercise greater discretion when constituting courts to hear appeals so that more cases may be heard by judges sitting alone or in pairs. The Lord Chancellor, former Lord Chancellors, Lords of Appeal in Ordinary and the presidents of the various divisions of the High Court are also ex officio members of the Court of Appeal and competent to hear appeals there. Under Lord Denning (who was Master of the Rolls from 1962 to 1982) the Court of Appeal acquired a reputation for being an innovative force in English law. Through its unconventional approach to precedent, it contributed to the process of law reform in many areas.

The growth in workload of the Court of Appeal, the anticipation of a further growth of cases as a result of the HRA and the analysis presented by the Woolf Report on Civil Justice prompted the Lord Chancellor in 1997 to set up an examination of the workings of the Court of Appeal under Sir Jeffrey Bowman. (Sir Jeffrey later undertook a review of the Crown Office List and recommended the creation of a specialized Administrative Court.) The Bowman Report led to a number of changes, including a reduction in the number of judges required to hear cases and the extension of the requirement that the right to appeal was not automatic but needed the permission of the Court. These changes are calculated to reduce the workload of the Court of Appeal, although they also inevitably limit access to the Court. The principle behind the new approach to the appeal mechanism appears to be that only a single substantive appeal route is needed and that opportunities for endlessly appealing decisions through the system should be curtailed.

Above the Court of Appeal is the House of Lords, which is the highest domestic court in the United Kingdom. Its function is to resolve the most important legal disputes and its workload has been given additional political significance by the role it has in relation to European Community law and in relation to human rights cases.

Judicial functions are exercised by an Appellate Committee of the House of Lords, which now sits in a committee room of the House rather than the chamber. Under the Administration of Justice (Appeals) Act of 1934, the right of appeal to the House of Lords is limited. Permission to appeal must be obtained either from the House of Lords itself (which delegates the question of whether to allow an appeal to an Appeals Committee) or from the Court of Appeal. Leave to appeal will usually only be granted when there is a substantial point of law in dispute.

The House of Lords' judicial functions originated when medieval monarchs delegated routine aspects of adjudication to members of the Great Council. It took time for the legislative and adjudicative functions to be separated, but it is clear that by the end of the sixteenth century the House of Lords was the pre-eminent court in England and Wales. Peers without judicial training participated in judicial proceedings until the middle of the nineteenth century, but this practice was effectively ended with the case of *O'Connell* in 1844.

Since that time the House of Lords has reserved its judicial functions for specialists, although the appointment of professional judges to undertake them had to wait until the Appellate Jurisdiction Act of 1876. That Act provided for the appointment of paid judges – Lords of Appeal in Ordinary – to cope with the judicial work at the highest level of the system. Their number has been raised over the years and now stands at 12 (see table 13.2). As well as these specially created law lords (who are given life peerages), any peer who has held high judicial office may sit on appeals to the House of Lords. Law lords retire at 70 but can hear cases until they are 75. The House of Lords normally hears case in panels but the selection of who is to sit on

Table 13.2 The law lords

Law lord	Date of birth
Lord Bingham of Cornhill	13.10.33
Lord Nicholls of Birkenhead	25.1.33
Lord Steyn	15.8.32
Lord Hoffmann	8.5.34
Lord Hope of Craighead	27.6.38
Lord Hutton	29.6.31
Lord Saville of Newdigate	20.3.36
Lord Hobhouse of Woodborough	31.1.32
Lord Millett	23.6.32
Lord Scott of Foscote	2.10.34
Lord Rodger of Earlsferry	18.9.44
Lord Walker of Gestingthorpe	17.3.38

Source: Lord Chancellor's Department (now the Department for Constitutional Affairs).

which panel is by convention delegated by the Lord Chancellor to the senior law lord.

The Lord Chancellor himself does not usually participate much in the routine judicial business of the House of Lords, not least because of his increased administrative and legislative workload. The question of whether the Lord Chancellor *should* hear cases is a different issue. For many Lord Chancellors, participating in the judicial workload of the House of Lords enabled them to shape the law and to keep in touch with the wider legal profession. Certainly Lord Irvine's immediate predecessors – Lord Hailsham and Lord Mackay – deliberately increased their participation in judicial work, reversing the trend towards minimal participation by the Lord Chancellor. Increasingly, however, problems with having a Lord Chancellor taking a full judicial role became apparent. The Lord Chancellor is part of the executive branch as well as part of the legislature, and his role was thought to offend the separation of powers and the independence of the judiciary. Numerous appeals arise in which the state has an interest and, although a Lord Chancellor may exclude himself from hearing such a case, there is no consistency in the matter. The passage of the 1998 HRA made the Lord Chancellor's position even more sensitive because Article 6 of the ECHR guarantees the right to a fair trial (*McGonnell* v. *UK* No. 28488/95; see box 2.13, p. 74). This article cast further doubt on the legality of the Lord Chancellor's participation not only in human rights cases, where clearly there is a potential conflict of interest, but also in any judicial proceedings. Doubts about the wisdom of allowing a Lord Chancellor to participate in judicial proceedings also arose on the grounds of competence. Although a Lord Chancellor had to have some legal background, he need not have had any immediate – or indeed any – judicial experience. Moreover, the very fact that he had been selected for high political office made it likely that his temperament and orientation would be more towards the political than the judicial realm.

Initially, Lord Irvine as Blair's Lord Chancellor resisted efforts to reform the Lord Chancellor's role, but the pressure for a review of the whole position became overwhelming by June 2003. At that point the decision to abolish the historic office of Lord Chancellor was announced, as was the intention to create a new Supreme Court to replace the law lords. Lord Irvine was replaced by Lord Falconer as Lord Chancellor for the transitional period before the reforms were fully implemented.

Thus, although the House of Lords for the time being remains the ultimate court of appeal in the British system, a major restructuring of the entire system of upper courts is in the offing. Even before the radical reforms of June 2003 were announced, recent constitutional developments – and the acquisition of a role in devolution cases – had given the Judicial Committee of the Privy Council greater salience. Currently, the law lords' workload is divided between these two bodies. Taken together, these two courts perform a number of important systemic and integrative roles for the legal systems of the UK, facilitating the provision of what has been called 'joined-up justice' (Le Sueur and Cornes, 2000). Reform of the judicial system will produce a single ultimate court of appeal which can combine the functions of the House of Lords and the Judicial Committee.

The criminal courts and the police

The criminal law is administered through a rather different system of courts from the civil law, and of course the detection and prosecution of crime involves the police. The whole structure of criminal law was radically overhauled in 1971, but concern about injustice in the system led to the establishment of a Royal Commission on Criminal Justice under Lord Runciman, which reported in 1993. More recently, the whole criminal law system has been reviewed by the Auld Commission and many of its recommendations were included in the 2003 Courts Act. One of the main features of that legislation is the creation of single integrated court structure for England and Wales.

The decision to prosecute in criminal cases in England and Wales is taken by a (now decentralized) Crown Prosecution Service (CPS), which was established in 1985. The CPS is headed by the Director of Public Prosecutions (DPP), who is responsible to the Attorney General, although the decision to prosecute is independent of political interference in all but a few areas where the Attorney General's consent is required. These include areas of extreme political sensitivity, for example decisions to prosecute under the Official Secrets Act. The DPP's work is decentralized but some categories of case will automatically be reviewed by the DPP. Although the system is generally regarded as free from political interference, controversy can occur if a case is dropped after the Attorney General's intervention or because there turns out to be insufficient evidence to secure a conviction.

The role of magistrates

One of the most peculiar features of the criminal law in England and Wales is the role played by the 30,000 or so unpaid magistrates or justices of the peace (JPs), who see a large proportion of all cases through from start to finish. In addition there were a small number of stipendiary magistrates, who dealt with cases in larger cities. A unified stipendiary bench was created in 2000 and stipendiary magistrates were given a change of title to district judges (magistrates' courts). As of 2003, there were 105 full-time such district judges.

The organization and operation of the magistracy and of the magistrates' courts are now governed by three comprehensive statutes – the Justice of the Peace Act 1979, the Magistrates Act 1980 and the Police and Magistrates' Courts Act 1994. In 1993 there was major political argument as government tried to extend its view of efficiency and value for money to the police and magistrates' courts, although bipartisan criticism forced amendment of the legislation. In 1992 responsibility for the administration of the magistrates' courts was transferred from the Home Office to the Lord Chancellor's Department. The 2003 Courts Act is designed to integrate their administration with that of the other criminal courts.

The lay magistracy has a long history that has been closely linked to that of local government. By the end of the sixteenth century there had evolved a system in which minor offences could be tried by appointed members of the gentry in the area, while more serious offences had to wait for visitations from the itinerant judges on assize.

Administrative functions, especially those concerned with the poor law, were also assigned to the magistracy. JPs were appointed on a county basis and would assemble four times a year in quarter sessions to perform their judicial duties. However, as the burden of work increased, magistrates developed the practice of dealing with lesser offences themselves without a jury at so-called petty sessions.

Magistrates' courts thus form the bottom rung of the judicial hierarchy but are linked in significant ways with the administrative system because of the variety of functions they perform. Magistrates also constitute the only point at which most citizens directly encounter the criminal justice system – not least because of their responsibility for dealing with motoring offences.

Yet although the system is long-established, it remains controversial. There are several arguments in favour of substantial lay participation in the administration of justice, not least the contention that such participation reinforces the idea that the prevention of crime and the application of punishment should involve the whole community. Lay participation enables the legal sanctions imposed on criminals to reflect the general values of the community. By involving the public in the sentencing process, the law can be rooted in a wider section of the society than would be the case if only professional lawyers were involved. In addition, there are important considerations of cost. Using unpaid lay magistrates makes the whole system much cheaper than a system staffed by professional judges. It is also likely to be difficult to find the right number of professional judges. Even though there are costs associated with lay magistrates (for example, for expenses and training), these are still small by comparison with a system that depended wholly on full-time judges. Moreover, there is some doubt about whether the personnel is available to replace the magistracy.

Despite these traditional arguments in favour of the lay magistracy, there is now considerable concern about the system. The most common argument deployed against the lay magistracy is that, far from enhancing the legitimacy of judicial administration, the bias in its composition undermines it. In no way does the magistracy reflect the social composition of modern Britain. There is a retirement age of 70, but magistrates are generally in the upper age bracket and overwhelmingly white and middle class. Although there is an equal gender balance, significant sections of society – the young, manual workers and ethnic minorities – are under-represented on the bench. No doubt part of the problem is – as with councillors – the difficulty of combining public service as a magistrate with full-time employment. But at present the corps of JPs appears skewed towards an unrepresentative sector of society.

The manner of appointment to the bench was in the past highly contentious because of the role political patronage played. The advisory committees that vet potential magistrates are carefully balanced to ensure that all political parties are represented. For a long time these committees were anonymous in an effort to protect them from lobbying by aspiring magistrates, but since 1992 their names have been published. Recommendations from the committees about magistrates' appointments are vetted by the Lord Chancellor, assisted by a secretary of commissions whose work is principally concerned with the appointment of district judges (magistrates' courts).

The lay magistracy may still be criticized for its lack of expertise. It is suggested, for example, that lay magistrates are prone to accept police evidence too easily and that they become too dependent on their professionally trained clerks, although studies have not confirmed this hypothesis. Much of the sting of these criticisms has been removed by a greater emphasis on training, which now underpins the system. Training is especially emphasized in the more specialized areas of magistrates' work. Service on juvenile courts, for example, involves enhanced training in such areas as sentencing, social welfare and psychology. Nevertheless, there must still be a suspicion that the justice that JPs administer is somewhat arbitrary and amateur. To some extent the remedy for the deficiencies in the system lies in the comprehensive appeals mechanism that exists and in the variety of professional expertise and welfare services available to the bench.

Crown courts and the process of criminal appeal

The trial of more serious crimes takes place at the level above magistrates' courts in what are known as crown courts. Crown courts were established by the Courts Act of 1971 and replaced the old system of assizes. They are staffed by High Court judges, circuit judges and recorders. Criminal offences are divided into two categories: those very serious offences such as murder which must be tried by a High Court judge; and those which would normally be tried by a circuit judge. Some offences may be released for trial by a circuit judge according to convenience and are known as 'either-way' offences. The system thus ensures that no area is subject to the peculiarities of a single judge and there is enough flexibility in the system to ensure a reasonable distribution of the workload.

Appeal from the crown courts in criminal matters is to the Court of Appeal (Criminal Division) and in very rare cases to the House of Lords. A general right of appeal in criminal matters was a twentieth-century innovation in the English legal structure. Indeed, the Court of Criminal Appeal was established only in 1907. It merged with the Court of Appeal in 1966. An appeal may be against conviction, on the grounds that conviction was wrong in law, or against the length of sentence. Usually appeals against sentence are on the grounds that the sentence was too harsh; but there now also exists a route whereby the Attorney General may appeal if a sentence is deemed too lenient.

Much of the controversy surrounding the courts from the 1970s and the 1980s was the result of a series of miscarriages of justice, for example in the case of the Birmingham Six and the Guildford Four, who were convicted of terrorist offences on what turned out to have been false evidence. Following the Runciman Commission, a Criminal Cases Review Commission was set up to allow independent referral to the Appeal Court of cases where there is doubt about the soundness of a conviction. Although about 4,000 cases have been reviewed, only a small number of convictions have been set aside.

The thrust of more recent reforms has been much more towards the efficient administration of courts and the removal of rules which may be seen as impeding the likelihood of a conviction. Thus the controversial 2003 Criminal Justice Bill sought to weaken the double jeopardy rule and to allow previous convictions to be admissible in court in certain circumstances. The bill also sought to restrict the right to a jury trial. Perhaps this attempt to strike a new balance in the name of efficiency is acceptable to the public at large in the effort to curb crime;

but there is no doubt that it involves compromising the protections available to the accused.

The Police

Law enforcement in any society relies heavily on an organized police force. The British experience of an organized police force dates from 1829, when Sir Robert Peel established the Metropolitan Police; in the succeeding decade both the counties and the boroughs established forces of their own. Although the development of police forces occurred speedily in the nineteenth century, the notion of an organized force took root slowly.

Policing was originally a local matter and police forces were organized around local authorities. For much of the nineteenth century there were over 200 separate police forces in the United Kingdom. During the twentieth century there was an evident need for rationalization and in 1960 the Royal Commission on Police urged the amalgamation of a number of forces, although it rejected the arguments for a national police force.

The implementation of the 1960 Royal Commission proposals and the subsequent Police Act of 1964 initiated a process of amalgamations so that by 2003 there were 52 police forces, of which 43 were in England and Wales, eight in Scotland and one in Northern Ireland (see table 13.3). (The Royal Ulster Constabulary was substantially reorganized as the Police Service of Northern Ireland under the Police (Northern Ireland) Act 2000 following the Patten Commission Report.) In addition there are several specialist forces, such as the Transport Police and the Ministry of Defence Police.

Table 13.3 Police forces in the UK

Year	England and Wales		Scotland		Ireland and Northern Ireland (NI only from 1930)	
	Number of forces	Police in post	Number of forces	Police in post	Number of forces	Police in post
1900	179	41,900	64	4,900	1	12,300
1910	190	49,600	63	5,600	1	11,900
1920	191	56,500	59	6,500	1	11,600
1930	183	58,000	49	6,600	1	2,800
1940	183	57,300	48	6,800	1	2,900
1950	129	62,600	33	7,200	1	2,800
1960	125	72,300	33	8,700	1	2,900
1970	47	92,700	20	11,200	1	3,800
1980	43	115,900	8	13,200	1	6,900
1990	43	125,646	8	13,981	1	8,243
1999	43	126,096	8	14,810	1	8,456
2002	43	129,603	8	15,324	1	6,947

Source: Figures derived from Butler and Butler (2000); Home Office; Scottish executive; Police Service of Northern Ireland.

Control and accountability for policing in England and Wales involves three key elements: the chief constable of the force (who exercises day-to-day responsibility), the local police authority (who provide local accountability) and the Home Secretary, who ensures that national standards and priorities are met. The relationship between these three has always been a sensitive one, not least because any suggestion that the government, or indeed a local authority, is giving political direction to the police tends to be seen as a threat to liberty. It is also sensitive because there is a need in a democracy to ensure that the individual police officer is accountable for his or her actions and that there is control of the general policing policy.

The chief constable who is responsible for operational decisions is at the cutting edge of policing. He or she is appointed by the local police authority and is accountable to it for the operation of the force. It is, however, unclear how far a local police authority can set the priorities of its own police force. For example, can a local police authority request its police force to give priority to detecting crimes of violence over other offences or to place a low emphasis on detecting the possession of soft drugs? What is clear is that there is a degree of discretion about how the police interpret the enforcement of the laws. Thus it was found that the police could not be compelled to enforce the law on obscene publications, nor were they obliged to devote resources to giving total protection to lorries that were being picketed by animal rights protesters. During the nineteenth century local authorities frequently gave their police forces instructions on prosecution policy, but this practice declined during the twentieth century. Then the general view developed that policing policies were not a proper subject for detailed supervision by local government, a view that was apparently reinforced by the common law doctrine that the relationship between a local authority and a chief constable was *not* one of master and servant. As a result, a local authority could not be sued for the wrongdoing of the local police force.

The triangular relationship between the police, the local authority and central executive (which is now governed by the Police Acts) has recently come under increasing pressure from central government, which is seeking to extend its role in policing arrangements at the expense of local control and, it is feared, of police discretion. For much of the twentieth century the Home Secretary's powers in relation to police forces outside the Metropolitan area were limited. The Home Secretary had powers of inspection and powers to withhold grant, but not much more. The Home Secretary also had to approve the appointment of a chief constable.

During the 1990s, however, successive governments intervened in the management of the police. A key change occurred in 1994, when the Police and Magistrates' Courts Act altered the composition of the police authorities (which had hitherto contained two-thirds local councillors and one-third magistrates) to add an 'independent' element of persons appointed by the Home Secretary. Police authorities after April 1995 became 17-member bodies composed of three magistrates, nine local authority members and five central government nominees. (Slightly larger police authorities were established for Devon and Cornwall, Greater Manchester, Powys and South Wales.) Although local councillors remained the single largest element on the police authority, the effect of the 1994 legislation (which made police authorities single-function statutory bodies) was to distance the management of the police from local government. It was clear that councillors' powers had been diluted, but more importantly that national government intended to play a much greater role in the formulation and monitoring of police policy. In 1996 the Police Act gave central government new powers to set performance targets for the police; and there were changes in financial arrangements that gave greater powers to the Home Secretary to determine the distribution of police grant. The Home Secretary may also under the 1996 Act require the inspectors of constabulary to carry out a report and demand reports from the police authority on any matter relating to its police functions.

The balance of power has tilted further towards central government since 1997 in response to Labour's concern with efficiency and the effective delivery of policy and new concerns about crime and terrorism. After the 2001 election a new standards unit within the Home Office was established in an effort to eradicate variations of performance between police forces. A wide-ranging white paper – *Policing a New Century: A Blueprint for Reform* – foreshadowed a raft of changes including strengthened power for the Home Secretary, greater use of auxiliary forces and a revamped complaints procedure. The Police Reform Act of 2002, though modified as a result of criticism from such groups as Liberty, the Association of Chief Police Officers (ACPO) and the Association of Police Authorities, all of whom expressed reservations about its centralizing aspects, reinforced the Home Secretary's powers in a number of ways, including giving the Home Secretary powers to intervene in the management of police forces.

Complaints against the police

Public confidence in the police depends in part on the existence of effective machinery for handling complaints against them. Until 1976 allegations would usually be dealt with by another force, but this system inevitably failed to reassure the public, especially in the light of a series of scandals. In 1976 a Police Complaints Board was established to provide an independent element in the process of reviewing complaints against the police; this was replaced by a Police Complaints Authority in 1985. The inclusion of an independent element had at first been bitterly opposed by the police. Even when instituted, the system had many defects. It did not hear all allegations, only the most serious, and it was seen as lacking autonomy and openness. Criticisms of the system were made by the Home Affairs Committee in 1997, but it was probably the soul-searching that followed the Stephen Lawrence Inquiry that provided the greatest impetus for reform (see box 13.3). The Police Reform Act of 2002 set up a new body – the Independent Police Complaints Commission – to improve the machinery for handling complaints. Specifically, it is designed to provide greater openness and will investigate all cases that fall into certain categories (basically, the most serious) as well as ones referred to it. It will have its own teams of inspectors and will include substantial elements from outside the police.

Public confidence

Public confidence in the legal system was badly dented in the 1970s and 1980s by the discovery of gross errors of justice and the exposure of corruption in a few police

Box 13.3   The Macpherson Report into the death of Stephen Lawrence

Stephen Lawrence, a young black teenager, was murdered at a bus stop in south London on 22 April 1993. The police inquiry into the murder was widely seen as negligent, failing to accept that the murder was racially motivated and failing to follow up witnesses properly. A five-year campaign by the Lawrence family for an inquiry into police handling of the case finally succeeded when Home Secretary Jack Straw set up an inquiry under Sir William Macpherson, a former High Court judge. Macpherson was asked to consider whether the police had been incompetent, racist or corrupt. The Macpherson Report, published in 1999, found no evidence of corruption but did find incompetence and institutional racism, defined as 'the collective failure of an organization to provide an appropriate and professional service to people because of their colour, culture or ethnic origin'.

Source: The Stephen Lawrence Inquiry: Report of an Inquiry by Sir William Macpherson of Cluny (London: The Stationery Office, 1999), http://www.archive.official-documents.co.uk/document/cm42/4262/4262.htm

forces. Ethnic minorities in particular were alienated as evidence emerged of discrimination and indeed, as the Macpherson Inquiry into the death of Stephen Lawrence found, what was termed 'institutionalized racism' in the Metropolitan police force. Since then, substantial efforts have been made to remedy the situation through recruitment and training. Whether these efforts will be enough to rebuild public confidence is unclear (see table 13.4).

Table 13.4   Public confidence in the police
Q: Are you satisfied or dissatisfied with the way your area is policed?

Year	Satisfied	Dissatisfied	No opinion	Net
	%	%	%	± %
1981	75	23	2	+52
1983	70	25	5	+45
1985	67	23	10	+44
1987	59	25	16	+34
1989 (Apr)	58	31	11	+27
1989 (Nov)	64	22	14	+42
1992	51	35	14	+16
1993 (Jan)	51	35	14	+16
1993 (Jul)	59	28	13	+31
1999	69	21	10	+31
2000 (Apr)	53	33	14	+20
2000 (Jul)	52	33	15	+19
2001	43	50	7	−7

Source: MORI, http://www.mori.com/digest/2002/c020315.shtml

Conclusions

The legal system and the role of the judiciary are currently undergoing a series of profound transformations as a result of constitutional change and the government's agenda of legal reform. On some fronts those changes are making the legal system more accessible to those who use it and more transparent. There is, however, a danger that some reforms made in the name of modernization and enhanced efficiency – for example, the radical changes to the rules of evidence in criminal trials – may be at the expense of civil liberties and protections for the individual. Similarly, while many of the modernizing reforms of the police can be justified in the name of operational effectiveness, they also carry the danger of shifting the balance towards central government and weakening long-standing assumptions about the management of the police.

The most significant change in the British political system is the enlarged and enhanced role that judges are acquiring as independent checks on the government and protectors of individual rights. How they exercise that role will have serious implications for the quality of the British political system. On the most favourable scenario, the United Kingdom's hitherto executive-dominated system will become more balanced and the judiciary will be able to defend due process and individual liberties more effectively than in the past. On a less favourable scenario, the scene is set for endless wrangles between politicians and judges over which of them has the greater legitimacy in relation to matters that touch on legal policy. Either way, there will be renewed pressure for the judiciary itself to become more open and accountable, though this pressure may stop short of importing such American devices as confirmation hearings. At the very least, we may expect the significant and tangible cultural changes in relation to the handling of legal issues within the political system, and indeed within the legal profession, to accelerate, even if the end point of those processes of change is less than clear-cut.

 Key Questions

1 Do you agree that the judiciary's role in the political system is likely to increase in future?
2 Should the judiciary be made more accountable to the public and, if so, how?
3 How far should the police be accountable at the local level?

 Further Reading

The role of the judges is covered in J. A. G. Griffiths, *The Politics of the Judiciary* (5th edn; London: Fontana, 1991) and in Robert Stevens, *The English Judges: Their Role in the Changing Constitution* (Oxford: Hart, 2002). David Pannick, *The Judges* (Oxford: Oxford University Press, 1988) is also worth reading on judicial character. David Robertson, *Judicial Discretion in the House of Lords* (Oxford: Oxford University Press, 1998) offers a scholarly interpretation of the role of the House of Lords.

Several articles address the changing relationship between law and politics. See, for example, C. Foster, 'The encroachment of the law on politics', *Parliamentary Affairs*, 53: 2 (2000); D. Williams, 'Bias: The judges and the separation of powers', *Public Law* (2000); D. Woodhouse, 'Politicians and the judiciary: A changing relationship', *Parliamentary Affairs*, 48: 3 (1995) and 'The law and politics: More power to the judges – and to the people?', *Parliamentary Affairs*, 54: 2 (2001). Judicial review is examined in S. Halliday, 'The influence of judicial review on bureaucratic decision-making', *Public Law* (2000) and in A. Le Sueur, 'The judicial review debate: From partnership to friction', *Government and Opposition*, 36: 1 (1996). Nevil Johnson, 'The judicial dimension in British politics', *West European Politics*, 21: 1 (1998) and Hugh Berrington (ed.), *Britain in the Nineties* (London: Frank Cass, 1998) offer a more general analysis. The Human Rights Act is well covered in F. Klug, *Values for a Godless Age: The Story of the UK's New Bill of Rights* (London: Penguin, 2002). M. Zander, *A Bill of Rights?* (London: Sweet and Maxwell, 1997) is also illuminating.

Dawn Oliver, 'Parliament, ministers and the law', *Parliamentary Affairs*, 47 (1994) looks at the impact of increasing judicial activism on government, while D. Wincott, 'A community of law? "European" law and judicial politics', *Government and Opposition*, 35: 1 (2000) covers the expansion of the judicial role from the perspective of European law.

 Websites

See also the list of general websites at the back of the book.

- www.dca.gov.uk – Department for Constitutional Affairs
- www.lawreports.co.uk – Law Reports
- www.echr.coe.int/Eng/BasicTexts.htm – European Convention on Human Rights
- www.cps.gov.uk – Crown Prosecution Service
- www.cjsonline.org – Criminal Justice System online
- www.courtservice.gov.uk – Court Service
- www.ccrc.gov.uk – Criminal Cases Review Commission
- www.lawcom.gov.uk/ – Law Commission
- www.magistrates-association.org.uk/ – Magistrates Association
- www.hmprisonservice.gov.uk/ – Prison Service
- www.police.uk – Police Services of the UK
- www.met.police.uk/ – Metropolitan Police
- www.acpo.police.uk/ – Association of Chief Police Officers

14 Accountability and the Control of Government

The modern state and its agencies take a vast number of decisions that affect the lives of individuals. In a democracy it is vital that citizens can feel confident that mechanisms exist for those decisions to be monitored and challenged if they go wrong. Democratic theory assumes that there will be procedures in place for exposing administrative error and governmental mistakes. At the broadest level, this means that there must be opportunities to subject the government to rigorous and public examination to see, for example, if public policy is being effectively made and if public money is being properly spent. At a lower level, there need to be rules which make the interactions between state and the citizen predictable. Finally, individuals who are affected by public decisions, for example in relation to tax, property or benefits, need to have independent channels through which they can challenge or appeal those decisions. The broader the reach of public policy, the more the need for effective and accessible appeal mechanisms.

Changing Expectations and Values

For a long time the United Kingdom looked primarily to Parliament to secure accountability rather than to other agencies such as the courts. The growth and complexity of the modern state (as evidenced by such cases as the 1954 Crichel Down affair; see box 14.1) cast doubt on Parliament's ability alone to exercise the scrutiny of executive power. Accordingly, new institutions such as ombudsmen have been developed to balance the executive; and the older ones – the courts, tribunals and Parliament itself – have sharpened their techniques and acquired more resources for controlling government decision making.

There has been a cultural shift towards greater openness and transparency in government which has greatly aided the cause of accountability. Recent constitutional reforms – especially devolution and the introduction of the Human Rights Act (HRA) – have changed the balance of power in the British state. The HRA in particular has immense potential to bring about greater transparency within the UK by strengthening the ability of the judiciary to review the decisions of public authorities and by obliging decision-making bodies to give reasons for their decisions. Equally importantly, the HRA is promoting a cultural transformation in which all governmental agencies and bodies with public responsibilities give greater prominence to civil rights issues in their thinking. In this chapter we review the

Box 14.1   The Crichel Down affair, 1954

The Crichel Down case was the cause of a major political controversy, prompting a re-examination of the methods available for investigating administrative error and the traditional doctrine of ministerial responsibility.

Crichel Down was a piece of land in Dorset which had been compulsorily purchased by the Air Ministry in 1937, though later transferred to the Ministry of Agriculture. In 1950 the land was no longer needed, but instead of allowing the original owner's family to repurchase it, the department pursued a policy of trying to let it. A campaign led by Commander Marten (the son-in-law of the original owner) gained support on the Conservative backbenches and was backed by the National Farmers Union. An inquiry seriously criticized the way the issue had been handled. After a debate in the House of Commons, the Minister of Agriculture Sir Thomas Dugdale resigned, taking responsibility for the actions of his civil servants. On one level this looked like a classic case of how the convention of ministerial responsibility should operate; but the civil servants were also publicly criticized (rather than shielded) and Dugdale's resignation was widely thought to have occurred because the prime minister could afford to let him go. During the debate the Home Secretary set out a series of rules of ministerial responsibility (the Maxwell-Fyfe rules). The affair underlined the danger of administrative error in the expanded British state and provoked new thinking about how best to protect against it. Concern about maladministration led first to the establishment of the Franks Committee on Tribunals and Inquiries, and later to the establishment of the Parliamentary Commissioner for Administration, or ombudsman.

structures of accountability more generally in order to try to obtain a total picture of the various ways in which public bodies are held responsible in the United Kingdom and the opportunities that individuals have to challenge governmental decision making.

On a number of fronts public attitudes towards decision making by public bodies have changed in recent years. There is greater emphasis on probity and procedural fairness and an expectation that decision makers will be able to justify their decisions. The Citizen's Charter placed a greater emphasis than before on the rights of consumers in terms of both being able to challenge decisions and making public bodies user friendly. Public authorities, like private bodies, have to be responsive to their customers.

Parliament

Parliament's ability to serve as the major mechanism for holding government accountable has long been open to question. As was noted in chapter 2, the vagueness of the convention of ministerial responsibility makes it highly uncertain when a minister will resign over policy errors. Internal party considerations rather than parliamentary ones forced Leon Brittan's resignation over the Westland affair (see box 5.5, p. 186). No minister resigned over the Matrix Churchill affair. It is true that ministers will more readily resign when issues of personal conduct are involved, as occurred in the case of Peter Mandelson (twice), Stephen Byers and Geoffrey Robinson. But a minister who has the support of his colleagues, especially of the prime minister, is likely to be able to withstand calls for resignation. Decisions to resign because a minister feels he or she was responsible for a policy error (as occurred with Lord Carrington over the Falklands) or on grounds of conscience (as occurred with Robin Cook over the war with Iraq) are rare.

The ability of the government to command the majority of Parliament's time and, above all, the pervasiveness of party and the control that gives to the executive mean that Parliament is very unlikely to act as a major counterbalance to the wide discretionary powers of the executive in the British system. Although select committees play an important scrutiny role, their coverage is patchy and they are not intended to operate as mechanisms for protecting the individual citizen from administrative error. Parliamentary questions may be used to expose some weaknesses in decision making, but they too are uneven in what they cover. They have also become too much a part of the adversarial gamesmanship to operate systematically as a check on government or as a channel which an aggrieved citizen can use to challenge a decision that affects him or her.

In addition to these long-standing weaknesses of Parliament, recent years have seen changes in the wider structure of decision making within the state that have further reduced Parliament's capacity to exert control over the decisions affecting citizens. Most notably, the scope of the government's own decision-making powers has been reduced by processes that have transferred decision-making power to supranational bodies such as the European Union or to devolved bodies such as the Scottish Parliament. As a result, many policy areas such as the environment are now largely outside not just Parliament's control, but the control of the nation state as a whole.

The fragmentation of executive structures within the UK and the greater use of agencies (discussed, respectively, in chapters 2 and 5) do not in themselves weaken accountability. But they mean that responsibility for decision making is diffused, and it is harder to follow the trail of a policy or administrative action. The attribution of blame (or credit) becomes more difficult and errors are likely to be exposed the further a decision is taken away from the centre. Other changes over recent years, for example contracting out and privatization, have obscured accountability.

From the perspective of the individual citizen, the multiplication of decision-making bodies and the frequent reorganization of their responsibilities are likely to be confusing and daunting. In many instances of administrative decision making, for example in relation to taxation decisions and welfare benefits, Parliament has made provision for formal channels of appeal. In some areas there is no formal appeal machinery and individuals who want to challenge decisions have to rely on the courts or the ombudsman.

Tribunals

In the last chapter we mentioned the way in which tribunals had developed as an alternative mechanism of dispute resolution to the ordinary courts and as a means for providing appeals in such important and contentious areas as welfare benefits, employment law and tax assessment (see box 14.2). There used to be a number of separate tribunals operating in the field of social security but in 2000, as part of a wide-ranging reform designed to speed the process of review, a single unified tribunal, the Appeals Service, replaced five separate tribunals: the Social Security Appeal Tribunal, the Medical Appeal Tribunal, the Disability Appeal Tribunal, the Child

Box 14.2 Examples of tribunals, 2003

- Agricultural Land Tribunals (DEFRA/Welsh Assembly) – Settle disputes between agricultural landlords and tenants, also drainage disputes between neighbours.
- Agricultural Arbitrators (DEFRA/Welsh Assembly) – Most cases relate to commercial rent review disputes.
- The Appeals Service (DWP) – The Service arranges and hears appeals on decisions on Social Security, Child Support, Vaccine Damage, Tax Credit and Compensation Recovery. The Appeals Service consists of two distinct bodies within a single organization. The first is a tribunal non-departmental public body with responsibility for the judicial functioning of appeals tribunals. It is headed by the president of appeals tribunals. The second is an executive agency of the DWP. At the head of the agency, with responsibility for the administration of appeals, is the chief executive.
- Care Standards Tribunal (DoH) – Encompasses the former Registered Homes Tribunal and the Protection of Children Act Tribunal. Deals with appeals under the Registered Homes Act 1984 in respect of independent residential care and nursing homes, and under the Children Act 1989 in respect of voluntary homes and registered children's homes.
- Civil Aviation Authority (DTLR) – Disputes in connection with regulation of airlines, air travel organizers and airports.
- Comptroller-General of Patents, Designs and Trade Marks (DTI) – Covers both the grant/registration of patents, trade marks and designs and also disputes on the cancellation of these rights, entitlement and licensing.
- Criminal Injuries Compensation Appeals Panel (Home Office) – Hears appeals against review decisions taken by the Criminal Injuries Compensation Authority on applications for compensation received from victims of crimes of violence.
- Director General of Fair Trading (DTI) – Hears representations made against a 'minded to refuse/revoke/suspend/grant in different terms' notice in respect of licences issued under the Consumer Credit Act 1974 and a 'notice of proposal' under the Estate Agents Act 1979.
- Employment Tribunals (DTI) – Hear appeals relating to employment rights matters including claims regarding unfair dismissal and discrimination.
- General Commissioners of Income Tax (LCD/DCA) – Hear and determine appeals concerning decisions of the Inland Revenue relating to income tax, corporation tax, capital gains tax and national insurance.
- Health Authorities Discipline Committees (DoH) – Hear cases of alleged breaches of terms of service by Family Health Service independent contractors (which could involve false claims for fees or expenses).
- Immigration Adjudicators (LCD/DCA) – Determine appeals against refusal to enter or remain in the United Kingdom and in asylum cases.
- Immigration Appeal Tribunal (LCD/DCA) – Hears appeals from determinations of Immigration Adjudicators on a point of fact or law, and against certain executive decisions to make deportation orders.

(Continues)

Box 14.2 *Continued*

- Information Commissioner (Home Office) – May impose various sanctions against data users who fail to comply with the standards of information handling required by the Data Protection Act 1984.
- Lands Tribunal (LCD/DCA) – Covers disputed claims for compensation for compulsory purchase of land; appeals from valuation tribunals in rating valuation cases; and discharge or modification of restrictive covenants affecting freehold land.
- Mental Health Review Tribunal (DoH) – Hears applications for discharge made by patients detained in hospital or a nursing home or detained under restrictions, and applications by patients who are made subject to 'supervised discharge'.
- Parking Adjudicators (DTLR) – National Parking Adjudication Service (outside London)/Parking and Traffic Appeals Service (London). Hear appeals against penalty charge notices (for unauthorized vehicle parking).
- Pensions Appeal Tribunals (LCD/DCA) – Hear appeals against decisions as to eligibility for (entitlement), or amount of (assessment), war pensions.
- Pensions Ombudsman (DWP) – Appointed under the Pension Schemes Act 1993 to investigate and decide complaints and disputes concerning occupational and personal pension schemes.
- Rent Assessment Panels (ODPM) – Constituted as Rent Assessment Committees to decide appeals against fair rent determinations by rent officers, and to determine a rent in the open market and under an assured tenancy, and as Leasehold Valuation Tribunals to adjudicate in disputes about the enfranchisement of the freehold and leasehold renewals, and in disputes about service charges, insurance and the appointment of managers.
- Schools Admission and Exclusion Appeal Panels (DfES) – Local education authorities constitute the panels to hear school admission appeals and exclusion appeals under the School Standards and Framework Act 1998.
- Social Security and Child Support Commissioners (LCD/DCA) – Determine appeals and applications for leave to appeal from decisions of the Appeals Service.
- Special Commissioners (LCD/DCA) – Hear and determine appeals concerning decisions of the Inland Revenue relating to all direct taxes, e.g. income tax, corporation tax, capital gains tax and capital transfer tax.
- Special Educational Needs and Disability Tribunal (DfES) – Hears parents' appeals against the decisions of local education authorities on assessments and statements of special educational needs.
- Traffic Commissioners (DTLR) – Make decisions concerning the grant, variation, revocation or suspension of goods and public service vehicle operator licences, and to deal with disciplinary matters affecting goods and public service vehicle operator licences.
- Transport Tribunal (LCD/DCA) – Hears appeals against decisions of Traffic Commissioners regarding goods and public service vehicle operator licences.
- Valuation Tribunals (ODPM) – Hear appeals concerning council tax, non-domestic rating and land drainage rates.
- VAT and Duties Tribunals (LCD/DCA) – Hear and determine appeals and applications concerning decisions of HM Customs and Excise relating to VAT, Customs and Excise duties, landfill tax and insurance premium tax.

Support Appeal Tribunal and the Vaccine Damage Appeal Tribunal. At the same time, the Appeals Service Agency was established as an executive agency to oversee the judicial functioning of these appeal tribunals. This tribunal now hears a quarter of all appeals.

This reform of the structure of social security appeals underlines some of the problems facing tribunals and other formal appeal mechanisms in modern Britain, not least the potential conflict between the needs of government, the needs of users and the requirements of procedural fairness. Tribunals, as noted in the last chapter, developed in an ad hoc and incremental way over the twentieth century and it was not until the mid-1950s that a general review took place, partly as a response to heightened awareness of the range of public decision-making powers affecting individuals in the modern state at the time of Crichel Down. That review – the Franks Report – was an important early effort to get to grips with the complexities of the modern state and to subject decision making to clear principles and rules. Franks recognized that the increased role of government even in 1957 had created the need to review the procedures that balanced the rights of individuals against the wider public interest. The report recognized also that while administration needed to be efficient in the sense of being able to secure policy objectives speedily, care had to be taken to show that where an individual's interest was affected, the case had been carefully considered. If this care was not demonstrated, Franks argued, the administrative process would not command public support and indeed would be unlikely to remain efficient in the long run. Franks identified values that he thought should mark the workings of tribunals. These values were openness, fairness and impartiality and they have come to play a major role in public thinking about the administrative process as a whole. The specific recommendations of the Franks Report were largely directed towards identifying the conditions that would make tribunals more clearly part of the machinery of justice. Franks also recommended that a supervisory body for tribunals be set up (the Council on Tribunals; see box 14.3) and that it report to the Lord Chancellor.

The Franks Report was the only general review of the tribunal system until the Leggatt Report of 2001, although the Council on Tribunals has monitored the system's efficacy through its annual and special reports. By the time of the 2001 Leggatt Report, tribunals had become even more significant and diverse than they were in the mid-1950s – the largest part of the civil justice system, handling over a million cases per year.

The diversity between tribunals was criticized by Leggatt, who contrasted their various types. The largest tribunal, the Appeals Service, is a relatively recent creation and is the result of the amalgamation of several tribunals dealing with benefits. Because it is so large (dealing with about one-quarter of all tribunal cases), it is provided with an extensive infrastructure and resources. Other tribunals, as Leggatt pointed out, do not have such capacity.

In the period since the Franks Report of 1957, concerns about tribunals have altered, reflecting different priorities on the part of government and different public agendas. Franks was especially anxious to ensure the independence and procedural fairness of tribunals. During the years after Franks, other concerns surfaced. The Conservative governments of 1979–97 were particularly eager to increase efficient and economic decision making, even at the expense of public confidence in the

Box 14.3   The role of the Council on Tribunals

The Franks Report concluded that 'openness, fairness and impartiality' should govern the work of tribunals. The Council on Tribunals, which was established following the Franks Report, believes that, to comply with these principles, tribunal proceedings need to display the following characteristics:

- be easily accessible to members of the public who would like the tribunal to deal with their case;
- be cheap, quick and as informal as possible;
- provide the right to an oral hearing;
- be held in public;
- conclude with the tribunal giving adequate reasons for its decisions;
- have time limits where necessary to prevent delay (although these limits should not be too short);
- be seen to be independent, impartial and fair to all.

The Council takes an overview of the work of tribunals including:

- delays in hearing cases
- ways in which tribunals can show their independence
- guidance literature about tribunals
- the qualifications of tribunal chairs and members
- accommodation and resources
- access for the disabled
- the role of tribunal clerks, listing and other administrative issues
- legal advice and representation (including legal aid)
- training of tribunal members
- readiness for the implementation of ECHR
- standards and performance targets

Source: Council on Tribunals, 2003.

quality of decision making by tribunals. For example, there was a tendency, roundly criticized by the Council on Tribunals in the 1980s and early 1990s, to exempt some tribunals from the duty to give reasons for a decision. Leggatt wanted to ensure that tribunals were responsive to the needs of users as much as to the needs of departments.

Inquiries

Inquiries can be used in situations where it is important that an extensive examination of the factual background occurs before a decision is taken and where it is important for different viewpoints to be heard. Legislation will often build in the requirement or possibility of an inquiry before a final decision is made. They are routinely used where the compulsory purchase or development of land is involved. An inquiry may be used in connection with a local authority's structure plan, or it can be used as an appeal mechanism against the recommendations of the Boundary Commissions for the redistribution of a parliamentary constituency. Inquiries about development projects that are environmentally sensitive now provide an opportunity for pressure groups as well as individuals to voice their objections, and planning inquiries, especially those into road development, have become the focus of much organized and well-publicized opposition in recent years. Indeed, it has been argued that the lack of formalized procedures at inquiries made it easier for the anti-road movement to hijack them (Dudley and Richardson, 1998).

In theory, inquiries provide information for the minister who must ultimately make the decision about whether a project should go ahead. They are thus an inherent part of the policy process. The scale of an inquiry can vary enormously depending on whether what is at issue is the siting of a new airport, a motorway or nuclear waste plant, on the one hand, or a much smaller development, on the other.

The Franks Report of 1957, which also covered inquiries, gave the Council on Tribunals different powers in relation to inquiries from those it gave in relation to tribunals. Tribunals, Franks thought, should properly be seen as part of the machinery for adjudication; inquiries were an integral part of the policy process involving ministerial discretion. Since ministers would be answerable to Parliament for the resolution of any conflict between private and public interests, ministers could not be entirely impartial in relation to an inquiry, though they could ensure that all the evidence relevant to a decision was heard. The taking of that evidence was the purpose of the inquiry. Thus, although it was important that the process of holding the inquiry was procedurally fair, there could be no guarantee that the evidence taken to an inquiry would determine the minister's decision. As the Council on Tribunals put it, 'the inquiry is modelled on judicial procedure, but it cannot lead to an equally objective decision. In the last resort the Minister must do what he thinks most expedient' (Second Report of the Council on Tribunals, 1961).

Nevertheless, the Council on Tribunals took as its mandate the application to inquiries and hearing of standards that would satisfy the average citizen of their fairness. Since the 1960s the courts have increasingly imposed standards of procedural fairness on the conduct of inquiries, while recognizing that ultimately the decision remained one of policy.

The passage of HRA resulted in a challenge to the way inquiries have been conducted in the UK. In a 2001 case that reached the House of Lords (*R. v. Secretary of State for the Environment ex parte Alconbury Development*), the very character of inquiries was at issue. It was alleged that when a planning decision was taken not by an inspector but by the Secretary of State, there was an interest in the outcome which meant that it could not be regarded as independent and impartial within the meaning of Article 6 (1) of HRA. The House of Lords, however, decided that HRA did not prevent the minister having the final say in planning applications because planning matters were essentially matters of policy and expediency, not of law. Moreover, it was felt that there existed a reasonable balance between matters of policy left to ministerial discretion and matters of procedural fairness in relation to the inquiry where the courts could control the exercise of discretionary power.

Inquiries may be statutory, where provision for an inquiry is made through legislation such as the Transport Acts, or non-statutory, where an inquiry is established by the executive using its inherent powers. A special category of inquiry is that constituted under the Tribunals of Inquiry (Evidence) Act of 1921. This allows Parliament to establish a tribunal to look into a public policy issue or catastrophe in a judicial manner detached from government or party interest. The use of the Tribunals of Inquiry (Evidence) Act of 1921 is relatively rare, although it has been employed for investigations into a range of policy errors and public disasters where it is important to make a complex factual background public, such as the Aberfan pit disaster, the Bloody Sunday incident, the Dunblane massacre and the discovery that a Manchester doctor, Harold Shipman, had killed a large number of patients (see box 14.4). An inquiry was also established to examine the complex background to the suicide of the government scientist Dr David Kelly in 2003 (see box 14.5 for

Box 14.4   Terms of reference of the Shipman Inquiry

The Shipman Inquiry was established under the Tribunals of Inquiry (Evidence) Act 1921. Its terms of reference were:

a.   After receiving the existing evidence and hearing such further evidence as necessary, to consider the extent of Harold Shipman's unlawful activities.

b.   To enquire into the actions of the statutory bodies, authorities, other organizations and responsible individuals concerned in the procedures and investigations which followed the deaths of those of Harold Shipman's patients who died in unlawful or suspicious circumstances.

c.   By reference to the case of Harold Shipman to enquire into the performance of the functions of those statutory bodies, authorities, other organizations and individuals with responsibility for monitoring primary care provision and the use of controlled drugs.

d.   Following those enquiries, to recommend what steps, if any, should be taken to protect patients in the future, and to report its findings to the Secretary of State for the Home Department and to the Secretary of State for Health.

Box 14.5   Some controversial inquiries

Inquiry and chairman		Topic
1989	Piper Alpha Disaster (Lord Cullen)	The cause of off-shore oil rig disaster.
1992	BCCI (Lord Bingham)	The collapse of the Bank of Credit and Commerce International.
1996	Sales of Arms to Iraq (Lord Scott)	Issues raised by the Matrix-Churchill trial.
1998	BSE (Lord Phillips)	The emergence of BSE and CJD and responses to them.
2001	Shipman Inquiry (Dame Janet Smith)	Issues raised by the conviction of a Manchester doctor for multiple murders.
2003	Hutton Inquiry (Lord Hutton)	Circumstances surrounding the death of a government scientist, Dr David Kelly.

examples of controversial inquiries). Transport accidents such as rail crashes tend to be examined under transport legislation and the procedurally contentious Scott investigation into the sale of arms to Iraq was examined by a non-statutory inquiry. Sometimes inquiries are forced upon government by pressure groups; sometimes – like Royal Commissions – they are a device to kick complex or embarrassing questions into the long grass.

The Role of Ombudsmen

One innovation to remedy Parliament's weakness in the investigation of cases where the individual is harmed by an administrative error of a public authority occurred in 1967, when the Parliamentary Commissioner Act established the office of the Parliamentary Commissioner for Administration, now the Parliamentary Ombudsman (the title changed in 1994). The catalyst for change was the 1961 Whyatt Report produced by Justice, the organization for administrative lawyers within the United Kingdom. This report recommended that the UK should adopt a modified version of the ombudsman system familiar in Scandinavia and introduced into New Zealand. The idea was initially rejected by the Conservative government but was taken up by the Labour Party prior to the 1964 general election. Ultimately, that commitment resulted both in the office of the Parliamentary Commissioner and in the introduction of a range of ombudsman-type bodies across the public and private sectors.

The Crichel Down affair of 1954 had underlined the difficulty in reversing faulty administrative decisions in the increasingly complex British state. The idea of the ombudsman was that the office should provide dedicated investigation of grievances against government departments. In this way, not merely would individuals in dispute with public authorities have a champion whom they could approach in a relatively simple and low-cost way, but the office would provide a spur to high standards of administration. Unfortunately, the system introduced in 1967 was initially extremely restrictive and much time and ingenuity have been required to overcome the limitations of the original legislation. Although the House of Commons of 1966 contained a number of MPs who appreciated the need to augment traditional constitutional mechanisms to improve accountability in the modern state, the new institution still seemed threatening to MPs' cherished role as defenders of their constituents. This fear was a powerful one, despite the difficulties increasingly facing individual backbench MPs in unravelling the complex workings of bureaucracy. As a result of the fear that one element of the MP's role would become redundant, the Parliamentary Commissioner for Administration was not allowed to handle complaints direct from the public. Instead, all complaints had to be referred from an MP.

The restriction of the so-called 'MP filter' distinguishes the UK's Parliamentary Ombudsman from the majority of foreign ombudsmen systems. The refusal to accept complaints directly from the public was designed to locate responsibility for the redress of grievances very firmly in the House of Commons; but it caused confusion among the public, especially once other public sector ombudsmen (for example in local government) did accept complaints directly. Significantly, both the Public Administration Committee (which absorbed the work of the Select Committee on the Parliamentary Commissioner for Administration in 1997) and the Parliamentary Ombudsman want this filter removed. It seems highly likely that direct access will be introduced if a series of proposals for reforming the office (notably by creating a collegial public sector ombudsman – i.e., effectively an ombudsman's office that would incorporate all the separate public service ombudsmen) contained in a 2000 Cabinet Office review are implemented.

One fear about direct access to the ombudsman's services is that the removal of the filter will lead to a further increase in workload. Although the number of complaints handled by the Parliamentary Ombudsman has varied over the years, 2001–2 saw the highest number of complaints on record – 2,139 compared with 1,721 in 2000–1, an increase of 24 per cent over the previous year (see figure 14.1). Despite a 7 per cent drop in staff, the Parliamentary Commissioner for Administration intervened in 54 per cent of complaints referred to it or 57 per cent of complaints within its jurisdiction. Both Parliament and the Parliamentary Ombudsman have emphasized the importance of dealing with complaints from the public as quickly as possible. Michael Buckley, who was Parliamentary Ombudsman until 2002, changed the working practices of the ombudsman's office towards the end of his term. Simpler and faster methods were employed so that many issues could be resolved quickly, moving away from the stark 'investigate or reject' culture (see box 14.6). Nevertheless, even with these reforms, investigations still take what may seem to a complainant an excessive amount of time: on average about 45 weeks in 1999–2000 as against 91 weeks in 1998–9.

There were at the beginning of its history a number of restrictions in the Parliamentary Ombudsman's jurisdiction. The office's remit is limited to cases of maladministration, which puts the emphasis firmly on procedural error rather than the merits of a case or individual rights. The notion of maladministration was initially illustrated by the so-called 'Crossman catalogue', which comprised examples of errors that would constitute maladministration. These included bias, neglect, inattention, delay, incompetence, ineptitude, perversity, turpitude or arbitrariness. Decisions that were simply unjust, unreasonable or oppressive in substance were

Box 14.6 Investigative methods of the Parliamentary Ombudsman

In April 2000 the Parliamentary Ombudsman effected a major reorganization to increase the speed with which it could handle complaints. The separate screening and investigation directorates were replaced by five separate directorates (later reduced to four). There was more delegation to staff and inspectors were appointed, each covering particular departments, agencies and other public sector bodies. A structure of investigators manages the progress of complaints and reports on investigations. Most importantly, the Parliamentary Ombudsman has varied the way in which complaints are handled to match the individual circumstances of a case and to resolve disputes early in the process without a statutory investigation and full report. This is done by making inquiries of a department as an alternative to starting an investigation so that a complaint can be settled quickly and efficiently. In an increasing proportion of cases it is possible to resolve complaints without a statutory report, instead sending a brief note to the MP and the body complained against setting out the findings.

Source: Parliamentary Commissioner for Administration, Annual Report 2000–1.

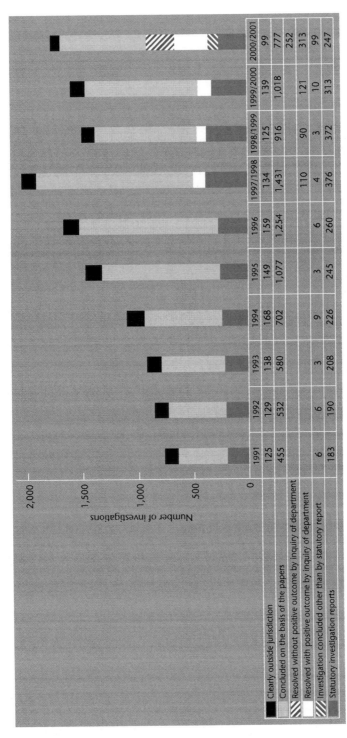

	1991	1992	1993	1994	1995	1996	1997/1998	1998/1999	1999/2000	2000/2001
Clearly outside jurisdiction	125	129	138	168	149	159	134	125	139	99
Concluded on the basis of the papers	455	532	580	702	1,077	1,254	1,431	916	1,018	777
Resolved without positive outcome by inquiry of department										252
Resolved with positive outcome by inquiry of department							110	90	121	313
Investigation concluded other than by statutory report	6	6	3	9	3	6	4	3	10	99
Statutory investigation reports	183	190	208	226	245	260	376	372	313	247

Number of investigations

Figure 14.1 The changing pattern of the Ombudsman's activities. A change in working practices has led to an increase in the number of investigations concluded other than by statutory report. In previous years discontinued investigations were often the result of natural circumstances such as the aggrieved taking court action rather than a conscientious decision by the Office to conclude the case as soon as is reasonable to do so.

apparently excluded from the ombudsman's jurisdiction provided that they were taken without maladministration. Over time, however, expectations about what constitutes maladministration have changed, especially in the light of the new emphasis on consumer rights. Thus in 1978 the Parliamentary Ombudsman declared that although it was not his job to substitute his judgement for that of a minister, he believed he already had the power to investigate unjust or oppressive governmental action. In the early 1990s, rather different examples of what would constitute maladministration were given by the Parliamentary Ombudsman (see box 14.7).

The areas which the Parliamentary Ombudsman can investigate are roughly those for which a parliamentary question would be accepted – mainly central government departments and agencies. The 1967 legislation excluded the Parliamentary Ombudsman from investigating complaints made against health authority decisions, decisions of the nationalized industries and the police. Civil service personnel questions were excluded from investigation, as were matters of a commercial or contractual nature. Some of these exclusions reflected the government's intention to tie the office to central government; others indicated the conception of the Parliamentary Ombudsman as a weapon for the ordinary citizen to use rather than as one which public employees could use against their employer or for one citizen to use against another.

Another complicating restriction in the early years of the Parliamentary Ombudsman's existence concerned the relationship between redress through the courts and complaints to the Parliamentary Commissioner for Administration. The ombudsman was not intended to investigate matters where there was recourse to the courts, unless taking legal action would be unduly burdensome. However, with the growth of judicial activism in the period since 1967, there is now a substantial degree of overlap between the Parliamentary Ombudsman and the courts. Indeed, the Parliamentary Ombudsman has commented on the extent to which the overlap between judicial remedies and those provided through his office can be problematic, not least because complainants may use an initial inquiry by the ombudsman to prepare the ground for litigation.

There were extensions of the Parliamentary Ombudsman's jurisdiction – for example, to cover complaints against consular officials and to enable those resident abroad to make complaints about the quality of assistance they had received. In 1993 the Parliamentary Ombudsman was given the task of policing the government's open government reforms. Although there is now freedom of information legislation, it is not being fully implemented until 2005. The Parliamentary Ombudsman thus retains for the moment the task of monitoring departmental compli-

Box 14.7 Maladministration

There is no simple definition of maladministration but the Parliamentary Ombudsman has stated that it includes such things as bias, rudeness, unwillingness to treat the complainant as a person with rights, refusal to answer reasonable questions and neglecting to inform someone, on request, of his or her rights or entitlements.

Source: *Insight*, October 2002 (Newsletter of the Parliamentary Ombudsman).

ance with the 1993 Code of Practice. As noted earlier, some of the gaps in the Parliamentary Ombudsman's early coverage were filled by the creation of specialist public sector ombudsmen for the health services in 1973 and local government in 1974 (see box 14.8).

The Parliamentary Ombudsman is also the Health Commissioner, although separate reports are issued in each capacity. After devolution separate jurisdictions were established for Scotland and Wales. The Parliamentary Ombudsman exercises this role but reports to the Scottish Parliament and the Welsh Assembly, respectively.

The idea of ombudsmen has been extended to the private sector to enhance consumer powers of redress (Seneviratne, 2002). Thus there are now ombudsmen for the insurance industry, banking, building societies, legal services, pensions, investments and rented housing. Some of these schemes were set up voluntarily, others as a result of statute.

Initial fears about how well the ombudsman would fit into the British administrative process largely explain the early restrictions on jurisprudence and powers imposed on the office. It also shaped the style adopted by the first ombudsman, Sir Edmund Compton. Sir Edmund had been Comptroller and Auditor General and his cautious approach to the new responsibilities paralleled the internal auditing functions of his office. Initially the ombudsman's office was seen as an instrument for aiding parliamentary control of the administration rather than as a wholly independent institution with its own lien to the public. It was also felt that complaints were best investigated by civil servants who were best able to understand departmental procedures. Since Sir Edmund's time ombudsmen have changed their style to reach out more widely to the public and to promote the role of the office as one of external

---

Box 14.8   Public and private sector ombudsman schemes, 2003

Estate Agents
Financial Ombudsman Services
Health Services: England
                   Scotland
                   Wales
Independent Housing Ombudsman
Legal Services Ombudsman
Local Government Ombudsman: England
                              Scotland
                              Wales
Northern Ireland Ombudsman
Northern Ireland Police Ombudsman
Parliamentary Ombudsman
Scottish Parliamentary Ombudsman
Welsh Administration Ombudsman
Pensions Ombudsman
Scottish Legal Services Ombudsman
Scottish Public Services Ombudsman
Telecommunications Ombudsman

accountability. In this, successive ombudsmen have been encouraged by the parliamentary select committees to which the office reports. It is also worth noting here that although the first appointments as Parliamentary Ombudsman were civil servants, this tradition has changed and appointments have been increasingly made from the ranks of lawyers. (The current Parliamentary Ombudsman is Ann Abraham, who was formerly Legal Services Ombudsman.) The government will consult the relevant select committee before making an appointment to the post. As of January 2003, there were 81 Parliamentary Ombudsman full-time-equivalent staff, not counting central support services, which are shared with the Health and Safety Commission. Although the majority of the Parliamentary Ombudsman's staff are still civil servants, many are now employees of the office rather than staff on secondment from another department. Since the early days, Parliamentary Ombudsmen have also become increasingly imaginative about publicizing their work by media appearances and the use of new technology, including email and websites.

The Parliamentary Ombudsman has no formal powers to overturn a departmental decision, but there is a strong convention that recommendations are implemented. The Parliamentary Commissioner may recommend that monetary compensation be paid and the amounts can vary from small sums to the very substantial amounts involved in the complex Barlow Clowes case. Sometimes all that is required is an apology. Recently, the Parliamentary Ombudsman has drawn attention to sometimes quite lengthy delays and foot-dragging before departments accept recommendations for redress. The ombudsman is keen that there should be a deadline for a departmental response to a finding of maladministration.

The popularity of the institution is explained by the fact that it is relatively simple to use and that it is free. It does, of course, have limitations and the proliferation of ombudsmen may lead to increased public confusion. The idea – proposed in the Collcutt Review – of a single 'one-stop shop' for complaints is probably the way forward, though no legislative action has as yet been forthcoming.

Administrative Law and Judicial Review

The central importance of the theory of ministerial responsibility in British constitutional thinking partly explains why the British ombudsman was established with such restrictive features. The central role of Parliament was also a factor in the relatively slow growth of judicial techniques for controlling and regulating administrative discretion. Judicial review of administrative action was relatively familiar at the level of local government, where powers were delegated. Starting in the 1960s, however, the courts began to take a much more active role in reviewing all public sector decisions, including national-level ones taken by ministers. Although this development met with opposition from politicians and administrators, it is unlikely that this trend will be reversed. Questions of legality and the possibility of legal challenge have become even more significant with the passage of the HRA, which strengthens significantly the obligations on public authorities to behave lawfully.

Judicial review is a process that addresses the lawfulness of a decision by asking, for example, whether the decision-making body was within its powers, whether it was procedurally fair, whether it was unreasonable and, since 1998, whether it was compatible with the HRA. (A decision might also now be challenged as to whether it was compatible with European Community law.) Judicial review had long been a familiar feature of local government, where the question of whether a local authority has the power to act in a given way is regularly challenged. What was novel from the 1960s onwards was the increasing tendency of the courts to review the use that ministers made of their discretion in taking decisions.

Appeals against an administrative decision can go to the merits of a decision only if Parliament has provided a mechanism for appeal. Sometimes, however, Parliament has not provided any appeal mechanism. Challenging the legality or procedural fairness of a decision is often an additional opportunity to overturn a decision, and sometimes the only available remedy.

The strengthening of judicial review in the United Kingdom since the 1960s was inevitably a somewhat piecemeal process and there was some variation in approach between different judges and courts. But as a result of judicial refinement of the law, as well as important reforms promoted by the Law Commission and successive governments, by the end of the twentieth century the UK had a recognizable and authoritative body of administrative law. It also in 2000 had an Administrative Court (see box 14.9).

The modern period of judicial review probably begins with the landmark case of *Ridge* v. *Baldwin* in 1964. In this case the judges extended the doctrine of natural justice so that it could be applied to administrative as well as judicial or quasi-judicial decisions. The distinction between categories of decision (administrative, judicial or quasi-judicial) seems to have been injected into British administrative law in the 1930s when the Donoughmore Committee examined the enormous growth of ministers' powers that took place with the expansion of government. The principles of natural justice the Donoughmore Committee asserted had to be observed in decisions that were judicial or quasi-judicial in character, but certain implications of those principles, for example the right to know the reasons for a decision, made them inappropriate for administrative decisions. Although the Franks Committee, a quarter of a century later, also underlined the significance of the principles in natural justice in areas where tribunals operated, it was not until the 1964 case of *Ridge* v. *Baldwin* that they were applied to *administrative* decisions. That extension had enormous consequences. The reluctance to extend the principles of natural justice to the administrative process before the 1960s reflects the historical concern to protect the governing process from the intrusive tentacles of the law.

In *Ridge* v. *Baldwin* a police authority's decision to dismiss a chief constable was held to be a nullity because he was afforded no opportunity to present his case to the authority before the decision was taken. Thus the police authority – the decision-making body – had failed to observe one of the fundamental rules of natural justice: that no party ought to be condemned unheard. Lord Reid, one of the judges who heard the case in the House of Lords, commented in his speech that the concept of natural justice was vague; but it did not follow that because a thing could not be cut and dried or nicely measured it did not exist. Lord Reid and his fellow law lords emphasized that the principles of natural justice were inherent in all legal thinking, even if they had to be applied to a host of new situations.

Judicial review developed rapidly after *Ridge* v. *Baldwin* as the judges refined their ability to ensure that ministers and other public bodies acted lawfully. This process

Box 14.9   Jurisdiction of the Administrative Court

- **Judicial review** – of decisions of inferior courts and tribunals, public bodies and persons exercising a public function. Criminal cases may arise from decisions of magistrates' courts or the Crown Court when it is acting in its appellate capacity.
- **Statutory appeals and applications** – the right given by certain statutes to challenge decisions of, e.g., ministers, local government, tribunals.
- **Appeals by way of case stated** – appeals against decisions of magistrates' courts and the Crown Court (predominantly criminal cases).
- **Applications for habeas corpus**
- **Applications for committal for contempt**
- **Applications for an order preventing a vexatious litigant from instituting or continuing proceedings without the leave of a judge**
- **Applications under the Coroners Act 1988**
- **Applications under the Drug Trafficking Act 1994 and the Criminal Justice Act 1988** – restraint orders etc. prior to criminal trial.

Some matters are required by statute or rules of Court to be heard by a Divisional Court (i.e., a court of two or more judges):

1   Applications for committal for contempt where the contempt (a) is committed in connection with (i) proceedings before a Queen's Bench Divisional Court, (ii) criminal proceedings (except where it is in the face of the court or disobedience to an order), (iii) proceedings in an inferior court or (b) is committed otherwise than in any proceedings.
2   Appeals from the Law Society Disciplinary Tribunal. Such appeals are heard by a three-judge court unless the Lord Chief Justice otherwise directs. By convention these appeals are heard by a Court presided over by the Lord Chief Justice.
3   Applications under s. 13 of the Coroners Act 1988 (with fiat of the Attorney General).
4   Applications for vexatious litigant orders under s. 42 of the Supreme Court Act 1981.
5   Applications relating to parliamentary and local government elections under the Representation of the People Acts (unless exercisable by a single judge by express statutory provision).

Others can be and usually are heard by a Divisional Court:

1   Applications for judicial review in a criminal cause or matter.
2   Applications for leave to apply for judicial review in a criminal cause or matter, after refusal by a single judge (whether on paper or after oral argument).
3   Appeals by way of case stated in a criminal cause or matter, whether from the Crown Court or from a magistrates' court.

The remaining matters in the Administrative Court List will generally be heard by a single judge.

involved the courts expanding the scope of judicial review of administrative decisions on substantive and procedural grounds and elucidating the constitutional and legal limits on discretionary power, although from the perspective of the decision makers – the civil servants and the ministers – this process came as something of a shock.

Situations where the duty to observe the principles of natural justice and the duty to act fairly have been applied are as varied as the range of decision-making bodies and decision-making situations within the modern state. Where the context is one involving some allegation of improper conduct or disciplinary sanction, the rules of natural justice – including the obligation to give each party a hearing and the rule against bias – are likely to be imposed strictly. Where there is simply a decision that may affect an individual or group of individuals – for example, the closure of a nursing home or care facility – the duty to act fairly may simply require that the decision-making authority provides time for consultation. Where there is a statutory requirement of consultation, the courts are likely to impose a strict requirement to ensure that the consultation is meaningful, for example by insisting that enough time and information be available for the consultation and that responses are taken into account (*R. v. North Devon and East Devon Health Authority ex parte Coughlin*, 1999).

Failure to act in accordance with the rules of natural justice is not the only reason why an administrative act may be challenged. Even more broadly, the courts may review the use of a discretionary power to see if it has been exercised reasonably. How the court interprets what is 'reasonable' has been getting more rigorous and less accommodating to public authorities over the last few years, so that again additional protections have been developed for an individual in conflict with a decision-making body. Moreover, it seems likely that the passage of the HRA will raise even higher the standard that a public body has to meet to show it was acting reasonably as the rather stricter test of proportionality used in the HRA and Strasbourg jurisprudence influences British courts.

Access to judicial review

One reform in the field of administrative law in the late 1970s transformed the ease with which individuals could use the courts to challenge governmental decisions. Until 1977 seeking judicial review of an administrative decision was a complex matter, confronting the litigant with a range of procedures such as an application for ordinary civil remedies or an application for a prerogative order of *certiorari* (to quash a faulty decision), of prohibition (to restrain the performance of an unlawful action) or of *mandamus* (to compel the performance of a legal duty). An application for the wrong remedy could mean that an action would fail altogether. The courts that granted review prior to 1977 could not award damages for a defective decision and it was frequently found that even when an application for review was successful, it was of little benefit to the aggrieved citizen.

These procedural deficiencies were reformed in 1977 by amendments to the rules of the Supreme Court (i.e., the British legal system). Applications for existing prerogative orders (*certiorari*, *mandamus* and prohibition) were replaced by a single procedure – Order 53, or an application for judicial review. And from 1977, an application could be combined with another application for other remedies, including the award of damages.

Although it was at first unclear what the impact of this change would be, the introduction of Order 53 (from October 2000, part 54 of the Civil Procedure Rules) had a substantial impact on the use of judicial review in the United Kingdom.

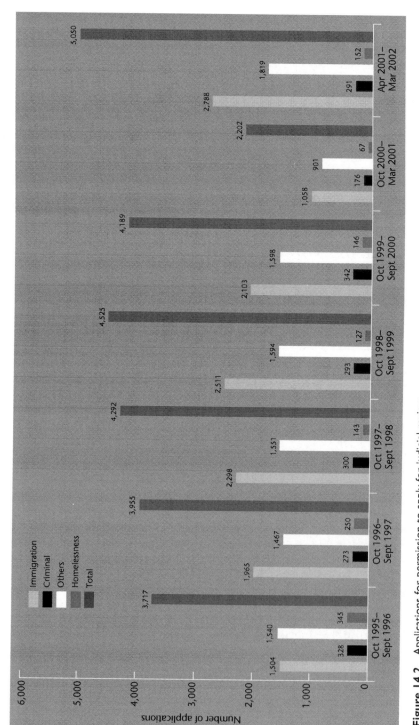

Figure 14.2 Applications for permission to apply for judicial review.

However, the increase in applications to courts for judicial review has placed severe strains on the legal system. The reorganization of the Crown List and the creation of an Administrative Court is one attempt to meet the need for additional expertise and judicial capacity in this burgeoning field (see figure 14.2).

Standing and remedies

The general rule is that the party must have sufficient interest in the matter to which the application relates to be granted standing. Standing is at the discretion of the court and a pressure group as well as the aggrieved party may be granted the right to judicial reviews.

There are a number of remedies available to the courts in seeking to redress administrative error. The court may quash a decision or issue an injunction to restrain an authority from acting unlawfully. It may issue a declaration of the rights of a litigant or it may make an order compelling an authority to fulfil its obligations. A court may award financial compensation. Other gaps in the coverage of administrative law have been closed in recent years. For example, it was long thought that British practice did not grant interim relief against the Crown. In the *Factortame* case, however, the European Court of Justice was unwilling to allow domestic law to prevent the protection of rights under Community law and rejected the idea that remedies could not be made available. In *M. v. Home Office*, 1994, an injunction was granted by a domestic court against a cabinet minister in a case where there was no element of European law. This case showed that in certain circumstances the courts would review the use of prerogative power and not just the use of powers granted under statute.

Conclusions

At the start of the twenty-first century the situation of the individual who wishes to challenge a government decision is stronger than ever before. New machinery in the form of the ombudsmen system has been successfully introduced and expanded. The courts have put in place a comprehensive system of administrative law and incrementally developed a powerful role for the judiciary in relation to administrative action. Judicial review, once unknown in the British system at the national level, is a regular fact of life. In particular, the passage of the HRA of 1998 has reinforced the judiciary in its effort to provide stronger legal controls on government decision making and contributed to a new climate in which individual rights are protected. In striking a balance between the needs of government and those of citizens in such areas as the construction of appeals machinery, the needs of users are gaining greater emphasis. On the other hand, there is little cause for complacency. The span of executive discretion is still extensive. There are areas of public policy making where scant opportunity for review exists or, if it does, is unsatisfactory. And pressures on time and cost sometimes preclude the effective use of the existing mechanisms. Nevertheless, this is an area where increasingly robust institutions have gained the power not merely to make improvements in the structure of accountability, but to ensure that issues associated with the protection of citizens' rights remain firmly on the political agenda.

Key Questions

1 Where are the weaknesses in the United Kingdom's system of accountability?
2 Are ombudsmen more effective than courts in checking maladministration?
3 Why does maladministration occur?

Further Reading

There are useful general works on accountability in the modern state. Especially insightful is Patrick Birkinshaw, *Grievances, Remedies and the State* (2nd edn; London: Sweet and Maxwell, 1994). Also highly relevant are P. Giddings, *Parliamentary Accountability: A Study of Parliament and Executive Agencies* (Basingstoke: Macmillan, 1995), Dawn Oliver and Gavin Drewry, *Public Service Reforms: Issues of Accountability and Public Law* (London: Pinter, 1996) and S. Weir and W. Hall, *The Untouchables: Power and Accountability in the Quango State* (London: Scarman Trust, 1996). More general overviews are provided by Samuel H. Beer, 'Strong government and democratic control', *Political Quarterly*, 70: 2 (1999), Gavin Drewry, 'Mr Major's Charter: Empowering the customer', *Public Law* (1993) and C. Hood, O. James and C. Scott, 'Regulation of government: Has it increased, is it increasing, should it be diminished?', *Public Administration*, 8: 2 (2000). Also pertinent is K. Jenkins, 'Effective government and effective accountability', *Political Quarterly*, 70: 2 (1999). T. Payne and C. Skelcher, 'Explaining less accountability: The growth of local quangos', *Public Administration*, 75: 2 (1997) looks beyond the national level. The ombudsman is covered in a number of works, including Mary Seneviratne, *Ombudsmen: Public Services and Administrative Justice* (London: Butterworth, 2002), Roy Gregory and Philip Giddings, *The Ombudsman, the Citizen, and Parliament* (London: Politicos, 2002) and P. Giddings, *Parliamentary Accountability: A Study of Parliament and Executive Agencies* (Basingstoke: Macmillan, 1995).

Websites

See also the list of general websites at the back of the book.

- www.ombudsman.org.uk/ – Parliamentary and Health Service Ombudsman
- www.scottishombudsman.org.uk/ – Scottish Public Services Ombudsman
- www.ombudsman.org.uk/pca/wales/ – Welsh Administration Ombudsman
- www.ni-ombudsman.org.uk/ – Northern Ireland Ombudsman
- www.lgo.org.uk/ – Local Government Ombudsman
- www.council-on-tribunals.gov.uk/ – Council on Tribunals
- www.searchuno.co.uk/Government/Inquiries/ – List of ongoing government inquiries

15 Beyond the Nation State

The discussion in earlier chapters has highlighted the distinctive features of the United Kingdom's system of government. Although much of that discussion was focused on government at the national level, it has been emphasized throughout the book that the ability of nation states to control many aspects of policy has been severely circumscribed in recent years. Constitutional changes *inside* nation states, such as devolution in the United Kingdom, have strengthened subnational authorities, altering the scope of central government control. Thus the devolution arrangements and regionalism that were discussed in chapter 12 have parallels in Spain and Italy, for example.

Changes at the supranational level are also highly important for governments. Many of the limitations on the nation state are a product of general trends in the world economy, which has become increasingly global in character, reducing the ability of individual states to control important aspects of their financial environment. As a result, many states have chosen voluntarily to pool sovereignty in a multinational organization and to delegate functions to the supranational level in the hope that working together across national borders will generate more effective policies. Taken together, these developments have led many commentators to highlight multi-level government as a major feature of many contemporary western states, including the British polity.

In this chapter we focus primarily on one particular dimension of multi-level government – the increasingly significant, yet highly complex, dimension of politics and policy making that exists because of the UK's membership of the European Union. Of course, as has been emphasized throughout, the UK is a member of many international organizations and agencies, including the Commonwealth, the North Atlantic Treaty Organization (NATO), the World Bank, the International Monetary Fund (IMF), the World Trade Organization (WTO) and the United Nations (where the UK is a permanent member of the Security Council). It is, however, the European Union which has the greatest potential to transform the political systems of its members.

Characterizing the United Kingdom's relationship with the European Union is itself problematic. Although there is an important tradition of analysing the European Union as an international actor, developments inside the EU and the extensive impact of Europe on the UK's government and politics increasingly make this approach inappropriate (Goetz and Hix, 2000). Accordingly, scholarly interest has shifted to focus attention on the extent to which the European

Union can be seen as a political system in its own right, as well as one which has consequences for the processes of government inside member states (Hix, 1999; Oliver, 2003). Thus in this chapter it is important to look at both the distinctive institutional arrangements of the European Union and the way they overlap and link with other institutions at the national level. The process of transferring policy competence from the national to the supranational level clearly affects policy outcomes and the style of policy making. But at a much more general level, it is also likely to affect our understanding of democratic government as a whole.

The European Union is in many respects a substantially different kind of organization to the other bodies of which the UK is a member. Not only are the scale and scope qualitatively different from those of other international organizations, but the goals and values of the EU and its methods of working are also novel in British experience. Although the need to secure agreement among several member states gives the European Union many of the familiar features of an intergovernmental organization, the EU now seeks to strengthen its own claims on the loyalties of the citizens of the various member states and to develop its capacity to act as a single political, presumably federal, system. As a result, not only is its impact on the processes of British government greater than that of other transnational institutions, but its aspirations and ambition also pose fundamental questions for the British system of government, as indeed they do for all the individual political systems within the European Union.

Why the European Union is Distinctive

Before examining the way in which the European Union's multiple institutions and processes interact with those of the United Kingdom, it is worth examining a little further those features of the EU that make it a distinctive entity. The first point we have noted is the sheer scale of the EU's activities and its impact on British life. This can be demonstrated by looking at the geographical reach, population and trading capacity of the EU in comparative context (see table 15.1). But it can also be grasped from looking at the extent of policy competences that the EU has acquired. While the European Union started as an organization specifically designed to promote competition and trade, it has developed a wide range of policy responsibilities in other areas, including the environment and social policy. The advent of monetary union with a common currency moved the European Union closer to statehood. Even the policy areas where national governments have most guarded their sovereignty – foreign policy and justice issues – have become the subject of increasing supranational collaboration.

A second distinctive feature of the European Union is its complex set of institutional structures and policy arrangements. In these structures there is much overlapping and diffusion of power, with no single centre of authority. These loose structures are able to accommodate a multiplicity of actors and interests. Indeed, some observers have seen the process of decision making at the level of the EU as fitting well the governance model (which was discussed in earlier chapters).

Thirdly, the European Union is unlike most supranational organizations (where relationships are mediated through national governments) in the extent to which the

Table 15.1 Distribution of trade in goods, UK, 2001

| | Value (million) | | | % | |
	Exports	Imports	Balance	Exports	Imports
European Union	111,315	116,497	−5,182	58.1	51.7
Other Western Europe	7,182	12,513	−5,331	3.7	5.6
North America	33,816	35,048	−1,232	17.6	1.6
Other OECD countries	10,914	17,418	−6,504	5.7	7.7
Oil-exporting countries	6,476	3,983	2,493	3.4	1.8
Rest of the world	21,941	39,719	−17,778	11.4	17.6
Total	191,644	225,178	−33,534	100.0	100.0

Source: Office for National Statistics, *UK 2003 Yearbook*, http://www.statistics.gov.uk/downloads/theme_compendia/UK2003/UK2003.pdf p. 363

EU seeks a progressively more direct relationship with the civil societies and citizens of its member states. The Treaty of Amsterdam of 1997 extended that direct relationship by making the citizens of all member states citizens of the European Union and thereby establishing in embryo the dual loyalty and identity found in federal systems. Increasingly, efforts have been directed towards making a reality of the free movement of peoples and developing a common approach to citizenship. Citizens of the European Union already have the right to vote for their representatives in the European Parliament and there are moves to give strong constitutional rights to citizens of the EU as part of the wider constitution-writing process being undertaken under the chairmanship of Valéry Giscard d'Estaing. Although the United Kingdom has resisted the development of a new charter of EU rights and has many reservations about the constitutional convention, there is little doubt that pressure for formal statements of rights and powers will continue, not least because of the implications of enlargement. In many ways the European Union obviously falls short of identifying itself as a single political community and the populations of the member states retain their national identities. Yet on some measures the structures of the European Union are already well advanced towards the federal model and display greater integration than those of well-established federations such as the United States (McKay, 1999, 2001). And while it would be difficult to claim that the EU had a strong civic culture of its own, there already exists in Brussels a diverse and extensive range of pressure groups, public interest groups and non-governmental organizations (NGOs) mobilizing on behalf of a variety of pan-European interests. Indeed, many of the public interest groups are subsidized by the EU itself.

The EU is also distinctive among international organizations in being able to act autonomously of its national members. While many EU initiatives require member state action for their implementation, much of the legislation of the EU has direct and immediate effect. Although the extent of European Union policy making varies from policy sector to policy sector in some areas – such as environmental policy making – the vast majority of legislation and regulation now emanates from the EU rather than the national level. The incremental transfer of policy making to the EU is controversial and there is a move to try to ensure that policy making does not automatically creep upwards. **Subsidiarity** – the principle that decisions should be taken at the

subsidiarity Theory which states that policy should be decided at the lowest level possible within the EU.

483

lowest possible level – often appears more honoured in the breach than in the observance, and a more powerful dynamic within the EU frequently seems to be one pushing policy towards the European level of decision making.

Most important of all, perhaps, in giving the European Union a distinctive and controversial character is its developmental quality. Although there is no agreement about the final goal of the European Union – whether its aim is confederation, federation or simply a closer union of nation states – it is a fast-moving process, not a static one, an 'experiment in motion' in Bomberg and Stubb's phrase (Bomberg and Stubb, 2003). Thus the goals, structures and processes of the European enterprise are constantly changing and evolving. Indeed, in many ways the structure of the European Union encourages dynamic transformation rather than stability. Individual states may try to set the agenda of integration, especially through the processes of hosting intergovernmental conferences (IGCs) or chairing the Council of Ministers. There is a competitive tension between the formal institutions of the EU – the Parliament, the Commission and the Council, and indeed the Court of Justice – that produces new initiatives. The institutions of the EU are receptive to a large number of interest groups and NGOs that will try to shape the agenda. Changes in the governments of member states are another source of change, generating new patterns of competition and conflict between the member states and between the institutions and actors within the EU.

The United Kingdom and the European Union

The development of the European Union has gone through several stages. While there is no space here to provide a detailed history of the EU or even of the UK's relationship with it, a few major turning points should be noted. Significant constitutional changes are decided at the IGCs, which punctuate the rhythm of EU history and mark the stages of its evolution (see box 15.1).

Periods of relative inactivity have interrupted periods of activism. New agendas have required a review of existing institutions and procedures and prompted treaty revision over the period from the earliest efforts at transnational cooperation.

The European Union had its origins in the attempts of France and Germany, influenced by the United States, to rebuild the shattered economic and political structures of Europe and especially to rebuild the German economy within the framework of an economically integrated and rationally planned western Europe. Jean Monnet, the head of the French Commissariat du Plan, and Robert Schuman, the French foreign minister, took the initiative in 1950 through the Schuman plan to pool the coal and steel resources of France and Germany. (Britain did not join the Coal and Steel Community in 1950, not least because of Labour's policies towards these industries, which were taken into public ownership.) This functional cooperation between states would, it was hoped, be mutually advantageous and have important by-products (spill-over effects) in promoting European cooperation. The Treaty of Paris of 1951 set up the European Coal and Steel Community (ECSC), which provided a model for the second sectoral community (Euratom) and the more wide-ranging European Economic Community (EEC). Both of these communities were created by treaties signed in Rome in 1957 (see box 15.1).

Box 15.1 EU treaties

Major treaties

- **Treaty establishing the European Coal and Steel Community(ECSC):** signed on 18 April 1951 in Paris, entered into force on 23 July 1952.
- **Treaty establishing the European Economic Community (EEC) and Treaty establishing the European Atomic Energy Community (Euratom):** signed on 25 March 1957 in Rome, entered into force on 1 January 1958. These treaties are often referred to as the 'Treaties of Rome'. When the term 'Treaty of Rome' is used, only the EEC Treaty is meant.
- **Treaty on European Union (Maastricht Treaty):** signed on 7 February 1992 in Maastricht, entered into force on 1 November 1993. It created the political union among member states and brought about considerable changes to the existing treaties. The treaty created the European Union, a concept comprising the European Communities (which had also been amended to the term European Community on the same occasion), as well as other forms of cooperation.

Other treaties

- **Merger Treaty:** signed on 8 April 1965 in Brussels, in force since 1 July 1967. Provided for a Single Commission and a Single Council of the then three European Communities.
- **Single European Act (SEA):** signed on 17 February 1986 in Luxembourg and The Hague, entered into force on 1 July 1987. Provided for the adaptations required for the achievement of the internal market.
- **Treaty of Amsterdam:** signed on 2 October 1997 in Amsterdam, entered into force on 1 May 1999. It amended and renumbered the EU and EC Treaties. Consolidated versions of the EU and EC Treaties are attached to it.
- **Treaty of Nice:** signed on 26 February 2001 in Nice, entered into force on 1 February 2003. It creates a framework for the expansion of the EU.

Source: Europa, the European Union Online, http://europa.eu.int/index_en.htm

These three treaties created close economic links between the six member states: France, Germany, Italy, Belgium, the Netherlands and Luxembourg. The aspirations of Jean Monnet and other founders of the EC certainly advocated a Europe that was politically as well as economically integrated. Given the political realities, however, they assumed that economic and technological cooperation within limited policy sectors would have to be the means to spread and encourage closer political integration.

The pattern of institutions created by the Treaty of Rome was inherited from the ECSC. It involved an independent supranational executive body in the form of a Commission (formerly a High Authority) which could initiate proposals but which was subject to the final determination of the Council of Ministers, which represented the member states. An indirectly elected Assembly and a range of consultative committees (most notably, the ECSC) existed to debate and advise on policy while a supranational Court was established to interpret the treaties and other relevant law.

Although the Treaty of Rome established new common institutions, the decision-making model that was adopted reflected earlier practice, with policy initiation

acquis communitaire The sum of rights and obligations derived from the whole body of European law, including the treaties and legislation of the European Union as well as decisions of the European Court of Justice.

powers located in the Commission and with the Council able to exercise final decision-making authority. In addition, the Treaty of Rome set up a number of other agencies – a European Investment Bank, a European Social Fund and a Regional Development Fund.

The UK initially rejected participation in the new European enterprise. The UK's long imperial history, her self-consciousness about her international role, including the special relationship with the United States, her dependence on overseas trade and her distinctive institutional traditions made her look with suspicion on the European project when it was first mooted. As an alternative Britain participated in forming other linkages, including a European Free Trade Area (EFTA). Even after the UK had taken the decision to seek membership of the EU, it was without great enthusiasm for the European idea with its federal overtones.

Doubts about the UK's commitment to the European Community, as well as fears that British membership would increase American influence in Europe and threaten French leadership, led French President Charles de Gaulle to veto Britain's application for membership twice – in 1963 and 1967. When the UK finally succeeded in joining the EC in 1973, it found a Community where the rules had already become well entrenched and where the procedures had developed without British input. New members had to accept all pre-existing Community obligations (technically known as **acquis communitaire**). In many respects, although the UK wished to be part of the EU for trade and diplomatic reasons, many of these pre-existing obligations and policies conflicted with British interests. Thus a central policy of the EC – the common agricultural policy (CAP) – was devised to protect the farming interest in countries such as France and Italy, which had large agricultural sectors. This policy accounts for about 50 per cent of current EU expenditure. This history made the UK a rather difficult country to integrate within the framework of the European Union – an 'awkward partner', in Stephen George's words (George, 1998). Yet the UK clearly intends to remain a member of the EU, even if she finds herself at odds with other members over such policies as the CAP and is not yet decided about taking the further step of joining the system of monetary union.

The original structures of cooperation between the six founding members of the Community were transformed into the EEC in 1958. The UK joined the EU in 1973, and Ireland and Denmark joined at the same time. Norway, which had been expected to join, did not do so following a referendum in which membership of the EU was rejected. The accession of the United Kingdom, Ireland and Denmark increased the EU's membership to nine. By January 1995, the European Union had further expanded to 15 – France, Germany, Belgium, the Netherlands, Italy, Luxembourg, the UK, Ireland, Denmark, Greece, Spain, Portugal, Austria, Finland and Sweden. At the time of writing, the EU is embarking upon a further round of enlargement, with 10 additional countries to join in 2004. Among the likely new members are Cyprus, the Czech Republic, Estonia, Hungary, Latvia, Lithuania, Malta, Poland, Slovakia and Slovenia (see map 15.1).

This enlargement will mark a radical new departure for the EU. The sheer number of potential new entrants – together with others waiting in the queue – seems likely to create greater diversity but also to complicate even further a highly fragmented policy process. For the first time also, the EU will include countries from eastern

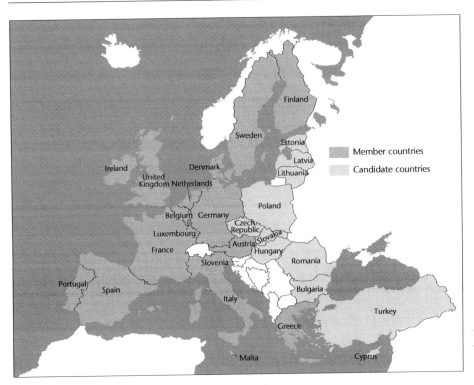

Map 15.1 EU members and candidates for membership.

Europe, many of whom have only recently established democracy following the collapse of communism. Not surprisingly, many of these candidate members have very substantial economic problems and their presence will again raise questions about the appropriateness of key EU policies, especially the CAP, which is designed to protect countries with a large agricultural sector, and the regional policy, which redistributes money from the richer countries to the poorer ones. Indeed, it is noticeable that this round of enlargement has not been characterized by the same requirements of economic and political stability that marked earlier enlargements.

The original Treaty of Rome of 1957 was substantially modified by the Single European Act of 1986, which paved the way for the single market. The determination to complete the creation of the single market by 1992 energized the European Union and boosted the integration process. The period of the 1970s and early 1980s has generally been seen as a time of stagnation within the Community, but the adoption of the single market programme revived its dynamism, although it also produced new tensions within member states, such as the United Kingdom, which were less firmly committed to closer monetary union or political integration. Following the completion of the single market process, wide-ranging changes to the European Union were introduced. The Treaty of European Union (or Maastricht Treaty) of 1992 radically revised the structures and decision-making processes of the European Community, expanding its concerns and promoting closer integration. The Maastricht Treaty widened the reach of the European Union by enacting the

Box 15.2 Pillarization of the European Union

The Maastricht Treaty of 1992 created three areas of activity known as pillars.

Pillar 1	Pillar 2	Pillar 3
European Community	Common foreign and security policy	Justice and home affairs
Most developed pillar. Covers most EU policy areas, including internal market competition, agriculture, EMU, immigration and asylum.	Member states try to develop common policies on foreign and security policy.	International and cross-border crime, police cooperation, criminal law.
Decision-making style: Supranational	*Decision-making style*: Primarily intergovernmental	*Decision-making style*: Usually intergovernmental

pillars/pillarization Structure of the European Union which emerged after the Maastricht Treaty (1992) and which distinguishes between the EU's different policy competences. The first pillar relates to the European Community competences, the second to the area of foreign and security policy, and the third to the area of justice and home affairs.

structure of **pillarization** and adding to the EC pillar two new areas of EU concern in foreign and security policy (the second pillar) and justice and home affairs (the third pillar) (see box 15.2). Although it was recognized that policy within these two pillars would be largely made through intergovernmental agreement rather than by the institutions of the European Union, the classification of new areas of development identified new areas for cooperation and, in a sense, the future agenda for integration. The Amsterdam Treaty of 1997 and the Nice Treaty of 2001 further reformed a number of the EU's political procedures and institutional arrangements prior to the major round of enlargement that begins in 2004. At every stage of the process of treaty revision, we can see not merely an expansion of the EU's competences into more policy fields and the refinement of the EU's aspirations. The process of treaty revision also reveals a range of tensions among the member states and between the institutions and the member states as they try to improve their bargaining position and powers. In some states – such as Ireland and Denmark – treaty revision triggers a referendum.

It is important to emphasize that, historically, the march towards a greater role for the European Union and a reduction in the power of individual nation states do not necessarily command universal enthusiasm among either the member states themselves or their publics. Scepticism about the EU vision is, of course, particularly marked in the United Kingdom, but it is not confined to this country. Although the federal idea was espoused by the so-called founding fathers of the European Union such as Jean Monnet and Robert Schuman, General de Gaulle, who was president of France from 1959 to 1969, was deeply hostile to federalism, preferring instead a Europe of nation states. Indeed, it was notable that the Maastricht Treaty generated controversy not merely in the UK but also in Denmark and France, where referendums to endorse the treaty changes were only narrowly passed. (In Denmark the first referendum resulted in the rejection of Maastricht.) In Germany the Maastricht Treaty was tested before the Constitutional Court. Some authors have noted the extent to which Maastricht itself gave rise to a period of increased scepticism about European integration, at least temporarily (Anderson and Eliassen, 2001). Although that scepticism has not entirely dissipated, new momentum has been provided by the enlargement agenda which in many respects transforms the concept of Europe and poses new problems for its governance. The contemporary dynamic of European integration indeed underlines the capacity of the EU to continue operating on a number of different levels – promoting enlargement, reforming structures and process, increasing the scope and depth of the delegation of policy from national governments while trying to strengthen its own democratic legitimacy. Two of the most profound questions facing the European Union and its member states are how to ensure that its expanded decision-making powers command legitimacy and how to graft democratic processes onto its structures.

Despite high-profile arguments about the future direction of the European Union, the UK's own policy processes have adapted to EU membership and, across a range of institutions and policy areas, EU membership has made a difference. The European dimension must be taken into account not just at the level of the executive and Parliament but also by local and regional governments, by the courts and by the bureaucracy. Political parties have also been profoundly affected by the need both to fight elections at the European level and to manage internal divisions caused by the issue of European integration. The addition of the European arena of decision making has required interest groups to adjust their tactics and has provided some, such as trade unions, with a valuable alternative arena in which to pursue their goals when – as in the Thatcher years – their position was weak at the national level. Thirty years of participation in the EU have thus produced a series of administrative and political changes in the UK to accommodate a new framework of decision making without entirely settling the issue of Britain's identification with the European project.

The United Kingdom initially saw membership of the EC primarily as an economic and trading association rather than as a mechanism for promoting closer political integration. Not surprisingly therefore, the UK has been much more enthusiastic about measures designed to facilitate trade between member states (for example, the measures taken to create the single market) than about efforts which appear to be building the infrastructure of a European polity. However, in the course of promoting the creation of the single market, the United Kingdom accepted pragmatically a number of institutional changes and substantial amendments to the founding treaties. Thus the Single European Act of 1986 brought about several changes in the institutions and procedures of the EC. It strengthened the role of the European Commission and extended the scope of the EU's competence even as far as foreign policy, an area hitherto jealously guarded by national governments. Moreover, the Single European Act introduced **qualified majority voting** instead of unanimity into the Council of Ministers, thereby making it theoretically more difficult for a single country to impede progress.

This expansion of competence was taken even further in the 1992 Treaty of European Union (the Maastricht Treaty). By the early 1990s also, the European Union had acquired an important

qualified majority voting (QMV) Weighted voting in the EU Council of Ministers.

social dimension. One of the UK's objections to the Maastricht Treaty centred on its enforcement of the Social Charter of 1989, which sought to give common protection to workers in relation to employment law. The then Conservative government took the view that there should be minimal regulation of the labour market and it accordingly negotiated an opt-out of the Social Charter. When Labour came to power in 1997, it accepted the Social Charter although it too is less than enthusiastic about many aspects of European social policy.

Another highly important aspect of Maastricht was the attempt to give more democratic and constitutional meaning to the European Union and to strengthen the relationship between the EU's political institutions and its citizens. This involved efforts to allow EU citizens to vote at elections in their country of residence – regardless of citizenship – and to provide better protection for citizens against maladministration by the introduction of a European ombudsman. The attempts to strengthen the democratic elements of the EU were on one level welcomed by the governments of member states. Yet there was, and is always, the concern that strengthening the political institutions of the EU, especially elaborating constitutional rights for citizens, moves the enterprise closer towards a federal political system and an alternative focus of loyalty for citizens.

The Decision-making Framework of the European Union

Thus far the institutional framework of the EU has been mentioned only in passing. It is, however, necessary to examine these institutions a little more closely because of the extent to which they shape the process of policy integration and constitute an important level of government that overlaps with national institutions. It must be remembered that the way these institutions work is not fixed but fluid: both their formal and informal procedures are highly adaptive. Rules governing voting, for example, may be amended by treaty revision, but so may the general powers of an institution. Informal pressures can also be exerted to change the way the formal rules and procedures operate in practice. More particularly, the decision-making structure of the Community is likely to be further reviewed and to have to adapt in the wake of enlargement, which will both multiply the number of actors on the EU scene and disrupt settled accommodations and understandings between existing actors.

The institutions of the European Union inevitably reflect the distinctive features of the European enterprise and do not compare precisely with the familiar concepts of legislature, executive and judiciary at the national level (see figure 15.1). They tend to display a tension between the national interests of member states and the supranational concerns and aspirations of the EU's leaders. They also tend to be highly fragmented because of the marked tendency for different policy sectors to operate separately. National and sectoral divisions can be seen within institutions and between them. The institutions themselves may at times display cooperation and at other times a competitive element. The competitive tension that exists between institutions may be seen in the relationship between the European Commission and the Council. These two bodies have been seen as constituting a dual executive within the EU (Hix, 1999), with the Council and the Commission both seeking to exercise a

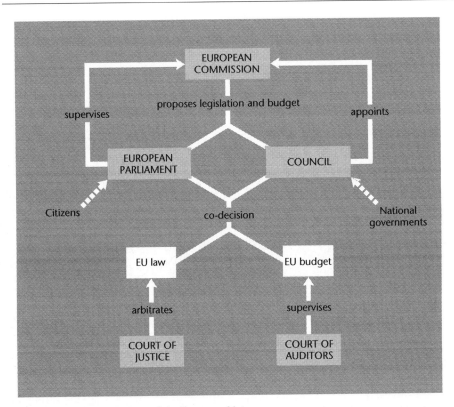

Figure 15.1 The institutions of the European Union.

leadership role. Competitive tension is also visible in the efforts of the European Parliament to carve out a more extensive and influential role for itself.

Similarly, the notion of legislation as it occurs in the EU is rather different from that found in member states. In the European Union there are several types of legislation. The first and most significant source of EU law is the treaties themselves. Subsidiary treaties may also be a source of law. Thus in 1977 the EC announced its intention to regard the European Convention on Human Rights (ECHR) as binding, so that its provisions could be directly applied in member states. Although the European Union has now declared itself in favour of a Charter of Fundamental Rights, the ECHR remains part of EU law.

Apart from treaties, the EU's policies are implemented through regulations, directives, decisions, recommendations and opinions (see box 15.3). All of these categories have a different status. Regulations are general in form and directly applicable. Directives specify a policy goal but leave the government to decide how to bring about the policy effect. They thus bind member states but are not usually enforceable through the courts until transposed into domestic law within the member states. This is usually done in the United Kingdom by secondary legislation, by Order in Council (Oliver, 2003). Decisions can be addressed either to private parties such as companies or to governments. Strictly speaking, only regulations,

Box 15.3   Types of European legislation

Community law may take the following forms:

- **Regulations**, which are directly applicable and binding in all EU member states without the need for any national implementing legislation.
- **Directives**, which bind member states as to the objectives to be achieved within a certain time limit while leaving the national authorities the choice of form and means to be used. Directives have to be implemented in national legislation in accordance with the procedures of the individual member states.
- **Decisions**, which are binding in all their aspects for those to whom they are addressed. Thus, decisions do not require national implementing legislation. A decision may be addressed to any or all member states, to enterprises or to individuals.
- **Recommendations** and **opinions**, which are not binding.

Source: European Commission, http://europa.eu.int/eur-lex/en/about/pap/process_and_players2.html#1

directives and decisions are legal instruments. However, in addition to these forms of legislation, policy may be promoted through opinions or the issuing of advisory notices.

The institutional framework and the decision-making processes of the EU are not static. They are the subject of debates and negotiations that are shot through with both national concerns and supranational considerations. Thus the Maastricht Treaty altered the institutional balance within the European Union by changing some of its procedures and structures. For example, the treaty continued the process of expanding the powers of the Parliament (which gained the power to confirm Commissioners) in an effort to make the system more democratic and accountable. Parliament's role in decision making was enhanced by the introduction of the co-decision-making procedure and by giving the Parliament the power to assent to international agreements. Subsequent treaties – Amsterdam and Nice – have made additional adjustments, and further major institutional change is foreshadowed in the IGC of 2004.

The Council

The Council (formerly known as the Council of Ministers) is still in many ways the key decision-making body within the European Union's system of government. The Council consists of a group of ministers (one from each member state), who meet regularly in Brussels. Unlike the situation in relation to Commission members (where members are supposed to promote the Community interest), it is expected that the individual Council members will defend their own country's interests.

The Council is not a body with a coherent identity. Its work is organized around policy sectors with different ministers attending the Council for their own policy agendas. Thus, although there is one formal Council, in practice there are many councils because of the Council's practice of convening in specialist groups comprising agriculture ministers, environment ministers or health ministers. In addition, there are groups with a wider remit, for example the General Affairs Council and the External Affairs Council. Not surprisingly, the fact that the Council's operation is structured around policy sectors makes coordination of policy across sectors a massive problem. The General Affairs Council, which could provide some integration, is generally too overloaded to be an effective coordinating body. The Council provides important leadership for the long-term goals of the Community and sets the agenda for treaty revision and significant developments such as enlargement. It also has the responsibility for seeing that policy is implemented in the member states. Since the Council must accept or reject proposals coming from the European Commission, it can set the pace of change within the Community. Because the ministers sent by each country differ according to the agenda, the Council has increasingly acquired its own bureaucracy, the most important element of which is the General Secretariat. There is a Secretary General and a staff of about 2,000. Moreover, because the work of the Council is complemented by the work of specialist and technical councils, there is a growing substructure of experts that now constitutes a formidable bureaucratic structure in its own right. COREPER, the Committee of Permanent Representatives, is the most important of these bureaucratic substructures and is itself a mix of national ambassadors from the individual states, diplomatic advisers and appropriate teams of civil servants who, like the Council, are committed to protecting their national interests. (COREPER operates in two sections, one dealing with foreign and economic policy and the other with general policy.)

This increasing involvement of Council-dominated bureaucrats in Community policy making interlocks national bureaucrats with the work of the Community. Although in some ways essential for continuity and expertise, the extent to which bureaucrats prepare and pre-empt decision making creates a decision-making style that is opaque and fragmented. The fact that the Council meets in secret may aid in securing a consensual decision but does not help the legitimacy of the process (Bunyan, 1999).

Initially the Council employed several different voting forms for different purposes – simple majority, qualified majority and unanimity – although in fact the norm within the Council is for matters to be decided by consensus where possible. The recognition of a country's right to veto legislation that conflicted with its national interest was embodied in the Luxembourg Accords of 1966. Although this protection was seen as valuable at the time, it clearly slowed the pace of integration and is now rarely used. Instead countries that wish to block an initiative will try to put together blocking coalitions, which in most circumstances will have the same effect and avoid isolating a single country.

The Single European Act extended the use of qualified majority voting (QMV) for a large number of subjects. The process was extended further by the Treaty of Nice. QMV is a system that, instead of giving each member one vote, weights the votes (see table 15.2). The qualified majority vote is 62; 26 votes are needed to block a decision. Most of the subjects for which QMV was initially allowed related to the internal market – for example, the free movement of goods and labour and the harmonization of laws designed to implement the internal market. This situation has now changed as QMV has been extended to apply to the majority of decisions. Majority voting obviously reduces the control that one country can exert over the decision-making process and makes the system as a whole more effective.

Table 15.2   Current (2003) weighting of votes in the European Union

Country	Votes
France	10
Germany	10
Italy	10
UK	10
Spain	8
Belgium	5
Greece	5
The Netherlands	5
Portugal	5
Austria	4
Sweden	4
Denmark	3
Ireland	3
Finland	3
Luxembourg	2
Total	87

Source: European Commission, http://europa.eu.int/scadplus/leg/en/cig/g4000q.htm#q1

Each member state takes control of the presidency of the Council by rotation on a six-monthly basis. This arrangement induces individual countries to try to promote a positive agenda for the period of their presidency. The negative impact is that it may lead to rushed decision making and a lack of continuity, which is only marginally offset by the institutionalization of the so-called troika of past, present and future presidents. As a result, it is likely that efforts will be made to amend the rotating presidency, probably at the 2004 summit. The House of Commons advocated change in its recent report on the EU's decision making, and certainly Tony Blair, among others, has been pushing for a permanent president, who could, if appointed, serve for five years and would give direction and continuity to the leadership of the EU.

Leadership within the Council is exercised by the president of the Council, a post that has become increasingly important since the 1970s. The role of the president of the Council was further strengthened by the formation in 1975 of the European Council (described below), which brings together heads of member governments on a regular basis. For the most part the meetings of the Council take place in secret, which makes accountability difficult. (It is also difficult because of the transient nature of the Council.) Yet the Council is still the final voice in the legislative process of the EU, and indeed many observers have seen the Council as growing in strength in relation to other elements of the Community.

The European Council

The European Council is the name given to the summits of heads of government that started informally in 1975 and now meet three or four times a year. These meetings were institutionalized by the Single European Act of 1986 and the European Council plays a useful role in coordinating the business of the Community, in agenda-setting, in promoting constitutional change and in providing leverage to overcome policy and institutional deadlocks. The individual countries take turns to host a European summit and this tends to give the host country an incentive to make their meeting significant. In the context of the UK's system of cabinet government, these meetings have tended to enhance the power of the prime minister. It is also important that the heightened profile of the European Council has strengthened the Council presidency *vis-à-vis* the other members, although the European Council has no executive powers of its own. Its powers and influence stem from its capacity to fashion compromises and set an agenda that fits with the other actors in the EU. Because it operates at a high political level, it is not a useful instrument for dealing with policy detail. However, Blair wishes to see its role enhanced.

The European Commission

The Commission is the second part of the dual executive of the European Union, but it is also crucially the body with sole responsibility for initiating European legislation, for managing the day-to-day affairs of the EU and for negotiating on the EU's behalf. New legislation will be drafted by officials but will then be agreed by the Commission, either by consensus or by simple majority. After the Commission has agreed draft legislation, it will be considered by the European Parliament and the Council. The Commission also plays a vital role at all stages of the policy process, and because of its long-term nature it is in many ways the key body within the EC. Although there is disagreement about how much independent power it exerts, the Commission has an influential role in agenda-setting and in implementing policy within the European Union.

The Commission has two separate elements roughly corresponding to its political and bureaucratic sides. The political side is composed of a college of 20 partisan politicians, one of whom is the president of the Commission. It meets weekly and operates on the basis of collective responsibility. The president has come to exercise an increasingly strong leadership role and plays a more active part in the distribution of portfolios between nationally nominated Commissioners. (The president can also veto a name put forward by a member state.) Individual members are allocated at present with some consideration as to the population of the member state, so that the larger states – Spain, Germany, Italy, France and the UK – each have two Commissioners. The prospect of major enlargement of the EU has focused attention on the size and structure of the Commission as well as on its role. Given that an entity in excess of 20 members is unlikely to be an effective decision-making body, there will inevitably be a rebalancing of membership.

The Commissioners are appointed by the member states, subject to general European Community approval. Since the Maastricht Treaty they are subject to confirmation by the European Parliament – a process like the Senate confirmation of judges in the United States. The Amsterdam Treaty gave the European Parliament the right to approve the nomination of the incoming Commission president, thereby extending the Parliament's role in the nomination process and making it likely that

cabinet A group of advisers (usually drawn from their home country) who support senior figures (e.g. the Commissioners) in the European Union.

the Commission will be more responsive to it. The Maastricht Treaty also gave the European Parliament the right to approve (and to sack) the Commission *as a whole*, but not to approve the president individually. After the approval of individual Commissioners, the European Parliament must then hold a second vote on the Commission as a college.

As the more permanent part of the Community executive machinery, the Commission is responsible for the most important preparatory stages of EU business: it drafts the budget and negotiates treaties, although confirmation is in the hands of the Council and the Parliament. The Commission also has important implementation and oversight powers, including the power to take other member states to the European Court of Justice for non-fulfilment of Community obligations. The Commission has a crucial role in the development of external policy, maintaining delegations in foreign states and conducting negotiations for the European Union, especially in relation to trade policy.

Commissioners take an oath of allegiance to the European Community. Under Article 10 of the Merger Treaty, they may neither seek nor take instructions from any government or any other body. Commissioners' loyalty is thus to the vision of an integrated Europe rather than to their own national government and, to that extent, they may find themselves at odds with the Council, which represents the member states more directly. Nevertheless, distinctions of national background do characterize the Commissioners, who are also inevitably divided on ideological lines. (They are for the most part high-profile former politicians, such as Britain's two current European Commissioners, Neil Kinnock and Chris Patten.)

It used to be thought that the European Commission enjoyed a strong security of tenure. Although individual countries could refuse to reappoint individual Commissioners and although the European Parliament had the power to dismiss the Commission as a whole, it was thought that this power was more theoretical than real. In 1999, however, following an attempt to censure the Santer Commission because of fraud, nepotism and mismanagement, the whole Commission resigned, pre-empting the possibility of a demand for its resignation. The Commission now serves a five-year term coterminous with the European Parliament.

The president of the Commission is supported by a permanent General Secretariat, which has a general responsibility for coordination within the Commission. The specialized work of the Commission is organized through 26 directorates. Each Commissioner is given responsibility for a particular policy department or directorate general, each of which will be headed on the administrative side by a director general and will have its own secretariat (see box 15.4). Which portfolio any particular Commissioner receives will depend to a large extent on internal bargaining. (The Parliament has no role in the allocation of portfolios.) Altogether, the Commission employs about 13,000 bureaucrats recruited for the most part by competitive examination from all the member states. The Commissioners all have their own *cabinets*, which are small, high-powered advisory bodies usually made up of individuals from the Commissioner's home country. In addition to the separately organized policy directorates, there are a number of services, such as legal services, which are organized horizontally across policy sectors.

Box 15.4 The directorates general

POLICIES
- Agriculture
- Competition
- Economic and Financial Affairs
- Education and Culture
- Employment and Social Affairs
- Energy and Transport
- Enterprise
- Environment
- Fisheries
- Health and Consumer Protection
- Information Society
- Internal Market
- Joint Research Centre
- Justice and Home Affairs
- Regional Policy
- Research
- Taxation and Customs Union

EXTERNAL RELATIONS
- Development
- Enlargement
- EuropeAid: Cooperation Office
- External Relations
- Humanitarian Aid Office: ECHO
- Trade

GENERAL SERVICES
- European Anti-Fraud Office
- Eurostat
- Press and Communication
- Publications Office
- Secretariat General

INTERNAL SERVICES
- Budget
- Financial Control
- Group of Policy Advisers
- Internal Audit Service
- Joint Interpreting and Conference Service
- Legal Service
- Personnel and Administration
- Translation Service

Coordination across the various policy sectors is sometimes very difficult. Until the Prodi Commission offices were relatively close together, which facilitated communication between departments. Since 1999 this physical proximity has been reduced, although the Commissioners are now in the same building as their director generals.

There is an obvious tendency for the powers of the Commission to expand, so much so that many have argued for the need to place formal limits on its role. This could be done by the creation of a watchdog to implement subsidiarity or by greater specification of the Commission's powers in a European constitution. Yet even if such additional checks were put in place, it would probably prove difficult and undesirable to curtail the activism of the Commission. A network of committees or **comitology** is designed to oversee the implementation of European law. While it may operate effectively, it does not necessarily allow very much general participation and, from the outside, seems to add yet another layer of bureaucracy to an already opaque and bureaucratized structure.

comitology Name given to the web of committees, primarily consisting of national officials, which monitors the implementation of policy.

The European Parliament

The European Parliament currently consists of 626 members, although enlargement will require readjustment of these numbers. Initially the European Parliament was known as the European Assembly and its members were not directly elected until 1979. As was seen in chapter 7, the UK's representatives are now elected for five years by proportional representation on a closed list system (see tables 15.3 and 15.4). The European Parliament sits in two centres: plenary meetings are held at Strasbourg, while committee meetings are held in Brussels.

The European Parliament's powers have been expanding so that its initial consultative role has evolved into one where it can claim the right to participate in policy making in a number of areas. Although the Maastricht and Amsterdam treaties both enhanced its powers, the European Parliament is ambitious to increase them further within the EU framework and to play a more active role. It is not primarily responsible for passing Community legislation – that function falls to the Commission. But it does have the power to amend draft legislation; and it has a significant amount of influence in the budgetary process. The European Parliament also has a general scrutiny role over the Commission, which it exercises through the right to put down questions and initiate general debates.

The European Parliament showed its potential to exercise a real check on the Commission in 1998, when it refused to discharge the 1996 budget. Concern, prompted by British representatives, had been mounting for some time about the

Table 15.3 UK turnout in European Parliament elections since 1979

Year	Turnout
1979	32.7
1984	32.6
1989	36.8
1994	36.8
1999	24.1

Source: Butler and Butler (2000), p. 514.

Table 15.4 UK parties in the European Parliament

Party	Number of MEPs
Conservatives	36
Labour	29
Liberal Democrats	10
Green Party	2
UK Independence Party	3
Scottish National Party	2
Plaid Cymru	2
Ulster Unionist Party	1
Social and Democratic Labour Party	1
Non-aligned (Rev. Ian Paisley)	1
TOTAL	87

financial management of European affairs. An independent committee produced a scathing report in 1999 and the whole Commission, headed by Jacques Santer, resigned.

The European Parliament has successfully extended its legislative role, first by the introduction of the cooperation procedure under the 1986 Single European Act, which gives greater consultation opportunities by adding new stages to the process of legislation, even though the final decision remains with the Council. The Maastricht Treaty introduced another new procedure, the co-decision procedure, according to which the European Parliament operates on an equal footing with the Council. Although initially reserved for a few areas, its role was greatly expanded by the Amsterdam Treaty to encompass 23 new areas, including such key domains as environmental policy, public health and equal opportunities. This procedure provides a way of counterbalancing the increasing volume of decisions taken by majority vote. Nevertheless, the procedures lack transparency and are alien to the way many member states, especially the UK, think about legislation.

The European Parliament has the important capability of vetoing enlargement and can use this potential power, as well as its power to endorse the budget, as a mechanism for exercising influence. (The European Parliament has very little control over revenue but may exercise extensive influence over EU spending; see box 15.5 for an overview of the budget process.) Although increasing, the powers of the European Parliament still appear weak by comparison with those of the Commission and Council. This imbalance, while it persists, will continue to place a question mark over the important issue of the system's democratic legitimacy, particularly as national Parliaments find it hard to monitor European legislation effectively. But efforts to strengthen the legislative powers of the European Parliament frequently provoke opposition in national Parliaments, especially given the perceived integrationist agenda of the European Parliament.

The European Parliament operates largely through its 17 standing committees, which roughly correspond to the structure of directorates in the Commission. The sectoral specialization of the committees reinforces the segmentation that pervades the whole European policy process. Politically, the European Parliament is arranged into blocks of ideologically organized parties rather than national groupings. At present there are ten groups, the two most important being the European People's Party (Christian Democrats) and European Democrats and the Party of European Socialists (see box 15.6). Some of these groups are very broad and loose and there are tensions within them. They are therefore by no means as cohesive as national parties, and indeed there is little formal discipline within groups. One feature of the European Parliament that initially made it somewhat alien to British practice was that instead of operating on strict party lines, issues were handled by the formation of cross-party alliances. Coordination is achieved through groups and subgroups as well as by temporary committees of inquiry. Moreover, in contrast to the shape of the House of Commons, which emphasizes its adversarial character, the European Parliament is arranged in a semi-circle.

Box 15.5   The budgetary process in the European Union

The budgetary procedure is set out in Article 272 of the EEC Treaty, which stipulates the sequence of stages and the time limits that must be respected by the two arms of the budgetary authority: the Council and Parliament. The budgetary procedure, as defined in the treaty, extends from 1 September to 31 December of the year preceding the budget year in question.

In practice, however, a 'pragmatic' timetable has been applied by the three institutions since 1977. The different stages of the procedure are now as follows:

- Establishment of the preliminary draft budget by the Commission and transmission to the budgetary authority by no later than 15 June. The preliminary draft can subsequently be amended by the Commission by means of a letter of amendment to allow for new information that was not available when the preliminary draft was established.
- Establishment of the draft budget by the Council. The Council conducts its first reading of the preliminary draft and, on this basis and after a conciliation meeting with a delegation from Parliament, establishes, before 31 July, the draft budget, which it sends to Parliament in the first half of September.
- First reading by Parliament. Parliament conducts its first reading in October on the basis of the Council's draft; amendments to non-compulsory expenditure require the votes of an absolute majority of members. Proposed modifications to compulsory expenditure require an absolute majority of votes cast when agreement on the amount of such expenditure is not reached at the ad hoc conciliation meeting.
- Second reading by the Council. The Council conducts this second reading during the third week of November, after a conciliation meeting with a delegation from Parliament. The draft budget is amended in the light of Parliament's amendments (non-compulsory expenditure) or proposed modifications (compulsory expenditure). The draft budget as amended is returned to Parliament around 22 November.
- Second reading by Parliament and adoption of the budget. As the Council has had the last word on compulsory expenditure, Parliament devotes most of its December part-session to reviewing non-compulsory expenditure, for which it can accept or refuse the Council's proposals. Acting by a majority of its members and three-fifths of the votes cast, Parliament then adopts the budget. The president of Parliament declares the budget adopted and it can then be implemented.

Source: European Commission, http://europa.eu.int/comm/budget/budget/index_en.htm#stages

The European Court of Justice

The European Union is a legally defined entity which assumes that major disputes will be settled by the European Court of Justice (ECJ), which is in a sense the constitutional court of the Community. The ECJ together with national courts exerts a powerful harmonizing influence through the legal process. The ECJ itself (which sits at Luxembourg) currently consists of 15 judges (one from each country) and has responsibility for interpreting and ensuring the effective implementation of European law (see box 15.7). Judges of the ECJ are appointed for overlapping six-year terms. If the Court is sitting in plenary session, a quorum is usually seven judges.

Box 15.6   Parties of the European Parliament by political group

The overwhelming majority of MEPs belong to a political group, although there are a few 'non-attached' members who include the Rev. Ian Paisley, one of Northern Ireland's 3 MEPs. To form a political group there must be at least 7 members drawn from more than one member state. Each group has a chair, a bureau and a secretariat. The groups are important to the way the Parliament works. They consider reports from the committees before votes in plenary session and play a key role in the agenda of parliamentary debate. The 1999 European elections saw the European People's Party and European Democrats (the centre-right grouping) become the largest group. The table below gives the groupings within the Parliament as of April 2003.

	Bel	Den	Ger	Gre	Spa	Fra	Ire	Ita	Lux	Neth	Aus	Por	Fin	Swe	UK	Total
PPE-DE	5	1	53	9	28	20	5	35	2	9	7	9	5	7	37	232
PSE	5	2	35	9	24	18	1	16	2	6	7	12	3	6	29	175
ELDR	5	6			2	1	1	8	1	8			5	4	11	52
GUE/NGL		3	7	7	4	15		2		1		2	1	3		49
Verts/ALE	7		4		4	9	2	6	1	4	2		1	2	6	44
UEN		1				4	6	10				2				23
EDD		3				9				3					3	18
NI	3				1	11		10			5				1	31
Total	25	16	99	25	63	87	15	87	6	31	21	25	15	22	87	624

PPE-DE, European People's Party (Christian Democrats) and European Democrats; PSE, Party of European Socialists; ELDR, European Liberal, Democrat and Reform Party; GUE/NGL, European United Left/Nordic Green Left; Verts/ALE, Greens/European Free Alliance; UEN, Union for Europe of the Nations Group; EDD, Group for a Europe of Democracies and Diversities; NI, Non-attached

Source: European Commission, http://wwwdb.europarl.eu.int/ep5/owa/
p_meps2.repartition?ipid = 0&ilg = EN&iorig = &imsg =

Although proceedings are open, decisions are given as though they were unanimous and there is no appeal against the Court's decision. One important feature of the work of the ECJ is the system of Advocates General. These are officials whose duty is to bring facts before the Court in a manner that is impartial rather than adversarial. Those facts will then be relied on by the Court but may be overruled. Another important part of the Court's procedures is the preliminary ruling, which allows national governments to request a ruling from the Court in order to inform their decision making.

With the expansion of EU business, the Court's workload inevitably increased. A new Court of First Instance was created in 1989 to hear limited classes of EC law cases, though not those involving the governments of member states. There is a process of appeal from the Court of First Instance to the full ECJ.

As was emphasized in chapter 1, the ECJ can be regarded not merely as the constitutional court of the European Union but also as the superior court of a new legal order of which the UK is a part, since it has the power to overrule cases from the House of Lords and indeed, as in the *Factortame* case, the power to overrule (or

Box 15.7   The European Court of Justice

The ECJ consists of 15 judges and nine Advocates General who are appointed for six years in mutual agreement by the governments of the member states. Every three years, some of the judges and Advocates General are replaced, but they are eligible for reappointment. From their number, the judges select the president of the Court for a three-year term. This person is also eligible for reappointment. The seat of the ECJ is in Luxembourg.

The ECJ may sit in plenary session but in practice only does this when asked to do so by a member state or institution that is party to the proceeding. Other cases are heard by panels of three, five or seven judges.

The Advocate General is an impartial and independent officer whose role is to support the Court by making reasoned submissions on cases brought before it.

The increasing workload of the ECJ created the need for a Court of First Instance, which has existed since 1989. This Court consists of 15 judges but has no permanent Advocates General. In some cases, one of the judges can be deployed as Advocate General. These judges are also appointed for a term of six years by common accord of the governments of the member states. As with the ECJ, the judges select a president from their number.

Source: Adapted from the ECJ website, www.curia.eu.int/en

disapply) statute. Put slightly differently, European law is part of the domestic law of the member states of the European Union.

The power of European law has been solidified and developed by a series of landmark judgements. In 1963 the *Van Gend en Loos* case enunciated the doctrine of direct effect and expounded the extent to which the European Union represented a new legal order. In 1964 *Costa* v. *ENEL* laid down the doctrine of the supremacy of European law. *Amministrazione della Finanze* v. *Simmenthal* in 1978 similarly asserted that national courts had to apply Community law and that where there was a conflict with national law, national law should be set aside.

Cases reach the ECJ by a number of routes. A country that is in breach of its European obligations may be referred to the ECJ by the European Commission (under Article 169). Or a case may be referred by a national judge in a system for a preliminary ruling under Article 177 of the Treaty of Rome. Finally, Article 173 allows review of the legality of actions of both the Council and the Commission. ECJ rulings are directly applicable in British courts. Maastricht and subsequent treaties have affected the powers of the ECJ by expanding the realm of Community competence and by allowing the ECJ to fine countries that fail to fulfil their European obligations.

One final point to bear in mind is that only a portion of the policy areas where there is a European dimension is governed by law. Where EU competence is well established, the legal framework will generally be dense – for example, in the field of competition policy, agriculture and product standards. In other areas, however, the role of the ECJ may be limited by the preference for non-legal instruments, such as intergovernmental cooperation, to develop policy.

Policy Making in the European Union

The institutional structure of the European Union is thus marked by complexity. The policy-making process of the EU is also highly complex, involving multiple actors and varying according to the policy sector. Thus in some areas – for example, the handling of trade and market regulation – some 80 per cent of the rules governing the policy sector emanate from the European Union. In other policy areas – education and foreign policy, for instance – the role of the EU is much less pronounced. Although there is no space here to describe the specifics of any policy area in detail, it is possible to highlight some characteristics of the EU policy process.

First, like so much else in the EU, the policy process exhibits a tension between national interest and supranational concerns. The style of policy making sometimes reflects the need to accommodate national interests, and sometimes it is more supranational depending on the subject matter. Foreign policy making, for example, is essentially intergovernmental. Even before the deep divisions within the Community over Iraq, achieving a common position on foreign policy was an arduous task. Secondly, the subject matter of European policy – especially its concern with trade and competition – means that the European Union is highly sensitive to interest group mobilization, while the fragmented institutions are vulnerable to interest group penetration. Thirdly, the need to secure consensus means that the policy process is marked by a high degree of coalition formation and bargaining, which is not always ideal for policy coherence. It does, however, aid representation. The policy process itself is sometimes ill-coordinated, unwieldy and cumbersome; but, by the same token, it can take account of numerous distinct interests. However, the need to reconcile differing interests, and indeed to bargain and broker them, creates a policy process that is neither open nor transparent.

The lack of transparency in the policy process is one feature contributing to the general image of remoteness and lack of legitimacy that the European Union has, at least among British voters. This aspect of the EU may well be more difficult to reform than the more obvious aspects of the **democratic deficit**, such as the lack of parliamentary power *vis-à-vis* the Council and Commission.

Conclusions

The European Union has become a major player on the international stage and its influence deeply affects the policies and politics of its member states. Debate rages about how best to characterize its operations – whether it should be seen as an intergovernmental organization or a supranational one, or whether its processes of decision making are best captured by the more fluid notion of governance. The problem of characterizing the European Union is that its procedures and institutions are constantly evolving, and in addition the formal account of how they operate is often at odds with informal behind-the-scenes practices. Whether the wholesale constitutional revision that is planned will create a more permanent set of structures is open to question. The European Union is inherently dynamic, not static. That in turn makes leadership difficult, though leadership is obviously also rendered

democratic deficit Phrase which refers to the accountability gap between European policy makers and the institutions that attempt to control them.

problematic by differences of vision about where the EU is headed. Legitimacy also remains a key problem for the European Union, both because its natural way of taking decisions fits uneasily into the existing pattern of British institutions and because its policies often seem exercises in bureaucratic gamesmanship. The legitimacy issue is one which must be addressed if the process of deepening integration is to continue and the United Kingdom is to play a full part in the European venture.

 ## Key Questions

1 How far is the European Union a genuinely supranational organization?
2 To what extent is there a battle for power between its institutions?
3 What if anything can be done about the democratic deficit in Europe?

 ## Further Reading

There is much invaluable background and analysis in S. George, *Britain and European Integration since 1945* (Oxford: Blackwell, 1996) and in the same author's *An Awkward Partner: Britain in the European Community* (3rd edn; Oxford: Oxford University Press, 1998). D. Urwin, *The Community of Europe: A History of European Integration since 1945* (London: Longman, 1991) is a useful survey.

J. McCormick, *Understanding the European Union: A Concise Introduction* (Basingstoke: Macmillan, 1999) provides a good introduction, as does Neill Nugent, *The Government and Politics of the European Union* (5th edn; Basingstoke: Palgrave, 2003). Jeremy Richardson (ed.), *European Union Power and Policy* (London: Routledge, 1998) is an excellent collection.

There are a number of works which look at different institutions of the European Union. The European Commission is covered in studies by Michelle Cini, *European Politics* (Oxford: Oxford University Press, 2003), Ken Endo, *The Presidency of the European Commission under Jacques Delors: The Politics of Shared Leadership* (Basingstoke: Macmillan, 1999), Laura Cram, *Policy-making in the European Union: Conceptual Lenses and the Integration Process* (London: Routledge, 1997) and Nugent, *Government and Politics of the European Union*. The European Parliament and elections are explored by Juliet Lodge (ed.), *The 1999 Elections to the European Parliament* (Basingstoke: Palgrave, 2001), Martin Westlake and David Butler, *British Politics and European Elections* (Basingstoke: Macmillan, 1999) and Julie Smith, *Europe's Elected Parliament* (Sheffield: Sheffield Academic Press, 1999). The European Court of Justice is examined in R. Dehouse, *The European Court of Justice: The Politics of Judicial Integration* (Basingstoke: Macmillan, 1998). Pressure groups are considered in the excellent study by Jeremy Richardson, cited above. Policy making is well covered in H. Wallace and W. Wallace, *Policy Making in the European Union* (4th edn; Oxford: Oxford University Press, 2000).

Parliament's relations with the European Union and the question of sovereignty more generally are the focus of P. Giddings and G. Drewry, *Westminster and Europe: The Impact of the European Union on the Westminster Parliament* (Basingstoke: Macmillan, 1996) and of P. Norton, *National Parliaments and the European Union* (London: Frank Cass, 1996). Paul Silk and R. Walters, *How Parliament Works* (4th edn; Harlow: Longman, 1998) has a detailed chapter on Europe. Shorter discussions may be found in A. Lester, 'Parliamentary sovereignty and the European Community', *Parliamentary Affairs*, 49 (1996) and in Ian Loveland, 'Parliamentary sovereignty and the European Community: The unfinished revolution', *Parliamentary Affairs*, 49: 4 (1996).

 Websites

See also the list of general websites at the back of the book.

Official websites

- www.europa.eu.int – European Commission
- www.cec.org.uk – European Commission in the UK
- www.europarl.eu.int – European Parliament
- www.ukrep.fco.gov.uk – UK Permanent Representation to the European Union
- www.ecb.int – European Central Bank
- www.coe.int – Council of Europe
- www.echr.coe.int – European Court of Human Rights
- www.echr.coe.int/Eng/BasicTexts.htm – European Convention on Human Rights
- www.curia.eu.int/en – European Court of Justice

Different attitudes to the European Union within the UK can be discovered from the websites of pressure groups concerned with contemporary controversies. See for example:

Pro-euro

- www.britainineurope.org.uk – Britain in Europe
- www.euromove.org.uk – European Movement
- www.euro.gov.uk – Get Ready for the Euro

Anti-euro and eurosceptic

- www.4sterling.org – 4 Sterling
- www.bfors.com – Business for Sterling
- web.ukonline.co.uk/keepthepound – Keep the Pound
- www.eurosceptic.com – Eurosceptic Portal
- www.independence.org.uk/home.shtml – UK Independence Party

Other international bodies

- www.thecommonwealth.org – Commonwealth
- www.g8.utoronto.ca/ – G8
- www.icj-cij.org – International Court of Justice
- www.imf.org – International Monetary Fund
- www.nato.int – North Atlantic Treaty Organization
- www.oecd.org – Organization for Economic Cooperation and Development
- www.un.org – United Nations
- www.worldbank.org – World Bank
- www.who.int – World Health Organization
- www.wto.org – World Trade Organization

16 Conclusion

The main focus of this book has been on the many ways in which the institutional framework of the United Kingdom has been transformed in recent years and how those changes have related to the values of the wider political system. It may at this point be worth noting that in the conclusion to the third edition (Peele, 1995), I suggested that one of the most significant puzzles about the British system of government was the extent to which there was any longer a good fit between the way the country was governed and its society and political culture. Clearly, there has been a concerted effort since 1997 to modernize and reform many aspects of British political life, but the question remains a pertinent one. In this final chapter, it may be helpful to explore a little more fully the likely direction of future change and to raise more explicitly the issue of the quality and functioning of the democratic system in Britain.

One of the reasons for the build-up of demand for extensive constitutional reform was the realization of how few checks and balances there were on the executive within the British system. Blair's agenda of constitutional reform has altered that situation to a very large extent. The introduction of devolved government for Scotland and Wales has diluted the centralization of the British state and created important new opportunities for policy divergence as well as encouraging the development of distinct political subsystems. The introduction of the Human Rights Act (HRA) has injected a much greater awareness of the values of rights into the administrative process and further strengthened pre-existing trends towards a greater role for legal institutions and the judges. Although there is no mechanism of entrenchment in the British system, it now seems very unlikely that either devolution or HRA could be repealed, although doubtless there will be room for argument about the detail of the system even under a Labour government. Put slightly differently, it is difficult to imagine a scenario in which an incoming Conservative government would contemplate a dilution of the powers of the Scottish Parliament or the Welsh Assembly, much less a repeal of HRA. That said, it is clear that if there were to be a change of government at Westminster, the practice of devolution at least would operate very differently.

What is less clear cut is whether the degree of reform that has been introduced is sufficient to adjust Britain's system to twenty-first-century needs or whether a further bout of radical institutional change is required. The ambitious agenda of constitutional reform and democratic modernization is only partially delivered. In Northern Ireland the 2003 elections (which saw the Paisley-led DUP become the largest single party in the Assembly) underlined the fragility of the moderate parties on both sides of the sectarian divide and the difficulty of framing a solution based on power sharing for a deeply divided society. Devolution has not noticeably intensified the desire to strengthen local government within the UK, and elected regional government will, if it comes, trigger further local government reform. House of Lords modernization stalled because a real counter-balancing chamber was too radical a step for the Commons to embrace. Radical reform of the House of Commons stalled in part at least because the existing politicians on both sides are too deeply imbued with party loyalty to create a world in which cross-party alliances would be more normal than before. The game of British politics is highly partisan. Meaningful parliamentary reform would require a degree of bipartisanship that is probably beyond the capacity of most MPs.

Even more problematic is the issue of electoral reform. This issue cuts right to the heart of the Westminster system and threatens the world view of most politicians (though not, of course, those of minority parties). It is, however, questionable whether either major party would adopt a move away from first past the post (FPTP) unless it is manifestly in that party's interest to change the system. But whether politicians who have been socialized into one system could work a new and more consensual, less adversarial one is an open question.

One of the most perplexing issues behind the discussion of whether there is an appetite or demand for more constitutional reform is the question of legitimacy. Have the reforms to the governmental structure made citizens more or less satisfied with their form of government or their politicians? Certainly, those who hoped that constitutional reform and institutional modernization would create greater democratic participation have been deeply disappointed. On almost every level from turnout to party membership, the public interest in politics appears to have diminished. It may be that neo-liberalism's emphasis on individual goals and private goods has been reinforced by scepticism about the motives of politicians. Whatever the cause, the result is not an encouraging one for those who believe that a healthy democracy requires widespread citizen engagement in its processes.

One solution that has been mooted to deal with the apparent alienation of the public from politics in Britain is the lowering of the voting age to 16. This suggestion, taken up by a coalition of pressure groups, parties and voluntary organizations in 2003, was fuelled in part by the argument that the political system had become unresponsive to the needs of younger people. Certainly, there was extensive evidence that non-voting was especially high among young voters and that pressure groups rather than orthodox parties were more likely to attract the interest of the young. Whether this extension of the franchise will reinvigorate the British polity or simply create another pool of non-voters is debatable, but the fact that the prime minister and the Lord Chancellor are seriously considering such a reform means that it is now firmly on the political agenda.

Making the polity more inclusive is obviously one possible way of overcoming a sense that the system has become unresponsive to its citizens. On the other hand, it would be a mistake to ignore the extent to which there have been significant changes in style of government in Britain. Even if they do not necessarily excite great electoral interest, these changes have altered the way in which the state is managed, making it more responsive to its citizens even without extensive voter activism. The mechanisms governing accountability and the redress of grievances have become more effective and more user friendly in recent years. Government has become more open and accessible, and areas that were long shrouded from public debate, such as the role of the prerogative and the handling of judicial appointments, have been subjected to greater scrutiny. And government has itself at all levels taken advantage of new technology to consult citizens about their policy preferences. Whether these advances are adequate substitutes for more direct involvement in political life is doubtful; but they represent a change in the style of government that is in many respects a substantial improvement.

Much of the alienation from politics stems of course from a feeling that there is very little that voters can do to control politicians; that it makes little difference who is in power. In one sense that sentiment has some accuracy because of the extent to which the nation state itself is subject to pressures beyond its control. The European Union and Britain's ambiguous relationship with it encapsulates the dilemma of modern British politics. Looked at from one angle, the European Union typifies remote bureaucracy and displays a massive democratic deficit in that much of what it does is not responsive to ordinary citizens. From another angle, the European Union, especially in its present phase of constitutional revision, is attempting to devise political arrangements that will be more appropriate to the globalized world of the twenty-first century than to one where nation states reigned supreme. The United Kingdom is thus in a very profound sense in a period of political transition. Its domestic political arrangements have been remoulded and may yet experience further refashioning. But that redesign of its democracy is taking place in the context of changes to the role of the nation state and the fabric of the European Union which inevitably dwarf domestic political considerations. Such change is at once both discomforting and exciting, and will create distinctly new patterns and processes in the governmental system of the United Kingdom. How quickly Britain's political elites and her citizens adapt to those new patterns and processes will be crucial to determining the quality of the country's democracy in the years ahead.

Appendix: Legal Cases

Amministrazione della Finanze v. Simmenthal (1978) ECR 629

Attorney General v. Guardian Newspapers (Spycatcher case) (1990) 1 AC

Attorney General v. Jonathan Cape (Crossman Diaries Case) (1975) 3 WLR

Beatty v. Gillbanks (1882) 3 AER 559

Bowman v. UK (1998) 26 EHRR

Brogan v. UK (1989) 11 EHRR

Bromley LBC v. GLC (1983) 1 AC

Bulmer (H.P.) Ltd v. J. Bollinger S.A. No. 2 (1974) 3 WLR

Conservative and Unionist Central Office v. Burrell (1982) 1 WLR

Conway v. Rimmer (1968) AC

Costa v. ENEL (1964) ECR 585

Council of Civil Service Unions v. Minister for the Civil Service (GCHQ case) (1985) AC 374

Douglas v. Hello Ltd (2000) QB 967

Edinburgh and Dalkeith Railway Company v. Wauchope (1842) 8 Cl and F 710

Entick v. Carrington (1795) 19 St Tr 1029

Francoviich v. Italy (1993) ECR 1

Garland v. British Rail (1983) 2 AC 751

Golder v. UK (1979–80) 1 EHRR 524

Gouriet v. Union of Post Office Workers (1978) AC

Hamilton v. Al Fayed No. 1 (2001) AC 395

Kirkless MBC v. Wickes Building Supplies Ltd (1993) AC 227

M. v. Home Office (1994) 1 AC 377

MacCormick v. Lord Advocate (1953) SC 396

O'Connell v. R. (1844) 11 Cl & F 155

O'Reilly v. Mackman (1983) 2 AC

Padfield v. Minister of Agriculture, Fisheries and Food (1968) AC 997

Pepper v. Hart (1993) AC 593

Pickstone v. *Freemans PLC* (1989) AC 66

R. v. *International Stock Exchange ex parte Else*(1993) 1 AER

R. v. *Secretary of State for Transport ex parte Factortame* No. 1 (1990) 2 AC 85

R. (on the application of H.) v. *Mental Health Review Tribunal for North and East London Region* (2001) 3 WLR 512

Ridge v. *Baldwin* (1964) AC 40

Secretary of State for Education and Science v. *Tameside MBC* (1977) AC (1014)

Starrs v. *Procurator Fiscal (Linlithgow)* (2000) JC 208

Sunday Times v. *UK* No. 1 (1979–80) 2 EHRR 245

Van Duyn v. *Home Office* (1975) 2 WLR 1038

Van Gend en Loos v. *Nederlandse Tariefcommissie* (1963) ECR 3

Key Concepts

Cross-references to further definitions in the list of key concepts are indicated in **bold**.

Accountability System of control and answerability which is seen as an inherent part of democratic and representative government. The mechanisms by which accountability is enforced vary, but may include political, legal and informal methods.

Acquis communitaire The sum of rights and obligations derived from the whole body of European law, including the treaties and legislation of the European Union as well as decisions of the European Court of Justice.

Act (of Parliament, of Scottish Parliament) Legislative measure which has passed through all its formal stages and become law. In the case of Westminster legislation, this means that normally a **bill** must be passed by both Houses of Parliament and must have received the **royal assent**. In the case of Scottish legislation, a bill must have gone through the Scottish Parliament and received the royal assent. The majority of **public legislation** is introduced by the government.

Acte clair Doctrine which allows national courts not to refer an issue of European law to the European Court of Justice because the answer to that issue is sufficiently clear. It is a technique which the UK courts have used to resist pressure from the ECJ.

Adversarial politics Style of politics in which the need to oppose government policy is emphasized rather than building consensus. Closely associated with the **Westminster**

model of parliamentary democracy and two-party dominance.

Advocacy rule Rule which prevents MPs and peers from raising a subject in Parliament in which they have a material interest. It was formulated after the 1995 **Nolan** Report but builds on resolutions of the House of Commons that have been in place since the late nineteenth century.

Affirmative nomination New selection process designed to give some security of tenure to sitting Labour MPs and to prevent constituency Labour parties removing MPs on ideological grounds.

Agencies/Next Steps Agencies/executive agencies Organizations created following the 1988 Ibbs Report to reform the civil service and produce greater executive efficiency. Effectively, these agencies are single-purpose bodies which operate at a degree of distance from the parent department. The minister retains responsibility for policy, but the chief executive of the agency is responsible for their day-to-day management.

Alternative vote (AV)/supplementary vote (SV) Voting method in which the elector indicates his or her preference among the candidates in the order 1, 2, 3 etc. If any candidate receives 50 per cent + 1 of the total vote on first count, that candidate is elected. If not, the candidate with the fewest first preferences is eliminated and that candidate's second preferences are redistributed.

The process continues until a candidate reaches 50 per cent + 1 of the vote.

Armstrong memorandum Memorandum issued by Sir Robert Armstrong, Cabinet Secretary and Head of the Home Civil Service from 1979 to 1988, in 1985 and revised in 1987. The memorandum was a response to the ethical problem faced by a civil servant who believed instructions given by a minister were improper or illegal. Such a case had arisen when Clive Ponting was prosecuted for leaking to an MP information that he believed showed the government had misled Parliament about the sinking of the *General Belgrano*, an Argentinian warship. The memorandum reiterated that civil servants had no identity distinct from that of the government of the day and insisted that civil servants' first recourse in cases of conscience was to their departmental civil service superior.

Asylum Process in which immigrants claim the right to stay in the United Kingdom because of political oppression or other threat in their home country. The increase in asylum seekers since the 1990s turned the issue into one of intense political controversy and generated successive revisions of the laws governing asylum. There was also criticism of the provisions for appeal against decisions to refuse asylum from the agencies with responsibility for the well-being of asylum seekers.

Backbencher Member of Parliament (or, by extension, of other legislative body such as the Scottish Parliament) who does not hold office in the government or have responsibility as an opposition spokesperson. At Westminster these MPs sit on the benches behind the frontbench spokespersons.

Barnett formula Formula named after Joel Barnett, Treasury Secretary in the late 1970s, for allocating public expenditure between England, Scotland, Wales and Northern Ireland. Originally introduced in 1888 as the **Goschen formula**, it allocated 11/80ths of public expenditure to Scotland. Under Joel Barnett that percentage was changed to 10/80ths. The Barnett formula is controversial because it is based on population rather than need.

Benchmarking Comparing the quality of products, services and practices against best practice – for example, using the best-performing local authorities as a guide to the standard of performance (or benchmark) that other local authorities are expected to achieve.

Bennites Left-of-centre group associated with Tony Benn (see box 1.5, p. 15), especially in the period 1979–83 when he was actively supportive of the Campaign for Labour Party Democracy's agenda of reform in the Labour Party.

Benthamism Moral and political doctrine developed by Jeremy Bentham (1748–1832) and the utilitarians which advocated that institutions should be judged on whether they advanced the greatest happiness of the greatest number. The doctrine was used to advocate reform of many aspects of British life in the nineteenth century and to justify the growth of governmental intervention in a number of areas.

Best Value The duty of continuous improvement for local authorities as set by the Local Government Act 1999. To fulfil Best Value requirements, councils must consult local people, review all their functions periodically, measure their performance and produce a performance plan which is audited by an independent auditor.

Bevanites Adherents of a loose left-wing group which formed around Aneurin Bevan (1897–1960) after his resignation as Secretary of State for Health in 1951. The group attacked the Labour leadership on domestic policy and on foreign policy, where it advocated unilateral nuclear disarmament. It had sufficient strength in the Labour Party to gain substantial representation on the NEC but ceased to be effective when Bevan himself abandoned the policy of unilateralism in 1957.

Beveridge Report Report published by a committee headed by William Beveridge in 1942 ('Social Insurance and Allied Services'), which provided the foundations of the 1945 Labour government's approach to the welfare state. The report, which was extremely popular, recommended a comprehensive welfare system that would cover citizens from the cradle to the grave. See box 3.10, p. 121.

Bill Legislative proposal that will normally be introduced by the government of the day (or Scottish executive). Bills are usually to be considered in principle and in detail. Amendments to bills may be made during legislative passage. After a bill has gone through all its parliamentary stages and receives the **royal assent**, it becomes law. See also **money bill**.

Bill of rights Statement of civil liberties or individual rights. The Bill of Rights of 1689 established parliamentary supremacy over the **Crown**. It did not, however, provide the kind of comprehensive statement of civil liberties found in many modern states. By incorporating most of the European Convention on Human Rights, the Human Rights Act of 1998 gives the UK a statement of rights and liberties.

Block grant Method of payment of grant from one authority to another that merges payments for different purposes in a way which allows the recipient body maximum discretion in the allocation of spending. Block grants have been employed in the UK since 1929 for a large portion of central government grant to local authorities and are used to transfer money to the devolved governments of Scotland and Wales.

Block vote Method of allocating votes at conference and in other Labour selection processes in which union delegates could cast the whole of their affiliated vote behind a proposal. It was the source of enormous power over Labour policy for a few trade union leaders, whose support would therefore be courted behind the scenes at conference.

Budget maximization An alleged tendency on the part of bureaucrats to maximize the budget allotted to their bureau/department to ensure status and influence, leading to the overproduction of public goods and services. This critique of **bureaucracy** is associated with public choice theorists, particularly Wil-

liam Niskanen, Gordon Tullock and James Buchanan.

Bureaucracy Government by administrative officers. Since the nineteenth century, the bureaucracy in the UK has been based on hierarchy and appointment on merit, an approach praised by Max Weber, who argued that this was the basis for rational administration. Weber, however, highlighted the potential for conflict between elected politicians and permanent civil servants. More recent critics of bureaucracy have criticized its wastefulness and tendency to pursue its own interests (see **budget maximization**).

Bureau-shaping An adaptation of the **budget maximization** critique of **bureaucracy**, the bureau-shaping approach argues that bureaucrats maximize prestige and influence not through increasing the size of their budget but by reshaping their bureaux. This allows senior bureaucrats to separate off routine implementation functions and to increase control over policy-making and managerial functions. The bureau-shaping model, developed by Dunleavy (1991), could be used to explain the creation of executive agencies within the UK.

Butskellism Phrase used by *The Economist* to capture the overlap between the economic policies pursued in the 1950s first by Labour's Chancellor of the Exchequer, Hugh Gaitskell, and then by the Conservative Chancellor R. A. Butler, who accepted many of the Keynesian theories of his predecessor.

By-law Subordinate legislation made by a local authority.

Cabinet government In Britain a form of government in which a group of senior ministers has executive responsibility. It is buttressed by the twin conventions of collective responsibility and individual **ministerial responsibility**. The way it works in practice has changed significantly over the years. Trends such as the enhanced power of the prime minister and the greater use of committees and informal procedures have caused many observers to argue that cabinet government has been so seriously undermined that it no longer serves as a useful description of how Britain is governed.

Cabinet A group of advisers (usually drawn from their home country) who support senior figures (e.g. the Commissioners) in the European Union.

Catch-all party A type of party which appeals to all voters rather than concentrating on one sector of society. Such parties tend to de-emphasize any ideological or rhetorical characteristics which would prevent them from maximizing their vote and they typically seek the centre-ground of politics. The term is associated with Kirchheimer and is widely used to explain the tactics of modern political parties such as New Labour.

Citizens' panel See **people's panel**.

Civil service In the UK the name given to the officials who are appointed to support the government, advising on policy and implementing it. Reform of the civil service in recent years has placed great emphasis on managerial skills.

Civil Service Code See box 5.2, p. 174.

Cohesion policy Regional policy introduced in 1973 as a way of equalizing the wealth of the regions within the EU and promoting economic integration. The cohesion policy uses the Cohesion Fund and structural funds to achieve this goal.

Collectivism General theory that social and economic policy should be organized for the good of the community as a whole rather than for private enterprise or individuals.

Comitology Name given to the web of committees, primarily consisting of national officials, which monitors the implementation of policy.

Committee stage Stage of a legislative measure at which it is considered in detail rather than in principle. Often carried out in a small committee rather than in the full legislative body, although in certain cases the whole legislative body may examine a bill in detail.

Community charge See **poll tax**.

Concentration of powers/separation of powers The extent to which powers within a state are divided between different institutions and people – especially between the executive, legislative and judicial powers – and the extent to which powers are concentrated in the same institutions and personnel. In a democracy it is often considered preferable to separate these powers, although in the UK they are largely concentrated through the cabinet, which is drawn for the most part from the House of Commons and controls it through the party system.

Concordat Agreement made between London and a devolved government as to how powers shall be exercised.

Consociationalism/consociational democracy Form of democracy that is often deemed more appropriate than **majoritarian democracy** for societies which are deeply segmented by race, religion or language. The purpose of consociational democracy is the accommodation of different identities within a common political structure, a goal that is usually achieved by such devices as **power sharing**, **proportional representation** and various minority safeguards both over policy and in relation to legal rights. The notion of consociational democracy appears to have special relevance to Northern Ireland, where the existence of two communities – Catholic and Protestant – makes majoritarian democracy inappropriate. The power-sharing arrangements of the Sunningdale Agreement (1973) and of the Good Friday Agreement (1998) reflect the desire to establish consociational democracy.

Contracting out (1) Process by which members of a trade union could avoid paying the political levy. (2) Process of delegating activities and services previously performed directly to third parties or private providers.

Convention Unwritten rules which govern political conduct but which do not have legal force. Their strength is that they are flexible, their weakness that they can be broken and are often unclear. Traditionally there has been a wide use of conventions in the British constitution, although the period since 1979 has seen an expansion of the use of written statements of practice.

Core executive A network of interdependent actors at the centre of government, who govern through building alliances rather than through command. The core executive includes the prime minister, ministers and senior civil servants and focuses on resource mobilization and informal contacts rather than on formal organizational structures.

Corporatism A system of government in which key interest groups representing labour and capital are included in the policy-making process. Although the state loses its autonomy, it gains the support of these groups in the implementation of policy as well as enhanced legitimacy.

Council tax Local tax on property which was introduced to replace the community charge or **poll tax**.

Cranleigh money See **short money**.

Critical elections A series of elections in which there are major long-term changes in voting behaviour and party alignment. See also **dealignment, realignment**.

Crown Monarch personally but usually used in a governmental context to refer to ministers and departments.

Crown privilege Rule which allows the **Crown** to refuse to answer questions or disclose documents if such disclosure would damage the national interest.

Dealignment Concept used to explain the decline of group identities, especially those based on social class, and the loosening of ties between political parties and distinct social groupings. See also **realignment**.

Decision Form of European legislation; see box 15.3, p. 492.

Declaration of incompatibility Declaration by the judges that a statutory provision is incompatible with the human rights protected under the Human Rights Act 1998.

Such a declaration does not in itself quash legislation, but it sends a strong signal to government that it should either amend the offending provision or justify its retention.

Decommissioning Process of putting weapons held by paramilitary forces in Northern Ireland beyond use.

Delegated legislation See **primary legislation/secondary legislation**.

Delegation Process by which a superior official or authority allows lower-level authorities or individuals to take decisions on their behalf.

Democratic deficit Phrase which refers to the **accountability** gap between European policy makers and the institutions that attempt to control them.

Deselection Process by which a constituency party removes a sitting MP. Deselection became controversial in the Labour Party during the 1970s and 1980s when it was systematically used to ensure that MPs adhered to their local parties' policy preferences rather than their own preferences or those of the leadership.

Devolution The transfer of legislative and executive powers to subordinate bodies within the state, e.g. the Scottish Parliament, the Welsh Assembly, the Northern Ireland Assembly 1921–72, the regions. Compare with **federalism**.

Dignified/efficient parts of the constitution A distinction made by Walter Bagehot in *The English Constitution* (1867) between those parts of the constitution where formal power resided (e.g. the **Crown**) and those parts where it was really located (e.g. the **cabinet**).

Direct action The use of tactics, which may be violent or non-violent, that bypass the normal institutions of representative government. Typically, these tactics involve some form of public protest such as a demonstration or march to publicize a cause. Direct action is associated especially with the emergence of radical social movements.

Direct democracy The use of instruments such as the initiative, **referendum** and recall which allow citizens a direct say in law making rather than simply delegating the authority to make laws to an elected body.

Direct effect The process by which European law comes into immediate effect and binds individuals and states. The Van Gend en Loos case (1963) clarified the doctrine of direct effect.

Directive Form of European legislation which is very widely used. It specifies the goals of a policy's objectives but allows individual member states discretion about the means to achieve those goals. See box 15.3, p. 492.

Disapplication Process by which a statute that does not comply with European Community law is effectively suspended.

Discretionary power A power vested in an administrative body or minister. Discretionary power is an essential tool of executive activity. Although broad, such powers are not unlimited and in recent years the courts have supervised their exercise increasingly closely to see, for example, if they have been used reasonably.

Disfranchisement Removal of the right to vote.

Dissent Disagreement and opposition which can appear at many different levels of the political system. One powerful measure of dissent within the context of an organized parliamentary party is the frequency with which MPs have voted against the instructions given by the leadership in a whipped division.

Dissolution Formal name given to the process of ending the life of one Parliament and calling a general election. Theoretically the decision is taken by the monarch, but in fact the choice is that of the prime minister of the day. The maximum life of a Parliament is five years in normal circumstances, although in exceptional circumstances Parliament may be continued.

Dual mandate System by which a person may be elected simultaneously for two authorities, e.g. the House of Commons and

the Scottish Parliament or the House of Commons and the European Parliament.

Early day motions Motions for debate put down by backbenchers in the House of Commons. There is no time allotted for the motions and their value is primarily as a way of expressing opinion on a controversial issue.

E-democracy Initiatives which allow electronic interaction between government and citizen using new technologies, and particularly the Internet. Includes online voting and use of e-mail.

Elective dictatorship Phrase coined by Lord Hailsham to refer to the ability under the British constitution of a party elected with only a small plurality of the votes or seats to exercise untrammelled power because of the absence of checks and balances on the executive.

Electoral college A body which is given the responsibility of electing to an office. The members of an electoral college will usually be selected to represent different parts of a wider constituency or they may be elected. This form of indirect election has been extensively used in the Labour Party for its leadership elections.

Electoral reform A term usually used to refer to moves to abandon Britain's **first past the post** or **simple plurality system**.

Emergency powers Those powers that are reserved to the government for use in a national emergency, which may involve the suspension of some human rights protection and the sidelining of normal legislative processes.

English question The broad question of whether devolution to Scotland, Wales and Northern Ireland should be complemented by a parallel devolved body for England or should be matched by a series of regional authorities.

Entrenchment Protections built into powers or functions so that, for example, a bill of rights might be repealed only by a two-thirds majority or after a **referendum**.

Erskine May Erskine May (1815–86) was clerk of the House of Commons between

1871 and 1886. His *Treatise upon the Law, Privileges and Usage of Parliament* (1844) effectively became the procedural bible of Parliament and is now in its 28th edition. See also *Hansard*.

Executive agencies See **agencies**.

Extradition Formal procedure for removing a person from one country usually to stand trial in another.

Fabianism Approach to political change that advocates gradual reform rather than revolution. Associated with a group of social reformers and intellectuals who founded the Fabian Society in 1884. Beatrice and Sidney Webb and George Bernard Shaw influenced the Liberals (**new liberalism**) as well as the early Labour Party.

Federalism A system of government in which power is divided constitutionally between a central authority and subordinate units such as states. It differs from **devolution** in that sovereignty is shared and the division of powers is symmetrical across the subnational units. Contemporary discussion of federalism within the UK centres on two issues: the future shape of the relationship between London and the devolved systems and the future shape of the relationship between the EU and the member states.

Financial Management Initiative (FMI) The system established in 1982 partly as a result of Rayner's efforts to improve management and decision making in government (see **Rayner scrutinies**). This improvement was to be achieved primarily by clarifying objectives and managerial lines of control.

First minister Equivalent of the prime minister in the devolved systems of Scotland, Wales and Northern Ireland.

First past the post (FPTP)/simple plurality system Electoral method in which the candidate who gets the most votes is declared the winner regardless of whether he or she had an absolute majority (50 per cent +) or not. The system is the one used in Westminster elections although widely seen as unfair to minorities.

Focus group A group which is used in public opinion polling and which involves intensive monitoring of attitudes over time through observation of group discussions and interviewing. It was used extensively by the Labour Party after 1994 to test policy options with swing voters. See also **people's panel**.

Franchise The right to vote. The franchise was gradually extended throughout the nineteenth and twentieth centuries, and by 1969 all those aged over 18, with a few exceptions, had the right to vote.

Frontbencher Member of Parliament (or, by extension, of other legislative body such as the Scottish Parliament) who holds office in the government or has responsibility as an opposition spokesperson. At Westminster these MPs sit on the frontbenches.

Globalization An umbrella term for the expansion of economic, political, cultural and environmental issues beyond national borders into issues of global importance.

Goschen formula See **Barnett formula**.

Governance A model of policy making which focuses not on formal governmental institutions but on policy making through bargaining and negotiation between governmental actors at the national level and private and voluntary sector bodies.

Grand Committees Committees of the House of Commons consisting of all MPs with constituencies in a defined area, sometimes supplemented by other members to make the composition of the House as a whole. A Scottish Grand Committee was set up in 1907, the Welsh Grand Committee in 1960 and the Northern Irish in 1994. During the period immediately prior to devolution, the Grand Committees were given powers to handle an extensive amount of parliamentary business affecting their area.

Green paper Statement of government thinking on issues raised by a public policy problem. Such a paper invites consultation and discussion. By comparison with a **white paper** it is used when government thinking is still at an early stage.

Hansard The official report of the proceedings in the House of Commons and the House of Lords. (Luke Hansard was a Commons printer who first published reports in 1812.) See also **Erskine May.**

Holistic government See **joined-up government.**

Hollowing out of the state Theory associated with Professor Rhodes and with B. G. Peters that organizational and structural changes to the state (decentralization, **devolution** and deconcentration) have changed fundamentally the nature of modern **governance.**

Hung Parliament/council Parliament or local authority in which no one party has sufficient support to form an administration by itself. Minority government or coalition government may follow from the election of a hung Parliament. Both have been rare at the national level, but Labour took office as a minority government in 1924 and 1929. The first Welsh Assembly elections created an Assembly (1999–2003) in which there was first a minority administration, then a formal coalition. Many local authorities are in a situation where no single party has overall control.

Hybrid legislation Used to refer to a **bill** which is part private and part public. See **private legislation** and **public legislation.**

Joined-up government Style of government which emphasizes that greater efficiency and effectiveness in policy making require greater integration at all levels and the reform of structural and other barriers that encourage fragmentation. The approach was endorsed by the Blair government on coming to power in 1997. Also called holistic government.

Joint committee Committee containing members of both Houses of Parliament, usually as a means of achieving better coordination.

Judicial review Process by which the courts scrutinize administrative or legislative acts to see if they are legal. In the UK, courts may examine an **Act of Parliament** to see if it conforms to the Human Rights Act or if it is in conflict with EU legislation. Subordinate legislation and administrative action are frequently reviewed by the courts.

Justiciability Term used to describe issues which properly fall within the jurisdiction of the courts. The concept is sometimes also used in a prescriptive manner to describe issues which are capable of being resolved by legal means and which therefore should be resolved by a court. Justiciable issues are often contrasted with 'political' or policy issues for which courts might seem inappropriate decision-making bodies.

Kilmuir rules Guidelines established by the Lord Chancellor, Lord Kilmuir, in 1955 restricting the freedom of judges to speak to the press. The restrictions were lifted in 1987 by the then Lord Chancellor, Lord McKay, and since then some judges have used the press to criticize government penal policy.

Line management The chain of command and accountability between managers and employees.

Lobby (1) Area in Parliament outside the chamber. (2) Group of people representing a particular political interest, e.g. the environmental lobby. (3) Collective name given to the press who are allowed into the Members' Lobby and who receive special briefings from the government.

Lobbying group See **lobby.**

Loyalist Term used of those within the Northern Ireland population (essentially the Protestant population) who wish the province to remain part of the United Kingdom and who are loyal to the **Crown.**

Majoritarian democracy A form of democracy in which the largest party following an election gains control of government, with no requirement to share power with smaller parties. Compare with **consociationalism.**

Maladministration Term used especially in relation to the jurisdiction of the Parliamentary Commissioner for Administration or Ombudsman. It was defined in 1967 by government minister Richard Crossman as 'bias, neglect, inattention, delay, incompetence, ineptitude, perversity, turpitude, arbitrariness and so on', but later interpretations have broadened it. Essentially, the term refers to errors in the process of decision making rather than in the substance of policy.

Mandate Endorsement of a party's policy platform gained through electoral success. Winning parties usually claim a mandate to govern, even though voters may not be well informed about their specific policy proposals.

Market testing The process of measuring public services against equivalent private sector provision to evaluate their cost-effectiveness and indicate ways to improve efficiency. This may include **contracting out** the service to the private sector if savings cannot be made in-house.

Mass membership party A form of political party which places emphasis on an extensive party membership for mobilizing votes and policy making. In mass membership parties there is usually a strong expectation that the members will play a significant role in the life of the party and not be subordinated to the parliamentary party.

Michigan model A model of voting behaviour developed at the University of Michigan's Survey Research Center in the 1950s which used survey data to test voters' attachments to political parties. The Michigan model placed considerable stress on the explanatory role of partisan identifications, arguing that attachments to one or other of the major parties were strong, predisposing electors to vote for the party with which they identified. This partisan identification was in turn the product of long-term political socialization.

Militant Tendency A Trotskyist party which used a policy of entryism to gain control of several local Labour parties in the 1970s. Militant was particularly powerful in Liverpool, where it dominated the Labour-controlled city council. After the 1983 election, Neil Kinnock pursued a policy of expulsion against Militant and it had declined as a force by the late 1980s.

Ministerial Code Essentially a handbook for ministers, which covers such issues as how to bring business to cabinet, relations with the media and ethical issues such as how to handle gifts. Although elements of the code date back to 1917, the modern document may be traced to Attlee's 1945 administration and the desire to promote efficient procedure in government. It was made public in 1992. Recently there has been some pressure to make the code enforceable against ministers, but at present it remains dependent on the prime minister for its implementation, an informal compendium of practice rather than a rulebook. (There is a separate Ministerial Code for Scotland.)

Ministerial responsibility The convention that ministers should be held accountable to Parliament for the conduct of their department. In recent years **accountability** has been interpreted as a requirement to give an account rather than to resign if problems occur.

Money bill A bill which involves the authorization of expenditure from government funds or seeks to raise money from taxes. Since the 1911 Parliament Act, money bills may not be amended by the House of Lords.

Multi-layered polity A model of policy making which focuses on bargaining and negotiation between governmental actors (at the national, subnational and supranational levels) and private and voluntary sector organizations. The model emphasizes the extent to which powers overlap in the modern state.

Multi-racial/multi-ethnic society Model of society which has within it a series of diverse groups and ethnicities all of which are accorded equal legitimacy and recognition.

Natural justice Rules of fair play which must be followed in a range of judicial and administrative circumstances. Key principles of natural justice include the rule against bias – that no one should be judge in his or her own cause – and that both parties in an argument should be heard. These rules have been adapted and elaborated by the courts and applied in administrative law.

Next Steps Agencies See **agencies**.

New Labour Name given to the Labour Party under the leadership of Tony Blair after 1994. As New Labour, the party repositioned itself in the centre of British politics, abandoning support for traditional Labour policies such as nationalization and high rates of taxation.

New liberalism Radical strand within British liberalism that emerged in the late nineteenth century and heavily influenced the Liberal governments of 1906–16. The new liberalism emphasized the positive role of the state and supported government intervention in the economy and in society, in contrast to the classical *laissez-faire* liberalism. Not to be confused with neo-liberalism, which was one strand in the movement to the right in the 1970s.

New public management (NPM) An umbrella term for the introduction of new forms of management into public administration in the 1980s, based on private sector values of risk taking, entrepreneurship, **market testing** and emphasis on results rather than traditional bureaucratic values of hierarchy and formality.

New right A term attached to the coalition of neo-liberal economists, philosophers and politicians who rose to prominence in the 1970s, advocating a reduced role for the state and a market-oriented, *laissez-faire* approach to economics. The term may also be used to refer to their organized supporters and is often associated with the policies of Margaret Thatcher in the UK and Ronald Reagan in the United States.

Night-watchman state Term associated with the political philosopher Robert Nozick (1974), who called for a minimal state that would provide nothing beyond a basic framework of laws and security for its citizens.

Nolan Lord Nolan chaired the Committee on Standards in Public Life from its inception in 1994 to 1997. The Committee's first report into standards in public life (the Nolan Report) recommended substantial restrictions on MPs working for outside interests, which were adopted by the Major government in 1995.

Non-governmental organization (NGO) A term usually applied to voluntary sector bodies and pressure groups to signal that, although they may provide public services and seek to shape government policy, they are formally separate from the state.

Non-ministerial departments Departments or boards with no ministerial head, e.g. the Inland Revenue.

Ombudsman Generic name given to an official who hears complaints against public authorities.

One-nation Toryism Style of Conservatism which dates from the 1950s and which emphasizes the importance of progressive social legislation in order to avoid class conflict. Its reformist stance looks to Disraeli for inspiration. Although it was to some extent eclipsed by Thatcherism within the Conservative Party, the tradition of 'one-nation' politics was provocatively claimed by Blair for New Labour.

Order paper The name given to the daily publication which gives the agenda of parliamentary proceedings for each sitting day.

Order in Council Decree or order made by the monarch with the advice of the Privy Council. The power to issue such orders effectively gives the executive a broad legislative power, although it is only used as an alternative to **primary legislation** in extreme circumstances. Orders in Council are widely used as a form of **delegated legislation**.

Opinion Form of European legislation; see box 15.3, p. 492.

Overlord system A system of organizing the **cabinet** used by Winston Churchill when he returned to government in 1951. Churchill wanted to reproduce for peacetime the style of government he had operated from 1940 to 1945. The idea was to have a small number of ministers (largely peers without constituency duties) overseeing several departments, but the system broke down in practice because of the difficulty of securing **accountability** and clear lines of control.

Pairing The practice of agreeing with a member of a different political party to be absent from Parliament, with the two absent votes cancelling each other out.

Parallel consent See **weighted consent**.

Paramilitary groups Umbrella term given to armed groups who regularly engage in terrorist activity. Most widely used in Northern Ireland to refer to the activities of, on the nationalist side, the Irish Republican Army (IRA) and its splinter groups and the Irish National Liberation Army (INLA), and, on the loyalist side, a number of groups such as the Ulster Volunteer Force (UVF), which dates from 1912, and the Ulster Defence Association (UDA), which dates from the 1970s.

Parliamentary privilege Immunity given to members of Parliament (and other legislative bodies) in order to enable them to work effectively. The phrase refers both to collective immunity, e.g. the right to control their own proceedings, and to long-standing immunity against suit for libel.

Parliamentary questions Written and oral questions from MPs and peers to ministers. Answers to written questions are printed in *Hansard*; oral questions are answered by ministers at departmental question time in the chamber.

Parliamentary sovereignty/parliamentary supremacy The doctrine that no outside body can overrule the will of Parliament, described by A. V. Dicey as one of the pillars of the British constitution. The doctrine has been challenged by membership of the EU, **devolution** and the extension of **judicial review** but remains formally central to the British constitution.

Participation See **political participation**.

Party cohesion The extent to which a political party votes together in legislative divisions.

Party political broadcast (PPB) A 3- to 5-minute television slot in which a political party can present its message to voters. Only major parties are eligible for PPBs.

Pay-roll vote Term used to refer to the large number of MPs who are either salaried members of the government or unpaid parliamentary private secretaries. These MPs may be expected automatically to vote for the government in the division lobbies rather than take an independent line.

Peerage General term given to group of nobles whose titles are conferred by the **Crown**. There are hereditary peers (whose titles pass to their heirs) and life peers. Until 1999 all hereditary peers and life peers of the UK could sit as members of the House of Lords, the second chamber of the British Parliament. After 1999 only a small number of hereditary peers could sit as members of the House of Lords as of right.

People's panel A representative panel of 5,000 people set up by the Labour government after the 1997 election as a way of testing responses to the government's proposed public service reform programme. It was dropped in 2002 when a Cabinet Office evaluation decided that its work had been done. See also **focus group**.

Performance indicators Criteria against which public bodies are judged. Local authorities, for example, may be measured against a set of **Best Value** performance indicators, and the results may be published in league tables. Failure to meet the required standard may lead to the imposition of penalties such as loss of grant or intervention by the Secretary of State.

Pillars/pillarization Structure of the European Union which emerged after the Maastricht Treaty (1992) and which distinguishes between the EU's different policy competences. The first pillar relates to the European Community competences, the second to the area of foreign and security policy, and the third to the area of justice and home affairs.

Plebiscitary democracy Form of democracy in which key issues are frequently put to a referendum rather than relying on representative institutions. While referendums may augment representative democracy, they may also be manipulated and used to enhance the power of individual leaders.

Pluralism The idea that power is and should be spread extensively through society and the political system. In political science, pluralists argue that as broad a spread of interest group activity as possible is necessary if democracy is to be maximized.

Political culture The attitudes, beliefs and values which underpin a political system, and which can help to account for the differences between countries with similar political institutions. The most famous study of political culture was undertaken by Almond and Verba (1963).

Political neutrality The duty of civil servants to serve the elected government of the day whatever its political complexion.

Political participation The engagement of the population in political action. There are various forms of participation ranging from voting through membership of parties and pressure groups to **direct action**.

Poll tax A form of local government taxation introduced in Britain in the late 1980s, formally called the community charge. The poll tax was levied on all adults rather than on a household basis, and was deeply unpopular.

Post-war consensus See box 3.1, p. 91.

Power sharing A system of government in which power is shared between different communities or segments of society.

Practice statement Directive issued on the authority of a court or its judges. Such a statement may relate to the way business will be handled or to the rules of interpretation which the court will follow.

Precedent Used in the legal system to indicate a rule laid down in one case which binds similar cases in future. Common law convention.

Precept The method by which a non-billing authority obtains income to cover its expenditure.

Pressure group An organization which is formed to promote a cause or interest. Such organizations have a limited agenda and do not themselves seek to govern the country, though they may run candidates for office as part of their general strategy to change public opinion and influence the policy process. Alternative terms may be interest groups or lobbying organizations.

Primary legislation/secondary legislation Acts of the Westminster and Scottish Parliaments constitute primary legislation. Secondary legislation (also called delegated legislation and statutory instruments) modifies the provisions of the Act in a way permitted by the original legislation – for example, by increasing the levels of benefit payment authorized by a Social Security Act.

Prime minister The head of the government and leader of the **cabinet**. A prime minister's position usually derives from his or her position as leader of the majority party in Parliament. The role is an extremely powerful one, although there are substantial variations in authority and style among individual holders of the office.

Prime minister's questions (PMQs) A 30-minute weekly session in the Commons in which the prime minister answers oral questions from MPs. Questions are not given in advance so the prime minister must be prepared to answer on a wide range of subjects.

Private Finance Initiative (PFI) The **contracting out** of large public sector capital projects to the private sector, often used to build hospitals and schools. Private companies may lease buildings back to the public sector over a period of 30 years or more.

Private legislation Legislative proposals which apply not to the whole country but to a section of it. Sometimes known as local and personal legislation.

Private member's bill (PMB)/private member's legislation Private members' bills are public bills introduced into Parliament by **backbench** MPs. A ballot process is used to decide which MPs will be allowed to introduce PMBs in a particular session. Few PMBs make it into the statute books to become legislation and die at the end of the session in a process colloquially known as the 'massacre of the innocents'.

Private office Office of a minister which consists of the group of personal staff serving him or her directly.

Private–public partnership See **public–private partnership**.

Privatization A term usually associated with the sale of shares in publicly owned industries to the private sector. Companies such as British Gas and British Telecom were sold off in this way during the 1980s.

Proportional representation (PR) Methods of election which attempt to ensure that the seats gained by each party accurately reflect their support in the electorate.

Prorogation The formal end to the Parliamentary year, which usually takes place in November.

Public legislation Legislation which applies generally rather than to some specific person or groups of people.

Public–private partnership (PPP) A joint venture between the public and private sectors, with investment often coming from the private sector and risk shared between the two sectors. Such partnerships may cover the management of services and small-scale enterprises as well as large-scale projects. Compare with **Private Finance Initiative**.

Public service agreements (PSAs) Performance targets negotiated between central government departments and the Treasury, or set for local government by central government. Future funding may depend on meeting the targets.

Purchaser–provider split Distinction which argues that it is more efficient to separate the purchase and regulation of a service from its direct provision.

Qualified majority voting (QMV) Weighted voting in the EU Council of Ministers.

Quango Publicly funded body operating at arm's length from a department. Quangos may perform executive, advisory or quasi-judicial functions. They have grown in number in recent years and are frequently criticized because they offer ministers extensive patronage and lack **accountability**.

Queen's Speech Address by the queen to Parliament, in which she states the government's legislative programme for the new session. The speech takes place in November at the start of a new parliamentary session, or after a general election.

Rates Local tax on property.

Ratification Process by which Parliament gives approval to an international treaty.

Rayner scrutinies Device used during Mrs Thatcher's premiership to bring private sector methods into government. Sir Derek Rayner was asked to establish an efficiency unit attached to the Prime Minister's Office. It conducted a series of ad hoc investigations of public sector practices and recommended a closer linkage between policy making, management and implementation.

Readings (of legislation) Stages at which legislative proposals are considered.

Realignment Concept used to analyse long-term shifts in the pattern of support in a competitive party system and which usually identifies a reconfiguration or fundamental change in the political loyalty of key social groups. See also **dealignment**.

Recommendation Form of European legislation; see box 15.3, p. 492.

Reference Request from a national court or tribunal for a preliminary ruling to the European Court of Justice on the interpretation of the European law and the validity of acts of the various EU bodies.

Referendum A vote of the national, regional or local electorate to settle a particular policy issue. Referendums have been an increasingly popular tool at local and regional level in the UK.

Regulation (1) Legislative instrument used by the European Community. Regulations are directly effective and specify both the goal of the regulation and the method of securing it (see box 15.3, p. 492). (2) System of rules applied to private bodies (especially to privatized industries) as a way of ensuring that they operate in a manner that conforms to the public interest.

Representative government System of government in which the people elect members of a legislature or other body to represent them.

Report stage The stage in a bill's passage when, following committee consideration, it is reported back to the House together with the committee's recommendations, which may be approved or rejected. The report stage may see the introduction of new amendments to the bill. Also called consideration stage.

Republican Term used of those within Northern Ireland who want the province to cease being an integral part of the United Kingdom and become part of a united Ireland. While most Republicans are Roman Catholics, by no means all Roman Catholics in Northern Ireland are Republicans.

Responsible government System of government in which the executive is formally answerable and accountable to the legislature, representative assembly or Parliament. The effectiveness of responsible government depends on a number of factors, including the resources of the legislature, the techniques of scrutiny available and the extent to which it itself is controlled by the executive through patronage or party discipline.

Rossi doctrine Doctrine associated with Sir Hugh Rossi MP, who when chair of the Environment Committee in the 1980s argued that in order to maximize their effectiveness, select committees should only investigate topics outside the mainstream of partisan debate. In this way, Rossi thought the select committees would avoid dividing on partisan lines. The logic of the Rossi doctrine was to confine select committees to non-controversial topics, and support for the doctrine has accordingly eroded.

Royal assent The final stage before a bill becomes law; the queen must signal her authorization of the bill before it can pass.

Royal prerogative Power which was exercised by the monarch without parliamentary oversight – such as the **ratification** of treaties and the issuing of passports. Most of these powers have now passed to the government and the prime minister.

Rule of law According to A. V. Dicey, the second pillar of the British constitution, alongside **parliamentary sovereignty**. The rule of law protects individuals from arbitrary government, requiring that all be equal before the law, and that government act in accordance with the law.

Salisbury convention The practice that the House of Lords will not vote down legislative proposals contained in the election manifesto of the winning party after an election.

Scott Report Report into the breaking of the embargo on the export of arms to Iraq, published in 1996. The report was highly critical of the government, accusing ministers and civil servants of misleading Parliament.

Second-order election An election other than a major national election (effectively, a general election in the UK). For example, in the UK, a local, regional or European election would all be second-order elections. First-order elections have the most salience with voters and are likely to affect the pattern of voting at second-order elections. Thus, voters in European and local elections may be casting their vote on the basis of national issues and personalities rather than European and local ones.

Secondary legislation See **primary legislation**.

Select committee Parliamentary committee which is established with a strong scrutiny role and which in the United Kingdom attempts to operate on a bipartisan basis.

Selective benefit A term used by Olson (1965) to describe a benefit provided to interest group members which is limited to members of that group, such as cheap insurance. Selective benefits can be contrasted with collective benefits, such as a cleaner environment, which are enjoyed by all members of society and cannot be restricted to group members.

Separation of powers See **concentration of powers**.

Service delivery agreement Sets out in more detail than a **public service agreement** the detailed outputs on which a department must focus to meet its targets.

Session Annual sitting of Parliament, usually from November to November.

Sewel convention/Sewel motion Procedural device named after Lord Sewel (a minister at the Foreign Office) which allows the Scottish Parliament to permit Westminster to make policy in an area devolved to the Scottish Parliament. When **devolution** was introduced, it was recognized that Westminster retained sovereignty so could in theory legislate for areas that were devolved. But the spirit of the devolution scheme meant that Westminster would rarely use this power unilaterally. However, it was also recognized that there might be occasions when Edinburgh would want Westminster to legislate on a topic that had been devolved. In that case, the device of a Sewel motion would apply in order to provide a legitimizing mechanism for Westminster's intervention.

Shadow cabinet The **frontbench** spokespersons of the major opposition party.

Sheriff In England, an administrative official appointed in each county by the monarch. In Scotland, a judicial office.

Short money A subsidy designed to help parties discharge their parliamentary duties. Known as Cranleigh money in the House of Lords.

Simple plurality system See **first past the post**.

Social democracy Political doctrine originally associated with Marxism but which has come to be associated with revisions of socialism that emphasize the possibility of gradual change rather than revolution. In Britain, the social democratic wing of the Labour Party explicitly criticized public ownership. In 1981 a split within the Labour Party brought about the creation of a separate Social Democratic Party, which later merged with the Liberals to form the Liberal Democrat Party.

Speaker The impartial officer who presides over the House of Commons.

Speaker's Conference All-party conference called to discuss matters which it is thought should be handled in a non-partisan way. Such conferences have frequently been used to deal with issues of **electoral reform**. The advent of the Electoral Commission in 2000 may make them less necessary.

Spin/spin doctor Term denoting the systematic attempt to influence the reception by the media and public of news and information. A spin doctor is one who is professionally concerned with ensuring that news and information are presented in the way that most benefits his or her client.

Standing committee Committee of the British Parliament used for a variety of legislative business, including the detailed consideration of **bills** and the handling of **delegated legislation**.

Standing orders Rules for the conduct of business of a legislative or other body.

Star Chamber Name given to the cabinet committee (MISC 62) which was established to arbitrate on public spending disputes.

Statute law The law which is contained in Acts of Parliament and **secondary legislation**, in contrast to the law which is contained in judicial **opinions**.

Statutory instrument (SI) The most important form of **secondary** or **delegated legislation** in the United Kingdom.

Stormont Site of the devolved Northern Ireland Parliament and administrative offices of the Northern Ireland government.

Strategic authority Authority such as the Greater London Authority which has powers to set long-term policy goals at a high level (usually in such areas as transport) but which has relatively few powers of direct service provision.

Strategic capacity Government's overall ability to plan, direct and deliver policy in the long term.

Sub judice rule Rule which prevents public discussion of an issue that is the subject of legal proceedings for fear of prejudicing the outcome.

Subsidiarity Theory which states that policy should be decided at the lowest level possible within the EU.

Supplementary vote See **alternative vote**.

Supply days Now called opposition days. These are the 20 days set aside in each session when the opposition selects the topics for parliamentary debate.

Surcharge Legal procedure by which elected councillors could be fined for excessive spending by their authorities.

Swing Summary measure used to calculate movement between elections. In its classical form, Butler or two-party swing measures the support for parties by calculating the average of the gain in the winning party's share of the vote between two elections and the losing party's deficit. Swing is a difficult measure to apply in multi-party situations and many analysts now prefer to use other measures to chart the flow of the vote.

Tactical voting Voting in which the elector casts his or her vote in a way which does not reflect his or her preferred option but which takes into account the candidates' relative strength. Thus a Labour supporter in a seat where the Liberal Democrats were the most effective challenger to the Conservatives might vote tactically for the Liberal Democrats.

Thatcherism Name given to the mix of free-market and populist policies associated with Margaret Thatcher.

Think tank Organization formed to conduct independent research and to press for the adoption of new policies. Think tanks became especially important in the period after 1970, when a clutch of organizations such as the Institute of Economic Affairs and the Centre for Policy Studies pushed for radical changes in social and economic policy and exerted intellectual influence on Conservative thinking. Think tanks associated with progressive and left-of-centre politics include Demos and the Institute of Public Policy Research.

Third way Doctrine associated with Anthony Giddens which argues for a new intellectual synthesis that transcends the ideological cleavage between capitalism and socialism and takes account of **globalization**. Third-way thinking had an impact on the policy choices of President Clinton and Tony Blair.

Tripartism Approach to economic policy making in the 1970s which emphasized the need for consensual agreements between the government, employers and unions.

Twinning Device of pairing constituencies and requiring that, in at least one of the two, a woman candidate be selected.

Ultra vires Doctrine which states that acts of a public authority must be within its legal powers. This means that there must be legal authority to perform a substantive function (e.g. operate a school) and that the local authority must comply with the procedural standards of administrative law. If the actions of a local authority are found to be ultra vires (beyond its powers), they are legally void. The doctrine has been seen as placing a brake on local authority enterprise.

Unilateralism Doctrine which states that the UK should renounce all its nuclear weapons regardless of what any other power does. The Campaign for Nuclear Disarmament has long promoted this cause and has found extensive support in the Labour Party.

Union state Concept used to denote the fact that although the UK is not a **federal** system and is seen by many as highly centralized, the arrangements and the character of the Act of Union with Scotland do not make it unambiguously a **unitary state**.

Unitary authority Local authorities which exercise all local powers, as opposed to authorities which split them between different tiers.

Unitary state State in which there is no constitutional division of sovereignty, as in a federation, but where all powers stem from a central authority. Contrast with **union state**.

Universal suffrage Grant of the right to vote to all adults without restrictions.

Usual channels Informal system by which the **whips** of the two major parties in Parliament arrange parliamentary business.

Volatility Electoral movement between elections which may involve a shift in support between parties and between voting and abstention.

Weighted consent System used in Northern Ireland to ensure that decisions on some issues require more than a simple majority and must achieve a level of cross-community agreement. Also known as parallel consent.

Welfare state State which recognizes an obligation to provide an extensive level of welfare services to its citizens.

West Lothian question The anomaly of Scottish, Welsh and Northern Irish MPs voting in Westminster on English issues, while English MPs are prevented by **devolution** from voting on Scottish, Welsh and Northern Irish issues.

The question was repeatedly raised by Tam Dalyell, West Lothian MP.

Westminster model System of parliamentary government found in the UK and a number of Commonwealth countries which has a number of distinct features and which contrasts with the parliamentary systems found in continental Europe. The government (which consists of a **prime minister** and cabinet) is formed from the majority party. The second largest party forms the opposition. Politics is **adversarial**. The British version is widely seen as promoting stable government, although its use of the **simple plurality system** is criticized for its unfairness to minorities.

Whip Name given to the officials who manage the supporters of their party in a legislature. Also the notice of business which requires attendance to vote with the party.

Whipped votes Votes or divisions in Parliament in which the party instructs its members how to vote.

White paper Document which sets out the government's thinking in a policy area. Although there is usually time for consultation before legislation is introduced, the proposals in a white paper are normally indicative of the government's intentions and much firmer than in a **green paper**.

Internet Resources

The Internet is a useful resource for students of modern British government. There are several websites that provide timely information and lively material on contemporary political issues. Websites change a good deal. Sometimes material is removed at short notice; sometimes websites disappear altogether. We have tried to ensure that the links given below and at the end of each chapter are still operative. The website associated with this book will provide further information on web resources.

Students should remember that the information contained on a website reflects the interests and perspective of the site provider.

- www.epolitix.com/ – Epolitix, general UK politics site
- www.psr.keele.ac.uk/ – Richard Kimber's Political Science Resource Pages, gateway into sites of interest to political scientists
- www.ukpolitics.org.uk/ – UK Politics, online magazine about UK politics
- www.ukpoliticsbrief.co.uk/ – Resource site for A-level students
- www.uk-p.org/ – Directory of UK political sites
- www.voxpolitics.com/ – Weblog of British politics
- www.politicos.co.uk – Politicos bookstore

Newspapers and other news sources

- www.guardian.co.uk – *Guardian*
- www.thetimes.co.uk – *The Times*
- www.independent.co.uk/ – *Independent*
- www.telegraph.co.uk – *Daily Telegraph*
- www.ft.com – *Financial Times*
- www.thescotsman.co.uk – *Scotsman*
- www.economist.co.uk – *The Economist*
- www.bbc.co.uk/politics – BBC political news
- www.channel4news.co.uk – Channel 4 news
- www.ananova.com – Ananova news

Think tanks

- www.adamsmith.org.uk – Adam Smith Institute
- www.catalyst-forum.org.uk – Catalyst Forum
- www.demos.co.uk – Demos
- www.fabian-society.org.uk – Fabian Society
- www.fpc.org.uk – Foreign Policy Centre
- www.ifs.org.uk – Institute for Fiscal Studies
- www.iea.org.uk – Institute of Economic Affairs
- www.ippr.org.uk – Institute for Public Policy Research
- www.smf.co.uk – Social Market Foundation

References and Bibliography

Adonis, A. (1993). *Parliament Today*. Manchester: Manchester University Press.

Adonis, A., Butler, D. and Travers, T. (1994). *Failure in British Government: The Politics of the Poll Tax*. Oxford: Oxford University Press.

Alderman, K. (1999). 'Revision of leadership election procedures in the Conservative Party', *Parliamentary Affairs*, 52: 2.

Almond, G. A. and Verba, S. (1963). *The Civic Culture*. Princeton, NJ: Princeton University Press.

Anderson, S. and Eliassen, K. (2001). *Making Policy in Europe*, 2nd edn. London: Sage.

Anderson, R., Heath, A. and Sinnott, R. (2002). 'Political knowledge and electoral choice', in L. Bennie, C. Rallings, J. Tonge and P. Webb (eds), *British Elections and Parties Yearbook*, vol. 12. London: Frank Cass.

Anderson, P. and Mann, N. (1997). *Safety First: The Making of New Labour*. London: Granta.

Andrews, L. (1999). *Wales Says Yes: The Inside Story of the Yes for Wales Referendum*. Bridgend, Wales: Seren.

Arthur, P. (2000). *Special Relationships: Britain, Ireland and the Northern Ireland Problem*. Belfast: Blackstaff.

Arthur, P. and Jeffrey, K. (1996). *Northern Ireland since 1968*, 2nd edn. Oxford: Blackwell.

Aughey, A. (2001). *Nationalism, Devolution and the Challenge to the United Kingdom State*. London: Pluto.

Bagehot, W. (1995). 'The English Constitution', in N. St John Stevas (ed.), *The Collected Works of Walter Bagehot*, vol. 5. London: Routledge.

Baker, A. (2000). *Prime Ministers and the Rule Book*. London: Politicos.

Baker, D. and Seawright, D. (eds) (1998). *Britain For and Against Europe: British Politics and the Question of European Integration*. Oxford: Oxford University Press.

Ballinger, C. (2002). 'The local battle, the cyber battle', in David E. Butler and D. Kavanagh (eds), *The British General Election of 2001*. Basingstoke: Palgrave.

Balogh, T. (1959). 'The apotheosis of the dilettante: The establishment of the mandarins', in H. Thomas (ed.), *The Establishment: A Symposium*. London: Anthony Blond.

Barberis, P. (ed.) (1997). *The Civil Service in an Era of Change*. Aldershot: Dartmouth.

Barker, A. (1982). *Quangos in Britain: Government and the Networks of Public Policy Making*. London: Macmillan.

Barnett, A. (1997). *This Time: Our Constitutional Revolution*. London: Vintage.

Beer, S. H. (1999). 'Strong government and democratic control', *Political Quarterly*, 70: 2.

Beetham, D., Byrne, I., Ngan, P. and Weir, S. (2002). *Democracy Under Blair: A Democratic Audit of the United Kingdom*. London: Politicos in association with Democratic Audit, Human Rights Centre, University of Essex.

Berrington, H. (ed.) (1998). *Britain in the Nineties: The Politics of Paradox*. London: Frank Cass.

Bew, P., Gibbon, P. and Patterson, H. (2002). *Northern Ireland 1921/2001: Political Forces and Social Classes*. London: Serif.

Birkinshaw, P. (1994). *Grievances, Remedies and the State*, 2nd edn. London: Sweet and Maxwell.

Blackburn, R. (1995). *The Electoral System in Britain*. London: Macmillan.

Blackburn, R. and Kennon, A. (eds) (2003). *Griffith and Ryle on Parliament: Functions, Practice and Procedures*. London: Sweet and Maxwell.

Blackburn, R. and Plant, R. (1999). *Institutional Reform: The Labour Government's Constitutional Reform Agenda*. London: Longman.

Blake, R. (1985). *Conservative Party from Peel to Thatcher*. London: Fontana.

Blumenthal, S. (1982). *The Permanent Campaign*. New York: Simon and Schuster.

Bogdanor, V. (1988). 'Britain and Europe: The myth of sovereignty', in Richard Holme and Michael Elliot (eds), *1688–1988: Time for a New Constitution*. Basingstoke: Macmillan.

Bogdanor, V. (1995). *The Monarchy and the Constitution*. Oxford: Clarendon Press.

Bogdanor, V. (1996a). 'Local government and the constitution', in V. Bogdanor, *Politics and the Constitution: Essays on British Government*. Aldershot: Dartmouth.

Bogdanor, V. (1996b). *Politics and the Constitution: Essays on British Government*. Aldershot: Dartmouth.

Bogdanor, V. (1997a). 'Ministerial accountability', *Parliamentary Affairs*, 50: 1.

Bogdanor, V. (1997b). *Power and the People: A Guide to Constitutional Reform*. London: Gollancz.

Bogdanor, V. (1999a). 'Devolution: Decentralisation or disintegration?', *Political Quarterly*, 70: 2.

Bogdanor, V. (1999b). 'Reform of the House of Lords: A sceptical view', *Political Quarterly*, 70: 4.

Bogdanor, V. (2001a). 'Civil service reform: A critique', *Political Quarterly*, 72: 3.

Bogdanor, V. (2001b). *Devolution in the United Kingdom*. Oxford: Oxford University Press.

Bogdanor, V. (ed.) (2003). *The British Constitution in the Twentieth Century*. Oxford: Clarendon Press.

Bomberg, E. and Stubb, A. (2003). *The European Union: How Does it Work?* Oxford: Oxford University Press.

Bonney, N. (2002). 'Scottish devolution: What lies beneath?', *Political Quarterly*, 73: 2.

Bradbury, J. and Mitchell, J. (2002). 'Devolution and territorial politics, stability, uncertainty and crisis', *Parliamentary Affairs*, 55: 2.

Brazier, A. (2003). *Parliament at the Apex: Parliamentary Scrutiny and Regulatory Bodies*. London: Hansard Society.

Brazier, R. (1988). *Constitutional Practice*. Oxford: Clarendon Press.

Bridges, Sir Edward (1950). *Portrait of a Profession: The Civil Service Tradition*. Cambridge: Cambridge University Press.

Brittan, S. (1971). *Steering the Economy*, rev. edn. Harmondsworth: Penguin.

Brown, A. et al. (1999). *The Scottish Electorate: The 1997 Election and Beyond*. Basingstoke: Macmillan.

Bruce, S. (1986). *God Save Ulster: The Religion and Politics of Paisleyism*. Oxford: Oxford University Press.

Bruce, S. (1992). *The Red Hand: Protestant Paramilitaries in Northern Ireland*. Oxford: Oxford University Press.

Bunyan, T. (1999). *Secrecy and Openness in the European Union*. London: Kogan Page.

Burch, M. and Holliday, I. (1996). *The British Cabinet System*. Hemel Hempstead: Prentice-Hall.

Burch, M. and Holliday, I. (1999). 'The prime minister's and cabinet offices: An executive office in all but name', *Parliamentary Affairs*, 52: 1.

Butler, D. E. (1963). *The Electoral System in Britain since 1918*, 2nd edn. Oxford: Clarendon Press.

Butler, D. E. and Butler, G. (2000). *Twentieth-century British Political Facts: 1900–2000*. Basingstoke: Macmillan.

Butler, D. E. and Kavanagh, D. (eds) (1997). *The British General Election of 1997*. Basingstoke: Macmillan.

Butler, D. E. and Kavanagh, D. (eds) (2002). *The British General Election of 2001*. Basingstoke: Palgrave.

Butler, D. E. and Stokes, D. (1970, 1974). *Political Change in Britain*. Basingstoke: Macmillan.

Byrne, P. (1997). *Social Movements in Britain*. London: Routledge.

Campbell, C. and Wilson, G. (1995). *The End of Whitehall*. Oxford: Blackwell.

Chandler, J. A. (2001). *Local Government Today*, 3rd edn. Manchester: Manchester University Press.

Chapman, R. A. (ed.) (1993). *Ethics in Public Service*. Edinburgh: Edinburgh University Press.

Child, S. (2001). *Politicos Guide to Election Practice and Law*. London: Politicos.

Child Poverty Action Group (2003). 'Child Poverty Figures Very Disappointing', London, 13 March.

Childs, D. (2001). *Britain since 1945: A Political History*, 5th edn. London: Routledge.

Chisholm, M. (2000). *Structural Reform in British Local Government: Rhetoric and Reality*. Manchester: Manchester University Press.

Cini, M. (ed.) (2003). *European Politics*. Oxford: Oxford University Press.

Clarke, M. and Stewart, J. D. (1992). *Citizens and Local Democracy Empowerment: A Theme for the 1990s*. Luton: Local Government Management Board.

Clifford, C., McMillan, A. and McLean, I. (1997). *The Organization of Central Government Departments: A History, 1064–1992*. Oxford: Nuffield College.

Coleman, S. (2000). *Electronic Media, Parliament and the People: Making Democracy Visible*. London: Hansard Society.

Coleman, S., Taylor, J. and Van De Donk, W. (1999). *Parliament in the Age of the Internet*. Oxford: Oxford University Press.

Collings, D. and Seldon, A. (2001). 'Conservatives in opposition', *Parliamentary Affairs*, 54: 4.

Commission on Strengthening Parliament (Norton Commission) (2000, July). *Strengthening Parliament*. London: Conservative Party.

Constitution Committee (2003). *2nd Report: Devolution and Inter-Institutional Relations in the UK*. HL28.

Conservative Party (1998). *The Fresh Future: The Conservative Party Renewed*. London: CCO Publications.

Coogan, T. (1995). *The Troubles: Ireland's Ordeal and the Search for Peace 1966–1995*. London: Hutchinson.

Cook, C. (2002). *A Short History of the Liberal Party, 1900-2001*, 6th edn. London: Macmillan.

Coulter, C. (1999). *Contemporary Northern Irish Society*. London: Pluto.

Cowley, P. (2001a). 'The Commons: Mr Blair's lapdog?', *Parliamentary Affairs*, 54: 4.

Cowley P. (2001b). *Revolts and Rebellions*. London: Politicos.

Cowley, P. (2002). 'Legislatures and assemblies', *Developments in British Politics*, 6.

Cowley, P. and Stuart, M. (2002). 'Mostly continuity, but more change than you'd think', *Parliamentary Affairs*, 55: 2.

Cowley, P. and Stuart, M. (2003). 'In place of strife? The PLP in government, 1997–2001', *Political Studies*, 51: 2.

Craig, F. W. S. (1989). *British Electoral Facts 1832–1987*, 5th edn. Aldershot: Dartmouth.

Cram, L. (1997). *Policy-making in the European Union: Conceptual Lenses and the Integration Process*. London: Routledge.

Crewe, I. (1985). 'Great Britain', in I. Crewe and D. Denver (eds), *Electoral Change in Western Democracies*. London: Croom Helm.

Crewe, I. (1993). 'Voting and the electorate', in P. Dunleavy, A. Gamble, I. Holliday and G. Peele (eds), *Developments in British Politics 4*. London: Macmillan.

Crewe, I. and Gosschalk, B. (1999). *Political Communications: Why Labour Won the General Election of 1997*. London: Frank Cass.

Crewe, I. and King, A. (1995). *SDP: The Life, Birth and Death of the Social Democratic Party*. Oxford: Oxford University Press.

Crick, M. (1986). *The March of Militant*, rev. edn. London: Faber.

Criddle, B. (1997). 'The candidates', in D. E. Butler and D. Kavanagh (eds), *The British General Election of 1997*. Basingstoke: Macmillan.

Criddle, B. (2002). 'The candidates', in D. E. Butler and D. Kavanagh (eds), *The British General Election of 2001*. Basingstoke: Palgrave.

Crowther Hunt, N. and Kellner, P. (1980). *The Civil Servants: An Enquiry into Britain's Ruling Class*. London: Macdonald.

Curtice, J. (2001). 'The electoral system: Biased to Blair', *Parliamentary Affairs*, 54: 3.

Daintith, T. and Page, A. (1999). *The Executive in the Constitution: Structure, Autonomy and Internal Control*. Oxford: Oxford University Press.

Deacon, D., Golding, P. and Billig, M. (2001). 'Press and broadcasting: "Real issues" and real coverage', *Parliamentary Affairs*, 54: 4.

Deakin, N. and Parry, R. (2000). *The Treasury and Social Policy*. Basingstoke: Palgrave.

Dehouse, R. (1998). *The European Court of Justice: The Politics of Judicial Integration*. Basingstoke: Macmillan.

Denham, A. and Garnett, M. (1999). 'Influence without responsibility? Think tanks in Britain', *Parliamentary Affairs*, 52: 1.

Denver, D. (1998). 'The British electorate in the 1990s', *West European Politics*, 21: 1.

Denver, D. (2003). *Elections and Voters in Britain*. Basingstoke: Palgrave.

Denver, D., Hands, G. and Henig, S. (1998). 'Triumph or targeting: Constituency campaigning in the 1997 election', in D. Denver, G. Hands and S. Henig (eds), *British Elections and Parties Review. Volume 8: The 1997 General Election*. London: Frank Cass.

Denver, D., Hands, G. and Henig, S. (2001). 'The impact of constituency campaigning in the 2001 general election', in D. Denver, G. Hands and S. Henig (eds), *British Elections and Parties Review. Volume 12: The 2001 General Election*. London: Frank Cass.

Dicey, A. V. (1995). *Introduction to the Law of the Constitution*, 10th edn. London: Macmillan.

Dixon, P. (2001). *Northern Ireland: The Politics of War and Peace*. Basingstoke: Palgrave.

Doherty, B. (1999). 'Paving the way: The rise of direct action against road-building and the changing character of British environmentalism', *Political Studies*, 47.

Doig, A. (2002). 'Sleaze fatigue in the house of ill-repute', *Parliamentary Affairs*, 55: 2.

Dowding, K. (1995). *The Civil Service*. London: Routledge.

Drewry, G. (1989). *The New Select Committees*. Oxford: Clarendon Press.

Drewry, G. (1993). 'Mr Major's Charter: Empowering the customer', *Public Law*.

Drewry, G. (1994). 'Revolution in Whitehall: The next steps and beyond', in J. Jowell and D. Oliver (eds), *The Changing Constitution*, 3rd edn. Oxford: Oxford University Press.

Dudley, G. and Richardson, J. (1998). 'Arenas without rules and the policy change process: Outsider groups in British politics', *Political Studies*, 46: 4.

Dummet, M. (1997). *Principles of Electoral Reform*. Oxford: Oxford University Press.

Dunleavy, P. (1991). *Democracy, Bureaucracy and Public Choice: Economic Explanations in Political Science*. London: Harvester Wheatsheaf.

Dunleavy, P. (2002). 'Elections and party politics', *Developments in British Politics*, 6.

Dunleavy, P. and Husbands, C. (1985). *British Democracy at the Crossroads: Voting and Party Competition in the 1980s*. London: Allen and Unwin.

Dunleavy, P. et al. (1999). 'Mixed electoral systems in Britain and the Jenkins Commission on Electoral Reform', *British Journal of Politics and International Relations*, 1: 1.

Duverger, M. (1954). *Political Parties: Their Organization and Activity in the Modern State*. London: Methuen.

Dyson, K. (1980). *The State Tradition in Western Europe: A Study of an Idea and an Institution*. Oxford: Martin Robertson.

Elcock, H. and Keating, M. (1998). *Remaking the Union: Devolution and British Politics in the 1990s*. London: Frank Cass.

Electoral Commission (2001). *Public Opinion and the General Election of 2001*. London: Electoral Commission.

Electoral Commission (2003). *Attitudes towards Voting and the Political Process*. London: Electoral Commission/MORI.

Elkit, J. and Reynolds, A. (2001). 'Analysing the impact of electoral administration on democratic politics', *Representation*, 38: 1 (Spring).

Endo, K. (1999). *The Presidency of the European Commission under Jacques Delors: The Politics of Shared Leadership*. Basingstoke: Macmillan.

Evans, G. (1999). 'Economics and politics revisited: Exploring the decline in Conservative support, 1992–95', *Political Studies*, 47: 1.

Evans, G. (ed.) (2001a). *The End of Class Politics?* Oxford: Oxford University Press.

Evans, G. (2001b). *For the Sake of Wales: Memoirs of Gwyn for Evans*. Caernarfon: Welsh Academic Press.

Evans, G. (2003). 'Political culture and voting participation', in P. Dunleavy, A. Gamble, R. Heffernan and G. Peele (eds), *Development in British Politics 7*. Basingstoke: Palgrave.

Evans, G. and Norris, P. (eds) (1999). *Critical Elections: British Parties and Voters in Long-term Perspective*. London: Sage.

Evans, G. and O'Leary, B. (2000). 'Northern Irish voters and the British–Irish Agreement', *Political Quarterly*, 71: 1.

Evans, P. (2002). *Handbook of House of Commons Procedure*, 3rd edn. London: Vacher Dodd.

Ewing, K. D. (2002). *Trade Unions, the Labour Party and Political Funding*. London: Catalyst Forum.

Ewing, K. D. and Gearty, C. A. (1990). *Freedom under Thatcher: Civil Liberties in Modern Britain*. Oxford: Clarendon Press.

Farrell, D. (1997). *Comparing Electoral Systems*. London: Prentice-Hall.

Fisher, J. (2002). 'Next step: State funding for the political parties?', *Political Quarterly*, 73: 4.

Flinders, M. (2002). 'Shifting the balance: Parliament, the executive and the British constitution', *Political Studies*, 50: 1.

Flynn, P. (1997). *Commons Knowledge: How to be a Backbencher*. Bridgend: Seren.

Flynn, P. (1999). *Dragons Led by Poodles: The Inside Story of a Labour Stitch Up*. London: Politicos.

Foley, M. (1999). *The Politics of the British Constitution*. Manchester: Manchester University Press.

Foley, M. (2000). *The British Presidency: Tony Blair and the Politics of Public Leadership*. Manchester: Manchester University Press.

Foster, C. (2000). 'The encroachment of the law on politics', *Parliamentary Affairs*, 53: 2.

Foster, C. D. and Plowden, F. J. (1996). *The State Under Stress: Can the Hollow State be Good Government?* Buckingham: Open University Press.

Foster, R. F. (1989). *Modern Ireland: 1600–1972*. Harmondsworth: Penguin.

Foster, R. F. (2000). *The Oxford Illustrated History of Ireland*. Oxford: Oxford University Press.

Franklin, M. N. (1985). *The Decline of Class Voting in Britain: Changes in the Basis of Electoral Choice, 1964–1983*. Oxford: Clarendon Press.

Fraser, D. (2000). 'The post-war consensus debate', *Parliamentary Affairs*, 53: 2.

Freeden, M. (1986). *The New Liberalism: An Ideology of Social Reform*. Oxford: Oxford University Press.

Freeden, M. (1996). *Ideologies and Political Theory: A Conceptual Approach*. Oxford: Oxford University Press.

Fry, G. (1969). *Statesmen in Disguise*. London: Macmillan.

Fry, G. (1979). *The Growth of Government: The Development of Ideas about the Role of the State and the Machinery and Functions of Government in Britain since 1780*. London: Frank Cass.

Gamble, A. (1988). *The Free Economy and the Strong State: The Politics of Thatcherism*. Basingstoke: Macmillan.

Garner, R. (2000). *Environmental Politics: Britain, Europe and the Global Environment*. Basingstoke: Palgrave.

Garner, R. and Kelly, R. (1998). *British Political Parties Today*. Manchester: Manchester University Press.

Gavin, N. (1996). 'The impact of television news on public perceptions of the economy and government, 1993–94', *Elections and Parties Yearbook 1996*. London: Frank Cass.

Geddes, A. and Tonge, J. (2002). *Labour's Second Landslide: The British General Election 2001*. Manchester: Manchester University Press.

George, S. (1996). *Britain and European Integration since 1945*. Oxford: Blackwell.

George, S. (1998). *An Awkward Partner: Britain in the European Community*, 3rd edn. Oxford: Oxford University Press.

George, S. and Bache, I. (2001). *Politics in the European Union*. Oxford: Oxford University Press.

Giddens, A. (1998). *The Third Way*. Cambridge: Polity.

Giddings, P. (1995). *Parliamentary Accountability: A Study of Parliament and Executive Agencies*. Basingstoke: Macmillan.

Giddings, P. and Drewry, G. (1996). *Westminster and Europe: The Impact of the European Union on the Westminster Parliament*. Basingstoke: Macmillan.

Gilmour, I. (1993). *Dancing with Dogma: Britain under Thatcherism*. London: Simon and Schuster.

Gilmour, I. (1997). *Whatever Happened to the Tories?* London: Fourth Estate.

Goetz, K. and Hix, S. (2000). *Europeanized Politics: European Integration and Political Systems*. Ilford: Frank Cass.

Goldsworthy, J. (1999). *The Sovereignty of Parliament: History and Philosophy*. Oxford: Oxford University Press.

Goldthorpe, J. H. (1968). *The Affluent Worker: Political Attitudes and Behaviour*. Cambridge: Cambridge University Press.

Goodhart, P. (1973). *The 1922: The Story of the Backbenchers' Committee*. Basingstoke: Macmillan.

Gould, P. (1999). *The Unfinished Revolution*. London: Little, Brown.

Government Statistical Service (2001). *Social Trends 2001*. London: HMSO.

Grant, W. (1995). *Pressure Groups, Politics and Democracy in Britain*. London: Phillip Allan.

Grant, W. (2000). *Pressure Groups and British Politics*. Basingstoke: Macmillan.

Grant, W. (2001). 'Pressure politics: From "insider" politics to direct action', *Parliamentary Affairs*, 54: 2.

Gray, A. and Jenkins, B. (2000). 'Government and administration', *Parliamentary Affairs*, 53: 2.

Greenleaf, W. H. (2003). *The British Political Tradition*. London: Routledge.

Gregory, R. and Giddings, P. (2002). *The Ombudsman, the Citizen and Parliament*. London: Politicos.

Griffiths, D. (2000). 'Writings on the margins: Welsh politics', *British Journal of Politics and International Studies*, 2: 1.

Griffiths, J. A. G. (1991). *The Politics of the Judiciary*, 5th edn. London: Fontana.

Hall, P. (1999). 'Social capital in Britain', *British Journal of Political Science*, 29: 3.

Halliday, S. (2000). 'The influence of judicial review on bureaucratic decision-making', *Public Law*.

Hansard Society (1992). *Making the Law: Report of the Hansard Society Commission on the Legislative Process*. London: Hansard Society.

Hansard Society Commission on Parliamentary Scrutiny (2001). *The Challenge for Parliament: Making Government Accountable*. London: Hansard Society.

Hansen, R. (2000). *Citizenship and Immigration in Post-war Britain: The Institutional Origins of a Multicultural Nation*. Oxford: Oxford University Press.

Harden, I. and Lewis, N. (1986). *The Noble Lie: The British Constitution and the Rule of Law*. London: Hutchinson.

Hart, H. L. A. (1972). *The Concept of Law*, repr. and rev. edn. Oxford: Clarendon Press.

Hart, J. (1992). *Proportional Representation: Critics of the British Electoral System, 1820–1945*. Oxford: Clarendon Press.

Hays, C. and Richards, D. (2000). 'The tangled webs of Westminster and Whitehall', *Public Administration*, 78: 1.

Hazell, R. (1999). *Constitutional Futures: A History of the Next Ten Years*. Oxford: Oxford University Press.

Hazell, R. (ed.) (2000). *The State of the Nations: The First Year of Devolution in the United Kingdom*. Thorverton, Devon: Imprint Academic.

Hazell, R. et al. (2002). 'The constitution: Coming in from the cold', *Parliamentary Affairs*, 55: 2.

Hazell, R. (ed.) (2003). *The State of the Nations: The Third Year of Devolution in the United Kingdom*. Exeter: Imprint Academic.

Headey, B. (1974). *British Cabinet Ministers*. London: Allen and Unwin.

Heath, A., Jowell, R. and Curtice, J. (1985). *How Britain Votes*. London: Pergamon.

Heath, A., Jowell, R. and Curtice, J. (1994). *Labour's Last Chance*. Aldershot: Dartmouth.

Heath, A., Jowell, R. and Curtice, J. (2001). *The Rise of New Labour*. Oxford: Oxford University Press.

Heclo, H. and Wildavsky, A. (1974). *The Private Government of Public Money: Community and Policy inside British Politics*. Basingstoke: Macmillan.

Heffernan, R. (2000). *New Labour and Thatcherism: Political Change in Britain*. Basingstoke: Macmillan.

Helm, D. (ed.) (1989). *The Economic Borders of the State*. Oxford: Oxford University Press.

Henig, S. and Baston, L. (2002). *The Political Map of Britain*. London: Politicos.

Hennessy, P. (1986). *Cabinet*. Oxford: Blackwell.

Hennessy, P. (1995). *The Hidden Wiring: Unearthing Britain's Constitution*. London: Gollancz.

Hennessy, P. (2001a). 'The Blair style and the requirements of twenty-first-century premiership', *Political Quarterly*, 7: 4.

Hennessy, P. (2001b). *The Prime Minister: The Office and its Holders since 1945*. London: Penguin.

Hennessy, P. (2001c). *Whitehall*, rev. edn. London: Fontana.

Hennessy, P. (2003). *The Secret State: Whitehall and the Cold War*, rev. edn. London: Gollancz.

Hennessy, P. and Anstey, C. (1992). 'The jewel in the constitution? The queen, Parliament and the royal prerogative', Glasgow, University of Strathclyde Department of Government.

Hennessy, T. (2001). *The Northern Ireland Peace Process: Ending the Troubles*. Dublin: Gill and Macmillan.

Himmelweit, H. T., Humphreys, P., Jaeger, M. and Ktaz, M. (1981). *How Voters Decide*. London: Academic Press.

Hix, S. (1999). *The Political System of the European Union*. Basingstoke: Palgrave.

Hood, C., James, O. and Scott, C. (2000). 'Regulation of government: Has it increased, is it increasing, should it be diminished?', *Public Administration*, 8: 2.

Horowitz, D. (1977). *The Courts and Social Policy*. Washington, DC: The Brookings Institution.

Hume, D. (1996). *The Ulster Unionist Party 1972–1992*. Lurgan: Ulster Society.

Hutton, W. (1996). *The State We're In*. London: Vintage.

James, S. (1999). *British Cabinet Government*. London: Routledge.

Jeffrys, K. (1993). *The Labour Party since 1945*. Basingstoke: Macmillan.

Jenkins, K. (1999). 'Effective government and effective accountability', *Political Quarterly*, 70: 2.

Jenkins, P. (1987). *Mrs Thatcher's Revolution: The Ending of the Socialist Era*. London: Cape.

Jennings, I. (1966). *The British Constitution*, 5th edn. Cambridge: Cambridge University Press.

Johnson, N. (1997). 'Opposition in the British political system', *Government and Opposition*, 32: 4.

Johnson, N. (1998). 'The judicial dimension in British politics', *West European Politics*, 21: 1.

Johnson, N. (2000). 'Then and now: The British constitution', *Political Studies*, 48: 1.

Johnston, R. J. and Pattie, C. *From Votes to Seats: The Operation of the British Electoral System since 1945*. Manchester: Manchester University Press.

Jones, N. (1996). *Soundbites and Spin Doctors: How Politicians Manipulate the Media and Vice Versa*. London: Indigo.

Jones, N. (1999). *Sultans of Spin: The Media and the New Labour Government*. London: Gollancz.

Jones, N. (2001). *Campaign 2001*. London: Politicos.

Jordan, A. (2002). 'Environmental policy', in P. Dunleavy, A. Gamble, R. Heffernan, I. Holliday and G. Peele (eds), *Developments in British Politics 6*. Basingstoke: Palgrave.

Jordan, G. (1994). *The British Administrative System: Principles versus Practice*. London: Routledge.

Jordan, G. (1998). 'Politics without parties', *Parliamentary Affairs*, 51: 3.

Jordan, G. and Richardson, J. J. (1997). *Governing Under Pressure*. Oxford: Blackwell.

Jowell, J. and Oliver, D. (eds) (2000). *The Changing Constitution*, 4th edn. Oxford: Oxford University Press.

Katz, R. S. and Mair, P. (1995). 'Changing models of party organization and party democracy: The emergence of the cartel party', *Party Politics*, 1.

Kaufman, G. (1997). *How to be a Minister*. London: Faber.

Kavanagh, D. (1995). *Election Campaigning: The New Marketing of Politics*. Oxford: Blackwell.

Kavanagh, D. and Richards, D. (2001). 'Departmentalism and joined-up government', *Parliamentary Affairs*, 54: 1.

Kavanagh, D. and Seldon, A. (1999). *The Powers Behind the Prime Minister*. London: HarperCollins.

Kellas, J. (1989). *The Scottish Political System*, 4th edn. Cambridge: Cambridge University Press.

Kelly, R. (1989). *Conservative Party Conferences: The Hidden System*. Manchester: Manchester University Press.

Kelly, R. (1998). 'Democratising the Tory Party', *Talking Politics*, 11: 1.

Kelly, R. (2001). 'Farewell conference, hello forum: The making of Labour and Tory policy', *Political Quarterly*, 72: 3.

King, A. (ed.) (1985). *The British Prime Minister*, 2nd edn. London: Macmillan.

King, A. (2001). *Does the United Kingdom Still Have a Constitution?* London: Sweet and Maxwell.

King, D. and Stoker, G. (1996). *Rethinking Local Democracy*. Basingstoke: Macmillan.

Kirchheimer, O. (1966). 'The transformation of western European party systems', in J. LaPalombara and M. Weiner (eds), *Political Parties and Political Development*. Princeton, NJ: Princeton University Press.

Klug, F. (1999). 'The Human Rights Act 1998, Pepper v. Hart and All That', *Public Law*.

Klug, F. (2002). *Values for a Godless Age: The Story of the UK's New Bill of Rights*. London: Penguin.

Knill, C. and Lehmkuhl, D. (2001). *The Europeanisation of National Administrations: Patterns of Institutional Change and Persistence*. Cambridge: Cambridge University Press.

Kogan, M. and Kogan, D. (1983). *The Battle for the Labour Party*, 2nd edn. London: Kogan Page.

Laborde, C. (2000). 'The concept of the state in British and French political thought', *Political Studies*, 48: 3 (June).

Labour Party (1999). *21st-Century Party*. London: The Labour Party.

Laffin, M., Thomas, A. and Webb, A. (2000). 'Intergovernmental relations after devolution: The National Assembly for Wales', *Political Quarterly*, 71: 2.

Leach, R. and Percy Smith, J. (2001). *Local Governance in Britain*. Basingstoke: Palgrave.

Leach, S. (1999). 'Introducing cabinets into British local government', *Parliamentary Affairs*, 52: 1.

Lee, J. M., Jones, G. W. and Burnham, J. (1998). *At the Centre of Whitehall: Advising the Prime Minister and Cabinet*. Basingstoke: Macmillan.

Lees-Marshment, J. (2001). *Political Marketing and British Political Parties*. Manchester: Manchester University Press.

Lent, A. (2001). *British Social Movements since 1945: Sex, Colour, Peace and Power*. Basingstoke: Palgrave.

Lester, A. (1996). 'Parliamentary sovereignty and the European Community', *Parliamentary Affairs*, 49.

Le Sueur, A. (1996). 'The judicial review debate: From partnership to friction', *Government and Opposition*, 36: 1.

Le Sueur, A. and Cornes, R. (2000). *What Do Top Courts Do?* London: The Constitution Unit.

Le Sueur, A. and Sunkin, M. (1997). *Public Law*. London: Longman.

Lodge, J. (ed.) (2001). *The 1999 Elections to the European Parliament*. Basingstoke: Palgrave.

Loughlin, J. (1995). *Ulster Unionism and British National Identity since 1885*. London: Pinter.

Loughlin, M. (1994). 'The restructuring of central–local government relations', in J. Jowell and D. Oliver (eds), *The Changing Constitution*, 3rd edn. Oxford: Oxford University Press.

Loveland, I. (1996). 'Parliamentary sovereignty and the European Community: The unfinished revolution', *Parliamentary Affairs*, 49: 4.

Lowndes, V., Stoker, G., Pratchett, L., Wilson, D., Leach, S. and Wingfield, M. (1998). *Enhancing Public Participation in Local Government*. London: DETR.

Ludlam, S., Taylor, A. and Allender, P. (2002). 'The impact of the Political Parties, Elections and Referendums Act 2002 on trade union campaigning in 2001', *Representations*, 38: 4 (Spring).

Lundberg, T. (2002). 'Putting a human face on proportional representation: Early experience of Scotland and Wales', *Representations*, 38: 4 (Spring).

Lynch, P. (2001). *Scottish Government and Politics: An Introduction*. Edinburgh: Edinburgh University Press.

McAllister, I. (1977). *The Northern Ireland Social and Democratic Party: Political Opposition in a Divided Society*. Basingstoke: Macmillan.

McAllister, L. (2000). 'Changing the landscape? The wider political lessons from recent elections in Wales', *Political Quarterly*, 71: 2.

McAllister, L. (2001). *Plaid Cymru: The Emergence of a Political Party*. Glasgow: Seren.

McCormick, J. (1999). *Understanding the European Union: A Concise Introduction*. Basingstoke: Macmillan.

McEldowney, J. F. (2002). *Public Law*, 3rd edn. London: Sweet and Maxwell.

McGarry, J. and O'Leary, B. (1995). *Explaining Northern Ireland*. Oxford: Oxford University Press.

McKay, D. (1999). *Federalism and the European Union: A Political Economy Perspective*. Oxford: Oxford University Press.

McKay, D. (2001). *Designing Europe: Comparative Lessons from the Federal Experience*. Oxford: Oxford University Press.

McKenzie, R. (1963). *British Political Parties*. London: Heinemann.

McKenzie, R. and Silver, A. (1968). *Angels in Marble: Working-class Conservatism in Urban England*. London: Heinemann.

McKibbin, R. (1974). *The Evolution of the Labour Party*. Oxford: Oxford University Press.

McKibbin, R. (1990). *The Ideologies of Class–Social Relations in Britain, 1880–1950*. Oxford: Oxford University Press.

Mackintosh, J. P. (1977). *The British Cabinet*, 3rd edn. London: Stevens.

McKittrick, D. (1994). *Endgame: The Search for Peace in Northern Ireland*. Belfast: Blackstaff.

McLean, I. (1999). 'Mr Asquith's unfinished business', *Political Quarterly*, 70: 4.

McLean, I. (1999). 'The Jenkins Commission and the implications of electoral reform for the UK constitution', *Government and Opposition*, 34: 2.

Majone, G. (1996). *Regulating Europe*. London: Routledge.

Mallie, E. and McKittrick, D. (1996). *The Fight for Peace: The Secret Story Behind the Irish Peace Process*. London: Heinemann.

Marquand, D. and Seldon, A. (1996). *The Ideas that Shaped Post-war Britain*. London: Fontana.

Marr, A. (1996). *Ruling Britannia*. London: Penguin.

Marsh, D. and Rhodes, R. A. W. (2001). *Networks in British Government*. Oxford: Clarendon Press.

Marsh, D., Richards, D. and Smith, M. J. (2001). *Changing Patterns of Governance in the UK: Reinventing Whitehall*. Basingstoke: Palgrave.

Marshall, G. (1957). *Parliamentary Sovereignty and the Commonwealth*. Oxford: Oxford University Press.

Marshall, G. (1984). *Constitutional Conventions*. Oxford: Oxford University Press.

Marshall, G. (ed.) (1989). *Ministerial Responsibility*. Oxford: Oxford University Press.

Mason, D. (2000). *Race and Ethnicity in Modern Britain*, 2nd edn. Oxford: Oxford University Press.

Meyer, A. (1990). *Stand Up and Be Counted*. London: Heinemann.

Minkin, L. (1978). *The Labour Conference: A Study of Intra-party Democracy*. London: Allen Lane.

Minkin, L. (1992). *The Contentious Alliance: Trade Unions and the Labour Party*. Edinburgh: Edinburgh University Press.

Moran, M. (2001). 'The rise of the regulatory state in Britain', *Parliamentary Affairs*, 54: 1 (January).

Morgan, K. O. (1981). *Rebirth of a Nation: Wales 1880–1980*. Oxford: Oxford University Press.

Morgan, K. O. (1999). *The People's Peace*. Oxford: Oxford University Press.

Morrison, J. (2001). *Reforming Britain: New Labour, New Constitution?* London: Pearson.

Morrissey, M. and Smyth, M. (2002). *Northern Ireland After the Good Friday Agreement: Victims' Grievance and Blame*. London: Pluto.

Mount, F. (1992). *The Constitution Now: Recovery or Decline?* London: Heinemann.

Mountfield, R. (1997). 'The new senior civil service: Managing the paradox', *Public Administration*, 75.

Mowlam, M. (2002). *Momentum: The Struggle for Peace, Politics and the People*. London: Hodder and Stoughton.

Mughan, A. (2000). *Media and the Presidentialization of Parliamentary Elections*. Basingstoke: Palgrave.

Mulholland, M. (2002). *Northern Ireland: A Very Short Introduction*. Oxford: Oxford University Press.

Murray, G. (1998). *John Hume and the SDLP*. Dublin: Irish Academic Press.

Nairn, T. (2000). *After Britain*. London: Granta.

Naughtie, J. (2002). *The Rivals: The Inside Story of a Political Marriage*, rev. ed. London: Fourth Estate.

Nicol, D. (2001). *EC Membership and the Judicialization of British Politics*. Oxford: Oxford University Press.

Niskanen, W. (1971). *Bureaucracy and Representative Government*. Chicago: Aldine Atherton.

Niskanen, W. (1973). *A Bureaucracy Servant or Master? Lessons from America*. London: Hobart Press.

Norris, P. (1990). *British By-elections: The Volatile Electorate*. Oxford: Oxford University Press.

Norris, P. (ed.) (1997a). *Britain Votes 1997*. Oxford: Oxford University Press.

Norris, P. (1997b). *Electoral Change in Britain since 1945*. Oxford: Blackwell.

Norris, P. (1999). *Critical Citizens: Global Support for Democratic Governance*. Oxford: Oxford University Press.

Norris, P. (ed.) (2001). *Britain Votes 2001*. Oxford: Oxford University Press.

Norris, P. (2002). *Virtuous Circle: Political Communications in Postindustrial Societies*. Cambridge: Cambridge University Press.

Norris, P., Curtice, J., Saunders, O. and Scammell, M. (1999). *On Message*. London: Sage.

Norton, P. (1992). *The Constitution: The Conservative Way Forward*. London: CPC.

Norton, P. (1993). *Does Parliament Matter?* London: Harvester Wheatsheaf.

Norton, P. (1996). *National Parliaments and the European Union*. London: Frank Cass.

Norton, P. and Wood, D. (1995). *Back from Westminster*. Lexington: University of Kentucky Press.

Nozick, R. (1974). *Anarchy, State and Utopia*. Oxford: Blackwell.

Nugent, N. (2003). *The Government and Politics of the European Union*, 5th edn. Basingstoke: Palgrave.

Office for National Statistics (1999). *Britain 1999*. London: HMSO.

Office for National Statistics (2002). *Handbook for National Statistics 2002*. London: Office for National Statistics.

Office for National Statistics (2003). *UK 2003 Yearbook*. London: HMSO.

Oliver, D. (1994). 'Parliament, ministers and the law', *Parliamentary Affairs*, 47.

Oliver, D. (2003). *Constitutional Reform in the United Kingdom*. Oxford: Oxford University Press.

Oliver, D. and Drewry, G. (1996). *Public Service Reforms: Issues of Accountability and Public Law*. London: Pinter.

Olson, M. (1965). *The Logic of Collective Action: Public Goods and the Theory of Groups*. Cambridge, MA: Harvard University Press.

Osborne, D. E. and Gaebler, T. (1992). *Reinventing Government: How the Entrepreneurial Spirit is Transforming the Public Sector*. Wokingham: Addison Wesley.

Page, E. C. (1999). 'The insider/outsider distinction: An empirical investigation', *British Journal of Politics and International Relations*, 1: 2.

Page, E. C. (2001). *Governing by Numbers: Delegated Legislation and Everyday Policymaking*. Oxford: Hart.

Panebianco, A. (1988). *Political Parties: Organization and Power*. Cambridge: Cambridge University Press.

Pannick, D. (1988). *The Judges*. Oxford: Oxford University Press.

Park, A., Curtice, J., Thomson, K., Jarvis, L. and Bromley, C. (2002). *British Social Attitudes: The 19th Report*. London: National Centre for Social Research.

Paterson, L., Brown, A., Curtis, J., Hinds, K., McCrone, D., Park, A., Sproston, K. and Surridge, P. (2001). *New Scotland, New Politics*. Edinburgh: Polygon.

Patterson, H. (1997). *The Politics of Illusion*. London: Lawrence and Wishart.

Payne, T. and Skelcher, C. (1997). 'Explaining less accountability: The growth of local quangos', *Public Administration*, 75: 2.

Peele, G. (1995). *Governing the UK*, 3rd edn. Oxford: Blackwell.

Peele, G. (1998). 'Towards "New Conservatives"? Organisational reform and the Conservative Party', *Political Quarterly*, 69: 2.

Pelling, H. (1996). *A Short History of the Labour Party*. Basingstoke: Macmillan.

Perri 6, Leat, D. et al. (2002). *Towards Holistic Governance*. Basingstoke: Palgrave.

Pilkinton, C. (1999). *The Civil Service Today*. Manchester: Manchester University Press.

Pimlott, B. (1989). 'The myth of consensus', in B. Pimlott, *Frustrate their Knavish Tricks: Writings on Biography, History and Politics*. London: HarperCollins.

Pimlott, B. (2002). *Governing London*. Oxford: Oxford University Press.

Pinto-Duschinsky, M. (1997). 'Tory troops are in worse state than feared', *The Times*, 6 June.

Pollitt, C. (1993). *Managerialism and the Public Services*. Oxford: Blackwell.

Porter, N. (1996). *Rethinking Unionism*. Belfast: Blackstaff.

Power, M. (1997). *The Audit Society: Rituals of Verification*. Oxford: Oxford University Press.

Public Administration, Select Committee on (2002–3). *On Target*.

Pulzer, P. (1967). *Political Representation and Elections in Britain*. London: Allen and Unwin.

Punnett, R. M. (1992). *Selecting the Party Leader: Britain in Comparative Perspective*. London: Harvester Wheatsheaf.

Putnam, R. D. (2000). *Bowling Alone: The Collapse and Revival of American Community*. New York: Simon and Schuster.

Putnam, R. D. (ed.) (2002). *Democracies in Flux: The Evolution of Social Capital in Contemporary Society*. Oxford: Oxford University Press.

Rallings, C. et al. (1999). 'An audit of local democracy in Britain: The evidence from local elections', *Parliamentary Affairs*, 52: 1.

Ramsden, J. (1978). *The Age of Balfour and Baldwin, 1902–1940*. London: Longman.

Rao, N. (2000). *Reviving Local Democracy: New Labour, New Politics?* Bristol: Policy.

Rawnsley, A. (2001). *Servants of the People: The Inside Story of New Labour*, rev. edn. Harmondsworth: Penguin.

Report of the Independent Commission on the Voting System (Jenkins Report) (1998). Cmnd 4090. London: HMSO.

Rhodes, R. A. W. (1994). 'The hollowing out of the state: The changing nature of the public service in Britain', *Political Quarterly*, 65.

Rhodes, R. A. W. (2000a). 'The governance narrative: Key findings and lessons from the ESRC's Whitehall programme', *Public Administration*, 78: 2.

Rhodes, R. A. W. (2000b). 'New Labour's civil service', *Political Quarterly*, 71: 2.

Rhodes, R. A. W. (2000c). 'New Labour's civil service: Summing-up joining-up', *Political Quarterly*, 71: 2.

Rhodes, R. A. W. and Dunleavy, P. (eds) (1995). *Prime Minister, Cabinet and Core Executive*. Basingstoke: Macmillan.

Rich, P. B. (1998). 'Ethnic politics and the Conservatives', in S. Saggar (ed.), *Race and British Electoral Politics*. London: University College Press.

Richard, I. and Welfare, D. (1999). *Unfinished Business: Reforming the House of Lords*. London: Vintage.

Richards, D. and Smith, M. (2000). 'The public service ethos and the role of the British civil service', *West European Politics*, 23: 3.

Richardson, J. J. (ed.) (1998). *European Union Power and Policy*. London: Routledge.

Richardson, J. J. (2000). 'Government, interest groups and policy change', *Political Studies*, 48: 5.

Riddell, P. (2000). *Parliament Under Blair*. London: Politicos.

Ridley, F. F. (1987). 'What are the duties and responsibilities of civil servants?', *Public Administration*, 65.

Ridley, F. F. and Doig, A. (eds) (1995). *Sleaze: Politicians, Private Interests and Public Reaction*. Oxford: Oxford University Press.

Ridley, F. F. and Jordan, G. (1998). *Protest Politics: Cause, Groups and Campaigns*. Oxford: Oxford University Press.

Rimington, S. (2001). *Open Secret: The Autobiography of the Director of MI5*. London: Hutchinson.

Robertson, D. (1998). *Judicial Discretion in the House of Lords*. Oxford: Oxford University Press.

Rose, R. (1987). *Ministers and Ministries*. Oxford: Clarendon Press.

Rose, R. (2001). *The Prime Minister in a Shrinking World*. Cambridge: Polity.

Routledge, P. (1998). *John Hume: A Biography*. London: HarperCollins.

Rush, M. (ed.) (1990). *Parliament and Pressure Politics*. Oxford: Clarendon Press.

Russell, M. (2001). 'What are second chambers for?', *Parliamentary Affairs*, 54: 3.

Saggar, S. (1992). *Race and Politics in Britain*. London: Harvester Wheatsheaf.

Saggar, S. (ed.) (1998). *Race and British Electoral Politics*. London: University College Press.

Salamon, L. (2002). *The Tools of Government: A Guide to the New Governance*. Oxford: Oxford University Press.

Sanders, D. (1991). 'Government popularity and the next general election', *Political Quarterly*, 62.

Sanders, D. (1996). 'Economic performance, management competence and the outcome of the next general election', *Political Studies*, 44.

Sanders, D. (1999). 'The dynamics of party preference change in Britain, 1991–96', *Political Studies*, 47: 2.

Sanders, D., Clarke, H., Stewart, M. and Whitely, P. (2001). 'The economy and voting', in P. Norris (ed.), *Britain Votes 2001*. Oxford: Oxford University Press.

Sarlvik, B. and Crewe, I. (1983). *Decade of Dealignment: The Conservative Victory of 1979 and the Electoral Trend since the 1970s*. Cambridge: Cambridge University Press.

Scammell, M. (1995). *Designer Politics*. London: Macmillan.

Scammell, M. (1999). 'Political marketing: Lessons for political science', *Political Studies*, 47: 4.

Scammell, M. and Semetko, H. (2000). *The Media, Journalism and Democracy*. Aldershot: Dartmouth.

Scarman, L. (1989). 'The shape of things to come: The shape of the future law and constitution in the United Kingdom', Warwick, University of Warwick.

Scott, R. (1996). 'Ministerial accountability', *Public Law*.

Searing, D. (1994). *Westminster's World: Understanding MPs' Roles*. Cambridge, MA: Harvard University Press.

Seaton, J. and Winetrobe, B. K. (1999). 'Modernising the Commons', *Political Quarterly*, 70: 2.

Seldon, A. and Ball, S. (eds) (1994). *Conservative Century: The Conservative Century since 1900*. Oxford: Oxford University Press.

Seneviratne, M. (2002). *Ombudsmen: Public Services and Administrative Justice*. London: Butterworth.

Seyd, P. (1987). *The Rise and Fall of the Labour Party*. Basingstoke: Macmillan Education.

Seyd, P. and Whitely, P. (1992). *Labour's Grass Roots: The Politics of Party Membership*. Oxford: Clarendon Press.

Seyd, P. and Whitely, P. (2002). *New Labour's Grass Roots: The Transformation of Labour Party Membership*. Basingstoke: Macmillan.

Seyd, P., Whitely, P. and Parry, J. (1996). *Labour and Conservative Party Members, 1990–1992: Social Characteristics, Political Attitudes and Activity*. Aldershot: Dartmouth.

Seyd, P., Whitely, P. and Richardson, J. (1994). *True Blues: The Politics of Conservative Party Membership*. Oxford: Clarendon Press.

Shaw, E. (1996). *The Labour Party since 1945: Old Labour, New Labour*. Oxford: Blackwell.

Shell, D. (1993). *The House of Lords at Work*. Oxford: Clarendon Press.

Shell, D. (1999). 'The future of the second chamber', *Political Quarterly*, 70: 4.

Shell, D. (2000). 'Labour and Lords reform', *Parliamentary Affairs*, 53: 2.

Silk, P. and Walters, R. (1998). *How Parliament Works*, 4th edn. Harlow: Longman.

Smith, D. E. (2000). 'A House for the future: Second chamber reform in the UK', *Government and Opposition*, 35: 3.

Smith, J. (1999). *Europe's Elected Parliament*. Sheffield: Sheffield Academic Press.

Smith, M. (1999). *The Core Executive in Britain*. Basingstoke: Macmillan.

Smith, M. and Spear, J. (1992). *The Changing Labour Party*. London: Routledge.

Standards in Public Life: First Report of the Committee on Standards in Public Life (the Nolan Committee) (1995). Cmnd 2850-1. London: HMSO.

Stevens, R. B. (2002). *The English Judges: Their Role in the Changing Constitution*. Oxford: Hart.

Stevenson, J. (1993). *Third Party Politics since 1945*. Oxford: Blackwell.

Stewart, A. T. Q. (1977). *The Narrow Ground: Aspects of Ulster 1609–1969*. London: Faber.

Stewart, J. (2000). *The Nature of British Local Government*. Basingstoke: Macmillan.

Stoker, G. (ed.) (1999). *The New Management of British Local Governance*. Basingstoke: Macmillan.

Stoker, G. (ed.) (2000). *The New Politics of British Local Governance*. Basingstoke: Macmillan.

Stone Sweet, A. (2000). *Governing with Judges: Constitutional Politics in Europe*. Oxford: Oxford University Press.

Sutherland, K. (ed.) (2000). *The Rape of the Constitution*. Thorverton, Devon: Imprint Academic.

Tate, T. (1983). 'Magistrates on trial', *The Listener*, 15 September.

Taylor, A. (2000). 'Hollowing out or filling in? Task-forces and the management of cross-cutting issues in British government', *British Journal of Politics and International Studies*, 2: 1.

Taylor, B. (2002a). *The Road to the Scottish Parliament*. Edinburgh: Edinburgh University Press.

Taylor, B. (2002b). *Scotland's Parliament: Triumph and Disaster*. Edinburgh: Edinburgh University Press.

Thain, C. (2002). 'Economic policy', in P. Dunleavy, A. Gamble, R. Heffernan, I. Holliday and G. Peele (eds), *Developments in British Politics 6*. Basingstoke: Palgrave.

Thain, P. and Wright, M. (1995). *The Treasury and Whitehall*. Oxford: Oxford University Press.

Theakston, K. (1987). *Junior Ministers in British Government*. Oxford: Blackwell.

Theakston, K. (1997). 'New Labour, New Whitehall?', *Public Policy and Administration*, 13.

Theakston, K. (1999). *Leadership in Whitehall*. Basingstoke: Macmillan.

Theakston, K. (ed.) (2000). *Bureaucrats and Leadership*. Basingstoke: Macmillan.

Thomas, G. (1998). *Prime Minister and Cabinet Today*. Manchester: Manchester University Press.

Thurlow, R. (1994). *The Secret State: British Internal Security in the Twentieth Century*. Oxford: Blackwell.

Tomkins, A. (1998). *The Constitution After Scott: The Constitution Unwrapped*. Oxford: Oxford University Press.

Tonge, J. (2002). *Northern Ireland: Conflict and Change*, 2nd edn. Harlow: Longman.

Townshend, C. (1983). *Political Violence in Ireland: Government and Resistance since 1848*. Oxford: Clarendon Press.

Travers, T. and Jones, G. W. (1997). *The New Government of London*. London: Rowntree.

Treasury Select Committee (2001). *HM Treasury 3rd Report HC73-1*.

Trench, A. (ed.) (2001). *The State of the Nations 2001*. Thorverton, Devon: Imprint Academic.

Urwin, D. (1991). *The Community of Europe: A History of European Integration since 1945*. London: Longman.

Van Zwanenburg, P. and Milstone, E. (2003). 'BSE: A paradigm of policy failure', *Political Quarterly*, 74: 1 (January–March).

Wakeham, Lord (2000). 'The Lords: Building a House for the future', *Political Quarterly*, 71: 3.

Wallace, H. and Wallace, W. (2000). *Policy Making in the European Union*, 4th edn. Oxford: Oxford University Press.

Warleigh, A. (2002). *Understanding European Union Institutions*. London: Routledge.

Webb, P. (2000). *The Modern British Party System*. London: Sage.

Webb, P. (2002). 'Parties and party systems: More continuity than change', *Parliamentary Affairs*, 54: 2.

Weir, S. and Hall, W. (1996). *The Untouchables: Power and Accountability in the Quango State*. London: Scarman Trust.

Westlake, M. and Butler, D. (1999). *British Politics and European Elections*. Basingstoke: Macmillan.

White, S. (ed.) (2001). *New Labour: The Progressive Future*. Basingstoke: Palgrave.

Whitely, P. and Seyd, P. (1998). 'The dynamics of party activism in Britain: A spiral of demobilization', *British Journal of Political Science*, 28: 1.

Whitely, P. and Seyd, P. (2002). *High-intensity Participation: The Dynamics of Party Activism in Britain*. Ann Arbor: University of Michigan Press.

Whyte, J. (1990). *Interpreting Northern Ireland*. Oxford: Oxford University Press.

Wigley, D. (2001). *Working for Wales*. Caernarfon: Welsh Academic Press.

Wilford, R. (ed.) (2001). *Aspects of the Belfast Agreement*. Oxford: Oxford University Press.

Williams, D. (2000). 'Bias: The judges and the separation of powers', *Public Law*.

Wilson, D. (2001). 'Local government: Balancing diversity and uniformity', *Parliamentary Affairs*, 54: 2.

Wilson, D. and Game, C. (2002). *Local Government in the United Kingdom*. Basingstoke: Palgrave/Macmillan.

Wilson, G. (1990). *Interest Groups*. Oxford: Blackwell.

Wilson, G. (2003). *Business and Politics: A Comparative Introduction*. Basingstoke: Palgrave/Macmillan.

Wilson, Sir Richard (1999). 'The civil service in the new millennium'. Lecture to City University London, 5 May.

Wilson, Sir Richard (2002). 'Portrait of a profession revisited', *Political Quarterly*, 73: 4.

Wincott, D. (2000). 'A community of law? "European" law and judicial politics', *Government and Opposition*, 35: 1.

Woodhouse, D. (1995). 'Politicians and the judiciary: A changing relationship', *Parliamentary Affairs*, 48: 3.

Woodhouse, D. (1997). 'Ministerial responsibility: Something old, something new', *Public Law*.

Woodhouse, D. (1998). 'The Parliamentary Commissioner for Standards: Lessons from the "Cash for Questions" Enquiry', *Parliamentary Affairs*, 51: 1.

Woodhouse, D. (1999). 'New Labour and a new constitutional settlement', *Parliamentary Affairs*, 52: 2.

Woodhouse, D. (2001). 'The law and politics: More power to the judges – and to the people?', *Parliamentary Affairs*, 54: 2.

Young, H. (1999). *This Blessed Plot: Britain and Europe from Churchill to Blair*, updated edn. Basingstoke: Macmillan.

Zander, M. (1997). *A Bill of Rights?* London: Sweet and Maxwell.

Index

Made in the USA
Lexington, KY
31 May 2017